THE ARCHITECTURE OF THE ECOLE DES BEAUX-ARTS

THE ARCHITECTURE OF THE ECOLE DES BEAUX-ARTS

Edited by

ARTHUR DREXLER

Essays by

RICHARD CHAFEE
ARTHUR DREXLER
NEIL LEVINE
DAVID VAN ZANTEN

THE MUSEUM OF MODERN ART
NEW YORK

Distributed by The MIT Press, Cambridge, Massachusetts

The publication of this book
has been made possible in part
by a generous grant from
The Graham Foundation for Advanced Studies
in The Fine Arts, Chicago.

The exhibition on which the book has been based,
"The Architecture of the Ecole des Beaux-Arts,"
was shown at The Museum of Modern Art, New York,
from October 29, 1975, through January 4, 1976,
and made possible through the generous support of the
National Endowment for the Arts,
Washington, D.C., a Federal agency.

Designed by Carl Laanes
Type set by Royal Composing Room Inc., New York, N.Y.
Printed by Rae Publishing Company, Inc., Cedar Grove, N.J.
Bound by Sendor Bindery, Inc., New York, N.Y.

The Museum of Modern Art
11 West 53 Street, New York, N.Y. 10019
Printed in the United States of America

Library of Congress Catalog Card Number 75-7649
ISBN 0-87070-244-0 (The Museum of Modern Art)
ISBN 0-262-04053-0 (The MIT Press)

CONTENTS

PREFACE
AND
ACKNOWLEDGMENTS

"The battle of modern architecture," Philip Johnson declared in 1952, "has long been won." His observation prefaced *Built in USA: Post-war Architecture*, a Museum of Modern Art catalog devoted to "the great post-war flowering of architecture in this country—which is so obvious around us." "With the mid-century," he concluded, "modern architecture has come of age."

By the end of the third quarter of the century, the theoretical basis of modern architecture is as much a collection of received opinions as were the doctrines it overthrew. We think we know what modern architecture is—although it is notoriously difficult to define—and how it differs from what preceded it; but we are no longer so certain as to what it should become and how it should be taught. And since history is written by the victors, the literature of the modern movement has helped to perpetuate confusion as to what was lost, let alone what the battle was about.

The triumph of modern architecture is inseparable from ideas given their clearest embodiment in the teaching and practice of the German Bauhaus, which replaced a French educational system that had evolved for over two hundred years. Ecole des Beaux-Arts practice before the first World War could not keep pace with Ecole theories, and that the theories themselves were preventing a reintegration is a historical judgment not likely to be reversed. The Ecole des Beaux-Arts seemed intent on solving what were no longer perceived as "real" problems. Defining—and solving—what seemed to be the right problems was the great achievement of the Bauhaus. Founded in 1919 and disrupted only fourteen years later by the upheaval of Nazism, the Bauhaus disappeared as an institution but flourished as a doctrine. It dominated architecture in America by effecting pervasive changes in education, and then, within the lifetimes of its protagonists, subsided without having generated its own succession.

Although Bauhaus ideas were as varied as the personalities of its faculty and its best students, our generalizations about what they thought they were doing are likely to be as partial as were those pronouncements made in the 1920s about the Ecole des Beaux-Arts. Nevertheless, we may observe that the Bauhaus began as a craft school, regarding craftsmanship as a necessary step toward the higher task of designing for machine production. Prompted in part by the supposed moral integrity of the craftsman as distinguished from the factory-hand, social concern was reinforced by a preference for treating form as simple geometric elements of unchanging value, at last enabling man's artifacts to be free of the shifting fashions of historical styles. The immutable nature of pure geometry was supposed to make it peculiarly well-suited to the demands of machine production, although there is nothing about machinery that inherently limits it to the replication of simple geometric forms. The result of this conjunction of ideas was, of course, the creation of a brilliant historic style, lucid in its reductionist simplicity but not necessarily simple in fact; reasonably responsive to the requirements of practical use (function); and most successful in the design of small-scale objects, particularly furniture. In architecture, its moralizing fixation on utility and industrial technique led to an anti-historical bias the consequences of which have yet to be fully understood, although they are all too painfully obvious wherever modern architecture has dealt with the urban environment. The modern movement has prided itself on its "urbanism," but to be anti-historical is to be anti-urban. The old architecture defined itself as the design of public buildings which, *pro bono publico*, quite naturally must be grand. The new architecture defined itself as the design of everything in the built environment—"total architecture," in Walter Gropius's alarming phrase—but perceived grandeur only as an instrument of oppression.

Fifty years ago redemption through design—*good* design—was the mystic hope hidden within the humane reordering of earthly things. Today, in architecture as in everything else, messianic fervor seems naive when it is not actually destructive. But architecture has yet to benefit from the sense of new possibilities generated by a relaxation of dogma. The kind of freedom achieved by Italian design in the '60s replaced moral imperatives with irony and humor, but not with new convictions, and it is scarcely surprising that once again architects agree about very little concerning the nature of their art. Indeed, if there is one thing about which they do agree, at least enough to sign manifestos and march on picket lines, it is the necessity of preserving what is left of Beaux-Arts architecture wherever it may be found. Reviled during the first quarter of the century, and forgotten until the '60s (when Louis Kahn's buildings and Kahn himself reminded us of the origin of some interesting ideas), the architecture taught and practiced by the Ecole des Beaux-Arts again rewards thoughtful study. We have rediscovered some of its problems.

Throughout the twentieth century, the planning concepts of the Ecole des Beaux-Arts have been the most readily accessible of all its productions. This was not only because of the formal interest of Beaux-Arts plans but because the majority of architects who reached professional maturity in the 1940s had received at least an American version of Beaux-Arts training. What remained incomprehensible to the modern movement—and for good reason—was the apparent unrelatedness, or independence, of elevation and section from the nature of the plan, despite the fact that a favorite Beaux-Arts theme was the correspondence of a building's exterior to its internal organization. Particularly disturbing was the eclectic use of historic styles, which during the last decade of the nineteenth century exploded in a frenzy of ornament and megalomania. And yet the Beaux-Arts was of course no more monolithic in its ideas and objectives than was the Bauhaus. Today, the variety of those ideas tends to clarify and enhance the underlying continuities. Some Beaux-Arts problems, among them the question of how to use the past, may perhaps be seen now as possibilities that are liberating rather than constraining. A more detached view of architecture as it was understood in the nineteenth century might also provoke a more rigorous critique of philosophical assumptions underlying the architecture of our own time. Now that modern experience so often contradicts modern faith, we would be well advised to reexamine our architectural pieties.

* * *

This book, like the exhibition that preceded it, presents some two hundred drawings for architectural projects. One hundred sixty of them were made by students at the Ecole des Beaux-Arts and represent virtually every type of assignment or competition organized by the school. The remaining forty drawings comprise those made by Henri Labrouste, who was first a student and then master of an atelier, for his Bibliothèque Sainte-Geneviève; by Charles Garnier and members of the office he established to produce his Paris Opéra; and by Viollet-le-Duc, also for the Opéra. A selection of executed buildings in France and the United States is shown in photographs. Apart from the American examples, the latest of which was completed in 1943, and some eighteenth-century projects significant for later developments, the survey is limited to what was done by French students and masters at the Ecole des Beaux-Arts during the nineteenth century.

Students were eligible for the Ecole if they were at least fifteen years old, or under thirty. They began with the *seconde classe,* in which they competed in the *concours d'émulation.* These alternated between an *esquisse*—a rough sketch for which up to twelve hours was allowed—and a *rendu*—the large-scale finished drawing for which one to three months were allowed. The *rendu* had to follow in all essentials the conception first proposed in its *esquisse.*

Two to four years were usually required for a student to accumulate enough credits to enter the *première classe.* The same system was followed again, usually for two to three years, after which the student should have accumulated enough credits to compete for the Grand Prix de Rome. The winner of the Grand Prix was entitled to five years of study under the auspices of the French Academy in Rome, and was provided with room and board and a small stipend. For each of his first three years he was required to submit an analytical study of an ancient monument. For his fourth year he had to submit a complete reconstruction of a major classical work. For his fifth year he was required to submit an original work designed to a program of his own invention.

Over the years numerous secondary prizes were developed for special interests, and students made increasingly large drawings as the century progressed. Monochrome ink washes were most often used, although at intervals color became popular and was permitted. In the *seconde classe* the student was required to attend a variety of lectures in theory, history, and construction, and learned to prepare construction drawings. Also required was drawing from life.

Work was done at ateliers located outside the precincts of the Ecole des Beaux-Arts. These were rented and organized by the students themselves, and the students had the right to invite a teacher of their own choice to serve as their *maître*. The teacher himself did not have to be a member of the faculty of the Ecole, nor—at least in principle—did he have to be a practicing architect. Some students found employment in their *maître's* office. From the *agence* operated by Charles Garnier to produce the drawings for his Paris Opéra, no fewer than four students emerged to win the Grand Prix, although Garnier was never the *maître* of an atelier.

The administrative and political history of the Ecole des Beaux-Arts, punctuated by government decrees and private vendettas and culminating in riots, belies the school's reputation for placid self-satisfaction. Such events are unintelligible unless we know what the arguments were about. Richard Chafee, an American architectural historian at the Courtauld Institute in London, has provided a detailed and enlightening account from which those who teach architecture may gain comfort.

The Ecole's capacity for deflecting, transforming, or absorbing heresies was not the least of its institutional accomplishments. Ideas changed. What the ideas were and why and how they changed are recounted by David Van Zanten, of the Department of the History of Art at the University of Pennsylvania. The information contained in Mr. Van Zanten's essay should make the range of Beaux-Arts theory accessible again, and will help to reacquaint us with what was once an indispensable vocabulary of critical discourse.

Discourse, or more specifically "readable architecture," is the principal theme of the essay by Neil Levine of the Department of Fine Arts at Harvard University; Henri Labrouste and the *Néo-Grec* preoccupation with signs and symbols are its subjects, examined with sympathetic imagination to reveal some surprising and peculiarly "modern" aspects of this architect's work.

The initial essay reviews the consequences for modern architecture of its thralldom to engineering, and to the related idea of a rational response to structure and function as the measure of architectural value, comparing in this context certain Beaux-Arts notions as they may seem to us now.

David Van Zanten and I made the selection of drawings for the book and the exhibition. The captions accompanying the illustrations were written by Ann Van Zanten, David Van Zanten, and myself. Unless otherwise specified the drawings reproduced in all but the initial essay are in the collection of the Ecole Nationale Supérieure des Beaux-Arts, Paris.

On behalf of the Museum I wish to thank M. Jean Bertin, Director of the Ecole Nationale Supérieure des Beaux-Arts, Paris. The exhibition and book would have been impossible without his enthusiastic interest and cooperation. Equally impossible would have been the research work in the storerooms of the Ecole if not for the active assistance of Mlle Annie Jacques, Librarian of the Ecole des Beaux-Arts, and her predecessor, Mme Bouleau-Rabaud.

We are also most grateful to M. Etienne Dennery, Administrateur de la Bibliothèque Nationale, and Mlle Martine Kahane, Conservateur de la Bibliothèque-Musée de l'Opéra, for making accessible Charles Garnier's Opéra drawings; and to M. Michel Parent, Inspecteur Général, and M. Jean-Pierre Guillen, of the Centre de Recherches sur les Monuments Historiques, for Viollet-le-Duc's drawings for the Paris Opéra competition. We are especially grateful to M. Léon Malcotte-Labrouste for making available Henri Labrouste's drawings for his fifth-year *envoi*. We also wish to thank M. J.-L. Vaudoyer for providing the plan of Marseilles Cathedral.

In New York research tasks were greatly facilitated by our good friend Adolf Placzek, Librarian of the Avery Architectural Library at Columbia University, and I particularly thank him for lending original photographic prints of the Chicago World's Columbian Exposition of 1893. Thanks are due also to the many people who have provided information and photographs from the following institutions: The Boston Public Library, the Burnham Library at the Art Institute of Chicago, the New York Public Library, the American Academy of Arts and Letters, the New York Historical Society, the Library of Congress, the National Archives, the Museum of the City of New York, the Chicago Historical Society, and the American Institute of Architects. We are also grateful to John F. Harbeson, Paul Sprague, and Richard Wurts for making available documents and photographs.

I wish particularly to thank Mary Jane Lightbown, Researcher in the Department of Architecture and Design, for her enterprising and persuasive efforts in assembling pictures and information; Kathryn Eno, Assistant to the Director in the same department, for her steadfast and resourceful handling of innumerable administrative details; Carl Laanes, whose book design has helped to clarify and enhance the material; and Mary Lea Bandy, whose editorial talents and sympathetic intelligence have been indispensable.

Arthur Drexler, *Director*
Department of Architecture and Design

THE ARCHITECTURE OF THE ECOLE DES BEAUX-ARTS

Charles Garnier. Opéra, Paris. Grand Stair Hall during construction.

ENGINEER'S ARCHITECTURE:
TRUTH
AND ITS CONSEQUENCES

Arthur Drexler

To visit Paris for the first or the twentieth time is to be surprised by history. The centuries take turns occupying a mental space larger than their buildings would justify; or they retreat from the conscious eye no matter how substantial their physical record. What fills the mind is not necessarily the best, or the most beautiful, or even the most interesting. When the cathedrals were white, Le Corbusier said, the world must have been fresh and bright and full of hope. Today in Paris the medieval cathedrals and much more are again "white," having been cleaned. Restored to vision, history is again possible. Now the gray note of futility is provided by skyscrapers.

Like unwanted guests at a party, or a glacier we hope may yet recede, the new Paris skyscrapers introduce authentic foreboding; but in the center of the city one thinks instead of the boulevards and the monumental set pieces, the vistas and the trees and the pervasive texture sustained like a dense orchestral sound: a work of art, a city revealed and completed, or invented, by the nineteenth century. Until the arrival of the skyscrapers nothing, not even the automobile, could destroy this built unity of urban context and event. Days and weeks may pass before one remembers Le Corbusier and the belligerent optimism with which he proposed to level so much of Paris to make room for eight glass towers. Through no fault of his he left Paris unmarked, except as he himself and then his disciples—and who has not been his disciple—infiltrated the city with those equivocal incidents of modern architecture by which the assertion of his theories refutes them. Relying upon the past as if it were an indulgent parent or some other inexhaustible resource, modernism's characteristic urban presence is not a building or a place, or even the ubiquitous glass wall made memorable by whatever it reflects; it is no tangible thing but rather the vague, disquieting suspicion that a wish from the childhood of modern architecture has come true, although we never really meant it to.

* * *

Art is a lie, Picasso declared. "We all know that Art is not truth. Art is a lie that makes us realize truth, at least the truth that is given us to understand. The artist must know the manner whereby to convince others of the truthfulness of his lies."[1] The "lie" whereby architecture most readily convinces us of its "truth" is that form responds to necessity. Which necessity, and which forms are appropriate to it, are questions each historical style answers

14

differently, but in all times the architect is sustained by the idea that his preference for certain kinds of form is validated by a force external to himself—the necessity imposed by society, or techniques, or nature, or God. Forms are manipulated in order to make explicit whichever of these external validations the architect affirms as the most satisfying explanation of the nature of existence. Architectural form is a fiction designed to reveal a truth. The futility of so much critical discourse results, first, from confusing the fiction with the truth, and second, accepting a conceptual truth as if it had the power to banish fiction from the world forever.

The history of the modern movement involves the effort to establish architecture on a necessity that would seem irrefutable because it seems self-evident—followed by the effort to escape the consequences. Who can deny that buildings have forms developed in response to materials and functions? They do and they should. And if different materials and functions should prove to be equally well accommodated by the same forms, how can one avoid shifting the choice of forms away from habits of use, or mere preference, toward the more sophisticated stasis of technique; that is, defining the value of built form according to its correspondence with the techniques of construction? It could scarcely be otherwise, if our guiding conceptual truth is that necessity is a matter of structural relations—from which it follows that when all else is removed the truth of architecture must seem identical with what cannot be subtracted: essential structure.

If, in pursuit of the absolute, we wish to exalt the act of building while devaluing its contingent forms, and the bewildering freedom contingency implies, then we will seek to purify techniques until they become the visible record of the act of building and nothing more. Proceeding by reduction, modern architecture is uniquely the Engineering Style. It is the art of the real—real structure—and its enemy has been the fictive body with which all previous styles have declared their values and expectations. Engineering was the purification of architecture necessary for the final solution—the solution to the problem of existence in historical time. "Objectivity" (*die neue Sachlichkeit*) begins by sorting out conflicting demands, but its aim is to end the conflict by producing the definitive building. Should that happen not styles merely but the historical process must come to an end.

Architecture may well seek to defy time by sheer physical endurance, but it cannot make time stop. We live in history, and believe ourselves ethically obliged to select, resolve, or abandon our problems according to our capacities to sustain life, not terminate it. When for architects modernism's conceptual truths seemed finally to exclude possibilities rather than embrace them, a saving impulse to escape the engineering or utilitarian style found expression in whatever would seem to contradict it—in a taste for contradiction as an end in itself. But before built form can be understood to embody contradiction, both the rule and its exception must be present and intelligible. Hence the characteristic problem for modern architecture in its post-Miesian phase: it acknowledges freedom by seeking to embody divergent possibilities (which it chooses to see as contradictions), but it has not yet dared to relinquish the reductionist imperative of the engineering style. Devised to tell the "truth" about necessity, its form language is now the only language available. And so it happens that the one necessity modern architecture cannot freely confront is the necessity for freedom.

If we did not have to live with the results, architecture would metamorphose into philosophy. Its physical manifestations would be three-dimensional models of truth intended, like the theologian's "disclosure model," to make the transitory bear witness to eternal Being. Tiny Alice, in Edward Albee's play, lives with and in such a disclosure model: her house and the model of itself it contains catch fire simultaneously. The mystery disclosed is that historical time has meaning on earth as in heaven, but we cannot tell whether the Model or the House has a prior claim on the management of reality.[2]

Architects are seldom interested in metaphysical questions, let alone those raised by three-dimensional models. They may accept enthusiastically the idea that among the "instruments of thought" language conditions and may even control what may be thought, but the proper instruments of their own thinking—drawings and models—remain largely unexamined. The model is regarded simply as the most convenient surrogate for a reality that cannot otherwise be apprehended whole and without distortion, where the reality is as yet insubstantial. Like the architecture it represents the model is thought to be "objective," meaning that it corresponds to "facts," which are taken for "truth." Its usefulness in shaping the built reality depends on its prior existence in time: a model made after the reality is achieved is useless except as representation. Of course the model is by no means the only efficient surrogate for the actual building, nor is there only one kind of model. Some models are analogs of mass only; others, of structure; some are meant to offer faithful representations of everything that will be seen. Mies van der Rohe, who knew how to draw, abandoned drawing for scale models that seem realistic, but which like his architecture carefully suppress certain elements in order to present an ideal—as in the model of Crown Hall at Illinois Institute of Technology—which the actual building can only corrupt (p. 16). Louis Kahn, whose preferred medium was drawing, also did not hesitate to limit models to partial representation. The model of his Mikveh Israel Synagogue tells us that his theme was mass, not simply because it was easier to construct without windows, or even because that is how he would have preferred to construct the real building. The model generated its own truth.

Whatever its instrumental role in the process of designing buildings, the

(opposite) Ludwig Mies van der Rohe. Crown Hall, Illinois Institute of Technology. Model, 1952; building, 1955.

The model represents all structural details; only a railing on the entrance platform is omitted. The photograph uses a viewpoint above the eye level of a pedestrian observer to reinforce the concept of transparency, which is further emphasized by a photographic backdrop of trees seen through the glass.

In the actual building, venetian blinds required to make the interior habitable appear as opaque white walls and destroy the intended transparency, but the building is nevertheless meant to be read as if it were the model.

(right) Louis I. Kahn. Mikveh Israel Synagogue, Philadelphia. Project, 1961–70. Model and perspective drawing. The Museum of Modern Art, New York.

The synagogue and a chapel (left and center of model) are compositions of rectangular and cylindrical masses, seemingly as impenetrable as a fortress. Their uniform surfaces and apparent weight, skillfully reinforced by the massive pedestal, make it clear that this is a study in dense sculptural form.

Drawings of the project reveal that the cylinders are hollow volumes meant to function as containers of light, for which purpose their surfaces are largely eroded by glazed openings. The model and the drawing describe architectural effects that are mutually exclusive.

model is seldom the first step. Most likely the architect begins by sketching plans, elevations, and perhaps perspectives; from these he will proceed to more precise drawings from which to build a model. In most schools of architecture today drawing understood as the rendering of light and shadow is a largely forgotten art, forgotten because the play of light and shadow no longer determines architectural form. Model-making is a decisive part of the curriculum, and it is to the requirements and possibilities of the model that students unconsciously respond when they do make drawings. Often a model concludes the design process, if only because it is understood at the outset that no real building will follow—the condition natural to students—but the model is not inevitably the last stage, nor is it necessarily the most advantageous embodiment of an architectural idea. Except for those whose commitment requires a style of presentation addressed to themselves and to other professionals, architects normally regard the visualization of a building and its presentation to the client as two separate problems. Presentation to the client often requires that models be supplemented by a "popular" visual language, for which drawing and photography in the illustrative modes common to advertising are especially suitable. One fixed image at pedestrian eye level may be most easily understood, and models are sometimes made expressly to be photographed or drawn from a single viewpoint. Because today few architects draw, this task is normally assigned to specialists, many of them itinerant, who "render" an image from information provided by plans, elevations, and models; and if a model does not exist some renderers will make one in order to draw it.

Most buildings today are known to students and laymen alike not from direct experience but from published photographs. When a building is finished and ready for publication, photography will often complete the visualizing process with a selective and hallucinating clarity that surpasses anything the architect may have achieved with his original studies. Interiors lend themselves particularly well to photographic editorializing, post facto, because they are so difficult to represent in drawings or models. The one-point perspective characteristic of much architectural photography in the 1950s made diverse modern buildings seem parts of a continuous image revealed in monthly installments, teaching us to see architecture as the photographer saw it. Photographs thus come to serve as exemplars at the very beginning of the design process, encouraging the student to draw effects of scale and perspective that can be seen only through a wide-angle lens with adjustments to eliminate vertical convergence.

Reacting against these distractions, the more thoughtful naturally turn back to "objective" modes of study. Chief among these is one whose special value is to anticipate the model: the axonometric drawing, which provides an image of three dimensions without the optical distortions of scenographic perspective.

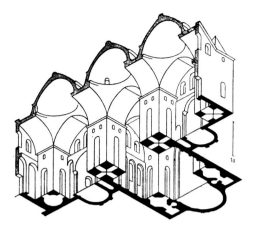

Auguste Choisy. Saint-Front de Périgueux. Plate 15 from *Histoire de l'architecture*, Paris, 1899, vol. II.

Choisy's famous *History* examined buildings of all cultures and times from the point of view of construction, other aspects being demoted to relative insignificance. Construction was illustrated by axonometric drawings whose merits he commented on in an introductory footnote:

"Graphic documents, sometimes simplified by the suppression of superfluous details are, for the most part, presented in axonometric projection, a system which has the clarity of the perspective and lends itself to direct measurement.

"In this system one single image, as lively and animated as the edifice itself, takes the place of abstract figuration broken into plan, section, and elevation.

"The reader has under his eyes at one time, the plan, the exterior of the edifice, its section and its interior dispositions."

In order to synthesize four kinds of information into one image, Choisy's axonometrics require a viewpoint that is physically impossible—most often from beneath the building. He exchanges one kind of abstraction for another, his own being better suited to a conception of architecture that would not have occurred to those whose buildings he analyzes.

Theo van Doesburg and Cornelis van Eesteren. Color Construction (Project for a Private House). 1922. The Museum of Modern Art, New York.

Detached, intersecting, and overlapping planes are shown as if floating in space, substituting a conceptual fantasy for the atmospheric distortions of scenographic perspective, or the information content of Choisy's structural analysis.

Axonometrics were first made popular by Auguste Choisy, who combined plan, sections, and elevations in one image in order to explain and compare different structural modes (*left*). For this purpose they are often quite useful, more so in fact than the remarkable models of French medieval buildings assembled for the same purpose by Viollet-le-Duc and now stored in the Musée des Monuments Français. A peculiarity of Choisy's method is that it works only when the observer is situated below the building, as if in the grave, looking up through the plan and into the large domed spaces that were Choisy's chief interest. Modern architecture retained this conceptual method but reversed the viewpoint, situating the observer in mid-air to look down on two elevations and the roof. Curiously, though this system pretends that the roof is an "elevation," it sacrifices simultaneous information about the plan (which modern architecture considers paramount) except insofar as the elements of a building may be extended upward from a ground plan intact, without vertical transformation and hence without the need for supplementary information. This is most easily done when interior space is no longer the focus of attention (whatever assertions are made to the contrary), and for modern architecture the most persuasive drawings of this kind were those made by such painter-architects as Theo van Doesburg and Cornelis van Eesteren (*above*). Whatever their conceptual departure from the realities of experiencing architectural form, the real merits of axonometric drawings are that they illustrate three-dimensional relationships without distortions of scale; they can

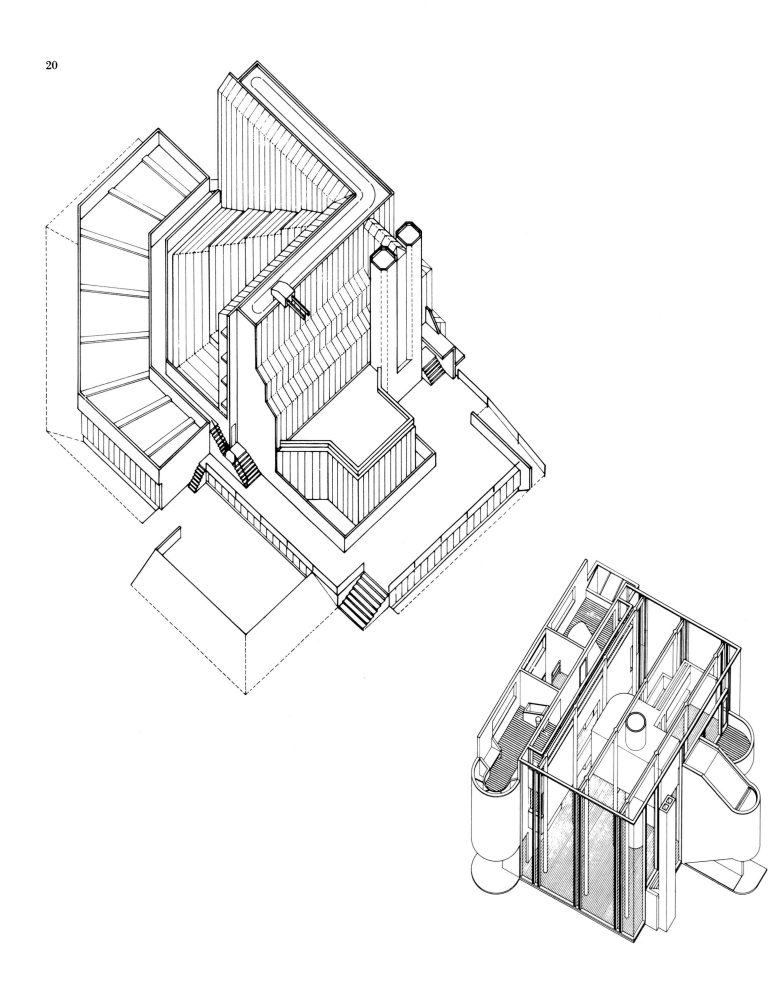

(above) James Stirling. Cambridge University History Building, Cambridge, England. Axonometric. 1964.

Because it keeps all dimensions to scale, axonometric drawing is particularly favored by mechanical engineers for the graphic description of geometric solids. Where architecture seeks to emulate the look of machinery, with complex shapes, chamfered corners, and movable bits of hardware, the axonometric seems to generate its own design solutions. A model can include more information, but only by sacrificing schematic elegance.

(below) Richard Meier. House in Pound Ridge, Connecticut. Axonometric. 1969.

Here the axonometric is used to reveal the inside of a complex three-story house, the roof of the building having been omitted. In all essentials this technique follows the conventions of Japanese scroll painting, wherein the "blown-away-roof" style made it possible to illustrate dramatic events going on in the rooms of a palace.

be drawn quickly and without special skills; and they look technical ("objective") to the degree that they do not look scenographic ("subjective"). They are thus the nearest that drawing can approach to the objectivity of a model.

Useful questions address themselves to the kinds of distortions, or emphases, both model-making and drawing engender. Since both modes of projecting architectural form are supposed to refer to something other than themselves, it must be asked in each case whether a model or a drawing is meant to describe a building as it actually will be; as it will be perceived; or as it ought to be perceived. Of these three distinct conditions, representations of architecture most often claim to be dealing with a building as it actually is or will be, when the fundamental preoccupation in our own as in other times is with the building as it *ought* to be perceived. The model or drawing is a set of instructions telling us what to look for and how to see it. Actualities of perception, which include the physiological limitations of sight, the fortuitous associations individual percipients carry in their heads, and such arbitrary but predictable interventions as moonlight and fog, modern architecture tends to dismiss as the sentimental concern of literary culture. If an Adrian Stokes were to write about office buildings and apartment houses in the self-revealing style of personal sensibility through which he "saw" Venice, his observations would be deemed embarrassing and irrelevant. We are no longer interested in the quality of an individual's perception, let alone entering the web of personal history that conditions response. We prefer instruction about any fact other than the fact of our own sensibility.

The guiding intention behind much modern architectural form and the images through which it is studied is to represent architecture as the product of another art: painting or sculpture. The celebrated modern reintegration of the arts depends on this kind of exchange: buildings whose forms are borrowed from, and approved because they are, abstract painting and sculpture; and painting and sculpture whose modes are admired because they resemble or incorporate the constructed realities of architecture. That art is made from art, despite contributions from economics, technology, social usage, philosophy, and religion, is a fact readily understood by artists if not by the practitioners of other callings. It may entail other things, but a work of art is art because it is not something else. We might therefore consider the possibility that continuity in the arts ought to stop short of transubstantiation: that architecture, for example, ceases to be architecture to the extent that it becomes painting or sculpture—even though the doctrinal history of the modern movement has involved the opposite assumption.

Examples abound. Mies van der Rohe's exhibition drawing for his 1921 glass skyscraper project seems to represent an undulating surface of some opaque material. The accompanying photographic montage, representing the same building as it would be seen on an imaginary site, offers an altogether

Ludwig Mies van der Rohe. Glass Skyscraper. 1921. Drawing *(left)*; photomontage with model *(right)*. The Museum of Modern Art, New York.

Prepared for an exhibition, the drawing renders the vertical mass of a skyscraper as if it were an irregularly fluted column made of an unidentifiable opaque substance.

The model is photographed from an angle that minimizes reflections on its faceted surface and emphasizes transparency. The tower is juxtaposed with rough models representing old buildings, and a background of over-scaled trees. The combination of images and the delicacy of the tower describe with seeming truthfulness an architecture impossible to realize, let alone inhabit.

different image based on the "realism" of a model (p. 23). Since the photographed model is juxtaposed with photographs of old buildings of Hansel and Gretel quaintness, it is fair to assume that the contrast between muddled opacity and diagrammatic transparency is the point of the image. But from neither the photograph nor the drawing would one deduce what Mies claimed to be the real point: "I discovered by working with actual glass models that the important thing is the play of reflections and not the effect of light and shadow as in ordinary buildings."[3] The drawing is meant to establish an association between the idea "skyscraper" and an abstract fragment of shadowed surface. Its possible use as architecture is hinted at by the dark patches, one of which may recall a sloping roof if we already know that it represents a building, and is explicitly stated by GLAS-HOCH-HAUS inscribed at the bottom to dispel any doubts. The point of the drawing is the surprising but not unprecedented suggestion that an impenetrable surface may also be architecture. From the elevation drawing alone one might not deduce the material and certainly not reflectivity as the determinant of form. From the photograph alone, the material might be correctly deduced but one would assume that transparency, not reflectivity, is the determinant. When Mies actually built glass skyscrapers neither reflectivity nor transparency determined their form, but rather "the effect of light and shadow as in ordinary buildings." Neither the beautiful drawing nor the photographed model conveys information as to what a glass building would really be like; their purpose, and their compelling power, is to persuade us that we ought to see and admire the particular qualities of certain kinds of images. More obviously than the model, the drawing does not "represent." It makes the act of drawing substitute for the real condition of a proposed architectural form. That we are persuaded to seek comparable effects in real buildings reminds us that "art is not truth."

Mies juxtaposed his schematic building with examples of the decaying past: as long as the old is still available, contrast with its decay makes more poignant the ideal of immutable crystalline structure. (In the winter of our decline, Spengler reminded his readers, engineering would attract the best minds.) But for Le Corbusier reductionism and efficiency were no more than advantageous propaganda, never entirely allowed to determine form. His 1927 study for the entrance elevation of the Stein House characteristically shows the wall as a paper-thin plane, like a stage flat from which windows might have been cut with a scissors, as Frank Lloyd Wright observed. But the openings are rendered as opaque lavender patches—not the most obvious way of indicating glass—and the sky, essential to this drawing, is like a blue wall on which Le Corbusier has hung a painting. A straightforward perspective drawing like that for the Moscow Centrosoyus office building suggests that its forms are the product of rational intentions, innocent of other mo-

Le Corbusier. Stein House (Villa Stein-De Monzie). Preliminary study, entrance facade. 1927. Fondation Le Corbusier, Paris.

Windows and doors are represented by patches of lavender and earth-red, regardless of actual materials, against a cream-colored wall and a bright blue sky.

Le Corbusier and Jeanneret. Centrosoyus (Central Office of the Union of Cooperatives of the U.S.S.R.). 1928–35. Perspective and model.

Wash tones are used in this relatively straightforward line drawing chiefly to indicate depth; black shadows help to clarify the separation of the three office blocks, although the shadows are inaccurately drawn for the intersection at the far right.

The roof of the model shows that the complex forms of stairs and an auditorium are the focus of the composition, although they are hidden by uncommunicative street elevations. The unity of the composition can be grasped only from above.

tives. Who would guess that its plan is a bas-relief incorporating elements of African sculpture, in the manner of Picasso and Lipchitz?

Le Corbusier's synthesis of engineering, folk idiom, and high art produced masterpieces, disguising those contradictions inherent in the reductionist aesthetic. But even before the Second World War architects had begun to break through the constraints of rationalism. Now, after exercises in Brutalism intended to retrieve effects of mass without seeming to abandon the rational logic of engineering, modern architecture has turned increasingly to a less unwieldy alternative derived from recent Minimal sculpture, whose most interesting aspect is reductionism made irrational. Since it already deals with conceptual ambiguities, Minimal sculpture makes architectural models of itself peculiarly hermetic, like a scientific hypothesis that renders physical embodiment beside the point. The rule preempts practice, in the progression academies so often follow. We have, Paul Valéry wrote in 1935, an aesthetics which

> was not deduced from observation of artistic phenomena, but arrived at by a dialectic method. It is a set of ideas, a variety of assertions originating in an analysis of the conceptions of the mind. The remarkable part of it is that our *classical aesthetics might exist without a single work of art:* in a sense it is quite independent of the existence of art. Dialectical in origin, it speculates on language, and if it speaks of observable artistic phenomena, it takes them as illustrations of rules in the application or breach, not as a point of departure.[4]

Whether they begin, mediate, or conclude the design process, the surrogates of built form now dominate it. Among surrogates the model is preeminent. Its effect on the architect's thought does not seem problematic because we still believe that when we think of the "reality" we have in mind an actual building. But when the primary object of the architect's deliberations is the model itself, the "real" building stands to it in the interesting but superfluous relationship of a giant copy of an egg to its miniature original. We would be unwise to dismiss this as inconsequential, when we are quick to recognize that for the nineteenth century, and for the Ecole des Beaux-Arts above all, it was the exquisite drawing that finally replaced the actualities it claimed to describe.

* * *

Nineteenth-century plans are more immediately appealing to the modern architect than the elevations and masses they imply. Because French theory eventually insisted on the primacy of the plan, and because that conviction has been reinforced by modern architecture, we read the plans and visualize buildings their architects never thought of. The appeal of such plans and their supposed clarity depend on an incomplete, and therefore inaccurate, response to qualities of graphic design. The plans we like best are those that resemble modern art. Utilitarian buildings provided some of the most interesting problems for the first two or three decades of the nineteenth century, and because the classical Orders were largely omitted in such problems their plans benefit, to the modern eye, by virtue of the repetition of a few simple elements: square and rectangular piers, unbroken walls, and occasional small accents either concentrated as apparently solid masses or extended as colonnades.

All of these elements are to be found in Louis-Ambroise Dubut's plan for Public Granaries, his 1797 Grand Prix project (pp. 31 and 126). His ideas retain the unmistakable stamp of Ledoux and Boullée, and in particular illustrate Boullée's dictum that the manner of envisioning architecture is pictorial. Above all, this building and its environs are scenography; its plan is its least persuasive aspect. The watercolor elevation is a painting of a townscape, and includes flanking groups of buildings and mountains, a softly clouded sky, a foreground of lively marine detail, smoking fires, and people at work or admiring the building. Although the scene has that air of deserted peacefulness we know from the landscape paintings of Claude and Poussin, there is nothing of melancholy about it; the observer can readily imagine the life of the community and the uses of particular buildings, and might well choose one of them as an agreeable place to live.

The rendering of the Granaries adheres strictly to the conventions of elevation drawing. This means that changes in plane produced by advancing or receding masses can be indicated only by cast shadows and minor variations of tone. But in the flanking buildings Dubut supplements elevations parallel to the picture plane with one-point perspective, so that he can illustrate side elevations. (The two groups of buildings each have their own vanishing point.) One recognizes a shift in professional, specialized intent, away from the painter's conventions of perspective to indicate the position of masses in space, toward the exclusive and accurate depiction of a frontal plane. In picturing the Granaries Dubut has denied himself the use of perspective just where it would have been most helpful scenographically: in making clear that the two central towers are closest to the observer, and that the central portion of the building is farthest away. In fact the upper tier of the central portion is on the opposite side of the building; it could not possibly be seen in conjunction with the facade unless the entire composition was shown in aerial perspective. The "accuracy" of the drawing obscures what we might have supposed to be its most important feature. The very contrast between the flanking groups in perspective and the frontally described Granaries tells us what we are supposed to look for. The ensemble provides a rudimentary vocabulary suggesting how background buildings, as they are still called, may avoid monotony. What differentiates the Granaries from the other buildings is a single variation on one theme: the basic element of the design is a square pier carrying a round-headed arch springing from impost plates; the variation, appearing on the upper floor, is a second round-headed arch within the larger one, but this time carried on small freestanding piers to produce a kind of Venetian window. Architecture is thus a matter of inflection achieved by embellishment, additively, and by diminution of scale. Dubut's plan, with its somewhat improbable reliance on a too skeletal masonry structure, offers clear but perfunctory modulations of space and circulation. Automatically the eye reads this plan as implying a modern cagelike transparency of elevation; the reality that interested Dubut is a pierced and decorated masonry shell.

No such disparity figures in the extraordinarily subtle and complex project of 1823 by Félix Duban, his Grand Prix entry for a Customshouse and Tollhouse. The dramatic elevation of this building as it would be seen from the waterfront is no less scenographic than Dubut's picture of his Granaries, although the building and its entourage of embankment and gardens are shown without reference to a related townscape. Another, more conventional elevation drawing shows the building as it would appear from the town, and two sections through the major and minor axes, as well as a detail section of part of the warehouse, all support a large plan drawing (pp. 32 and 146–47). No one of these drawings is entirely intelligible without reference to all the others, and certainly from the plan alone it would be impossible to deduce the ingenious orchestration Duban composes from the functional requirements of the program. The analogy with music is justified. Duban's plan follows sonata allegro form—exposition, development, recapitulation—but with the advantage peculiar to architecture that the sequence may be experienced both forward and backward, as it were, depending on which side of the building one chooses as its beginning. The preferred sequence is chosen for us by Duban. The problem called for a Customshouse and Tollhouse able to receive and discharge cargo from both the river the building abuts and the town it faces. Following a convention of plan drawings he places the "main" town entrance at the bottom of the sheet. (His competitors chose to reverse the order of importance; pp. 148–49).

The motif of doubled entrances, by water and by land, Duban elaborates along his major axis. Entrance from the town is through a kind of triumphal arch opening directly onto a covered street; at the opposite side of the building entrance from the water is by means of a canal, which passes through another triumphal arch and flows down a street open to the sky. Both streets lead to a rectangular water basin extending along the minor axis and surrounded by the warehouse, and both streets contain twin opposing facades midway down their lengths: on the town side these are the colonnaded entrances to administrative blocks; on the water side they are the loggia-like entrances to customs offices and stables.

The cruciform configuration with its two additional transverse bars is con-

Louis-Ambroise Dubut. Public Granaries. 1797. Left and right sides of elevation drawing.

Dubut flanks his own building with views of an imaginary town whose architectural vocabulary ranges from Roman temples to simple, box-like structures, with and without the classical Orders. Collectively they demonstrate the adjustment of formal resources to signify value. Derived substantially from Ledoux, these buildings also suggest the orderly but picturesque groupings of German Romantic Classicism. Perspective is essential to their presentation, but presumably in the interest of an ideal accuracy Dubut eliminates perspective from the elevation of his granaries. The entire drawing is shown opposite; a color reproduction appears on pp. 126–27.

(opposite below) School of Piero della Francesca. Architectural Study. National Gallery, Urbino.

This painting illustrates Alberti's specifications for the chief piazza in his ideal city. The main feature of most of the buildings is a portico for shade and shelter; a round temple dominates the public square. In this as in similar Renaissance compositions perspective is used consistently throughout.

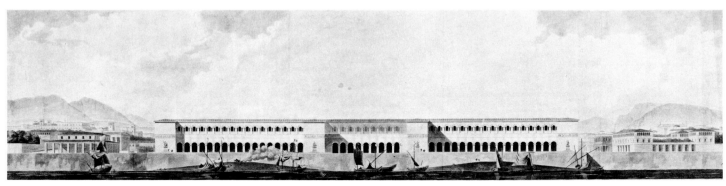

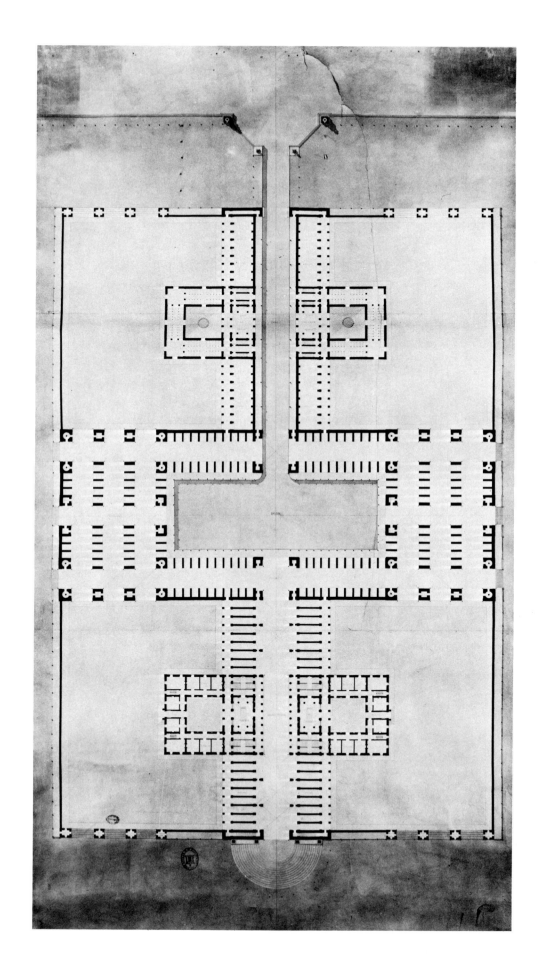

Félix Duban. Customshouse and Tollhouse. 1823. Plan.

This is one of two plan drawings in Duban's presentation. A second plan including the layout of the site is illustrated with sections and elevations on pp. 146–47.

tained within low boundary walls misleadingly drawn in the same dark *poché* used for the building proper. Adherence to this draftsman's convention was not mandatory: its use here has more to do with Duban's desire to enclose his composition of squares and lines, even at the cost of being unable to differentiate the relative heights of the masses they represent. The elevation drawings also have their characteristic problem of wall elements, actually distant from each other, seeming to inhabit the same plane. For example, the entrance elevation suggests that the triumphal arch is no more than a portico projecting from the main three-story block. But the plan reveals that what appears to be the main block is in fact at least 100 feet behind the arch and, moreover, is not at all the main block: it is the administration wing, which on the ground-level plan appears as two separate units, but which the elevation discloses to be unified by the addition of a third story straddling the major axis. The tripled giant arch motif repeated at each side, on the elevation drawing, is in fact still farther back and is part of the transverse wall of the warehouse. Formal implications of symmetry notwithstanding, Duban has chosen to make the administration block, not the central warehouse, the highest element in the composition—presumably because it is the only element that could be perceived as such when approached from the town.

A similar mingling of planes occurs in the elevation of the entire complex as it appears from the water. From this drawing and the longitudinal section one learns that the water level is one full story below the grade level of the plan. The embankment therefore adds an additional story to the composition, and one observes that entrance to the canal is under an arched bridge of the same masonry as the embankment itself. Some fifty feet beyond it the bridge is repeated, and this time it carries the large triumphal arch motif. (Both bridges are visible at the extreme left of the longitudinal section, but are arbitrarily omitted from the plan.) The service wings flanking the canal correspond to the administration block but are the lowest, not the highest, roofed enclosures in the entire composition; only those portions aligned with the workshops bordering the canal are slightly higher (as shown by their facades in the longitudinal section). More than the elevation, the longitudinal section makes clear that the symmetrical disposition of masses in plan is countered by an asymmetrical development of their heights.

Duban's primary interest is the unexpected juxtaposition of major and minor scales, and the usual difficulty of indicating relative depths in elevation drawings is actually incorporated into the conception and used to generate its thematic development. Thus the major scale, stated by the void of the giant arch, is derived from the width and the two-story height of the circulation system. The minor scale, stated by the width of the piers, is derived from the depth of a storage bay. The width of a storage bay gives the still smaller interval at which the pier-and-arch is repeated. Turning the circulation

34

system 90° at the ends of the warehouse block and repeating it three times juxtaposes the largest and smallest units and produces the most dramatic manipulation of scale in the entire composition. But this cannot be deduced from the ground level plan alone, because the lower parts of the transverse warehouse walls are shown as solids. Only the elevation on the water side shows these walls to be entirely open on their upper tier, and pierced by at least three windows below (their round-headed tops just visible behind the stable blocks).

Duban's conception clearly depends on a straightforward analysis of function and structure. The elements he works with have their origin in Roman utilitarian building, but their development is prompted by his method of visualizing them. A model or a perspective would make the relationships easier to understand, but would omit just those juxtapositions, fictitious but conceptually decisive, that are inseparable from the form language of elevation drawings.

Utilitarian buildings are easier to design than those that acknowledge non-utilitarian social values. The only great public space in Duban's scheme is its central water basin; the circulation system generates almost everything else. Symbolic expression is part of the value of the giant arch, but Duban evidently felt no need to pursue more explicit associations with civil authority. When the problem is precisely to make explicit the social value attached to buildings, the architect's task is simplified if society is in agreement as to the meaning and value of its institutions. An instructive example is Henri Labrouste's Grand Prix project of 1824 for a *Tribunal de Cassation*, a kind of high court which, it was explained, was even more important than a Palais de Justice. Besides describing the required accommodation the program instructed students to use a "noble and severe" style. Labrouste responded with a Greek portico overlayed on blank walls, and with a single colonnade centered on each of the other elevations (p. 157). Noble, severe, and direct if not simple-minded, the plan contrasts elongated rectangles with square courtyards. The staccato rhythm of colonnades enhances certain rooms and mediates transitions. Labrouste's drawing style heightens this conception by rendering walls and columns with careful monochrome washes; apart from detail there is little to divert the eye, but to read the fine detail requires the concentration one would devote to a document. The notion of justice is meant to be conveyed by severity; that is, from what has been withheld rather than from what has been given.

Besides the mandatory plan, elevation, and section drawings, Labrouste submitted another sheet joining in one beautiful composition an enlarged plan of the glass-roofed atrium with a roof plan of the whole building painted in delicate values of gray, yellow, and tan (p. 158). Both these images are superfluous to an understanding of the project, and the plan fragment in par-

Pompeii. House of Lucretius Fronto, detail of a mural. A.D. 50–60.

Painted on the wall of a *tablinum*, the cage-like structures in the upper part of this mural recall the pavilions and trellises of garden architecture. The second and fourth of the four successive styles of Roman wall painting were concerned in various ways with suggesting an imaginary world on the other side of a wall; the third style dealt with an impossible architecture of thin lines and infinite space. In some cases masks and temple facades imply a religious content or evoke the stage of a theater; in others the fantasy of dematerialization was pursued for its own sake.

ticular misrepresents it; but in combination they are emblematic of Labrouste's temperament: subtle, tenacious, protestant, and capable of inducing guilt in architects less fastidious. For Labrouste architecture was a matter of intensification: in this case of volume through elongation, and of surface through minute detail; but his refinement and "purity" had little to do with his later well-known interest in iron construction. He was not a twentieth-century engineer martyred to nineteenth-century historicism, as he is made to appear in Sigfried Giedion's canonization. On the contrary, he was predisposed to influences scarcely associated with the constraints of rationalism. Pompeian wall paintings, which he studied and drew while in Italy, apparently influenced him deeply. It was the impulse to dematerialize architecture that energized the weightless, whimsical stage decor portrayed in the later Pompeian styles. Dematerialization of structure—without the mystic meaning it had for Gothic architecture but with something of its original Roman fantasy—is vital to Labrouste's Bibliothèques Sainte-Geneviève and Nationale, where Pompeian columns like threads best express his "whim of iron." Painting, or more precisely a kind of visual surrealism possible only to painting, was perhaps more congenial to Labrouste's notion of architecture than was architecture itself.

Labrouste's drawing style for his Ecole projects does not generate architectural ideas, except in the sense that a meticulous technique is in his case more comfortable with flat expanses of sparsely decorated surface. The surviving drawings for the interior of the Bibliothèque Sainte-Geneviève lack even this compatability; they are handsome and clear enough, but they do not elaborate or intensify the thought behind the design. Indeed they tend to obscure it, as if Labrouste were not quite willing to acknowledge all his motives. They might have been made for him by other accomplished draftsmen skilled in rendering small detail: for example, Guadet, whose 1864 Grand Prix for a

Hospice in the Alps is interesting chiefly for the interior of its chapel, where surfaces are divided and embellished through strong, opaque color; or Blondel, whose 1868 *rendu* for the Portal of a Church uses fine black lines filled in with transparent washes (pp. 257, 289). The seemingly sun-drenched yellow ocher of this elevation is a pictorial effect independent of the design. Blondel's sense of atmosphere calls for a particular quality of light and perhaps even a time of day, but the abundant detail makes few concessions to the subjective experience the drawing suggests.

Not until the advent of Charles Garnier's bravura style does the pictorial generation of architectural form again become decisive. Of all nineteenth-century French architecture Garnier's is the most difficult to understand today. It is of no help that his formidable planning skill could make a building work in perfect harmony with the demands of its program, or that his declared concern for "sincerity" required exterior massing to reflect interior realities. These characteristics make him more of a proto-modern than did his willingness to use whatever suited his purpose: it is his purpose we reject. Garnier regarded himself not as a technician manipulating quantities of materials, but as a psychologist whose role was to observe and accommodate human behavior through the medium of architecture. In this respect he anticipated those architects and sociologists whose recent clear-eyed appraisals of public housing, and the anti-social behavior it so often encourages, have forced us to question the relationship between built form and the response it elicits. That relationship Garnier regarded as the beginning of architecture.

For Garnier as for the society he served, the behavior to be encouraged and the opportunities available to him were those that facilitated social pleasures. His best and most famous building, the Paris Opéra, is an essay in the pleasure of opulence confirmed by worldly approval. Opulence, like Shakespeare's Cleopatra, makes hungry where it most satisfies: too much is not enough. Garnier's architectural occasion—the most important opera house in France—was qualified by those conditions of society that relate certain pleasures to certain people. By the 1920s and '30s in the United States, architectural opulence, if not the ceremony that once accompanied it, had become a pleasure available to everyone through the advent of the movie palace. But opulence as an architectural virtue has made its way since the First World War steadily downward through the cultural strata of society: today it is the exclusive province of the uninstructed. Moreover, we no longer know how to achieve it even when we think it might be desirable, not because we have grown more sophisticated but because the far more wasteful kinds of entertainment available to us have the advantage of being ephemeral. Thus our difficulties in responding to Garnier's Paris Opéra include our own ambivalent attitudes about what constitutes acceptable extravagance, and our conviction that in architecture it must be disguised. "We will have simplicity,"

Mies is supposed to have remarked, "no matter how much it costs."[5]

The circumstances under which Garnier won the competition for the Opéra, the excellence of his plan, and his own statements about it are examined at length elsewhere in this book (pp. 261*ff.*). What is of interest here is his conception of architectural ornament and the drawings produced in his atelier to study its effects. A model of the Opéra and full-size mock-ups of certain details were kept in the office Garnier established at the construction site, and no doubt both the progress of the work and occasional changes were recorded on the models; but the scale and quantity of the detail guaranteed that it could be designed only in drawings.

Among the drawings reproduced in this book, the preliminary elevation best states the underlying architectural theme Garnier borrowed from classical Rome, as already transformed by Bramante and Michelangelo, and by Claude Perrault for the east front of the Louvre. As the studies progressed this theme was reinforced and sometimes disguised: those parts of the building that address themselves to public ceremony invariably combine a skeletal network of giant-order columns with parapets and entablatures on a foreground plane, behind which is a second plane combining smaller-scale columns and perforated wall surfaces. Ornament is added or subtracted as the studies evolve, apparently alternating between a desire to clarify or to blur the separation between the two planes. An example is the ornament in the frieze, immediately above the giant order of double columns, in the loggia of the principal facade. The frieze ornament is present in the preliminary drawing (p. 263), more detailed in the crisp watercolor study (p. 276), and subdued in the finished building (p. 437). In the drawings the broken surface of this frieze forces it back onto the plane of the secondary wall system, lightens the visual weight of the whole entablature, and emphasizes line rather than mass. In the finished building the calmer surface seems to move forward to become part of a heavy entablature, with the effect that relative diminution of ornament makes the composition weightier.

The theme of doubled motifs is repeated in the great stair hall. Twin columns here carry two tiers of semicircular arches; the second plane is the perimeter wall of the surrounding gallery. Although smooth the columns are multicolored, and the consequent agitation of their surfaces blends with the dense detail between the arches above and on the wall behind them. Both the scale of the ornament and its quantity are expanded throughout this most public space, and if the skeletal network is emphasized in the final drawings and even in photographs, the actual experience is less one of columns than of wall. Garnier's fantasia of the sumptuous required that columns expand to make another kind of surface.

Perhaps the most evocative drawing is one in which ornament is suggested with deliberate imprecision, avoiding sharp outlines and conveying the effect of incessant surface modulation relieved only by openings cut into it—but since two of these openings are filled by mirrors they would reflect the same modulation on another plane (p. 275). What we are shown is an elaborate setting for two couples costumed and posed in a style recalling Constantin Guys (whose sketches of Parisian life were the subject of a book Baudelaire published in 1863). This painterly image is like an illustration to a romance: "...the overture had begun, yet Isabel and Léon lingered in the Grand Foyer, unaware that at that moment the two people who could assure their happiness were..." The human presence is essential to Garnier's architecture. While the drawings quite often show people, they omit the sculpture with which the major spaces were later permanently inhabited, so to speak, and it is the sculpture that contributes so heavily to our discomfort. Simpering nymphs are always odd, but less demanding when airborne or safely at rest on cornices; one does not expect to find them at one's elbow, like hostesses (p. 438).

The more commodious the space in which to linger, the more elaborate the detail. Thus the stair hall is like a plaza surrounded by streets, all encased in ornament signaling the appropriate rate of movement. Only when Garnier wants movement to be quick does he eliminate ornament entirely, as in the plain embrasures of the doors. Ornament is supplemented by other devices suggesting movement: the compound curves of the stair itself, echoed in the projecting balconies overlooking the hall, in the dome, and in the flattened arches used for the ceilings of the Grand Foyer. The alternation between these asymmetrically flowing curves and the stabilized semicircular arches contributes to the effect of animation, but it also creates uncomfortable disparities ornament cannot resolve. In part this is because baroque movement is superimposed on a network of essentially static forms, and the more violently such quasi-structural details as the uppermost tier of archivolts in the stair hall are enlarged and elaborated, the more jarring their effect.

Color is used to lock the parts together, and it is finally the color of the drawings that focuses attention on the difference between what Garnier avowed and the architectural character he actually achieved. Whether they are improvisations or finished studies the drawings exhibit a continuous evolution toward darker, more somber color. From Garnier's written account one would suppose that he intended the air of festivity to be sustained by the bright shimmering colors of Bavarian Rococo. Instead he follows not only the architectural settings for ceremony in the paintings of Veronese (whom Garnier himself cited), but also a color scheme that darkens the Italian painter's palette. It is the color lithographs published by Garnier after the building was completed that present the most accurate record of its original appearance, and in these an undertone vaguely sensed in the building becomes its manifest content (p. 432). The emotional resonance of this work is more complicated than the qualities Garnier advertised with such cheerfulness. The Opéra has an undertone of malaise that belies public festivity. Dark gold and dark brown, and scarlet bitten with acidulous blue and malachite green, are the psychologizing colors of portraiture, not decoration, and like a portrait the building admits to an anxiety that is finally and irremediably private.

Garnier's building is a series of tableaux best studied in elevational fragments. For managing the movement of crowds the plan could scarcely be improved, but because the building is a compact mass and its major spaces are themselves parts of a circulation system, the plan does not exhibit those linear qualities of graphic design characteristic of circulation developed as an independent network. The practical advantages of such independence include flexibility (notwithstanding the limits implied by symmetry) and an organizational clarity that still makes such buildings a pleasure to use. The disadvantage is that the circulation system tends to become so large and so elaborately articulated that it outweighs everything else. Although this tendency characterized school work more than professional practice, it is also true that generous horizontal extension was often the only practical means of accommodating complex programs, when elevators were lacking and artificial light was problematic. Less readily understandable was the tendency to impose on individual rooms the scale and character of the circulation system. At its most compulsive, the preoccupation with grid patterns generated by crossed axes suppressed variety and contrast in interior spaces, despite ample precedents from classical Rome and, for that matter, eighteenth-century planning in both France and England. The more dominant the circulation grid the more it resembles the plaid-like patterns of a Mondrian painting, overwhelming or crowding out the life it is supposed to sustain but yielding graphic rhythms of hypnotic intensity.

Such single-mindedness was of course not inevitable. The program of Victor Baltard's 1833 Grand Prix for a Military School afforded a planning opportunity he was quick to grasp. Seven longitudinal and nine transverse axes in the main block are as insistent as compulsion could make them, but what is remarkable about the plan is its use of the required lecture halls to make nine semicircular battlements on three elevations (p. 190). It is noteworthy because the Ecole's axial planning tends to absorb such disparate volumes, concealing them on elevations but expressing them, more often, as centralized, domical masses. Intersections at crossing axes become critical points in modulating scale and marking the change in direction. One line of development, indicated by Honoré Daumet's Grand Prix of 1855 for a Conservatory, explores some of the possibilities of changing directional emphasis on the upper floor (p. 224). In doing this Daumet introduces a second set of pavilion-like termini that fall in the middle rather than at the ends of the several axes. Neither elevations nor section drawings adequately convey the complexity

Daumet achieves with this relatively simple device—it can be grasped only from a roof plan—and indeed the elevation drawing misleads not only with the usual juxtaposing of planes that are far removed from each other, but also by suggesting symmetry at a scale so large that it could never be seen as such. The device of intersecting linear masses that change directional emphasis from level to level, with varying degrees of architectural incident at key points of intersection, is an Ecole interpretation that has greater affinities with the temple and palace architecture of the Orient than with Rome. It was carried over into such examples of axial planning as Frank Lloyd Wright's Imperial Hotel, which employed symmetrically disposed axes, terminal pavilions, and alternations of directional emphasis, but rather than maintain their separateness Wright added the cantilevered horizontal roofs of the Orient in order to weave the component parts together.

Daumet's Conservatory and Wright's Imperial Hotel also have in common several major spaces of public assembly, flanked by less interesting lines of repetitive cell-like spaces for private use. The program of Paul Bigot's 1900 Grand Prix for a Thermal Bath and Casino is so extravagantly devoted to large public spaces that it is clearly intended—at least in Bigot's interpretation—as a pretext for the virtuoso manipulation of their shapes, sequence, and connection (p. 318). His most interesting result is the dissolution of form, especially in the central gambling Casino, and in the partly open-air complex of theaters and gardens to its right on the plan. In the Casino alone Bigot juxtaposes some eighteen different secondary spaces with a large central hall, mediating the transitions by enormous masonry piers whose shapes respond to the different configurations that surround them. The complexity of spatial relationships and the interweaving of several different structural scales produces a plan pattern as intricate as a Persian rug. From this plan, however, Bigot derives clumsy elevations in a pastiche of basilicas, domes, and minarets. His interest is focused on the aesthetics of the plan, and even such archaic pictorial devices as trees drawn in aerial perspective, with trailing shadows, are thrown in to sustain the patterns of clustered dots that seem to be in the process of exploding. Reflecting a preoccupation of the Ecole at the end of the century, Bigot's essay recapitulates Piranesi's fanciful plan of Rome, conceptualizing the plan as free play—the plan as ornament—but without a commensurate interpretation of mass and volume. That the program itself is absurd, although not necessarily more so than that for a hotel in Las Vegas, is beside the point. Bigot and his fellow students were absorbed in an exploration of form—specifically, one that involved structural masses as "residual" but active elements—not unlike current student exercises in plan diagonals with their consequent residual spaces, as derived from work by Louis Kahn. For Kahn such intricacies were justified by an alleged improvement in the quality of accommodation, expected to result from the

Frank Lloyd Wright. Imperial Hotel, Tokyo. 1915–22. Plan.

The massing of the building employs major and minor axes, terminated by pavilion-like projections. Square and rectangular masonry piers are used for some walls and circulation corridors. Although symmetrical in layout, symmetry is largely abandoned at the intersections of the various elements where Wright characteristically elides the transition from one space to the next. The rhythm and weight assigned to the various axes change from the ground floor to the upper level, and all the parts are tied together by numerous stringcourses and the overhanging roofs.

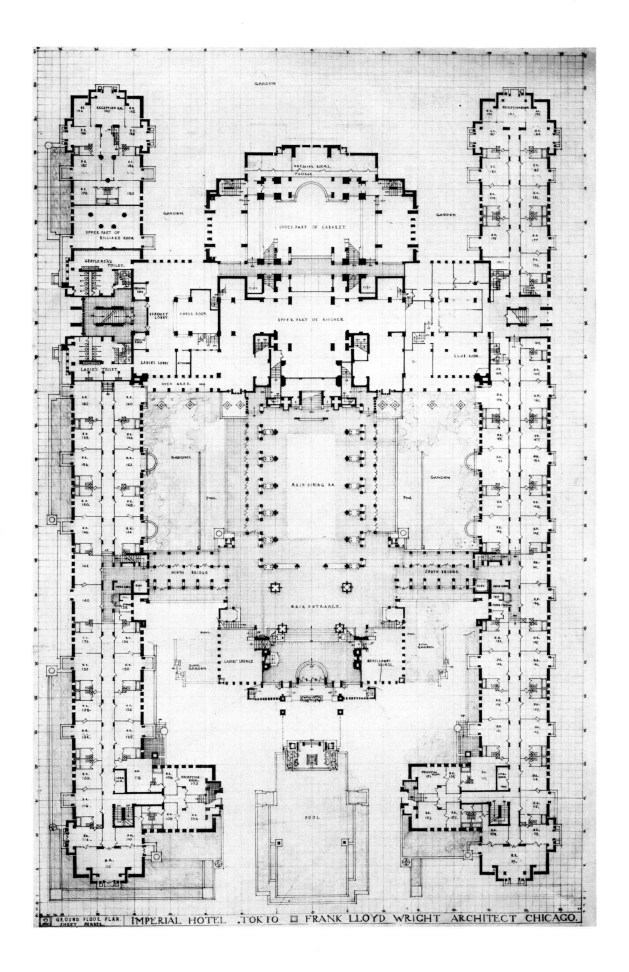

GROUND FLOOR PLAN. IMPERIAL HOTEL . TOKIO ▢ FRANK LLOYD WRIGHT ARCHITECT CHICAGO.

particularization of each element. For Bigot the justifications did not need to be labored, and his spaces are determined only by considerations of contrast and scale.

Where the small size of a building or some peculiarity of the program forced a circulation system into a subordinate role, the Ecole generated paradigms more compatible with modern constraints. An excellent example is François-Louis Boulanger's 1834 *rendu* for a Library (p. 181). Here the point of the circulation system is to limit or prevent rather than encourage access. The long main room is divided into five equal bays by transverse walls meeting in semicircular arches, and each groin-vaulted bay is lighted by high semicircular windows. Lining the walls of each section is a three-story wood gallery for book storage, treated as an insert of cabinet work with its own details and its appropriate scale. Behind these wood linings is a masonry double-wall system for interior access—what might be described in modern terms as "working-walls"—and behind these are reading rooms overlooking enclosed gardens. In plan, the double-walled main block of this building makes a "modern" graphic entity by virtue of its repetition of shapes and its contrast of line weights, so that the eye tends to discount the perimeter arcade as superfluous. But the walled gardens are of course the view that makes the reading rooms so agreeable. That Boulanger was uncertain of the proper relationship between the perimeter rooms and their view is clear from the manner in which his plan renders reading-room windows: besides being too small they are toned to blend with, rather than open up, the heavy outer wall. Graphic in origin, the problem is inseparable from the manner of drawing the doubled masonry shell: one of its two thick black lines "belongs" simultaneously to the central core and to the perimeter rooms. Thus the windowed outer wall can have no echo in the doubled core walls unless their uniformity is disrupted, which Boulanger chose to avoid for reasons of graphic purity. But the interest of this plan depends less on Boulanger's talent than on the possibilities suggested by an underlying formal clarity of purpose. One of these possibilities is the distinction between internal and external—between two aspects of "truth." Thus the uncommunicative facade is meant to announce the presence of a public benefit without advertising its internal workings; on these terms Boulanger scarcely makes the most of his opportunity. Another possibility, more skillfully exploited, is the easy manipulation of scale. In this the logic of classical architecture sustains Boulanger and seems almost to guarantee admirable results.

* * *

Until the advent of the utilitarian engineering style, architecture always and everywhere insisted upon the distinction between itself and building. The former is the domain of freedom of action, conscious choice, and ulterior motives; the latter is the domain of minimum effort in response to external necessity. The modern movement continues this distinction in practice—it cannot be suppressed—but has maintained that the distinction is theoretically invalid: architecture is art; if art decides the outcome the ethical integrity of building is somehow compromised; better therefore to suppress art. If art cannot be suppressed it should imitate building, because art delights in metaphors and the honest speech of building has been imagined to do without them. By that virtue architecture expected to free itself, first from the historic styles whose fixed forms inhibited new responses to new problems, and ultimately from the notion of style itself. Structural technique alone emerged as the interwoven thread whereby the diversity of styles could be understood as a unified manifestation of human purpose. For every other aspect attention focused on whatever makes the styles differ from each other, ignoring the one assumption on which all of them rest, including our own: architecture entails a conscious effort to establish a hierarchy of values.

The effort to decide what is important—to declare value—is something about which we have no choice. It is a function of human intelligence, and to suppose that its difficulties can be avoided is to advocate that we make ourselves stupid. Making our choices intelligible demands a flexibility of architectural speech that accepts the distinction between form and content: the medium is *not* the message, except when we no longer know what we wish to say. Even when what we wish to say is precisely that the medium *is* the message, we end by making the medium disclose a message we have in fact brought to it. When we know what we wish to say we begin to choose our words, exposing our desire to accept or avoid responsibility for what we say. In the sense that architecture is a language, modern architecture has been embarrassed by the usages of articulate speech. As John Summerson observed, it attempts to avoid the subjunctive: that which is grammatically subordinate and possibly contrary to fact, as when one prefers to say "if I were" rather than "I am." We prefer architecture to speak of and through the "real," which we understand has its root and flower in structural technique. Having denied to architecture its fictive body, we limit ourselves to such complications of truth as can be forced from structure and surface, or from the unwarranted enlargement of the insignificant. Virtuoso displays of technique and monodic form, divorced from problems of value, are among the achievements of modern architecture for which we pay a high price. It is no accident that we encounter great difficulties in the management of scale—difficulties so great that we tend to celebrate our failures by declaring scalelessness to be just what we set out to achieve.

All problems of composition in modern architecture culminate in problems of scale. The size of things in themselves and in relation to each other affects the management of form, in buildings of all kinds and in all places, from

pastoral to urban. The modern movement considers scale to be a peculiarly urban problem, and most often a problem of insufficiency. Failures of urban planning are characteristically attributed to making buildings too small, rather than to any problem inherent in our conception of architecture. The megastructure, an idea which gains ascendancy when utopian thought overtakes reality, was championed by Le Corbusier in the early '30s and taken up again by other architects in the '50s and '60s, despite all the evidence available by then to suggest that as a response to various urban ailments the megastructure might be the cure that finally kills. One advantage of arguments in favor of the megastructure, used by Le Corbusier but ignored by other architects, is that by generating built form so encompassing that it replaces the natural landscape, decisions as to the substance of architecture are indefinitely postponed because they are made to seem frivolous. Thus Le Corbusier's 1928 proposal for a linear structure like a multistory superhighway incorporates duplex "villas" in traditional North African as well as modern industrial styles, absurdity being regarded as one of the rewards of the

Le Corbusier. Project for a Road-Building: Algiers. 1930–34.

Le Corbusier noted that while governments are able to overcome all obstacles affecting superhighways, they falter when faced with problems of urban renewal. His solution was to combine roads and buildings, producing a variation on the linear city concept. His first proposals (for Rio de Janiero) called for a fourteen-mile-long, fourteen-story-high, continuous serpentine building. For Algiers he proposed many such structures to link dispersed communities. Each has one

highway on the roof and one on an intermediate level. The double-height floors would be built and owned by the state as *"terrains artificiels."* Private individuals would obtain long-term leases and then build within the structure whatever they wanted. Thus Le Corbusier's sketch includes a villa with horseshoe arches and small balconies in the manner of North African folk architecture. What was meant as a witticism is in fact a critique: the megabuilding would have to tolerate the superfluous, since that is what it renders everything other than itself.

system. Because not even the most authoritarian societies have yet found the resources or indeed the reason for building such megastructures, architects advocating them are able to attribute to politicians a paralyzing lack of imagination in dealing with urban problems at a truly modern scale, while at the same time they are able to avoid dealing with problems generated by their own notions of scale and form.

For most cultures the decisive intention in the management of architectural form is to convey the idea of stability, wholeness, and value. Even where form is cellular and additive, producing numerous distinct components of a single building, the organization of parts proceeds according to a sense of stability which places the heaviest and largest at the center. It requires that the transition to the perimeter be gradual and intelligible, and the latter requirement is most often satisfied by symmetry. The inherently static nature of such composition has usually implied a complementary animation of the component parts. Against this the modern movement asserted the advantages of asymmetry as a more straightforward response to function. But the consequences of an a priori commitment to asymmetry are that it tends to render the relationship between component parts unintelligible: the dynamic balance which may in fact be present can be perceived only from the plan, the model, or an aerial view. The experience of the building itself is least likely to reveal its order, unless the intent be specifically to thwart the experience of wholeness. The history of architecture does offer some profoundly beautiful buildings that do have just this intent, but they are not from our own industrial culture. The asymmetrical, deliberately fragmented and incomplete architecture of large private houses at various periods of Chinese and Japanese history is the expression of a quasi-religious, quietist view of man's place in the natural world. Such buildings are inconceivable apart from their gardens, within which they are only sheltering incidents.

No such world view determines the modern Western use of asymmetry, which seeks out restlessness as proof of dynamic intelligence transforming the natural world. In its secondary levels of organization asymmetry replaces minor animation, in the context of a larger stability, with an unbroken, metronomic rhythm imposed throughout all levels of detail. Mindless regularity, first justified as the straightforward response to the mass production of industrial building components, then becomes an end in itself. Misconceptions about scale, at their most trivial but exasperating, can be illustrated by the abuse of the adjective *human*. Thus the dividing up of a perimeter wall in a large office building is predetermined by the dimensions an individual human requires for an inhabitable room, one, two, or three identical modules of window providing the acceptable minimum. Beginning with a module most closely related to human size, the effect of its reiteration over a facade several hundred feet wide and perhaps fifty stories tall is of course inhuman, in the sense that individual identity is submerged and ultimately lost in the formation of an infantry parade. Inseparable from the notion of architecture as "problem-solving"—the problem is always supposed to have been generated by technology—is the notion that once a solution has been found it is universally applicable. It was precisely the willful enlargement of a few selected components into a larger than human scale that maintained both identity and coherence in the classical composition the modern movement rejected, although it must be said that Le Corbusier, from his 1938 proposal for a skyscraper in Algiers to his Secretariat Building at Chandigarh, never abandoned the search for modern equivalents to classical usage.

For some of our urban problems the form language and the compositional methods of classical architecture are beside the point, even though most efforts to transcend modern theory revert to classical imagery. Thus John Barrington Bayley's proposal for the renewal of New York City's Columbus Circle begins with the clear understanding that the real problem is the crea-

John Barrington Bayley. A New Opera House, Theater, and Forum, with Halls for Public Assembly and Civic Reception on Columbus Circle designed in The New Roman Style. 1958.

The classicizing impulse understands architecture's primary role as the creation of the public place, and it makes the assumption that modern societies, whether capitalist or socialist, might yet have the will to clarify the distinction between public and private. Bayley's ambitious and witty proposal contains ingenious solutions to an actual problem. Although its "New Roman Style" is not the only possible embodiment of his ideas, its insistence on the non-utilitarian serves his purpose. For the urban development occasioned by Lincoln Center (built several blocks northwest of New York City's Columbus Circle) Bayley proposed the Circle itself as a more logical site for redevelopment. He begins with the insertion of a public place in the form of a gigantic two-level gallery, centered on an existing monument and designed at a scale that presupposes public financing. Within and around this public place are theaters, television studios, restaurants, and shops, inserted into building blocks financed by private enterprise or by a combination of public and private agencies. The architectural sequence reflects the social purpose: an outdoor public room, opening onto theaters and restaurants conceived essentially as interior "private" spaces, the whole complex serving to enhance the park and the districts it serves.

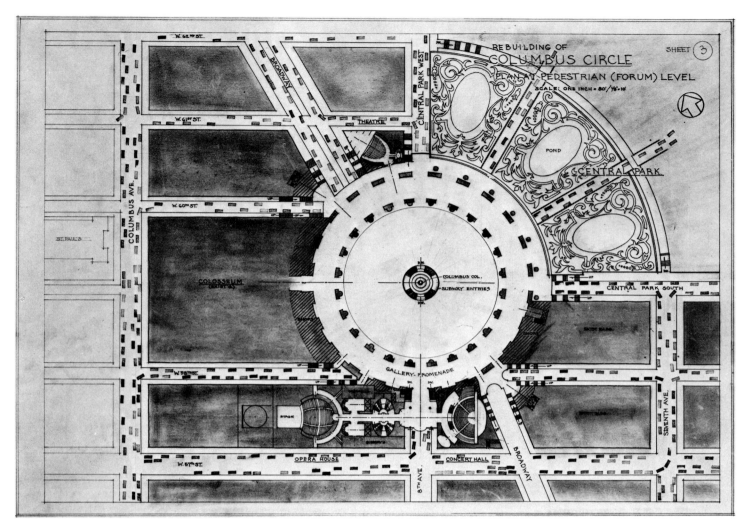

tion of a public place, which presupposes a distinction between public and
private. The circular forum and galleria flanked by relatively minor private
development accepts the distinction and uses Renaissance details to make it
unmistakably clear (p. 48). The public place cannot be construed as merely
utilitarian: it has a value above and beyond mere use. The logic of Bayley's
response might well be accepted today by many architects who would at the
same time reject his reliance on classical form. But they would encounter
decisive psychological difficulties in evolving a new language of form and
detail, capable of informing the observer that he is in a place to be valued
differently from the way one values a factory or a mechanical appliance. The
obvious difficulty is that the form language of reductionism, no matter what
structural complications are introduced into it, cannot cope with decisions
regarding scale because scale properly understood is a hierarchy of values.

John Summerson's collection of essays called *Heavenly Mansions* provides
a most useful discussion of this problem.[6] Summerson observed that the elements of classical architecture—a base with columns supporting a lintel or an
arch—make up a frame around a void. This unit constitutes an aedicule: a
miniature container, like a shrine, that imitates or represents a building. In a
sense it is a model of a building. Its formal function is to indicate a hierarchy

Bayley. A New Opera House, Theater, and Forum, with Halls for Public Assembly and Civic Reception.

of importance through its intrinsic size, its location, and perhaps through variations in the arrangement of its components. Summerson's thesis was that the classical aedicule did not vanish with the Roman world but reappeared transformed in Gothic architecture. In a cathedral its closer (but still fictive) correspondence to structural reality seems to have prevented the nineteenth century from recognizing the underlying continuity of Gothic architecture with Roman—partly because the nineteenth century preferred to see the Gothic cathedral as an exercise in engineering. Despite the profound differences, Gothic cathedrals are not the antithesis of Roman architecture; they are the realization of a metaphysical content prefigured in Roman decoration. Both modes of building use the aedicule to contain the very small within the very large; both modes vary the components of the aedicule and the manner in which they are juxtaposed.

Since the formal function of the aedicule is to frame a void, independently of true structure and true void, the abandonment of the function is reflected in the language of architectural criticism. Most of the terms developed by the Ecole des Beaux-Arts have survived in one form or another; students still make a *parti* and still deal with the graphic problems of solid and void, dark and light, in the *poché* of a plan. *Marche* is no longer in common use: instead one talks of Le Corbusier's *promenade architecturale,* or Philip Johnson's "processional." *Encadrement,* however, has vanished—because we no longer use a fictive frame around a void. Indeed, one sure sign by which half-hearted acceptance or misunderstanding of the modern idiom could be recognized, early in the twentieth century, was a projecting frame around a window or an entrance. The device was correctly associated with the stripped-down classicism with which Beaux-Arts architects of an older generation sought to counter the emerging modern style.

One consequence of seeing continuity, rather than irreconcilable oppositions, in the historic Western styles is that they cease to demand conflicting loyalties. The question of choice which so plagued the nineteenth century falls away. But what we may now see as the common ground of all historic styles is not structure, as radical thought in the nineteenth and twentieth centuries concluded, but rather the built metaphorical image by which value is declared. If we consider it from Summerson's viewpoint, Roman construction evolved toward an image that its masonry techniques could not fully achieve except symbolically. That image entailed the dematerialization of structure, as in the architectural fantasies of Pompeian wall painting. Steel and reinforced concrete have made it possible for us to achieve dematerialization directly. When we want columns as thin as pipes, we do not have to resort to such metaphors as the clustered stone columns and other linear devices of Gothic architecture—as Summerson noted, we use pipes. Because we no longer need the subjunctive "as if" to realize this particular fantasy, we have supposed

that we no longer need, and must now forbid, the fictions a subjunctive order allows. But we cannot forbid the fictive mode. "As if" breaks through: the banished metaphor returns to destroy its rational master. If we wish to deal with the metaphor we must confront its meaning.

Our fantasy now is to escape from dematerialization, which we associate not with the world to come but with the disorienting technological world of the here and now. The new image of hope is earthbound; Le Corbusier's Chapel of Notre Dame du Haut at Ronchamp is its fertile body. Beneath its stucco skin and rubble fat is a concrete skeleton; an incision beneath the swollen roof lets us glimpse the hidden skeletal truth. Because the entire building is a metaphor, intelligent response must ultimately address itself to the meaning Le Corbusier intends. Ronchamp identifies the space and structure of faith with corporeality. Its assertion—spirit *is* flesh—proposes a direction for faith that would be rejected if preached from the pulpit. One can admire even the most beautiful work of art while rejecting its premises, and this fact of experience should help us take responsibility for the premises we covertly smuggle into our aesthetics, as well as those we avow. It is true that

Le Corbusier. Notre Dame du Haut, Ronchamp, France. 1950–54.

The significant post-modern fantasy of architectural form makes mass and weight serve as symbolic assertions of the free spirit, contradicting the earlier rationalist commitment to a determinist architecture based on structural and economic necessities. Like his Marseilles apartment house, which first indicated this reaction, Le Corbusier's chapel at Ronchamp employs rough finishes and gratuitous bulk concealing a light skeletal structure. Since 1945, and perhaps in subconscious response to wartime German fortifications, this fascination with weight and density has opposed the architecture of light, transparent, idealized structure. Rejecting utilitarian values, it has opened the way to historicizing references but with the proviso that borrowed forms come from cultures other than our own.

art is not ethics, and the history of criticism has taught us not to confuse the two. But that does not mean that moral arguments have no bearing on questions of art. It means that the rational rebuke to a moral argument is a better moral argument.

The ethical injunctions of modern architecture merit close attention because the metaphor often insisted upon for its social value—the image of a building as an efficient machine, for instance—often conceals another meaning we would denounce on moral grounds if it were to be admitted to consciousness. Simplicity, for example, connotes virtue in architecture as in life: probity, forethought, restraint, humility. These modes of behavior can be sustained in the face of adversity because, unlike its utilitarian counterfeit, moral simplicity addresses itself to a source of value which it believes is beyond earthly existence. When the idea of simplicity takes the force of a moral injunction applied to the fashioning of buildings and artifacts, the avowed equation of simplicity with goodness obscures a less obvious connection: goodness is constraint; the ultimate good is the ultimate constraint; the ultimate good brings life to an end. Thus the Shaker community forbade sexual intercourse between its married adherents, extinguishing itself in consummate piety and good design. Shaker buildings and artifacts are undeniably simple and often beautiful, but intelligent appreciation eventually recoils from distortions, wrought in the name of simplicity, which signify death.

Among them is the prohibition against ornament, which the Shakers, like other ascetics before them, correctly equated with freedom and hence with dangerous play. The modern prohibition against ornament perversely equates it with crime or law-breaking ("Ornament und Verbrechen," the title of Adolf Loos's essay), offering for our guidance in art and life a judgment that conceals a deeper but familiar meaning: freedom is sin. For those still willing to risk damnation, ornament is further forbidden by practical reason, which fortifies the moral argument with expense. Ornament can be suppressed, but if thrown out it returns with a vengeance, seeking to convert all form into ornamental play. The loss of ornament, like the loss of the architectural subjunctive, has impoverished our architecture beyond any advantage simplicity can return. But its restoration does not depend on its being made inexpensive, or even on an allocation of funds that would find the expense justified. It depends on valuing the connection between ornament and freedom, and providing for it the moral space, so to speak, in which the free will can play. That is not to be accomplished by usurping the space that belongs to some other province of reality, which is what we now habitually attempt, any more than it is to be accomplished by replacing arbitrary simplicity with arbitrary complexity.

Western thought defines the categories of experience as threefold: God; Man; World. The distinguishing maneuver of philosophy is to assert the unity of existence by explaining that two of the categories are really "nothing other" than the third. Significant insight is attributed to whatever persuasive case can be made for the preeminence of one or another category. For science, Man and God alike are special conditions of the material World. For theology, Man and World are manifestations explicable only by reference to God. To modern variants of Idealism, God and World are subsumed under Man, whose consciousness sustains their existence. To explain something by declaring it to be something else is to argue from a metaphor as if it were a fact. Like art, such arguments may enrich experience but they explain nothing. When they have enough imaginative force to suppress any one of the categories of experience, they contribute to confusion. One can practice architecture without being perturbed by these considerations, but one may also fail to notice how the confusion of categories affects our idea of what is architecturally good.

The history of modern architecture is the history of the architect's attitude toward freedom and necessity. It evolves in the context of scientific determinism, which sees the material World as the sum total of existence, displacing Man and God, and made manageable only by the technological achievements the nineteenth century admired—and feared. Confronted with a determinism inimical to Man, God, and World alike, Frank Lloyd Wright sought the immanence of each in the other, declaring them to be one. His synthesis, intended to forestall the loss of freedom consequent to determinism, opposed the physicists' model of existence with a model derived from biology. His notion of organic unity depended on an equilibrium between the constraints of existence and the assertions of his own will; like Schopenhauer, it was the will he equated with the value of the individual. Translated into actual buildings, this meant that a fictive mode as such was superfluous, because *any* embodiment of the "real" is necessarily "fictive." The "real" and the "fictive" cannot be cut apart and must not be allowed to thrive at each other's expense. For Wright, form cannot *follow* function because the unity of fictive and real, of freedom and constraint, require that "form and function are one." In this Heraclitean tension the assertions of the will and the demands of necessity are like the inseparable components of the sprung bow. When Wright could sustain the tension he created some of the most sublime works in the history of architecture, reaching, as he put it, the truth that transcends the facts. But equilibrium achieved as an act of the will is inherently unstable. The string or the bow breaks; assertions of the will become willfulness, difficult to distinguish from mere excess. That is the outcome Wright may have had in mind when he observed that "every great thing is too much of whatever it is."

For Le Corbusier as for most other Europeans architectural freedom is to be found in the arms of necessity. Like a Faustian hero embracing his destiny, the architect willing to embrace constraints will be rewarded with freedoms whose existence he never suspected. Thus Le Corbusier's famous 1914 diagram concerns what is given: thin columns carrying concrete slabs—these alone are predetermined. By this small concession to necessity the stage is set for every architectural freedom: windows, facades, plan, everything to be disposed according to heroic impulse. All that is required for the sake of coherence is that the role of the structural component be made visible, and somehow implicit when not visible. This in turn requires a certain random eccentricity in the disposition of free elements, which otherwise may fall short of their ideal freedom. Horizontal ribbon windows, for example, may be a considerable inconvenience, but without them the free facade might fail to proclaim its independence from structural necessity. For a while Le Corbusier's ingenuity and wit sustained the illusion of coherence, producing until the Second World War beautiful buildings remarkable for their formal invention, generated with elements ultimately dependent on the reductionist logic of structure. But after the war both fixed structure and free form are made to repudiate the logic of reductionism. The truth of engineering yields to the fictions of poetry, and the poetry is no longer about the beauty of machines or even of geometry: it is a meditation on an archaic Golden Age whose monuments he seemed to be re-creating. Those who continue to accept Le Corbusier's original view of the nature of architecture understandably confine themselves to his work in the '20s and '30s: after that his thought begins to resemble Frank Lloyd Wright's, despite the apparent differences in formal resources.

Mies van der Rohe began with a conception of the plan as play: walls freed from their inhibiting role as the limit of a fixed volume, arranged in patterns whose ornamental value is most readily grasped from the two-dimensional plan, but which in three dimensions still clearly signify dispositions unconstrained by necessity. That is why Mies rejected them. His search for unity in the categories of experience came to rest on World—that is to say, on existence explained as the structure of matter. To limit freedom Mies next introduced a separate structural order, as in the combination of freely manipulated wall and roof planes with the regular, stabilizing disposition of columns in his Barcelona Pavilion. For a while he explored, and was satisfied with, the equilibrium of his architectural symbols for freedom and necessity. Then his 1942 project for a Concert Hall intensified the symbolical roles of both the free, space-defining plane and the predetermined, seemingly immutable structure. In one oracular image he shows the gigantic trusses of an airplane hangar enclosing a vast space in which flat and curved planes are suspended (p. 54). By asserting structure as a still more rigorously defined necessity, Mies expanded the realm of freedom, at least in theory. And once again he recoiled from the implications of greater freedom because, if the role of certain elements is to embody freedom, they will sooner or later assume shapes that contradict, and assert their preeminence over, the category of structural

necessity to which they are counterpoised. There is no reason why such freely chosen shapes should not evolve toward the arbitrary; indeed reason suggests that they should.

The implications of this possibility were first examined by Philip Johnson in 1951. His response was to design a building consisting of a single room almost filled by a suspended dome, like a plaster lampshade with hanging pendentive legs. This was a shape Johnson additionally savored because it recalls those historic circumstances when a pendentive dome represented a triumph of structural technique. In his first version of this idea, most of the drawings for which have been lost, Johnson made the walls of the building out of closely spaced vertical wood members, their reiteration affording a mix of structure and transparency that corresponded to the roof truss of Mies's Concert Hall. Against this, the suspended plaster dome, with its hanging legs curved back to imply completion of a sphere, as well as to signal that the dome could not possibly stand on its own feet, unmistakably occupied the category of freedom—which includes the capricious. In the context of an architectural vocabulary valuing necessity over freedom, Johnson reversed the priorities of determinism and made the representation of freedom force necessity to yield. In his second version of the idea (*right*), a brick-walled chapel projected for Vassar College, he blurred the categorical distinctions and thereby weakened the argument (because the structural role of the brick wall with its rounded corners is less clear) and his subsequent efforts to build variations on the theme diluted it still more.

Inevitable to the representation of freedom is the recollection of history.

Ludwig Mies van der Rohe. Project for a Concert Hall. 1942. The Museum of Modern Art, New York.

Prompted by his earlier studies for a museum with a suspended acoustical ceiling, Mies here carried the idea of free planes floating in space to its logical conclusion. These elements are shown superimposed on a photograph of the interior of an airplane hangar whose roof truss represents a structural and economic necessity. Against that acknowledged constraint, the floating planes and the Maillol sculpture oppose the gratuitous acts of the artist.

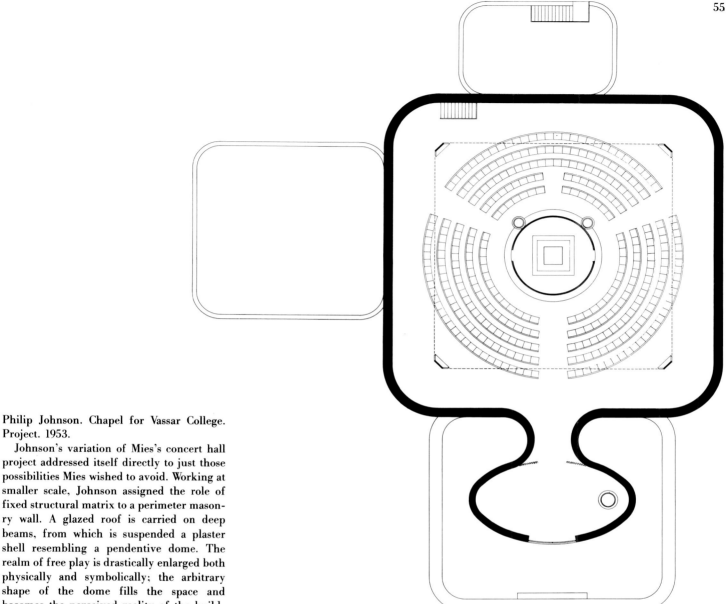

Philip Johnson. Chapel for Vassar College. Project. 1953.

Johnson's variation of Mies's concert hall project addressed itself directly to just those possibilities Mies wished to avoid. Working at smaller scale, Johnson assigned the role of fixed structural matrix to a perimeter masonry wall. A glazed roof is carried on deep beams, from which is suspended a plaster shell resembling a pendentive dome. The realm of free play is drastically enlarged both physically and symbolically; the arbitrary shape of the dome fills the space and becomes the perceived reality of the building. Although not inevitable, the reference to history is compatible with an anti-determinist conception of architectural form.

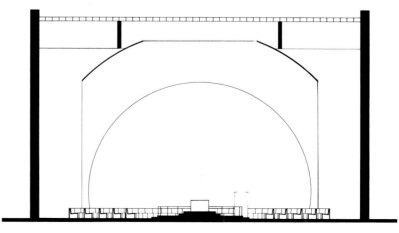

Necessity, confined to its own category, cannot exclude knowledge. But Johnson's later experiments with history proceeded chiefly by paraphrasing the forms of obsolete structural systems, which the economics of necessity will no longer tolerate, without clarifying their fictive role. The exaggerated mass of the columns used in his Dumbarton Oaks Museum, or the massive blocks seemingly supported on arches (but in fact suspended from hidden steel trusses) of his annex to the Boston Public Library, remain explicable only within the parameters of the engineering aesthetic. To the extent that they break through those parameters their implausibility renders suspect the admirable impulse to enrich form.

Johnson's earlier insight was recapitulated by Louis Kahn, and again the desire to enrich form involved history. Kahn's gnomic utterances on the nature of materials, whereby brick "wants to be" in a certain way, do not merely echo Frank Lloyd Wright. They are addressed not toward organic unity but toward the clarification of distinct categories. That is the ethical ground of his aesthetic preference for mass separated into discrete, even redundant, elements. Unity in Kahn's work is the product of a largely subjective feeling for the compatibility of materials and forms. They neither correspond to necessity nor deny it. Instead, Kahn sought the enrichment of form through an ever more scrupulous discrimination of the events that generate it. As each possibility is sorted out and developed, his work achieves an intricacy more apparent in plan than in three dimensions, and often more desirable in theory than in reality. These plans recall, and may have been prompted by, Roman architecture both in its original manifestations, especially as they came to be understood by archaeological research in the 1950s and '60s, and in its nineteenth-century Beaux-Arts interpretations. Among the most successful of his formal inventions are those which deal with light. Having justified them as necessary to physical or mental well-being, and therefore functional, he developed forms nevertheless meant to be understood as at least relatively free, and with such forms he himself felt freer to retrieve history.

And yet Kahn, who recognized and enjoyed his own affinity with classical

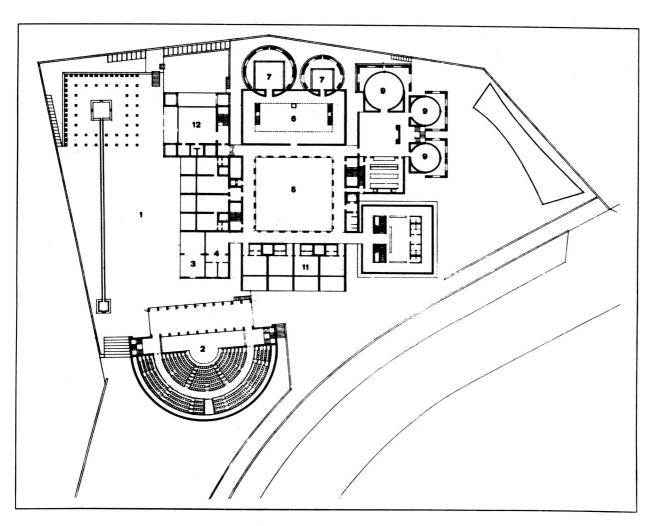

architecture and the Ecole des Beaux-Arts, hesitated to avail himself of all the implications of his own philosophy. For example, a corridor in a Kahn building, no matter how clearly defined in plan, stops well short of becoming what a corridor "wants to be." In this particular his sense of architectural opportunity was not so different from that of many architects whose work has been thought opposed to his. The comparison can be illustrated with the suburban office building, a type of problem analogous to the more farfetched extravaganzas of the Ecole des Beaux-Arts. (Between "A House for a Rich Banker in Paris" and a house for a rich corporation in the suburbs, it is the modern version on which greater resources are lavished.) The impeccable examples of this type by Skidmore, Owings and Merrill, among others, are recognized by virtue of their skillful planning as being *en famille* with their Beaux-Arts predecessors, although they curiously neglect the same element Kahn neglected: the axial corridor, which remains residual and formally mute. And even where Kahn's "wants to be" addressed itself to the design of a window, an architectural event he found more sympathetic, his response was ambivalent: a window apparently wanted to be no more than the absence of wall, even if he had to build a special wall to absent it from. The identity of the window could not be separated from that of its wall, which Kahn conceived as the window's bond to necessity (p. 57). Nevertheless his architecture has been rightly understood as a courageous effort to reexamine the spectrum of possibilities: his work opens the post-modern because it refuses to accept reductionism as its measure of value.

* * *

That our architecture is not all we might wish for, and that its effects are not universally admired, are issues by now familiar to the layman as well as the professional. To confront these problems is neither to lament the loss of innocence nor to betray a heroic mission; rather it is to suggest a perspective that might free energy for a different kind of integration. The test of theorizing does not depend on immediate practical applications, but theory can be readily tested in the classroom, by the manner in which architecture is taught. A conception of architecture that seeks to clarify the distinction between freedom and necessity, assigning to each its proper realm, would soon require more suitable and more diverse means of visualizing its thought than the hegemony of the model allows. Drawing as scenography is an art that would have to be learned again, bringing with it the desire to design something that can in fact be drawn.

Even the most intellectually inert recognize a change in the pervasive climate of opinion—in what must still be described clumsily as the zeitgeist. Part of the difficulty of coming to grips with the change, for professional architects perhaps even more than for students, is the fear that some things wholly admirable in modern architecture may yet be abandoned, where this is not at issue. In its early years the modern movement prompted an allegiance that transcended mere enthusiasm and approached religious fervor. Promising release from a past perceived as burdensome, the new architecture expected an end to injustice, with new patterns of life finding their own space and form. Most of us now understand that architecture is the least suitable instrument with which to achieve social justice. Without abandoning other responsibilities, we might yet wish to concentrate on what architecture and architecture alone can provide, leaving reform or revolution to those better equipped. "Everything begins as a *mystique* and ends as a *politique*," Charles Péguy remarked.[7] Just now architecture could do with less *politique*; whether we can or will reformulate the *mystique* is a subject for debate. Reductionist philosophies of architecture do not have a mandate from heaven, and yet we do not know what other values we wish to assert, let alone how to assert them. But already it is possible to suggest, if only with evidence provided from outside the realm of architecture, that the dominant utilitarian view of existence is being challenged from within its own technological disciplines. If the possibilities of non-reductive form were to be examined, their manifestations might well bypass the historical revivalism architects fear: they might culminate in a non-reductive interpretation of technology itself. Introspection and a little good humor could lead modern architecture out of its resentment, and allow us to continue the exploration of freedom.

Salles des Etudes Antiques, Ecole des Beaux-Arts. *See p. 78.*

THE TEACHING OF ARCHITECTURE
AT THE
ECOLE DES BEAUX-ARTS

Richard Chafee

The Académie Royale d'Architecture

The Ecole des Beaux-Arts in Paris taught architecture from 1819 until 1968. The school was not newly formed in 1819, however; rather it had been transformed between 1793 and 1819 from the schools of the Académie Royale de Peinture et de Sculpture and the Académie Royale d'Architecture. Some of the arrangement of teaching architecture survived from the Ancien Régime.

Royal academies proliferated during the reign of Louis XIV, for they were one of Colbert's means of centralizing the power of the king.[1] In 1635, during the reign of Louis XIII, Richelieu had set the precedent with the Académie Française, a gathering of literary men who were to compose a dictionary and a grammar and thus to regulate the language. In 1648 Mazarin founded the Académie Royale de Peinture et de Sculpture, and then in the '60s Colbert, Mazarin's successor as minister of Louis XIV, established a number of them: in 1661, the Académie Royale de Dance; in 1663, the Académie Royale des Inscriptions et Belles Lettres, for historical scholarship and archaeology; in 1666, the Académie Royale des Sciences; also in 1666, the Académie de France à Rome, for advanced study of the arts; in 1669, the Académie Royale de Musique; and finally, in 1671, the Académie Royale d'Architecture.

The purpose of this Academy, like that of the others, was study. The eminent architects whom the king had named academicians met once a week to share their learning; their discussions were intended to solve architectural problems. Records of the Academy's meetings were kept from the first, for it was assumed that these conferences would bring forth a more exact knowledge and a more correct theory.[2] The Academy would thus increase the glory of the king; more specifically, it often was asked to advise him on matters concerning royal buildings. So that young architects of the realm might benefit from its studies, the Academy conducted a school. Public lectures were given, initially two days a week, on theory of architecture, by François Blondel (1617-86), the first professor and director of the Academy, and also on arithmetic, geometry, mechanics, military architecture, fortifications, perspective, and stonecutting.[3] By 1717 the lectures had become a course lasting two or three years with the session from November to September. A single professor gave two two-hour lessons a week, the first on practical geometry, the second on the different notions, rules, and practices of architecture—in all, a course on the principles of architecture and the knowledge needed for its practice. The lectures were public, but the title of *élève* was reserved for a limited number of students.[4]

The Academy of Architecture and the Academy of Painting and Sculpture offered Colbert a means of attacking the medieval guilds, which were not under direct royal control. The academies attracted architects, painters, and sculptors by elevating these men in the hierarchy of society from the rank of craftsmen to that of philosophers. The word "academy" suggests the great philosopher of antiquity, Plato, as well as the academies of the Italian Renaissance with their humanist learning. Transplanted, as it were, from Italy, academies took root in France and thrived, but they did not entirely replace the medieval guilds. Academicians continued to have apprentices to whom they taught their art. An *élève* of the Academy of Architecture learned to design not there but in the workshop, the atelier, of his master. (Among the changes the Renaissance had brought about, the workshop was no longer at the construction site, the *chantier*, but had become a studio, an atelier; accordingly drawing became the first skill for the student of architecture to learn.) The student's drawing board was in the atelier, not at the Academy's *école*. At the Academy his lessons were mostly lectures; what was taught there was material communicable in words.

This academic doctrine was, in twentieth-century terminology, rationalist; it was characterized by a complete trust in, to use a more eighteenth-century word, reason; and at least at first the Academy's trust was so complete as to make reason a seventeenth-century absolute.[5] The Academy sought to evolve universal principles of architecture. It took for granted that it could do this and assumed that making these principles would be a reasonable activity and that the principles themselves would be likewise reasonable. The Academy assumed that formulating these principles was the way to make architecture perfect; for instance, if there could be a rule of proportion, it would result in perfect beauty. The touchstones of these principles were what had long been regarded as the best examples: for proportion, the five Orders; in general, the greatest buildings and texts of Roman antiquity and the Italian Renaissance. All these were reason materialized. Yet on close inspection the Academy found even them not beyond criticism. Late Renaissance as well as some Roman architects were accused in the Academy of being insufficiently reasonable, of being libertine. Thus, Palladio "took liberties with the profiles. . . ."[6]

In its early years the Academy was Platonist in its belief in absolutes. Of course the members were not all of one mind on questions of doctrine; they could never resolve the problem of whether beauty is absolute or capable of change. When the argument arose at one of the first meetings, most of the academicians supported François Blondel, not Claude Perrault, and the

Academy founded its aesthetic on the unchanging.[7] It never was interested in the transitory, for instance, in decoration.

François Blondel stamped his personality on the new Academy. As a Platonist, he believed in universals and thus in teachable doctrine. Having been trained in the mathematics of military engineering, his own mind was rational and systematic. So was his teaching, which he made available to posterity by publishing his *Cours d'architecture*.[8] He built little, yet his rationalism and his belief in the eternal validity of classical models can be seen in his best-known work, a triumphal arch, the Porte Saint-Denis of 1671 in Paris. After Blondel's death in 1686, Philippe de La Hire, who had also been trained in mathematics, became professor, and the values that the Academy tried to instill in its students remained the same. After La Hire's death in 1718, there were more than half a dozen professors until a teacher as great as François Blondel was appointed to the chair in 1762. He too was a Blondel, a distant relation: Jacques-François Blondel (1705–74).[9] He was determined to teach. In 1743, twelve years before he was admitted to the Academy, he had opened the first independent school of architecture in Paris, with the Academy reluctantly acknowledging that such a school might be useful. His academic point of view is recorded in his famous books, *L'Architecture française* of 1752–56 and the *Cours d'architecture* of 1771–77, a revision of lectures he had first given in 1750.

Like François Blondel, J.-F. Blondel urged students to reason logically and to learn from classical examples. "Classical," however, meant to J.-F. Blondel not only Roman antiquity and the Italian Renaissance but also the French classical tradition that had been established by Pierre Lescot and Philibert de l'Orme, perfected (in his opinion) by François Mansart, and maintained by Jules Hardouin Mansart, Claude Perrault, and François Blondel. J.-F. Blondel disapproved of the Rococo architecture of the first half of the century as capricious. Architects, he thought, should act reasonably, and it was reasonable to respect the good old traditions. Yet he was less absolute in his beliefs than François Blondel had been. The younger man believed that the masterpieces of antique architecture should not simply be copied, for all the circumstances were different. People's needs, customs, and politics; construction materials; the climate; even the gods—all had changed, and consequently architects had to create a different architecture. To do so they needed to study classical masterpieces so as to learn logical thought. Recognizing that circumstances determine architecture, Blondel acknowledged that beauty is changing, not absolute, but he also believed beauty to be derived from long-appreciated ideas. In effect he was like his contemporary, Ange-Jacques Gabriel: the two men redirected the course of French architecture to that of the French seventeenth-century tradition, a tradition they valued as having the best source and being reasonable.

Until the Revolution, the Academy of Architecture did not fundamentally change.[10] But it did grow in size.[11] Originally, in 1671, there were eight members. In 1699 new regulations divided the membership into two classes of seven architects each, plus a professor and a secretary—in all sixteen. In 1728 the king raised the number to thirty-two and in 1756 divided the thirty-two evenly between the two classes. Although not in control of its regulations, the Academy to an extent governed itself: for example, when a member died, the Academy proposed three possible successors to the king, and he appointed one of them.[12] At its meetings in the first half of the eighteenth century the Academy continued to discuss the five Orders, seeking to define the ideal proportions of each and failing to reach a conclusion, basically because of disagreement as to whether or not beauty is absolute. Planning was a subject of less interest and construction of still less. In the second half of the century the priority was reversed. The Academy gradually lost interest in theoretical questions and turned instead, at a time when knowledge of physics and chemistry was increasing, to construction.[13] The members heard technical reports on ways of building (timber engineering and masonry vaulting), on the behavior of materials (cement, stone, iron), on plumbing, heating, and lighting. They grew interested in Gothic architecture and sought to understand the logic of its construction. In those same years, with pictures of Greek ruins beginning to circulate, some academicians began to build in a new kind of classical style.

Design competitions, which for two and a half centuries were to be the most important part of French architectural education, began modestly in the early eighteenth century. In 1717, regulations of the Academy stated the intention of establishing an annual competition for students and of awarding a gold and a silver medal. (In 1701–02, there had been one inconclusive competition, initiated and judged by the minister in charge of the Academy, the Surintendant des Bâtiments. Unable to decide which of two designs was better, he had lots drawn for the first prize. In 1703, pressed by the Surintendant, the Academy began a second competition, but in the minutes of the meetings there is no mention of ending or judgment. Evidently, the academicians preferred to devote their meetings entirely to other matters and did so, until presented with the regulations of 1717.) In 1720 the first of the regular, annual competitions took place—it was an exercise at the end of the school year—and the award was first bestowed: a silver medal bearing portraits of the king and the regent.[14] In the school of the Academy of Painting and Sculpture, winners of the end-of-the-year prizes had for a long time been getting not just a medal each, but also the right to study, at the expense of the state, at the French Academy in Rome. When the Academy of Architecture was established in 1671, François Blondel had announced that the king intended to create a similar prize in architecture with, likewise, a stipend to

Rome. Blondel had spoken too soon: for the next half-century, the Surintendant selected young architects for Rome. In 1725, though, he sent to Rome the student of architecture who had won the fifth annual prize, and gradually *le prix*, as the Academy at first referred to it, became the Rome prize. But during the Ancien Régime the architectural prize never carried the right to go to Rome: in the late 1760s Marigny, the minister in charge, quarreling with the Academy, refused to send to Rome the prize-winners, but instead sent young architects of his own choice; and as late as 1781 Marigny's successor stated that a stipend for Rome was not a right of the prize-winner, but was a favor granted by the king.

The number of students of architecture grew. In 1717 there were twenty-eight in the Academy's school, in 1746, forty-seven. With more students, more competitions and prizes were in order. In 1763 Marigny created the *prix d'émulation*, to be awarded after monthly competitions that were easier than those for the annual prize. The monthly competitions were practice for the annual competition for the Grand Prix, as the end-of-the-year prize came to be called.[15]

In the eighteenth century, the appointment to the Academy in Rome was for three years, and during that time the architects made drawings of antiquities and of their own designs. In the 1780s, the Academy began requiring its *pensionnaires* in Rome each to make a detailed study of an antique building that the Academy considered important, and to send the study to Paris for preservation in the Academy's library.[16] The first student to be under this obligation persuaded the Academy to let him make *relevés* of the Pantheon. Thereafter, the arrival of the *envois de Rome* in Paris became a regular annual event, like the competition for the Grand Prix. In effect, the Grand Prix marked in youth an architect whom the Academy judged to hold great promise. Many winners did become eminent, and decades after the Grand Prix they customarily gained the further honor of election to the Academy (first accorded in 1741 to P.-E. LeBon, Grand Prix in 1725).[17]

The Suppression of the Academy and Reemergence of Its School

During the Revolution, the royal academies were suppressed. The struggle against them was led by the painter Jacques-Louis David (1748–1825), for whom the archenemy was the Académie Royale de Peinture et Sculpture. Because of his obstinacy, what began in 1789 as a complaint by some young painters and sculptors became in 1793 an onslaught by the revolutionary government against all the academies.[18] The Académie Royale d'Architecture was never at the center of the struggle, and there is evidence that David approved of the work of the professor of architecture, who continued to teach after the suppression of the academies. The academic tradition no longer remained without rivals, however; other pedagogies appeared. What happened to the academies is as follows.

In September 1789, several months after the creation of the National Assembly and the fall of the Bastille, dissatisfied young artists issued a pamphlet to make public their trifling grievances.[19] They demanded that students be permitted to sketch from classical antique models, and that professors' protégés be excluded from the Academy's special classes for medal-winners. The pamphlet was impolite, calling the officers of the Academy "blind protectors of rampant mediocrity."[20] It was out of order, for the officers had the responsibility of governing the Academy, and students were expected to stay in their place. David, who had been accepted into the Academy in 1783, took up the cause of the malcontents. After several months of public quarreling, which reached a climax on February 25, 1790, when some of the dissidents went before the Paris Commune and denounced the Academy of Painting and Sculpture as opposed to equality and liberty, the Academy compromised. On March 6, it named David to a commission to reform the statutes.[21]

Talk of reform was in the air that month: in an address to the National Assembly, Angiviller, the Directeur Général des Bâtiments, invited the Royal Academy of Architecture to inspect its statutes with an eye for reform.[22] On April 27, 1790, seven months after the agitation in the Academy of Painting and Sculpture had begun, students of the Academy of Architecture made a few demands: the right to be present at Academy meetings (especially those in which academicians judged student work and conferred prizes), and changes in the rules of the competition for the Prix de Rome.[23] On June 14, the Academy of Architecture decided to begin reviewing its statutes.[24]

David, meanwhile, was showing that he was not at all pacified by the compromise of the Academy of Painting and Sculpture. At once he made more demands, and on June 28, 1790, he led a delegation that complained to the National Assembly.[25] The Assembly ordered the Academy to revise its statutes, the Academy's Secrétaire Perpétuel published a defense of the existing rules,[26] and on September 21, the dissident artists proposed to the National Assembly statutes for an Académie Centrale de Peinture, Sculpture, Gravure, et Architecture.[27] This proposal seemed to David not enough of a break with tradition, and showing himself to be more radical than those whose cause he had been championing, he set off on his own and created an organization to rival the Royal Academy of Painting and Sculpture: the Commune des Arts. On September 29, in its first meeting, the Commune des Arts demanded that the National Assembly dissolve the Royal Academy of Painting and Sculpture.[28] On February 14, 1791, the Royal Academy of Architecture delivered the review of its statutes begun the preceding June. At the same time, a minority of the architectural academicians proposed a centralized Académie Nationale des Arts like that suggested five months earlier by the dissident painters and sculptors.[29]

During 1791 the quarrel seemed to be subsiding into a literary dispute. The Secrétaire Perpétuel of the Academy of Painting and Sculpture published a second and third defense of his Academy,[30] and Quatremère de Quincy argued in two books against the traditional way of teaching design.[31] Marat insulted the Académie Royale des Sciences and the Académie Française in his small book, *Les Charlatans modernes, ou lettres sur le charlatanisme académique.*[32] David, however, wanted more action, and on August 19, 1791, he sent the National Assembly a letter, which other academicians also signed, claiming that the public exhibition of academicians' painting and sculpture maintained the Academy's privilege of exclusiveness.[33] The Academy would not fight. Two days later it opened its Salon to all artists.[34] In the last month of the year, the Academy of Architecture, in testimony to the municipality of Paris about the state of the Academy's goods, asserted its loyalty to the king.[35] The architectural academicians seem to have felt sure that the clamorous threats of disruption were all past.

In the summer of 1792 the Academy of Painting and Sculpture elected David Professeur Adjoint, and he accepted the appointment.[36] Such inconsistency raises doubts as to his principles. In the autumn in another, more ominous election, David became a Député in the new government of France, the National Convention.[37] That body appointed him to its Committee of Public Instruction.[38] With new power he returned to the attack. On November 11, he led a group of artists before the Convention to demand that the academies of painting and sculpture and of architecture be abolished, but that their schools be provisionally saved. The official record alludes to David:

> After this petition, a Member places on the desk his patent as an Academician, and asks that the Academies of the Arts be abolished.

The Convention referred consideration of the demand to its Committee of Public Instruction.[39]

A fortnight later, when the post of director of the French Academy in Rome became vacant, the Academy of Painting and Sculpture named, as was its right, a replacement. It chose Joseph-Benoît Suvée, to whom in 1771 it had awarded the Grand Prix for painting.[40] David hated Suvée, "the most inveterate of aristocrats . . . the horrible Suvée, Suvée the ignoramus."[41] In 1771 the Academy had changed its mind when judging the Grand Prix competition and had not, as it had first intended, given the prize to David.[42] David never forgot. Now he showed his strength. On November 25, 1792:

> The National Convention, after having heard its Committee . . . decrees:
>
> > Art. I. The office of director of the French Academy . . . established in Rome, is abolished. This establishment is placed under the immediate supervision of the agent of France. . . .

III. The National Convention suspends, as of this date, in all the academies of
France, all replacements and all nominations.[43]

In January 1793, the Convention brought the king to trial, condemned,
and guillotined him. David voted for execution.[44]

In April 1793 came David's turn, as Professeur Adjoint, to supervise the
life class, and the Academy sent him the usual invitation. David dismissed it
with the words:

I was formerly of the Academy.

David, deputy to the National Convention.[45]

But many members of the Convention were not as hostile to the royal
academies as was he, for they recognized that the academies had work to do.
The decree of November 25, 1792, forbidding all academies to fill empty seats
hindered the Royal Academy of Science in completing the task assigned to it
several years before by the revolutionary government—the creation of a
metric system. Thus, on May 17, 1793, the Convention authorized "tem-
porarily the Academy of Science . . . to fill vacancies in its membership."[46]

During July and August of 1793, David stormed and took his Bastille. On
July 1, he persuaded the Convention to separate the question of the
academies from the more general question of educational reform.[47] Then, on
the same day,

on the proposal of one of its Members, the National Convention decrees that the
Committee of Public Instruction will submit to it, within eight days, a report on
the abolition of the Academy of Painting, Sculpture. . . . [48]

On July 4, the Convention recognized David's Commune des Arts as the
only artistic society;[49] the Commune figuratively usurped the place of the
Academy. On July 18, there was actual usurpation: members of the Commune broke into and occupied the quarters of the Royal Academy of Painting
and Sculpture in the Louvre.[50]

Such disorder was alarming. On July 17 and 18, the great scientist
Lavoisier wrote to Lakanal, a deputy in the Convention, to defend the
Academy of Science, "so that the temple of science remain standing amid so
many ruins." He argued that the Academy was deserving:

Even under the Ancien Régime, the sciences were in some way organized as a
republic, and . . . a kind of respect had protected the sanctuary of science
against the invasions of despotism.

And it was necessary:

Tightly bound to the continued life of the Academy . . . is . . . one of the most
beautiful enterprises that have been conducted for the happiness of man, . . .
the establishment of universal standards.[51]

But even Lavoisier could not ward off the attack. On July 25, David got
still more power: he was elected secretary to the Convention.[52] On August 3,
on behalf of the Committee of Public Instruction, he announced that he was

preparing a report on the suppression of "all the corporations of the arts," and on August 5 the whole Convention began to debate the question.[53] That day the Academy of Architecture, aroused and afraid, moved forward the date of judging the competition for the Grand Prix. It was the students who asked for this change of schedule;[54] in the midst of turmoil, they were supporting the work of their Academy. Challenged, David put a stop to that work. On August 7:

> The National Convention, after having heard the report of its Committee of Public Instruction, decrees:
>
>> Art. I. There shall be a postponement in judging the prizes of the academies of painting, sculpture, and architecture....
>>
>> II. The Committee of Public Instruction shall present without delay the mode by which the prizes shall be judged....
>>
>> III. The sketches and the works of artists presented for these competitions shall be immediately transported and displayed in the rooms of the Commune des Arts....[55]

The next day the Committee of Public Instruction issued the report it had been preparing for five days.[56] After another member spoke for the Committee, David gave a fervent discourse "on the need to abolish the academies."[57] They are the "last shelters of all the aristocracies." Just as

> the policy of kings is to maintain the balance of crowns, the policy of the academies is to maintain the balance of talents.

They employ cruel means "to smother budding talents" and take "monastic revenge" against any young man whose natural gifts put him beyond their tyranny. To illustrate these charges, David told four lurid stories: one of an "animal" in the Académie Française, three of "monsters" in the Academy of Painting and Sculpture. He justified this emphasis:

> I shall dwell most particularly on the Academy of Painting and Sculpture; to speak of one Academy is to speak of them all; in all, it is always the same spirit, in all, the same men.

He ended his tirade with a call for extermination:

> In the name of mankind, in the name of justice, for the love of art, and above all for the young, let us destroy, let us annihilate these too deadly academies, which can no longer remain under a free regime. As academician, I have done my duty. You decide.

At once the deputies did:

> The National Convention, after having heard its Committee of Public Instruction, decrees the following:
>
>> Art. I. All the academies and literary societies, licensed or endowed by the nation, are abolished....[58]

On the night of August 16–17, 1793, the quarters of all the academies were sealed.[59] The royal academies were finished.

But a week later the government admitted its need for the school of the late Academy of Architecture. On August 24, 1793, the Minister of the Interior wrote to the Committee of Public Instruction, "the school of architecture is of immense utility."[60] He proposed that the school continue to exist with the same Secrétaire Perpétuel and the same teachers. Because previously in March and April the Convention, acknowledging a responsibility, had allocated funds for education, the minister now had the money to pay for his proposals.[61] Thus the school of the Royal Academy of Architecture reopened in the autumn of 1793. During the summer recess it had lost its name and its quarters, but Julien-David Leroy (1724–1803), who had been appointed Professeur Adjoint in 1762 and Professeur in 1774, was teaching again,[62] if in a different chamber in the Louvre.[63] David Leroy enlisted as his associate Antoine-Laurent-Thomas Vaudoyer (1756–1846), and to judge student work he organized a jury with Percier and Fontaine as chairmen. (Whether the state in fact paid for this teaching is a question; legend has it that David Leroy and Vaudoyer met the school's expenses until the autumn of 1795.)[64] On September 29, 1793, the Convention decreed the provisional reopening of the school of the Academy of Painting and Sculpture.[65] The suppression of the academies had not held these two schools down for long.

Although J.-L. David had said that all the academies equally deserved to be suppressed, he may have been predisposed in favor of the Academy of Architecture. He evidently approved of its professor, David Leroy. David had always counted architects among his friends: his maternal uncle was the academician Pierre Desmaisons; an older friend was M.-J. Sedaine, who became secretary of the Royal Academy of Architecture; and A.-C. Hubert, winner of the Prix de Rome of 1784, was both friend and brother-in-law.[66] David Leroy, too, seems to have been a friend; the painter also may have respected the professor as one of the patriarchs of French Neoclassicism.

David Leroy's great accomplishment had been to reveal the appearance of Greek architecture. As a Grand Prix *pensionnaire* at the French Academy in Rome, he had visited Athens in 1754–55, and in 1758 he rushed into print his book, *Les Ruines des plus beaux monuments de la Grèce*.[67] It consists of descriptions and pictures (both picturesque sketches and measured drawings) of Athenian buildings; these were the first measured drawings of Athenian buildings to be published. When David Leroy arrived in Greece, the Englishmen Stuart and Revett had already been there for three years making their drawings of these and other buildings, but they did not issue their first volume until 1762, and not until 1787 did they bring out their second, which shows the buildings on the Acropolis.[68] Their book in time supplanted David Leroy's because their illustrations are more numerous, more detailed, and more precise, but for nearly two decades David Leroy's book alone showed the most famous Greek buildings. His book also set the course of his own career: from 1762 onward he lectured at the Academy's school on architectural theory and history. Student designs from this period reflect a new awareness of Greek architecture.[69] As J.-L. David reached maturity, he shed the Baroque and Rococo characteristics that he had been taught as a student, and he became profoundly Neoclassical. His great paintings of the 1780s— *The Oath of the Horatii, The Death of Socrates, The Lictors Bringing Home to Brutus the Bodies of His Sons*—are Neoclassical in style and subject matter. David intended these paintings to be moral: in order to improve eighteenth-century mankind, he portrayed antique virtue.[70] These acts of virtue take place in antique architecture. It is all imaginary architecture: David was seeking not archaeological accuracy but settings that would intensify his dramas.[71] His preparatory sketches for paintings show that he made his architecture increasingly Neoclassical: for instance, in a preliminary sketch for the *Horatii*, the columns are slender with bases and fluting, like Baroque columns;[72] but in the final painting they are stocky, baseless, and smooth—a kind of Tuscan Doric that is, in effect, more robust.[73] David obviously was aware of current thinking about the Doric column.[74] An imaginary Neoclassical architecture fitted his purpose, and his purpose was to revive classical virtue. Thus he may well have respected David Leroy's work.

Whatever the reasons for the bond between them, the fact is that J.-L. David, after bringing down the academies, expressed confidence in the academician David Leroy. In the autumn of 1793 the Convention, on the advice of its Committee of Public Instruction, abolished the Commune des Arts, which had antagonized David personally.[75] For the function of judging important artistic competitions, such as those for the Salons and the Prix de Rome, the Convention appointed a jury.[76] It was not composed solely of painters, sculptors, and architects, as had been the Commune des Arts and royal academies; instead, it evinced the new equality. Of its fifty-five members, twelve were painters, seven were sculptors, and nine were architects. The other twenty-seven included a *constructeur* (Jean-Baptiste Rondelet), three actors, a dealer in paintings, four men of letters, and the commanding general of the revolutionary armies. One of the architects was David Leroy.[77]

Again, a few months later, David tapped David Leroy. On January 5, 1794, the painter had been elected president of the Convention, and on the sixteenth of the month (27 nivôse an II), that body, having heard the report by its Committee of Public Instruction, named a committee to care for the museum. This *conservatoire* consisted of ten men: four painters, two sculptors, two antiquaries, and two architects, of whom one was David Leroy.[78]

Thus, because of the patronage of J.-L. David during the period when he was in effect dictator of the arts in France, David Leroy was able to give to the school of architecture a continuity between the Ancien and Nouveau Régimes. In the years immediately following the suppression of the academies, the number of students that he taught was actually very small. Today, another school established in Paris in those same years is better known — the Ecole Polytechnique. Its architectural reputation is due to Jean-Nicolas-Louis Durand (1760–1834), its professor of architecture from 1795 to 1830, whose books were influential for a generation and continue to be of historical importance.[79] But the Ecole Polytechnique was not an architecture school, although it seemed at first as if it might become one.[80] The school arose in response to the crises of 1793, when the French felt threatened with invasion across every border. Engineers were needed to erect fortifications and to maintain roads on which French armies could march to the frontiers, and yet in that year the school of civil engineering, the Ecole des Ponts et Chaussées (which had been in existence since 1747), was, like all the other schools of the Ancien Régime, in such chaos that the future supply of engineers was most uncertain. The Convention saw the need and listened to the proposal of a group of scholars, led by the geometrician Gaspard Monge, that there should be a new school of civil and military engineering in Paris. Monge and his colleagues also had in mind another purpose: preserving the study of higher mathematics and the abstract sciences. The immediate need was urgent, though, and on March 11, 1794 (21 ventôse an II), the Convention created a Committee of Public Works and decreed, "This Committee shall be in charge of the establishment of a Central School of Public Works."[81] The Convention named as one of the two commissioners the architect Rondelet, who had in 1789 suggested to the National Assembly the establishment of an *école pratique* to train the architects and engineers necessary for public building. The opening of the Ecole Centrale des Travaux Publics was fixed for December 1, 1794 (10 frimaire an III). In January 1795, the government ordered that some architectural drawings and models be transferred from the sealed Académie Royale d'Architecture to the new school.[82] The Ecole Centrale des Travaux Publics began to take the place of the Ecole des Ponts et Chaussées, of several little provincial royal schools of military engineering, and of the school of the abolished Academy of Architecture.

At the beginning of the next academic year, on September 1, 1795 (15 fructidor an III), the Convention decreed that the school's name be changed to the Ecole Polytechnique. It was a telling change. Monge persuaded the Députés that instead of replacing the old schools of applied technology with a single new one, the Convention should reorganize the old schools and make the new one a school of abstract studies of the highest quality, applicable to all technological fields. The Convention, on October 22, 1795 (30 vendémaire an IV), after a fortnight of debate about education, issued a decree that precisely defined the new purpose. The Ecole Polytechnique

> is intended to train students for the artillery service; military engineering;
> bridges & highways & civil constructions; the mines; the building of ships and

vessels; topography; & at the same time for the free practicing of those professions which require a knowledge of mathematics & physics.[83]

This decree gave the Ecole Polytechnique its name and form. (At about the time of the decree, Rondelet left the school's administration.) From then on, the school prepared students in two intense years for the schools of Artillerie, Génie Militaire, Ponts et Chaussées, Mines, Génie Maritime, Télégraphie, Aeronautique, and so on. Napoleon put the *polytechniciens* into uniform, which they have worn since. Many of them went on to be officers, and a score (including Joffre and Foch) Maréchals de France. Other former students are the mathematician Henri Poincaré, the chemist J.-L. Gay-Lussac, and the philosopher Auguste Comte. After the decree of 1795, the subjects of instruction at the Ecole Polytechnique became the general notions common to the various technologies, higher mathematics, chemistry and physics, and also principles of architecture. From the beginning, there has been a professor of architecture; Durand, Léonce Reynaud, Emmanuel Brune, Auguste Choisy, and Gustave Umbdenstock are the best known. Of these men the most famous is Durand, who published his teaching in two books, *Recueil et parallèle des édifices en tout genre, anciens et modernes*, Paris, 1800, and *Précis des leçons d'architecture données à l'école polytechnique*, two volumes, Paris, 1802 and 1805. The latter was probably the most widely read manual on architectural composition of its time and remained in print until 1840.[84] Its success may have been due to its simplicity. Durand saw that the plans and elevations of the simple geometric shapes of Neoclassical architecture could easily be represented on a grid of regularly spaced lines intersecting at right angles. This kind of representation suggests a kind of composition. The reason for the simplicity, Durand writes in his preface, is that engineers need to learn architecture but have little time to do so.[85] At the Ecole Polytechnique, the course taught by Durand and the professors after him was but an introduction to the subject. Only a few of Durand's students became well-known architects: the father and son Hubert and Charles Rohault de Fleury, and more important, Emile-Jacques Gilbert. Each of these three later studied architecture at David Leroy's school or its successor.

Three days after its decree concerning the Ecole Polytechnique, on October 25, 1795 (3 brumaire an IV), the Convention issued a long decree "on the organization of public instruction."[86] In the hierarchy thus established, David Leroy's became the single important school of architecture. Title III, Article I proclaimed, "In the republic there shall be schools especially dedicated to the study of . . ." and the decree then listed ten schools, such as astronomy, medicine, political science, and music. The ninth was "of painting, of sculpture, of architecture." David Leroy's school was thus given a name—L'Ecole Spéciale de l'Architecture—and was joined in name to the Ecole Spéciale de la Peinture et de la Sculpture to form a single school of art.

The same decree organizing public instruction created the Institut National des Sciences et des Arts.

> It is intended: I. to perfect the sciences & the arts through uninterrupted researches, by the publication of discoveries, by correspondence with learned and foreign societies; 2. to follow ... scientific & literary work intended for the general utility & the glory of the republic.

Thus the Institut was brought into being in 1795 in order to assume another of the tasks of the abolished royal academies—study. This task was redefined, though, in the optimistic language of the revolutionary epoch. A member of the Convention, the historian Daunou, said that the Institut would "reassemble and unite all the branches of instruction"; it would be a "living Encyclopedia."[87] To unite knowledge, the most learned men were to be united in one body. The Institut, at its foundation, was restricted to 144 members divided into three classes: (1) the physical sciences and mathematics, (2) the moral sciences and politics, (3) literature and the beaux-arts. Six of the members of the third class were to be architects.[88] The six architects who were named to the Institut in 1795 had all belonged to the Royal Academy of Architecture; they were another link between the old and new bodies.[89] The Institut from the first was responsible for designating the winners of the Prix de Rome, briefly the task of the now-defunct Commune des Arts.[90]

The Consulate and Empire were a time of unfulfilled hopes for architectural education—and architecture too. Napoleon would have liked to build more grand monuments than Louis XIV had, but France could not afford both to dispatch armies across Europe and to erect palaces at home. One vast project, commissioned in 1802 under the supervision of Percier and Fontaine, was for a complex of governmental and educational buildings along the Left Bank across the center of Paris. An Ecole des Beaux-Arts was to be housed there; its design was assigned to A.-J.-B.-G. de Gisors. After years of proposals, he and Poyet and Damesme, who were designing the adjacent building for the university, jointly planned a palace for the two faculties. The cornerstone was placed on August 15, 1812. Two months later Napoleon was turned back from Moscow; his time for building palaces ended.[91]

The reality of architectural education was humble; David Leroy's school in its first decade (1793–1802) admitted only thirty-seven students.[92] The course, like that in the abolished Royal Academy of Architecture, consisted of faculty lectures and student designs.[93] Three forgotten men, de Machy, Mauduit, and Rieux, lectured on perspective, mathematics, and stereotomy (stonecutting). David Leroy lectured one hour a week on, in the words of the annual program,

> the history of architecture and of the theory of the different branches of this art, the Orders, the buildings erected by the peoples of antiquity and the works of Vitruvius, Palladio, Scamozzi and Vignola....

In his lectures he

> applied himself to making known the kind of male architecture [*architecture mâle*] he had for a long time admired in Greece, the architecture the Athenians had put to great use during the centuries when they were proud to be a free people, and that seems to fit particularly well the materials we possess.[94]

Students submitted architectural designs for monthly judgments, and the jury awarded medals. The best students competed for the Grand Prix de Rome, which the Institut began judging in 1797. (For three years, 1793–96, the *concours* and prize had been suspended because of the difficulty of travel to Rome.)[95] As before the Revolution, each student learned to design not in the Ecole but in an architect's atelier. (Of the ateliers the most influential was Percier's.)

The little school in the Louvre even lacked a precise name, as is shown by a decree of October 11, 1801 (19 vendémaire an IX):

> Art. I. The School of Painting, Sculpture, and Architecture shall be transferred to the Collège Mazarin, which shall take the name Palais des Beaux-Arts.
>
> Art. II. The Professors attached to this School shall be lodged in this Palais. . . .[96]

In that year more than ninety artists and their families were still living and working in the Louvre in apartments that had been granted by the king; the reason for ordering artists and art school out was to clear space for a museum. The school, or more truly, schools were slow to leave. During the year 1803, accommodation for the School of Architecture was prepared in the building to which it had been assigned, Le Vau's Collège des Quatre Nations; alterations to and care of it had been made the responsibility of David Leroy's associate, Vaudoyer. By mid-autumn of 1803 the School of Architecture had crossed the Seine. A decree of March 20, 1805, ordered the Institut also to move from the Louvre into Le Vau's palace. It went in February 1807 and remains there to this day. (A possibly inadvertent use of the plural in the decree of March 20, 1805, indicates the partial unity of the art school, united in administration, divided in teaching; the decree mentions "Les écoles spéciales de Peinture, Sculpture et Architecture.")[97] The School of Painting and Sculpture, in spite of repeated governmental orders, did not vacate its quarters in the Louvre until it was expelled one day in April 1807. The next day it was with the School of Architecture.[98]

Napoleon was able to realize most of his intentions concerning the Institut.[99] He reorganized it. The decree of January 23, 1803 (3 pluviose an XI), redivided the former three classes into four and enlarged the total membership.[100] The first remained the Classe des Sciences, Physiques et Mathématiques. Because Napoleon did not like the ideologists of the Revolution, he abolished the former second class (moral sciences and politics) and replaced it with the Classe de la Langue et de la Littérature Française. The former third class (literature and the beaux-arts) was divided in two, the Classe d'Histoire et de Littérature Ancienne and the Classe des Beaux-Arts. The total membership was raised to 165, but the number of architects remained six. Napoleon would have liked to rename the four classes academies—Académie des Sciences, Académie Française, Académie des Inscriptions et Belles-Lettres, and Académie des Beaux-Arts—but he was persuaded that such an allusion to the suppressed royal academies would antagonize many French citizens. After the restoration of the monarchy, Louis XVIII did change the names, thereby both preserving the Institut, one of the most worthy accomplishments of the Revolution, and reviving the names of some of the seventeenth-century academies, to recall the splendor of Louis XIV. In the words of the royal decree of March 28, 1816, the purpose of renaming the classes of the Institut was "to tie their past glory to the glory they have acquired."[101]

The name for the fourth class—the Académie des Beaux-Arts—does not echo the name of any one suppressed royal academy; in this class Napoleon had brought together several kinds of artists: painters, sculptors, architects, engravers, and composers of music. Each of these groups had been formed into a section of the class—Section d'Architecture, Section de Peinture, and so on. Louis XVIII increased the size of this class from 28 to 40;[102] thus, the number of architects rose from 6 to 8, and 8 it has remained ever since. These were the only changes to the Institut made by Louis XVIII, and later only one other important change occurred. In 1832 the class abolished by Napoleon was reestablished as the Académie des Sciences Morales et Politiques.[103] The membership in the whole Institut de France became 206 (plus 3 Sécretaires Perpétuels).[104]

Such continuity has had advantages and disadvantages. A disadvantage of the Institut, unforeseen by its founders but often noted in this century, has been its unchanging size in the midst of a growing national population. Before the Revolution, proportionately more French architects, painters, sculptors, literary men, and scientists were in academies. For the artists represented in the Académie des Beaux-Arts of the Institut, both variables in the proportion have changed. For example, in 1789 the Royal Academy of Architecture had places for thirty-two architects, but today, for countless more architects, there are only eight seats in the Institut. Thus, whereas before the Revolution exchanges of architectural ideas were likely to take place in the Royal Academy, in the nineteenth and twentieth centuries such exchanges have increasingly occurred outside the Institut, isolating it more and more from the main questions of the age. But this criticism is taking us far beyond 1803, the year in which Napoleon reformed the Institut and the Ecole Spéciale d'Architecture left the Louvre.

David Leroy died that year, 1803. He was succeeded in the School of Architecture by the man had chosen, his former student and loyal disciple, Léon

Dufourny (1754–1818).[105] Dufourny had lived in Italy from 1782 to 1795, and at Palermo in 1790 he had built an Ecole de Botanique, whose main building was a Neoclassical little block with a dome, a central octagonal space, and at the entrance a peristyle of four Doric columns with bases (an old-fashioned detail). At the School of Architecture, Dufourny lectured about architectural writings, ancient and modern, and about the monuments he had visited and the casts of antique ornament he had collected. Like David Leroy, he urged Greek classicism upon his students. David Leroy's associate, A.-L.-T. Vaudoyer, also remained on the staff. In 1807 he was officially named Archiviste-Secrétaire of the school, and in 1810 he began to be paid for the job.[106] In 1806, teaching stereotomy became the responsibility of Rondelet, who was no longer associated with the Ecole Polytechnique.[107] An indication of what he taught is in his book, *Traité théorique et pratique de l'art de bâtir*, of 1812–c.1814; it was reprinted for the eighth time in 1838. There continued to be professors of perspective and of mathematics. In the year of Dufourny's death, the chair of architecture went to Louis-Pierre Baltard (1764–1846), who had been a student of Antoine-François Peyre at the school of the Royal Academy of Architecture.[108] Baltard was of the generation that, inspired by Hellenistic and Roman temples in the Near East, dreamed of creating immense classical buildings; his Palais de Justice in Lyons of 1834 is fronted by a row of thirty-four Corinthian columns.

The number of students increased markedly: six admissions in 1803, thirty-eight in 1818.[109] The Ecole Spéciale d'Architecture thus endured, and it maintained continuity from the suppressed Académie Royale d'Architecture to the soon-to-be-established Ecole des Beaux-Arts.

The Ecole des Beaux-Arts and the Ateliers

After the restoration of the monarchy, the schools—or school—of architecture, painting, and sculpture moved from the Collège des Quatre Nations to nearby buildings, which before the Revolution had been the Couvent des Petits-Augustins. This monastery, which like all other church property was seized by the revolutionary government in 1789, became the Musée des Monuments Français of the archaeologist Alexandre Lenoir; there he installed the religious sculpture and architectural fragments that he had rescued from destruction.[110] Lenoir's museum did not last long: on April 24, 1816, Louis XVIII commanded in a royal order that the museum be closed and its monuments be returned to their previous owners. The buildings and grounds were then assigned in an order of December 18, 1816, to the "Ecole Royale et Spéciale des Beaux-Arts." The special schools were brought together now in name and were called, possibly for the first time, "des Beaux-Arts."[111]

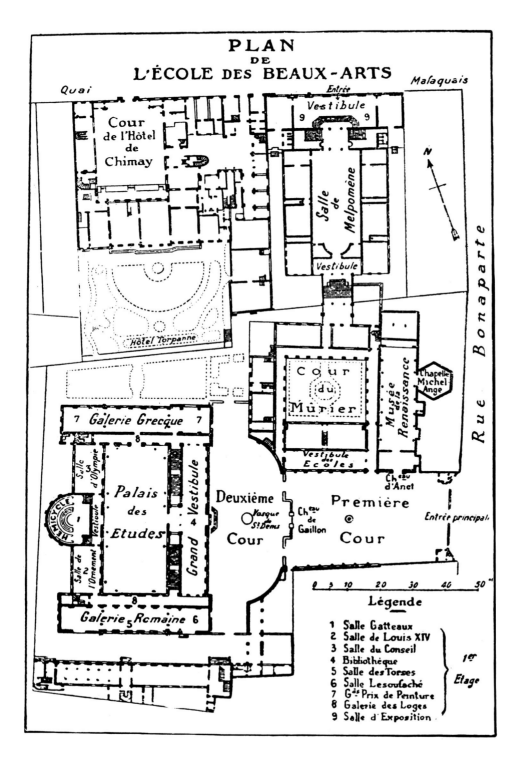

PLAN
DE
L'ÉCOLE DES BEAUX-ARTS

Quai   Malaquais

Cour
de l'Hôtel
de
Chimay

Entrée
Vestibule
9   9

Salle
de
Melpomène

Vestibule

N

Hôtel Torpanne

Cour
du
Mûrier

Musée de la Renaissance

Chapelle
Michel
Ange

7 Galerie Grecque 7
8

Palais
des
Etudes

Salle d'Olympie
3
Salle de l'Ornement
2
Salle
1
HÉMICYCLE
Vestibule
Grand Vestibule

Deuxième
Cour

Vasque de
St Denis
Chau de
Gaillon

Première
Cour

Vestibule des Écoles

Chau
d'Anet

Entrée principale

Galerie Romaine 6
8   5

0 5 10   20   30   40   50 m

Légende

1 Salle Gatteaux
2 Salle de Louis XIV
3 Salle du Conseil
4 Bibliothèque
5 Salle des Torses
6 Salle Lesoufaché
7 Gᵈˢ Prix de Peinture
8 Galerie des Loges
9 Salle d'Exposition

1ᵉʳ
Etage

Rue Bonaparte

Félix Duban. Ecole des Beaux-Arts, Paris. 1832-64. Overall plan *(left)*. Palais des Etudes: plan *(opposite)*, facade and forecourt showing Arc de Gaillon *(following pages)*.

From 1819 to 1968 "Beaux-Arts" architecture was taught in the buildings adapted for the use of the Ecole des Beaux-Arts by Félix Duban (1797–1870; student of François Debret, Grand Prix of 1823). The building history was complex; only one section, that on the Quai Malaquais containing the Salle Melpomène, was completely the work of Duban. Before this extension onto the quai in 1858–62, the Ecole was restricted to the Rue Bonaparte site of the seventeenth-century Monastery of the Petits-Augustins, which comprised a chapel, a cloister, and a garden. After the Revolution and the confiscation of Church property, the monastery had served as Alexandre Lenoir's Musée des Monuments Français, and after that institution's dissolution in 1816 the spaces were still encumbered with the French Gothic and Renaissance architectural monuments that he had brought there for preservation.

The monastery was appropriated for the use of the Ecole in 1816. François Debret, Duban's brother-in-law and a *maître d'atelier*, designed a large building to occupy the only open area of the monastic garden as well as the narrow three-story Bâtiment des Loges *(lower left on plan)* for the sequestration of students during competitions. Although all the foundations of the principal building were in place, only its southern wing was complete in 1832, when Debret was replaced as architect by Duban. Duban reorganized the whole site, placing the daily lecture and drawing courses in the old cloister, redesigning Debret's unfinished structure as the "Palais des Etudes" (containing a library, a ceremonial amphitheater, and a museum of casts and student work), and arranging the spaces around the buildings as a series of courtyards defined by the remnants of Lenoir's museum, most notably the "Arc de Gaillon," thought to have been designed by Fra Giocondo, and the frontispiece of the Château at Anet, by Philibert de l'Orme.

The detailing of the new facades was Early

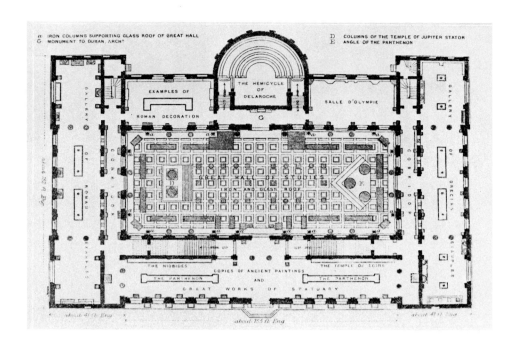

Renaissance Italian, harmonizing, Duban wrote, with the "lines and forms" of Lenoir's fragments. The more conservative professors at the Ecole des Beaux-Arts blocked approval of Duban's design, in part because of his integration of these Gothic and Renaissance remains, "whose taste may not be entirely in harmony with the principles of antique architecture." Eventually a compromise was reached, Duban chastening the detailing of the facade of the Palais des Etudes but being permitted to retain the architectural fragments in place. The work was executed during the years 1834–40. Duban remained the architect of the Ecole buildings and subsequently executed the Quai Malaquais extension for exhibition space (1858–62), painted the old monastic cloister in the style of a Pompeian garden (1864), and covered over the courtyard of the Palais des Etudes with an iron-and-glass roof to permit the display of plaster casts (p. 60). The walls of the courtyard were painted in strong *Néo-Grec* patterns by Ernest-Georges Coquart, Duban's successor as architect, in 1874.

As the controversy over Duban's initial design points up, the home of the Ecole des Beaux-Arts was a polemical building, a Romantic rather than a classical one. As is also evident, it could not be as clear a statement as its partisans would have wished. Duban had to accommodate his design to preexisting structures, and his facade of the Palais des Etudes even then was altered at the demand of the professors. And finally Duban's own ideas were not yet clearly formulated. The greatest significance of Duban's early work at the Ecole lies simply in his preservation of the remains of Lenoir's museum, which by their very presence suggested an alternative to the Greco-Roman tradition.

The most memorable parts of the Ecole des Beaux-Arts are the forecourts, laid out by Duban in 1832–40, leading to the Palais des Etudes from the Rue Bonaparte. These were an exercise in *mise-en-scène* and the arrangement of the *marche*, not involving general theories, but testing instead Duban's handling of space and one's voyage through it. From the Rue Bonaparte, the visitor looks

In fact, not all of Lenoir's collection was returned: the most impressive of the many remaining pieces of architecture are the entrance facade of Philibert de l'Orme's Château d'Anet and the portico of the Château de Gaillon. The Ecole took years to move. Until 1830 most of its activity remained in the Collège des Quatre Nations,[112] and not until 1839 was it entirely settled in its new main building, the Palais des Beaux-Arts or Palais (or Musée) des Etudes.[113] Construction of this building had begun in the early 1820s with plans by François Debret, but only one wing was complete in 1832, when Jacques-Félix Duban became architect. He got the rest up in five years and gave this Italianate *palazzo* his personal character. Between the facade and the Rue Bonaparte he arranged an outer and an inner forecourt in which he placed most of the fragments surviving from the Musée des Monuments Français. Between 1858 and 1862 he added another sizable building, the facade of which overlooks the Seine. Thus, Duban formed the principal parts of the school's physical environment. In 1884, the Ecole completed its physical growth on this site when the state acquired the house next door, the eighteenth-century Hôtel de Chimay.

But this is getting ahead of the story. Soon after ordering the Ecole to make its last move, the king gave to the administration and curriculum of the school a shape that remained substantially unchanged, except for a few years after the reform of November 1863, for more than one and a half centuries. The royal order of August 4, 1819, formally united the special schools of architecture, painting, and sculpture into an "Ecole Royale des Beaux-Arts."[114] (Regulations earlier in that year, issued on April 17, still referred to the "Ecole d'Architecture.")[115] Yet, from 1819 onward, the Section d'Architecture of the Ecole des Beaux-Arts was separate from the Sections de Peinture et de Sculpture. Students of architecture had their own faculty and their own curriculum. This curriculum was fully defined in the regulations

80

through a grill into an outer forecourt closed by the open screen of the Arc de Gaillon, behind which the mass of the Palais des Etudes appears precisely framed by the forecourt's lateral walls, its silhouette defined by a delicate iron openwork cresting (*opposite*).

After crossing the outer, public forecourt and penetrating the Arc de Gaillon, the broader extent of the facade of the Palais (*above*) presents itself in a space opened up by two half-hemicycles in the inner forecourt walls. The facade is framed by two vistas,

through screens of architectural fragments at each corner, into gardens flanking it on the north and south. Entering the door, one crosses a single chamber occupying the whole of the front wing, passes between two straight staircases leading to the painted loggias overlooking the courtyard on the second story, traverses the courtyard and arrives at the amphitheater on whose long curved wall Paul Delaroche depicted an imaginary assembly of the greatest artists of modern times, seemingly in attendance at the ceremonies of the Ecole.

of December 27, 1823.[116] All subsequent regulations were modeled on those of 1823 and merely modified them. Rather than summarizing these regulations, let us instead follow a would-be architect through the school.[117]

The structure was like a step-pyramid, with a top big enough for only one man. Below were four steps. The lowest of these was preparation for admission; above it was second class; higher yet was first class; and almost at the top was competition for the Grand Prix. Each student climbed at his own speed as high as he could.

First, the young man (or, from the end of the century on, young woman)[118] found a master, the *patron* of an atelier. People seem to have got into the atelier of their first choice. There the student learned architecture.

Once in an atelier, the would-be architect enrolled at the Ecole des Beaux-Arts on the list of *aspirants*. For this registration the only requirements were a letter of introduction from a known artist, almost always the *patron* of the atelier (a requirement dropped in 1863), and a document certifying that the candidate was between fifteen and thirty years old. French citizens presented birth certificates, foreigners, a letter of introduction from their ambassadors. The *aspirant à l'Ecole des Beaux-Arts* then began preparing for the school's entrance exams, which tested (both on paper and orally) mathematics, descriptive geometry, history (from 1864 on), drawing (from 1867 on), usually of a cast of ornament, and most important architectural design. An *aspirant* might prepare for the mathematical exams by hiring a tutor, for the architectural exam by making designs using Ecole programs. And he would help older students in the atelier with their drawings.

The Ecole gave its *aspirants* the privileges of reading in the school library, sketching the casts in the school's collection, and listening to all lectures. From the early 1820s on, there were lectures in theory of architecture, history of architecture, construction, perspective, and mathematics; by 1900 there were more than twice as many courses, including physics and chemistry, descriptive geometry, building law, general history, and French architecture.

Admission exams were at first given annually, then, from 1865 on, semi-annually. The number of students of architecture accepted increased from on the average thirty-seven a year in the 1820s to ninety-seven a year in the 1890s, and the number continued to grow. An *aspirant* could sit for the exams as many times as he wished, until he reached his thirtieth birthday.[119] Most Frenchmen needed about two years of preparation to get into the school. Foreigners, from the late nineteenth century on, tended to take less time, for most of them came from architectural schools in their own lands.

Admitted into the Ecole itself, the student entered the second class. He was now entitled to call himself an *élève de l'Ecole des Beaux-Arts*. The Ecole charged no tuition and was open to anyone, French or foreign, between fifteen and thirty years old who could pass the entrance exams. The curriculum for the second class consisted of *concours* and of the lectures that *aspirants* were allowed to attend. None of these lectures were compulsory at any stage of the curriculum. Only those on scientific subjects were followed by exams, and a student could prepare for the exams without hearing the lectures. Only the lectures about construction seem to have been dutifully attended; many of the others seem to have been ignored. *Concours d'émulation* (competitions) were the method by which students' designs were judged. The largest number of these *concours* were in architectural composition, and they were of two kinds: *esquisses* (sketches) and *projets rendus* (rendered projects). Programs were issued monthly, *esquisses* alternating with *projets rendus*. (The professor of theory wrote these programs, and thus his was the most important chair in the Section d'Architecture.) Sketch *concours* required one drawing submitted after twelve hours of study; those for *projets rendus* usually required three larger drawings, submitted after two months. Programs that were repeatedly used in the second class were, for *projets rendus*, a small school, an assembly hall, a small railroad station, and so on; for *esquisses*, often a part of a building assigned as a *projet rendu* such as the facade of a small public building, a small house, or a village fountain. From about 1876 on, students commenced their architectural *concours* with a third kind, *éléments analytiques*, of which two examples were required. The elements to be analyzed were Doric, Ionic, or Corinthian; the single drawing required for each of these *concours* had the purpose of introducing the student to classical architecture, whose parts were considered to be the source of both architectural proportions and decorative motifs.

Of as much importance as architectural composition was construction. Every year from 1823 to 1868 there were four construction *concours*, one for stone, one for iron, one for wood, and one for *construction générale*, each lasting about four months (p. 215). To be promoted to the first class, a student had to get credit in each of these four *concours* (and also in a *concours* in mathematics, in one in perspective, and in several in architectural composition). The regulations of November 1867 made construction into a single *concours*, lasting three months, with knowledge of mathematics, descriptive geometry, and stereotomy the prerequisite. By the latter decades of the century, students in the second class usually needed at least a year for their scientific studies: for the written (and drawn) exercises, the exams, and the *concours* in mathematics, descriptive geometry, stereotomy, and perspective, and for the construction exams and the construction *concours*. The construction *concours* required about a dozen drawings, showing how a projected building would be put together, with attention to the detailing of stone, iron, and wood, and with mathematical calculation that the building would stand. Passing the construction requirement seems to have been the hardest task in the second class.

Students entering *concours* worked in small cubicles—*en loges*—where they had twelve hours in which to study the program and draw their preliminary sketches. Drawing by L.-B. Bonnier, from de Penanrum, Roux, and Delaire, *Les Architectes élèves de l'Ecole des Beaux-Arts, 1819–94*, Paris, 1895.

Some minor *concours* became further obligations. *Dessin* was added to the curriculum between 1855 and 1859.[120] The *dessins* drawn by the student were of classical ornament and of the human figure, or more precisely of a cast of an antique statue of the human figure. In 1883 this single *concours* was divided in three called together *l'enseignement simultanée des trois arts*; in the Section d'Architecture the three *concours* were in drawing ornament, drawing a cast of the human figure, and modeling a bas-relief of ornament. Also in the Sections de Peinture et de Sculpture there were new *concours* for studying what the regulations[121] called the "elements" of the three arts: for painters a *concours* in modeling the figure, for sculptors a *concours* in drawing the figure, and for both painters and sculptors a *concours* in composing a work of architecture. The regulations of 1883 added to the schedule of architectural *concours* in the second class the history of architecture, long the subject of lectures. Known by students as archaeology, it required a drawing or two of a building or part of a building. In the '80s and '90s this was likely to be antique Greek or Roman, but in the twentieth century more likely to be medieval or Renaissance French.

These, then, were all the subjects of *concours* in the second class by 1900, and this curriculum remained almost unchanged until 1968. Because students could progress each at his own speed, a student had to enroll for every *concours* he wished to enter. For architectural *concours* the process of enrollment was remarkable. In a special building, parallel to and south of Duban's "Palais des Etudes," the student would sign his name in the book of registrations for *concours* and would receive a copy of the program. He then went into a small cubicle—in French, one says he went *en loge*—and there he had twelve hours in which to study the program, and if he wished to draw a small preliminary sketch recording the essential form of his architectural design. All the students *en loge* for a *concours* could talk together, but no one else was allowed to join them (*above*). If a student wished to take part in the *concours*, he would when he left the building give his sketch to the guard, who acknowledged receipt in the registration book. Once out, the student could not return. He would take a tracing of his sketch back to his atelier, where with the criticism of his *patron* he would develop his idea. Ultimately, if the student wanted to, he would prepare drawings for submission on an appointed date to the school for judgment. The jury compared each student's preliminary sketch with his final entry, for the two had to reflect the same idea. If they did not, the jury declared the submission out of the competition, *hors de concours*, and for that *concours* the student would get no credit. The purpose of this complicated arrangement was to insure that each student thought for himself, that he did not have his work done for him by his *patron*. Students often were judged *hors de concours*, often they were simply failed by the jury, and often they registered for *concours* but did not submit final drawings or even a preliminary sketch. Many students found it worthwhile every month to enroll for an architectural *concours*, get the program, and try that day to conceive of a building, even if there was no time for further study. The very number of *esquisses* and *projets rendus* that were offered kept architecture at the center of the second class's curriculum.[121a]

To remain in the Ecole a student needed only to do one or two *concours* a year. If he did none, his name was struck off the list of students; for readmission, he had to take the entrance exams again. A student could do as many *concours* as he wanted, until he reached the age of thirty. Most students had part-time paying jobs. Promotion did not occur after a set period of time, as it does in American schools, but rather after the student in the second class had fulfilled his various obligations and had collected enough of the numerical points (called *valeurs*) with which the Ecole graded *concours*. (The Ecole also awarded prizes, the *prix d'émulation*, which were *médailles* for some *concours* and *mentions* for others.)[122] The better the jury considered a design to be, the more points the competitor got. It was possible for a student who passed all his other requirements to win promotion after only one *projet rendu*, but usually students presented several *projets rendus* and several *esquisses* and had two of each accepted. Once in a great while, a student would complete the second-class work in a year, but most needed two to four years. Some never got beyond that class, but slipped away from the school to work for a living full-time. In the nineteenth century they had a higher status than that of many architects, for if a former student could rightfully call himself both an architect and an *ancien élève de l'Ecole des Beaux-Arts*, probably the latter title meant more. In France, from the time of the Revolution until 1940, anyone who wished to be known as an architect needed only to buy a patent, and some so-called architects were but pretentious entrepreneurs.[123] Outside France in those years, an architect who had studied at the Ecole in Paris won respect simply for having been there.

Students who were promoted entered the first class. There the curriculum was like that of the second but with greater emphasis on the annual six *esquisses* and six *projets rendus* that were the architectural *concours*. A student could take part in as many of these as he wished, until his thirtieth birthday.

Their programs were more complicated than those of the second class: typical subjects of first-class *projets rendus* were schools, museums, hotels, theaters, and large houses (p. 289); *esquisses* might be parts of a larger building (such as an entrance way, or a single bay in a palatial hall) or small buildings with one purpose (such as a boutique or a clock tower, p. 189). From 1883 on, there were also minor *concours* in drawing the human figure, in modeling ornament, and in the history of architecture. And for the students of the first class there were the Ecole's annual *grand concours*, which carried as prizes not only *valeurs* and *médailles* but also money. The oldest of these, the Concours Rougevin (named for its endower), began in 1857; it was for ornament in an architectural context, as, for example, a tomb. In 1881 began another *grand concours*, the Godeboeuf, which was for an architectural work of a special nature, such as an elevator cab (p. 306). First-class students were required each year to participate in one or two minor or *grand concours*.

The fourth step up the school pyramid was competition for the Grand Prix de Rome. (The prize that in the eighteenth century was usually called the *prix*, and in the first half of the nineteenth the Grand Prix, came in the second half of the nineteenth century to be known as the Grand Prix de Rome.)[124] It was the goal of the best students, and the competition for it was the most important *concours* of the year. The judgment was reported by the architectural press, the exhibition of drawings in the school's Salle Melpomène attracted the public, and the publication of reproductions of the winners' drawings spread their influence. The *concours* for the Grand Prix was open to any French citizen between fifteen and thirty years old, but not to foreigners. In principle, someone who was in no way connected to the Ecole des Beaux-Arts could win the prize, but in practice the winner was nearly always a student in the Ecole's first class. An exception was Jacques Carlu, later professor of architecture at the Massachussetts Institute of Technology, who won the Grand Prix in 1919 when he was in the second class. The entire competition was conducted not by the Ecole des Beaux-Arts but by the Académie des Beaux-Arts of the Institut de France; thus, the Ecole did not control the culmination of its own educational program.

The competition for the Grand Prix de Rome occupied almost half the year. In fact, it was not one *concours* but three.[125] Early in March came the first trial, which was open to all applicants: twelve hours *en loge* to draw an *esquisse*. One year the program was for an addition to a palace; customarily this first *esquisse* let each competitor show his brilliance in designing a facade. The second stage of the competition took place within the week: twenty-four hours *en loge* for another *esquisse* that customarily required solving a complicated problem in planning, such as a building to house a university in a city. This second trial was for only thirty people: as many of the competitors from the third stage of the *concours* in previous years as might wish to try again, plus, to bring the number to thirty, the competitors whose designs had been judged best in the twelve-hour trial of a few days before.[126] The architects in the Académie des Beaux-Arts of the Institut de France judged the first and second trials. Immediately after the second, this jury named eight winners (from 1864 on, ten winners) allowed into the third trial, the competition proper, which began at once and lasted until the end of July. The program was usually for a monumental public building of a kind that only the state would be likely to erect; for example, there were museums (of art, natural history, and so on, p. 241), hospices (in the Alps or by the Mediterranean, p. 255), universities or analogous schools of higher education (a conservatory of music, a military or naval academy, a school of medicine or of arts and crafts, pp. 190, 192, 224), embassies (or a palace for the governor of a French colony), and cathedrals. The final stage of the *concours* for the Grand Prix was like the architectural *concours* conducted by the Ecole in that each competitor was obliged to make a preliminary sketch and not digress too far from it. The jury compared the final drawings with this preliminary sketch; if they were not in accord, their maker was declared *hors de concours*.[127]

During the four months of the competition proper, each of the rivals got close attention from his *patron*, not only because everyone wanted to win the Grand Prix, but also because making these designs was a chance for architectural speculation. In effect, the Institut and behind it, the state, encouraged theorizing by the most talented young designers. As the day of presentation approached, each competitor's atelier became a team of assistants, producing the final versions of the many drawings. These sheets grew larger and larger during the nineteenth century. By 1880 some elevations were more than twenty-six feet long.

The final judgment was complicated. First, the eight architects in the Académie des Beaux-Arts decided which projects, if any, deserved the first, second, and third prizes; and then this decision was reported to the entire Academy, that is to say, to the painters, sculptors, engravers, and musicians who, with the architects, made up the membership. The whole Academy then voted. Nearly always the Academy made the decision of the architects final (likewise it usually made final the decision of the artists in each of the other sections for the Grand Prix in that particular art), but it could do otherwise. It had the last word.

The winner of the Grand Prix de Rome was marked by the Academy as the most promising architect of the year. He was then sent to the French Academy in Rome for four or five years, at the expense of the government, in order to learn the lessons of antiquity. Upon his return to France, he was likely to be made an Architecte du Gouvernement, and thereafter in the employ of the state he would be responsible for a public building, such as the national library or one of the national palaces. He would see to the maintenance of his building and, if necessary, to its alteration or enlargement. He might well teach, perhaps as *patron* of an atelier and even as a professor at the Ecole des Beaux-Arts. He was not through competing, for he would hope in time for the highest honor: election by the Academy to its Section d'Architecture. Almost without exception, the architects in the Academy in the nineteenth century were winners of the Grand Prix de Rome, but because there were only eight chairs for architects in the Academy and because each member held his chair for life, someone just back from Rome could expect to wait for decades before being nominated for election.

The old age of academicians affected the Ecole des Beaux-Arts. Every year the Academy judged the most influential *concours*, and naturally the standards by which these eight old men made judgment were old-fashioned. Thus, although the *concours* for the Grand Prix could be taken as an opportunity for innovation, the competitors, knowing that the jurors were old men, tended to present familiar ideas. As a result, the pace of change in French architecture in the nineteenth and early twentieth centuries was slower than that in England or America.

The winner of the Grand Prix de Rome stood, so to speak, at the top of the Ecole's pyramid. Only one man a year could reach the height; some people were for years just below, among the eight or ten competitors in the final stage of the *concours*. Léon Vaudoyer, Jules André, Léon Ginain, L.-M.-H. Sortais, and René Patouillard-Demoraine each won the Grand Prix on his fifth attempt. Other men tried as many times without success. Constant Moyaux and Tony Garnier each won in his sixth competition, and Jean-Louis Pascal in his seventh. Edmond Paulin was *en loge* four months every year from 1868 through 1875; at last, on his eighth try, he won.

The winner of the Grand Prix was likely to be almost thirty years old. (From November 1863 to February 1870, the maximum age of the competitors was lowered to twenty-five.) The average student at the Ecole des Beaux-Arts knew by the time he was in the first class whether or not he had any chance of winning the top prize. If he decided that he lacked the necessary talent (or if he was one of these who tried and failed to get the prize), he would simply leave the Ecole when he felt ready to go. The culmination of the course was for only one man. Until 1867 this prize was the only termination of the curriculum other than the age limit. No students graduated, in the sense that the word is commonly understood in America. In November 1867 a diploma was instituted, but for twenty years it had no effect. Before dealing with that change, however, let us turn our attention to the places outside the Ecole where students learned architecture—ateliers.

An atelier is a studio; an architectural atelier is a drafting room. Every student of architecture at the Ecole des Beaux-Arts learned to design in an architectural atelier. The Ecole's teaching of design was limited to lecturing, issuing programs, and judging *concours.* (The judgments were never an educational experience, as at their best they became in American architectural schools in the twentieth century, because during judgments at the Ecole des Beaux-Arts only the jurors were present.) At the Ecole, everyone in the Section d'Architecture was registered as—and thought of himself as—the student of an architect. He might be the architect's only student, and when that was the case the atelier was likely to be the place in which the architect was designing his buildings and making the drawings required for construction. The student there was like the pupil of one of the architects in the Académie Royale before the Revolution, or like the apprentice of an English or American architect of the time, but in France such students seem not to have signed contracts equivalent to the English articles of apprenticeship. The student was sometimes the architect's employee. Or he might be the architect's son; in the nineteenth century the medieval tradition of a son taking up his father's work remained stronger than it does today.

But the single student in an atelier was the exception; most of the Ecole students chose to group together. A statistical study made in 1852 will serve as an illustration.[128] During the school year 1851–52, of the 281 students enrolled in the Section d'Architecture, the average number presenting drawings in each architectural *concours* was 112. These 112 students were in 37 ateliers. But 55 of them were in 3 ateliers—25 in Blouet's, 17 in Lebas's, and 13 in Labrouste's. Another 25 were in 5 other ateliers. In other words, most of the students were in a few of the ateliers. These large ateliers were not architectural offices; they were private schools of architecture. The architect who directed such an atelier did not do his own designs there for projects that were his commissions; that work he and his employees did in his office, called his *agence.* The purpose of the large ateliers was solely teaching.

The attraction of the ateliers was twofold: an experienced master offering guidance, and a company of students sharing their learning. The master's experience was likely to consist not only of his buildings but also of a rarer accomplishment—a Grand Prix de Rome. That prize and all the years needed to get it had attached the winner to atelier life. Prize-winning students often become teachers. The atelier the winner directed might be the one in which he had studied, or he might teach in another, perhaps of his own founding. In any case, he hoped in turn to be training winners of the Grand Prix. People naturally want to learn from someone they know to be excellent: the master's own prize marked his excellence in design; his students' prizes marked his excellence in teaching. Not surprisingly, French students were attracted to the ateliers that were currently capturing the Prix de Rome, if only because those were the ateliers where the best students were exchanging ideas. (Foreigners, not being eligible for the prize, were less affected by it; they tended to enter ateliers in which there were fellow countrymen.) Had a statistical study like

Victor Laloux surrounded by his students, in a courtyard of the Ecole des Beaux-Arts, 1890–91.

that of 1852 been made a generation later, it would have shown many more students of architecture distributed among fewer ateliers. In fact, from the mid-1860s on, nearly all Ecole students belonged to the big teaching ateliers. Many of these establishments were to endure for decades and some for more than a century.[129] By 1900 such an atelier was probably three times as large as it had been at mid-century, containing from thirty to eighty students (*above*).

The ateliers were in the neighborhood of the Ecole des Beaux-Arts on the Left Bank. The needs were few: space enough for drawing boards for all the students, big windows for light, water for mixing colors, and a low rent. The water was cold, and the only heat in the winter came from coal-burning stoves. Emile Vaudremer's atelier (which in the 1870s was on the Rue du Bac)[130] is described in a letter Louis Sullivan wrote home in December 1874:

> It is the damnedest pigstie I ever got into. First it's cold, and then when you light the fire it smokes so that it nearly puts your eyes out, and you have to open the windows, which makes a devil of a draft, which is not to be recommended for people with a cold.[131]

Laloux's atelier was unusual in being in an impressive building, a handsome eighteenth-century house at 8 Rue d'Assas, where students pinned their drawings onto walls paneled with Louis-Quinze woodwork, and where the stairway had such broad treads and low risers that, one student remembered, "you sort of fell upstairs, it was so comfortable."[132] The atelier Pascal, which was perhaps the largest at the turn of the century, was then at 20 Rue Mazarine, where on the ground floor there was a junk shop; Pascal's students, up two flights of dilapidated stairs in the courtyard, worked in the top three stories of the building (and chased each other on the roofs around the chimney pots).[133] Three architectural ateliers were, from 1863 on, in the Ecole's own buildings. (They were near the Cour du Murier until the acquisition of the Hôtel de Chimay, when they moved into its wings.) These ateliers,

Students in an atelier at the turn of the century.

which were established by the reform of 1863, were not, strictly speaking, private schools of architecture; they were *ateliers officiels*, whereas the others were *ateliers libres*, free in the sense that they were privately, not officially, controlled. The *ateliers officiels* were, in effect if not in intent, very much like the *ateliers libres* (*above*). A description by an architect who completed his studies in 1903 fits any one of them:

> The ateliers ... occupy quarters in old buildings where cheapness and dirt keep company. A crowd of students is not a desirable neighbor: they sing much, often through the night. The walls of the rooms are decorated with caricatures and pictures until a dark somber tone is attained that accords well with the dirt, dishevelment, and confusion of the place. The lighting is by candle, each man furnishing his one or two candles that are stuck to the board on which he is working. The air of the room is close, for there is no ventilation. Silence never prevails. Jokes fly back and forth, snatches of songs, excerpts from operas, at times even a mass may be sung, yet amid the confusion and the babble—strange as it may seem—work proceeds.[134]

The organization of the ateliers was remarkable. Each was governed not by the architect whose name it carried but by the students themselves. They elected one of the group, usually a long-time member, to be their *massier*. He administrated the atelier, collecting modest dues from each member and paying the atelier's costs: the rent, coal for the stoves, oil for lamps (if they were being used instead of candles), a few books (if the atelier had an architectural library), and most important a fee to the architect in charge. (The architects in charge of the *ateliers officiels* were paid by the state. It was said in 1871 that students in those ateliers paid no dues, but there is evidence that by 1906 they too were paying.)[135] The responsibility of the *massier* in some ateliers even included accepting new members,[136] but more often, at least in the nineteenth century, the *patron* kept for himself the task of interviewing appli-

Judging a competition. Drawing by L.-B. Bonnier, from Delaire, *Les Architectes élèves de l'Ecole des Beaux-Arts, 1793–1907*, Paris, 1907.

cants. (The young Julian Clarence Levi was taken to meet the *patron* Scellier de Gisors one morning in 1898 at half past seven.)[137] Accepted into the atelier he had chosen, each member found a hierarchy of students old and new, *anciens* and *nouveaux*. As the newest of the new, he and others joining the atelier at the same time would have to undergo an initiation, which might consist merely of "dodging wet sponges, and singing the 'Boulanger March' standing upon a drawing board."[138] More often the initiation was a duel in which the contestants, naked, were each armed with a bucket of paint and a long brush. Afterward the newest members would swear to observe the atelier rules and would buy food and drink for the group.

The *anciens* and the *nouveaux* helped one another. The *anciens*, some of whom would have been in the atelier nearer ten years than five, gave the benefit of their experience to the *nouveaux* by criticizing designs, not in formal sessions but in the endless exchange of ideas about architecture that was the intellectual life of the atelier. The *nouveaux* assisted the *anciens* with presentation drawings: tracing shadows on facades, repeating patterns of ornament, and inking plans. The *nouveaux* usually did this hard work nonstop, day and night, shortly before each *concours* reached its end. The term used for carrying out this work was to *négrifier*. If an *ancien* in the atelier reached the last stage of the *concours* for the Grand Prix, all the men he needed would become his "assistants." Thus, for months, the *nouveaux* would have their hands in the development of a complex project, and the competitor, like an architect with an office, would keep in mind not only his design but also the efficient management of his staff.

Students rushing drawings to the Ecole in a cart, called a *charette*. Drawing by Charles Collens, from "The Beaux-Arts in 1900," *AIA Journal*, 1947.

Members of each atelier also worked together in lesser *concours*. Whenever drawings were due, people on the Left Bank could see the last steps in these shared efforts. Outside the ateliers, students would load their designs onto little handcarts that they would drag through the streets to the courtyard of the Ecole. This kind of cart, commonly used for all sorts of light haulage in Paris, was called a *charette*; thus, being *en charette* came to mean not only the rush to the Ecole (*right*), but also before that, the long hours of last-minute work in the atelier. At the Ecole, the drawings were delivered to the Salle Melpomène, where later the judgment took place (*opposite*). The guard who received the drawings stamped an identifying number on each; for the sake of fairness, the designers' names were kept from the jury.

If the jury awarded a *mention* or *médaille* to someone in the atelier, the whole group would be proud; if an *ancien* in the atelier brought back the

Projects on exhibit in the Salle Melpomène, between the two world wars.

Students registering drawings in the Salle Melpomène. From Alexis Lemaistre, *L'Ecole des Beaux-Arts dessinée et racontée par un élève*, Paris, 1889.

Grand Prix, the *esprit de corps* was intense. Each atelier was in rivalry with all the others. Consequently, especially in the nineteenth century, it was most unusual for a student to set foot in any atelier other than his own. Sometimes a *nouveau* during his initiation would be sent to another atelier to borrow something, such as a compass that draws volutes (which no compass will do). The unsuspecting visitor would probably get a bucket of water on his head.

A *patron* would make a call on his atelier two or three times a week. When he was seen approaching, all the schoolboy hilarity suddenly ceased. The visits were conducted with a formality utterly alien to our current notion of the teacher-student relationship. Memoirs by their students give us glimpses of those teachers in another age.

Of Emmanuel Pontremoli in the 1920s:

> He would come into the quietly waiting room (warned by a scout), take off his hat, lay his fur-lined coat on a filthy table, go to a drawing board, the men then all around him, and begin pointing out the doubtful and danger spots, generally ignoring the author, addressing the whole group about the progress of the world, as entailed in this little piece of architecture. At the end, "See to that for me," and he would move on to the next place. At the end of twenty or forty crits in the gloom, at the dim drafting lights, he would go to the sty of a sink and wash his hands at the cold water tap. . . .[139]

Of Jules André in the 1880s, as Pontremoli remembered him:

> Old André would appear there on the days he chose, he would pass quietly from table to table, from stool to stool, speaking little, never taking a pencil nor making a sketch, content with a wave of the hand or a rub of the thumb; in a silent language he would show us what had to be developed, enlarged, reduced in order to give a better look and nobler proportions to our drawings and facades; with a glance he would judge our sketches and show us the way to further development.[140]

Of Léon Jaussely in 1919:

> When he had arrived . . . he had been greeted with profound ceremonial respect. He had moved from table to table, with the *élèves* grouped behind him with bated breath—not one word or other sound disturbing his criticism. Every word was treasured (the older men would interpret his critique later, for the benefit of all). . . . When he came to my *esquisse* . . . he vigorously illustrated his commentary on proportions with a diagrammatic sketch no larger than a small postage stamp. I got the point.[141]

Of Jean-Louis Pascal in the 1870s:

> In the atelier it did not seem to take him an instant to realize the possibilities of any sketch that his pupil might put before him, and he always left us either happily convinced that our sketch was not worth further trouble, or with our eyes opened to artistic possibilities in it of which we had not dreamed, giving us courage to go through the days and nights required to make finished drawings. He had a wonderful power of accepting the conception of his pupil and helping him to develop it in his own way. . . .[142]

Of Victor Laloux at the turn of the century:

> Followed by his pupils, he went from table to table, giving his criticism to each student in turn; having made the rounds, he would bow, put on his silk hat and quietly leave the room, but no sooner was the door shut than pandemonium would break loose and a noisy discussion of what he had said follow.[143]

Thus, it could be said, architecture was taught at the Ecole des Beaux-Arts, for the *patrons* truly were the *professeurs d'architecture*, as they officially were titled. They transmitted their theories of architecture in the most effective way, face to face with their students, talking about those students' designs. So long as the atelier system worked well, the students almost without exception revered the *patrons*, and the term *patron* curiously expresses this relationship. Students did not speak of the architect in charge of the atelier as the *professeur*, the *directeur*, or the *chef*, as they might have done; only rarely, in circumstances inviting special respect, did they call him *maître*. Instead, he was the *patron*, a word that suggests, as one student wrote, "a bond of friendship."[144] Among the meanings of the word *patron* in French are protector (a patron-saint) and head of a business (the colloquial equivalent in America might be "the boss" and in England "the governor"). The word *patron* struck a note of familiarity.

The atelier system was effective in the nineteenth century partly because of economics. Students could afford to pay the rents of large, if primitively lit and heated, ateliers. *Patrons* could afford to teach regularly and often; they seem to have lived comfortably if modestly on their various incomes — atelier fees, government salaries to those responsible for public buildings, and a few private commissions. In the twentieth century, between the wars, there were signs that the system was being strained. The number of students seemed to enlarge faster than did the floor area of the ateliers. In an atelier in 1850, there were likely to be twenty students with plenty of room, the *nouveaux* working among the *anciens* and thus all constantly helping one another. By 1925 there might be more than a hundred students, and the very number led to some separation of classes. The Ecole schedule further caused separation: for a long time first-class *concours* were due one month and second-class the next. In large, crowded ateliers, one class tended to stay away when the other most needed space for drawings. Naturally, such ateliers lost unity. Also, by the 1930s many of the *patrons* had one or two assistants, who often did most of the teaching. (Were the *patrons'* finances too becoming strained?) The system was becoming less personal. The old loyalty in each atelier to the *patron* was divided and weakened.

A student could change ateliers if he wished, but in the nineteenth century this was almost unheard-of. More often, a whole atelier (or a large part of one) changed *patrons*. In 1853 after the death of the *patron* Blouet, it was the students in the atelier who chose Gilbert as his successor.[145] In 1856 Henri Labrouste announced to his students that he would no longer be a *patron*. According to a student who was there, Labrouste hesitated to name his successor. The majority of the students proposed Jules André; Labrouste accepted but with little enthusiasm. The other students, even less enthusiastic, then went to Viollet-le-Duc and asked him to become their *patron*, and he accepted.[146] In 1867, the Ecole appointed André as *patron* of one of the ateliers in the school, and he closed his *atelier libre*. Most of his students followed him, but some, not wanting to enter an *atelier officiel*, asked Coquart to open an atelier for them, and he did.[147] In 1890, after André died, the students in his *atelier officiel* asked that his successor be Laloux, who had long been unofficial assistant and during André's fatal illness was in effect *patron*. The school (and government) refused the request and appointed Moyaux. Nearly all André's students then walked out, taking much of the furniture with them, and rented an atelier for themselves and Laloux.[148] In 1923, a group of students who felt that the Ecole and the ateliers were isolated from the stirrings of modernism asked Le Corbusier to teach them architecture. He refused but sent them to Auguste Perret, who was willing and thus in early 1924 became a *patron*.[149]

In the 1930s, individuals did begin to change ateliers. It was another ominous sign, for these students took to moving into ateliers whose *patrons*, it was rumored, were influential within the Institut.[150] Producing the winner of a Grand Prix had from the first established the reputation of an atelier, and more winners kept its reputation great. Both students and new *patrons* were periodically demoralized by the belief that only work from a few large ateliers with old *patrons* would be rewarded. In the 1840s and '50s this had been the case. Although Henri Labrouste directed one of the most popular ateliers, not one of his students ever won the Grand Prix, and eventually he gave up teaching, convinced that the Institut was prejudiced against his rationalism and in favor of the old-fashioned classicism of Lebas. Again, after the First World War, the Institut seemed willing to accept only old-fashioned classicism (which was quite different from the classicism of the mid-nineteenth century), rejecting anything influenced by the new ideas of those men we call modern. In the 1920s and '30s, the Grand Prix de Rome was carried off by students of Laloux six times, by students of Roger Expert never. The students of Perret in the '20s decided that their work in the second and first classes had little chance of being accepted even by the school jury.

In the decades between the founding of the Third Republic and the outbreak of the First World War, when the fame of the Ecole was at its greatest, perhaps deservedly so, the differences among *patrons* were not so divisive. Their teaching was not uniform, because their artistic personalities differed, as did their interests. Jules André, for instance, had, as his first principle, circulation: attention to circulation was the way to make the requirements of a program into an equilibrium of architectural solids and voids.[151] André's pupil Laloux concentrated on the organization of a plan, with an intuitive balancing and proportioning of each part so as to contribute to the whole. He let his students leave facades until the last minute; one remembered him saying, "You can put forty good facades on a good plan, but without a good plan you cannot have a good facade."[152] Pascal urged logic, not intuition. He taught simplification: rational plans and decorous elevations. His ideal was architecture that was and looked distinguished.[153] Gaston Redon, brother of the painter Odilon, was known for his interest in decoration.[154] Jaussely was concerned with planning not only buildings but also cities, and was city planner of Barcelona after the First World War. In the teaching of all the *patrons*, two constants are evident: the importance of the plan, and the importance of a vague quality often called "character." In the nineteenth century, it was taken for granted that plans were symmetrical; in the twentieth, symmetry became an issue. A building with character was one that fulfilled its purpose; character was the expression of this fulfillment. A student at the school in the 1880s put it this way:

> The point on which French architects stand preeminent is planning, and in the School special attention is given to planning. Each plan is prepared with due regard to the requirements of the particular building it is intended for, composed with the greatest deference to proportion and symmetry, and the elevations follow as natural consequents. The principle of all the design is that every building shall have its own character, as a natural development of the use it is put to.[155]

The Reform of 1863 and Later Changes

The reform of the Ecole des Beaux-Arts that was decreed by Napoleon III on November 13, 1863, occasioned the greatest disturbance to architectural education in France between the suppression of the royal academies in 1793 and the riots in 1968. The reform of 1863 was the result of a controversy that had persisted for nearly three and a half decades, and it caused an uproar at the Ecole that echoed in architectural journals for almost another ten years. But when all was said and done, the school was much the same. The reformers had failed to make the changes they wanted most. Later changes that caused little fuss—most important, the introduction of the *diplôme*—proved in time to be of greater effect.

The controversy revolved around two architects: Henri Labrouste (1801–75) and Eugène-Emmanuel Viollet-le-Duc (1814–79).[156] It began in 1829 when the fourth- and fifth-year *envois de Rome* of the *pensionnaires* Henri Labrouste and Félix Duban—a restoration of the Greek temples at Paestum (p. 361) and a design for a Protestant church—provoked the wrath of the Secrétaire Perpétuel of the Académie des Beaux-Arts, Quatremère de Quincy. Quatremère fought all his life for one cause—idealized classical art. In the early 1790s, to hasten the revival of that style, he allied himself with the painter David and attacked the Académie Royale de Peinture et Sculpture; from 1816 to 1839, as Secrétaire Perpétuel of the successor to that Academy, he defended idealized classicism against what he saw as a new enemy—Romanticism (and especially Romantic painting). A forceful personality, he made the most of his position and controlled not only the Académie des Beaux-Arts but also the Ecole des Beaux-Arts, the Académie de France à Rome, and the Conseil des Bâtiments Civils. Thus he controlled the teaching of art, the exhibiting of works in the Salons, the awarding of prizes, and the granting of official commissions. Labrouste's and Duban's *envois* did not adhere to what had become official classical doctrine, and Quatremère severely rebuked the young men. The director of the French Academy in Rome came to the defense, and a quarrel ensued that was bitter and not entirely confidential.[157]

Labrouste returned to Paris in 1830, shortly before the July Revolution that deposed Charles X and made Louis-Philippe king. Within days the young architect received a letter from some discontented students of Vaudoyer and Lebas, asking him to become a *patron*. In August he opened an atelier. Soon Duban, who had been home for over a year, acquired an atelier of his own. He had for several months been assisting Debret, his *patron* and brother-in-law, when in the autumn twenty-five of Debret's twenty-eight students decided that Duban alone should be their master. The atelier split in two.[158] Labrouste's atelier was to become more important than Duban's, if only because Labrouste's was to become much larger, in fact one of the largest. Also, for the twenty-six years it was to remain open, it was to be the place of greatest opposition, within the circle of the Ecole, to the orthodoxy of the Academy.

In the summer of the July Revolution, students at the schools of law and of medicine and at the Ecole des Beaux-Arts were demonstrating, demanding changes in the government's educational and professional policies. Labrouste and Duban supported their demands and in August signed a petition that called upon the government to make numerous changes, specifically: to open the *concours* for the Grand Prix to all qualified students, to include students in all juries, to display projects both before and after judgments, to restrict the authority of the Conseil des Bâtiments Civils to technical (as opposed to aesthetic) matters, to grant public commissions only to trained architects, and to restrict each architect to only one major government commission at a time.[159] Some members of the new government were sympathetic to the young architects in Labrouste's and Duban's group, and on January 25, 1831, the Minister of the Interior established a Commission des Beaux-Arts to suggest changes in the regulations of the Ecole des Beaux-Arts and of the Académie de France à Rome, and in the relation between these two schools and the Académie des Beaux-Arts.[160] He named to this commission artists of all persuasions, from Quatremère (and all the artists in the Academy) to Delacroix, and including Duban and Labrouste. All the academicians at once refused to serve. The other commissioners did meet, and on October 31, 1831, they completed a report, which was sent to the Academy for comment. That body refused to cooperate, and after months of bureaucratic quibbling, by which time the impetus of the events of 1830 had been lost, the report was put aside to be forgotten.

Labrouste paid a penalty for opposing the Academy: his career did not advance as fast as did those of his contemporaries. Quatremère retired as Secrétaire Perpétuel only in 1839, the year of his eighty-fourth birthday. Labrouste was not entrusted with the design of an important public building until the last years of the 1830s, when he received the commission for the Bibliothèque Sainte-Geneviève, the building that was to bring him lasting fame (p. 335). He put much of his energy into his teaching, but none of his students won the Grand Prix, the second prize, or the third prize. The departure of Quatremère made the Academy no more approving. By 1856 Labrouste had had enough of teaching, and in May of that year he closed his atelier, and his students went their separate ways. About fifteen of them persuaded Viollet-le-Duc to become their *patron*. Thereby, it could be said, the opposition to the orthodoxy of the Academy was taken outside the circle of the Ecole. Labrouste's career remained in that circle: he began as a student at the Ecole, he won the Grand Prix de Rome, and he ended as a member of the Institut. As the architects of his generation reached the age for this final honor, the more conventional were elected first: in 1850 Abel Blouet (who had become professor of theory at the Ecole in 1846), in 1853 Emile Gilbert, in 1854 Alphonse de Gisors and Duban, in 1855 Hector Lefuel, in 1863 Victor Baltard, and in 1866 Louis Duc. Last of all came the most original: in 1867, when he was sixty-six, Labrouste was elected to one of the eight places.

Viollet-le-Duc neither began at the Ecole des Beaux-Arts nor ended in the Institut.[161] Among the boys learning architecture in the ateliers in Paris in the years when he was studying, he was most unusual, perhaps unique, in not wanting to be at the Ecole. Architects who were friends of his family—Percier and Fontaine, Visconti, and others—urged him to study there, but he was determined to go his own way. In 1831, at the age of seventeen, he set off on the first of his trips through France to study and draw medieval buildings. In 1836–37, having seen much of his own country, he visited Italy. In December 1839 came the opportunity that launched his career: Prosper Mérimée (the author of *Carmen*), a friend of the family who had become Inspecteur Général des Monuments Historiques, designated young Viollet-le-Duc architect in charge of restoring the abbey church at Vézelay. It was the first of his many restorations, among which are the cathedrals of Paris, Troyes, Amiens, Chartres, Laon, and Reims, the abbey church at Saint-Denis, the church of Saint-Sernin at Toulouse, the palace of the Popes and the city ramparts at Avignon, and the city of Carcassonne. Named in 1853 Inspecteur Général des Edifices Diocésans (a post subordinate to Mérimée's), Viollet-le-Duc saw to it that the great Gothic buildings of France were preserved. Furthermore, in years of analyzing medieval vaults and buttresses, he became convinced that this rational structural system should be the basis for the development of architecture in the nineteenth century, and in his many writings—most important, in his *Dictionnaire raisonné de l'architecture française du XIe au XVIe siècle*, published from 1854 to 1868—he sought to transmit his learning and persuade his readers of its relevance.

The Academy, however, saw Gothic architecture as only for the past. In 1846 the Academy delivered a memoir on the subject; the pronouncement confirmed the disrespect for that body Viollet-le-Duc had long felt.[162] It was the considered opinion of the Academy that new churches should not be Gothic, because Gothic churches were not the proper expression of Christianity, Gothic architecture never having penetrated Rome. The memoir appealed for the invention of a new, nineteenth-century art instead of a revival, but the reasoning showed that the academicians assumed that the new architecture would be an extension of the classical tradition.[163] Among others, an outraged Viollet-le-Duc replied, defending the Gothic revival and attacking the Academy. Thereafter, every few years, he attacked again. For example, in a long article called "A Word on Architecture in 1852," he assailed both the Academy and the Ecole.[164] In all epochs that have produced original and beautiful work, he asserted, as if it were a fact, artists have been solely responsible for creating their art and have not been dependent upon a sovereign, a minister, or an academy. Today art is debased, he claimed; the trouble is that teaching is by the Ecole, an exclusive coterie that isolates itself from our customs. We artists, he proposed, should direct the study of art, perhaps found another school. Such writings provoked further argument.

Viollet-le-Duc's atelier opened in the autumn of 1856 at 1 Rue Bonaparte, just up the street from the Ecole. Characteristically, he took pen in hand and began to write for his pupils lectures that he planned to publish as *Entretiens sur l'architecture*.[165] Very soon he found that conducting an atelier was not what he had expected. He read the first of his lectures, into which he had concentrated his theories, but he could see little effect in the drawings on his students' boards. He grew impatient with these people; his own work interested him more. He came to the atelier at irregular intervals. Arriving once after many days away, he discovered caricatures of himself; shocked, he walked out and never returned. The students dispersed. In all, the atelier lasted only months, and it had remained small. (There was one brilliant student, Anatole de Baudot, and he joined the staff of his master's office.)

Viollet-le-Duc continued to think about education and to write his *Entretiens*, in addition to accomplishing his vast works of restoration. A pronouncement by the Académie des Beaux-Arts in 1858 aroused his ire again, and again he gave vent to his feelings in print.[166] In 1862 he published further articles attacking the Academy and the Ecole.[167] Meanwhile, he was being heard with increasing respect in important places. Viollet-le-Duc had been introduced to the empress, Eugénie, by Mérimée, a friend of hers and of her mother, before the *coup d'état* of 1852. The architect got along well with Napoleon and became a favorite of Eugénie. During the imperial years, he visited the Château at Compiègne, where the court was in residence in autumn and early winter, for weeks at a time; he showed a talent for organizing the amateur theatricals with which the court entertained itself. When in Paris, he frequented the weekly salon of Napoleon's cousin, Princess Mathilde, whose lover was the emperor's Surintendant des Beaux-Arts, the Comte de Nieuwerkerke. Members of the Bonapartist circle commissioned Viollet-le-Duc to design châteaux. The grandest of these, commissioned in 1858 and in construction all through the 1860s, was a summer residence for the imperial family at Pierrefonds. It pleased the emperor.

In the court of the Second Empire, Viollet-le-Duc urged that the teaching of art be reformed. He got what he wanted. On November 13, 1863, the government issued a report that Nieuwerkerke had made to Vaillant, Ministre de la Maison de l'Empereur et des Beaux-Arts. Nieuwerkerke so much as damned the Ecole for insufficiency and proposed drastic changes. With the report the government issued a decree, signed by Napoleon and on his behalf by Vaillant, thoroughly reorganizing the Ecole.[168] The major changes were as follows. Four of the six professors were discharged. A larger number of chairs were set up, and new professors were named. The post of director of the Ecole was established; he was made responsible to the Ministre des Beaux-Arts. Official ateliers were created, three in architecture, and a *professeur chef d'atelier* was put in charge of each. The maximum age of admission to the Ecole and of competition for the Grand Prix de Rome was lowered from thirty to twenty-five. The second prize in the Grand Prix competition was abolished. The Académie des Beaux-Arts lost its right to conduct the competition; writing the program became one duty of a new Conseil Supérieur d'Enseignement, and judging the task of a special jury. The prize itself was changed from five to four years on a government pension; two years in Rome, two years in travel elsewhere. The director of the French Academy in Rome was made responsible to the Ministre des Beaux-Arts.

The purpose of this decree was at once clear; the government was seizing control of the Ecole des Beaux-Arts and the Academy in Rome from the Académie des Beaux-Arts. A storm burst. Artists, critics, and academicians deluged periodicals with polemics. The former professors of the Ecole together wrote the emperor an open letter of protest.[169] Likewise, the Académie des Beaux-Arts objected, defending its "moral tutelage" of the French Academy in Rome and asserting that part of the decree was illegal.[170] Vaillant replied; the Academy argued back, and called in its lawyers; the legal proceedings went on into the summer of 1864.[171] Several hundred students signed a protest to the new Conseil Supérieur d'Enseignement and to the emperor. The government retreated slightly. On December 6, 1863, Napoleon decreed, as "a testimony to his benevolent solicitude for students," that the maximum age of Grand Prix competitors would not be lowered from thirty until 1867; in each of the intervening three years, if the winner was older than twenty-five, another Grand Prix would be awarded to a competitor younger than that.[172] The students got this one compromise.[173] The big changes remained, though. On January 14, 1864, regulations implementing the decree of November 13, 1863, were issued, and at the same time appeared the program of forthcoming lectures by the new professors.[174]

Professors became the main, if symbolic, issue, the center of the storm. Before the reform, each professor who lectured at the Ecole had customarily held his chair for life, and when a chair was empty, the other professors had recommended a new occupant to the government minister, with the certainty that the recommendation would be followed. The decree of November 13, 1863, ended the professors' de facto control of their own company. The government strongly objected to three of the five professors who had been responsible for lecturing to students of architecture: J.-B.-C. Lesueur (1794–1883), who had been professor of Théorie de l'Architecture, the most important chair because its holder wrote the programs for the school's architectural *concours*; Hippolyte Lebas (1782–1867), who had been professor of Histoire de l'Architecture; and A.-M.-F. Jaÿ (1789–1871), who had been professor of Construction. These men not only lost their chairs; two of the chairs were abolished and the third was renamed. Simon-Claude Constant-Dufeux (1801–71), who had been professor of Perspective, was also dismissed, but the government appointed him to another position, probably because he was younger and more active. Furthermore, he was one of the architects who, influenced by Labrouste, had come to be known as the *Néo-Grecs*. The government made Constant-Dufeux *professeur chef* of one of the *ateliers officiels* of architecture that were opened within the school, free of charge to students. These new ateliers obviously were intended to put the private ateliers out of business. Constant-Dufeux's income before the reform had come partly from the government for lecturing and partly from his private atelier; now the government was paying him to compete with himself! He did, keeping his old atelier open and seeing its prosperity decline. The other two official *patrons* were less well known at the Ecole. Alexis Paccard was architect in charge of the palace at Fontainebleau and a favorite of the empress; when young he had been in the atelier of the old-fashioned classicist Lebas and had in 1841 won the Grand Prix. Jean-Charles Laisné,[175] who had won a second Grand Prix in 1844, belonged to the Commission des Monuments Historiques and Service des Edifices Diocésans and thus was a subordinate of Viollet-le-Duc, whose friend he had been since boyhood. Perhaps the government intended that these three official *patrons* would represent the three main schools of architectural thought: classical, *Néo-Grec*, and Gothic.[176]

The professors charged with lecturing aroused more excitement. The government named eight men to new professorships and decreed that the increased number of lecture courses would henceforth be obligatory, but that the course in anatomy would not be required of architects.[177] Several of the new professors were notable. In the chair of geology, physics, and chemistry was the great scientist Pasteur, who was then making the studies of fermentation that led to his proof of the existence of germs; his appointment brought approval from all sides. Eugène Millet, the new professor of Administration et Comptabilité, Construction et Application sur les Chantiers, was a more partisan choice; originally a student of Labrouste, he had become a disciple of Viollet-le-Duc. The man designated Professeur de l'Histoire de l'Art et Esthétique—the most important professor, who would be intellectual leader of all sections of the school—stirred up the strongest feeling, for he was Viollet-le-Duc. The foremost medievalist was to be enthroned in the most classical of schools.

His first lecture, on January 29, 1864, was awaited with high anticipation. It was a fiasco. Viollet-le-Duc's point that day was that each great art shows the forces of the civilization that produced it, and as examples of those forces he spoke about Hindu divinities and Greek myths. Unfortunately, he read his lecture in a dull voice and bored his audience with lists of divinities and the plots of familiar myths. The hall was full of dignitaries—artists, scholars, and government officials including Nieuwerkerke, the Surintendant des Beaux-Arts—plus, let in last, students, a few of whom continually murmured, coughed, and stomped. After the lecture, Viollet-le-Duc managed to slip away unseen, but Nieuwerkerke and his attendants had to walk back to the Louvre. As they did so, they were followed through the Rue Bonaparte, alongside the river, and across the Pont des Arts by a crowd of noisy students, who taunted the Surintendant with a song about Mathilde and encouraged themselves with that old call to arms against tyranny, "La Marseillaise." The second lecture by Viollet-le-Duc caused further uproar. Only students were admitted, and their noise was riotous. Afterward, they surged out of the school's courtyard into the street to harass their enemy. There was a similar riot during and after each of the following lectures, until, after the seventh one of March 18, 1864, Viollet-le-Duc resigned.[178]

Although no one knew it yet, the government's campaign to take over the Ecole des Beaux-Arts was lost. The leader of the reformers had gone into retreat, and behind him he left no one with his zeal and, indeed, few defenders of his policies. In his absence, the Conseil Supérieur d'Enseignement assumed importance. It was a creation of the reform: a council of fourteen men from outside the Ecole to oversee the teaching there. The two architects whom the government had named in November 1863 to the Conseil were Hector Lefuel, architect of the New Louvre, and Alphonse de Gisors, architect in charge of enlarging the Luxembourg. Neither was a follower of Viollet-le-Duc; both had come out of the Ecole, Lefuel with the Grand Prix in 1839 (p. 194) and de Gisors with the second prize in 1823 (p. 149). It is said that most members of this committee found its tasks boring; and that although neither Lefuel nor de Gisors was president or vice-president, together they actually took control of the Conseil to get the school back to work.[179]

One by one, the reforms were canceled. Lecture courses were once again not required. This requirement, first announced in the decree of November 13, 1863, and further defined in the regulations of January 14, 1864, as an obligatory composition to examine the subject of the history of art and aesthetics, was effectively negated in the spring of 1864 by an exemption granted to all students.[180] Thereafter, no one mentioned such an obligation. Lesueur, who on November 13, 1863, had been stripped of his responsibility for *concours* and of his title of Professeur de Théorie, was by June 8, 1864, again signing *concours* programs as "professor in charge of organizing the competition."[181] (One might ask who had put him in charge.) In July, though, it may have seemed that the government was reasserting its authority. On the twenty-first of that month, the imperial Conseil d'Etat rejected the final appeal of the Académie des Beaux-Arts and declared the decree of November 13, 1863, fully legal; but for the government the victory was hollow.[182] In August, the *concours* for the Grand Prix de Rome was judged by the new jury designated in place of the Academy. Following the letter of the law of November 13, the jurors did not give second prizes. For architecture, painting, and sculpture, however, they awarded after the Grand Prix something they called an *accessit*.[183] On October 26, the government named to Viollet-le-Duc's chair the famous historian Taine, and on January 20, 1865, he gave his first lecture.[184] Before, during, and after, there was applause. The *Revue Générale de l'Architecture* reported, "He left the Ecole courtyard to frenetic cries and bravos; a tide of enthusiastic students ran through the streets as he drove away. In acclaiming today's professor, people seemed to want to prolong the protest against yesterday's."[185] In the spring of 1865, Viollet-le-Duc's disciple Millet resigned as professor of construction. His replacement was Baude, an engineer of the Ponts et Chaussées and thus identified with neither Viollet-le-Duc nor the Académie des Beaux-Arts.[186] On February 19, 1870, the maximum age of competitors for the Grand Prix de Rome was raised again by imperial decree to thirty.[187] After the collapse of the Empire and the establishment of the Republic, a presidential decree of November 13, 1871, returned to the Academy control of the Grand Prix de Rome. (Writing the *concours* programs again became the academicians' privilege and so did judging, but a third of the jury thenceforth consisted of artists from outside the Academy.)[188]

Finally, on May 6, 1874, a decree reorganizing the Ecole returned the maximum age of studies and thus of admission to thirty; furthermore, the decree set up again the chair of theory of architecture.[189] Into it went Lesueur, by then nearly eighty. In that same year the *Revue*, recalling the reform of 1863 and the subsequent events, reminded its readers that it had not been free to say all it had wished. In fear of suppression, it had stayed within the limits imposed by the law.[190]

What, then, were the lasting effects of the reform of 1863? The administration of the Ecole was altered, but the change was inconsequential, for the government ceased meddling and left the day-to-day running of the Ecole to the administrators and professors. The *ateliers officiels* continued to exist, but they did not put the private ateliers out of business. The new ones became almost indistinguishable from the old, different only in that when a new *patron* was needed for an *atelier officiel*, the authorities of the Ecole made the choice. Thus, the *ateliers officiels* were not controlled as much by their students and *patron* as were the outside ateliers. Nearly a century later, the *ateliers officiels* would become more important than the *ateliers privés*. The other enduring change introduced by the reform of 1863 was the increased number of optional lecture courses.[191]

The *diplôme*, quietly instituted by the government in 1867, changed the nature of architectural studies at the Ecole more than did the whole reform of 1863, but for its first two decades the innovation made no difference at all. According to the school regulations of November 27, 1867, a diploma was to be awarded to each of an unlimited number of winners of a special annual competition, open to students credited with about two years' worth of *concours* in the first class. Each competitor was to conceive and develop his project as if it was to be built.[192] The authorities intended that the *diplôme* would be a sign of architectural proficiency and a culmination of studies less exclusive than the Grand Prix de Rome.

The students, however, largely ignored the new opportunity. The best were after the Grand Prix, and nearly all the others seem to have been satisfied with the title *élève de l'Ecole des Beaux-Arts*. A *diplôme* was not worth the time and trouble. On June 27, 1887, however, it gained value. That day the government awarded a *diplôme* to each of the living winners of the Grand Prix de Rome in architecture, and the Rome prize then gave the *diplôme* luster. The next year it became more attractive. Instead of the same program being assigned to all the competitors, as had been done previously, each competitor gained the right to propose his own program. Thereafter, ordinarily competent students no longer drifted away from the Section d'Architecture after a few years, but rather stayed longer (in all, usually five to seven years), entered more *concours*, and finally worked several months on an individual project in hopes of gaining the title Architecte D.P. L.G. (*diplômé par le gouvernement*). By the mid-1890s the *diplôme* had become the goal of architectural studies at the Ecole.

A few years after the *diplôme*, another innovation was introduced: *ateliers préparatoires*, which prepared beginners for admission to the Ecole by teaching mathematics, drawing, and, especially, architectural design. One of the first preparatory ateliers was founded by J. Pillet in 1869.[193] He was too early, though; *aspirants* took to using these places only in the mid-1880s. From then on, people usually transferred from a preparatory to a regular atelier just after being admitted to the Ecole. Among the most popular of the *ateliers préparatoires* were Guicestre's in the late '80s, Duray's from the late '80s through the '90s, that of Godefroy and Freynet in the '90s and after the turn of the century, and those of Chifflot and of Umbdenstock in the twentieth century until the First World War. (Shortly before the war Umbdenstock enlarged his atelier to include students in the school. Godefroy after the war became a *patron* of an ordinary atelier.)

Another change that was occurring in the Section d'Architecture in these decades was an increase in the number of prizes. Some of these were awarded after special competitions open to students in the first class—the *grand concours*, of which by the 1920s there were a dozen or more, conducted either by the Ecole or by the Académie des Beaux-Arts. Each of these prizes was financial, the annual interest from individual gifts of capital. (Americans endowed several prizes; first, one established by architects from the school and awarded annually from 1889 on, the *prix de la reconnaissance des architectes américains*.) Besides the prizes for special *concours*, there came into being about a dozen more, similarly endowed, for students in both classes with a large number of *valeurs*, that is to say, with high grades.[194]

The reason for these new prizes—and for the *ateliers préparatoires* also—was the sheer growth in numbers of students. In the Section d'Architecture in the school year 1851–52, there were 281 enrolled. In 1890–91, there were 606. In 1906–07, there were 950.[195] This change in size eventually caused a loss of the informality of the earlier years.

The *diplôme*, preparatory ateliers, and prizes can be seen as a loss of this informality—or as a raising of standards and encouragement of better work. At the time, these changes seemed all for the better. In that peaceful era, nearly half a century long, between the founding of the Third Republic and the outbreak of the First World War, the Ecole was in good health. No great controversies upset it, and it was contented. In its ateliers, the classical tradition was vigorous. Furthermore, after the ill-feelings of 1863 were forgotten, students read Viollet-le-Duc's books without prejudice, in hopes of synthesizing his theories with classicism. In 1901–04 the professor of theory, Julien Guadet, published in four volumes the great treatise of the school's academic classicism, *Eléments et théorie de l'architecture*.[196] During those prosperous decades, buildings by architects from the Ecole were going up not only in France but throughout the French Empire, from Dakar to Saigon, and elsewhere all around the world, from Glasgow to Rio de Janeiro, from Bucharest to Berkeley. In English-speaking lands, a certain kind of architecture came to be called Beaux-Arts, and the name has stuck.

The First World War took the lives of 480 students and former students of the Ecole des Beaux-Arts.[197] This number includes people from all sections of the school: architects, painters, sculptors, and engravers. (More than half the students in the school usually were in the Section d'Architecture.) When the school reopened at the end of the war, every atelier felt the loss. Many men were gone, and the continuity from *nouveau* to *ancien* within each atelier had been broken. During the 1920s, however, the school recovered, with a resilience that from our viewpoint seems awesome. (Awesome too, it must be said, was the regeneration of architectural education across the Rhine.)

In the early 1930s the Ecole made the first addition to its physical plant since the 1880s; to get more drafting rooms, it erected a few blocks away, on the Rue Jacques-Callot, a six-story building designed by Roger Expert in the style of the time—with a rounded corner and horizontal bands of windows. The new building went up to house *ateliers extérieurs* of architecture.[198] Some of them were in trouble. With more students they needed more space, but in the late 1920s rents on the Left Bank had become expensive. In providing quarters, the state, which paid for the building, took some responsibility for the *ateliers libres*. They were becoming quasi-official.

Another problem apparent by the early '30s could not be solved by government funds: the architects leading the Ecole and the Academy were on the defensive. Ideas attracting worldwide notice were no longer coming from their circle but from other countries, especially Germany (until Hitler forced such thinkers out), and from a foreigner practicing in Paris, whose hatred of the Ecole and the Academy was as fierce as Viollet-le-Duc's had been. The defensiveness of some of the *patrons* was felt in their ateliers: it was almost taboo to study the works of certain architects, in particular Le Corbusier.

The Second World War made the problems graver. French architects were isolated by five years of Nazi occupation, and when they were free again, they found themselves out of touch with architectural thought outside their country. Making matters worse was a shortage of money. There was little for education, and nothing for enlarging the quarters of the Ecole des Beaux-Arts. But the number of students grew ceaselessly: in 1921–21 there had been about 1,100 in the Ecole's Section d'Architecture; in 1967–68, there were 2,780.[199] Throughout higher education in postwar France, the student population increased greatly. At the Ecole the number of architecture students took a sudden jump when, after the war, the school incorporated the *aspirants* into the student body as a new *classe préparatoire*. One thus could claim that the increase was somewhat illusory, for the *aspirants*, though uncounted, had always been there. But in 1949 the Ecole established an official *atelier préparatoire*, and room was found for students who formerly would have worked elsewhere. Renting large studios in the Latin Quarter became more and more difficult. In the '50s the Ecole acknowledged this by assuming responsibility for some of the big old *ateliers extérieurs*. One by one, their *patrons* were put on the payroll of the Ecole, each as a *professeur chef d'atelier*, and nearly all their students moved into the buildings of the Ecole, where the new *ateliers officiels* were installed: Noël Lemaresquier's in 1953, Georges Dengler's in 1955, Ottelo Zavaroni's in 1957. More students were now in *ateliers officiels* than in *ateliers libres*. It was no longer economically possible for an architect to open an atelier in Paris for a few students who were dissatisfied with their instruction. The flexibility of the nineteenth-century system of architectural education was gone; economic necessity in the mid-twentieth century caused a more rigid centralization.

In the late '50s the French economy recovered, but the Ecole and its students continued to feel a shortage of money. The neighborhood on the Left Bank grew fashionable, and living there grew correspondingly expensive; the cheap Latin Quarter with its carefree artists was as much of the past as the opera *La Bohème*. The Ecole itself was neglected by the state, and the neglect showed. In the '60s during the presidency of Charles de Gaulle, when on the initiative of the Minister of Cultural Affairs, André Malraux, the buildings of Paris were washed clean, the government left the Ecole des Beaux-Arts unwashed, its stones grimy with soot. In these shabby buildings ambitious students of architecture were obliged to compete for *valeurs* and for prizes that also had become bitter reminders of the school's poverty. The Prix Rougevin, for example, in 1907 carried with it 600 francs (then $125); in 1963 the same prize, after repeated devaluations of the franc, was worth six francs (less than $1.25).[200] Such a reward is demoralizing. The most ambitious students persisted, as they will, but ordinary students were questioning the purpose of these *concours*, of all *concours*, indeed, of their architectural education. Among students elsewhere in Paris, there were stronger feelings of cynicism toward their studies and of alienation from the life for which these studies were supposed to prepare.

In May 1968, rioting erupted in the University of Paris. For several months there had been a strike, led by students of sociology, at the new branch of the University located in Nanterre: when the police intervened, there was an uproar, and on May 2 the Faculty at Nanterre was closed. The next day the Faculties of Arts and of Sciences in Paris also were closed. On May 6, barricades against the police began to go up in the Latin Quarter. On May 8, the students of the Ecole des Beaux-Arts seized the school's buildings; other students that month occupied the Sorbonne and the theater of the Odéon. During the night of June 26–27, police forcibly dislodged the occupants of the Ecole. That summer, however, the students prevented the *concours* for the Grand Prix from being held, and that autumn the school from reopening. On December 6, 1968, a decree, signed by de Gaulle and Malraux, removed responsibility for the teaching of architecture from the Ecole des Beaux-Arts.

The same decree reorganized architectural education in France.[201] The *concours* for the Grand Prix de Rome was abolished. The centralized Section d'Architecture of the Ecole des Beaux-Arts was replaced by a number of autonomous units, named Unités Pédagogiques, eight of which are in Paris. Each Unité Pédagogique can teach architecture in the way it wants; each can establish its own curriculum. However, the duration of studies is the same in all of them: six years. There is no longer an admission exam, as there was for the Section d'Architecture of the Ecole; admission is open to any student with a *baccalauréat*, the degree the government awards to those who pass the difficult examinations at the end of the equivalent of the American high school. On the faculties of the Unités Pédagogiques are more than a dozen architects who used to be *patrons*; also there are many new young men.

One of the eight Unités Pédagogiques in Paris, U.P. 4, remains particularly close in spirit to the abolished Section d'Architecture of the Ecole, and thus it continues to assume that architecture is a fine art. In ateliers under the supervision of *patrons*, the students make designs for judgment. The ateliers are all, so to speak, *officiels*; they are in the buildings provided by the state. Four of the patrons were formerly in charge of *ateliers officiels* at the Ecole: Lemaresquier, Dengler, Zavaroni, and Michel Marot. Another Parisian Unité Pédagogique, U.P. 7, grew from the atelier Perret-Remondet. Inspired by the buildings and theories of Auguste Perret, it considers structure to be the determinant of architectural form. Consequently, the curriculum emphasizes the study of modern structural systems that use steel and concrete. The largest Unité Pédagogique in Paris, U.P. 6, is most directly the result of the events of 1968 and keeps alive the spirit of that May. It is the most ideological. Convinced that architecture is determined by society, it seems to concern itself with the latter as much as with the former. The aim of many of its members is to reform society along Marxist lines.

It is too soon to judge the effectiveness of the teaching of any of these establishments; the basis for such judgment should be the architecture of former students, and the first generation is only recently out of school. In the eight Unités Pédagogiques in Paris, there are now more than twice as many students as there were in the Section d'Architecture in its final year. These new institutions seem as distant from the Ecole des Beaux-Arts in its greatest years during the nineteenth century and until 1914 as the Ecole was from the school of the Académie Royale d'Architecture. Indeed, the break of 1968 seems more complete than was that of 1793.

Peyre. *Bâtiment qui contiendroit les Académies.* Plan. See p. 113.

ARCHITECTURAL COMPOSITION
AT THE ECOLE DES BEAUX-ARTS
FROM CHARLES PERCIER
TO CHARLES GARNIER

David Van Zanten

French academic architecture passed through three distinct phases. First was a formative period, extending roughly from the founding of the Académie Royale d'Architecture in 1671 to the French Revolution in 1789. During these years the institutions constituting the academic system itself—the Institut de France, the Ecole des Beaux-Arts, and the Académie de France à Rome— either had not yet been created or were not yet efficiently organized. The theories they were to propagate, however, were being formulated in the discussions at the Academy of Architecture and, toward the end of the eighteenth century, in the lessons given in the ateliers and schools of Jacques-François Blondel, David Leroy, and Etienne-Louis Boullée. Principles of composition were being refined in the yearly prize competition, administered by the Academy, which was to become the *Concours du Grand Prix de Rome.* This tradition of architectural composition continued, basically unaltered, into the nineteenth century: the designs produced for the Grand Prix were to remain the most respected, and the most conservative, manifestation of French academicism.

The second phase extended from the establishment of the academic institutions at the turn of the nineteenth century to the tumultuous and fruitful decade of the 1860s. It was this period in which the twelve-to-fifteen-year course of study undertaken by the best students proved to be the most meaningful, and in which all factions of the French architectural profession—those headed by Charles Percier, Henri Labrouste, Charles Garnier, and, for a few months in 1863–64, Eugène-Emmanuel Viollet-le-Duc— sought a place within the system. Relations were strained, but everyone sought to work within the existing structure.

The third phase commenced in the 1870s, the outcome of the events of the previous decade. The success of the French academic system appeared impressive and exemplary. Foreign architectural students were attracted to the school in great numbers and returned home to create local varieties of Beaux-Arts curricula. There slowly came into being the idea that there existed a single, all-encompassing Beaux-Arts system. At the same time, however, this seems to have marked the beginning of a decline in France as the Ecole became, in fact, exclusive and ossified. Viollet-le-Duc's efforts to work within the school ended in 1864; thenceforth his writings addressed the public directly. By 1920 the system could in no way accommodate the ideas of Le

Corbusier. Yet in 1901 Julien Guadet, professor of theory at the Ecole, wrote: "The originality of our school may be defined in a word: it is the most liberal there is in the world."[1] He went on to say that he would teach only that which was "incontestable."[2] Unfortunately, what Guadet had come to think "incontestable" seemed so only from his very distinct point of view.

Composition was the French academic system's term for what it considered the essential act of architectural design. What *composition* signified was not so much the design of ornament or of facades, but of whole buildings, conceived as three-dimensional entities and seen together in plan, section, and elevation. But this was a very particular use of the word, which only became general during the last half of the nineteenth century.[3] As the concept of architectural composition coalesced, so the word emerged as distinct from two more specific terms denoting "planning": *distribution* and *disposition*. Thus Léonce Reynaud could write in his *Traité d'architecture* of 1850–57:

> An apartment, for example, is well *distribué* if all the rooms which compose it are placed in the order most favorable for the uses for which they are to serve, . . . but it may be at the same time badly *disposé* if one has not taken every possible advantage of the site, if one or several rooms do not have the forms and dimensions needed, if the walls and openings are so made as to complicate execution instead of simplifying it, and if, finally, the *composition* of the interior does not manifest itself on the exterior by means of a satisfactory configuration.[4]

Indeed, *Distribution* appeared as the heading of the discussion of what we assume to be composition in Germain Boffrand's *Livre d'architecture* (1745),[5] in Jacques-François Blondel's *Cours d'architecture* (1771–77),[6] and again in Antoine-Chrysostome Quatremère de Quincy's dictionary, *Architecture* (1788–1825).[7] The *Dictionnaire de l'Académie française* of 1835 defined *distribuer* as "to apportion between several"; *disposer*, "to arrange, to put things in a certain order"; and *composer*, "to form, to make a whole out of several parts."[8] This change in terminology from *distribution* and *disposition* to *composition* would seem to imply that what had at the beginning of the century been an act of division and setting out in order, had by the end of the century become an act of unification.

At the same time that composition gained architectural significance, a new term became prominent in the vocabulary of the professors of the Ecole: *parti*. Georges Gromort wrote:

> In the genesis of a plan, the choice of the *parti* is of greater importance—especially at the outset—than what I shall call *composition pure*. This latter is mostly a matter of the adjustment of the elements, while the *parti* plays the role of inspiration in musical composition and applies principally to the layout and relative importance given to the elements. . . . The role of *composition pure* is to link together, to make effective, to unite into a whole. It is primarily the agent of connection. It will create, in order to lead one to the various parts—to these

Marie-Joseph Peyre. *Bâtiment qui contiendroit les Académies* (Building To House the Academies). 1756. *Envoi de Rome*. Plan, elevation, and section.

Published in 1765, this project was actually drawn up by Peyre while he was a *pensionnaire* in Rome and sent to the French Academy at that time. The plan is richly varied with slight internal asymmetries. The great entrance colonnade and the central dome are consistent features in mid-eighteenth-century student projects, but later in the century the Baroque curves of Peyre's building would give way to more rectilinear designs, such as Percier's project of 1786 (p. 125). The section uses an eighteenth-century convention of turning the center line 90° at the center of the building, in order to show one long and one short axis together.

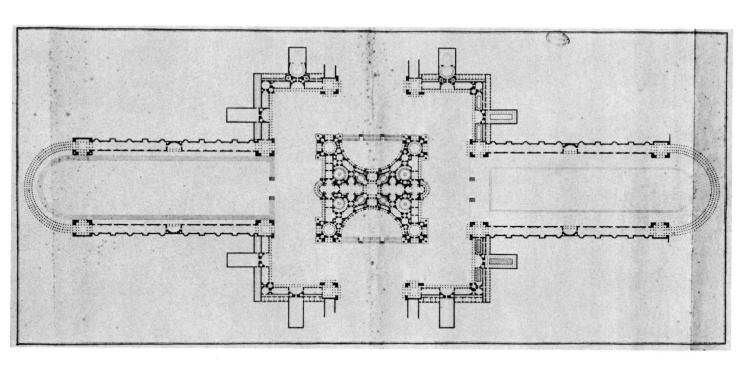

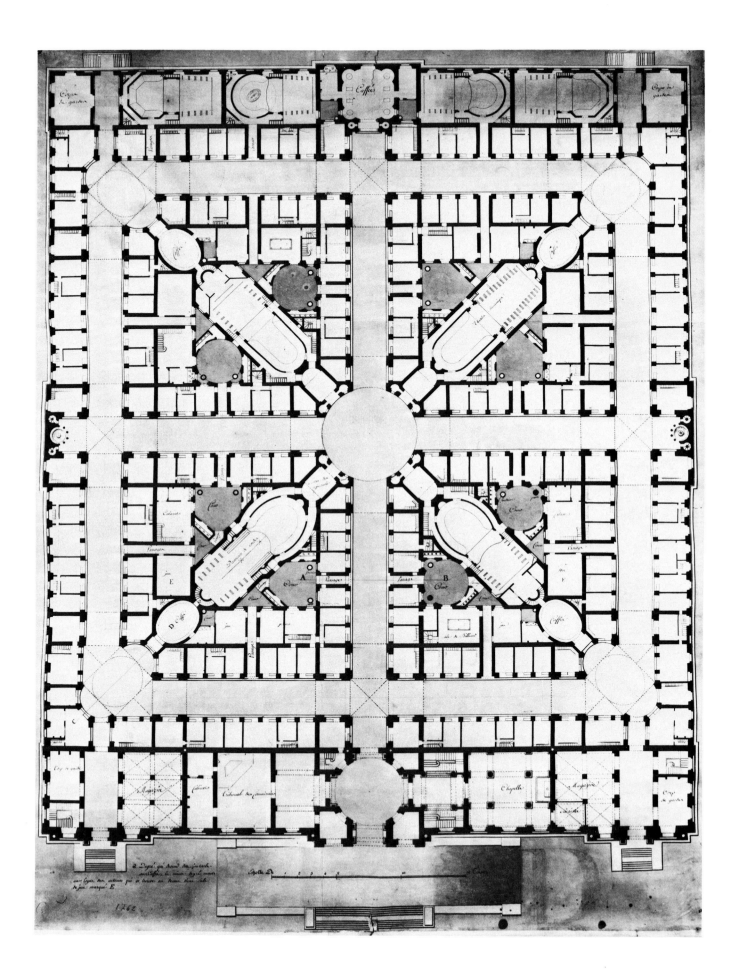

Antoine-François Peyre. *Foire couverte* (Covered Fair). 1762. 1ᵉʳ Prix. Plan.

Peyre's plan creates an ingenious circulation pattern by laying an *étoile* of four theaters and cafés on a simple grid of shops, joining them at the center and corners.

rooms, to these libraries, to these auditoria—a whole network of vestibules, of staircases, of covered or open courts, or corridors, all of which we designate by the word *circulations*. . . . It is the more or less graceful articulation of this network which to a great extent determines the building's appearance.[9]

That is, composition has to do with the presentation of architectural ideas, but not with the generation of these architectural ideas themselves. These ideas, furthermore, are *partis*, choices (from *prendre parti*, to make a choice, take a stand). Being seen as choices, these generative ideas were not taught at the Ecole itself, but a range of theories and convictions was available to the students in the ateliers. In his dictionary, *Architecture*, written at the beginning of the nineteenth century, Quatremère de Quincy had used *conception* where, a century later, Gromort would speak of *parti*.[10] There is a vast difference between these two words: Quatremère's denotes a *première idée*, a creation of the artist's own mind. It assumes that art ideas are all natural and of the same system. Gromort's placement of choice as the first act of the design process manifests the eclectic position taken by the Ecole at the end of the century. The Ecole's assertion of the importance of composition reflects its belief that it had discovered a method of architectural presentation nonetheless valid whatever the choice made. It was this institutionalization of the "battle of the styles" and this confidence in the suppleness of a certain method of composition that inspired Guadet to call the Ecole "la plus libérale qu'il y ait au monde."[11]

Thus "Beaux-Arts" denotes not a style, but rather a technique. By 1900, however, composition had become an end in itself; the liberal preference for compromise had produced an architecture that was, literally, superficial—dealing with surface, avoiding substance.[12] It was therefore to be overthrown during the 1920s by an architecture so committed to making substantive points that today the profession's complaint is not about complacency but about puritanism—ironically sustained by habit long after the battle against "Beaux-Arts" composition had been won. Late nineteenth-century Beaux-Arts composition, however, came almost as a relief at the end of a century of architectural turmoil, in which its principles evolved at the time of—almost in spite of—a collision of precisely the *partis pris* it sought to neutralize.

The Era of Percier

Il est simple en marche et sagement distribué.
Académie des Beaux-Arts, *Registre des concours*, 1829

The materials with which the Ecole student composed were precisely congruent interior spaces and exterior volumes. Although he admitted that this system was impractical in terms of construction and heating, Blondel in his

Louis-Alexandre Trouard. *Un Collège.* 1780. 1er Prix. Plan and elevation.

This project defeated Durand's entry for *le prix*, as it was then known. The two are derived from classic plan types used at the Ecole, Trouard's from an *étoile*, Durand's from crossed axes contained by a larger figure (in this case a hexagon to fit the triangular site). Trouard's *parti* is developed to indicate the nature of different parts of the building, through their varied heights and angles of appearance.

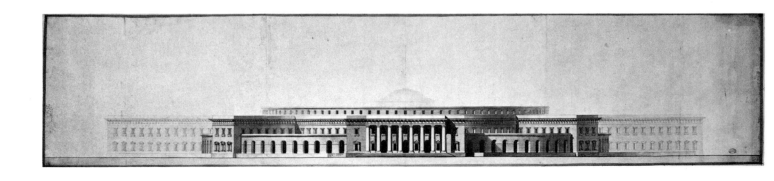

Jean-Nicolas-Louis Durand. *Un Collège.* 1780.
2e Prix. Plan and elevation.

Although it appears more ingenious in the
use of its site, Durand's solution yields less
interesting and varied elevations than those
of its competitor. Durand's course of architecture at the Ecole Polytechnique was later
founded on examples from the Ecole des
Beaux-Arts.

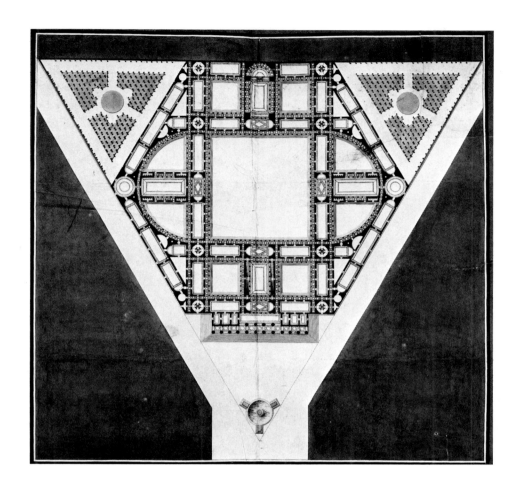

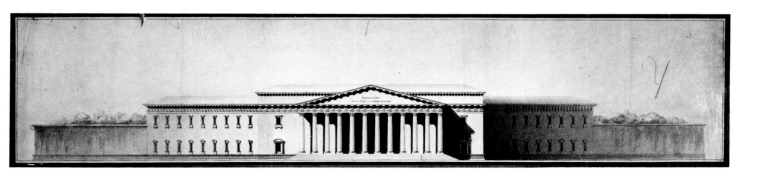

Cours d'architecture of 1771–77 counseled the laying out of a monumental building on one story with rooms of various heights, "the exterior and the interior agreeing perfectly one with the other."[13] Later, in 1832, Antoine-Laurent-Thomas Vaudoyer phrased the idea thus: "The walls of a monument are only its natural envelope; they are to the edifice that they enclose what drapery is to the statue that it covers."[14] Finally Charles Garnier, in 1871, presented this as the essential moral and philosophical "law" of architecture: "A great first principle, a principle of reason and truth. It is the requisite: that the exterior masses, the composition of the outside, indicate the interior plane, the composition of the inside. . . ."[15]

The manner in which the student arranged these spaces and volumes was to group them along axes, symmetrically and pyramidally. The basic solution for the composition of a monumental building on an unencumbered site (the sort of building and site usually specified at the Ecole) was discovered almost at once: two axes embodied in two enfilades and intersecting at right angles at a major central space, the whole compressed inside a circumscribed rectangle. This solution indeed was implicit in the problem. Its first appearance—evidently in Antoine-François Peyre's Premier Prix project for a *Foire couverte* (Covered Fair) of 1762 (p. 114), perhaps based on Luigi Vanvitelli's palace at Caserta (1752 *ff.*)[16]—immediately raised a problem that was to survive into the twentieth century: how to establish a direction in the design, a front and a back. Gromort wrote that an axis is infinite in only one direction: "One enters a truly beautiful building from only one direction, and in this direction entrance is never too generous."[17] French Baroque planning was essentially directional, based on the sequence of *cour d'honneur* (forecourt), *corps de logis* (principal block), garden. This paradigm blended with the biaxially symmetrical Caserta type in the Grand Prix designs, of which the most straightforward example is Hector Lefuel's 1839 project for a *Hôtel de Ville* (p. 194). Lefuel here clearly stated the cross-in-a-rectangle configuration, then merely rubbed out one arm of the cross to create a *cour d'honneur*, transforming the side of the circumscribed rectangle into a public loggia, and the two lateral arms of the inscribed cross into a *corps de logis* marked at its center by a tall tower.

A smoother and more frequently used solution was to treat the *cour d'honneur* as the open center of a cross-axis plan contained in two concentric rectangles, the whole front side removed, and each of the three remaining sides on the court with a central feature marking three centrifugal enfilades. In the Grand Prix projects one can see this configuration slowly emerging from the simple *cour d'honneur–corps de logis* paradigm, from Paul-Guillaume Lemoine's *Ecole de Médecine* (1775) to Bénard's *Palais de Justice* (1782) to Simon Vallot's *Ecole des Beaux-Arts* (1800). The basic technique for elaborating these paradigms was repetition: for the simple cross-in-a-rec-

Charles Percier. *Une Ménagerie d'un Souverain* (Menagerie for a Sovereign). 1783. 2ᵉ Prix. Site plan.

Percier's site plan, combining squares within squares with three great exedrae, placed second to Vaudoyer's more complex project (p. 122). The placement of the required amphitheater and pavilion is the opposite of Vaudoyer's, and the circulation around them is somewhat more clearly established; yet as a whole the project lacks the sweeping grandeur of its competitor's solution.

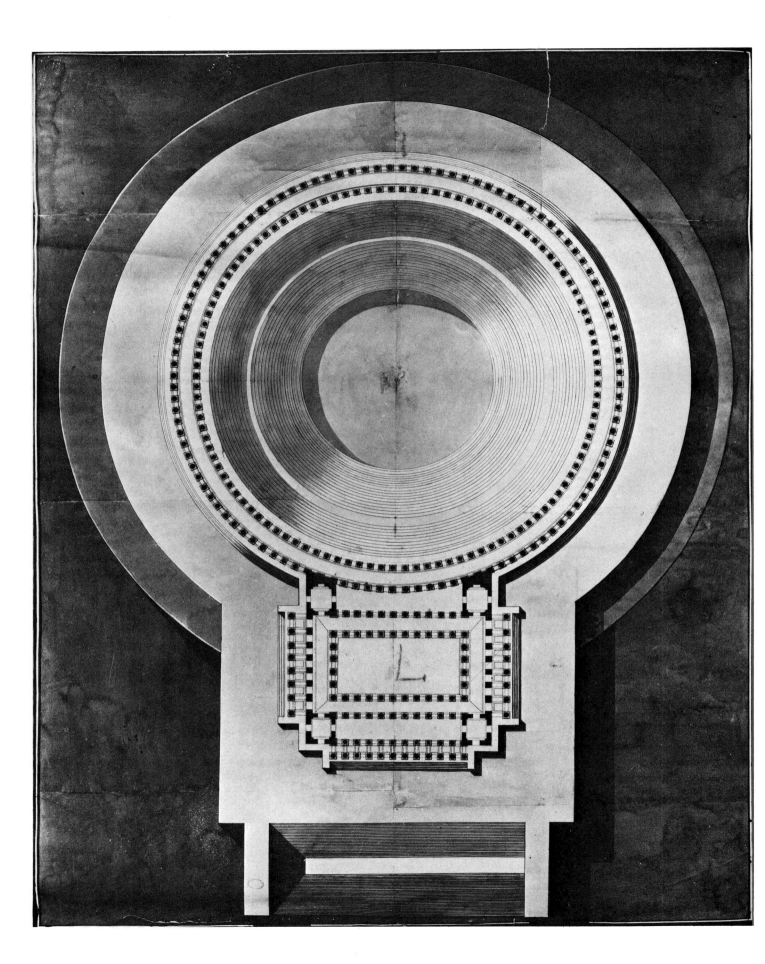

Percier. *Une Ménagerie d'un Souverain.*
Amphitheater plan *(opposite)* and section
(top); pavilion elevation *(above)* and section
(right).

Because of its position in the complex, the
amphitheater takes the directional plan of a
Roman pantheon rather than a colosseum.
Percier's delicate pavilion, drawn in his
characteristically light rendering style, shows
his enjoyment of elegant details in an otherwise grandiose project. The pavilion is romanticized by the addition of an underground grotto, which relates to the extensive
use of water throughout the project. His entire conception is generally less severe than
that of Vaudoyer and suggests the genius for
decoration that characterized his later work.

Antoine-Laurent-Thomas Vaudoyer. *Une Ménagerie d'un Souverain* (Menagerie for a Sovereign). 1783. 1ᵉʳ Prix. Site plan and section *(opposite)*; amphitheater plan and pantheon section *(right)*.

Vaudoyer was to become one of the great teachers and theorists of the Ecole. His plan for a menagerie is based on an *étoile*. It runs through a great circular plaza surrounded by circular and square subsidiary spaces, each of which has its own cross-axes. The enormous central amphitheater provides a severely simple focal point and at the same time seems to generate the project's circular *parti*. The section reveals the project's essential Romanism as well as its directional orientation from a lowered entry court at one side to the raised pavilion at the other. The pavilion is a small pantheon in a square, which is the form Percier applied to his winning *prix* project three years later (p. 125).

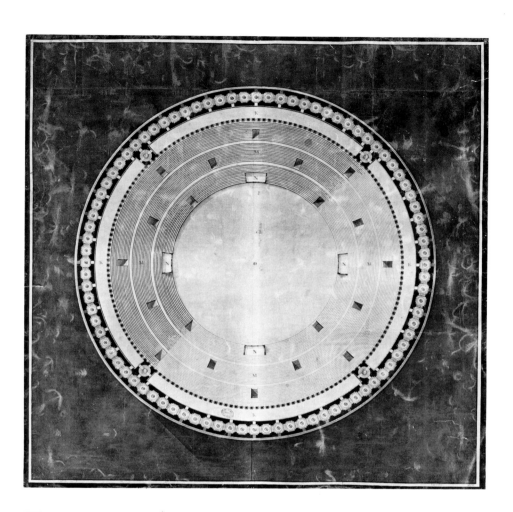

tangle configuration, the student added concentric rectangles and extended the enfilades through them; for the *cour d'honneur–corps de logis* model, he added forecourts, producing a plan like that of the Palace at Versailles.

The tension one sees in the Grand Prix projects between biaxially symmetrical planning and directional layouts is characteristic of a basic conflict in Beaux-Arts composition: that between the purity of the geometric pattern and the circumstantial distortions required for the fulfillment of the given function and for the expression of that function. In the Beaux-Arts system, the building had to be usable in a general sense and had to be recognizable for the sort of building it was. Achille Leclère's 1808 project for *Bains publics* (Public Baths) is identifiable as such by its central motif, an ancient Roman thermal hall (here open to view, as it would not have been in an ancient bathing complex). Lefuel's 1839 *Hôtel de Ville* (p. 195) is recognizable by the huge *loge publique* across its facade, behind which rise clock tower and belfry; its articulation with pavilions, rustication, and pilasters refers to seventeenth-century French paradigms.[18] This characterization became increasingly specific as the nineteenth century progressed. Individual rooms took on strict, practical, identifiable forms, as one sees in the amphitheaters of Honoré Daumet's 1855 Grand Prix design for a *Conservatoire de musique et de déclamation* (p. 224). By the end of the century the student had even to devise a plausible structural system, as is evident in the 1891 Grand Prix competition for a *Gare centrale de chemin de fer* (p. 302). Yet the tightness and consistency of the abstract plan pattern had to be preserved, and the managing of conflicts had to be graceful. There was an academic cliché that John Vredenburgh Van Pelt, an American student at the Ecole des Beaux-Arts, put into the mouth of his *patron* Henri-Adolphe-Auguste Deglane: "The architect can never have perfection. He must always choose between two evils."[19]

What permitted Beaux-Arts composition to make these compromises without losing its coherence was a number of specific techniques developed at the end of the eighteenth century. These techniques are neatly summed up in Charles Percier's celebrated Grand Prix design for a Building for Assembling the Academies, 1786 (*right*). In comparison with the more typically Baroque plans produced earlier in the century—for example, Mathurin Crucy's *Bains publics* of 1774 or Marie-Joseph Peyre's *Académie*, executed when he was a *pensionnaire* in Rome in 1756 (p. 113)—Percier's project seems remarkably understated. It is almost perfectly biaxially symmetrical. Instead of the sequence of strongly contrasting plan forms of Crucy and Peyre—round, square, oval, octagonal—Percier uses only rectangles, except for a single broad circle at the center, echoed by four small semicircles set in the corners of the square. Percier's rectangular system adheres to a pattern: a central space surrounded by four narrow rectangular spaces that overlap at the corners to form squares. This pattern appears in Percier's plan at two scales, that

Charles Percier. *Un Edifice à rassembler les Académies* (A Building for Assembling the Academies). 1786. 1er Prix. Plan, section, and elevation.

Percier here creates a system of interlocking routes of circulation between groups of major rooms, passing directly along the two axes of the plan and around the central rotunda. The facade owes a great deal to Boullée's project for a museum of three years earlier. Of the original drawings, all but the plan of Percier's project are now lost; facade and section are therefore shown in an engraving. The section reveals the alternation of large rooms and circulation spaces across the building.

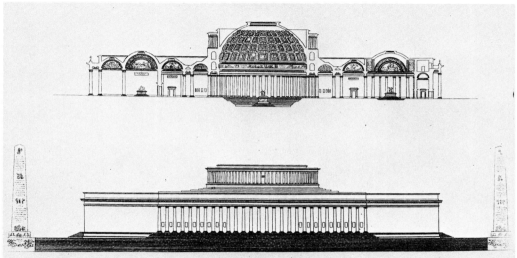

Louis-Ambroise Dubut. *Greniers publics* (Public Granaries). 1797. 1er Grand Prix. Elevation and section.

The elevation of this project by Dubut, a student of Ledoux, with its extensive and handsomely rendered colored landscape, foreshadows the ideal revolutionary city of Ledoux's 1804 version of the *Ville de Chaux*. The inscription in the center of the facade reads, "Under these vast arcades can Providence maintain equal abundance forever."

The utilitarian character of this project for public granaries accords well with Ledoux's vocabulary of semicircular arches and square piers, which are here adopted by Dubut. Such forms later appeared in the Napoleonic markets and *abattoirs* erected throughout Paris.

Dubut composed a plan that seems unusually complex among Grand Prix projects of the time. The building is essentially a five-aisled gallery broken by a central opening on the water side; by an administration block at the center of the opposite side; and by minor entrances centered on each of the two other sides without any corresponding change of elevation.

Dubut. *Greniers publics*. Plan.

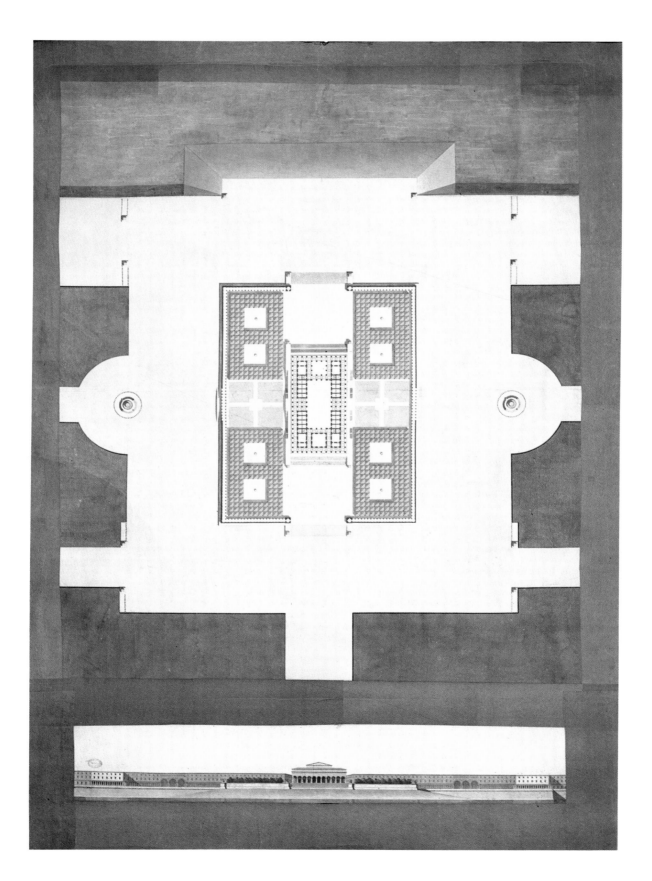

Joseph Clémence. *Bourse pour une ville maritime* (Bourse for a Maritime City). 1798. 1ᵉʳ Grand Prix. Plan and elevation.

This project is laid out on crossed axes, which encompass both the building and an ensemble of trees on a raised platform. Orientation of the building toward the sea is established by the single asymmetry of open and closed square rooms to the front and rear of its plan. Unusually young for a Grand Prix winner, Clémence was only twenty-two when he drew this project.

of the whole wing and that of the single room. Furthermore, all the forms of the plan are made to adhere to a modular grid stated in the four colonnades across the four facades, unifying the elements in these two scales by numerical proportion.

By bringing all of his spaces to rectangles, and forming them into rectangle-within-rectangle figures, Percier permitted his spaces to link together smoothly, to interpenetrate. The outer rectangle of the figure is always shared with the neighboring figure. When three such figures are set side by side, as they are laterally and longitudinally in Percier's plan, it is unclear whether one should read the resulting configuration as two interlocking rectangles, as four rectangles overlapping at the center square, or as four rectangles set around the sides of the central square. Percier thus bound his plan together and introduced a play of ambiguity through the use of the modular grid, of consistently rectangular spaces, and of the rectangle-within-rectangle figure. He in fact essentially altered the elemental Caserta paradigm of crossed enfilades circumscribed within a rectangle: his system created axes along the lines of juncture of the forms as well as through their centers, permitting his pattern to read not as four squares like Caserta, but as nine (counting the four unarticulated squares in the corners between the wings).

Percier was not the inventor of these compositional techniques, although his rendition of them in this Grand Prix design was exceptionally clear and successful. There was a source in an actual building in Paris conceived in the 1750s: Jacques-Germain Soufflot's church of Sainte-Geneviève, the present-day Panthéon. Its plan is a similar cross-shaped configuration of five squares-within-squares, modular, reading as overlapping rectangles. Predominance is given to the central space by suppressing the inner square (suggesting it, instead, by the diagonal piers at the corners). Articulation and church-like character are given to this very abstract plan by the vaulting system, which makes it clear that the plan is to be read as five separate units, four wings subordinated to a central domical space.[20]

Percier's configuration was something new in the Renaissance tradition and introduced possibilities important to Beaux-Arts composition. The reduction of almost all the spaces to rectangles adhering to a continuous modular grid greatly increased the ease with which they might be combined and manipulated. Furthermore, the rectangle-within-rectangle figure produced a system of communication quite different from that of the Renaissance and Baroque enfilade. It introduced a web of multiple readings over the surface of the plan and created a system of secondary axes along the lines of juncture of the principal spaces of the enfilades. These secondary axes also became lines of movement and of sight—a phenomenon vividly demonstrated by a visit to the Panthéon—enfilades of a sort, not monumental, but rather varied and picturesque spaces between the monumental spaces. And these secondary axes were also, conveniently but secondarily, corridors. The rectangle-within-rectangle figure and the overlapping of the outer rectangles introduced the possibility of the separation of functioning spaces and communications, which by the time of Guadet (1901) had become one of the cardinal rules of Beaux-Arts composition.[21]

* * *

The Revolution and the subsequent Napoleonic reorganization of France were accompanied by the emergence of a new generation of architects and *maîtres d'ateliers*, most notably Charles Percier, who returned from Rome in 1791. At the same time the student projects produced for the *Concours du Grand Prix de Rome* after its reestablishment in 1797 evince a new, distinctly Spartan simplicity and urban consciousness, fostered in part by the programs that now specified such structures as *Greniers publiques* (Public Granaries, 1797, p. 126) or a *Bourse* (Stock Exchange, p. 128). Joseph Clémence's winning project for the latter is remarkable for its clarity and simplicity. The program specified four spaces: a "large hall where traders can meet," a "vestibule where the guards will be stationed," a room for the stockbrokers, and an uncertain number of individual offices. Clémence's solution adhered closely to a grid stated not only by the columns of the circumferential peristyle but also by the pattern of squares covering the floor spaces—what in the ateliers was termed the *mosaïque*. All the spaces are rectangular. Each major space is placed in a rectangle one bay larger on each side, creating surrounding, overlapping "corridor" spaces. Within this framework the monumental enfilades of internal spaces have been worked out. The core, a rectangle five bays by eleven, is rendered as a single barrel-vaulted space. Two vestibules, each three bays wide, connect the core to the exterior along its secondary axis; a similar pair of halls opens along its primary axis. On this primary axis, however, Clémence introduced the one asymmetry of his composition, to give his building a front and a back: the central three bays of these halls are opened as an atrium on one side and closed to form a chamber—that of the stockbrokers—on the other. Thus Clémence with the slightest change of configuration created a hierarchical sequence of rooms: atrium, main hall, office of the stockbrokers.

The primary and secondary axes are restrained and the building's form disciplined by the imposition of a rectangular peristyle. The spaces in the four corners between this peristyle and the primary and secondary enfilades are filled with small closed offices and committee rooms. The constraining peristyle gives the building as a whole the paradigmatic civil basilica form established by Palladio at Vicenza (at least as he represented his Basilica in his *Quattro Libri dell'Architettura*), recommended by Quatremère and repeated several times around the turn of the nineteenth century.[22]

André-Marie Chatillon. *Une Eglise cathédrale* (A Cathedral Church). 1809. 1er Grand Prix. Plan.

This highly abstract plan by a student of Percier shows to what length the *parti* of crossed axes in a rectangle could be taken. The entry and apse of the church are distinguished only by the colonnade of the former and the exedra within the latter.

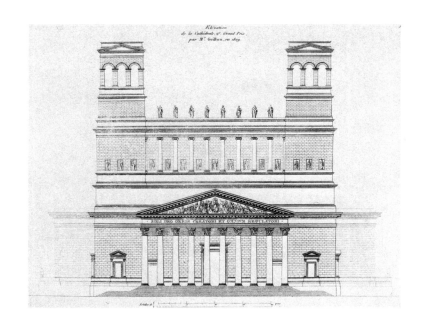

(opposite) Chatillon. *Une Eglise cathédrale.* Elevation and section.

The placement of the towers, resulting from the *parti* of the plan, was unusual for the contemporary basilican projects that Chatillon took as his model. So, too, was the central dome, although it was specified in the program. The section shows the Early Christian basilical form that Chatillon adopted for his interior.

(right) Jean-Louis Grillon. *Une Eglise cathédrale.* 1809. 2e Grand Prix. Elevation and plan.

Defeated by the far more abstract design of Chatillon, Grillon's cathedral project, reproduced here from engravings, has a compact plan that nevertheless resembles traditional church forms in its ambulatory and transepts. The elevation is based on the facade of Saint-Sulpice in Paris, as completed by Chalgrin in the late eighteenth century.

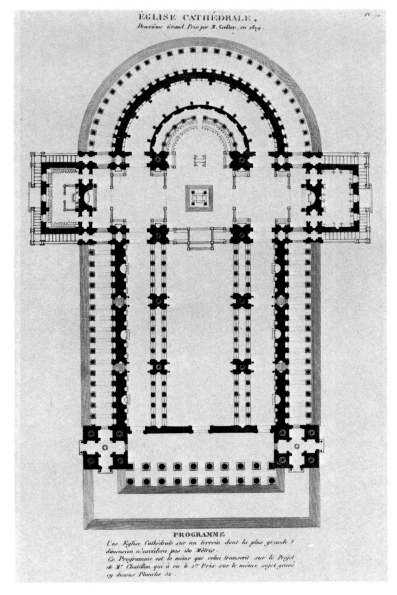

Similar in the effect of its plan to Clémence's *Bourse* is André-Marie Chatillon's Grand Prix project of 1809 for an *Eglise cathédrale* (p. 131). Both are modular and almost perfectly biaxially symmetrical. Indeed, in certain respects, Chatillon's project is closer to Clémence's earlier design than to the winner of the Deuxième Grand Prix of 1809. This project (p. 133), by Jean-Louis Grillon, is not nearly as abstract: the plan is clearly that of a church because of the expansive apsidal termination at one end and the tower-flanked portico at the other. The cross-axis is clearly a transept because of its placement off-center, nearer the apse, which divides the nave unequally and accommodates the unequal proportion of clergy to congregation.

It was precisely these distinctions that Chatillon denied in the evenness and symmetry of his design, but that he subtly permitted to emerge in his details. At a distance, Chatillon's cathedral plan appears to be a simple rectangle on which are superimposed two narrower, longer rectangles along its primary and secondary axes. The four projections from the central rectangle thus formed are approximately equal in accentation, yet in their details they reveal themselves to be several quite different things: a portico, an ambulatory, and two towers. They are hieroglyphs for these architectural forms within a strict general system of notation. The ambulatory resembles the portico in its shape, size, and cascading steps, but is defined by solid black lines (walls) instead of black dots (columns) and is linked to the interior space in a different way. The towers, too, echo the portico in their dotted exterior perimeters crowning massive ranges of steps, but their interiors are filled with thick walls in concentric squares, implying a tall superstructure.

What has just been said of Chatillon's plan applies as well to his elevation, a series of symmetrically arranged rectangular solids orbiting around a central cylindrical mass and terminating in an unarticulated hemisphere. The colonnaded rectangular solid serving as a portico is recognizable as such by its pediment; those solids serving as towers, by their open upper belfry stages. By comparison, the forms of Grillon's facade, like those of his plan, are more overt and also less consistent within the overall geometry of the design and smaller in scale. Chatillon, not Grillon, won the Premier Grand Prix in 1809 because he achieved a very tight, harmonious pattern in ink and wash that, while embodying forms necessary to the communication of the building's practical nature as a church, enhanced rather than competed with its purely geometric quality. Whether the clergy would ever have been numerous enough to fill the back half of the nave, or the congregation small enough to be squeezed into the front half, was beside the point.

* * *

Chatillon's solution stood in contrast with the ideal church types put forward by contemporary theorists of architecture, notably Quatremère de Quincy,

Antoine-François-Girard Bury. *Observatoire.* 1802. *Concours d'émulation, rendu.* Plan *(opposite)*; elevation and section *(following pages)*.

This *rendu* by a twenty-two-year-old student of Percier and Fontaine recalls projects by Boullée and A.-L.-T. Vaudoyer. The monochrome wash is a handsome example of draftsmanship of the end of the eighteenth century (the background tone is distorted by creases in the paper). The plan uses eighteenth-century conventions of color to indicate different levels. Telescoping forms and astrological decorations symbolize the function. The staircase core is surrounded by a library of several stories, which in turn is ringed by workrooms on the ground floor and instrument rooms on the main floor. Both this project and another by Bury two years later (p. 141) show a delight in the abstraction of the sectional view.

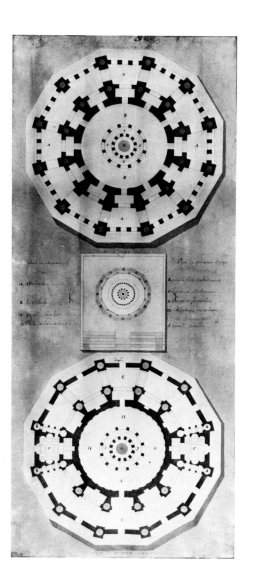

Secrétaire Perpétuel of the Academy from 1816 to 1839. A series of ideal church forms had been conceived and experimented with during the eighteenth century, as has been abundantly documented.[23] Architectural theorists sought to deal simultaneously with the discovery of the Greek temple, with an increasing awareness of structure in architectural conceptualization, and with a growing consciousness of the distinctiveness of Christianity and French civilization. Their efforts to imagine a new Christian church type, characterized by internal colonnades part Greek and part Gothic, but no longer Roman, reached their culmination in the church type conceived by Quatremère and published in his *Architecture* (1788–1825). He derived his ideal church plan from the Early Christian basilica (specifically, from San Paolo fuori le Mura in Rome): a single vessel embracing a nave and aisles separated by colonnades.[24] As a point of departure it is not surprising: Jean-François-Thérèse Chalgrin had established the type with his church of Saint-Philippe-du-Roule begun in Paris in 1765. What is significant is the way in which Quatremère derived an extraordinarily pure and consistent form from it. First, he asserted that just as arches had to rest on piers, and lintels on columns, so a basilica with its colonnades had to have lintels and a flat ceiling (not a vaulted one like that of Chalgrin's church). Second, just as the structural system had to be integral, so the exterior masses had all to be of one sort; there could be no dome or towers. Of domes he remarked, "...What does this placement of one building on top of another signify? To what end this circular temple placed on a square temple, its exterior mass seeming only made to decorate the approaches to a city, its interior architecture too seeming only to belong to the aerial regions?"[25] Of towers, "Imagining a temple as it can and should be on the exterior, towers or belfries are as out of place at the chevet as at the main facade, and I doubt not the day will come for sacred buildings to be entirely freed of these constructions so foreign to them."[26]

Both Chatillon's and Grillon's designs of 1809 were vaulted, domed, and towered. Indeed, the program demanded the towers and permitted the dome — "One is free to use or to reject a domical crowning." The same was true the next time a cathedral was the subject of the Grand Prix competition, in 1837, after Quatremère had been Secrétaire Perpétuel for twenty years. Indeed, a Grand Prix cathedral design without vaults, domes, and towers seems unthinkable because it was an exercise, not in theory or detailing, but in composition, in the manipulation of spaces and volumes. Composition was to be learned in the atelier; for Chatillon, that meant the atelier of Percier, who carried on the eighteenth-century tradition of his teacher and colleague, David Leroy. The latter's *Histoire de la disposition et des formes différentes des temples des chrétiens*, of 1765, was refuted at length by Quatremère in his discussion of churches.

* * *

Bury. *Observatoire.* Elevation and section.

The Ecole des Beaux-Arts as a school organization slowly grew to maturity during the years from 1792 to 1840—from Leroy's and Vaudoyer's almost clandestine courses to the inauguration of the buildings on the Rue Bonaparte with their lecture halls, *loges*, and collections dedicated specifically to the use of the institution. Student exercises matured with it, in both the increasingly well-organized *projets rendus* of the *concours* (p. 140) and the Grand Prix designs. The simplicity of the solutions of Clémence and Chatillon evolved into the mannered subtlety of the Grand Prix projects of Félix Duban and Henri Labrouste during the 1820s (pp. 146, 157), then into the complex projects of Victor Baltard and Charles-Victor Famin during the '30s (pp. 190, 192). The same development can be observed in the *concours d'émulation* designs.

There is, however, an important complication in this development, for the history of architectural ideas was not so polite as to mature at precisely the same rate as the doctrine of the Ecole and Académie des Beaux-Arts. Ideas appeared in France during the 1820s and '30s that could not be embraced by the system we have analyzed in the turn-of-the-century Grand Prix compositions. They originally appeared among the students' work, in the fourth- and fifth-year *envois* of the *pensionnaires* at Rome, beginning with those of Duban and Labrouste of 1828 and 1829. These projects, meant to summarize all that the best students had learned during a decade and a half at the Ecole, horrified the Academy.[27] The ideas these designs embodied were banned from the Grand Prix competition until the end of the century, although they did appear in the *concours d'émulation* in the late 1840s. In the 1830s the Academy and, to a lesser extent, the Ecole had become conservative.

Ironically, it was these same radicals, Duban and Labrouste, who produced the most celebrated exercises in the conventional genres of the competitions before going to Rome. Later publications of the Grand Prix designs begin with their projects, of 1823 and 1824, respectively.[28] Both designs adhere to the cross-in-a-rectangle configuration, as do several of the losing designs in those competitions. Both of the winning projects, however, are extraordinary for their simplicity of form, their tightness and evenness of accentation, and their articulation. Duban built up the plan of his *Hôtel des douanes* (Customshouse, p. 148) entirely from rectangles, in contrast to the more diffuse compositions of octagons and ovals offered by his competitors Jean-Louis-Victor Grisart and Alphonse de Gisors (pp. 148–49). These rectangles Duban united by making the secondary blocks—the administration and stable buildings—echo closely the rectangular doughnut configuration of the warehouse block in the center, and by enclosing all three blocks in a broad walled precinct. Similar to this stark, compressed plan layout is Duban's treatment of the elevations of the warehouse block: the block is broken up into an openwork of massive piers and large voids, powerful both as a pattern on paper and as an expression of a practical building type. Thus the warehouse block decisively dominates the

André-Marie Chatillon. *Salle de Concert.* 1803. *Concours d'émulation, rendu.* Elevation, section, and plans.

For his concert hall, Chatillon adopts a classic *parti* (the Theater of Marcellus), which joins a semicircular amphitheater to rectangular vestibules. The parts are interlocked by a smooth circulation system and by the secondary amphitheater space within the rectangular mass.

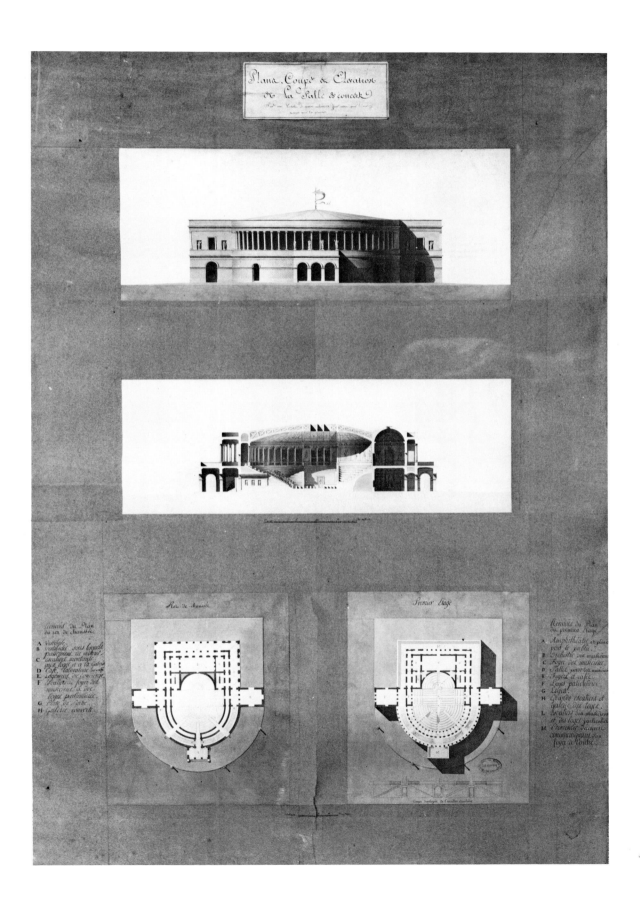

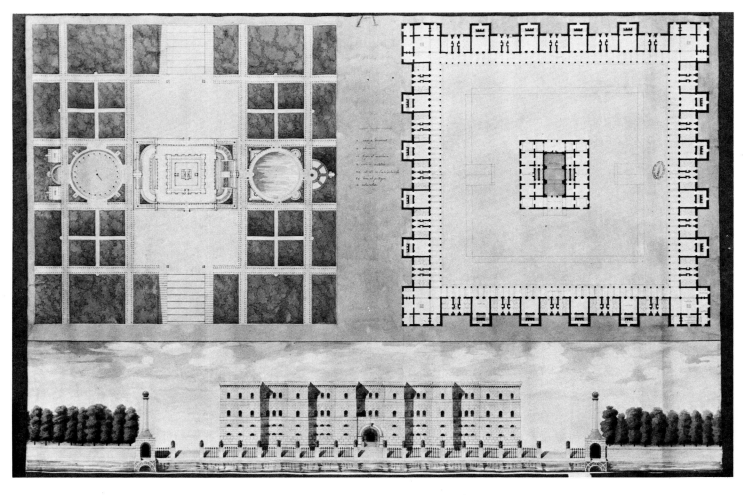

composition, as does no one part in the projects of Grisart and de Gisors, and communicates the building's nature as a place to store goods.

Labrouste's *Tribunal de Cassation* (Supreme Court) of 1824 is even tighter and simpler (p. 156). Indeed, Duban's *Hôtel des douanes* seems baroque and extravagant next to it. All the elements in Labrouste's design are contained in an encompassing square, except for the portico marking the principal entrance. A competitor, Félix-Victor Lepreux (p. 154), utilized almost the same disposition of parts, but he revealed his lack of Labrouste's decisiveness by permitting all four axes to project from the mass and by placing all the courtrooms on three sides of a small central space. Labrouste laid the courtrooms out side by side, facing a spacious *salle des pas perdus* (great hall), and the axes of the two secondary courtrooms opened into cloisters in the corners of the plan, spaces unutilized by Lepreux. Labrouste's project is remarkable for the simplicity and ease with which it solved a problem Lepreux's failed to solve with its more insistent articulation. Léon Vaudoyer's project, awarded the Deuxième Second Grand Prix, becomes complex to the point of confusion.

In the 1830s there came another series of brilliant student projects, followed in the 1840s by a falling off in the Grand Prix designs and a decisive change in the character of the *concours d'émulation* drawings. The 1830s thus seems to have witnessed the last baroque manifestation of late eighteenth-century composition as it was taught in the ateliers of the Napoleonic masters' students—

Antoine-François-Girard Bury. *Hôtel pour loger les vélites* (Barracks for Light Infantry). 1804. *Concours d'émulation, rendu.* Site plan, plan, and elevation.

This project provides lodging and drill grounds for four companies of special troops. The lodgings of the brigade leader and the eating facilities occupy the core structure, the lodgings of officers are in the corner bastions, and a company of troops occupies each of the four sides. This is the form of a Roman *praetorium*, which is then augmented by secondary buildings, exercise fields, and a swimming pool.

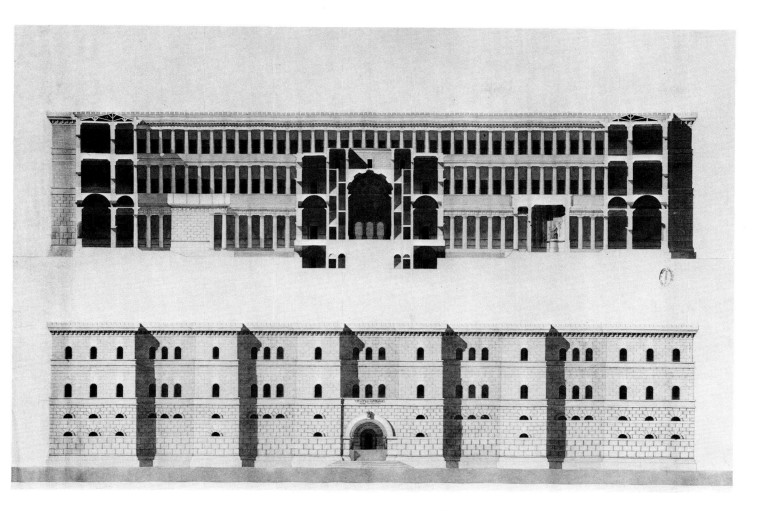

Bury. *Hôtel pour loger les vélites.* Section and elevation.

The fortress-like exterior contrasts strikingly with the porticoes of the interior. The great Roman audience hall is shown in section, with a temple to an unspecified hero on either side. The whole is a typically Napoleonic image of a military facility.

Achille Leclère, Jean-Nicolas Huyot, André-Marie Chatillon, and Hippolyte Lebas.[29]

Two Grand Prix projects that in their complexity and composite nature necessarily stretched the conventional paradigms to their limits are those of Victor Baltard (1833, p. 190) and Charles-Victor Famin (1835, p. 193). Both Baltard and Famin chose to give the constituent elements of their designs practical and thereby characteristic forms, and consequently they tried to unify them by a looser handling of axes, rectangles, and echoing forms. Baltard's design for an *Ecole militaire* frankly admits that its spaces divide into at least two distinct series: a cloister with a chapel and classrooms, and a *cour d'honneur* with administrative offices. The two are linked by an assembly hall. The cloister is an improvement over the medieval university courts that it imitates in having the surrounding classrooms separated by courts to let in more light and air, and it is adapted to a military regimen by opening into a second, outer peristyle to surrounding exercise fields. This outer peristyle also provides the means for linking the two parts of the entire ensemble, for its axes continue into the administration section and become the peristyle of the *cour d'honneur:* in the process it is transformed from outward-facing to inward-facing. This understated, unifying rectangle is the element out from or in from which the administration building and the classrooms evolve.

By comparison, Famin's *Ecole de médecine* is simpler. It comprises four disparate parts—the hospital in the traditional cross-form of Filarete's Ospedale Maggiore at Milan, the classrooms, the principal amphitheater, and the museum and library. Famin arranged these elements around a court, but his way of unifying them was to suggest the paradigmatic interlocking rectangles, crossing at the court. The classrooms were split to form two symmetrical side masses; the museum and library were similarly split and placed in the front corners of the figure to enframe a *cour d'honneur.*

* * *

Famin's *Ecole de médecine* was typical of early nineteenth-century Beaux-Arts composition exercises: the pattern of its spaces, though expansive, consistent, and simple, was not especially practical, particularly in splitting the classroom and library-museum spaces. Later, in 1901, Guadet wrote of the early Grand Prix designs: "There you will find a great number of plans conceived as a longitudinal axis and a transverse axis cutting the plan into four absolutely superposable quarters—not one pilaster more nor less. This is not symmetry, it is nonsense."[30] They had only come to seem nonsensical, however, after the Beaux-Arts system, having encountered the ideas first of Labrouste and Duban, then of Garnier, had reached maturity. These early nineteenth-century projects were a first attempt to conceptualize in terms of spaces and volumes and were necessarily one-sided and exaggerated.

We have forgotten what an impressive accomplishment architectural composition seemed at the turn of the nineteenth century. At that time, order and axes, the linking of interior space and gardens, and the creation of vast ensembles of architectural masses represented the conquest of reason and enlightenment over medieval fear and confusion. Percier and Fontaine, in the lengthy text of their *Résidences de souverains* of 1833, characterized the medieval palace as "a chaotic pile of buildings where military chiefs, become masters and owners by force of arms, live constantly at war with their subjects and their neighbors."[31] Much as sixteenth-century French architects tried to regularize building, "some power other than their own was needed to bring about this adoption of a new type of planning [*distribution*], and thereby to change the habits and mores. . . ." This momentous change, begun during the reign of Louis XIV, was reflected architecturally in "a better arrangement [*disposition*], planning on a larger scale, in sum, a reasoned ensemble. . . ." But it was only in the last half of the eighteenth century that architecture, linking itself closely to science and society, came to maturity and produced Soufflot's Panthéon, Victor Louis's Bordeaux theater, and Jacques Gondoin's Ecole de Chirurgie. Nothing built since the Revolution had surpassed these models, concluded Percier and Fontaine: they remained paradigms for architecture in the 1830s.

Auguste-Jean-Marie Guénepin. Arch of Titus, Rome. Restoration. 1810. Fourth-year *envoi.*

Guénepin's reconstruction is typical of early archaeological student *envois*. The subject is a simple and often-copied Roman decorative monument, and the treatment makes it clear that a *chiaroscuro* study of architectural detailing was Guénepin's primary concern. The illustration shows the drawing, one of a set, bound into a book.

SENATVS
POPVLVSQVEROMANVS
DIVO TO·DIVI VESPASIANI·F
VESPASIANO·AVGVSTO

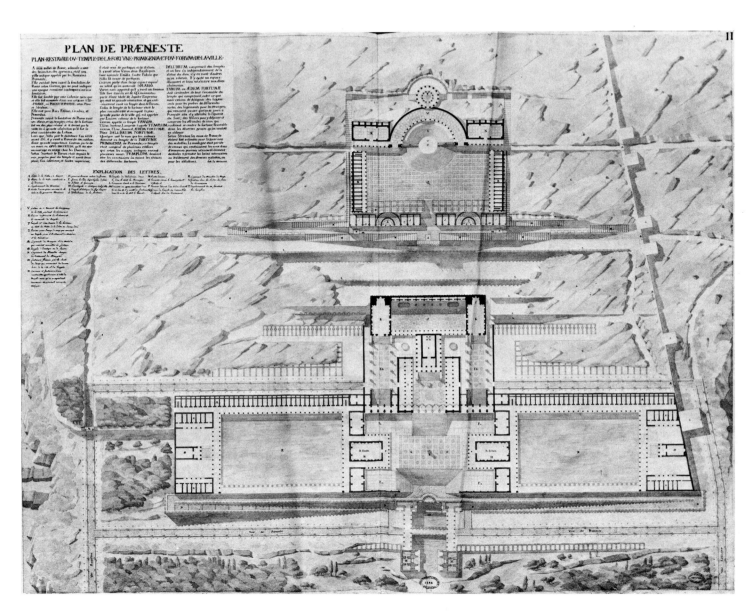

Jean-Nicolas Huyot. Temple of Fortune at Praeneste. Restoration. 1811. Fourth-year *envoi*. Site plan.

One of the most celebrated archaeological studies by a Grand Prix laureate, this restoration established a new level of precision in research and rendering, far higher than that of Guénepin the year before (p. 143). Huyot was appointed professor of history at the Ecole in 1819.

Huyot. Temple of Fortune at Praeneste. Restoration. Elevation.

The Roman precinct at Praeneste, huge and dramatically sited but built-over and difficult to reconstruct, had been the subject of architectural restorations since the Renaissance. Although restrained in its use of decoration, Huyot's handling of wall planes and spaces is skillful and imaginative, demonstrating why Labrouste was to call him one of the best planners of his generation.

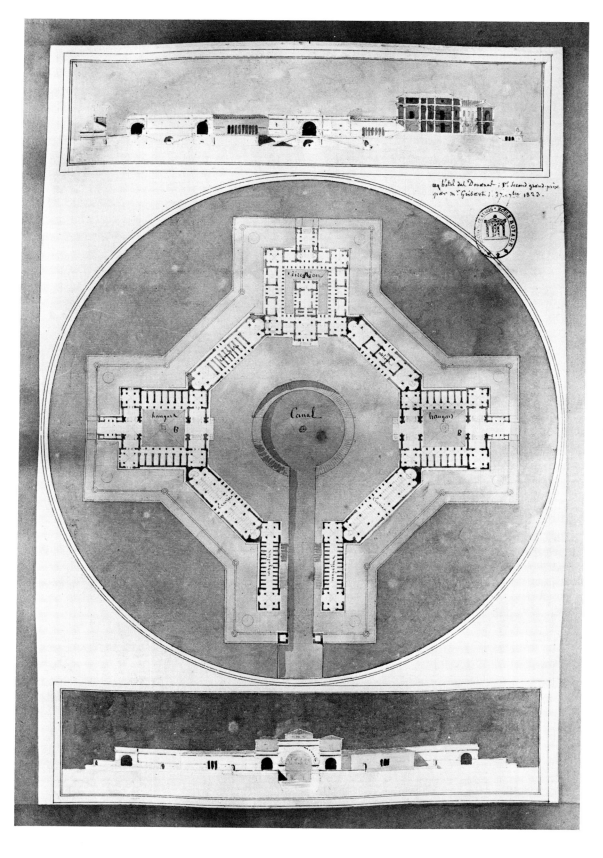

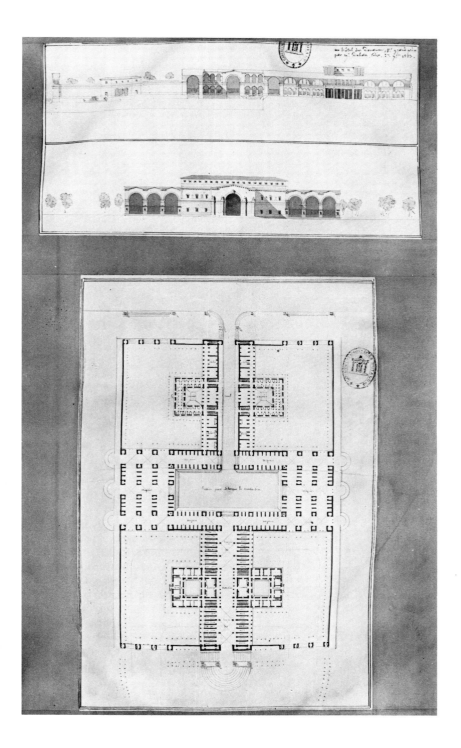

(left) Félix Duban. *Hôtel des douanes et de l'octroi.*
(right) Jean-Louis-Victor Grisart. *Hôtel des douanes et de l'octroi.*
(opposite) Alphonse de Gisors. *Hôtel des douanes et de l'octroi.* 1823. *Esquisses* for the Grand Prix.

Of these three *esquisses* for the Grand Prix competition of 1823, Duban's design is clearly the simplest in form, tightly embracing the canal and basin; the most consistent in scale with its system of wide vaulted bays; and the most expressive with the warehouse clearly dominant.

Grisart, by creating a large open space around the central canal basin, puts a void rather than a volume at the center of his design. The surrounding forms are broken into many smaller parts no one of which clearly dominates the composition. De Gisor's project sacrifices compactness of plan for a monumental terraced layout in elevation.

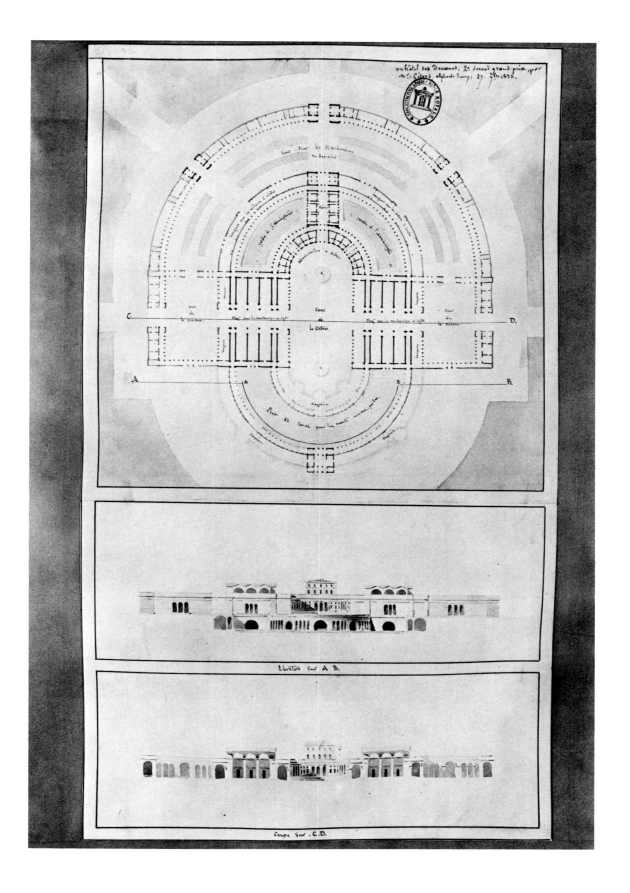

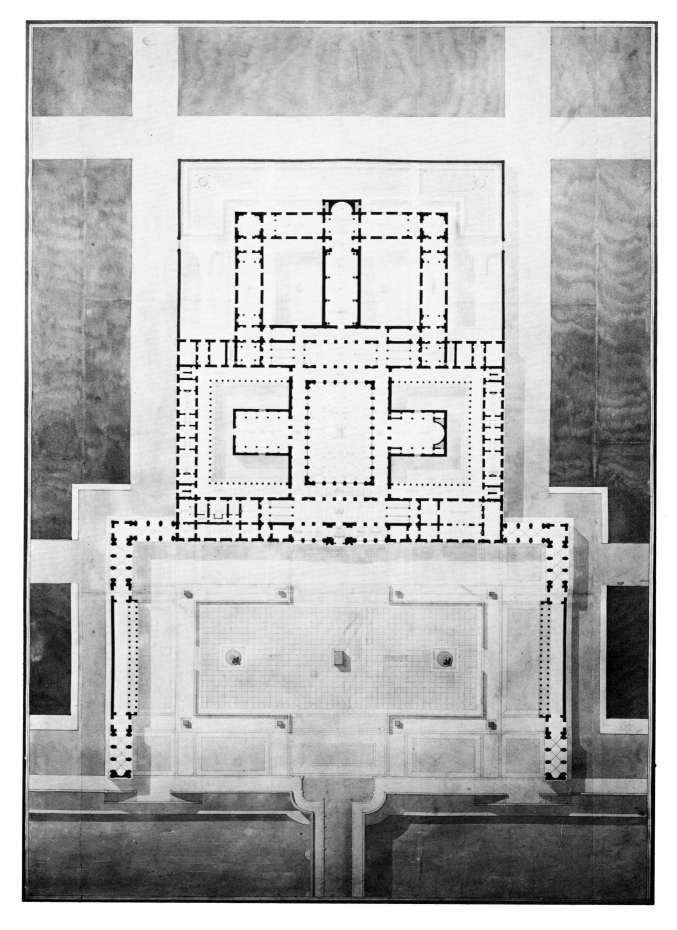

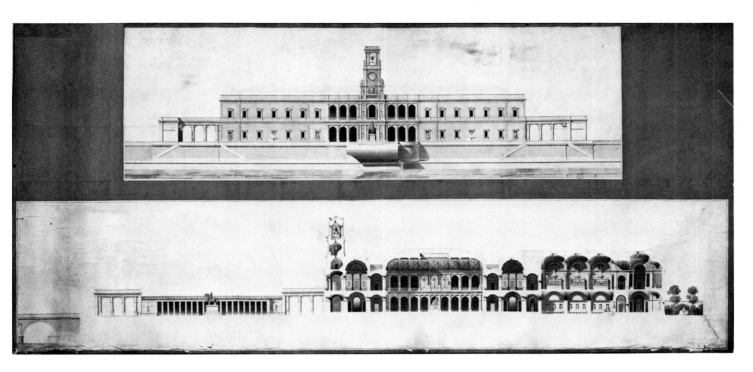

Louis Duc. *Un Hôtel de Ville pour Paris* (A City Hall for Paris). 1825. 1ᵉʳ Grand Prix. Plan of second floor, elevation, and section.

Duc's plan is of much greater clarity than its competitors', but by subordinating the location of the staircases to the visual unity of a two-storied central space, it loses some smoothness in its circulation pattern. The central pavilion shows a new interest in a Renaissance mode, and the section reveals Duc's emphasis of the upper floor to give it some of the Renaissance character of the entry pavilion. This upper floor was devoted to public rooms and to the lodgings of the prefect, while the lower floor was for city offices and archives.

This idea that planning was a recent French innovation was frequently encountered during the late eighteenth and early nineteenth centuries. Jacques-François Blondel in the fourth volume of his *Cours d'architecture* (1773) remarked that *distribution* was "unknown to our ancient architects," but "those at the beginning of this century knew how to refine it into art."[32] Later he stated, "No one is unaware that we owe this facet of the art to Jules Hardouin Mansart."

The architectural effect sought, the particular experience that these buildings were meant to embody, was made explicit in the *Histoire de la disposition et des formes que les Chrétiens ont données à leurs temples, depuis le regne de Constantin le Grand, jusqu'à nos jours* (1764) by David Leroy. Soufflot's disciple and Percier's master, Leroy had been professor at the school of the Académie Royale de l'Architecture and its Revolutionary successor. Leroy ended his treatise with a description of Soufflot's church of Sainte-Geneviève and Contant d'Ivry's contemporary and similar project for the Madeleine. This he led up to with a discussion of the visual effects of colonnades:

> When we wish to appreciate the whole of a colonnade, we are obliged to stand back a certain distance in order to take in the whole of it, and as we move about the separate masses of the building change very little in relation to each other. When we approach it a different spectacle strikes us: the overall form escapes us, but our proximity to the columns makes up for this, and the changes which the spectator now observes in the *tableaux* of which he is the creator in moving about [*qu'il est le maître de se créer en changeant de lieu*] are more striking, more rapid, and more varied. And if the spectator enters under the colonnade itself, an entirely new sight offers itself to his eyes with every step he takes, because of the relationship of the columns to the objects they reveal, whether a landscape, the picturesque massing of the houses of a city, or the magnificence of an interior.[33]

This manner of experiencing a building Leroy applied to Soufflot's and Contant d'Ivry's churches of Sainte-Geneviève and the Madeleine—both in 1764 only projects.

> One sees from their plans that the spectator will be able to perceive the whole of the interior at one time, regardless of precisely where he is imagined to stand, and that the columns, at each step he takes, will successively conceal different parts of the decoration of the church. This change of *tableaux* [*changement de tableaux*] is not only affected by the columns which are very close to the spectator, but also by all those which he can perceive, and if light animates the interior of these buildings, I am emboldened to say that there will result an enchanting spectacle of which we can only form a feeble idea.

It has already been noted how this conception of the church in terms of composition clashed with Quatremère de Quincy's conception in terms of the Orders and their consistent elaboration. Leroy had not acknowledged the con-

Simon-Claude Constant-Dufeux. *Un Lazaret* (A Quarantine Hospital). 1829. 1ᵉʳ Grand Prix. Plan.

Constant-Dufeux had already worked as *inspecteur* on a variety of Parisian constructions by the time he won the Grand Prix. His project for a *lazaret* was greatly admired by the jury, and particularly by Percier, for its clarity and originality of composition. His plan is singularly abstract and repetitive in its arrangement of forms.

Un Lazareth
Constant
1.ᵉʳ g.ᵈ Prix année 1839

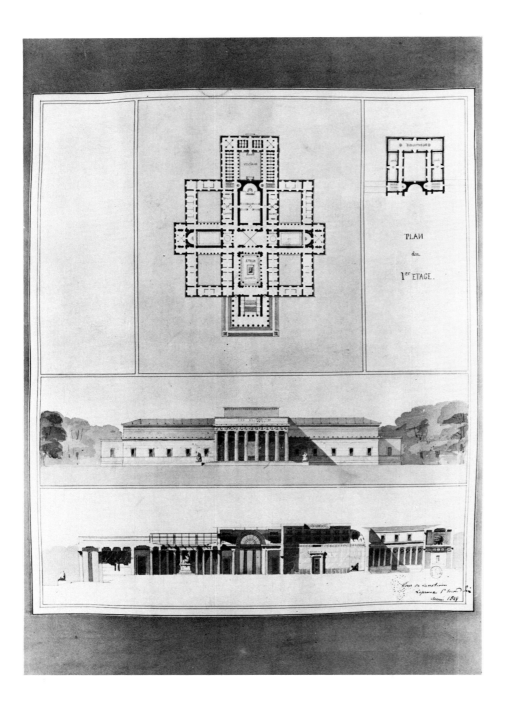

PLAN
du
1er ETAGE.

(left) Félix-Victor Lepreux. *Tribunal de Cassation* (Supreme Court).
(opposite) Léon Vaudoyer. *Tribunal de Cassation*. 1824. *Esquisses* for the Grand Prix.

The program of the competition of 1824, for which Henri Labrouste received the 1er Grand Prix, was for a Supreme Court. Lepreux's design defines some of the major spaces more assertively than does Labrouste's (pp. 156–58) and shows them on the exterior by making them protrude from the rectangular mass. The resulting plan, which has none of the subtlety and richness of Labrouste's, leaves the courtyards in the corners, out of the flow of the enfilades, and provides a restricted central space at the meeting of the four major elements.

Vaudoyer tries to deal with the problem urbanistically by adding two successive forecourts and a complex public space around the building, to which its masses and secondary entrances respond. The result is an unusually interesting design whose only "weakness" is the complexity Vaudoyer consciously sought to introduce.

PLACE   PUBLIQUE.

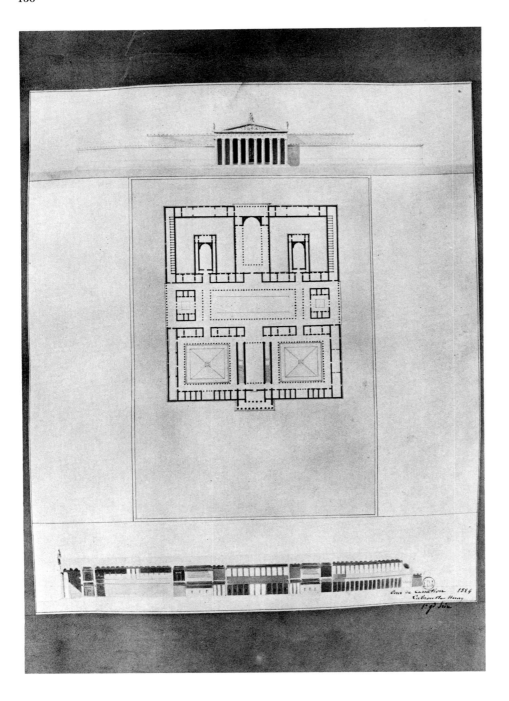

Henri Labrouste. *Tribunal de Cassation.* 1824. *Esquisse* for the Grand Prix.

Labrouste produces an unusually simple general configuration as well as a complex juxtaposition of axes and spaces. Within the plan's stark confining rectangle of exterior wall, the varied spaces preserved mirror symmetry to left and right of the central axis, but develop unexpectedly as the sequence changes from bottom to top. The Section d'Architecture awarded Labrouste's project the 2ᵉ Grand Prix, preferring that of Lepreux, but the order was reversed when the Académie des Beaux-Arts voted as a whole, Huyot and Percier supporting Labrouste.

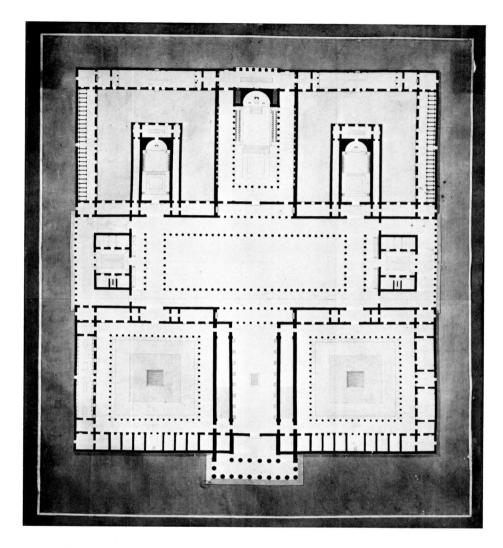

Henri Labrouste. *Tribunal de Cassation* (Supreme Court). 1824. 1er Grand Prix. Plan, facade, and section.

The program of this *concours* demanded three court rooms, one larger than the other two, each with a private meeting room and offices for the president and vice-president of the courts. There were also to be a central atrium and a variety of offices. The two courtyards and the long entrance hall are Labrouste's idea. The program pointed out that because a Tribunal de Cassation was superior to a Palais de Justice, an "antique style," "noble and severe," would express its distinctive character, "without conflicting with our customs." Labrouste responded with a design in the simplest fifth-century Greek vocabulary.

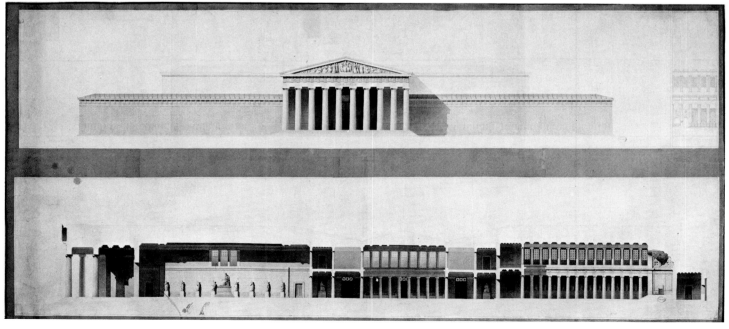

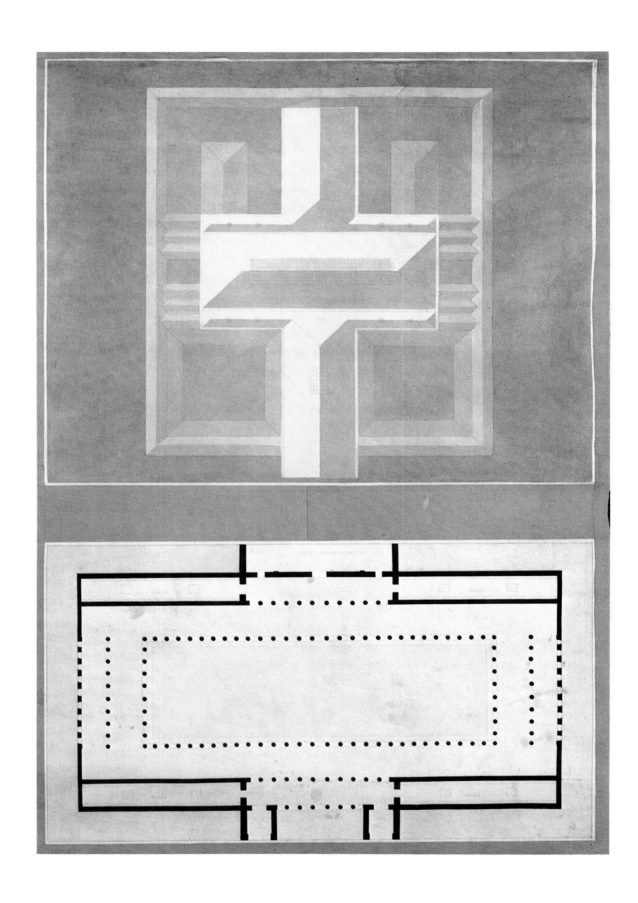

Labrouste. *Tribunal de Cassation.* Roof plan. This sheet was not required by the program, the competitors not usually being asked to submit such details as a roof layout. Even more superfluous is the inclusion, on the same drawing, of the enlarged fragment of the plan. But the combined images, with their contrasting ranges of tonal value, yield a work of graphic art uncommonly subtle even for this period of the Ecole's history.

flict of his ideas and the theory of the Orders, but during the 1780s another prominent *maître d'atelier,* Etienne-Louis Boullée, did so in his *Essai sur l'architecture.*[34] Boullée directly denied the importance of columns and the Orders, suggesting instead that the building masses themselves are the elements of architecture, and for them to have order, they must be disposed symmetrically in a precisely responding pattern. "In architecture, faults in proportion are sensible to any great degree only to connoisseurs. It is clear that proportion is not the first law from which emanates the constituent principles of the art. . . . The first law of architecture and that which establishes its constituent principles" is "regularity." "It is as improper to stray from symmetry in this art as it is to stray from the law of harmonic proportion in the art of music."[35]

The proportions and the details of the Orders formed the basis of the expression of character in the classical conception of architecture. Boullée's rejection of the Orders meant that the expression of character must be lodged in another architectural element, and Boullée proposed that that element was the overall impression of the building experienced in light and shade—in a word, the *tableau.* Among his suggestions he proposed four architectural modes based on the four seasons, systems of visual effects as consistent as the Orders they replace, though in different terms. "In these *tableaux* [the landscape] preserves the character special and proper to [each season], to the extent that nothing is inconsistent in effect, in form, or in color, and that all possible relationships are in flawless accord, analogy and harmony."[36] He compared his *Metropole* and his *Monument to Issac Newton* to the effects of summer: "The light, spreading itself everywhere in nature, is at its most effective; . . . this vivifying light appears scattered over a prodigious multitude of objects, among them shapes of the greatest beauty glimmering from the flash of the liveliest colors and at the peak of maturity; and . . . from this beautiful assembly [of effects]: the ceremonious *tableau* of magnificence." Fall, "by the extreme variety of objects, by the contrast of light and shadow, by the picturesque and dissimilar shapes, by the irregular and bizarre quality of the mixed and checkered colors," in its appearance suggested to Boullée cafés, fairs, promenades, health baths and informal theaters. The effect of winter, its "dark and sad" light, when "shapes are hard and angular," he found appropriate to sepulchral monuments. These Boullée made display "the skeleton of architecture by means of a wall totally bare," and he employed "the image of buried architecture through the use of squat proportions, sunken and concealed in the earth," as well as "light-absorbing" materials to communicate the "black *tableau* of shadows depicted by the effects of shadows even blacker." It is not surprising that on the first page of his manuscript Boullée wrote, *ed io anche son pittore* (I also am a painter).[37]

As presented here, this conception of architecture in terms of *tableaux* of

building masses and interior spaces was an eighteenth-century phenomenon, first stated by Leroy of the generation of Soufflot, and then by Boullée of the following generation. But it persisted through the Empire and the Restoration and down to the Romantic revolution around 1830. It is assumed in the works and writings of Percier and Fontaine.[38] It is stated explicitly in the writings of A.-L.-T. Vaudoyer, secretary of the Ecole des Beaux-Arts and *patron* of both Henri Labrouste and Léon Vaudoyer. In a discourse delivered before the Académie des Beaux-Arts in 1832, Vaudoyer presented architectural expression as the creation of *tableaux* and compared the architect's enterprise with that of the author of the illustrated Renaissance fantasy *Hypnerotomachia Poliphili.*

Architect unknown. Iron Bridge. *Projet de construction, serrurerie.*

Many of the early iron construction projects at the Ecole were devoted to urban river bridges. Their ironwork and forms were usually simple, but these projects provided the opportunity for great shows of draftsmanship concentrating on the *mise en pages* of the drawing, the distribution of pink and blue-gray washes, and the representation of cast shadows.

When one looks at a masterpiece of history painting, one forgets that one is facing a picture; one finds oneself amid the scene represented, one shares the sorrow or joy of the characters, one divines and hears their conversation.

Music invites the same response.

And monumental architecture, architecture that is art, arrives at the same end; the material that comprises it is forgotten, when the architect who has produced it has deeply probed the human heart and sees how the human heart is affected by places under different circumstances; when he studies within himself the varying emotions he has experienced when seeing, caught by surprise or upon reflection, under a clear and luminous sky or a dark and sad horizon, the curious combinations of effects, of certain places, of this great universe. When this artist produces the same impression by means of imitation, we have what cannot be expressed in words, let alone be reduced to principle.

[The architect's] spirit takes fire and is transported into a domain of elevated and vivid illusions. His heated imagination yields a kind of delirium, or better, an ecstasy; he penetrates new and unknown places, he passes through magnificent palaces, enchanted gardens, cool and mysterious grottoes; and a dream, like a second *Hypnerotomachia Poliphili*, a vision, causes him to experience successively diverse sensations; here a rich and imposing architecture brings him to recognize a temple to the deity; further on a majestic but simpler building, severe in character, open and easy of access, discloses the seat of justice.

Beyond an antique bastion, built up of high walls flanked by towers, their openings few and small, and encircled by a wide moat, across which a drawbridge falls from time to time, tells him that here, in this frightening monument, is the abode of crime.[39]

* * *

Little of what has just been cited appeared in formal printed treatises.[40] If we were to seek to understand the Beaux-Arts compositions produced during the early nineteenth century through the best-known theoretical works of that time, we would have to refer to the works of Quatremère and J.-N.-L. Durand, in which we would find little to enlighten us. Composition was taught in the ateliers. What there is to be known about it is to be found in the manuscripts of the *patrons*—and in their vocabulary.

Some of the most interesting, but cryptic, documents of academicians' ideas are the *motifs pour jugement*, the reasons recorded each year in the *Registre des concours* for the award of the Grand Prix.[41] The critiques adhered to stylized formulas no more than four or five sentences in length; toward the middle of the century, they were often merely a sentence. Emile Vaudremer's project (p. 221), for example, is recorded to have been chosen by the Section d'Architecture for the Premier Grand Prix in 1854 because "it offers a great deal of simplicity in its plan and much character in the elevation and section."[42] Yet in general the words of the critiques were carefully chosen. In a description of the character of a project of 1828, the word *grave* had been crossed out and *tranquille* written in its place, to read, *d'un caractère tranquille.*

The handling of the Orders and of detailing was rarely mentioned, and if so, at the end. First came the layout—*disposition*—and second the character—*caractère*—of the elevation.[43] Among the words used to describe the *disposition* we find an otherwise unfamiliar technical term: *marche.* The critique of the Premier Grand Prix design of 1828 began by citing its *marche simple.* This phrase reappeared in the critiques of the Premier Grand Prix

Théodore Labrouste. Temple of Vesta at Tivoli. Restoration. 1829. Second-year *envoi.* Elevation and section.

Sent to Paris in the same year as Duc's massive restoration of the Colosseum, this modest analytical study of a Roman temple at Tivoli by the brother of Henri Labrouste was accompanied by separate colored renderings of the Etruscan tomb paintings at Tarquinia. In this project painted decoration is made an illusionistic expansion of the interior space.

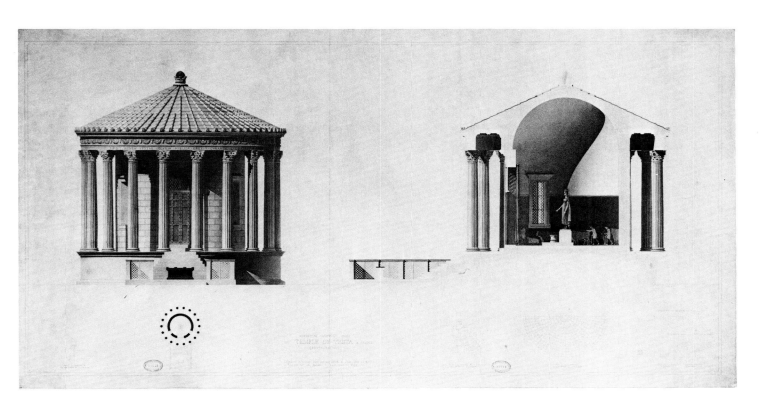

project of 1829 and of the Deuxième Grand Prix designs of 1831 and 1838.

The word *marche* meant, literally, "spot where the foot is placed," "action of placing one foot forward, then the other, to proceed in some direction,"[44] as in the marching of troops. Figuratively, as a "manner of proceeding according to a certain order," it was commonly used to denote the sequence of images in a poem or of action in a novel, the progress of a piece of music or of the moves in a game of chess. Most nineteenth-century dictionaries of the French language in general and of artistic terms in particular went no further than this. The *Dictionnaire des arts de dessin* of J.-B.-B. Boutard (1826, second edition 1832), however, cited a specific use of it in painting: *"Marche,* used in speaking of the composition of a painting to signify the order in which the figures, groups, masses of light and shadow, the sequence of planes of a picture are presented, how they follow one another, and are linked together." He described the *marche* of a painting as following the *ligne de la composition,* of which he wrote:

> One calls lines [*lignes*] in a landscape the broad planes, the masses of trees, the groups of buildings, the chains of mountains, the groups of clouds which the eye can embrace in nature and traverse successively. The sequence of the lines, chosen or imagined by the painter in an order in accord with the rules of pictorial representation [*ordonnance pittoresque*] is the *ligne de la composition* of the painting.[45]

Thus in painting during the 1820s and '30s the word *marche* seems to have

ELEVATION SUR UNE ÉCHELLE DE 0M05 P.M.

TEMPLE D'HERCULE A CORA
ÉTAT ACTUEL

Théodore Labrouste. Temple of Hercules at Cora. Restoration. 1831. Fourth-year *envoi*. Actual state and elevation. *See also pp. 380–81.*

In his reconstruction of this Republican Roman temple, Théodore Labrouste adds an awning, garlands, palm fronds and weapons strapped to its architectural members, in addition to the ex-votos and painted mural decorations that had appeared tentatively in his second-year *envoi*. The noble architectural ensemble thus clothed begins to seem a sort of primitive fetish accurately expressing, as Labrouste and his brother Henri thought, the nature of Republican Roman religion.

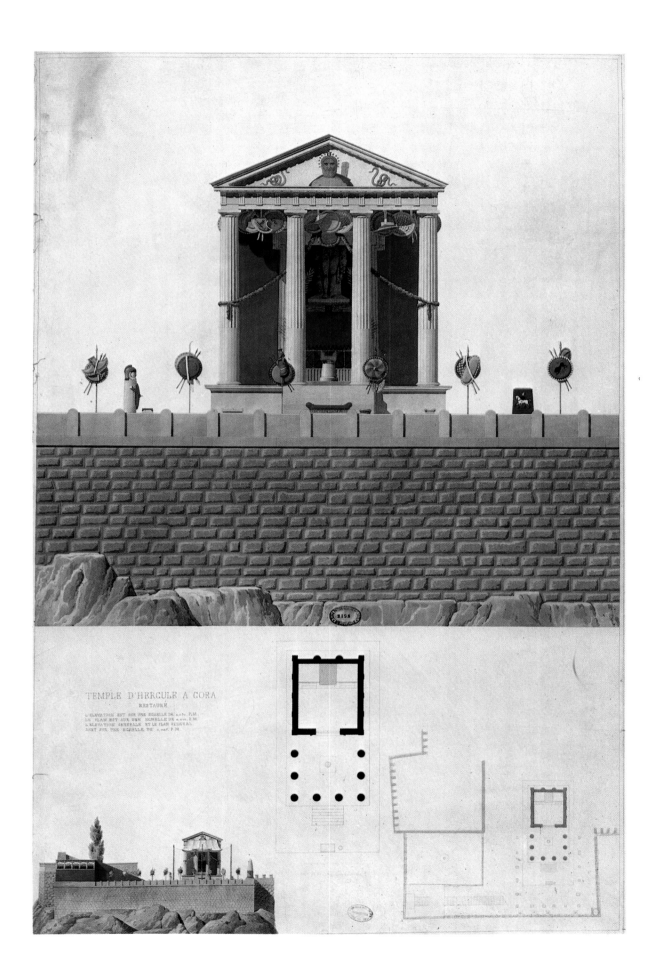

TEMPLE D'HERCULE A CORA
RESTAURÉ

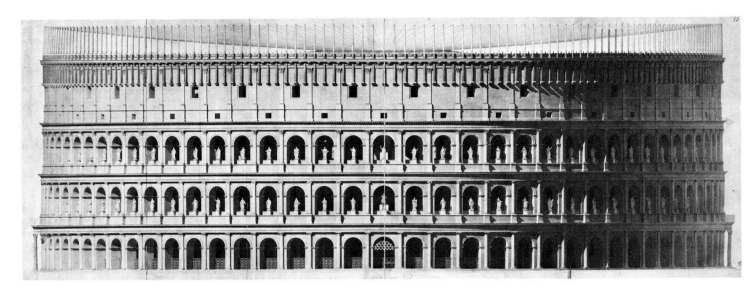

Louis Duc. Colosseum, Rome. Restoration. 1829. Fourth-year *envoi*. Elevation, structural detail, and capital details *(opposite and following pages)*.

Executed by a close friend of Henri Labrouste the year after his Paestum study (pp. 361 *ff.*), this reconstruction of the Colosseum applies Labrouste's structural analysis to a complex Roman building, reintroducing the problems of planning that had occupied *pensionnaires* since Huyot's great Praeneste study (pp. 144–45). Duc, however, emphasized the structural envelope rather than the spaces enclosed by it and included an extraordinarily precise and voluminous documentation.

In his examination of the Colosseum, Duc concluded that Roman detailing had more subtly inflected curves and less consistent forms than had been thought during the seventeenth and eighteenth centuries. Duc's friend Léonce Reynaud wrote of these details in 1835 in the *Encyclopédie nouvelle*: "These Orders are treated with a firmness and simplicity of line that is appropriate to the use of the building, to its dimensions, and to the materials of which it is built. Accordingly, the Doric Order is without triglyphs; the Ionic capitals are without the usual spiral fillet; the leaves of the Corinthian capitals are not detailed, and so on. This is a remarkable document of the latitude that the artists of antiquity knew how to take and the intelligence with which they employed it in modifying the Orders consecrated by use...."

Duc. Colosseum, Rome. Capital details. Ionic, second level.

168

Doric, first level.

Corinthian, third level.

Corinthian, fourth level.

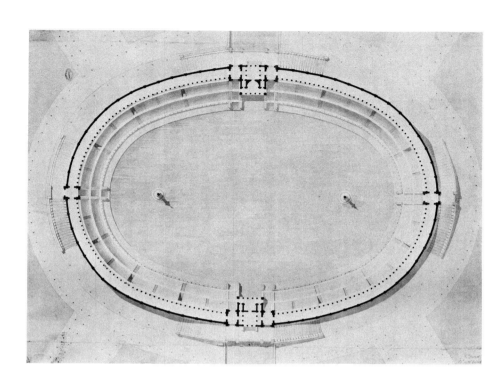

Victor Baltard. *Naumachie* (Water Circus).
1830. *Concours d'émulation, rendu.* Plan,
elevations, and section.

A "Water Circus" was the kind of Ecole
program much criticized by the press and by
radical architects for its lack of relation to
nineteenth-century problems. The author of
the program was Baltard's father and master,
Louis-Pierre Baltard, an eighteenth-century
theorist who had outlived his appropriate
milieu by at least thirty years. Today the
program and its solution may be compared
with similarly extravagant sports facilities.
Roman in conception, it is rendered with dry
elegance.

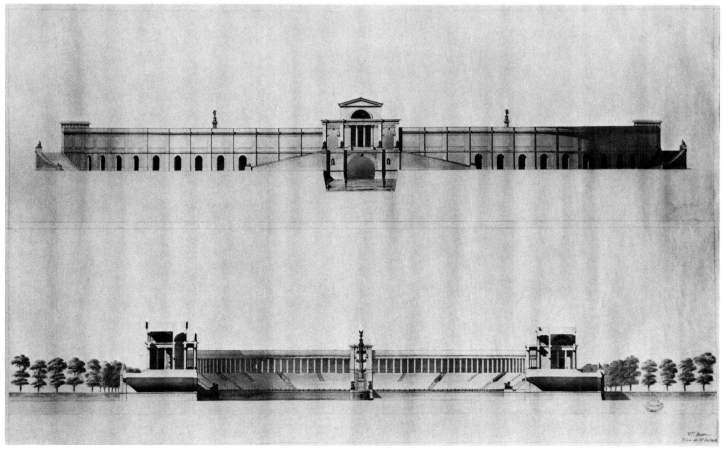

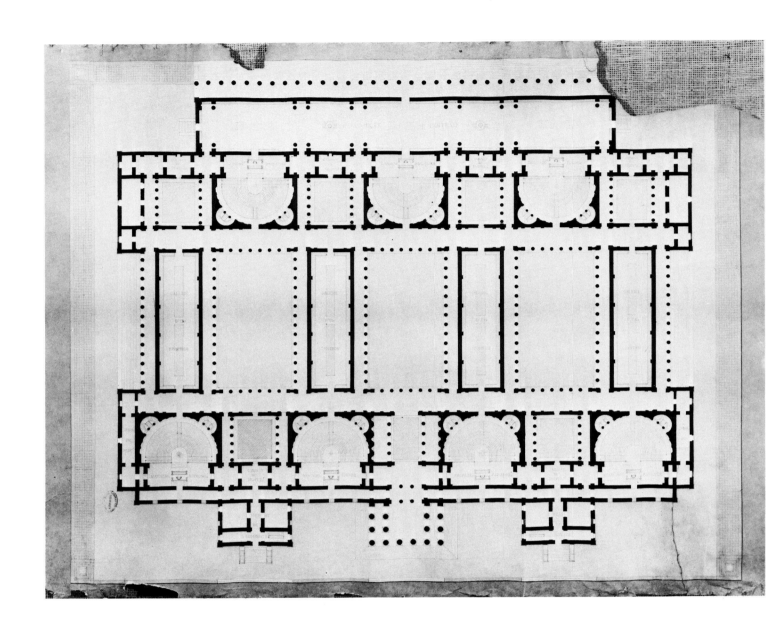

Victor Baltard. *Collège.* 1830. *Concours d'émulation, rendu.* Plan, elevation, and section.

The notable feature of this project is its compact and carefully distributed plan. The four lecture halls to the entry side are for classes in science and the arts and, therefore, open onto four exhibition galleries which, together with three courtyards, occupy the middle range. The three halls at the rear are for history, language, poetry, and philosophy, and thus are linked to the library. The two pavilions flanking the entrance house administration and concierge.

Baltard inherited his excellent planning from the eighteenth-century tradition of the Ecole, but he also continued a conservative pattern in his facades and interiors. The Roman work of the Romantic students of the 1820s was yet to have its impact on student projects at the Ecole.

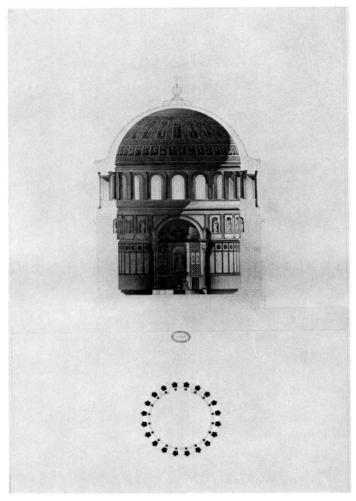

Théodore Labrouste. *Baptistère*. 1832. Fifth-year *envoi*. Elevation, section, and plans.

A Grand Prix winner's final *envoi* was to be an original design based on a program of his own conception, summarizing everything he had learned during his twelve- or fifteen-year architectural education. Like several of the fifth-year *envois* produced around 1830, this baptistery is simple in its planning and massing, but raises the basic issue of the expression of Christian content in classical architecture, here worked out in terms of a circular, domed configuration. In the interior, Christian character is expressed through the decoration, which is essentially Early Christian in style—a delicate polychrome marble revetment embracing an hieratic arrangement of holy images in sculpture, mosaic, and paint.

Joseph Nicolle. *Monument aux illustres Français* (Monument to Illustrious Frenchmen). 1833. *Concours d'émulation, rendu.* Elevation.

The form of this monument recalls late eighteenth- and early nineteenth-century models, though it addresses a problem important to the Romantic circle of Nicolle's master, Duban. It reads in three zones of different character: from far off in general form and in the huge personification of France with French cities at her feet; from close up in the open loggia at the base with its entries and niches like triumphal arches; and from very close as one might climb up to read the inscriptions. Nicolle later became a famous radical *maître d'atelier* and from 1856–70 was art director at the Sèvres porcelain works.

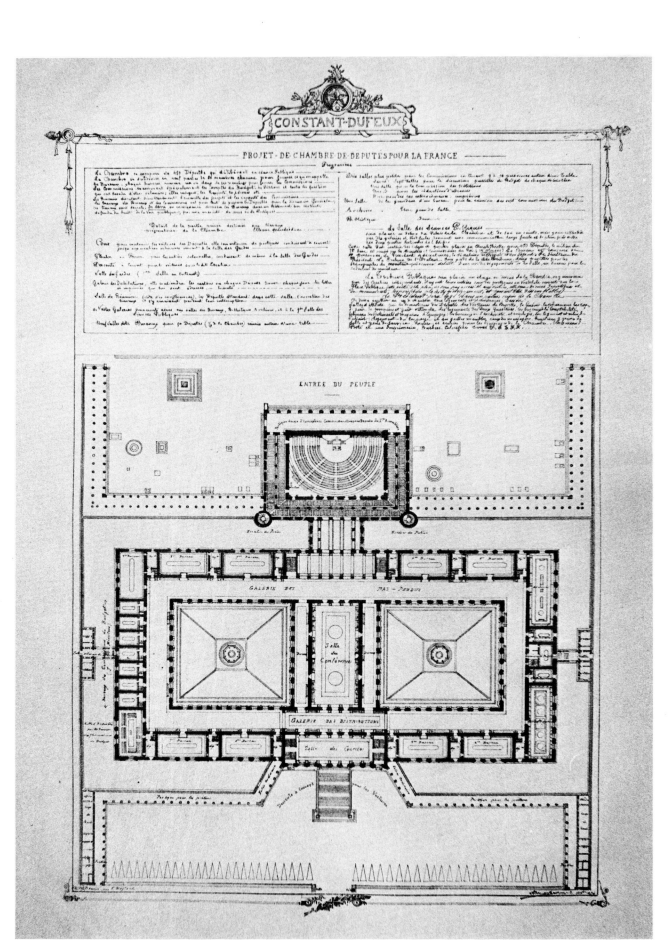

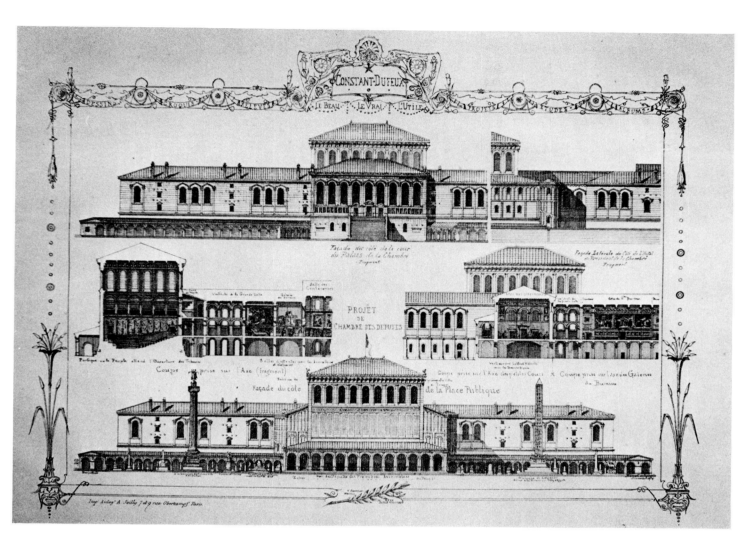

Simon-Claude Constant-Dufeux. *Chambre des Députés* (Chamber of Deputies). 1834. Fifth-year *envoi*. Plan and elevations.

This fifth-year *envoi*, reproduced here from lithographs, was thought by the Academy to be a contradiction of both the talent evidenced by Constant-Dufeux in his Grand Prix project and the goals of a student's sojourn in Rome. The plan, which has a people's entry and a legislative hall on one side, and a deputies' entry leading to galleries and conference rooms on the other, was considered ill-disposed and inappropriate to a building of such importance. Constant-Dufeux's admirers saw this arrangement as a rational solution to a practical problem.

His eclectic design was termed "of an uncertain style" by the Academy, which also deplored his avoidance of the Classical models he had been sent to study in Rome. Like the contemporary archaeological restorations of Constant-Dufeux's companions in Rome, this building is decorated with inscriptions of laws and dedications to great men, while elements of a variety of styles have been adopted for its structural detailing. In spite of initial official displeasure with his work, Constant-Dufeux served as professor of perspective at the Ecole des Beaux-Arts from 1845 to 1863, a position he used for extensive philosophizing on the history and principles of art.

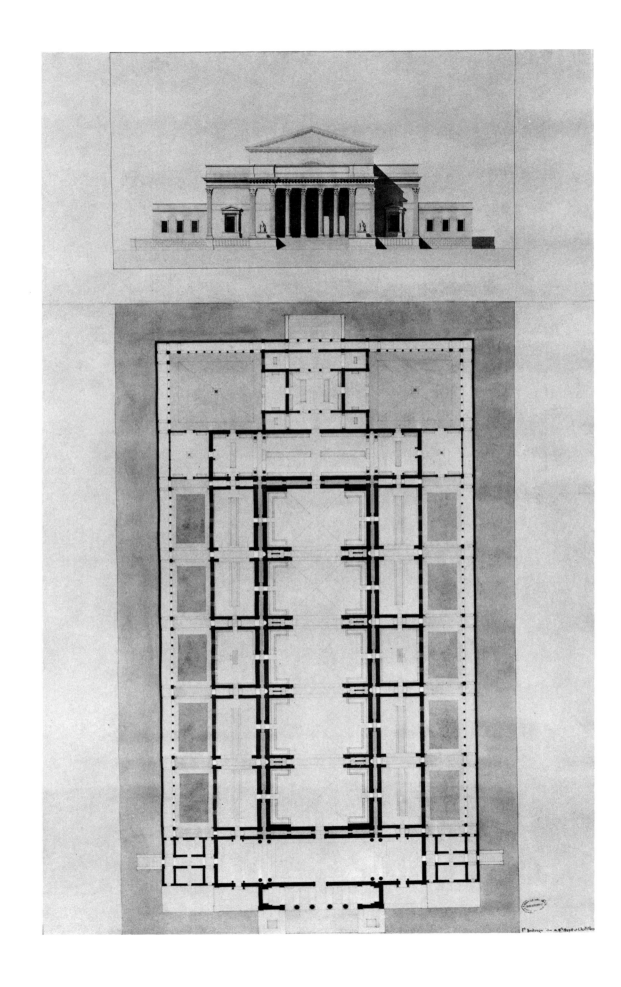

François-Louis Boulanger. *Bibliothèque.* 1834.
Concours d'émulation, rendu. Plan, elevation, and sections.

This library project is an example of the
ability of a student at the Ecole to produce an
elegant plan of basic geometric forms with
simple articulations. Several similar library
plans appear among the *projets rendus* of the
period. The longitudinal section adapts a
Roman Bath paradigm to form a great hall
lined with books.

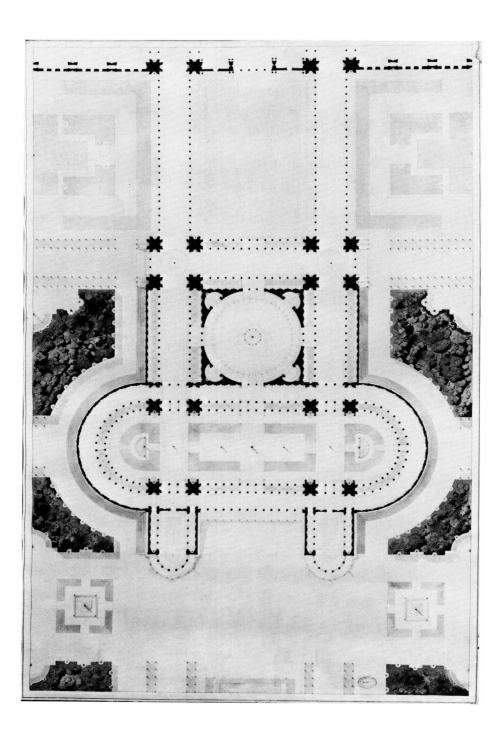

François-Louis Boulanger. *Jardin d'hiver* (Winter Garden). 1835. *Concours d'émulation, rendu*. Plan, elevation, and section.

This pavilion was probably specified to be attached to a palace or great private house. Fragments of Roman Bath forms are modified and combined here to create a series of varied spaces on different levels: some closed, some glazed, and some colonnaded. The delicate tones of the wash are unusual for projects before the 1840s.

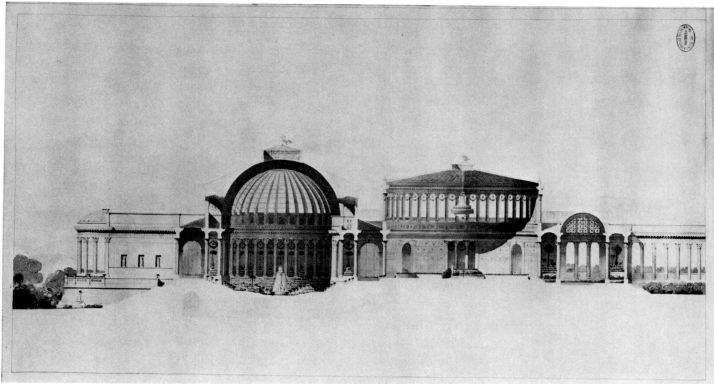

Boulanger. *Jardin d'hiver.* Sections.

designated, among other things, the sequence of fictive spaces represented, proceeding back into space.

One could guess with some assurance in what sense the Section d'Architecture used the word *marche* when criticizing the Grand Prix designs, but Boutard documented it more closely, evidently basing himself on informal studio usage. It must have denoted the experience of the building under analysis imagined as if one were walking and looking down the principal enfilade. *Marche* did not mean the abstract layout of the plan, for which the Section d'Architecture used the term *parti.* Like *marche, parti* was derived from a common phrase, *prendre parti* (to take a stand).[46] When applied to architectural composition, *parti* designated the conceptual disposition of parts decided upon by the designer at the outset: whether a fountain be freestanding or against a wall;[47] whether a tomb be an aedicula containing a statue or a closed architectural mass;[48] whether a theater foyer have a main staircase at the center or two at the sides.[49] The *parti* pertained to the architect, the *marche* to his design. Thus the Section d'Architecture could note, on the one hand, the "originality" of a competitor's *parti* and, on the other, the "grandeur" and "simplicity" of his project's *marche.*

Beaux-Arts composition at the outset was concerned with masses rather than detailing, with those masses as containers of space, and with those spaces as experienced when walked through. A Beaux-Arts building was designed from the inside out. The irony in this is that of all the national schools of nineteenth-century architecture the French would seem the most guilty of practicing drawing as an end in itself. Yet their buildings were conceived and judged as if imagined in their complete state. The Beaux-Arts designers were like musicians, whose reliance upon musical notation reflected confidence in their ability to imagine the music notated, not any myopic love of musical notation in its own right. Despite the polish of the Grand Prix drawings, no nineteenth-century Beaux-Arts design is known to have won the prize on the basis of its rendering alone; despite perspective being banned from the submissions, the projects were always analyzed in terms of a sort of ambulatory perspective.

Quatremère, supposedly dictator of the Academy's policy while he was Secrétaire Perpétuel (1816–39), recognized *marche* in his dictionary only as designating the steps of a staircase. Indeed, his publications on architecture and his discourses before the Academy did not reflect the redefinition of the classical doctrine cited in the works of the *maîtres d'atelier* (who were members of the Academy as well).[50] Architecture's model for imitation, to Quatremère's mind, was still Laugier's primitive hut, and thus its primary element was the Order. We have seen what this meant in terms of the conception of an ideal church type: the trabeated system of the hut had to be used consistently, and any element foreign to it—vault, tower, or dome—was dismissed.

Gabriel Davioud. *Eglise.* 1845. *Concours d'émulation, rendu.* Plan, elevation, and section.

Davioud's church is one of the first prize-winning projects of a student of the Romantic ateliers, in this case that of Léon Vaudoyer. It also shows a new interest in medieval architecture, though in a bold and eclectic treatment which reflects contemporary controversy over the development of a nineteenth-century Gothic style in France. Davioud's drawings also show a change in style from those of the 1830s and a new use of strong color, hitherto restricted to reconstruction drawings. The simple plan is still a fairly conservative drawing and should be compared with the rich, colored *poché* of Villain's church plan of 1849 (p. 202).

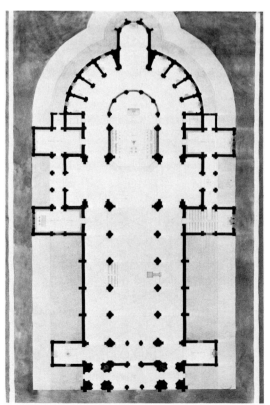

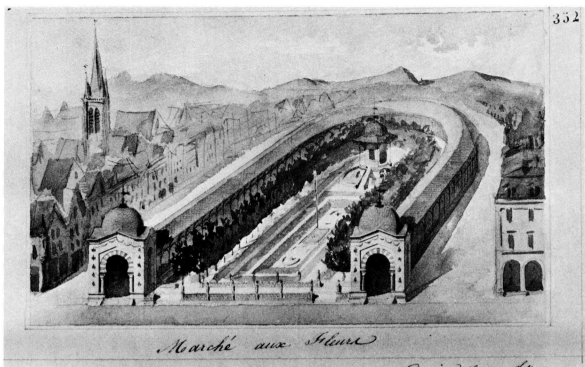

Marché aux Fleurs

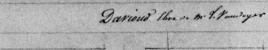

(opposite) Gabriel Davioud. *Marché aux fleurs* (Flower Market). 1848. *Concours d'émulation, esquisse.*

The *esquisses* of the *concours d'émulation* were drawn in the *loges* in a limited amount of time and were therefore usually projects for small buildings or monuments. In the 1840s, these *esquisses* began to reflect the "revolutions" generated by archaeological reconstructions in the '20s and '30s, and of Romantic architecture outside the Ecole. Davioud's flower market shows Moorish pavilions leading to a light iron structure.

(right) Gabriel-Auguste Ancelet. *Fontaine.* 1848. *Concours d'émulation, esquisse.*

The program of this *concours* called for a fountain at a roadside oasis in Algeria and required that it provide shade as well as water. Ancelet, nineteen years old at the time, responded with this stone, iron, and cloth structure, which is conceived in a "local" style inflected with *Néo-Grec* detailing.

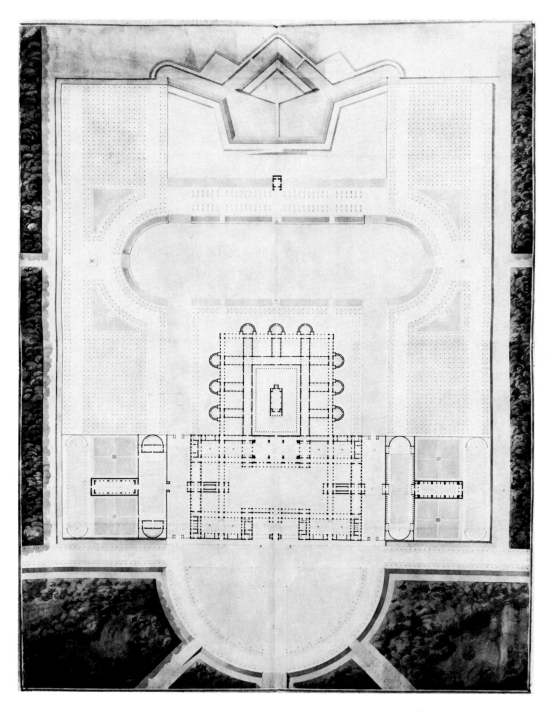

Victor Baltard. *Une Ecole militaire.* 1833. 1ᵉʳ
Grand Prix. Plan and section.

Baltard's plan seems almost of the eighteenth century in its rigid abstraction (and its
style of rendering), yet it also plays on the
connotations of the program by using
auditoria like bastions around one wing of the
school. The project includes teaching and
dormitory facilities in the center and a riding
and a swimming school to either side, as well
as covered and open exercise areas.

The section reads from the edge of the dor-
mitories at the left, cutting through the main
assembly hall and the chapel, with its tower,
and extending to a gallery and auditorium on
the right.

He recognized the existence of a secondary realm of architectural effects in which architecture was considered a "mode of expression or representation," used "to make perceptible either the intellectual ideas through the sensations it has the power to arouse in us, or the distinct qualities of each building through the agreement of all its forms with its use and nature."[51]

This realm, which seems distinctly like that of Vaudoyer's and Boullée's thinking, Quatremère designated as "relative" and characterized as distinct from a higher, "ideal" realm: "I would see between them the same distance that one places in sculpture and painting between ideal beauty [*beau idéal*] and imitative beauty [*beau imitatif*]." The one architectural form that manifested ideal beauty was the Greek temple, because of its closeness to the primitive hut. Indeed, Quatremère characterized the Doric temple as the most elevated architectural paradigm, because among all Greek temple types it reproduced the primitive hut the most precisely, and he saw all subsequent building as a steady decline as this paradigm was modified:

> Of the three Orders of architecture, that which . . . has the most *character* is the Doric—that is, the primitive Order in which the manifestation of the framework and of the constituent types of the art is most forcefully and plainly stated and rendered. Because of this, Greek architecture . . . has more *character* than Roman architecture where the . . . imprint of these types begins to disappear and becomes confused. Because of this, modern architecture has been steadily losing *character*, as the faithful imitation of the types of framing has gone on disappearing and changing to the point of being no longer recognizable.[52]

To Quatremère, this paradigm was architecture's universal and eternal ideal.[53] It was to the elucidation of this simple type that most of his theoretical writings on architecture were devoted; it was by this measure that he judged contemporaneous architecture. In his eulogies of Léon Dufourny and Eloy-Etienne de Labarre, it was their handling of the Orders that he discussed.[54] Yet when the eulogies were read at the public meetings of the Academy in 1822 and 1833, architecture students disrupted the meetings in protest.

These students seem simply to have ignored the ideas of another contemporary theorist, J.-N.-L. Durand, professor of architecture at the Ecole Polytechnique from 1795 to 1830, who published his lectures in several editions beginning in 1802. He competed for the Prix de Rome four times, winning the Deuxième Prix (p. 117) in 1780 (as a student of Perronnet, although he worked in the atelier of Boullée). When in 1793 the Republican government held a series of competitions for the design of public buildings, Durand, in partnership with Jean-Thomas Thibault, won the majority of the prizes.[55] Typical plans published in the second volume of Durand's *Précis des leçons d'architecture donnés à l'Ecole polytechnique* (1805) include at least two copied from Grand Prix projects: Clémence's *Bourse* of 1798 and Percier's Building for the Academies of 1786.

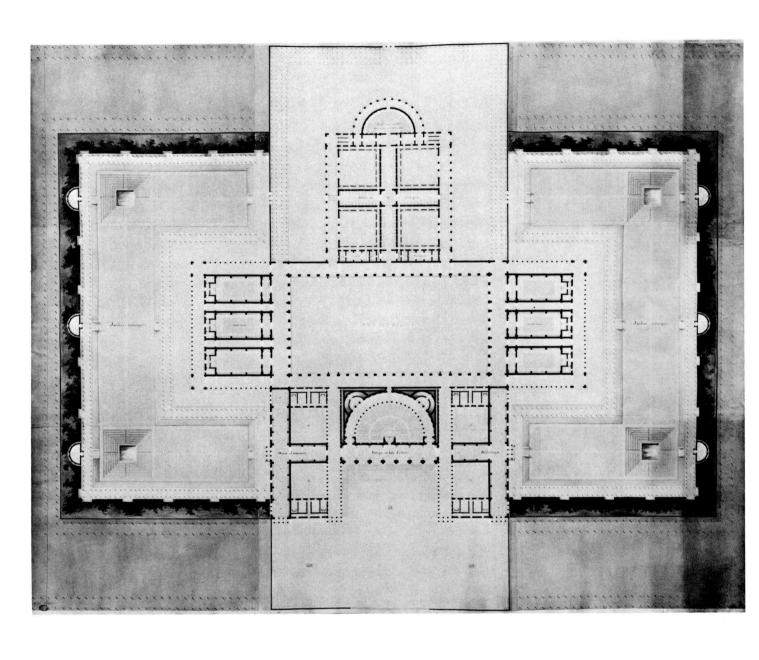

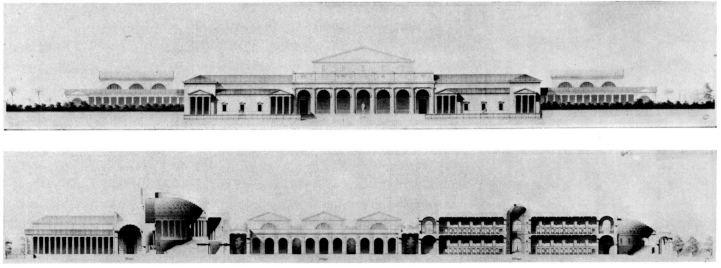

Charles-Victor Famin. *Une Ecole de médecine et de chirurgie* (A Medical and Surgical School). 1835. 1er Grand Prix. Plan, elevation, and section.

This plan combines classrooms, a library and museum, and a working hospital in a smooth interlocking of rectangles within two crossed axes. The exedrae on the edge of the botanical gardens that surround the school are dissection rooms, which the program required be well out of sight of the hospital. The elevation provides separate entrances to main amphitheater, library, museum, and main corridors. The buildings to either side are classrooms, which open onto the central courtyard. Famin neatly divides his building into zones for theory *(bottom)*, practice *(center)*, and clinic *(top)*, all of which give onto a central court bordered by arcades.

The text of Durand's book makes it clear that he did not share the academicians' belief in architecture as the imitation of a natural model. The only justification that he recognized for architectural forms was the efficient enclosure of specified spaces. Imitation was an intellectualization, justifiable only as giving pleasure in the analysis of architectural beauty. "Whether one consults reason or examines the monuments, it is plain that to give pleasure could never have been the object of architecture, nor could architectural decoration. Public and private good, the happiness and protection of individuals and society, such is the object of architecture."[56] The projects published in the *Partie graphique*, the third volume of his *Précis* (1821), no longer serve a specific purpose; they are simply arrangements of spaces.[57] In that volume he spoke at length of the necessity to think abstractly, to sketch with signs and numbers, to avoid copies and images of existing buildings. His method was to "decompose" and "analyze" historical and traditional architecture as a series of elements—loggias, porches, vestibules, rooms, stairways, galleries, courts—physical entities, without sensational or symbolic implications. These he recast according to a modular grid and an elemental vocabulary of columns, walls, flat ceilings and vaults, and then synthesized along patterns of axes to generate ensembles. The resulting buildings, he insisted, were magnificent in their stark simplicity and expressed their function by the mere fact of physically embodying it: "All the beauties that one perceives in or seeks to introduce into architectural decoration arise naturally from a plan that encompasses fitness and economy."[58]

Durand's system would have been impossible without the late eighteenth-century compositional techniques of the reduction of all spaces to rectangles, of the grid, and of the use of simple configurations of axes; his confidence that his results would give visual satisfaction presupposed Boullée's investigations into massing and chiaroscuro. But Durand's intentions were quite different: he separated the techniques from their ends; he taught what Vaudoyer termed *execution* but not *invention*. In the second edition of his *Précis* (1817) he expressed surprise that composition "had never been treated in any text or course. . . ."[59] The reason seems to have been that by *composition* Durand meant the techniques that the academicians took for granted and that the students learned in the ateliers. For example, the studies of country house composition made by Louis-Ambroise Dubut (a student of Ledoux) while he was a *pensionnaire* in Rome and published in his *Architecture civile* in 1803 illustrate, without explaining in words, the same principles as Durand. Since only Durand, teaching engineers, had any purpose in codifying these techniques, they remained uncodified at the Ecole until the turn of the twentieth century, when the professors again sought to communicate composition to outsiders, abstracting it from a national tradition to create an "international style."[60]

194

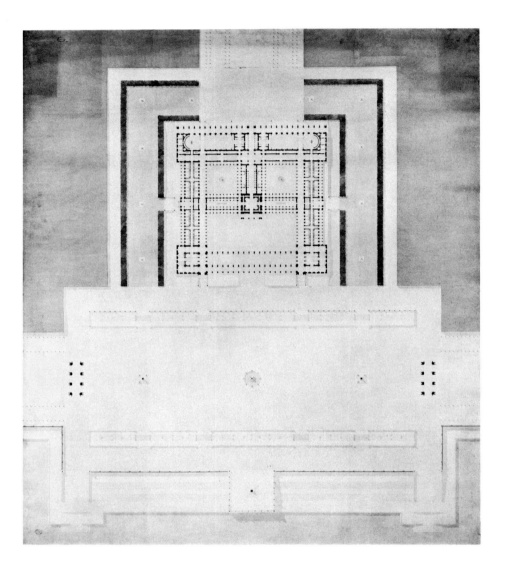

Hector Lefuel. *Hôtel de Ville* (City Hall). 1839. 1ᵉʳ Grand Prix. Plan, elevation, and section.

In contrast to Louis Duc's Grand Prix project of 1825 following a similar program (pp. 150–51), Lefuel's solution is compact and strongly accented as well as simple and broad in its *marche*. Lefuel places his two principal ceremonial chambers on a common axis across the back facade. They are approached by a monumental staircase leading up from a domed chamber inside the tall central tower. This chamber is entered from a broad forecourt closed on the facade by a vast *loge publique*. The small Renaissance campanile that Duc had used to express the specific character of his *Hôtel de Ville* has become in Lefuel's design a vast ziggurat, and the Renaissance motifs have been multiplied, including now the mansarded roofs of the recently restored Paris Hôtel de Ville (as well as the project for the completion of the Palais de Justice presented in 1836 by Lefuel's master, Huyot).

The Era of Duban, Labrouste, and Vaudoyer

The author of the design for the Catholic church in Hamburg,
having to cover a large space, has decided to vault it. . . .
The vaults once agreed upon, the architect has deduced from
them the overall and detailed arrangements of his building.
Félix Narjoux, *Notes de voyage d'un architecte,* 1876

While the Grand Prix projects of the 1840s continued in the established mold, but seemingly with less and less imagination and conviction, a major change was taking place in Parisian architecture. A group of young architects led by the Grand Prix laureates Abel Blouet, Emile Gilbert, Félix Duban, Henri Labrouste, Louis Duc, and Léon Vaudoyer had evolved a new conception of building while they were *pensionnaires* in Rome in the '20s.[61] Upon their return to Paris around 1830, Duban, Labrouste, and Vaudoyer opened ateliers to teach their ideas. (Blouet also opened an atelier, but he carefully sought to avoid polemical issues.)[62] During the following decades they erected a series of buildings that forcefully demonstrated their point of view: Gilbert's asylum at Charenton (1834–45), Labrouste's Bibliothèque Sainte-Geneviève (1838–50, p. 335), Vaudoyer's Marseilles Cathedral (1845–93, p. 425), Duc's Palais de Justice (1840–79 and after, p. 428)—not to mention Duban's completion of the buildings of the Ecole des Beaux-Arts itself (1832–64, p. 78). As has been noted, it was in the 1830s that one encountered for the first time the conservatism that eventually came to seem one of the basic characteristics of the Beaux-Arts system. The winning Grand Prix designs, which were judged by the Academy, were never to reflect the influence of these architects' ideas with any decisiveness.[63]

The monthly *concours d'émulation* at the Ecole itself, however, which were judged by the professors and a jury of twenty architects, did reflect this influence. In 1845 Simon-Claude Constant-Dufeux, a younger member of the circle, was elected professor of perspective; in 1846 both A.-L.-T. Vaudoyer and Louis-Pierre Baltard died, and Blouet replaced the latter as professor of theory. Nonetheless, the only students from the radical ateliers consistently to win medals were Gabriel Davioud and Henri Espérandieu, protégés of Léon Vaudoyer, the best connected of the young architects. Four Grand Prix winners—Charles-Victor Famin (1835), Arthur-Stanislas Diet (1853), Julien Guadet (1864), and Edmond-Jean-Baptiste Paulin (1875)—started their training in one of these three ateliers, and only one—Albert-Félix-Théophile Thomas (1870, student of Vaudoyer)—was crowned while he was under such patronage.[64]

The few projects emanating from these ateliers that did win the *concours d'émulation* (and thus were preserved at the Ecole des Beaux-Arts) reveal how easily they could be recognized and discriminated against by the jury. One of the first projects to win, though only a *deuxième médaille*, was by a student of Duban, Joseph Nicolle (p. 177). One's uneasiness before this *Monument aux illustres Français* (Monument to Illustrious Frenchmen) of 1833—a dramatic, repetitive pyramid of fragments—is not lessened by the inscriptions identifying the statues: POURQUOI, MANGEOIR, COBALT, MAUVAIS CHAT.

More subtle and also more fundamental in its transgression of the traditional limits of Ecole design was a series of projects from the late 1840s, most notably a *projet rendu* for a *Bourse* by Gabriel Davioud (pp. 209–10). The plan of this *Bourse* is indecisive in *marche*, without an emphatic central axis along which the spaces open. Instead, five equally accented axes start off from the nine wide bays of the facade, and it is the two inner lateral axes, not the central one, that continue through the whole structure to the back entrance hall. The three masses that compose the building are separate and contrasting rather than blended into a single composite form. The proportions of these masses, their openings, and their detailing are heterogeneous. The decorative vocabulary seems fourteenth-century Italian, a mixture of Gothic and classical. Indicated in the broad facade loggia are temporary wooden shops erected between the buttresses and public announcements or advertisements affixed to the walls, undignified signs of hard public use never before seen in a winning Ecole project. In the drawings the walls and spaces are simply and monotonously delineated, and their *poché* (silhouette) is unattractive; these are not especially beautiful sheets.

Yet behind this disorder and lack of decorum—in terms of the tradition of premiated student work at the Ecole—Davioud's *Bourse* displays a very strict order of a new sort. It is clear in the facade loggia. Intruding into the very center of the space is a central row of piers. These piers support a double row of groined vaults whose lateral thrusts are taken up by two rows of deep buttresses across the front and back of the chamber. The longitudinal thrusts are resisted by two pairs of thick-walled "reading rooms" filling the end bays. Similarly, the variously scaled openings of the facade are appropriate to their function: broad, segmental doorways for the storerooms in the basement; small windows (illuminating "divans" within) for the "reading rooms"; wide openings for the loggia.

Similarly, the iron-ribbed ceiling of the trading room, itself tacked on almost circumstantially behind the loggia, is held in place by a thick masonry arcade buttressed by walls in the peripheral offices, the thrust carried across the corridors by arches. The structural system of the trading floor, like that of the loggia, embraces that whole portion of the building, the spaces within which seem to have been partitioned off after this structural form had been determined.

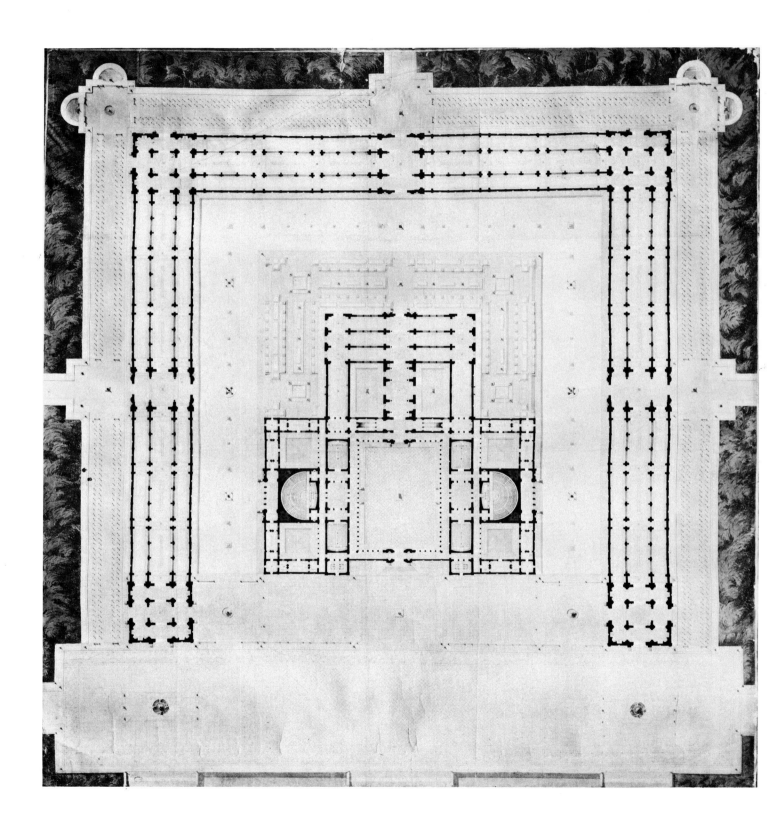

Charles Garnier. *Conservatoire des arts et
métiers, avec galeries pour les expositions des
produits de l'industrie* (School of Arts and
Trades, with Galleries for Expositions of Industrial Products). 1848. 1er Grand Prix.
Plan, elevation, and section.

Garnier, then twenty-three years old, was
said to have won on the merits of his plan
from the moment his *esquisse* was judged. He
was the only *logiste* who successfully handled
the differentiation of the galleries (the large
U-shaped building), which were to be open
to the public, from the central school building. The latter's interlocking axes organize
lecture and demonstration halls and library
rooms with circulation areas.

The elevation shows how Garnier articu-
lates his secondary buildings as a gallery by
means of a broad, two-storied entry and
large, high windows, while for the main
school building he uses a *parti* similar to that
of the facade of the Palais des Etudes of the
Ecole des Beaux-Arts (p. 80). Garnier tries to
enliven the interior surfaces of his courtyard,
but these show little of the baroque quality
that later emerged in his work. The section is
taken through the teaching museum.

Gabriel-Auguste Ancelet. *Monument dans l'Ile Sainte-Hélène à Napoléon 1er* (Monument to Napoleon on the Island of Saint Helena). 1849. *Concours d'émulation, rendu.* Section, plan, and elevation.

In a typically complex *Néo-Grec* conceit, this monument, cut out of the living rock of the island itself, represents an empty imperial throne guarded by lions and an eagle. The throne is placed on top of a sarcophagus covered with a shroud and bearing images pertaining to the emperor's life, carved as a continuous relief. A fortified bastion protects the ensemble at its base. The detailing is incised and angular, responding to the material of which it is made. Its "style" is a mélange of the Egyptian, Assyrian, Etruscan, and Byzantine.

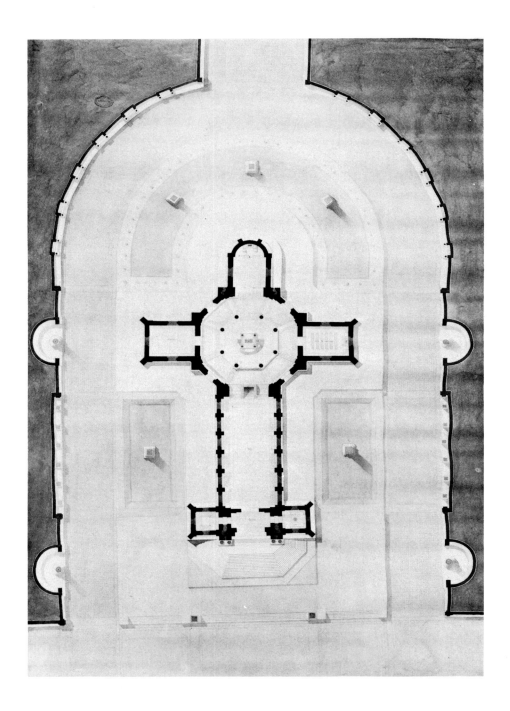

Edouard-Auguste Villain. *Eglise paroissiale* (Parish Church). 1849. *Concours d'émulation, rendu.* Plans, elevation, and section.

This project suggests a Northern Italian site because of the use of vivid Lombardic brick and an Italian Romanesque style. It reflects the current interest in medieval styles and the ideas of Blouet, professor of theory, and the Romantic circle in the use of local polychromatic materials. Villain treats these elements with a balanced and refined touch, which slightly reduces the force of the Romantic conception.

Villain's plans are notable for the strong distinction of principal space, transepts, and towers. Like the elevation and section, they are drawn in handsome, deep-toned watercolor.

A comparison of Davioud's *première médaille Bourse* design with Edmond-Auguste Villain's *deuxième médaille* in the same competition (pp. 205–06) vividly demonstrates how the student of Vaudoyer sacrificed the *marche* for the abstract integrity of the structural organism. Villain's design unfolds itself along a central axis, firmly and generously laid out. Starting at a boat landing, poetically mirrored in the placid waters of a broad river, one mounts two ramps to a quai into which the warehouses are excavated (this convenient watercourse is nowhere mentioned in the program). From here the visitor passes up a broad flight of steps flanked by fountains (compare this with Davioud's stairs!), crosses a shallow loggia, and penetrates through an opening of three linked arches onto the trading floor. There the viewer's gaze is embraced by a great round arch in the opposite wall within which, beyond a screen of columns, is placed the office of the stockbrokers. The *poché* of Villain's plan sheet is elegant. The Roman detailing of the elevations is equally attractive. The trading floor, which with its three thermae windows discreetly states its nature as a public hall, clearly dominates the composition of masses: the loggia is its base and preparation, as is the quai that Villain added to the program, permitting his design to pyramid grandly. The spatial conception, the massing, the decorative vocabulary, and the rendering all adhere to the conventions of the Ecole—and very elegantly. Yet Davioud's project won.

Davioud provided little in the way of subtlety of plan, massing, or decoration to conceal the fact that his *Bourse* is essentially two separate structural organisms appropriate to the building's two basic activities: hectic trading in a centralized space and leisurely conversation in an open loggia. The river and the quai were Villain's addition to the program; the "reading rooms" with their "divans" were Davioud's. Ludovic Vitet in his critique of the Paris Bourse by Brongniart defined the problem in Davioud's terms: a hall for trading and a portico for repose.[65] But it had never occurred to Brongniart or Vitet (or Clémence) to break out of the closed rectangular geometry of the basilica paradigm and make the loggia a thing in itself, thus making the form multiple and its reading sequential. Likewise Davioud's openings and details on the facade take their scale and meaning from their individual functions, not from an a priori total configuration.

All of which makes it surprising to confront the *Eglise paroissiale* with which Villain won a *première médaille* in that same year, 1849 (p. 202). It seems, in fact, to have taken up Davioud's composition-in-parts, structurally expressive surfaces, and convincing structural organism (entirely in masonry, however, with no use of iron). Yet when one compares it with Davioud's *Eglise* of 1845 (p. 187), one quality becomes evident immediately: Davioud's insistent crudeness of spatial division, proportion, and detailing. Villain's project is colorful and elegant, the *marche* broad and varied, his walls and spaces in-

Edouard-Auguste Villain. *Bourse* (Stock Exchange). 1849. *Concours d'émulation, rendu.* Plan.

Villain was twenty years old in 1849 and thus six years younger than Davioud, who took the *première médaille* in this *concours*. His plan subordinates the loggia to the trading room and establishes an insistent central axis which, however, cannot be traversed for the building's full length.

Villain. *Bourse.* Elevation and section.

The trading floor clearly dominates this composition, the loggia and the quai being treated as entourage, terracing up to this central feature. The ships' prows and anchors in the decoration identify the building as one devoted to commerce. The ceiling of the trading floor is supported by an iron armature concealed beneath an elaborate plaster ceiling, appearing only at the skylight.

terestingly formed. In 1849 Villain also won a third medal, for a *Cour de Cassation* closely resembling his *Bourse* design; his radicalism, like that of Ancelet (p. 210), was a matter of the decorative surface, not of rudimentary principles. Already one sees what was to come to a head with Guadet's Grand Prix design of 1864 (p. 256): the use of Labrouste's ideas to create a sort of updated rustic mode, applicable in certain less monumental buildings, but always disciplined by the rules of composition, proportion, and detailing.

* * *

The model for Davioud's *Bourse*, at least its loggia, is obvious: Labrouste's Bibliothèque Sainte-Geneviève, which stood virtually complete in 1849 (p. 335).[66] Here too the *marche* is sacrificed to the display of the integrity of the structural system, and the regularity of the pattern of openings across the facade is subordinate to the expression of the nature of the spaces within. Both Labrouste's reading room (p. 345) and Davioud's loggia comprise a central spine of piers supporting two ranges of vaults ringed by a girdle of deep masonry buttresses. Labrouste's piers and vaults, however, are of iron, a material that Davioud only used in the vault of his trading floor. Yet certain of the preliminary studies for the library do show buttressed stone vaults, suggesting that Davioud had studied this rejected solution as well as the completed building.

Labrouste's facade implies the internal disposition. The piers, joined at their summits by arches, are the organizing features, and they are identical, like the bays of the structural system that engenders them. Between them are recessed masonry curtain walls decorated to read as clearly separate elements. Above the curtain walls these bays are open, creating the expansive arched windows of the reading room, while small slits below light equally small storage rooms that ring that space. Medium-sized windows in the basement-like first story light the stacks located on that floor.

Seen in terms of early nineteenth-century composition, Labrouste's Bibliothèque Sainte-Geneviève, like Davioud's *Bourse*, is meager of access, inexpressive and repetitive in its space and massing, and unbalanced in the pattern of its facade openings. But, unlike a student project, Labrouste's library was built, and thus can be visited, walked through, and worked in. And when doing so, one is impressed by two contrasting experiences. First, that of confinement: in the reading room there are neither monumental exit passages nor windows at eye level to lead the mind out of the space. Indeed the columns occupying the center of the room prevent one from commanding its perspective; it presents itself simply as a series of identical bays, arranged in the agonizing proportion of four to nineteen. Second, that of expansion, a conceptual experience: all along the wall are the books that to the Romantic mind opened deep mental vistas into history and science. To make this explicit, Labrouste decorated the vestibule of the Bibliothèque Sainte-Geneviève (p. 341) with illusionistic paintings representing a mythical landscape of treetops and blue sky on the side walls, behind busts of great scholars and artists. He explained some of his intentions in a letter to the *Revue Générale de l'Architecture* of 1852:

> I would very much have desired that a large space planted with big trees and decorated with statues were laid out in front of the building, to shield it from the noise of the street outside and prepare those who came there for contemplation. A beautiful garden would undoubtedly have been an appropriate introduction to a building devoted to study, but the tightness of the site did not permit such an arrangement and it had to be foregone. Thus the garden which I would have loved to traverse in order to arrive at this monument I painted on the walls of the vestibule, the only intermediary space between the public square and the library. My painted garden is not so fine as beautiful *allées* of chestnut and plane trees, but it has the advantage of offering trees always green and always in bloom; . . . without regard for the climate of Paris. I can, in this fertile soil of the imagination, plant trees of all regions, and place next to Bernard the palm of the Orient, near Racine orange trees in flower, behind La Fontaine the oak and the rose, and next to Poussin the myrtle and the laurel.[67]

These paintings, in a sense, were the mental images that the rows of multicolored bindings making up the walls of the reading room conjured up in Labrouste's imagination. The ceiling of the vestibule was once painted sky blue, continuing the sky of the murals and transforming the light, painted green iron members of the exposed ceiling structure into the arches of a pergola under which one traversed Labrouste's painted garden.[68]

The weakening of form in Labrouste's architecture was balanced by a strengthening of illusion. The world of illusion painted onto and cut into the surfaces of the naked structural organism of the Bibliothèque Sainte-Geneviève exercised a powerful effect on younger architects around 1848. It eventually came to be a fashion, called the *Néo-Grec*.[69] At the Ecole des Beaux-Arts, a student of Victor Baltard, Gabriel-Auguste Ancelet, began winning *concours d'émulation* with what was popularly regarded as that mode of design in 1848 (p. 189).[70] His most extraordinary work was a *projet rendu* of 1849, *Monument dans l'Ile Sainte-Hélène à Napoléon 1er* (Monument to Napoleon on the Island of Saint Helena, p. 201). Here are present all the characteristics of *Néo-Grec* design: over-scaled angular forms; stylized incised decoration; an ornamental vocabulary partly of anecdotal narrative scenes, partly of primitive symbols, partly of the decorative elaboration of the constituent materials; and a "style" simultaneously Egyptian, Assyrian, and Byzantine. And like most *Néo-Grec* productions it must be "read," each part taken into account in sequence.

When seen from the sea, the whole of Saint Helena appears transformed into a monument to Napoleon, for it is not built on the island, but rather is

Gabriel Davioud. *Bourse* (Stock Exchange). 1849. *Concours d'émulation, rendu*. Plan.

This project should be compared with Villain's (p. 205), which won the *deuxième médaille* in this competition. Davioud's plan falls into three distinct parts: the loggia on the facade, the trading floor, and the Tribunal de Commerce (Chamber of Commerce) at the back. There is no very pronounced central axis linking them. The *poché* is simple and inelegant.

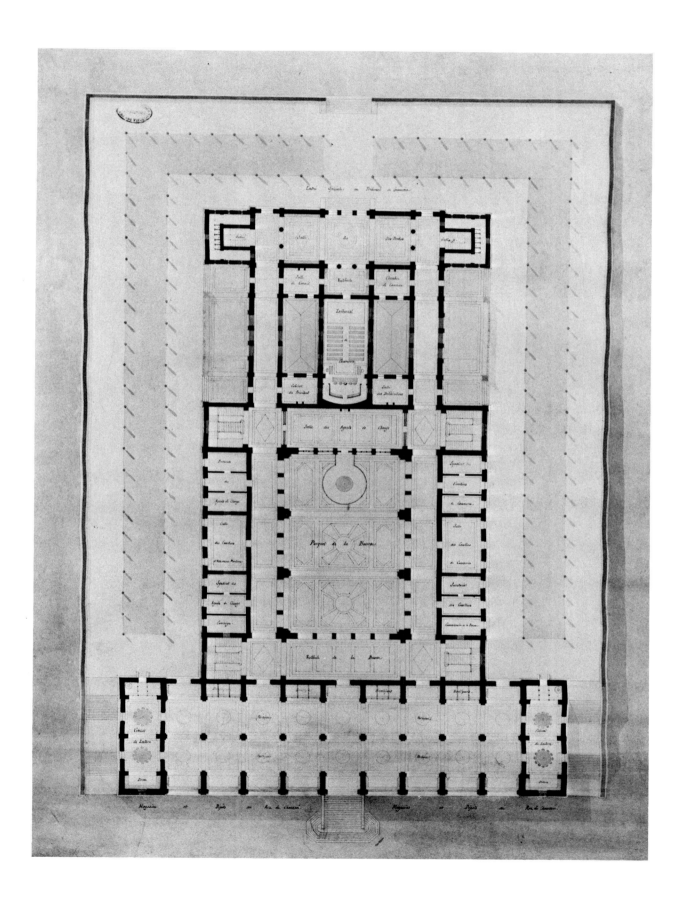

211

Davioud. *Bourse.* Elevation and section.
The loggia and the trading room read as separate, contrasting forms. The general lines of the articulation recall fourteenth-century Florentine architecture, but the actual details are so simplified and geometricized as to be unclassifiable. Unlike Villain, Davioud sees a *bourse* as a very stark, business-like place. Public notices are shown affixed to the walls of the loggia. The ceiling of the trading floor is supported by exposed iron elements.

sculpted into it like the statues of Abu Simbel. The rock of the island's seaward cliffs has been cut back into a great plane surface out of which emerges a throne resting on a two-tiered podium, empty but guarded by four freestanding lions and an eagle. This throne-podium is made to rest on a huge rectangular block of stone—a sarcophagus of Egyptian solidity—draped with a shroud held in place by rosettes that cause the fictive material to gather at the points where they penetrate it. This juxtaposition of throne and sarcophagus is conceptual; the sarcophagus represents death, the throne the memory of Napoleon's great deeds (or the possibility of his return—was Ancelet a supporter of Napoleon III?) On the surface of the sarcophagus is a continuous narrative relief of the events of Napoleon's career, in front of which his scepter seems to float.

Imagined as if sailing toward the fortified bastions that guard its base, one may experience the monument at another scale, that of the human visitor. One may mount up to the sarcophagus to find a chapel flanked by two custodians' shelters, made to seem miniscule by the scale of the monument. Here one may read the story in the narrative reliefs, then one may climb to the throne-podium and mount it by a stairway inserted into its stepped base. On the wall of the podium one may read a long memorial inscription and enter a second chamber cut into the rock, probably a tomb chamber.

Thus there are two parts to the image (the funereal base and the memorial throne) and two scales in its representation (those of the island as a whole and of the human visitor). The project's relationship to the imagery of the Bibliothèque Sainte-Geneviève is indirect—except on the level of "touch"—since it is a carved monument rather than an architectural space. Both the project and the library, however, were attempts to get past the existing conventions of style, symbolism, and the relationship of the monument to man. Style is not a vocabulary to which one is restricted, but rather is one associative system among many that one may manipulate with motifs. Symbols are not hieroglyphs in a system of notation; they are derived from direct experience and are shared by many societies. And as far as possible both form and rendering are engendered by the site and by the materials at hand.

Ancelet went on to win the Grand Prix in 1851, at the extraordinarily early age of twenty-two, with a project on a conventional plan, neither *Néo-Grec* nor Roman, but fifteenth-century Italian in style. He proceeded through the *cursus honorum*, building little, restoring much (notably the Château at Pau), and ending with election to the Academy in 1892. Upon Ancelet's death in 1896, Paul Nénot devoted a considerable part of his necrology to his student projects, remarking significantly: "And this was in 1849, when Ancelet was barely twenty years old!"[71] Ancelet was a young student when he produced these *Néo-Grec* projects. He had not invented the style, however, Labrouste had, and the events of 1848–51 seem to have helped spread it.

Pont sur un chemin de fer

Buillard

Élève de M. Gallard.

(opposite) Charles-Gustave Huillard. *Pont sur un chemin de fer* (Bridge over a Railway). *(right)* Emile Vaudremer. *Pont sur un chemin de fer.* 1852. *Concours d'émulation, esquisses.*

The program of this *concours* specified a site in a garden cut by a new railway line, and required not only a means to cross the track but also a place to watch in comfort as the trains passed. Huillard placed first, using the maximum of two pavilions and a covered gallery allowed by the program, and taking advantage of the gallery to show off an elegant iron structure.

Vaudremer's bridge is far more modest in scale and conservative in style than that of Huillard. It takes the *parti* of a viewing stand rather than a pleasure pavilion.

391

The next great effusion of the *Néo-Grec* came during the 1870s, after the Franco-Prussian War and the Commune. To understand it one must first comprehend, on the one hand, Labrouste's effort to enrich and make more specific architectural expression, and on the other, contemporary French society's periodic plunges into the political and philosophical unknown.

* * *

Ancelet's *rendu* dealt primarily with decoration, whereas Labrouste's Bibliothèque Sainte-Geneviève dealt with decoration in the context of structural and spatial composition. In order to describe Labrouste's method of conceptualization, new words and formulas were invented. For example, L. Radoux (a student of both Duban and Labrouste and a *proscrit* of 1851) described the procedure of Labrouste's student Eugène Millet when designing in this manner:

> He undertook a new construction with the ease of a sculptor modeling in clay or of a painter roughing out a sketch. . . . He would proceed always from the simple to the complex. . . . He would turn his attention first to the skeleton [*ossature*] and when he had weighed and balanced [*raisonnée et equilibrée*] all its parts, he dressed [*habillait*] his building as needs and function would dictate and according to resources at hand, but always allowing, under the folds of the attire, the means to divine a healthy and vigorous form.[72]

One now spoke less about spaces formed and the character of the elevation than about the *ossature,* how it was *equilibrée,* how then it was *habillée.* If one were to analyze a building of this sort, one should proceed as Félix Narjoux did here:

> The author of the design for the Catholic church in Hamburg, having to cover a large space, has decided to vault it. . . . The vaults once agreed upon, the architect has deduced from them the overall and detailed arrangements of his building.[73]

There was one man who took this approach to its ultimate conclusion: Viollet-le-Duc. It was to him that some of Labrouste's students went when he closed his atelier in 1856. Soon afterward, in 1863, Viollet-le-Duc was one of the instigators of the most determined attempt to break the Academy's control over the educational system.

The twelfth and thirteenth of Viollet-le-Duc's twenty *Entretiens sur l'architecture* treated as a loose series the famous *Marché couvert* (Covered Market) and iron-and-stone vaulted halls today often reproduced.[74] The problem he posed for himself was to create characteristic nineteenth-century architectural spaces from masonry and iron in combination. The culmination of the series served as the frontispiece of chapter twelve of the *Entretiens,* a "salle voûtée" (vaulted hall), dated 1864 on the plate (p. 227).

In Viollet-le-Duc's "salle voûtée," it is hardly necessary to point out that,

René-Robert Millet. *Maison en bois* (House in Wood). 1852. Sheet from an album of the general construction course.

This drawing is by a student from a liberal atelier, who chose to fully express his wooden structure rather than to show it stuccoed over, as did the more conservative students. The general construction course taught the structural detailing of wood, stone, brick, and iron.

215

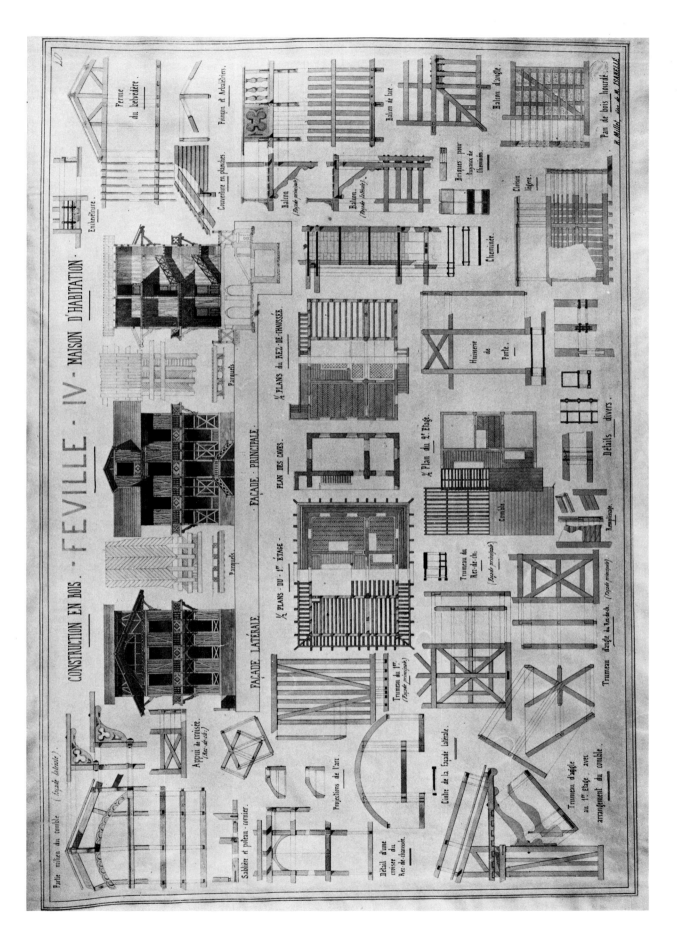

CONSTRUCTION EN BOIS. — FEUILLE - IV - MAISON D'HABITATION.

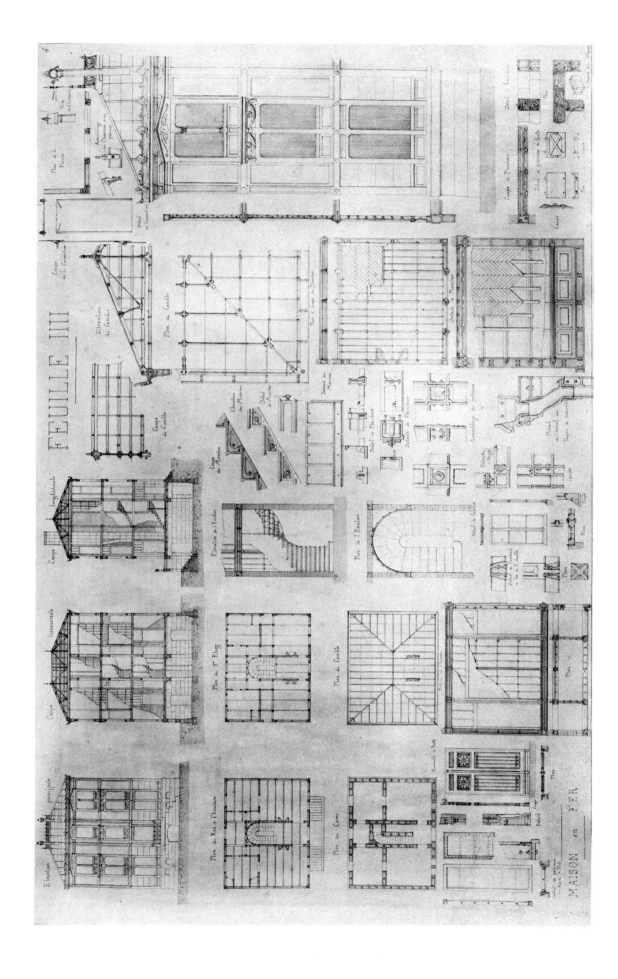

FEUILLE III

MAISON en FER

Louis-Clementin Bruyère. *Maison en fer* (House in Iron). 1852. Sheet from an album of the general construction course.

This project shows a house entirely in cast and wrought iron, with cast decoration derived from carved stone motifs.

like Davioud's *Bourse* and Labrouste's Bibliothèque Sainte-Geneviève, the *marche* is of little consequence. It is a vaulted hall and not much more: one enters and ascends to the balconies through tight, awkward vestibules and stairways. The only aesthetic experience is to be found in contemplating the all-encompassing vault system of the major space. What is unique about Viollet-le-Duc's project, in comparison with those of Davioud and Labrouste, is the consistently three-dimensional geometry of the structure. The vault that determines the plan describes, in fact, half of a regular polyhedron, the iron ribs defining the edges of the solid and the masonry forming the sides. Viollet-le-Duc emphasized this fact, reproducing the geometric solid opposite the plan and section of the building, just as he related all of the structural configurations of the twelfth *Entretien* to geometric figures. This polyhedral vault physically contains most of the building, and what it does not so contain—the modular dimensions and hexagonal shapes of the secondary spaces—is directly derived from its geometry.

Viollet-le-Duc compared the polyhedral form of his "salle voûtée" to a natural crystal, noting: "Most of the polyhedrons produced by crystallization offer arrangements of planes that favor the use of great sections of metalwork to cover extensive areas, as well as shapes of a very satisfying appearance. When it comes to using new materials, one must miss no opportunity and look everywhere for instruction, particularly among the natural principles of creation, from which, if we too are to create, we could never derive too much inspiration."[75]

Viollet-le-Duc explained what he meant by this in the article "Style" in the eighth volume of his *Dictionnaire raisonné*, published in 1866. He repeated his basic definition in italics several times in the course of the essay: *"Le style est la manifestation d'un idéal établi sur un principe"* (Style is the manifestation of an ideal founded on a principle). To demonstrate what he meant by a *principe*, he presented a discussion of geodesy, the geometric configuration of the structure of the terrestrial globe. "Please forgive this digression, which indeed is only apparent, for what we are about to say is tightly linked to our art, and especially our art during the medieval period."[76] He ended his summary of geodesy with the remark, "Here is the example that is given us, and that we must follow when, with the aid of our intelligence, we pretend to create." He wrote this in 1864, during a period in which he devoted his summers to a lengthy geological study of Mont Blanc (he published his findings twelve years later as a book, *Le Massif de Mont Blanc*). He explained why he, an architect, undertook this enterprise:

> In fact, our globe is nothing other than a great building, all the parts of which have a reason for being; its surface takes on the forms commanded by imperious laws and followed according to a logical order.
>
> To subject a group of mountains to intensive analysis, to study how they were

formed and what brings about their erosion, to recognize the prevailing factors in their elevation, the conditions of resistance and endurance in the face of atmospheric forces, to compile a chronological record of their past, all of this is, in effect, to undertake on a grand scale a methodical labor of analysis, analogous to that undertaken by the practicing architect or archaeologist who establishes his calculations according to the study of monuments.[77]

This "sublime" image is superficially reminiscent of the theory shared by Boullée and A.-L.-T. Vaudoyer that architecture had a model for imitation in nature. But there is a vast difference: Viollet-le-Duc materialized and mechanized what to Boullée and Vaudoyer had been the mysterious emanation of God. The concepts of *invention* and *imitation* were transformed. Invention has become reason; imitation is seen in terms of process rather than form. On inspiration Viollet-le-Duc had written in 1866:

What we call the imagination is only one side of our mind. It is the part of the mind that is still active while the body sleeps, and makes us witness in dreams to scenes so bizarre a procession of impossible facts that bear no connections one with the other. This part of ourselves does not sleep in its turn while we are awake, but it is ruled by what we call reason. We are not the masters of our imagination, as it is forever distracting us, turning us away from present occupations, and as it seems to escape and wander freely about while we sleep. But we are the masters of our reason; reason belongs to us, we nourish it, we cultivate it, . . . we succeed in making an attentive guardian of it, one who tunes the machine and bestows the conditions of life and duration to its output.[78]

And Viollet-le-Duc's analogy of architecture and geology made one specific point: that his was, in a sense, a Copernican point of view. In the period from

219

Charles Garnier. Temple of Jupiter, Aegina. Restoration. 1852. Fourth-year *envoi*. Section.

The establishment of the Ecole Française at Athens in 1846 immediately produced a series of studies of the great Greek monuments. Garnier's seems extraordinary for its insistent polychromy, but it differs from the *envois* produced around 1830 in its lack of structural detail studies and of ex-votos and other attachments. This was drawn at a time when the refinements of the Greek temples were being documented and published, especially by C. R. Cockerell and F. C. Penrose.

Boullée to Vaudoyer, a building had been conceived in terms of its *marche*—like the medieval universe, from the standpoint of the human occupant. In Viollet-le-Duc's epoch, it was conceived abstractly, from everywhere and nowhere all at once—like the earth itself in Copernican astronomy, as an abstract diagram of natural forces. Davioud's *Bourse*, Labrouste's Bibliothèque Sainte-Geneviève, and Viollet-le-Duc's "salle voûtée" all assumed a sense of abstraction and extrahuman perspective in order to be comprehensible. The beauty of these designs is comparable to that of the most typical creations of nineteenth-century logic, Cuvier's skeletal reconstructions, for example.

* * *

Ironically, the radical ideas that ultimately produced the Bibliothèque Sainte-Geneviève and its parallels evolved under Academy patronage in Rome around 1830. There the six leaders of the movement (the consecutive Grand Prix winners Blouet, Gilbert, Duban, Labrouste, Duc, and Vaudoyer) recruited the laureates of the four following years, Théodore Labrouste (Henri's older brother), Marie-Antoine Delannoy, S.-C. Constant-Dufeux, and Pierre-Joseph Garrez.

The regulations of the French Academy in Rome specified that the architecture students send back to Paris analytical studies of ancient architecture during their first three years, a complete reconstruction of a significant monument in the fourth, and an original composition on a program of their own conception in the fifth.[79] The trouble between the *pensionnaires* and the Academy in Paris began with the fourth-year *envois*, which began to show a conception of ancient architecture quite contrary to that taught by the academicians. It started quietly enough with Blouet's painstaking study of 1825 of the Baths of Caracalla, carried out during actual excavations, which so impressed the Academy that they had it published.[80] Gilbert's fourth-year project, a reconstruction of the Temple of Jupiter at Ostia of 1826, puzzled the Academy because he seemed to be able to reconstruct so much from such very meager remains.[81] But it was Labrouste's restoration of the three Greek temples at Paestum of 1828–29 (pp. 357*ff.*) that caused the break: Quatremère criticized Labrouste severely, refused to read his defense, and after heated arguments the director of the Academy in Rome, Horace Vernet, tendered his resignation in protest.[82] The issue was again *imitation* and the modes.

Looking at these three Doric Greek temples—examples of what Quatremère was in those very years presenting as the imitation of a mythical wooden prototype—Labrouste reconstructed them simply as practical, rational stone structures. One of the three, he even proposed, was not a temple at all, but a "portique," a stoa for public meetings.[83] His sheets are studies of

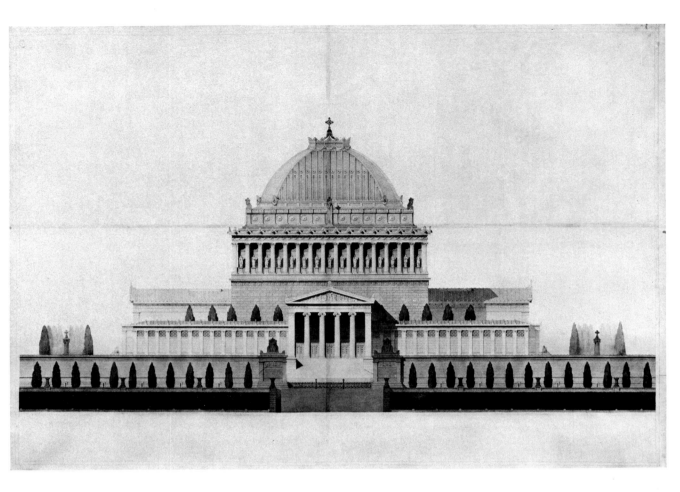

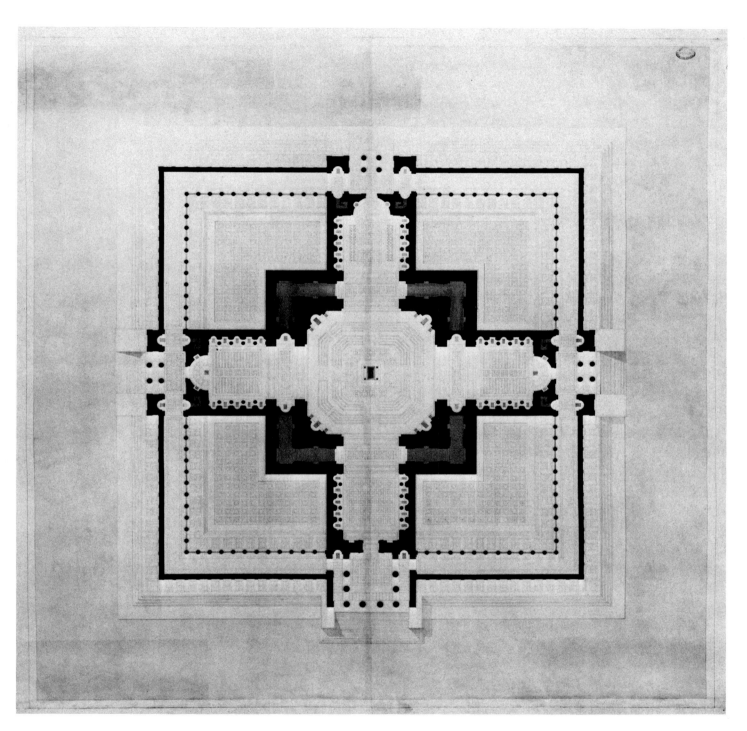

Emile Vaudremer. *Un Edifice consacré à la sépulture des Souverains d'un grand Empire* (A Building Consecrated to the Burial of the Rulers of a Great Empire). 1854. Second Premier. Plan, elevation, and section.

Vaudremer's project was voted the 1er Grand Prix by the Section d'Architecture of the Academy, but the decision was over-turned when the Academy voted as a whole. The strange royal herms around the dome and the low-relief floral decoration mark this as one of several *Néo-Grec* projects completed by the *logistes* of that year, most of which were modeled on the Mausoleum of Halicarnassus.

The plan, which was considered "well-dis-posed" by the jury, shows the main floor of the building. The section shows the principal space, which was to be used for funeral and memorial services. The central funerary monument recalls some of the projects of 1841 for Napoleon's tomb. The walls are decorated with rich but somber colors. Sketched in below are the actual tombs.

structural details rather than of molding profiles and parallels of the three Doric Orders. Instead of accepting the Academy's view that meaning was expressed through the constituent structural members of the temples themselves, Labrouste reconstructed an ephemeral decorative coating, applied in paint and in objects attached to the structural skeleton and now irrevocably lost.[84] The cautious reconstruction of painted graffiti and attached shields, which Labrouste restricted to the "portique" of his 1828–29 envoi, by 1831 in his brother Théodore's reconstruction of the Republican Roman temples at Cora had become murals and awnings and heaps of votive objects, totally disrupting and concealing the forms of the building (p. 165). In 1832 Delannoy sent his restoration of the Tiber Island (p. 170), extending this treatment to an entire quarter of ancient Rome. In 1833 Garrez's third-year envoi, a reconstruction of four early Roman temples, inspired the Academy to pronounce at the annual public prize ceremonies, "These temples are disfigured by the colors so bizarrely applied that one is prevented from judging their proportions."[85]

Along with these archaeological studies were sent the fifth-year envois, which were proposals for contemporary buildings and consequently no less threatening to the Parisian academic doctrine. In 1829 Duban sent with Labrouste's Paestum drawings a design for a Protestant church, not only twitting the clericalism of the Restoration monarchy, but also basing himself on studies made in Germany and Switzerland, whose architectural monuments were considered neither classical nor Classical.[86] In 1830 Labrouste's project for a Bridge to Unite France and Italy (p. 396) arrived with its meager proportions, stark surfaces, and anecdotal ornamentation. In 1830 Duc's envoi of a monument to the revolutionaries killed in February of that year compelled the Academy to remark in the annual public meeting, "The Academy regrets not being able to accord the same praise [as that granted to Vaudoyer's fourth-year reconstruction] to the project sent by M. Duc for his work of the fifth year."[87] Their grumbling continued in the reviews of Vaudoyer's belfry of 1831—"One wishes that this pensionnaire ... had chosen a project in which he could apply the grand and beautiful studies that he has made in Italy"—of Théodore Labrouste's Baptistery of 1832 (p. 176), and of Delannoy's Triumphal Monument Commemorating the Conquest of Algeria of 1833—"The Academy thinks that this pensionnaire has not sufficiently comprehended the character of the monument."[88] In 1834, with the arrival of Constant-Dufeux's Chamber of Deputies (p. 179), the Academy's public criticism grew sharper:

> We regret that, for his fifth year, M. Dufeux has come up with nothing but a project for a Chamber of Deputies to which he has failed to give any of the features characteristic of such a building. Undoubtedly there are ingenious combinations in the working together of varied parts, but what strikes one at

first glance is an outward appearance that proclaims anything but a Chamber of Deputies. Certain parts resemble fortress walls, others greenhouses, orangeries, pleasure pavilions. It makes, all the same, some very pretty watercolors.[89]

In 1835 came Garrez's project for a grain storehouse (unpublished and now lost): "The plan of this project shows a good arrangement, but this alone cannot excuse the bizarreness of the elevations and sections!"[90] The *Journal des Artistes* commented, "One can hardly conceive a project so little in harmony with common sense."[91] But the Romantic critic Théophile Thoré singled it out for praise: "He has made a real warehouse, vast and well formed [*bien coupée*]. As to style, it is a mélange of the round arch and the segmental, responding to the requirements of the situation. Upon his return from Rome M. Garrez will no doubt join with the young artists who are working to introduce into architecture a modern form and to harmonize it with our customs."[92]

* * *

A major source for understanding what was going on in this circle during the 1830s are the numerous Romantic periodicals published in that decade by various groups.[93] They precede the founding of the first exclusively architectural periodical in France, the *Revue Générale de l'Architecture*, in 1840, and present theories of building from several different points of view. Among certain of the Saint-Simonian enterprises, there emerged a consistent and realistic doctrine from the pen of Léon Vaudoyer, working in concert with his friends the architect and *polytechnicien* Léonce Reynaud and the critics Hippolyte Fortoul and Thoré.[94]

The eighteenth-century doctrine of Laugier and Quatremère had been formulated in terms of Greco-Roman architecture, on the assumption that this architecture manifested a universal, eternal ideal. The doctrine of Vaudoyer and his collaborators during the 1830s, on the contrary, embraced the whole history of architecture, on the assumption that history is evolutionary and that each age has a separate, distinct ideal. In architecture, the basis of theorizing was not a temporally static interpretation of the system of the Greek temple, but was instead a historical interpretation of transitions—of syntheses—meant to define the mechanism of evolution in building. The specific transitions identified as significant were those from Greco-Roman to Byzantine (from pagan to Christian) and from Gothic to Renaissance (from spiritual to rational). The roots of the Western tradition were seen as lying in the architecture of Egypt, Greece, and Rome, but these architectures were seen to have been rendered historical documents by successive syntheses, first with those of Christianity, then of Renaissance humanism. The whole doctrine sought to explain, not the distant ideal of an almost mythical architecture of the childhood of man, but the real buildings that surrounded Frenchmen in the decade of the 1830s.

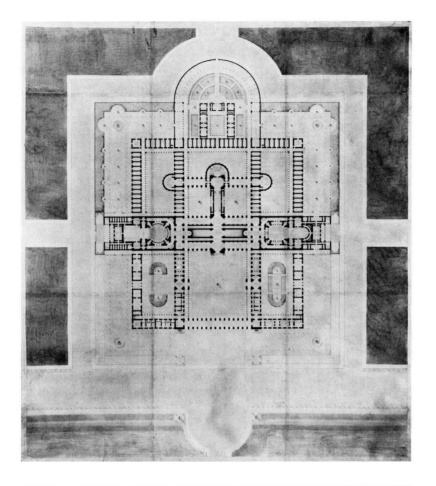

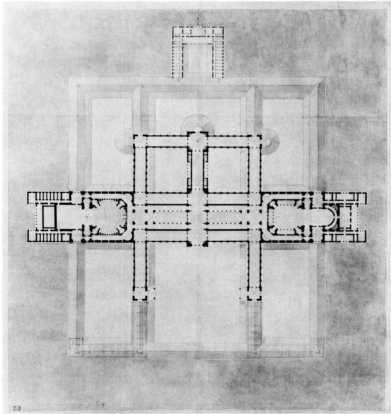

Honoré Daumet. *Un Conservatoire de musique et de déclamation* (A Conservatory of Music and Oratory). 1855. 1er Grand Prix. Plans of first and second stories, elevation, and section.

Daumet's plan, one of the greatest among mid-century Grands Prix, is composed on the traditional cross-axes in square *parti*, but it is enriched by stretching out one axis for two large theaters, and by inserting a subsidiary cross-axis for three smaller auditoria. The second-story plan changes emphasis to the secondary axes. A comparison with Charles Garnier's Grand Prix of 1848 (p. 199) shows how lively and complex is Daumet's conception. Daumet later restored and expanded the Château of Chantilly (pp. 444–47), where he manipulated existing fragments into an elegant plan.

Daumet's elevation is the first to be articulated by varying the forms of the pavilions and the surfaces of the wings, and by creating such a pronounced tiered effect of open and closed surfaces at different depths. It also exhibits a few subtle asymmetries which reflect interior arrangements. The overall effect is one of well-controlled variety in a unified mass. The section shows the full longitudinal extent of the building and emphasizes the circulation areas.

Léonce Reynaud, writing in 1835, defined the successive historical systems of architecture according to their characteristic structural organisms.[95] Egyptian and Greek systems of trabeated architecture were elaborations of the post and lintel form, Egyptian building reflecting the heavier proportions of stone, Greek building the lighter proportions of wooden constructions. The first crisis in the evolution of Western architecture that Reynaud perceived occurred when the arch and vault were introduced into Roman architecture, but were left unexpressed under a clothing of Greek trabeated forms. The resolution of that contradiction came with Christianity, in the Constantinian basilicas and the Byzantine churches: the pier supporting the arch became a column, and the entablature and other trappings of the Order were replaced by the moldings of the semicircular arches of the arcade, repeated in the forms of the vaults and cupolas, which were articulated as forms in their own right. "A new art and a new religion appeared; the Christian religion needed buildings. Since no tradition imposed predetermined forms on that religion, it availed itself of those indicated by the most advanced science. The Christians thus almost always employed arcades on columns."[96] Léon Vaudoyer, in 1842, phased this as the *affranchissement de l'arcade* (the emancipation of the arcade):

> In using the ancient basilica as the model for their first temples, the Christians did not copy the treatment of the Orders [*ordonnance*]. . . . They customarily used columns as the support and springing of the arcades, which they substituted for the monolithic lintels of pagan antiquity. At first these columns were those that the antique monuments provided, and that were designed to bear the architraves; . . . but soon they felt the need to modify the proportions and to substitute a new form of capital, better adapted to their new function. Then later the system of arcade construction, which had been applied in principle only to join isolated points of support, was generalized and gave birth to a general system of vaulting. So it is that Byzantine art was engendered while Italy was still holding faithfully to its first Latin basilicas, the layout of which she was later to transmit to the West.[97]

This idea implied that, in fact, Gothic was not a distinct style, but the extreme manifestation of the "emancipation of the arcade" in Early Christian architecture, an implication insisted upon by Reynaud, Vaudoyer, and Fortoul.[98]

The second crisis came at the end of the Gothic period, when, with the weakening of the intellectual hegemony of the Church, European architects became fascinated with the simplicity, the regulated system, and the broad, clearly defined spaces of Roman building. According to Reynaud,

> Had architecture only to satisfy the prescriptions of science and material needs, it would be hard to imagine that modern societies would have been able to forego a system of construction as perfected as that of the Middle Ages in favor of a return to an earlier and consequently less perfect system. But in the brief

Eugène-Emmanuel Viollet-le-Duc. "Salle voûtée" (Vaulted Hall). 1864. From *Entretiens sur l'architecture*, vol. II. chap. 12, figs. 16–18. Polyhedron, section, plan, and perspective.

The "salle voûtée" exemplifies Viollet-le-Duc's speculations on the role of crystalline structure and the nature of materials in architectural design. Although the structure is scrupulously worked out, the space is difficult of access and lacking in hierarchical order, and is thus the antithesis of the concepts of spatial progression taught at the Ecole.

The plan and section show the polyhedral form on which the "salle voûtée" is based; they also emphasize the preeminence of structure over circulation in this project. It is this order of considerations that so strikingly separates Viollet-le-Duc's project for the Paris Opéra (pp. 282–85) from that of Charles Garnier, with its central staircase motif (pp. 263 ff.).

summary we have just given, we have been looking at architecture from only one side and we must not forget that it is also an art. It is as art that it exercises its greatest influence and, in this respect, it depends entirely upon the tastes and passions of different peoples. Each architectural system, it is true, corresponds largely to a certain set of ideas and is highly qualified to produce certain impressions; [a system] must be abandoned when these ideas have changed and these impressions are no longer relevant. When, therefore, at the end of the Middle Ages, the Christian religion began to lose the authority it had till then exercised, the architecture it had developed and affirmed was rejected. Society, feeling at the time the need to relink the entire chain of its tradition, which for so long its religious concerns had put out of mind, was carried by a great current back toward Greek and Roman antiquity. . . . Since, too, all the arts were developing rapidly and numerous buildings were being erected everywhere, only a very short lapse of time was necessary for the establishment of a distinctive system of architecture—the architecture of the Renaissance. Its methods of construction, less sophisticated and less bold than in the system that had just been laid aside, were nonetheless simpler and more elegant. The buildings had still something Gothic in them; they had the same layout and the same general proportions. All the needs that had called them into being were openly expressed; all the proprieties duly observed. These were still Gothic buildings, but with purer and more graceful forms, overlaid as it were by an alien veil, a veil rich and diaphanous, which decorated without concealing. There was a delightful blending of art and naiveté in all this architecture, an exquisite taste and a great refinement. There was even originality, the borrowing from antiquity notwithstanding; for, if some details had been imitated, they had been brought together in a new way; there had been nothing servile in the copying, and especial care was taken not to alter in any way the general forms called for by the customs of the time.[99]

The break between the Middle Ages and the Renaissance, however, was placed not at the start of Brunelleschi's career, but at the beginning of the fourteenth century, Vaudoyer identifying the critical moment as that of the planning of Florence Cathedral:

In the layout of its nave, the Cathedral of Florence derives essentially from the vast Roman constructions such as the Thermae and the Basilica of Constantine. It possesses their grandeur, nobleness, and simplicity. From its main dome, flanked by secondary cupolas, one may assume that it was conceived on the model of the churches of the East. It consistently preserves nothing from the churches of the West, not even the bell tower. The one raised later on the side of this vast church was the work of Giotto, who had brought about the same change in painting that Arnolfo had in architecture.[100]

The implication of this architectural Pre-Raphaelitism[101] is that the High Renaissance with its rules was the beginning of a decline rather than a point of perfection. Vaudoyer said as much of Florence Cathedral;[102] earlier, Reynaud had written:

> The principle of imitation, however, had been laid down and was followed to its ultimate conclusion. After having borrowed some motifs from the monuments of antiquity, they tried to imitate the structural uses and effects of these details, and came in the end to look upon the ancient monuments as absolute types of beauty [*types absolus de beauté*]. . . . They made conventions yield to form, and they modified the form taken as model so as not to stray too far from the conventions. Architecture became something mysterious and fated; it had immutable rules and precepts and it firmly imposed them. This explains the introduction into our midst of the open porticoes, terraces, and small windows to replace the covered porches, high roofs, and big openings of the Middle Ages. While these new arrangements were appropriate to neither our customs nor our climate, they did approximate the buildings of Greece and Rome. The result has been in recent years to see our churches, stock exchanges, theaters, tollgates, even guardhouses take on the form and attire of antique temples.[103]

Here we arrive back at the theory of *imitation*, this time refuted as a misunderstanding of the nature of architecture, whose forms are pictured as determined by structure, plan, and climate, first and foremost, and as such changing from society to society, from region to region, successively evolving new ideals.[104] Thus modern architecture, like that of the Romans at the time of Constantine, must emerge from its shell of borrowed conventions and create a distinctive system. Fortoul, the non-architect of the group, was bold enough to try to state in words what that new system should be: one based on the round arch, but with a system of coordinated relationships like that of the systems of proportions of the Greek Orders. The key, to him, was "to discover within curvilinear [round-arched] architecture itself a canon [*régulateur*], which could render the angles of the arcs sensible to the eye, and permit them to coordinate the entire form of the building."[105] More enlightening than Fortoul's vague words, however, is the building Vaudoyer designed during the decade 1845–55 to embody his solution: Marseilles Cathedral (p. 425).[106]

Examining this building makes evident what Reynaud, Vaudoyer, and Fortoul meant by relinking the entire chain of tradition and by responding to the demands of structure, custom, and climate. It is clearly an arched, rather than a trabeated, organism. The forms were borrowed from Roman, Byzantine, and Romanesque architecture: the three vaulted spaces of the nave and the triumphal arch of the facade came from the first source, the domes from the second, and the apsidal chapels and facade towers from the third. This was not, however, a static mélange of borrowings, either historically or formally. It was not Vaudoyer who combined the Roman thermal hall with the three arms of an Eastern centralized church, it was Arnolfo di Cambio in Florence Cathedral. Vaudoyer borrowed not from Rome and the Middle Ages, but from what he considered to be the first building of the Renaissance. Thus, instead of seeing the individual forms Vaudoyer used, we should perceive the conceptual manner in which he put them together. Indeed, Vaudoyer did not precisely follow Arnolfo, for he stated the three-quarter centralized configuration only in his domes, permitting his plan to take on a complex form, which its radiating apses, western towers, and its prominent chapel to the Virgin—the cult of whom achieved great importance in the nineteenth century—identify as French and modern. The building summarized the history of architecture in the sense that its abstract configuration showed clearly the historical evolution through which its type coalesced: first the separately conceived Roman, Byzantine, and Romanesque forms, then the combination of these forms in the Renaissance, and finally their adaptation in France in the nineteenth century.

These plan forms, however, are not abstract geometric volumes of space, they are the insides of a series of structural organisms whose piers and vaults have been carefully made evident both inside and out. Each major surface is divided into a central plane, set within the thicker piers and arches that form its skeletal framework at its edges—even the arcades between the piers on the interior reappear as blind arcading along the exterior of the nave. The surfaces are the X ray of the structural organism, but also have a presence of their own asserted by the green and white horizontal striping of the masonry, its colorfulness and materials suggestive of the weather and quarries of Marseilles. This polychrome surface is the "veil, rich and diaphanous, which decorated without concealing" that Reynaud had perceived in Renaissance architecture in his essay of 1835.

Marseilles Cathedral was Vaudoyer's solution to the problem formulated by the Romantics in the 1830s. It is frankly "eclectic," a term applied to their own work by Vaudoyer and Reynaud, who accepted the Saint-Simonian belief in the historical alternation of "organic" and "critical" ages. (Their own epoch, they believed, was a "critical" one.)[107] It is different from Labrouste's earlier Bibliothèque Sainte-Geneviève (p. 335), which is without overt references to historical sources, composite form, and plasticity in articulation. Yet Labrouste's unitary form also embraces the history of the library, from the "portique" at Paestum with the history of the city written on its walls to the Vatican Library with its stone vaults and central spine of piers. Labrouste for his abstract and cryptic details drew upon the whole history of ornament and symbols. The Bibliothèque Sainte-Geneviève is the abstraction of what Marseilles Cathedral literally embodies.

Between these two poles are a great many other solutions. Davioud in his little *projet rendu* (p. 187) accepted Vaudoyer's overt eclecticism, but played down his plasticity and rejected his compressing of form to create composite configurations. Louis Duc, Vaudoyer's contemporary as *pensionnaire* in

Rome, erected his mighty Rue de Harlay wing of the Palais de Justice (1852–69, p. 428) with all Vaudoyer's plasticity and more, combining slightly Gothic vaults with slightly Greek columns, but retaining a unitary, repetitive form.[108] Viollet-le-Duc accepted the structural doctrine, expressed plastically, but believed that one should adhere to a single style rather than to a modern mélange. Constant-Dufeux and César Daly (editor of the *Revue*) seem to have codified Labrouste's hermetic ideas and made them even more obscure.

* * *

Our problem, the modern historian sometimes thinks, is to discover the mainstream of the evolution of French architecture from Percier to Garnier. It is evident both in the eclectic vocabulary of Garnier's architecture and in his rejection of *imitation* (he never mentioned it) that something momentous did happen in the intervening years. We might phrase our question thus: Was the basic cause Labrouste? Viollet-le-Duc? Duban, Duc, and Vaudoyer? But in fact we are talking about a revolution in thinking in which the only stable element was the momentous event that caused this diversity of new ideas to arise in reaction. That momentous event in architecture during the 1830s seems to have been the simultaneous discovery that architecture in itself was a physical, structural entity, not inhabited by any physical ideal; and that it had no eternal form, but evolved in form with the passage of time and from place to place. This, of course, was the Romantic realization, and architecture's crisis during the 1830s paralleled that of literature and painting.

In the practical terms of composition—of planning and massing—the arrival of Romanticism at the Ecole des Beaux-Arts meant a change of emphasis in the student projects, from the space enclosed to the structural organism enclosing it, from the achievement of a gracious *marche* to the assemblage of clearly separate parts. The plan of such a Romantic student project was merely the section of its structural organism taken horizontally at floor level, just as the section of Labrouste's "portique" at Paestum was a slice taken down its axis without taking into account the columns as they then appeared (p. 362). What really went on was in the three-dimensional organism of that structure, which could only be represented as a crystal diagram or in perspective.[109] The ultimate solution was found by the engineer Auguste Choisy, professor at the Ecole des Ponts et Chaussées, in the uptilted isometric sections with which he illustrated his *Histoire de l'architecture* of 1899 (p. 18). Whether the structural skeleton should be articulated in the traditional system of moldings and plasticity, or in a new abstract system meant to make evident the inert material being articulated; whether to communicate ideas with a vocabulary of traditional motifs of historical architecture, or to invent a system of signs both more precise and more cryptic—these were questions the Romantic architects debated among themselves.

The Era of Charles Garnier

But what will be the dimensions of this foyer?
To answer this question, one has to study
the way people promenade.
Charles Garnier, *Le Théâtre*, 1871

The *concours d'émulation* projects seem practical and relevant, whereas the Grand Prix projects seem impossible and megalomaniac. This, however, is an important oversimplification: for beginning with Haussmann and culminating with turn-of-the-century Imperialism, the scale of society's building enterprises caught up with that of the Academy's programs. Among the most famous Grand Prix winners of the last four decades of the nineteenth century, many—including Emile Bénard, Paul Nénot, Victor Laloux, Charles-Louis Girault, and Tony Garnier—actually designed ensembles that were as grandiose as their prize projects—the University of California campus in Berkeley, the League of Nations headquarters in Geneva, the Gare du Quai d'Orsay (p. 460) and the Petit Palais (p. 456) in Paris, and various public works in Lyons. The Academy was teaching urbanism without really knowing it, at a time when it had come to be the principal challenge facing architecture. And in this respect the Grand Prix, rather than the *concours d'émulation*, achieved primary importance among the student exercises.

* * *

Jean-Louis Pascal's winning Grand Prix project of 1866 is clearly an extraordinary work, and it was one of the best known and most controversial of the century (p. 236).[110] Its designer became an eminent architect of the Third Republic and the *patron* of one of the principal ateliers of the period. His design embodied a new sort of academicism, yet it came at a moment of often violent upheaval. The program with which Pascal had to work reflected the last effort of Viollet-le-Duc and his friends to change the Ecole.

The building specified by the program was *Un Hôtel à Paris pour riche banquier* (A Town House in Paris for a Rich Banker). This building was to include the dwelling of the banker, his bank, two dwellings for his two sons (with the suggestion that one was married and the other a bachelor) and extensive stables and kitchens. The site was not only described, it was described at great length.[111] It was in a new, wealthy quarter of Paris, along one of the new boulevards with which Haussmann was just then reorganizing the city. The back of the site gave onto a park into which the banker had the right of access and into which his house could look. Two party walls 88 feet in length delimited the street facades at each end. (The shape of the site was so complex and irregular that, for the first time in the history of the Grand Prix competition, a small site plan had to be provided to the *logistes.*)

Two of the plot's six sides are unimportant—those partly masked by the party walls. The sides giving on the park and onto the small square formed by the crossing of the two streets in front are of primary importance, the sides along the two streets of secondary importance. Here the clarity of the problem ends. Each of the two primary and the two secondary facades differs, and the relative importance of one to another is ambiguous. The facade on the square is the obvious place for the principal feature of the composition, yet its actual width is only 59 feet. It is only on the rear facade, facing the park, that the building can really unfold itself, but this facade should be subordinate to the street front. Similarly, one of the facades on the streets is 558 feet long and faces a boulevard 131 feet in width, while the other facade fronts on a thoroughfare only 82 feet wide yet is 728 feet in length.

The same studied—indeed, bedeviling—complexity and ambiguity appear in the enumeration of the spaces to be provided. These might be divided into three pairs of descending hierarchical importance: the banker's dwelling and his bank, the sons' two dwellings, the kitchens, and the stables. The problem becomes one of arranging these pairs within themselves. Should the central feature be the banker's house, or his bank? The sons' houses should somehow flank the central feature, but should they be asymmetrical, one house for the family, the other for the bachelor?

All of which makes this a revolutionary program, and not simply because it was for an everyday problem. (One critic compared it to giving as the program for the Grand Prix in painting or sculpture, "the family of a financier taking chocolate" or "the same financier wishing his wife a Happy New Year."[112] Anatole de Baudot, student of both Labrouste and Viollet-le-Duc, commented differently on the program: "By its very nature, by the intelligent way it has been presented, it invites the competitors to put aside the routine of the vague and the impossible and to take up once and for all the way of reality.")[113] By forcing the *logistes* to choose between making the principal feature the bank or the banker, between facing the building inward or outward, and by imposing an inalterably asymmetrical site, the program sought to make them profoundly rethink the program and to basically alter the rules of composition. Jean-Louis Batigny and Edouard-Charles Weyland placed the bank in the center of their compositions, facing on the square; all the other *logistes* placed the banker there.[114] Batigny placed both of the sons' dwellings on the longer side of the plot; Weyland placed all three dwellings on the garden front; the rest placed the sons' houses on either side of the banker's; and so on.

It was rare for the competition to elicit such a variety of basic solutions. It evidently was meant to answer the primary criticism made of the Grand Prix competition since the turn of the nineteenth century: that it tested the student's technical knowledge of composition, not his fundamental intelligence, which could only be demonstrated by reformulating the program.[115] Percier, Viollet-le-Duc, and Guadet emphasized the primary importance of the program.[116] The competitors had always had to choose what to emphasize and what to make subordinate, but never before 1866 had such a philosophical decision been required as choosing between the man and the institution, the banker and the bank. And there were no helpful precedents among previous Grand Prix projects.

The elevation of Emile Bénard's project (p. 239) is distinctive for the simple reason that the elevation he chose to render is that of the street facade, thus more closed and severe than Pascal's elevation (p. 237), which represents the garden facade.[117] The challenge in the competition was to generate from the program a configuration expressive of the function of the building, but the opportunities for a display of richness and imagination lay only around the back. That is, Pascal adopted a trick (the program specified that an elevation be submitted, but not of which side), as did seven other of the ten competitors. Bénard and Batigny alone really faced the problem. Bénard was credited in general with fulfilling the program most scrupulously. But he received the *deuxième accessit*; the Premier Grand Prix de Rome went to Pascal.[118] Jules Bouchet explained in his review of the designs:

> Among the ten competitors, M. Bénard is certainly the one who has most scrupulously studied, understood, and rendered the distinguishing conditions set by the title: "A Town House in Paris for a Rich Banker." The fine studies of M. Bénard do have every feature appropriate to the bourgeois opulence that must needs deny itself the elegant and noble sumptuousness of royal residences.
>
> But we must hasten to add before going further, this apparent and entirely relative superiority of M. Bénard is in reality only a rather deceptive mirage owing to the somewhat limited nature of a program that is more sympathetic to M. Bénard's youthful talent than to the mature, fuller, and greater learning of M. Pascal. To judge otherwise than has been done would have been quite regrettable, but nevertheless we note that respect of, and conformity to, the program have not been uppermost in the minds of the judges.[119]

The issue, then, in the judgment of the Grand Prix designs in 1866 seems to have been what Bouchet called "great and exceptional monumental arrangements." And, as becomes evident when one compares Bénard's submission with those of Pascal and others, what Bouchet meant was a positive quality: Bénard's design is not radical, merely pedestrian. Alfred Normand called it *étudié maigrement.*[120]

The other submissions were complex and picturesque in a way that was new to the realm of the Grand Prix competition. Almost all the competitors, having chosen to represent the garden rather than the street facade, introduced round and octagonal pavilions with elaborate roof structures, placed amid complicated patterns of advancing and receding building planes, some at the 120° angle imposed by the site. The problem was to make a convincing whole from these elements. Pascal used only two pavilions, but raised them up to give their open silhouettes full play, broadening them at their bases to harmonize with the broad planes of the three principal building masses that embrace them. De Baudot called these effective but unfamiliar forms "pagodas." By making them belvederes rather than forms derived from the Louvre with the accompanying royal connotations, Pascal gave his design an appropriate bourgeois, domestic appearance, as he did in the treatment of the main blocks. Yet the dimensions of the individual parts of Pascal's scheme are larger than those of the other submissions, scaling the parts to the whole. Pascal's five-part composition has a unity and decisiveness that, for instance, Weyland's nine-part configuration lacks.

Pascal's plan, moreover, is brilliant—and not just as ink washes on paper (p. 236).[121] In order for it to work, Pascal had to simplify the complex and perverse program. He accomplished this by making the *hôtels* of the two sons almost identical and by suppressing nearly completely the bank (it is, in fact, the semicircular court on the right of the *cour d'honneur*, echoing the stables similarly located to the left of the court). Just as in his choice of elevations, Pascal here cheated a bit, but produced a magnificent work of his own.

The beauty and novelty of Pascal's plan result from the rhythm of its forms, the use of 60° and 120° angles and curves, seemingly imposed by the site. The square *cour d'honneur* lies just below the center of the sheet. It engenders four semicircles on its four sides: the two broad half-circles of the stables and the bank to the right and left, the entrance exedra fitted into the narrow "prow" of the site below, and the tighter curves of the grand staircase above. It is the traditional *parti* of two interlocking rectangles transformed here into two interlocking ovals, and thereby greatly animated. The semicircle at the top, the grand staircase, permits the axes of the porticoes flanking the *cour d'honneur* to pass on either side—gaining momentum as they penetrate the *corps de logis* through apsidal chambers—and to terminate in a spacious lateral enfilade of salons generating two semicircular *jardins d'hiver* at each end. Parallel to the axis of the salons, the axis of the entrance hall is extended past the curves of the stables and the bank—containing them as the salons do the grand staircase—and terminates in two tight, round chambers. These, in turn, twist the axis and split it, creating two new pairs of axes, set at 120° to each other and to the axis of the entrance hall. One of each pair becomes the axis of the main enfilade of one son's dwelling, the other debouches into the street through an apsidal portico. In fact, this latter system of axes has become separate from, and of a character different from, that of the *cour d'honneur* it embraces. It traces a line of movement that starts at the

236

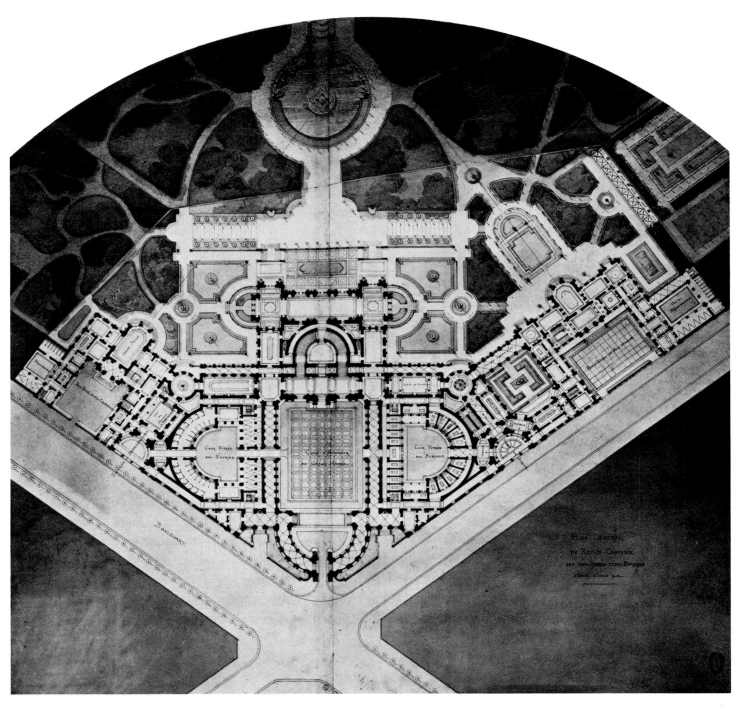

Jean-Louis Pascal. *Un Hôtel à Paris pour riche banquier* (A Town House in Paris for a Rich Banker). 1866. 1ᵉʳ Grand Prix. Plan, elevation, and section.

Only in 1866 was so complicated and irregular a site specified for a Grand Prix competition. Undaunted by this challenge to the principles of symmetrical planning, twenty-three-year-old Pascal oriented his plan toward the garden and suppressed as nearly as possible any unequal distribution of masses implied by the program. His use of angles turning on round hinge points was considered to be particularly ingenious. The main house is at the center, the house for a bachelor son is to the left, and the bank and house for a married son are to the right.

Eight of the ten *logistes* chose to render the garden facade, which Pascal characterized with Second Empire bourgeois lavishness. The two cupolas top the round spaces, which facilitate a smooth change of direction. The richness of color and detailing of the sections resembles that of the drawings for the Paris Opéra (pp. 263 *ff.*). Like several other Grand Prix winners of the 1860s, Pascal worked in Garnier's *agence*.

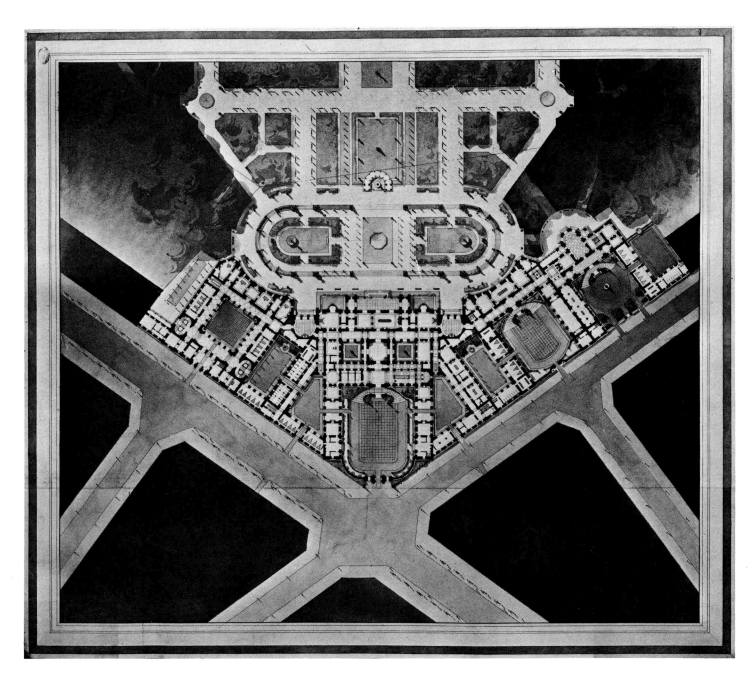

Emile Bénard. *Un Hôtel à Paris pour riche banquier* (A Town House in Paris for a Rich Banker). 1866. *2ᵉ accessit*. Plan, elevation of street facade, section, elevation of garden facade.

Bénard was one of the two *logistes* who fulfilled this difficult program more scrupulously by rendering the street facade and allowing program requirements to be expressed asymmetrically both inside and out. His plan is less ingenious than that of Pascal; his great *jardin d'hiver* at the center of the garden facade is the most distinguished feature of the project.

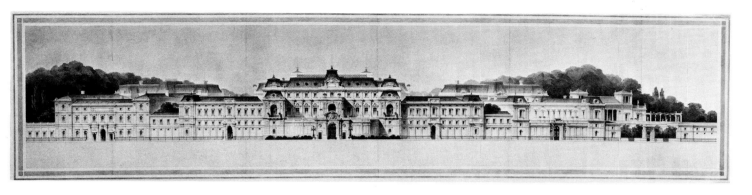

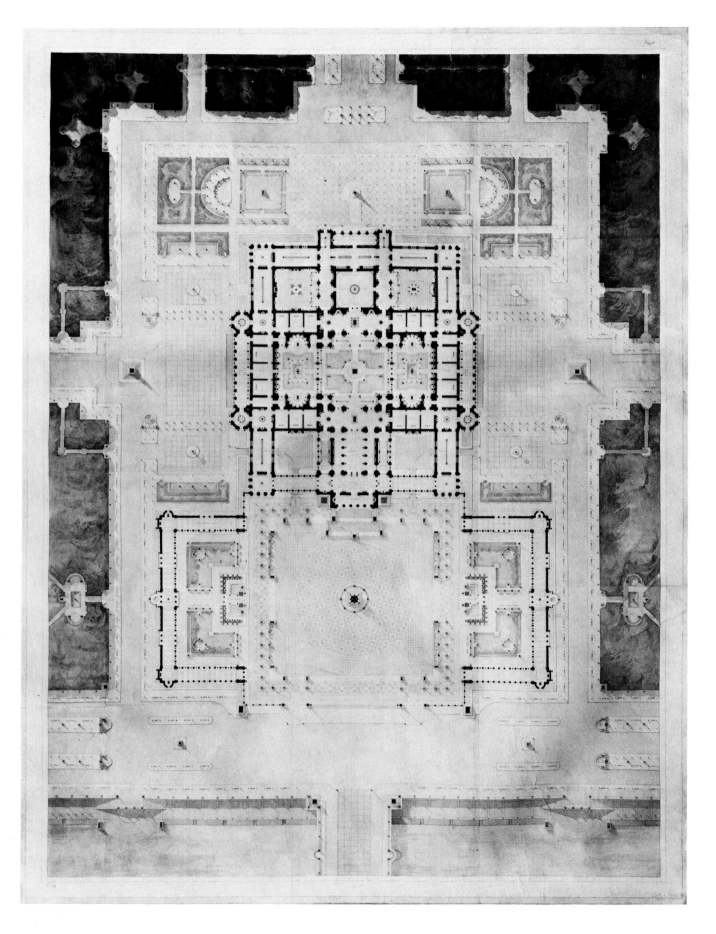

Emile Bénard. *Un Palais pour l'exposition des Beaux-Arts* (A Palace for an Exhibition of Fine Arts). 1867. 1ᵉʳ Grand Prix. Plan, elevation, and section.

This submission was considered far superior to its competitors. The program required rooms of varied shapes for the exhibition of works of art in various mediums. Its plan is a clear and simple arrangement of crossed axes in a rectangle, yet the interior is much enlivened by exedrae and small connecting rooms. Although the elevation employs precise classical details, these are joined in a complex and baroque arrangement that relies on screening colonnades for much of its depth and variety. This facade was copied for museums in Chicago three times between the 1890s and 1930s (p. 474).

The section shows a continuity of indoor and outdoor exhibition space. The interior detailing, with its screens of arcades and colonnades, is quite strange and original among Grand Prix projects, but it probably derives in part from Bénard's work at Garnier's *agence* for the Paris Opéra. The lower story at the rear is a service entrance.

apsidal entrances and fans out through the building at the round rooms. In these two round chambers—the forms carried up into the belvederes essential for the success of the elevations—are the beginnings of Beaux-Arts planning in its late nineteenth-century, urbanistic sense. They are the hinges upon which the three disparate parts of the composition turn and are linked together. They engender a system of enfilades that overlays that of the traditional internal communications of the individual parts and unites them in terms of circulation. This ensemble, like most Grand Prix projects, is not a building but a complex, and Pascal has demonstrated the urbanistic advantages of Beaux-Arts planning that were to make the system of such great importance by the turn of the century.

* * *

The competition of 1866 witnessed the culmination of an effort to change the academic methods of conceptualization by the circle of Duban, Labrouste, and Viollet-le-Duc, working through the competition programs. It also witnessed the defeat of this effort by a new generation of students with a revitalized sense of monumental design. The jury of the Grand Prix competition during the years 1864–71 was carefully divided between the "conservative" and "liberal" factions, yet the more conservative students carried away almost all the prizes because of their talent and weight of numbers.

Abel Blouet had tried to effect such a change through the programs he provided for the *concours d'émulation* while he was professor of theory at the Ecole (1846–53). His friend Henri Labrouste had always emphasized the importance of the program.[122] When César Daly asked Labrouste to review the student work at the Ecole for the *Revue Générale de l'Architecture*, Labrouste concerned himself chiefly with the criticism of the programs.[123] It is thus not surprising that the elections of Blouet, Gilbert, and Duban to the Academy, in 1850, 1853, and 1854, respectively, were immediately followed by changes in the types of programs for the Grand Prix competition.[124]

The system used to select the program during the 1850s and early 1860s was complex. The eight members of the Section d'Architecture met in May of each year, having prepared complete programs, which they laid before the group. Three were chosen from these eight by vote, then one of the three definitively selected by lot. As a result of this system, the same program could be submitted by a member year after year until selected. For example, Jakob-Ignaz Hittorff suggested a *Palais pour le gouverneur de l'Algérie destiné aussi à la demeure temporaire du Souverain* (Palace for the Governor of Algeria Serving Also as the Temporary Residence of the Sovereign) in 1854; 1856; 1858; 1861, when it was one of the three voted for the lottery; and 1862, when it was finally selected as the actual program.[125] Duban suggested a *Palais de l'ambassade française à Constantinople* (Palace for the French Em-

Emmanuel Brune. *L'Escalier principal d'un palais d'un Souverain* (Principal Staircase of the Palace of a Sovereign). 1863. 1ᵉʳ Grand Prix. Elevation and plans *(following pages)*.

The unusual program of this *concours*, which addressed itself to only a fragment of a building, was criticized by the contemporary press, and the winning project was not reproduced in publications of Grand Prix projects at that time. The elevation locates the staircase in a facade of Brune's own invention.

The first-story plan shows, as required by the program, the stairway rising from a vestibule that opens onto a porte cochère, a reception room, and a chapel. The stairway leads to second-story galleries and to two ramps that descend to a garden. The exedra at the turn of the stair was particularly liked by the jury.

Brune. *L'Escalier principal d'un palais d'un Souverain.* First- and second-story plans.

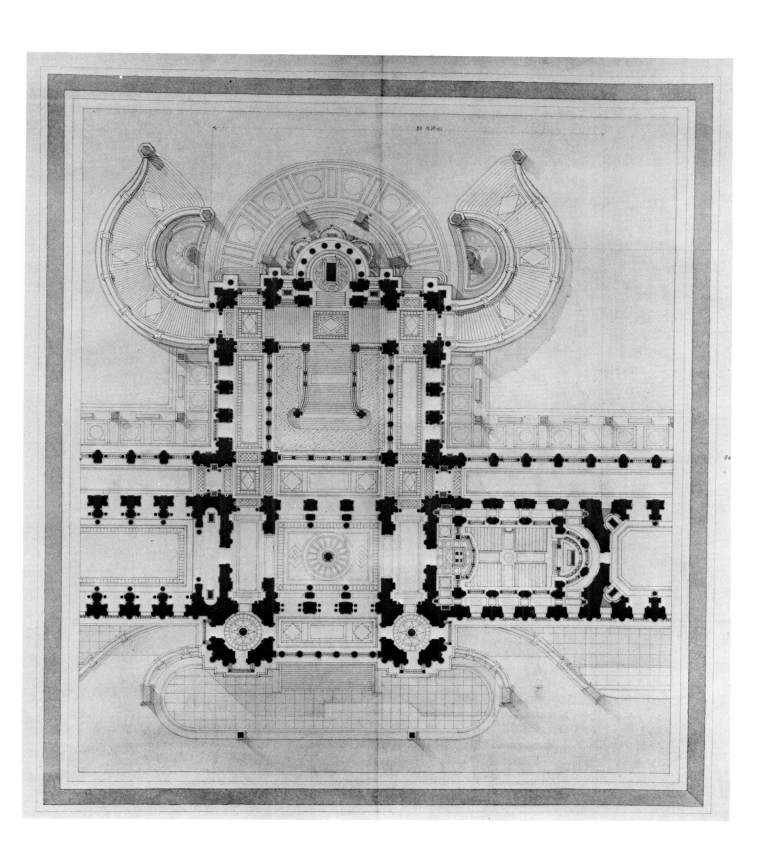

80 Mètres

Brune. *L'Escalier principal d'un palais d'un Souverain*. Section.

The longitudinal section shows to what extent Brune was influenced by early drawings for the Paris Opéra, whose facade and grand staircase are recalled in Brune's detailing. The rich, colorful drawing style associated with Garnier is also new in Grand Prix projects. There is, too, an obvious debt to Lefuel's Nouvel Louvre begun in 1853.

Brune. *L'Escalier principal d'un palais d'un Souverain.* Section and perspective.

The transverse section shows the chapel, which draws on eighteenth-century models for its organization. The perspective, which is unfinished, is the result of an unusual requirement given only in 1863 and 1864; it may have been prompted by the ideas of Viollet-le-Duc, who later in 1863 was made professor of theory at the Ecole.

bassy in Constantinople) in 1854; 1855; and 1856, when it became the definitive program of the competition. Duban was also designer of the program for a *Hôpital Impériale pour invalides de la marine* (Imperial Hospital for Naval Invalids), which was accepted upon first submission in 1858. Gilbert in 1861 and 1862 submitted what sounds like the most radical program, an *Edifice pour l'exposition universelle* (Building for the World's Fair), but it was never voted even one of the three for the lottery.[126]

Compared with the program of 1866, Duban's of 1856, for an *Ambassade française à Constantinople,* a simple ceremonial building on an open site, seems rather conventional. It is interesting, however, to compare it with Hittorff's design for a *Palais pour le gouverneur de l'Algérie.* Hittorff's program specified a truly vast ensemble: there was to be a plaza for military reviews, a triumphal arch, offices for the government bureaucracy, a reception suite for the Emperor, another reception suite for the governor, a chapel, a theater, kitchens, stables, belvederes, gardens, and so on. Duban's program was much shorter, specifying only a reception suite and residence for the ambassador, a chapel and offices for the transaction of embassy business, as well as kitchens and stables. The contrast is even greater between their respective remarks about how the buildings were to be rendered. Hittorff specified:

> The building is to combine an imposing grandeur and high magnificence; the competitors are to apply the principles of the beautiful forms from the ages of Pericles, Augustus, and Leo X. By simple and natural means, in the exterior appearance of the terraces, the vaults and cupolas, the relative smallness of the windows, the particular form of the loggias, the introduction of belvederes, and finally the introduction of abundant water and Southern vegetation, they will attempt to achieve the expression of a character valid for the edifice and the region: in a word, the goal is to exhibit to the imagination of the Algerian tribesmen the high degree of perfection of our industry and arts.

The projects desired were to be typically vast, abstract Grand Prix designs, classical rather than typically French and vaguely Mediterranean rather than typically Algerian (indeed, the Algerians are described as primitive tribesmen). Duban, on the other hand, specified that "the architectural forms honored in France will be reproduced in their loftiest sense, although differences of climate and materials stamp them with a special character." He emphasized the importance of taking advantage of the site, the steep slopes along the Bosporus. He reminded the competitors, "The materials of the region are particularly adapted to the construction of light vaults. Malta and the Cyclades furnish stone and marble of all sorts." That is, he urged them to ponder the contrasting forms of French and Constantinopolitan architecture, the first in terms of aesthetic (indeed, essential geometric) types, the second in the more materialist terms of climate and construction. He evidently sought to encourage the creation of a distinctive and carefully thought-out synthesis, like that in Vaudoyer's Marseilles Cathedral designed the year before (p. 425).

Duban's program was much simpler in its planning but much more complex in the factors that it attempted to make the competitors consider. It was addressed to the powers of reason; Hittorff's, to those of the imagination. The institution of the twenty-four-hour *esquisse* gave the Grand Prix competitors no time to think, a fact that had been pointed out repeatedly since the beginning of the nineteenth century.[127] This system rendered such a program as Duban's ineffectual, but already in 1855 Duban himself had fostered a change in the regulations that increased the time allotted for the *esquisse* among the architect competitors to ten days.[128] This, even more effectively than his programs, should have worked to alter the tradition of Grand Prix design.

It was up to the students, however, to take advantage of Duban's changes. What actually happened during the late 1850s presaged Pascal's conduct in 1866. The winning design of 1856, by Lebas's student Edmond Guillaume, is distinctively French only in its reproduction of a specific motif—the arched pediment of Libéral Bruant's Hôtel des Invalides—in the center of its facade. It is Constantinopolitan only in the open side of its principal enfilade. It looks like a typical Grand Prix design: the inflections that Guillaume gave to that set vocabulary—belvederes, open loggias—operate on a different level from the inflections of structural form and colored surface that Vaudoyer used in Marseilles Cathedral, and that Villain had already used in 1849 in his winning *Eglise paroissiale* project for the *concours d'émulation* (p. 203).

The great disappointment for Duban and his friends came in 1862, when Emmanuel Brune and Victor Dutert actually submitted projects that were "Algerian" in style, in response to Hittorff's program, and lost to the dreariest conventional project by François-Wilbrod Chabrol.[129] And as is evident in Hittorff's program, such a conventional rendering was what the Academy had demanded. The radicals, especially Viollet-le-Duc, realized that change could only come by breaking the Academy's control over the Grand Prix competition, and in 1863, partly as a result of the public outcry over the results of the previous year's competition, the system was reorganized. What is fascinating is that three years afterward, in 1866, Pascal won the Grand Prix by proving the conventional vocabulary supple enough to solve a problem purposely hostile to it.

* * *

The complex, essentially domestic subject and the irregular site of the 1866 competition had helped justify some of Pascal's innovations, but they also made his design atypical among Grand Prix projects. For the compositional ideas that it embodied to achieve the status of paradigms in the tradition of the competition, the ideas had to be incorporated into a monumental public building on an unrestricted site. In spite of the efforts of Duban in the 1850s, this was to continue to be the format down to 1968. Alfred Normand had explained apropos of the 1866 competition program:

> What the students of the Ecole des Beaux-Arts need for such a competition [the Grand Prix] and for training and accustoming the artist to the most difficult architectural conceptions is a program that specifies large layouts [*de grandes dispositions*] as required for a large monument. He who can do more can do less, and the student who will have proven his capacities in a project of this sort will have proven that he is capable of producing real art and that he will have no trouble composing, if need be, the residence of a rich banker.[130]

The program of 1867 specified a monumental building on an open site, a *Palais pour l'exposition des Beaux-Arts* (Palace for an Exhibition of Fine Arts), part of a larger industrial exposition, but isolated on all sides.[131] It is not an entirely abstract subject: 1867 was the year of the second French Exposition Universelle. The design and the judging necessarily took account of the strange oval iron-and-glass structure on the Champs de Mars, the conception, it has recently been shown, of the entrepreneur Frédéric Leplay.[132] What architects (even the radical Léopold-Amédée Hardy)[133] would have preferred is seen in the exposition building of 1878: rectangular, with galleries punctuated by a hierarchical arrangement of pavilions.[134] This is essentially the same as the *projets rendus* submitted in 1853 by Boitte and Rougevin for an *Exposition des Arts et de l'Industrie*.[135] Furthermore, the subject of the 1867 competition is a pavilion not for the whole exposition, but for only the most monumental part, the Department of Fine Arts. (In 1855 the fine arts had been given a separate, much more compressed structure on the Avenue Montaigne, designed by Hector Lefuel and clothed in masonry.)

The problem for the competitors was deciding to what extent the building should be a museum of the traditional sort, and to what extent it should be the new sort of vast iron-and-glass exposition building. Bénard, this time the Premier Grand Prix winner, treated it as an exposition building, monumentalized and inserted into the most traditional Grand Prix paradigm, two interlocking rectangles (p. 240), which we had first encountered in Percier's design of 1786 (p. 125). In the breadth and regularity of its pattern, Bénard's rendition recalls Percier's, and it seems Neoclassical and archaicizing in its details.[136]

Bénard's plan, in spite of its superficial Neoclassicism, continued and brought to fruition the developments of the 1860s. It differs from Percier's plan in the binding together of the five squares on the principal axes, and in the great animation both of the form of the spaces and of their representation on the sheet through exedras, rotundas, and a wide variety of wall treatments handled with richness and control. Bénard's *marche* is, in fact, simpler than

Percier's; whereas the lines on Bénard's plan sheet from a distance read as two interlocking rectangles, the spaces they define would be experienced as one great space running across the building from side to side, preceded by an atrium and followed by a cloister. One element in Bénard's project, evident in the elevations, was totally foreign to Percier's version of the paradigm: the use of pavilions to divide the building's masses into contrasting vertical and horizontal volumes. Like the blending of space in Bénard's plan, this was a source of an impression of *mouvement*—of a counterpoint of visual rhythms resulting from the overlaying of two different systems—which imparted that quality to the Grand Prix designs of the 1860s that we call baroque no matter what the historical style clothing the project. This pavilion treatment had evolved slowly in the Grand Prix tradition, appearing first in Lefuel's strange *Hôtel de Ville* of 1839 (p. 195) and maturing in Daumet's subtly staccato *Conservatoire de Musique* of 1855 (p. 225), which should be compared with Diet's quite static, pavilioned *Musée pour une capitale* (Museum for a Capital City) of 1853. Pavilions are important to Guadet's *Hospice dans les Alpes* (Hospice in the Alps) of 1864 (p. 256), Gerhard's and Noguet's *Vaste Hôtellerie pour des voyageurs* (Great Hostelry for Travelers) of 1865, and Pascal's *Hôtel* of 1866 (p. 237). Yet in all these cases the pavilions seem foreign elements dotted around a conventional composition of static horizontal blocks to enliven the ensemble. What is significant about Bénard's design of 1867 is that he broadened his pavilions and compressed his wings so that his building finally coalesced into a consistent series of blocky forms, all variations on a single type. The dominating horizontal wings of Guadet's and Pascal's projects have in Bénard's elevation literally disappeared into thin air by being reduced to open columnar screens. The central mass rises to a tall iron-and-glass square domical crown, echoing the corner pavilions of the facade and the pairs of pavilions marking the center of the side elevations. These pavilions are the essence of the building, firmly defined at their corners and in their roofs, responding to each other across the terraces and colonnades of the ensemble, which fill in between and set off these features. Working within the tradition of the Grand Prix designs, Bénard managed to basically alter the vocabulary and accent.

If Bénard's plan (p. 240) is laid next to that of Garnier's Opéra (p. 433), it becomes evident why the latter was often compared to a Grand Prix design, [137] and why the former managed to rise above the mannerism of its tradition. The two plans are based upon the same paradigm: two interlocking rectangles, which intersect at a major space bleeding in front into an atrium with banks of stairways at its side, externally defined and internally unified by a generous girdling avenue of circulation. In elevation (pp. 241, 434), the masses of the four main axes push out beyond the circumscribed corridor to terminate in pavilions at the sides, echoing the dome crowning the composition, and in a broad flat block at the front. Garnier's design, of course, pre-dates Bénard's; it was conceived in 1860–61 and its facade scaffolding removed on August 15, 1867 (five days after the Grand Prix designs of that year were judged). Garnier's problem in adapting a paradigm from the academic genre was to render it buildable, a feat he accomplished by reducing the number of parts while elaborating and interrelating the treatment of them. In so doing Garnier provided the impetus for the ideas that Bénard so brilliantly brought back to the academic sphere.

* * *

The innovations of the Grand Prix projects of the 1860s seem extraordinary when one considers the largely unexceptional work of the *maîtres d'atelier* who trained the winners: Jules André, Alexis Paccard, Charles Questel, Hippolyte Lebas.[138] There was, however, a place of incubation for the students' ideas, one of the largest and most active places of architectural endeavor of the century: Charles Garnier's *agence* for the Paris Opéra. Between 1862 and 1875 it is said to have produced some 33,000 drawings to keep pace with the rapid construction of that monument. The Grand Prix laureates Guadet, Noguet, Pascal, Bénard, Scellier de Gisors, and Paul Nénot all worked there, as did J.-L. Batigny, winner of both a *deuxième* and a *premier accessit*.[139] Guadet, Pascal, and Nénot later wrote glowingly of the camaraderie of the *agence*.[140] Garnier they called *le grand chef*.[141] Garnier himself took credit for his assistants' later success in the Grand Prix competition: "I would ask for nothing more than to believe it and I would like to persuade myself that the successive victories my young collaborators won would not have been so frequent without the influence of the sort of school I had established."[142] Not only were many of the Grand Prix laureates actually working in Garnier's *agence*, but also the detail drawings themselves were lithographed and circulated; by 1867 one could purchase whole sets of almost 350 sheets.[143] (This practice was not unprecedented.) Although the facade was masked with scaffolding until late summer 1867, its design was well known in the ateliers from its commencement in 1862.

The Opéra's impact on the Grand Prix designs is already clear in Emmanuel Brune's winning project of 1863 (p. 243), of which some details were borrowed directly from Garnier's building. The successive projects of the decade witnessed the gradual digestion of his paradigm, from the copying of motifs to the adoption of compositional principles. Guadet used pavilions to move the eye back and forth across the space of his project. Pascal bound his design together with a system of impelling enfilades. Bénard made an academic translation of the Opéra's masses and spaces.

Garnier in 1871 published an exposition of the organization of his building in his book *Le Théâtre*. It is structured as a series of reflections on theaters in

Julien Guadet. *Un Hospice dans les Alpes* (A Hospice in the Alps). 1864. 1er Grand Prix. Plan.

Guadet was to become the great theorist of the Ecole at the turn of the century. His plan for a hospice, although thought unexceptional at the time, does neatly apply a traditional *parti* to the church and monastic facilities, while lodging and services for voyagers are terraced down the hillside.

Guadet. *Un Hospice dans les Alpes.* Elevation; section of chapel.

Although no indication of style was given in the program, Guadet chose a medievalizing work, the first of its kind for a Grand Prix. The severe style of the subsidiary buildings recalls much institutional architecture of the time, while the chapel reflects the work of the Gothicist architects of the 1850s and '60s. The jury that selected this project included several students and friends of Labrouste and Viollet-le-Duc.

The detailing of the section of the chapel has Tuscan arches and almost Byzantine polychromed decoration of Greek crosses and saints and martyrs. The colors are among the richest used in the Grand Prix drawings of the period.

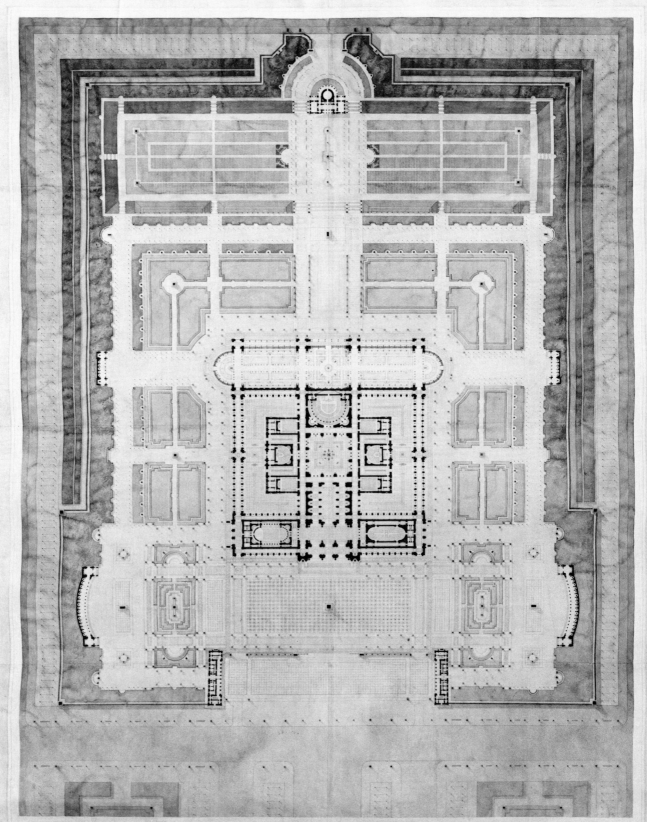

Paul-Henri Nénot. *Un Athénée pour une ville capitale* (An Atheneum for a Capital City). 1877. 1ᵉʳ Grand Prix. Plan, elevation, and section.

The program for this atheneum called for great meeting areas, auditoria and halls for teaching, a large library, and a greenhouse for botanical exhibits. A contemporary review called Nénot's project less brilliant than others, but more logical and condensed, as the simple, compact plan of the main building indicates. Because of the broad front wings, the elevation suggests a far larger structure than the plan reveals. Nevertheless, the entry pavilion, which leads to the main enfilade, is articulated as a complete building facade in itself. This center facade draws precise classical detailing into a composition of baroque complexity.

The last of the students to win a Grand Prix after working in Garnier's *agence* for the Paris Opéra, Nénot delineated a less colorful interior than those of the Grand Prix projects of the 1860s. There is a noticeable modulation of spaces for meeting and study apparent in the section. The hall of casts is a variation on the glass-roofed courts of the Ecole des Beaux-Arts (p. 60), in which the two casts of columns shown in the drawing were installed in 1873.

Nénot. *Un Athénée pour une ville capitale.* Facade detail.

This detail of a central bay of the facade, as required by the program, demonstrates the comparatively dry rendering style of the 1870s applied to a rich arrangement of classical elements.

general, although he admitted that it was but an apology for his own design. In contrast to Viollet-le-Duc's explanation of his "salle voûtée," Garnier did not explain theaters in terms of their abstract spatial geometry, but rather in terms of the operagoer attending a performance. His chapters are, in sequence: "Covered Entries," "Vestibules," "Stairways," "Foyers and Galleries," "Chambers of the Chief of State," "Auditoria and Dependencies." In the first chapter he insisted on the necessity and comfort of covered vehicle entries; in the second he developed this into a conception of arrival at the theater, simultaneously in terms of social usage, physical comfort, and architectural form. He divided the arriving theatergoers into four groups: the carriage-borne and the pedestrian, with tickets and without. He placed the carriage entry at the side and the pedestrian entry at the facade, linked the two flows and diverted them to the auditorium through a great stair hall in the center; but he placed around this hall, along the lateral facades, two long corridors open to the pedestrian and carriage entries at their ends, where tickets can be bought without disrupting the graceful passage of subscribers to their boxes.

This short description of Garnier's plan misses the sensitivity to the whole ceremony of opera attendance, which is the substance of Garnier's text:

> Pedestrians holding tickets arrive at the main steps, climb them, and go toward the doorways of the facade, immediate entry into the theater being already possible through these outer doors. But such direct entry would deprive the arrivals of the chance to catch their breath, or, quietly now and indoors, to get out their tickets, buy a program or some other publication, or to find all in all a place between getting to the theater [*marche extérieure*] and staying [*séjour intérieur*]. To allow for this useful and desirable pause, it is wise to establish something of a portico at the main entrance, a porch or gallery that would also serve as shelter for theater personnel stationed at the doors. Under this gallery, the arrivals, now protected from the elements, would be able to remove their walking clothes, look for their tickets, and then go into the theater, free from all such petty concerns.[144]

From here the pedestrian theatergoers pass through double doors into a heated outer vestibule:

> This room is what one might call a place to pause [*lieu de repos*] for those arriving at the theater. Here is a place for meeting friends. Here, at last inside, one is not or need not be in a rush to take one's seat; one can wait a moment or two or walk around a bit. But for this pause to be even more pleasant and for one's assurance to be all the more complete, one ought to be able to see, from this introductory vestibule, the flight of stairs and the ticket booths. One knows at this point where one is going to go; there is no mistaking the way one will take, and the certainty permits you to be in no hurry. Indeed it invites you not to be.[145]

From here the pedestrians penetrate past the ticket-takers into the stair hall,

Charles Garnier. Opéra, Paris. Preliminary project. 1861. Facade. Bibliothèque-Musée de l'Opéra, Paris.

This design, drawn two months after Garnier officially received the commission for the Opéra and approved on August 20, 1861, shows approximately the same massing as the completed building (p. 437). In the final version, the domes and the peak of the roof were heightened, a ramp was added to the Emperor's Pavilion, and much of the decoration was altered and enriched. Drawings for Garnier's winning competition project have not been preserved, and this seems to be among the earliest of the surviving Opéra drawings.

Garnier *(agence)*. Opéra. Emperor's Pavilion. *(above)* Study of elevations, plan. 1861–63. Bibliothèque-Musée de l'Opéra, Paris.

This study, one of some 33,000 drawings produced by Garnier's assistants in the *agence* established especially for the Opéra, retains the same articulation of the side wall as earlier projects. Now, however, it heightens the dome of the Emperor's Pavilion and adds a regal decoration of eagles and a most important new element, a carriage ramp. The ramp distinguishes the pavilion from its counterpart yet does not contradict the building's basic bilateral symmetry. This drawing conveys more of the richness of the finished building than do earlier studies.

(opposite above) Garnier *(agence)*. Emperor's Pavilion. Working drawing of the crown of the dome. October 24, 1864. Bibliothèque-Musée de l'Opéra, Paris.

This working drawing, which shows a detail essentially as it was built, is typical of those produced by the *agence*. The drawings were usually copied in pencil from Garnier's detailed ink studies and were then approved by him for execution. Many of Garnier's assistants were also students at the Ecole.

(right) Garnier *(agence)*. Emperor's Pavilion. Ink study of the entrance. Bibliothèque-Musée de l'Opéra, Paris.

This is a study for one of the two portals on the carriage ramp of the Emperor's Pavilion, which lead to a central rotunda below the main Salon. Although this was executed, much of the decoration of the Emperor's Pavilion was never completed, for the Opéra did not open until after Napoleon III fell from power.

Garnier. Opéra. Preliminary project. 1861. Side elevation. Bibliothèque-Musée de l'Opéra, Paris.

Somewhat different from the project showing the facade, approved in August 1861, this version may be slightly earlier. In the building as constructed, the pilasters on the side walls were replaced by circular niches with busts, and the side pavilion and corners were more clearly emphasized in both mass and decoration than they are here. The comparatively dull wall surfaces and the pale washes suggest that this drawing was intended to be worked over and elaborated, as was done on some parts of the sheet.

where they meet the flow of the carriage-borne theatergoers who have alighted under cover at the lateral porte cochère and gathered in the basement rotunda, under the auditorium, before proceeding up the first flight of the grand staircase to the main floor. This rotunda serves for the carriage-borne the same function as the outer vestibule for the pedestrians, but somewhat differently:

> Then the theatergoers should pass into a large vestibule, rather spacious, well lighted and provided with mirrors, where the ladies can adjust their finery before offering themselves to the waiting eyes of the public. This vestibule performs the function for those coming by carriage that the grand vestibule, described above, performs for those coming by foot. . . . But these vestibules must differ in appearance. The first, as I have said, is a sort of *salle des pas perdus*; the second is rather a *grand salon* meant for the most elegant portion of society. Ladies rarely come to a great theater on foot, and, if the pedestrian vestibule is rather given over to men, the opposite is so for this new *grand salon*, which is particularly given over to the ladies, not that they will be there alone, but because they will be in the majority. One realizes consequently that the decorative character of the two different vestibules must be different in keeping with their differing functions, and that if the first must have a plainer, more imposing look, the second must appear more intimate and more elegant.[146]

From the *grand salon* of the carriage entrance these more elegant theatergoers mount to the *salle des pas perdus* of the pedestrians and confront the two principal flights of Garnier's great staircase: rising to the caryatid-flanked entry to the boxes, dividing and passing on each side to the *piano nobile* and the *premières loges*. It stands in a tall chamber open on all four sides through a double-layered arcade, which embraces two levels of iron balconies serving the cheaper seats of the *deuxièmes, troisièmes,* and *quatrièmes loges*. One mounts to these through banks of staircases behind. The "plebians" in the upper tiers can watch the "patricians" progress to their boxes, as can the "patricians" themselves, because the double-layered arcade contains balconies for spectators, three steps down from the *piano nobile*.

> No one used to think that apart from the spectacle of the plays enacted the view of broad staircases crowded with people was a spectacle of pomp and elegance too. But today, luxury is spreading, comfort is demanded everywhere, and there are those who love to see the movement of a varied and elegant crowd, who follow the emptying of a great theater with interest. Ease of communications is now a necessity. The eyes, as well as the mind, bid for satisfaction and pleasure. It all imposes on the architect broad and monumental arrangements with vast and commodious stairways. . . . There will be profit and advantage for everyone, therefore, if the big central stairway is a place of luxury and movement, if ornament is distributed elegantly, if the animation that rules the steps is an interesting and varied spectacle. With the lateral walls of the staircase arranged to be

Garnier. Opéra. Plan of *étage des baignoires* (amphitheater and dress circle boxes) from *Le Nouvel Opéra*.

This plan is one of a set drawn after construction and printed in Garnier's book *Le Nouvel Opéra*, of 1878–80. It is from this level, one story above the street, that the principal flight of the grand staircase rises, and from which the arriving operagoer first beholds the splendor of the building's central public space. It is also the level at which the carriages arriving at the Emperor's Pavilion *(left)* would have set down their passengers, well above the street and away from the threat of assassins.

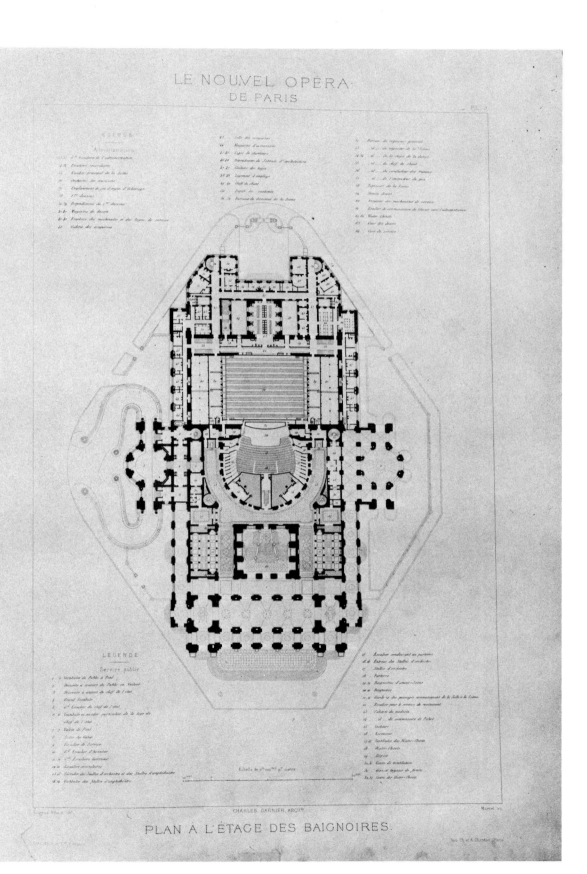

LE NOUVEL OPÉRA
DE PARIS

PLAN A L'ÉTAGE DES BAIGNOIRES

(above) Garnier (agence). Opéra. Grand Foyer. Study of the longitudinal section. 1861–63. Bibliothèque-Musée de l'Opéra, Paris.

This section, taken facing out through the facade of the building, corresponds to the disposition shown in the preliminary studies of the summer of 1861. It is organized in much the same way as later studies and as the finished room, but it does not yet show the degree of elegance and assurance for which Garnier's baroque decorations became famous.

(opposite) Garnier. Opéra. Grand Foyer. Ink study of a detail of the north wall. Bibliothèque-Musée de l'Opéra, Paris.

The bay shown here closely resembles the final form of the bays of the Grand Foyer, and this beautiful, detailed ink drawing was probably executed by Garnier as a model for final working drawings for that room. The arrangement of the curtain, beyond which would be the avant-foyer and the great stair hall, recalls the effect achieved by Garnier in the trompe-l'oeil painted curtain for the stage (p. 441).

left open, all the people walking about on each floor will be able, as they like, to entertain themselves by the view of the great hall and by the incessant comings and goings of the crowd up and down the stairs. . . . Finally, by arranging fabrics and wall hangings, candelabra, girandoles, and chandeliers, as well as marble and flowers, color everywhere, one makes of this ensemble a brilliant and sumptuous composition, which recalls in real life certain of the resplendent tableaus that Veronese fixed on his canvases. The sparkling light, . . . the animated and smiling faces there, . . . the greetings exchanged, all will have an air of festivity and pleasure, and without realizing what is owed to architecture for the magic effect, everyone does, through good feeling, pay homage to this great art, so mighty in its manifestations, so noble in its effects.[147]

Garnier continued in the same vein in *Le Théâtre* to treat the Emperor's pavilion, the auditorium, the foyers—"But what will be the dimensions of this foyer? To answer the question, one has to study the way people promenade. Most of the time theatergoers stroll together only in twos. . . ."[148]

* * *

A similar description of the cramped circulation and cranky detailing of Viollet-le-Duc's "salle voûtée"(p. 227) or Davioud's *Bourse* (p. 209), not to mention one of the two theaters Davioud erected on the Place du Châtelet beginning in 1860, would simply be embarrassing. These buildings were not designed from Garnier's standpoint. Viollet-le-Duc's own project for the Opéra competition (p. 282), although strikingly close to Garnier's in basic configuration, lacks the monumental path of movement from street to box that was Garnier's primary concern (p. 269). The essence of the contrast is in the stairways: Viollet-le-Duc's project is a warren of stairs of various sizes and shapes, all narrow, gravitating toward the corners of the plan. Garnier divided his into two classes, the processional and the functional; he made the first bind the spaces of the building together from basement to attic, and he set the second, concentrated in spacious banks, to serve it at either side, providing the audience for his Veronesque tableau.

The two men knew each other: Garnier, a poor boy from the Rue Mouffetard, had worked for Viollet-le-Duc as a draftsman during the 1840s. They knew how they differed. Viollet-le-Duc's son, editor of the *Gazette des Architectes et du Bâtiment,* wrote of Garnier's Opéra that it was a *projet d'école,* "that is to say, one of those projects one believes unbuildable."[149] The auditorium, he wrote, "seems made for the staircase and not the staircase for the auditorium." The style seemed imprecise, "a mixture of all architectures"; the silhouette, he predicted, would prove ineffective. All of which is irrelevant, and the latter point grossly mistaken, when the building is experienced as Garnier intended it to be. In 1867, Garnier summarized the problem inherent in Viollet-le-Duc's Opéra project more accurately:

Garnier *(agence).* Opéra. Grand Foyer. Working drawing of the transverse section. Bibliothèque-Musée de l'Opéra, Paris.

Features of working drawings like this one were sometimes greatly altered in the finished structure. At the ends of the foyer, the *oeils-de-boeuf* with busts were eliminated to make room for murals by Paul Baudry, and the bust of Napoleon III was replaced by an urn after his fall from power.

NOUVEL OPÉRA

COUPE TRANSVERSALE SUR LE FOYER ET SUR L'UN DES SALONS A L'EXTREMITÉ

ECHELLE DE 0,10 P.M

NOUVEL OPERA
DE PARIS

GRAND ESCALIER D'HONNEUR

(opposite) Garnier *(agence)*. Opéra. Studies for the Grand Stair Hall and principal facade. 1861. Bibliothèque-Musée de l'Opéra, Paris.

Drawings in colored washes were made for the Opéra principally for two reasons: for presentation, and for study of polychromatic decoration. These studies for the grand staircase and part of the facade are addressed to two of the most important and most colorfully detailed parts of the building. The polychromy of the interior was designed for a rich appearance under the artificial light of an evening performance, while that of the facade was intended to help articulate the three-dimensionality of the facade and to read well from a range of distances.

(right) Garnier *(agence)*. Study of light standard and banners. Bibliothèque-Musée de l'Opéra, Paris.

The *agence* not only designed light standards and street furniture, but also planned to incorporate flagpoles into many of the lighting fixtures so that they could be hung with banners on festive occasions. Light standards similar to the one shown here appear today, but it is uncertain whether the banners were executed.

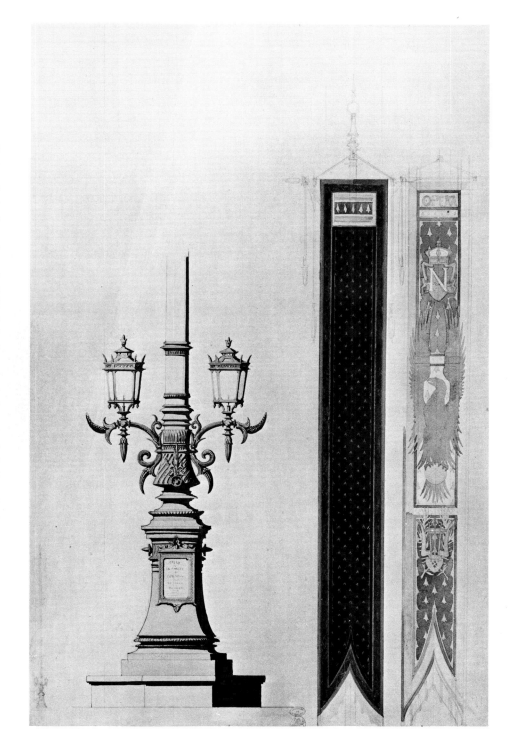

The principles he approves, the precepts he provides, are often abandoned in his own compositions where the bizarre dominates. These are perhaps not indifferent works, but they are heterogeneous, and they stir up confusion in the mind: one seeks the reason and the purpose, . . . one finds only compromises between what the author attacks and what he defends.[150]

Inhabiting a world of architectural theorists, Garnier formulated a defense of his architecture in terms of *mise en scène* and *le comfortable*. At the end of *Le Théâtre*, he stated what he saw as the basic law of architecture, the "principle of reason and sincerity" quoted at the beginning of this essay: that the exterior volumes should perfectly express the interior spaces. The Opéra, he asserted, carefully adheres to that law: first comes the flytower, seeming as large as it in fact is; then the auditorium separately expressed in front; finally the vestibules and corridors around and below these forms. At this point, had Garnier been of Labrouste's and Viollet-le-Duc's persuasion, he would have proceeded to demonstrate how each volume was crystallized into a specific structural organism and how its details were reasoned out of that context. But instead there are no comments at all on structure and only this on detailing: "Regarding decoration as such, and regarding what ordering and style to adopt, there is no guide other than the inspiration and will of the one who is doing the building; the decorative art has such independence and freedom that it is impossible to submit it to fixed rules."[151]

Garnier's "law" of expressive volumes came at the end of his abstract reasoning, not at the beginning. One clothed these volumes as one saw fit; in the realm of decoration, "one falls into the vague, . . . one falls into the sentimental."[152] For Garnier it was what came before the manifestation of plan as volumes that was the object of the architect's reasoning: the first four hundred pages of his book were devoted to the experience of passing through the theater, gracefully and comfortably. This social phenomenon Garnier rationalized with all the skill that Labrouste and Viollet-le-Duc had shown when, learning from the abstract analytical methods of nineteenth-century philosophy and science, they reasoned out a building as a quantity of matter. Viollet-le-Duc's first step in the analysis of his "salle voûtée" was to compare it to a crystal. In his introductory chapter to *Le Théâtre* Garnier started with an examination of the human institution of theater. He understood it not as something restricted to the stage, but as the fundamental social relationship: "Put two or three people together and right away the theater exists. Two talk for a moment with each other, they become the actors; a third watches them and listens, he is the spectator; what is said is the poem; the place where the conversation takes place, that is the stage. . . . Everything that happens in the world is, in sum, but theater and representation. . . . See and be seen, hear and be heard, that is the inevitable circle of humanity; to be author or spectator, that is the vital human fate; that is the end and at the same time the means."[153] Seven years later in his book *Le Nouvel Opéra de Paris*, Garnier reminded ladies attending the Opéra: "Everyone gains from what is stupidly called *coquetterie*, which is, in fact, nothing other than art, the most serious art, and the most charming as well, the art of dressing oneself with grace, of walking with distinction, of smiling with finesse."[154] As he imagined the Opéra accommodating and responding to the spectacle of the theatergoers, so he justified its appearance in terms of them, more as a work of tailoring than of building: "Why is it, Gentlemen, that you slip on your black tailcoat and put on a white tie! Why is it, Ladies, that you appear at the Opéra, your shoulders bare, diamonds at your neck, flowers on your head, and silk draped about you! You love the sparkle of your eyes and the grace of your smile, you are, in a word, beautiful, and you could consent to take your elegance, your charm, your finery into a monument that would not for its part be in gala attire to receive you?"[155] The architecture that results is not one of literary symbols or structural geometry, but one of scenes, of taking part in the actions that they enclose, of responding almost as does a person's face in conversation. In 1878 Garnier justified the unexpected polychromy of the Opéra facade: "That the great masses be tinted pale and monochrome in order to sharply contrast silhouettes against sky and background is well and good, but why even so should we be shocked to find warm and brilliantly colored areas coming to cheer and brighten the general mass, just as hair, lips, and especially the eyes cheer and brighten the human face?"[156]

The logical culmination of Garnier's characterization of architecture as setting and participant in a spectacle is his assertion of the primacy of personality in the act of conception: "The style I employ is my own; it is that of my own will and my own inspiration; it is the style of my times that I produce and affirm; it is my personality that I lay bare, but which moves with the current of our productions. And my work, whatever it may be, will certainly leave its imprint in the manifestations of a style that will be recognized when its time comes."[157] The admission—indeed, imposition—of the *moi* is a constant theme in his writing:

> The "I" is not so hateful a word as one likes to say it is, and, all in all, I prefer the open, direct "I" to the disguised "I" of more than one writer. In matters of science and theory, it is the personality . . . that stirs minds to passion, and if an author speaks, a thinker writes, the sayings or writings gain or lose force and power depending upon the individuality of their authors.[158]

In response to Viollet-le-Duc's assertion that taste is unconscious reason, Garnier asserted that reason is only significant after intuition has established a general framework, and that reasoning is a temptation to be suppressed by the strong artistic personality:

> Theories often have as their end the explanation of what has already been done; but they could sometimes be very dangerous if one were to listen to them before

Charles Garnier. Funeral of Victor Hugo. 1885. Studies for a public monument and decoration of the Arc de Triomphe. Bibliothèque-Musée de l'Opéra, Paris.

This study for a monument to Hugo uses a *parti* familiar in student projects and in the memorials that were spread about France after the Franco-Prussian War. The decoration of *fêtes* and funerals was a frequent assignment for major French architects, and in 1885 Garnier was appointed architect of the public funeral of Victor Hugo. The study for the draping of the Arc de Triomphe, beneath which Hugo's catafalque was set, shows the nature of Garnier's sketching style. Unlike the dry drawings of the eighteenth century or the delicate and precise drawings of the Romantics, it shows a loose, swift, and heavy use of ink, appropriate to the emotional approach to design that Garnier defended in his writings.

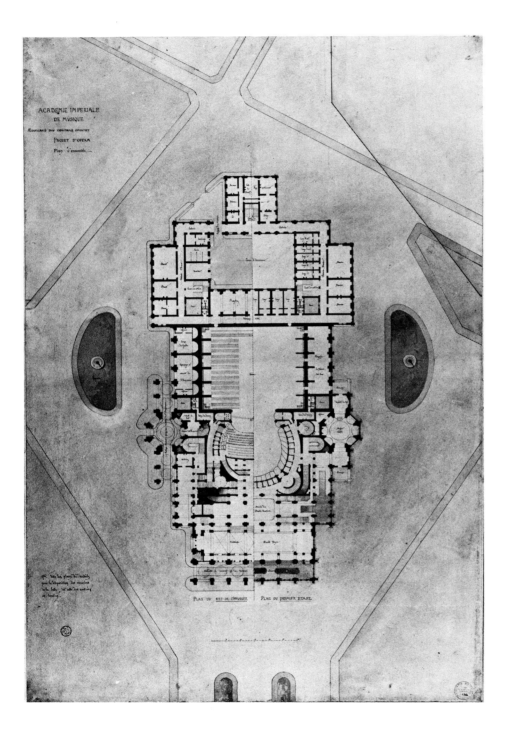

ACADEMIE IMPERIALE
DE MVSIQVE

PLAN DV REZ-DE-CHAVSSEE   PLAN DV PREMIER ETAGE

Eugène-Emmanuel Viollet-le-Duc. Opéra,
Paris. Competition project. 1861. Composite
plan (ground floor, *left*; main floor, *right*);
front and side elevations. Centre de
Recherches sur les Monuments Historiques,
Palais de Chaillot, Paris.

For the plan of his competition project for
the Opéra, Viollet-le-Duc adopted essentially
the same *parti* that Garnier was to use for the
building as constructed. The basic differences lie in the treatment of circulation.
Viollet-le-Duc makes little provision for
pedestrian entry to the building; and once
inside, the operagoer would have been confronted with a confusing and unimpressive
selection of stairways, with little indication of
access to the main *salle* or of the location of
secondary *salons*.

The exterior of Viollet-le-Duc's project is
severely articulated, with only a little variation from the lightly decorated entry
pavilions and region of the main *salle* to the
plain, buttressed walls of the backstage and
the almost residential block of the administration and opera company. Although the exterior walls reflect the uses of the interior,
the massing largely contradicts the interior
disposition of spaces (see the section on the
following page).

ACADEMIE IMPERIALE DE MUSIQUE

PROJET D'OPERA

Facade Principale

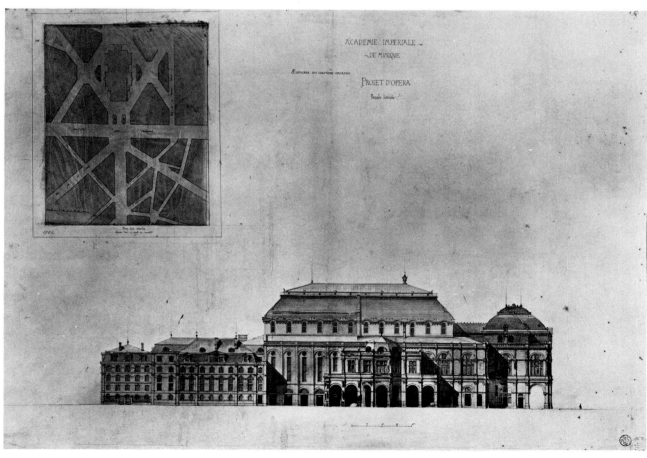

ACADEMIE IMPERIALE DE MVSIQVE

PROJET D'OPERA

Facade latérale

284

Viollet-le-Duc. Opéra, Paris. Competition project. 1861. Section, interior detail, and perspective. Centre de Recherches sur les Monuments Historiques, Palais de Chaillot, Paris.

The section reveals a complete separation of interior space and exterior profile, in contrast to Garnier's final solution. It also emphasizes the lack of clarity in circulation and in access to the various levels of seating, which is the greatest weakness of the project. The lower floor is entirely without decoration, while the upper floor is given a restrained, Romanized version of Viollet-le-Duc's often rich, medieval sculpture and polychromy.

The perspective of Viollet-le-Duc's project for the Opéra is justly celebrated, for its broad masses and insistent articulation seem to convey a governing principle of organic structure. Nevertheless, Viollet-le-Duc here contradicted many of his own theories (apart from the unworkable plan), and he failed to provide what was wanted: the exuberant pavilion of entertainment that Garnier made the crown of Second Empire Paris.

setting to work. From the first the artist has to compose and even execute without overly troubling himself with these axioms and dogmatic rationalizations. . . . Sometimes when I take up my pencil to compose, I feel invaded by these theoretical ideas that rise before me like a schoolteacher confronting a child who has made a mistake; but I assure you that instead of trying to reason at such times, I chase them from me as best I can, till feelings alone, and nothing else, guide my eyes, my hand, and my thoughts.[159]

This sounds like A.-L.-T. Vaudoyer's assertion of the primacy of *invention* over *execution*. Garnier, however, neither recognized any Platonic ideal nor expected any help from any force outside of his own spirit. His intuition was entirely earthbound, more so indeed than Viollet-le-Duc's reason:

> This intuition, in fact, is simply the habit of directing one's thought toward a particular end: it is the outcome of long and persevering study, whose progress is often unseen. It is, in effect, a kind of instinct that makes itself felt almost unconsciously over the keys of the piano. . . . Exactly that which makes the hand sure and the eye decisive is the very introduction into the brain of all the indispensable doctrines and their existence there, embodied, set in place, and ready to manifest themselves when they are needed.[160]

* * *

Garnier's is an essentially objective architecture: the constituent interior volumes engender the exterior massing; the decorative vocabulary is one of specific historical forms selected because they are appropriate to the associations of operagoing. Quatremère de Quincy would not have applauded it; its form and expression are not controlled by the Orders. But we know that the most dogmatic of the Romantics did not applaud it either: the exterior of the Opéra is only an approximate expression of the interior (the auditorium has been exaggerated in size and the stair hall suppressed); the building's style has been selected for reasons of particular personal sentiments rather than on the basis of a general historical theory. Its form is, in the last analysis, intuitively derived. But while Garnier's architecture is neither classical nor Romantic, it does conform to some system: that of composition, as it was defined by Gromort. It is in order to balance and pace the objective facts of the Opéra as they are presented to the visitor that Garnier has inflected the building's forms, softening them, decorating them, composing them. It is all summed up in the grand staircase that the Romantics so disliked, invisible from the exterior but completely dominating the presentation of the interior, so effectively composed for the visitors' eyes.

The opening of the Opéra at the beginning of the Third Republic was accompanied by a general effort to establish an architecture of this same sort: objective, eclectic, but also intuitive and composed. Within the Ecole de Beaux-Arts itself the movement's protagonist was Jules André. Of his doctrine

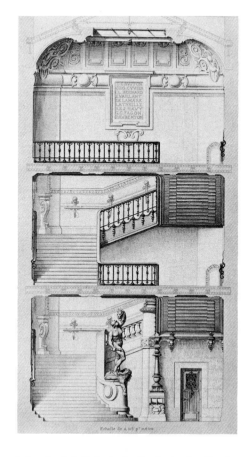

Jules André. Galerie de Zoologie, Jardin des Plantes, Paris. 1872–85. Section of main staircase. From *Revue Générale de l'Architecture*, Paris, 1885.

André has concealed the iron members of the ceiling and the stair treads under a plaster surface, which nonetheless expresses their presence with its ribbing and rippling. He did this to beautify the raw facts of the structure without denying them. The decorative motifs are *Néo-Grec*: André had been Labrouste's *inspecteur* at the Bibliothèque Nationale.

and his method we unfortunately know little,[161] but his Galerie de Zoologie in the Jardin des Plantes (1872–85) stands as their expression in built form.[162] The notices of the building in the *Revue Générale de l'Architecture* occasioned some telling remarks. In 1883 F. Monmory observed of the iron ceilings of the north galleries:

> The skeleton, frankly articulated, is covered with forms underneath which one divines the metal, but which moderate [*amortissent*] its stiffness [*raideur*] and soften [*adoucissent*] its sharpness [*âpreté*]. The architect has here applied the procedure of nature: the sight of the human body charms us because of its envelope which, while letting us divine the bone structure and the muscles, saves us the revulsion [*répugnance*] inspired by the anatomical model [*écorché*] or the fright [*effroi*] inspired by the skeleton [*squelette*].[163]

Monmory does not question the principle of revealing on the exterior the facts of the interior—Garnier's "principle of reason and sincerity"—but he suggests that a too direct application of it would result in a building like an *écorché* or a *squelette*, productive of feelings like *répugnance* and *effroi*. To avoid this he proposes that the architect, like André, should *amortisser* and *adoucir* the *raideur* and *âpreté* of these objective facts by means of an envelope like the human skin, suggesting but not displaying the inner organization. His choice of words and use of the analogy of biological and architectural forms were henceforth to be repeated endlessly at the Ecole.

In 1885 Monmory again reviewed the Galerie de Zoologie. Evidently the point he had made two years earlier had stirred up contention, for he devotes five paragraphs to a restatement and explanation:

> Does the common man need to know the particular shape which has been chosen for the joists supporting the ceiling, to know the thickness of the sheets of iron and the angle-pieces of the beams which constitute the structural skeleton, to count the bolts and rivets which hold these pieces together? Was this structure constructed for engineers to come and study the smallest details? Certainly not! In this case, besides the naturalist attracted by the richness of the collections, there will be the shopkeeper, the clerk, the pensioner, etc., come here to usefully occupy their time or simply drawn by curiosity. It is external form that will please this public and not the presentation—absolute to the point of brutality [*absolue jusqu'à la rudesse*], of the system of construction based on the use of specific materials.[164]

Here we see that there has been a change in the audience to which architecture is addressed and a consequent change in the manner in which things are presented to it. In a sense Romantic rationalism was indeed addressed to the "engineer come to study the smallest details" and the man of science generally: he comprised the Romantic élite, the Saint-Simonian priesthood, the Postivist modern man. E.-J. Delécluze in 1855 recalled his father explaining the French Revolution to him when he was a boy: "The Revolution destroys all distinctions among men. Henceforth there will only be one, that which aptitude for science and education place between the ignorant and the intelligent. Therefore work hard if you wish to distinguish yourself; there is no other nobility."[165] Since its inception the Revolution had failed four times: 1814, 1830, 1848, and 1871. A new world of sorts had come into being, different from the former one of rank and traditional faith, yet not the organized, organic, scientific one imagined by the Romantic rationalists and utopians. It was a world of shopkeepers, clerks, and pensioners; nouveau-riche operagoers and trivialities, as contemporary Parisian writers and painters clearly recognized. Everything was to remain quiet until the turn of the century when, with Hérriot and Tony Garnier and the last works of Zola, with Bergson and Picasso, a new revolution was to be conceived—one which the Ecole des Beaux-Arts, at ease at last with what appeared to be the perfect compromise, finally was unable to accommodate.[166]

Paul Blondel. *Portail d'église* (Portal of a Church). 1868. *Concours d'émulation, rendu.* Elevation.

This extraordinary rendering, which shows a particular mastery of light and shadow, is the work of a twenty-one-year-old student. Its lush, eclectic detailing reflects such Second Empire Parisian churches as Théodore Ballu's La Trinité of 1861–67.

* * *

Society in various ways preserves as a basic rite of renewal the sacrifice of the father or the king. The architecture of the nineteenth century was slain on the altar during the 1920s, and society since has felt the equally traditional guilt concomitant with its act. For all the concern with distinguishing the twentieth from the nineteenth century, there continues to be an undercurrent of belief that the two epochs stand together, father and son, against a very different world, one which existed down to the end of the eighteenth century. There is a tradition of interpretation of modern architecture, begun by Emile Kaufmann's *Von Ledoux bis Le Corbusier* (1933) and carried on by Colin Rowe, which holds that there is in fact a common mentality characteristic of all European architecture since 1775 and that its essential element is the concept of composition.[167] Kaufmann believed that Ledoux translated the revolutionary ideas of Rousseau and the Sturm und Drang into an architecture composed of self-contained, intrinsically meaningful geometric forms, "fitted together like children's blocks."[168] He saw Ledoux's discovery of "architectural autonomy" submerged—but never destroyed—by the irrelevancies of nineteenth-century historicism, finally reemerging in the architecture of Le Corbusier and his contemporaries.[169] Rowe has been more subtle, if less poetic: he does not dismiss historicism as irrelevant nor does he present the composed architecture of 1775 as the same as that of Le Corbusier.[170] Instead he perceives the idea of composition (together with the balancing idea of character) as having been formulated around 1800; then becoming the object of a reaction at mid-century, when the building's objective organism was accepted as the truest container of beauty (equated with character); and finally being resuscitated in the 1870s as the only way of imposing order upon what had become an architecture of "characteristic particles." That is, he perceives a dialectical evolution,

manifesting in the context of modern architecture the apparently eternal conflict of form and process. The trace of development is spiral, so that the architecture of the 1920s "curiously paralleled" that of mid-century Romanticism while being distinct from it in rejecting the idea of character.

Rowe's construct, although formulated in the context of English architecture, illuminates what we have seen taking place in France. There an architecture of Orders was replaced by one of composed spatial *tableaux* during the last half of the eighteenth century. The supposed artificialities of this, in turn, gave way at mid-century to such designs as Davioud's *Bourse* of 1849, its structural and spatial expression *absolue jusqu'à la rudesse*, declaring by its baldness that "if he is in earnest his work will not be deficient in character."[171] Finally Charles Garnier emerged, reestablishing an architecture of composed *tableaux* and intuitive effects, although now within the framework of the objective facts of plan and structure.

Yet there is something uneasy about the introduction of the English parallel and the obviously unequal comparison of Davioud's student project with Garnier's vast and elaborate building. One has to look for a French equivalent to real English High Victorian "ugliness." Thus this paltry project by Davioud has been emphasized because nothing more impressive was so bald—because Labrouste's Bibliothèque Sainte-Geneviève and Vaudoyer's Marseilles Cathedral were not the Opéra's diametrical opposites. The arching of the iron members of the Bibliothèque Sainte-Geneviève's reading room ceiling and the modulation of the contrasting volumes at Marseilles reveal belief in the composition and inflection of forms. The French were never able to be ugly in the artful way of Pugin or Butterfield: the bold admission of an architectural fact (for example, that an iron ceiling is made of straight elements) was in the end impossible for Labrouste. It was left for the Rhinelander Hittorff to show iron as iron in the Gare du Nord (1858–62), then to bluntly clothe it in a curtain of Greek columns. Labrouste's ultimate iron interior in contrast is a total fantasy: the cloth-like white domes of the Bibliothèque Nationale reading room, billowing up over the readers' heads, are held aloft by a fictive breeze blowing across a space illusionistically opening out into verdant sunny gardens on three sides (p. 431).[172] The slim Pompeian columns seem to tie the ceiling down rather than to hold it up. This is indeed an objective structural metaphor, but by replacing load and support with expansion and levitation it becomes free and lyrical—unlike the earthbound metaphors of Davioud and Viollet-le-Duc. The Veronese-like *tableaux* of Garnier's Opéra are gross by comparison. Labrouste was not Pugin or Butterfield. It is when one tries to set parallels that one senses the general peculiarity of French architecture: lyrical, nostalgic, precious, subtle, professional, and immensely urbane.

Emile Bénard. Villa Madama, Rome. Restoration. 1871. Fourth-year *envoi*. Plan and elevation *(following pages)*.

By 1871 an unfinished Renaissance monument, Raphael's Villa Madama, could be made the subject of archaeological analysis, reflecting a significant broadening of what the Academy held to be exemplary. Bénard reconstructed the gardens and the left half of the villa proper from the few surviving drawings and from his imagination. Unlike Percier (*Choix des plus célèbres maisons de plaisance*, 1809), Bénard made the villa asymmetrical, visualizing it as a Baroque progression of contrasting spaces on both axes. The gardens are similarly Baroque in their complexity, scale, and articulation.

Formigé. *Une Gare de chemin de fer.* Plan and facade detail.

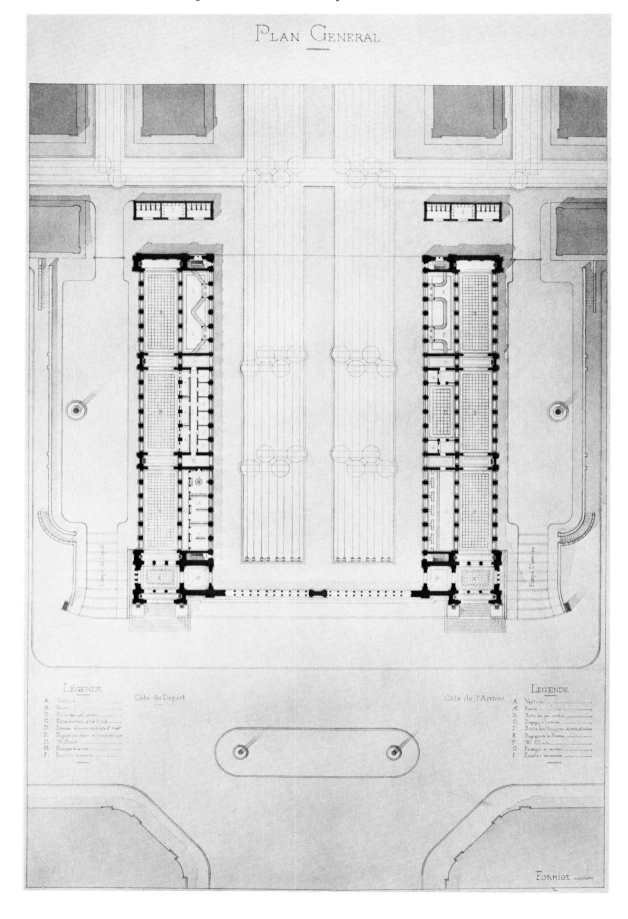

AGRICVLTVRE

AVRATION DV PARTHENON

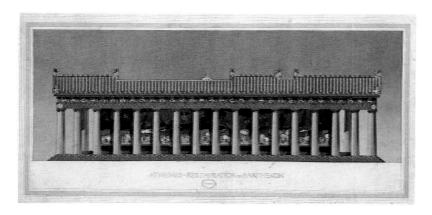

Edouard Loviot. Parthenon, Athens, Restoration. 1881. Fourth-year *envoi*. Elevation and detail.

The study of ancient Greek architectural polychromy by 1881 has become a matter of design rather than of archaeology; there is little here that was not already known in 1830. The structural and symbolic considerations of the earlier *envois* have likewise been put aside. Motifs and coloring are reminiscent of the painted decorations executed in the glass-roofed court at the Ecole des Beaux-Arts by Coquart in 1874 (p. 60) and presage the work of Otto Wagner in Vienna at the turn of the century.

The section *(preceding page)* is remarkable for the way it expands the interior space of the cella through the huge mythological murals, which are on the scale of the chryselephantine cult statue, their blue and black coloring—picked out with thin gold lines—in harmony with the dim lighting of the space.

(opposite) Henri-Thomas-Edouard Eustache. *Une Gare centrale de chemin de fer avec un vaste hôtel* (A Central Railway Station with a Large Hotel). 1891. 1ᵉʳ Grand Prix. Plan.

The plan of this railway station introduces a great *salle des pas perdus* between the departure and arrival areas for the sale of tickets, as required by the program. It also demonstrates the difficulties encountered by the *logistes* in relating the hotel space, here divided into two buildings *(at bottom on plan)* to the station.

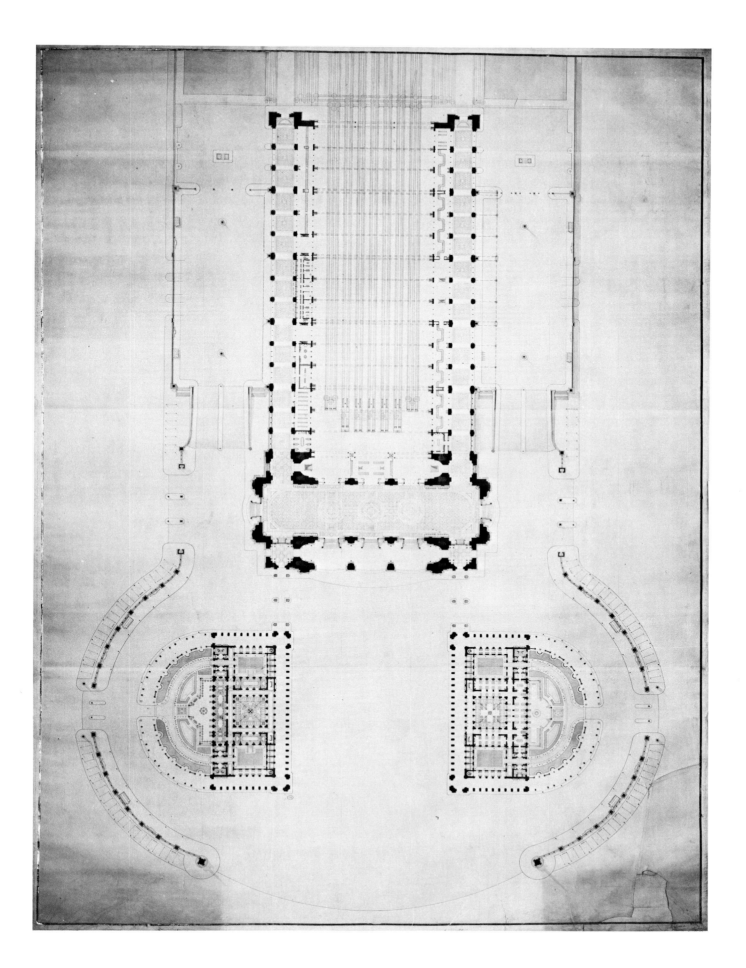

Eustache. *Une Gare centrale de chemin de fer.* Elevation and section.

Eustache's project (with a twenty-foot-wide elevation drawing) addressed itself primarily to the problems of entry and the expression of iron, as well as to the internal scale relationships of such a building. This project may be compared with Laloux's Gare du Quai d'Orsay (pp. 460–63), which it precedes by several years but does not equal in terms of organization.

Alphonse Gougeon. *Une Grande Factorerie dans l'Alaska* (A Large Trading Post in Alaska). 1896. Prix de Reconnaissance des Architectes Américains. Elevation.

This project adapts a traditional tiered arrangement of wings with a central tower to what the student imagined to be a "local" style in wood. The handsome and facile monochrome wash is typical of student drawings of the 1890s.

(*opposite*) Lucien Bardey. *Cabine d'ascenseur* (Elevator Cage). 1890. Prix Godeboeuf.

Many of the projects for the Prix Godeboeuf were for programs designed to meet "modern" problems. This elevator cage, which won its *concours,* is apparently pushed by a hydraulic jack and runs along the poles at the sides. Square in plan, it is surmounted by four arched ribs meeting at the center to carry a light topped by a winged Eros.

(*right*) Julien-Maxime-Stéphane Doumic. *Lustre électrique* (Electric Chandelier). 1891. Prix Godeboeuf.

Doumic, a student of Laloux, won a first prize with this project. Its style recalls *fin-de-siècle* jewelry, as compared with the baroque fixtures at the Paris Opéra twenty-five years earlier.

Joseph-Eugène-Armand Duquesne. *Pile de pont* (Suspension Bridge). 1895. Prix Godeboeuf. Detail.

Duquesne's suspension bridge, which took a first prize, emphasizes delicate detail. It should be compared with the pylons of the Manhattan Bridge in New York (completed in 1912), designed by the American Beaux-Arts firm of Carrère and Hastings.

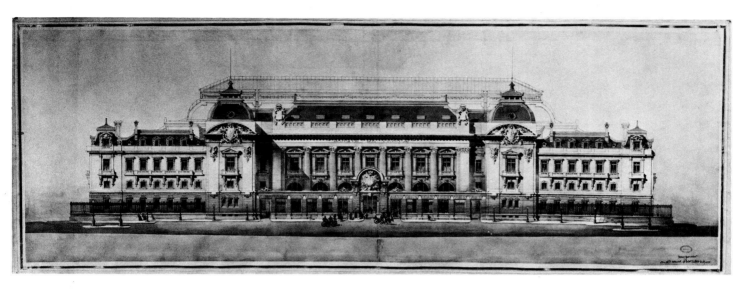

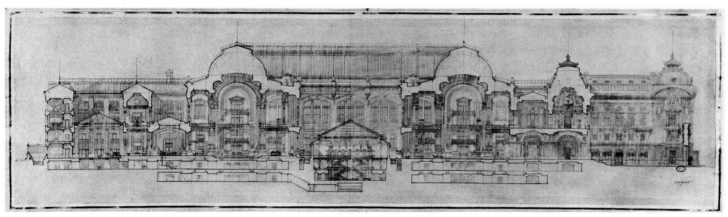

Tony Garnier. *Un Hôtel pour le siège central d'une Banque d'Etat* (A Building for the Central Headquarters of a State Bank). 1899. 1er Grand Prix. Elevation and section: first- and second-story plans *(following pages)*.

Garnier's elevation resembles some of the great Parisian banks of the last quarter of the century. The wings that are to house the bank governors, however, are articulated in a more residential mode and there is a straightforward institutional treatment of the inner wall surfaces. Besides all the offices required for banking transactions, the plan includes postal and telephone services at the main entrance, the governors' lodgings and a great central vault sunk into the open courtyard.

The section, which is an unfinished drawing without the monochrome wash, shows Garnier's most ingenious detail: the central vault is glass-roofed and visible to all in the bank, but it is accessible only by a passage from the director's office. Although essentially based on the traditional crossed axes in a rectangle, the plans show the lively articulation of masses and the freedom of line characteristic of projects of this time.

310

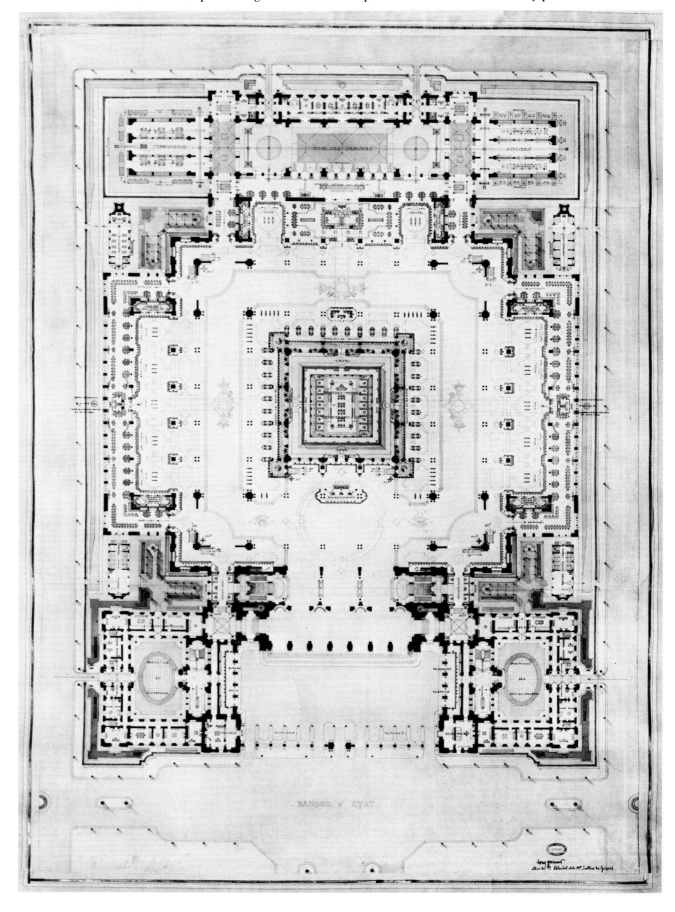

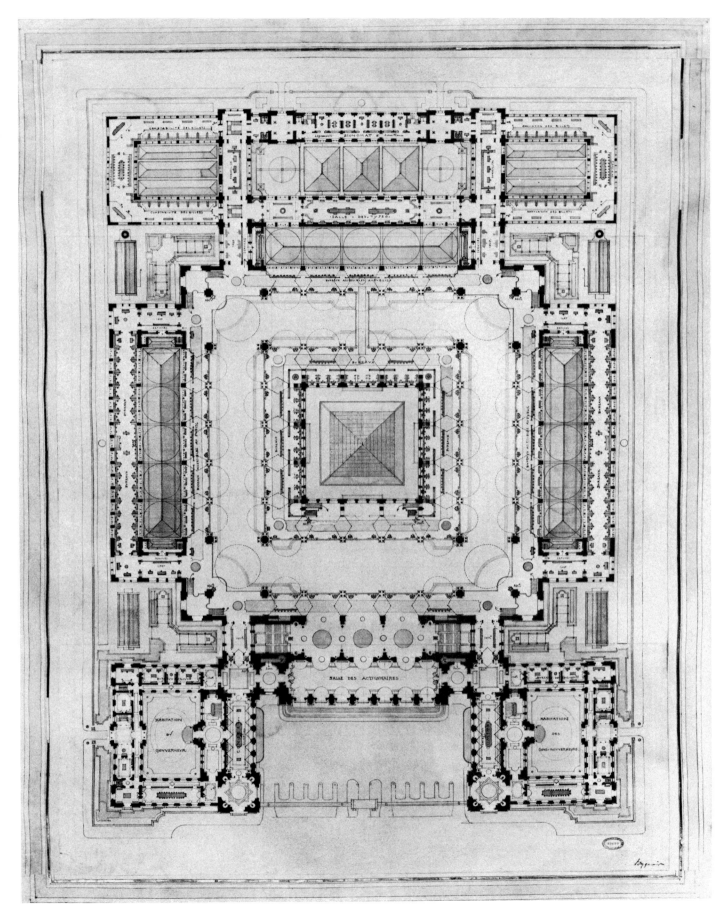

Louis-Hippolyte Boileau. *Casino.* 1897. Prix Achille Leclère, *1re médaille.* Plan and elevations *(following pages).*

This entertaining project was drawn when Boileau, a son and grandson of architects, was nineteen years old. The elevation drawings show a throng of pleasure seekers—presumably gamblers—ascending a gigantic flight of stairs through a stupendous grotto, which serves as the monumental base to a festive but somewhat anti-climactic pavilion of stone, iron, and glass. It is flanked by lighthouses and backed by an enormous formal garden decorated with fountains and bandstands. The plan shows the fine, nervous lines and radiating masses typical of student projects of the late 1890s, and the brushwork of the elevation drawings suggests a sympathetic interest in what contemporary painters were doing.

Boileau. *Casino*. Front elevation.

Joseph-Eugène-Armand Duquesne. *Une
Eglise votive dans un lieu de Pèlerinage
célèbre* (A Votive Church in a Celebrated
Place of Pilgrimage). 1897. 1er Grand Prix.
Side elevation: front elevation and plan
(following pages).

Duquesne's project suggests accretion over
time by joining Sienese, Florentine, and
French Gothic styles in the principal buildings. The area at the base of the hillside is for
pilgrims' lodgings; above it is a cloister, and
above that is the great pilgrimage church
with subsidiary chapels. This elevation drawing with its rich monochrome wash includes a
loosely brushed and unusually tempestuous
background.

RESTAVRATION
ECHELLE · 0.03 · P·M·

POMPEI · MAISON

DV · CENTENAIRE

Jules-Léon Chifflot. House of the Centenarian at Pompeii. Restoration. 1903. Fourth-year *envoi*. Section.

Like Loviot's 1881 restoration of the Parthenon, Chifflot's extensive and celebrated studies of Pompeii are exercises in colored decoration. This beguiling view into the private garden of a Pompeian house proposes an environment in which most people would enjoy finding themselves.

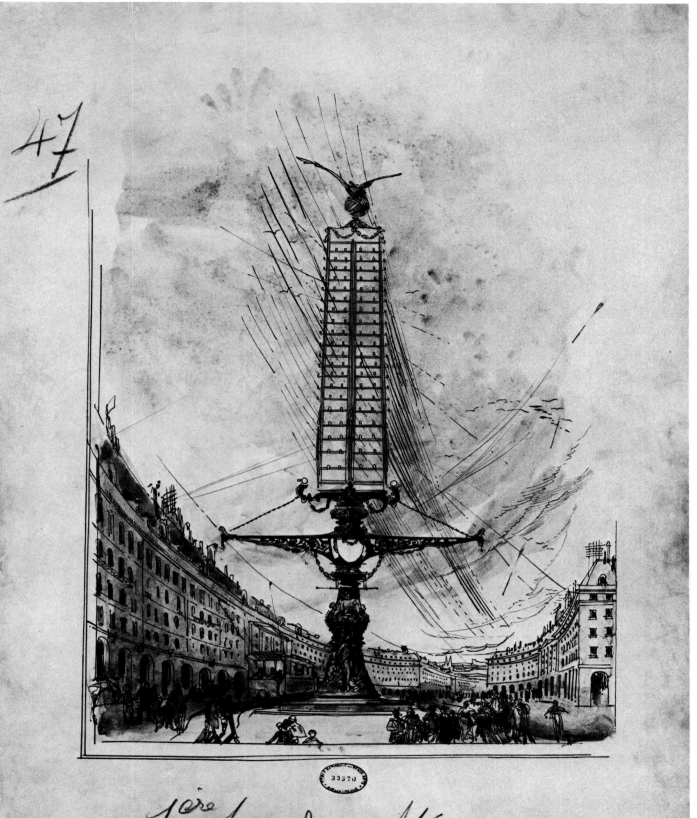

Janin. *Une Heurse* (A Utility Pole).

(preceding page) Georges-Fernand Janin.
Une Heurse (A Utility Pole).
(opposite) Joseph-Eugène-Louis Madeline.
Une Heurse. 1906. *Concours d'émulation, es-quisses.*
These two drawings for the same program are attempts to meet the burgeoning requirements of telephone, telegraph, and electric wires at the turn of the century. Both students interpreted these additions to the city as monumental street decorations. Janin, whose draftsmanship was greatly admired by his contemporaries, worked briefly for Daniel Burnham and did some important drawings for his Chicago Plan. Madeline became a *maître d'atelier* popular with American students.

Labrouste. Bibliothèque Sainte-Geneviève, Paris. Stair Hall.

THE ROMANTIC IDEA OF
ARCHITECTURAL LEGIBILITY:
HENRI LABROUSTE
AND THE NEO-GREC

Neil Levine

Reading the Bibliothèque Sainte-Geneviève

The drawings produced by the students at the Ecole des Beaux-Arts in the nineteenth century are extraordinarily beautiful. For a long time since, their formal display of virtuosity has seemed to most twentieth-century architects and art historians to betoken a lack of meaningful content perfectly exemplifying the stultified classical tradition that the students were supposed to embrace. Though rarely unrolled and examined in detail, the series of projects for the coveted Grand Prix de Rome were assumed to exhibit merely a set of conventional classical rules of composition—symmetry, axiality, and the use of the Orders for ponderated order—which appeared to prove the uselessness of looking into the issue more deeply. This opinion was naturally bolstered by an Anglo-German-American historical equation of Gothicism and radicality, which drew support from the nineteenth century itself. John Ruskin, in his Edinburgh lectures on architecture and painting of 1853, posed the question that, when applied to architecture, has been disturbing ever since:

> Of all the wastes of time and sense which modernism has invented . . . none are so ridiculous as the endeavor to represent past history. What do you suppose our descendants will care for our imaginations of the events of former days? Suppose the Greeks, instead of representing their own warriors as they fought at Marathon, had left us nothing but their imaginations of Egyptian battles. . . . What fools we should have thought them! . . . And that is precisely what our descendants will feel towards us, so far as our grand historical and classical schools are concerned. What do we care, they will say, what those nineteenth-century people fancied about Greek and Roman history! If they had left us a few plain and rational [structures] . . . , we should have thanked them. Well, but, you will say, we *have*. . . . Yes, you have indeed, and that is the only histor[y] [architecture] . . . that you either have or can have; but you don't c[are for] historical [architecture]. . . . You don't thank the men who do it; yo[u] upon them and dissuade them from it, and tell them they don'[t] grand schools.[1]

The problem of assigning value to the products of the [⌐] transcends the question of student work alone and relationship between what was produced by a studen[t] an architect in his late thirties. The career of Henri Labr[ouste] student and an architect, is a case in point, for the appreciation of his work in both the past century and in ours reveals in the most profound way that myopia described by Ruskin.

Led by architectural historians such as Sigfried Giedion, most twentieth-century observers have claimed to see in Labrouste's first and greatest building, the Bibliothèque Sainte-Geneviève (1838–50), just what Ruskin called a "plain" and "rational" structure (p. 335). Labrouste's use of an exposed iron framework for the internal structure of the reading room and his equally rationalized system of distinguishing the supporting from supported and infilling members of its masonry facade have caused most historians to see in that building a rejection of the idea of classicizing pomposity and a premonition of what has been called the engineer's aesthetic. Labrouste's library is thereby disassociated from its more ornate contemporaries, and its apparent rationalism is placed in a falsely symmetrical opposition to them, just as the Ecole Polytechnique is to the Ecole des Beaux-Arts. The real problem, however, is shoved under the table. The actual form of the building is stripped of its meaning. For Giedion, "Labrouste's chief accomplishment in this library rests in the manner in which the iron construction is balanced in itself, so that it puts no stress on the walls. The achievement of just such a hovering equilibrium became the chief task for engineers in the second half of the nineteenth century."[2] To preserve the building's prescient quality of utilitarian instrumentality, Giedion had to delete from his reconstruction of Labrouste's intention any mention of the decorative forms by which the structure of the library makes itself manifest as art, in a word, its clothing. Labrouste had, in fact, by 1830 set this idea before the students of his atelier as his main intention: "As soon as they know the first principles of construction, I tell them that they must derive from the construction itself a reasoned, expressive ornamentation. I tell them repeatedly that the arts have the power to embellish everything."[3]

Curiously, Viollet-le-Duc, whom one would suppose would have admired Labrouste's solution to the problem of using iron in monumental buildings, found no words of praise on this score for either Labrouste's first library or his later, now better-known, Bibliothèque Nationale (reading room, 1857/58–68; p. 430). In 1869–70, soon after the latter building was opened to the public, Viollet-le-Duc wrote, "What has never been tried anywhere with intelligence is the simultaneous use of metal and masonry." "Until now," he noted, it has "been tried only timidly and, it must be said, without having achieved any successful results. . . . To substitute a cast-iron shaft for a column of granite, marble, or stone is not bad, but one must admit it can hardly considered an innovation."[4] Despite this conclusion he claimed that rouste's work evinced a remarkably "proud and independent mind . . . ed with . . . fecund principles,"[5] which nurtured and remained the foundation for his own later brand of rationalism. He even professed to see in Labrouste's apparently conventional student work at the Ecole in Paris and the Academy in Rome (1819–29) the first glimmerings of that radical "originality and . . . independence": "even at the Ecole, he had . . . displayed certain ideas that were subversive of the established order and he tended toward what we called then, thirty years ago, *rationalism*."[6] As a result of such radicality, Viollet-le-Duc stated, as Ruskin predicted, that Labrouste was hardly "thanked" and that his ideas were considered not to "belong to the grand schools": Labrouste's students "received neither *médailles* nor *mentions*. . . . The students obtained no jobs anywhere. . . . Their teacher received nothing and just managed to get by on what his atelier brought in, because he had no private means," and members of the Academy "no longer considered him one of its students."[7]

Viollet-le-Duc claimed that Labrouste's ideas were "combatted" by the Academy, that he was "persecuted," "spurned," and "reduced to eking out the barest existence," that he was "doomed to ostracism," a sentence they only lifted near the end of his life.[8] Since, in his own view, Labrouste's radicality did not reside in his use of iron, then how can we explain all the fuss? Indeed, such a question goes right to the heart of the matter, for its response is equally a response to the limited appraisal of Labrouste's work by technologically oriented twentieth-century historians. For Giedion, "as in the English mills and warehouses, the iron construction of Labrouste's library is enclosed in the stonework of the exterior" but, unfortunately, "thick masonry walls still remain."[9] How, given Giedion's criterion, can one possibly distinguish between a rationally structured warehouse and Labrouste's first library? Indeed, given that criterion, Labrouste's work seems overladen with extraneous ornamental matter. But that was not the nineteenth-century view of the situation. Viollet-le-Duc described the art of architecture as the clothing of a structure with decorative artistic form: "*l'architecture, c'est . . . la structure revêtue d'une forme d'art.*"[10] Those forms of significant decoration should not be chosen from a restricted set of conventionalized correlatives for structure (the classical types) but should be derived from an analysis of the actual propensities of the materials and methods of construction in relation to the *idea* that the building is to express: "Art is the form given to an idea, and the artist the one who, in creating the form, succeeds in getting that very idea across to his fellow men."[11]

Meaningful expression was the real issue facing the nineteenth-century architect. The question of style was only a subset of that problem. With an apparently unlimited variety of forms available, the dilemma was how to ascribe meaning to any one, how to ensure its comprehension. For the classical architect, the limitations placed on what forms could be considered typical and appropriate circumscribed the content of those forms and ensured their signification. For the nineteenth-century architect, that ideal ground had been transgressed by a new consciousness of history, which undermined the classical illusion of a naturally based coherence of form and content. César Daly (1811–94), the founder of France's first and major architectural magazine, the *Revue Générale de l'Architecture et des Travaux Publics*, and its editor for fifty years, constantly proclaimed that the ideal classical concordance of form and content was no longer realizable, and that it had been just an article of absolutist faith all along:

> For a long time European societies have borrowed from the same source, antiquity. But as a result of this agreement in favor of the classical source, and due to an insufficient study of history, there developed a school claiming, in France perhaps more than elsewhere, to have formulated nothing less than the *absolute* doctrine of art . . . without regard for real life . . . , the country, the race, or the era . . . [or] the materials used; and thus the monuments of the age of Augustus were presented . . . as the only ones embodying the true principles.[12]

Daly described the classical doctrine as "false," "detrimental," and "boring" and claimed that up to 1830 it had had the most inhibitory effect on the expression of "real" meaning in architecture. In Daly's view the deposition of classicism had, by 1830, revealed to young architects the fundamental problem with which they had to cope: how to give meaning to forms once the denotative limits placed upon them by classical thought had been rendered meaningless. He described it in the following way:

> [Today] the forms that constitute a sort of alphabet of our art seem to have lost precise meaning, or at least to have no longer the same meaning for everybody.[13]
>
> . . . How times have changed for us architects, and how often painful is this situation for architecture!
>
> . . . Modern society, powerless to express through art a harmony among souls that no longer exists, and powerless to attribute a fixed meaning, the same for everybody, to the fundamental forms of architecture . . . [is] without the power to create, and is constrained to borrow.[14]

For Daly the answer did not lie in short-circuiting history. That would merely have compounded the erroneous classical belief in ideal and eternal truths, since this act of proscription would have become conscious. The answer lay in hooking up to all branches of the historical tree in the hopes of synthesizing some really fictitious, *i.e.*, artistic, harmony. Using forms inherited from the past while admitting them to be stripped of significance was the situation faced by nineteenth-century architects. The nineteenth century no longer felt that harmonious balance between form and content that was their definition of classicism and thus felt themselves to be cut off from the tradition of classicism.

There is no longer any use in considering any of the products of nineteenth-century architecture classical. To designate some as classical and some as not involves the same kind of historical schizophrenia as trying to understand such a building as the Bibliothèque Sainte-Geneviève without taking into account its deliberately *applied*, historically derived decorative forms. These forms describe its meaning and constitute its legible character. The very idea of formal application as a way of literally describing meaning in stone was an anti-classical procedure. In order to understand nineteenth-century French architecture we must dispense with the word classical as a descriptive term applying to style and, at the same time, accept its disinherited forms applied to buildings as supplying to them contextual meaning. We must begin to read history in, not out. The Beaux-Arts is neither as monolithic a structure nor as homogeneous a system of design as its classical appearance would lead one to believe.

The history of nineteenth-century French architecture is much more complex than we have previously wanted to admit. It has generally been assumed that French architecture underwent a major change in the eighteenth century during the pre-Revolutionary years and that nothing of consequence happened during the Romantic decades of the second quarter of the nineteenth century. Historians have assumed that eighteenth-century Neoclassicism, since called Romantic-Classicism, merely degenerated or, at the very least, was simply straightjacketed into an uneventful academic tenure throughout the following century. That misreading of history provided the veneer of classicism. Yet that is not how the nineteenth century itself perceived its own history. Julien Guadet, professor of theory at the Ecole des Beaux-Arts from 1894 until his death in 1908, would surely have liked to see the tradition of classicism, which he claimed to represent, as an unbroken chain of events. In his lectures, published in his *Eléments et théorie de l'architecture* (1901–04), even he was forced to admit the contrary to be true. He described French architecture of the early eighteenth century as signaling a change:

> Under the aging Louis XIV . . . the French mind had undergone a change; where there had been proud independence, there was now superstitious regard for authority, narrow devotion to the rules, the cult of despotism. . . .

and he saw the academicization of the classical ideal reach its conclusion in the nineteenth century and the school's modern tradition develop in the 1830s and '40s in reaction to that:

> For a century, and throughout the world, the arts, and above all architecture, have been enfeebled by their subordination to archaeology; . . . in almost every other country, architecture is nothing more than an archaeological expression, a servile adaptation of illogical anachronisms. . . . In Munich, they conjure up utilitarian Parthenons. . . .
>
> France alone finally resisted, and thus there is still a French school! Even we were about to fall asleep under the pneumatic engine. At the beginning of the century, the only aesthetic was to create, a priori, a Roman building—at least

that was the intention—till this Procrustean bed began to torture modern lives and requirements.... Happily, proud artists—our masters—saw and made us see that independence does not consist in a change of livery, and our art gradually set itself free from the prevailing paleontology.[15]

Guadet's first *maître d'atelier* was Henri Labrouste. He entered Labrouste's atelier in 1853 and remained there until the summer of 1856, when Labrouste, discouraged by the Academy's continued ostracism, finally decided to close it. By mid-1856, Guadet had not been promoted and had received only one *mention* in composition. He later explained that Labrouste's teaching totally rejected the classical idealism which, by the time Labrouste opened his atelier in 1830, had been codified into rigid formulae by such proponents of eighteenth-century Neoclassicism as Charles Percier, Louis-Pierre Baltard, Thomas Vaudoyer, Hippolyte Lebas, and J.-B.-C. Lesueur. Anarchy and confusion followed in the wake of Labrouste's overturning these values:

> [Henri Labrouste's atelier] created ... a revolutionary, sometimes anarchic school; ... he wanted to free his students from the livery of Percier's art ... which he himself ... proudly cast aside.
>
> ... They might not have always understood, but they became fanatic over what they thought they understood.... Where the teacher would express aesthetic dissent, his students readily conceived savage hatreds: Lebas, Lesueur were not leaders of another school, they were enemies capable of any crime, who out of sheer bad faith refused to renounce their errors. Had Labrouste wished their heads, I believe that they would have been brought to him the next day by a guileless enthusiast.[16]

The opening of Labrouste's atelier in 1830 was a response to the call of a group of students from the Vaudoyer-Lebas atelier who saw no meaning in what they were being taught there. Notwithstanding its major significance, the break was but one symptom of the development of a new attitude toward architecture, which both irrevocably sundered any connection between the nineteenth century and the classical past and revalued the meaning of classicism itself. The movement of which Labrouste was a part was considered throughout the nineteenth century to be the architectural counterpart to the Romantic revolution in painting and, most particularly, in literature: "Architecture, like the other arts, had its men of 1830.... The romanticism of architecture came to life in the very heart of our academized Ecole. The Dubans, the Ducs, the Vaudoyers, the Labroustes above all, set out to do battle with the official classicism and to force it to capitulate."[17]

Along with Labrouste, Félix Duban, Louis Duc, and Léon Vaudoyer were usually singled out as the leaders of that Romantic rebellion against the idealism of Neoclassicism. Although the style they developed could never be defined in simple historicist terms, its rationally expressive character came to be seen as the basis for all of later French architecture, whether medievalizing or classicizing in form. Throughout the middle four decades of the century, their work was called Romantic or Rationalist. By the end of the '60s, it came to be called *Néo-Grec*, which, as Charles Garnier remarked, "was Greek in name only."[18] The *Néo-Grec* was, above all, considered to be the "distinctive expression" of "modern" French architecture.[19] The appellation connoted a peculiar, almost indefinable synthesis of crypto-Gothic and quasi-classical qualities.[20] The *Néo-Grec* was viewed as a revival of the Greek spirit of rationally developed, emotionally charged expression rather than simply a reapplication of Greek forms. It appears to be more than coincidence that during the time when it was first developing, but before it received a stylistic definition, the term *néo-grec* was used to refer to Byzantine and Romanesque architecture.[21] In its frankly exposed arcuated form, descriptively surfaced by glittering, legible imagery, *néo-grec* architecture was considered to be the cradle of modern architecture. As a reaction against the Roman academicization of Greek forms, Byzantine architecture gave evidence of a true revival of the Greek spirit, if not of its forms.[22] The analogy between the earlier *néo-grec* and the later *Néo-Grec* was based on their similar transitional characters, each being seen as a moment of change from a revived though moribund classicism to a more fully developed stage of Gothicism.[23]

In an article first published in 1861 in *Atlantic Monthly* and republished thirty-two years later as the first article of a book with the same title, *Greek Lines*, Henry Van Brunt described the *Néo-Grec* as having liberated French architectural training and practice from the restricting rules of classicism:

> One of the most remarkable peculiarities of this school was that it seemed to encourage the expression of individual traits in architects; . . . and to free the spirit of the designers from the impediments of conventionalism. Indeed, when Greek lines were first received in the Paris *ateliers*, the architects were so much impressed by the freedom which the use of these lines gave to all the processes of design, when compared with the restrictions of practice under the Roman academic system, that the new dispensation was called a style, and christened Romantique, to distinguish it from what was conventionally called classic. . . .
>
> The neo-Grec . . . [was] confined to no rigid types of external form. . . .[24]

The term Greek lines referred to the unconventional, astringently expressive means by which *Néo-Grec* surfaces were given a precise narrative content:

> Antique prejudices, bent into rigid conformity with antique rubrics, are often shocked at the strange innovations of these new Dissenters from the faith of Palladio and Philibert Delorme, shocked at the naked humanity in the new works, and would cover it with the conventional fig-leaves prescribed in the homilies of Vignola. Laymen, accustomed to the cold proprieties of the old Renaissance, and habituated to the formalities of the five orders, the prudish decorum of Italian window-dressings and pediments and pilasters and scrolls, are apt to be surprised at such strange dispositions of unprecedented and hereti-

cal features, that the intention of the building in which they occur is at once patent to the most casual observer, and the story of its destination told with the eloquence of a poetical and monumental language. . . . the blessed renovations of the *Romantique* . . . [sweep] away the dust and cobwebs which ages of prejudice have spread thickly around the magnificent art of architecture.[25]

Van Brunt declared that the *Néo-Grec* had "an influence far more thorough and healthy than had hitherto been experienced in the whole history of Art."[26] That is a pretty powerful statement. It can only be understood if one accepts the fact that the *Néo-Grec* meant the replacement of classicism by a new way of thinking about architectural form and content.

The *Néo-Grec* reaction against classicism was (1) a rejection of the classical containment of generic meaning in the exclusive forms of one style or set of types; (2) a replacement of ideal nature by real history as a more inclusive source for forms; and (3) a systematic rather than mythological view of history. Consequently, *Néo-Grec* architects were the first to make the radical distinction between structural principle and decorative form. In demanding that forms of decoration be rationally induced from the materials and methods of construction as well as from the specifications of the program, the *Néo-Grec* architects acknowledged the distinction between appearance and reality as simply a matter of fact, and therefore saw the process of design as the *decoration of construction*. This contravened the classical belief in appearance as reality, wherein the process of design was seen as the *construction of decoration*. The classical ideal of apparent formal homogeneity was replaced by the reality of structural differentiation. The classical belief in the inherent content of apparently consistent forms was replaced by a discursive application of forms that could only take on adherent meaning in context.

The fundamental change was the replacement of the rhetorical form of classical architectural discourse by a more literal and descriptive syntax of form. The ground for its figures of speech was legibility rather than eloquence. Eloquence was a byproduct of the elegant application of those figures of speech to the idea of the building they were called upon to express, and all illusions were rendered real by their allusions to history. In acknowledging a basic disjunction between form and content, the substantiality of structure and the insubstantiality of clothing form, the *Néo-Grec* offered a new literary syntax of expression, which answered the nineteenth century's profoundly moving realization that it was no longer possible to embody ideas in eternally meaningful forms.

The sources and evolution of the *Néo-Grec* are complex and have not yet been historically documented. At the time, the movement was felt to be a "bolt from the blue," a development "without precedents."[27] Three events, however, were usually singled out in describing its intersection with and effect upon the training and practice of architecture. Its emergence in projects by students at the Ecole was claimed by Van Brunt to have happened well after its initial impulse had been felt elsewhere:

> For some time the designs of the new school were not recognized in the competitions of the Ecole des Beaux-Arts; but when, in the course of Nature, some two or three of the more strenuous and bigoted professors of Palladio's golden rules were removed from the scene of contest, the *Romantique* [*Néo-Grec*] ... was received at length into the bosom of the architectural church, and now [1861] it may be justly deemed *the distinctive architectural expression of French Art.*[28]

Van Brunt was referring to the coeval deaths in 1846 of Louis-Pierre Baltard, professor of theory at the Ecole since 1818, and Thomas Vaudoyer, Secrétaire Archiviste of the Ecole and, in collaboration with his nephew Hippolyte Lebas, a leading *patron* in the earlier part of the century. It was they, along with other classicists of their generation, who were most shocked by the first public manifestation of *Néo-Grec* ideas, Henri Labrouste's fourth-year *envoi* from the French Academy in Rome. Van Brunt considered his restoration of the temples of Paestum of 1828–29 to have been the crucial event:

> Labrouste ... surprised the grave professors of the Academy, Le Bas, Baltard, and the rest, by presenting ... carefully elaborated drawings of the temples. ... Witnessing, with pious horror, the grave departures from their rules contained in the drawings of their former favorite, they charged him with error.

But what Labroust had perceived was, as Van Brunt noted, "a remarkable freedom from the restraints of his school" on which "was founded the new Renaissance in France."[29]

The *Néo-Grec* idea of literary expression first achieved form in Labrouste's Bibliothèque Sainte-Geneviève (p. 335). Until Garnier's Opéra (pp. 432–41), this building was considered to be the most important work produced by the young Romantic generation and had the most profound effect on all subsequent architectural design in France. In 1893, Van Brunt wrote that "most of the important buildings which have been erected in France within the last fifty years" were based on *Néo-Grec* thought.[30] The choice of fifty years was not fortuitous, for the Bibliothèque Sainte-Geneviève was begun in 1843 and, by 1861, Van Brunt described it as "the most important work with pure Greek lines, and perhaps the most exquisite, while it is one of the most serious of modern buildings."[31] He saw "the lore of the classics and the knowledge of the natural world, idealized and harmonized by affectionate study, ... built up in its walls" so that "*internally* and *externally*, it is a work of the highest Art."[32] Student projects from 1847 to 1853 directly reflect the way in which Labrouste first applied *Néo-Grec* thought to the reconstitution of architectural meaning in stone and iron. It was, significantly, in 1847 that the construction of the Bibliothèque Sainte-Geneviève was completed, both internally and externally, and that he turned his thoughts to its decoration. That surface retold the "lore of the classics" in a new form—one first realistically outlined in his restoration of Paestum of almost twenty years before. The *Néo-Grec*, as Labrouste showed, demands a reading of its decorative surfaces.

* * *

Throughout the past century and a quarter, the Bibliothèque Sainte-Geneviève has been seen as a strange mixture of a portentous modernism clothed in retrogressively historical forms. Its exterior *(opposite)* has been likened to the Doge's Palace in Venice, Alberti's Tempio Malatestiano in Rimini, and Michelozzo's *quattrocento* Banco Mediceo in Milan; whereas the interior of its reading room (p. 345) has usually been compared to the thirteenth-century Gothic refectory of the former Abbaye de Saint-Martin-des-Champs in Paris. It is all of these and none of these. The inscribed inset panels of its facing give it the appearance of a late Egyptian temple like the one of Hathor at Denderah. The cool, dark, illusionistically open space of its vestibule (p. 341) is like an Egyptian hypostyle hall, with its ceiling, depicting a sky, raised above the piers on impost blocks. With the upper spaces between the piers of its side walls filled with illusionistic paintings of trees, forming a background for the procession of busts of famous authors, artists, and scientists, the vestibule is also like a classical stoa or, more precisely, like one depicted in a Pompeian interior. The planes of the exterior facing of the building illusionistically flip in and out like those in Roman wall paintings. The rear wall of the stairwell carries on its surface a full-scale copy by the Balze brothers of Raphael's *School of Athens*. And the reading room itself, girded round by its continuous arcade, can be seen not only as a Gothic "vessel" but also as a canvas-canopied version of the French Renaissance court of the Château at Saint-Germain-en-Laye, which in turn might be understood by reference to the fourth-year restoration of the interior of the Roman Colosseum by Labrouste's colleague Louis Duc (p. 166). The historical indicators of the meaning of Labrouste's library are disconcertingly legion. No one stylistic container really works.

Labrouste was appointed architect of the Bibliothèque Sainte-Geneviève on June 6, 1838. On November 29, he was commissioned to design a new building for the former Bibliothèque des Génovéfains, which until then was located on the upper floor of the Lycée Henri IV directly behind the Panthéon to the east.[33] Prior to the Revolution, it had been the home of the Couvent des Génovéfains. The site given to Labrouste, on the north flank of the Place du Panthéon, was extremely long and narrow. The building is approximately 278 by 69 feet. It is 19 bays long and 4 bays wide, established on a grid of 13 feet 11 inches on-center. The "exiguity" of the site, as Labrouste himself said, allowed for no possibility of a forecourt, which, "planted with big trees and decorated with statues," might have been "laid out in front of the building, to shield it from the noise of the street outside and prepare those who came

Henri Labrouste. Bibliothèque Sainte-Geneviève, Paris. 1838–50.

In 1838, eight years after his return from a sojourn in Rome as a Grand Prix laureate, Henri Labrouste received his first major appointment as architect of the Bibliothèque Sainte-Geneviève. He seems to have settled fairly quickly on a general *parti* but experimented with both stone and iron vaults, details of the facade, and made constant alterations of details as the building was erected.

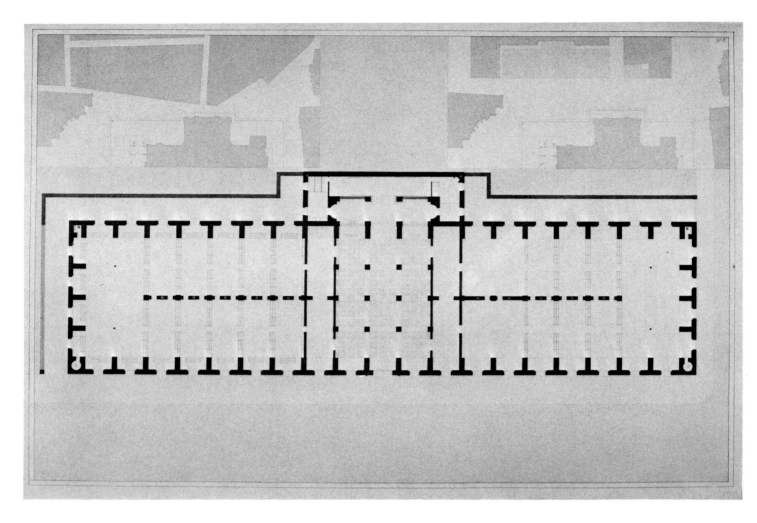

Labrouste. Bibliothèque Sainte-Geneviève, Paris. *(above)* Site plan and plan of ground floor; *(opposite)* plan of second floor. 1850. Bibliothèque Nationale, Paris.

The lower story houses the library stacks; the reading room is on the upper floor.

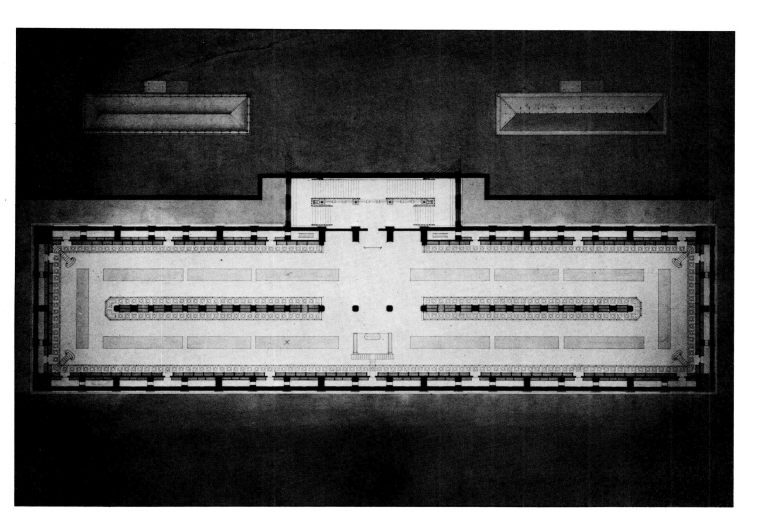

there for contemplation."[34] Instead, Labrouste decorated the deep vestibule of the library itself as an illusionistic garden, which, in his words, would have "the advantage of offering trees always green and always in bloom . . . without regard for the climate of Paris . . . in this fertile soil of the imagination."[35] That imaginative dematerialization of the structure was only designed in 1847–48 and executed in the following two years. It is but one part of Labrouste's decorative program, which gives meaning to a construction that was rationally determined by its site and materials.

It was in response to the constricted site that Labrouste immediately arrived at his *parti* of a long narrow rectangle encased by a double tier of continuous closed arcades that are self-buttressing (pp. 336–37). Externally, the ground-level arcade is masked; the upper arcade is rendered half-blind by panels slightly inset. In the reading room the piers are perpendicularly posed to the main volume of space, which is delineated by a single spine of cast-iron columns down its center. In what surely must be the first jotting down of that premise, two sketch plans on the back of a letter postmarked November 28, 1838, the *parti* was immediately defined.[36] Given the site but also given the fact that Labrouste could easily have vaulted the space without internal supports, his decision to divide the room in half with a central spine of columns suggests a predilection for the plan-type represented by such Greek temples as Hera I at Paestum and such utilitarian accommodations as the Gothic refectory. For Labrouste, the appropriateness of such a solution would have been reinforced by the fact that in the same year, 1838, his friend Léon Vaudoyer was planning to restore the refectory of the former Abbaye de Saint-Martin-des-Champs as the library of the Conservatoire des Arts et Métiers (executed 1845–52). In a series of further sketches and studies dating from 1838–39, Labrouste never veered from the *parti*, but connected it with the idea of using iron for its internal supports. It had been decided by the Minister of Public Education, Salvandy, that the library would be open at night and therefore be lit by gas. The use of iron was obviously an answer to the problem of fireproofing. But, as Labrouste explained when he submitted his project, that was only a secondary, partial reason.[37] His prime reason was spatial. He wanted the main reading room to be open, evenly lit in the daytime, and well-ventilated. The open arcades of masonry let in light from all four sides. As a continuous, Roman viaduct-like series of fins set perpendicular to the space, they cut down the glare, and like an internalized row of Gothic buttresses, they provide a minimal sense of encasement. The internal iron supports are as dematerialized as in any Gothic hall and allow for a spatial and psychological freedom in the reading room, which fully occupies the upper floor.

The stairwell, reached through the vestibule, which cuts the library in half on the ground floor, is merely a box tacked onto the rear (p. 324). The idea of a centrally located spine of columns was Labrouste's way of giving to the

Labrouste. Bibliothèque Sainte-Geneviève, Paris. Elevation detail and section of wall. 1850. Bibliothèque Nationale, Paris.

The building comprises two stories, expressed on the exterior as a simple base into which windows are cut, and as an arcade partially filled with screen walls. The names of authors inscribed on the screen walls provide an idealized representation of the contents of the library, which is ranged on shelves behind the walls.

Labrouste. Bibliothèque Sainte-Geneviève, Paris. *(above)* Elevation and section of vestibule wall. 1850. Bibliothèque Nationale, Paris. *(right)* Vestibule.

Labrouste used decoration to make a significant journey of the passage from the street to the reading room. Lamps flanking the entrance suggest knowledge, as well as the fact that the library was the first in Paris to be gaslit and therefore open at night. The vestibule, with its mural decorations of trees and trellis-like ironwork, serves, as Labrouste noted, to recreate the real garden through which he would have liked readers to pass as they entered the library.

Labrouste. Bibliothèque Sainte-Geneviève, Paris. Vestibule.

One enters through the center of the lower story, traverses the depth of the building through the vestibule, and mounts the stairs to reach the reading room.

volume of the reading room a modulation that would be utilitarian in quality and a definition that would be secular and nonhierarchical in character.

The project that Labrouste submitted just about one year after the commission was an outline of his basic idea for the building. It would only be rendered once the construction was completed. Labrouste finished the set of plans for the library on December 15, 1839, and submitted his project to the Ministry of Public Works on December 19. It was reviewed by the Conseil des Bâtiments Civils in January 1840, and approved by the Conseil at that time. Because of a lack of funds, however, the project was shelved until 1842.

Labrouste's unaltered project for the Bibliothèque Sainte-Geneviève was finally submitted and approved by the legislature in 1843. Work was begun on August 1, 1843, and all masonry construction was substantially completed by November 26, 1846. In May 1846, Labrouste began studying the question of the iron structure that was to form the main floor, and work on it was completed, except for the vestibule, in the following year. Labrouste began designing the iron skeleton that was to be the exposed framework of the reading room on September 19, 1846. Throughout the winter of 1846–47, he produced a number of studies in which he elaborated its form, working from his original idea of a round arch within a gable, which he then heightened by a clerestory, until he arrived finally at the form of a double arch supporting two barrel vaults (p. 344). On-site construction began on August 3, 1847. The vaults and the roof were completed by early 1848.

It was only at this point that Labrouste turned his attention to the question of defining the iconographic program of the building by designing the carved and painted images that were to be incised in or applied to its structural surfaces. Between late 1847 and December 1850, when the building was turned over to the Ministry of Public Education, Labrouste designed and had executed the inscribed names of authors on the upper panels of the facade; the garland that defines the full extent of its lower story; the black cast-iron paterae that bolt the lower and upper stone surfaces to the internal iron structure; the iron arches, painted impost-blocks, illusionistic trees and sky, and busts of the vestibule; the painted and stuccoed decoration of the stairwell, the dedicatory plaque, and the copy of the *School of Athens* on its rear wall; and the painting of the voussoirs of the arches of the stone arcade and plaster vault of the reading room as well as the heads of Night and Day carved into the stone piers that anchor the iron columns of the reading room in place. All this was done *in situ*, by eye, so to speak. It was not until the cast bronze door of the library actually was put in place, between August 23 and 28, 1850, that Labrouste worked out the final designs for the illusionistic "lamps of learning" that were to be carved on the jambs of the entrance. That final touch was completed just about four months before the library was opened to the public on February 4, 1851.

Labrouste. Bibliothèque Sainte-Geneviève, Paris. *(above)* Elevation and section of Reading Room. 1850. Bibliothèque Nationale, Paris. *(right)* Reading Room.

The Bibliothèque Sainte-Geneviève has often been viewed in this century as an innovative iron structure, hidden in a stone shell whose "conservatism" was demanded by the times. It is clear that Labrouste saw the building as a whole made up of parts necessarily different in character. Yet the exterior and interior intermesh and complement one another, with the piers of the exterior arcade becoming the buttresses of the interior iron structure, and with the iron structure bolted to the facade by paterae which become part of the exterior decorative scheme, illusionistically supporting stone garlands. Rather than being simply an example of technical progress or stylistic stasis, the library is Labrouste's solution to the problem of the institutional building, which by its form, arrangement, and decoration conveys the manner and meaning of its use.

The Bibliothèque Sainte-Geneviève was immediately perceived as "the work of a reformist . . . [a work that], from the point of view of progress in the art, is a major creation, the most important without question among all those completed within recent years."[38] It never received from architects and critics the same unanimity of approval accorded Garnier's later Opéra. Ironically, just that which was felt by many observers at the time to be lacking in its conception, a classical gravity and pomp, was just what most twentieth-century historians have seen as compromising its modernism. César Daly, who as editor of the *Revue Générale de l'Architecture* was a fervent supporter of Labrouste and the spokesman for the *Néo-Grec* movement, called the library not only a "monument, but a fundamental work."[39] Félix Pigeory, a student of Leclère at the Ecole in the mid-1830s, stated, in his more conservative *Revue des Beaux-Arts*, that "M. Labrouste outbids his confreres by a bizarre mixture [of forms]."[40] In describing the building in the *Paris-Guide* of 1867, Théodore de Banville remarked that at the time of its completion "M. Labrouste was often branded with the epithet 'fantasist' " and de Banville offered the opinion that that was because there is "something of the primitive" about the building which "perforce makes an abstraction of known styles."[41] Whether liked or disliked, it was this quality of anti-classical stylophobia, expressed in the library's realistic form, that disturbed or appealed to most critics. The critic F. Barrière wrote in the *Journal des Débats* on December 31, 1850: "And the exterior effect! . . . It is something else again, that exterior, it has a look you have to get used to." "To each building, a style, a character, forms in relation to its purpose. That is what M. Henri Labrouste has grasped so wisely."[42] The critic for *The Builder* wrote in 1850:

> It is a curiosity of its kind, being quite original in design, and not to be compared to any other building that we are acquainted with. The facade is simple—we would say plain—having little ornament and less variety, and is relieved almost solely by the multitude of names of celebrated authors, of all times and countries, which are cut in tablets let into the walls on every side, and nearly covering them. . . . Above and below . . . are festoons of flowers . . . : beyond this nothing can exceed the severe plainness and originality of the building.
>
> We might find fault—who cannot? who has not? But so long as there is no glaring impropriety of style, so long as proportion is not absolutely outraged, . . . we feel that we ought to be pleased at the effort. The edifice is peculiar, is original—and we like it for that. It will not please everybody, how can it?—when one is enamoured with the Gothic, another with the Grecian, a third with the Roman or Italian . . . ! We would rather see [as here] a little more originality than that interminable system of copying, which, by enforcing strict rule, and limiting within certain bounds, what is boundless and ever varying, drags genius always in the mire of imitation. . . . It is time to be tolerant in all things, in order to be more perfect, more exact, and more capable.[43]

In January 1851, Henry Trianon, who was later to become the administrator of the Bibliothèque Sainte-Geneviève, gave the following layman's opinion in *L'Illustration:* "If we take the exterior of the new Bibliothèque Sainte-Geneviève as grounds for judgment, M. Labrouste, who is accused of an exaggerated taste for innovation—let us be blunt, for romanticism—seems not at all to disdain the fundamental rules of the architectonic tradition."[44] But Trianon was really more in the know than that, because at the time he was a librarian at the Bibliothèque Sainte-Geneviève. He had known Labrouste throughout the construction of the building, and his explanation of the work must surely be taken as a statement of Labrouste's own intentions:

> He is of the opinion that originality consists even more in the use than in the creation of forms. But he does not believe . . . that the law and the prophets are contained in Vitruvius and in Barozzi da Vignola, and that outside their two names there is no salvation. To him, all architecture, subject only to conditions relating to the customs and climate specific to each country, seems a single field where no flower may be systematically disdained. . . . He gives free rein to the genius of the artist.[45]

Labrouste's Romantic openness to all of history and his rational concentration on the principles taught by history rather than its rules and forms gave to the new library an allure of composure and a diagrammatic leanness that could no longer be considered classical. He had replaced eighteenth-century classical eclecticism by a new and more positive form of syncretism. The fusion of forms and meaning involved in that new equation made the building appear simple yet hermetic. Later, A.-N. Bailly, who replaced Labrouste at the Academy in 1875, remarked that upon completion "the work produced a sense of astonishment that gave rise to a wide divergence of opinions."[46] Echoing Bailly, Emile Trélat wrote that "public opinion seized upon his monument and let bursts of passions rule its judgment. He had fanatic admirers and fanatic detractors. The work deserved this two-fold explosion."[47]

One might conclude from all these critiques that Labrouste's library was of such an astonishing new simplicity and plainness that most people debated its merits or demerits in terms of the classical criteria by which it was supposedly informed without being able to interpret the new informational process on which its significance rested. Such a conclusion is more or less reinforced by Achille Hermant's puzzled review of the building written for *L'Artiste* soon after it was finished.[48] He found the facade's repetitive inscriptions "rather puerile" and "something shocking" about the contrasts in the materialistic expression of the vestibule. He blamed this on Labrouste's too "rigorous" adherence to the *Néo-Grec* doctrine "that architecture is nothing but decorated construction." He thought that by refusing to admit the a priori and ideal power of certain forms to represent the exalted idea of a library as a temple of learning, Labrouste had "transgressed certain imprescriptible rules":

The character of a building cannot be measured only by its purpose; the idea it represents in the eyes of the public is part of it, the essential part of it. Materially speaking, a library can be merely a place in which to store books . . . ; but is that all? Certainly not; for it is also a place containing the noblest of riches; the treasury where the most precious possessions of mankind are kept, the works of genius. . . . And, in an age where men are drawn to knowledge, as they once were drawn to faith, perhaps there is no monument of a higher order. Is it that the artist failed to endow his creation with the grandiose character that so great a program demands? That is what, I think, the public instinctively reproaches him for.

Hermant claimed that the public "sees and feels before it reasons" and that Labrouste did not provide enough traditional indices of stylistic coherence for the public to be able to understand the library. For them, it had to be based on a preconceived image of a temple of learning. Consequently, the qualities by which its character is expressed "are, in a way, to be appreciated only by the initiate."

The hermeticism of expression that resulted from Labrouste's most rigorous application of *Néo-Grec* principles provoked an immediate reaction by Louis Duc, one of Labrouste's former colleagues in Rome. His Vestibule des Assises (the Salle de Harlay) for the Palais de Justice, with its major facade on the Place Dauphine (pp. 428–29), was a conscious critique of Labrouste's library. By giving plasticity to Labrouste's conception, with the superposition of a giant Order as an explicitly applied character of style over a paneled, arcuated substructure, Duc consciously acknowledged Labrouste's precedent and, to a second generation of more conservative young architects such as Garnier and André, showed how to overcome what they felt to be the flatness and inertness of Labrouste's work. The Vestibule was designed in 1856 and begun in 1857. In a letter of 1856, written perhaps to Duban, Duc described his own intention as a reaction to Labrouste's work:

My esteem and admiration for the arch are not less vivid than for the Order; it is just that they are of a totally different nature.

First, I set forth as a principle that one must not take the place of the other: the Order belongs to poetry, it is lyrical, it speaks nobly, declaims and sings.

The arch belongs to prose, it is positive, it toils, serves and carries.

The Order is noble, it is a master, it commands; the arch is plebeian, a servant, it obeys.

The arch is nothing in itself as a term of art. It counts only when a new element, alien to it, is superimposed, the ornamentation. . . .

By itself, the arch is powerless to constitute an architecture; the arch is only a means of construction. . . .

. . . the poetry of the Order [must] come to complement the material necessity of the arch. . . .

If one were to grant the equivalence of the Order and the arch, and not the supremacy of the former over the latter, then, utilitarian demands being constantly present, the realm at first shared would pass exclusively to the arch and make one forget the artistic law of the Order. . . .

. . . Without the Order, what could our monuments be? . . .

For once the Order is suppressed, what confusion results! The strangest proportions, . . . an incoherent ensemble which might for an instant stun . . . the eye, but never charm it.

. . . Without these last vestiges of poetic essence, only inert material masses would remain.[49]

Louis Duc's Vestibule des Assises clearly revivifies Labrouste's Bibliothèque Sainte-Geneviève, but it does so by an applied device, the colossal Hellenistic Order. Duc admitted the Order to be but a "fiction" or "lie" and yet claimed it to be the "essence" of architecture.[50] He rejected the classical idea that the Order was the outcome of a process of "imitation" and claimed it to be merely a "fictional translation" of an idea of grandeur and nobility. Such a self-conscious, prosaic understanding of the "vestigial, poetic" content of the Order can only be understood as a post-classical act of reattribution of meaning.

Labrouste's library was the first French building to discard the Order, or any of its surrogate forms, as the means for ordering a building. In the vestibule, the tall stolid piers are "shockingly" contrasted to what Hermant called the "meagerness" of the cast-iron arches. As those are segments of an extremely large circle, they take the illusionistic form of a beam consistent with the hypostylar image of the whole and thereby seem all the more disproportionate. In the reading room, the willowy cast-iron columns have their capitals set not at 90° to the space but rather diagonally in relation to the lines of the arches. This crypto-Gothic definition reinforces one's perception of the columns as dropped anchor-lines rather than gravity-resisting supports.

On the facade, Labrouste's rejection of the subsuming and singular power of the Order is perhaps less obvious. In his report to the Conseil des Bâtiments Civils in January 1840, when the project was reviewed, the Inspecteur-Général Auguste Caristie claimed that the building lacked a certain homogeneity and gravity of style because it did not appear to be of a single piece.[51] He felt that the ground floor and the upper floor had no plastically ordered connection one to the other—an apt observation—and he suggested Labrouste correct that fault. It was never corrected by Labrouste, who obviously intended the building to be read that way. To him, the ordering of parts was not plastically revealed in the overall image of any one fictive unifying force. Where that would normally occur in a classical building, at the corners or at the entrance, Labrouste purposely denied such a reading. The entrance (p. 335) is merely a cut in the lower wall, an ellipsis or punctuation break. The covering plane of the ground floor is merely a revetment clamped into place by the cast-iron paterae and strung along the extent of the street by the line of the attached garland. At the corner, it becomes clear that the plane is only an extended surface veiling the really abstract and underlying order of the building. At the corner, the plane of the lowering revetting wall turns sharply and the swag is distended in space. The revealed pier of the upper arcade emerges into view behind that lower plane at exactly the same depth as that described by the window reveals of the lower story. It thus becomes clear that the upper arcade is merely the revealed, opened-up version of the supporting lower arcade, which in reality is the background support to which the facing of the lower story is attached. Everything about the structure of the building is thereby made known without being plastically represented in fictional equivalents. That had been the power and purpose of the Order or any of its surrogate forms such as quoining. Set between the porticoes of Soufflot's Faculté de Droit and Panthéon, the stretched skin of the library is both a thin casing and the descriptive edge of a porous volume. It is as if the *scena frons* were pulled aside to allow the real drama of a wall to take place on its own terms, as Hugo demanded for the drama itself:

> What could be more unbelievable or more absurd than that . . . peristyle . . . that banal spot where our tragedies obligingly take place. . . . On the stage what we see in a way is only the elbows of the action; its hands are elsewhere. . . . Grave characters, placed like the ancient chorus between the drama and us, come to tell us what is happening in the temple, in the palace . . . so that we are often tempted to cry out, "Really! Well then take us there! That is where the fun must be, it must be worth seeing!" To which the answer would certainly be, "Maybe you would be amused or interested, but that is not the point; we are the guardians of the dignity of the French Melpomene." There you are![52]

In his Preface to *Cromwell* of 1827, Victor Hugo described the need to relieve theater of its conventional forms of representation, based as they were on the three unities of time, place, and action, to allow the real story to be told in its own terms. Daly, as we shall see, related the Romantic rejection of the three unities to the denial of the unifying power of the Orders. The Order was to classical architecture what the "grave character" was to classical theater; the peristyle was the interlocutory chorus. The Order gave the classical building its nobility and unified its theme by the modal inflection of character it represented. In the Bibliothèque Sainte-Geneviève, Labrouste was the first to show that the content of architecture could no longer be the plastically qualified transformation of the word into stone but just its literal transcription—the descriptive naming on its surface of the actual content of thought contained therein in books of printed words. As Labrouste himself said, the principal exterior decoration of the library became the word, not the Order, and its interior decoration, the books:

On the building's facade, in the part of the upper story corresponding to the interior shelves containing the books, are inscribed in large characters the names of the principal authors and writers whose works are preserved in the library. This monumental catalogue is the principal decoration of the facade, just as the books themselves are the most beautiful ornament of the interior.[53]

There are 27 inscribed panels: 4 on the west face, 19 across the south, and 4 on the east face. In all, they contain 810 names. Labrouste conceived the idea for decorating the exterior facing of the reading room bookshelves shortly after the popular uprising known as the June Days had overturned the Provisional Government, which had taken over power from Louis-Philippe in the February Revolution of 1848. On August 1, 1848, Labrouste formally submitted to the Minister of Public Works a proposal to inscribe the 27 panels with the names of authors of books contained in the library collection. This idea was approved on August 24, and the job was begun by the *sculpteur-graveur* Deutsch on September 30. Deutsch completed the task on November 21, two and a half weeks after the promulgation of the Constitution of the Second Republic (November 4). At the same time, Deutsch also inscribed the date "1848" on the small stone patera in the keystone of the arched entrance.

The first name on the first panel at the northwest corner of the library is Moses. The last name on the last panel at the northeast corner of the library is that of the Swedish chemist Berzelius, who died in 1848. The inscriptions thereby circumscribe on the library's three visible faces the entire history of the world from monotheism to scientism. The 409th name, directly over the central date 1848, is that of the Byzantine writer and professor of philosophy, Psellus (1018–79). Considered the "prince of philosophers," he was the forerunner of the Renaissance Neoplatonists. His name thus marks the meeting of East and West and locates it temporally at the millenium. The name "Psellus" marks the central historical stage of metaphysics which, as Auguste Comte outlined in his *Discours sur l'ensemble du positivisme* of July 1848, succeeded that of monotheism and preceded that of scientism.

The 810 inscribed names on Labrouste's library illustrate a democratic all-inclusiveness. The date 1848 gave the whole a Republican definition soon after the Second Republic's Constitution was actually drawn up. The continuous panels are contained within repetitive arches like those of a Roman aqueduct of the Republican period. The panels themselves are inscribed like the sides of the Roman perpetual calendar that Labrouste had seen and drawn in the Museum of Naples in 1826. (The calendar is a solid marble block perpetually reminding the observer of the closed cycle of the natural seasons.) Labrouste's inscribed panels face an open volume and transcribe onto its exposed faces the progressive development of historical change. The meaning of that progress is open to all who can read.

Just six months after Deutsch finished carving the name of Berzelius, Auguste Comte launched his religion of humanity in April 1849, with the publication of a *Calendrier positiviste ou système général de commémoration publique destiné surtout à la transition finale de la grande république occidentale.* As finally incorporated in his *Catéchisme positiviste* of 1852, it was a new calendar that, in graphic form, was intended to provide the adherents to his religion with a new verbal catechism "ou Tableau Concret de la Préparation Humaine."[54] Each month was "rechristened" with the name of one of history's most important figures. The first month was called *Moïse.* Each day was also given the name of a great man. The last month, that of the scientists, was named *Bichat,* and *Berzelius* was the twentieth of Bichat. In the form of a Socratic dialogue between the priest of the religion of humanity and a new woman convert, Comte had the priest, in his *Catéchisme positiviste,* explain that by the daily consultation of the calendar, she would learn the historical law of evolution, and it would reveal to her the constant progress of humanity toward a more universal understanding of man's own divine nature "as we are being led toward a greater synthesis . . . [and] to becoming more capable of sympathy."[55]

Comte's "concrete guide" to human progress is simply a series of names — words with adherent meanings — which, like those inscribed on the surface of Labrouste's library, were supposed to call forth an associated intellectual-emotional response. The freedom of the present was to be achieved in the mnemonic presence of the past. The form of the discourse is ventriloquistic, infusing new meaning into the mute images culled from the past. The parallel with the nineteenth-century architect's use of a vocabulary of historically derived forms for the same purpose is obvious. Comte's calendar was supposed to function by actual pronouncement. On the printed page, it looks like the extended form of Labrouste's facade. Like Comte, Labrouste offered his pantheonic lesson in stone as words to be read. It is significant that all the historical forms that Labrouste used to give meaning to his library were, like words imprinted on paper, added to the blank surfaces of the building's structure after its actual construction had been completed.

The idea of using inscriptions on a building was not new in 1848. Boullée and Durand among others had also covered some of their revolutionary projects with words and names, but they used the idea as a rhetorical device, replacing the Order in effect. To Labrouste, it was the less rhetorical form of literary expression, as revealed in the abstract, rational, and reflexive relationship between the printed word and its adherent meaning, that was intended to dominate architectonic form. The abstract relationships between the discrete elements of his facade are defined as the content of the construction. Almost all critics at the time understood this. They all remarked on the way the exterior translates with absolute fidelity the interior arrangement:

how the lower revetting wall is a protective encasing; how the inset panels of the upper arcade denote the backsides of the bookshelves; how the names inscribed on the surface externalize those on the spines of the books; and how the horizontal friezes and little wedged windows describe the actual hollow wall construction, where, between the piers of the arcade, a service passage and extra bookshelf space are located (p. 339). The little windows light the passage; the lower frieze marks the point where the gallery level abuts the panel; and the upper frieze indicates the top of the bookshelves placed against the panel on the gallery level.

The descriptive expression of the library is not that simple, however; otherwise it would not have demanded, as Hermant said, a specially initiated audience to understand it. One of the initiates in the *Néo-Grec* circle was Léon Danjoy, whom Trélat described as wanting to "make stone speak as a book speaks" (p. 408). In what must surely be taken as a drawing representing his impressions of the Bibliothèque Sainte-Geneviève, Danjoy revealed that the building was understood by some to have a much more complicated meaning (p. 354). He gave the drawing to Labrouste, probably soon after the library was completed.[56] It was an imaginative response to a poetic stimulus, a *composition* not intended for building, but rather created in reaction to a built idea. In its recomposed form, one of the figures (Danjoy?) appears to be explaining its meaning to the other (Labrouste?). Or is it the other way around? Everything in Danjoy's drawing is fused. The caryatids along the inset side walls are posed like those of the Erectheion, but they are Egyptoid in scale. The scale of the whole is weird and very similar to that of Labrouste's vestibule. The caryatids support medieval turrets. Between the figures, as in the library's vestibule, are painted depictions of trees. Below that level a Byzantinoid row of saints replaces Labrouste's classical busts. The upper turrets are Etruscan red; the caryatids are pale yellow limestone. The female figures at the far end, who guard the bronze doors opening into the treasure-house of books, are elongated fusions of the Hera of Samos and the twelfth-century statue-columns on the west facade of Chartres. All the caryatids seem to float like mermaids and to be connected to their grounds by a watery veil of seaweed. They are, like the piers in the library's vestibule, disconnected from the ceiling, which here is an iron-and-glass roof open to the sky.

Danjoy's imagery is an elaboration and thus an explanation of Labrouste's. He saw the whole building in terms of "that fertile soil of the imagination," which Labrouste could only allow himself to enter discreetly. Yet, even there, the fluidity of Danjoy's *composition* is undercut by the more basic *Néo-Grec* distinction between construction and decoration that could never in reality permit an organic image of movement and life. In Danjoy's drawing, the discontinuities between vertical supports, horizontal partitions, and overhead release are ultimately not too different from the library's more materially

Léon Danjoy. Architectural Composition. Undated. Private collection, Paris.

Among the Romantic architects and their followers, Léon Danjoy was famous as a great draftsman of architectural fantasies. This watercolor drawing, dedicated to his friend Henri Labrouste, is similar in conception to the illusionistic and symbolic decoration of the vestibule at the Bibliothèque Sainte-Geneviève. It appears to have been inspired by the library, for through the open door at the rear of the great hall one can glimpse part of a vast set of bookshelves.

grounded distinctions of parts. Both are really mechanistic images, powerful and overriding. Danjoy's purely mental operation allowed him more freedom for fusion. His drawing condenses into one multilayered volume what in Labrouste's library actually takes place in a spatial sequence. Danjoy's *composition* recreates Labrouste's vestibule as a volume set within a more open framework. That preliminary space is, like Labrouste's vestibule, a dark preparatory narthex. It is a protectively guarded chamber like a cave. It barely reveals the institutional holdings of books behind the great bronze doors. It is, again like Labrouste's vestibule, an entrance to a storehouse of knowledge, girding and enclosing yet upwardly open as a premonition of the effect of knowledge itself. Danjoy's narthex is itself inset within the more ethereal world of knowledge described by the birds seen flying in the sky.

Danjoy's *composition* fuses into one image the archetypes of dark cave, structured hut, and open tent. In Labrouste's library, after passing through the monochromatic veil of the exterior facing, the observer-user passes through the same archetypal images from dark to light, which correspond to the stages in the progress of human thought in architecture. Those layers of experience are literally described by their historical signs. Our first perception is that of a closed box, incised with words and symbols, like the exterior of the Egyptian temple at Denderah. This is an immutable, public facing. The vestibule, acting as a hypostyle hall, overlays the further historical levels of Greco-Roman antiquity: the peripatetic stoa, the Etruscan tomb, the Pompeian atrium and bath. The stairway leads up through the illusionistic world of Renaissance knowledge, the *School of Athens*. The upper reading room completes the historical cycle by referring to the source of that nineteenth-century sense of the universal openness of the spatial experience in architecture, the Gothic Middle Ages. Thus, the whole is finally read as a sequence of signs, and the historical thread is rewoven into a new kind of architectural fabric, as intricate and as ethereal as the original Byzantine synthesis of spirituality and materiality. And, as in a Byzantine church, the imagery is supposed to be read; in the case of Labrouste's building, the reading in motion is directed toward the actual goal of reading *in situ*.

The succession of historical prototypes responds to the very progress the nineteenth century saw in the evolution of the mediums of artistic form as bearer of significant information. The external facing—the material enclosure carrying on its surface the record of its holdings—is the primary art form, architecture. It subsumes the engraved word unto itself. Its panels are like those first graven tablets given by God to humanity; they end up looking like scientific charts, or rather they began as such. The internal movement through the library recapitulates that evolutionary process only outlined in architecture.

The vestibule introduces us to the world of the spoken word, not declamatory but hushed. The busts along its "walls" are those of French artists, writers, scientists, and philosophers; and, like those of ancient Greece and Rome, they are perceived against the illusion of outdoor space. It is the oral world of a culture now succeeded, the secondary level of artistic progress in which primary information is now carried by sculpture. The stairwell introduces us to the further illusion and more profound dematerialization of artistic information in the world of painting. That world, represented by the *School of Athens,* is located on the same level, the same historical layer, as the world of the printed word. The real arches opposite the illusionistic ones of Raphael open into the completely ethereal world of literature. In that new mental space of the nineteenth century, all architectural illusions of representational objectivity disappear in the face of the real light and space needed for the totally abstract and subjective task of gaining information through reading. The entire structure of the building is literary. Both our reading of history and of the present are thus subjectively conjoined in our real experience of the past emerging out of the present. Its evolutive nature suffuses the structure of the whole. The form of the building carries the burden of history not simply on its surface, but as a programmatic fact of local characterization that is engendered in the stark, mute presence of material form. In 1831, in his novel *Notre-Dame de Paris 1482,* Victor Hugo described the Romantic perception of architectural form as an act of reading the "building-as-book." In the eighth and definitive edition, which appeared in December 1832, Hugo added three chapters, one of which he entitled "This will kill that." "This" refers to the book and "that" to the building. In a prefatory note, he explained that this chapter described his conclusion as to the "present decadence of architecture and . . . the death, almost inevitable today, of this sovereign art [*art-roi*]."[57] That conclusion was based on the idea that literature, through the proliferation of the printed book, had sapped architecture of its powers of expression. Were architecture to regain any significant form, it would have to do so under the dominion of the printed word:

The book will kill the building. . . .

. . . the book of stone, so solid and durable, would give place to the book of paper, even more solid and durable. . . . The printing press will kill architecture.

. . . The printed book, the building's cankerworm, now sucks and devours it.

. . . The great poem, the great building, the masterpiece of mankind will no longer be built, it will be printed.

And from now on . . . architecture . . . will submit to the law of literature which literature first took from it.[58]

It was the appearance and disappearance of a word that predicated, as Hugo said, the reality of his book and the message of its sovereignty over architecture. The Greek word 'ΑΝΑΓΚΗ, which he had noticed on the internal wall of one of the towers of Notre-Dame, he placed on the first page of his novel to indicate to his contemporaries the need to preserve and restore the fast-disappearing Gothic buildings of France. The word itself means necessity, overriding constraint. The inscription was alarmingly fragmentary, and its form thus implied impotence, loss of power. It spoke its own fate: it disappeared from the building within the short span of two visits by Hugo. The individually rendered word was weaker than the building on which it was imprinted. But by 1831 the tables had turned. The building itself was showing signs of crumbling. It had already lost much of its encyclopedic content with the destruction of its sculptural decoration during the Ancien Régime and the Revolution of 1789. Emblematic of the disappearance of France's medieval architecture, the mechanically printed word gave evidence of its being more powerful and more durable than the building itself. It would predominate and thus protect the weakened form of the building by appealing for its restoration.

Two years before, Labrouste had already arrived at a similar conclusion. He believed that the rhetorical foundation of the classical language of architecture had cracked under the real weight of what Hugo was later to call "real history."[59] In 1828–29, as part of his fourth-year *envoi* from Rome, Labrouste submitted a restoration of one of the temples at Paestum, which was inspired by a similar idea of the role of graffiti. And just a little more than two years later, it was the young Labrouste whom Hugo asked to proofread and criticize the chapter "This will kill that" which he was about to add to complete *Notre-Dame de Paris*.[60]

Henri Labrouste's Restoration of Paestum (1828–29): The Romantic Rejection of the Classical Trinity

According to the Academy's regulations drawn up in 1819 and revised in 1820, the Grand Prix assured a French student a stipend to live and study in Italy for five years. His home base was to be the French Academy in Rome, located in the Villa Medici. In the final version of the regulations, it was stated that the *pensionnaires* "will travel through several parts of Italy in order to become acquainted with the different styles, the varied arrangements of the monuments, and the means of construction employed."[61] By that the Academy did not mean what we mean by different styles. Rome and its antique monuments were to be the "essential counterbalance" of their studies.[62] The study of Renaissance examples would only reinforce the continuity of the classical tradition, and thus the *pensionnaires* would "realize . . . the importance of keeping French architecture on the path that the architects of the Renaissance laid out for it in having returned it to the principles of antique architecture."[63] A student was obliged to send back to Paris each year a series of drawings, based on his study of antique monuments, which would show to the Academy that he was indeed following in the footsteps of the Renaissance masters. The *envois* were graduated in importance; in the fourth-year *envoi*, the student's understanding of the value of classical architecture was to be most clearly seen.

The *envois* were first exhibited at the Villa Medici in the spring of each year and then sent to Paris for exhibition at the Academy in the fall. The Academy reviewed the progress of each student's work, sent a report back to Rome, and delivered an abridged version of the report at its Séance Publique Annuelle toward the end of the year.

The work of the *pensionnaire's* first three years was considered as a unit and was to comprise "analytic studies" of details drawn almost exclusively from Roman remains. In the regulations drafted by Quatremère while he was Secrétaire Perpétuel, the Academy stipulated that these were to be "studies of details drawn from the most beautiful antique monuments, chosen by him with the approval of the Director [of the Academy in Rome]."[64] In the third year, these were to be supplemented "either by a portion of an antique building from which the details will be taken, or from any other building of his choice." In the all-important fourth year, the *pensionnaire* was to present a complete restoration of an antique building: "Flat projections of an antique Italian monument . . . sketched and rendered from the monument as it presently stands . . . and of its restoration . . . as he conceives it . . . [accompanied by] a *précis historique* of its antiquity and construction."

Henri Labrouste entered the atelier of Thomas Vaudoyer and Hippolyte Lebas in 1818 and was admitted to the Ecole in 1819. He won the Deuxième Grand Prix in 1821 and the Premier Grand Prix in 1824. He arrived in Rome in January 1825. For his first-year *envoi*, Labrouste submitted seven drawings of the Temple of Antoninus and Faustina in Rome (1825–26); for his second-year *envoi*, seven drawings of details from the Column of Trajan, the Column of Marcus Aurelius, and the Arch of Titus, all in Rome, and the Arch of Trajan at Benevento (1826–27); and, for his third-year *envoi*, five drawings comparing the Colosseum and the Theater of Marcellus (1827–28). All these studies were favorably received at the Academy. For his fourth-year restoration, Labrouste chose the site of Paestum, and executed twenty-three drawings in 1828–29, which showed the buildings in their "present state" and as restored (pp. 361 *ff.*). The Academy found things to criticize in most of the drawings, except those of the Orders, and claimed that Labrouste's explanatory text, the *précis historique*, was full of "curious findings."[65] Labrouste had made several trips in 1826 and 1828 to Paestum and one long trip to Sicily in order to study the architecture of Magna Graecia. He was the first *pensionnaire* of the Academy to devote his fourth-year to a restoration of a Greek site and the last for another decade and a half. In fact, soon after the drawings were exhibited in Rome, but before they were shown in Paris, the Academy, led by Quatremère, launched a campaign to prohibit travel outside of Rome by students prior to their fourth year and to restrict its scope thereafter.[66] Quatremère claimed that this would prevent "a great number of abuses" for, faced with examples of architecture other than the Roman or Renaissance models (say, Greek or Etruscan), the student might arrive at incorrect interpretations not informed by "preconceived judgments, fixed" by the study of Roman exemplars. It is just this which Labrouste's restoration of Paestum represented in the eyes of the Academy:

> At the end of the Restoration . . . architects . . . lived quietly amid ordered and unquestioned ideas. . . . One would go nicely off to Italy to measure and remeasure the Roman buildings. But, doing nothing other than that and always laboring over the same monuments, critical correction was lacking and, in the end, one's knowledge remained quite incomplete. . . .
>
> It was from out of this very proper, very stiff milieu that the young Grand Prix Henri Labrouste came to Rome. . . . Upon arriving on that old, antique soil . . . he was startled; he collected his thoughts, he became the attentive, honest observer. . . . The monuments and sites [Paestum] revealed so many things that contradicted what he had been shown before! They raised so many questions for which he had not been prepared! *What I have been taught, he thought, is well and good! But what I come to understand and feel in the presence of these buildings, is better! I shall speak of nothing else from now on.*
>
> The whole of M. Labrouste's work and life is revealed in this decisive development.[67]

Twentieth-century scholarship has recited the events involved in the rediscovery of Greek art and architecture in the latter part of the eighteenth century and assumed that its influence on that period was as crucial as the events involved in the rediscovery of Gothic art and architecture were for the nineteenth century. Consequently, it has been assumed that the nineteenth-century involvement with Greek archaeology was just a Neoclassical hangover. It is important to realize that the nineteenth-century French Academy did not see the situation in such black-and-white terms. Throughout the late 1820s and '30s, the reports by the Academy insinuated that too early an exposure to Greek architecture could be as debilitating as any exposure at all to the Gothic. In its view, Greek architecture was, however ideal, but the earliest stage of classicism, its infancy. The Academy never praised a student's choice of Greek remains as an example for his *envoi* with the same enthusiasm it reserved for Roman choices. It particularly regretted the type of archaeological guesswork that developed in the attempt to restore such partial remains: "to investigate customs to the detriment of observing the grand conceptions" of Rome was to forsake the study of beautiful "forms and of proportions."[68] For their decorative motifs, the students turned to

Etruscan and Roman Republican examples, which the Academy claimed to be undeveloped forms of art.[69] Quatremère claimed that it sufficed to study the monuments of Rome to see the basis for everything else: "By studying the same monuments, [the young architect can] assimilate the principles in diverse ways. A small number of works have served as models for generations. They have acquired a sort of natural right."[70] Furthermore, since classical art was but the imitation of nature, and since that made manifest eternal, constant values, then why search for different versions of the same thing? "The Academy . . . spurns the mania of this false point of view, which considers invention to be innovation—as if artistic imitation, being nothing other than that of Nature, could invent a new Nature—as if Nature, being infinite, could lack for new aspects in the eyes of those with the proper genius to see and to grasp her innumerable characteristics."[71]

Quatremère and the Academy associated invention and innovation with the Romantic idea of freedom. That, in turn, was associated with a new interest on the part of their own students in Rome with what they considered the infantile stages of art. That interest and the obvious conclusions drawn from it were first made manifest in their own bailiwick in Henri Labrouste's restoration of the temples of Paestum. By 1830, its influence had already been felt in his brother Théodore's fourth-year restoration of the Roman Republican temples at Cora (pp. 380–81), and by the following year in M.-A. Delannoy's fourth-year restoration of the Tiber Island (pp. 170–71). Once having seen both the early and later Imperial forms of Roman architecture infected by the same Romantic attitude, the Academy finally declared in its report of 1835 that only the study of Roman architecture in its full-blown magnificence could "possibly safeguard the artist's taste against every temporary aberration the innovational mania gives rise to." What they saw as a temporary inroad on classical thought, developing in the heat of the Romantic movement of 1830, was to have much more long-lasting effects than they believed possible at the time. It was, in turn, to nurture that other more obvious form of anti-classicism, the so-called Gothic revival of the '40s and '50s.

That a radical gesture should be made in historical guise was not unusual in the nineteenth century; that it should occur in the classical context is characteristically French. Unlike the near-contemporary development of Romantic Rationalism in England, the rejection of classicism in France was not at first directly associated with the revival of the Gothic. The *Néo-Grec* transcended the question of style as the bearer of essential architectural meaning. It reached beyond the classicists' distinction between the Classical and the Gothic, or the rational and the picturesque. In posing the problem outside the classical framework of general or ideal form and demanding that the specific facts of program, materials, and methods of construction serve as the basis for each application of universal principles of composition, the latter were freed

Henri Labrouste. Temple of Hera I ("Portique"), Paestum. Restoration. 1828–29. Fourth-year *envoi*. Elevation and plan.

In his restoration of this building, Labrouste omitted the pediments, added two interior walls for which there was no direct evidence, and gave the whole a hipped roof, thereby rejecting the possibility that it might have been a temple. He envisioned it instead as a place for public meetings and notices, and he called it a "portique" in contradistinction to the eighteenth-century description of it as a basilica.

Labrouste. Temple of Hera I ("Portique"),
Paestum. Restoration. Sections and perspective.

Labrouste took his longitudinal section
through the precise center of the columns,
showing nothing of their decorative surfaces
and thus making them appear simple stone
supports. The consistency of the architectural surfaces is further disrupted by the inscriptions on the front column and on the
walls relating to civic affairs, and by the military trophies hanging from the upper architectural members.

from a priori formal equivalents. Thus Alfred Darcel could, in 1857, quite naturally see the anti-idealist connections between the *Néo-Grecs* and the so-called Gothic revivalists:

> Disorder . . . had invaded the camp of the classicists; the need to return to the sources and principles of architecture, which had caused some to take the medieval road, led others all the way to Greece. We have come, therefore, to find both the Greek and the Gothic treated with horror and cursed, all in the name of the architecture that flourished in Rome at the time of the first Caesars.
>
> Equally indifferent to all this, either side followed its own path and sought to give to stone or wood, iron or bronze, the form appropriate to each material, one side drawing prototypes from the century of Saint Louis and the other from that of Alcibiades."[72]

Writing in the heat of debate with Ernest Beulé, who succeeded Halévy as Secrétaire Perpétuel of the Academy in 1862, and inspired by Beulé's attacks on the Gothic,[73] Darcel simply abridged his chronology a bit in order to give that added status of seniority to his own cause. César Daly, however, more fully explained what everybody, including Viollet-le-Duc and Lassus, agreed to be the idiosyncratic manner in which nineteenth-century French architects had broken the hegemony of classical absolutism:

> [Since the end of the Middle Ages] European societies have borrowed from the same source, antiquity. But as a result of this agreement in favor of the classical source, and due to an insufficient study of history, there developed a school claiming, in France perhaps more than elsewhere, to have formulated nothing less than the *absolute* doctrine of art: in literature, the three unities, without regard for real life; in painting and sculpture, the same general conditions of harmony and style, without regard for the country, the race, or the era; in architecture, the same proportions, whatever the materials used; and thus the monuments of the age of Augustus were presented . . . as the only ones embodying the true principles. In the presence of these doctrinal excesses, so detrimental to the legitimate and desirable influence of *true antiquity*, and amid this heavy darkness of an ill-conceived fanaticism, a blazing constellation suddenly appeared in the architectural skies of France. *It came to us, however, from the city of Augustus, and was launched from the classical "foyer" of Paris.* It was at the moment when, under the general name of *Romanticism*, a reaction was making itself felt against the doctrinal excesses of the classical school, . . . excesses that were breeding the false in art and weariness in the soul. This constellation . . . bore the names of Duban, Duc, Labrouste, and Vaudoyer.[74]

Without getting embroiled in the controversy as to which of the four was the real force in changing the situation,[75] we can safely say that the one event that publicly emerged from the "city of Augustus" and that nineteenth-century French architectural historians later referred to as the turning point in the development of ideas was Labrouste's restoration of the temples at

Paestum. Viollet-le-Duc described the project as "purely and simply a revolution, on a few sheets of double-elephant paper."[76] Reflecting the opinion generally held by 1861, Van Brunt traced the birth of the *Néo-Grec* to this event:

> While in Italy, [Henri Labrouste's] attention was directed to the Greek temples of Paestum. Trained, as he had been, in the strictest academic architecture of the Renaissance, he was struck by many points of difference between these temples and the Palladian formulae which had hitherto held despotic sway over his studies. . . . he perceived a remarkable freedom from the restraints of his school. . . . Labrouste . . . surprised the grave professors of the Academy, Le Bas, Baltard, and the rest, by presenting to them, as the result of his studies, carefully elaborated drawings of the temples of Paestum. Witnessing, with pious horror, the grave departures from their rules contained in the drawings of their former favorite, they charged him with error. . . . True to their prejudices, their eyes did not penetrate beyond the outward type. . . . It was in vain that poor Labrouste upheld the accuracy of his work. . . . The professors still maintained the integrity of their long-established ordinances, and, to disprove the assertions of the young pretender, even sent a commission to examine the temples in question. The result was a confirmation of the fact, the ridicule of Paris, the consequent branding of the young artist as an architectural *heretic*, and a continued persecution of him by the Ecole des Beaux-Arts. Undaunted, however, Labrouste established an *atelier*, in Paris, to which flocked many intelligent students, sympathizing with the courage which could be so strong in the conviction of truth as to brave in its defence the displeasure of the powerful hierarchy of the School.
>
> Thus was founded the new Renaissance in France. . . .[77]

Labrouste's restoration of Paestum seems to have gathered around itself an aura of religious dissension. Van Brunt described it as a "revelation." Mainly as a result of this project and the events surrounding its censure by the Academy, Labrouste returned to Paris in early 1830 as a triumphant Romantic hero. He was paraded through the streets of Left-Bank Paris on the shoulders of dissident students during the July Revolution and was then petitioned by them to form an atelier.[78] The project itself, received by the Academy on August 5, 1829, and exhibited in Paris from August 24 through October 3, 1829, caused the single greatest flurry of architectural controversy in France until Viollet-le-Duc's attempted reform of the Ecole in 1863.[79] It directly resulted in (1) the open warfare between the Director of the Academy in Rome, Horace Vernet, and the Secrétaire Perpétuel of the Academy in Paris, Quatremère, because Vernet defended Labrouste against Quatremère's criticisms and formed the commission that went to Paestum to verify Labrouste's findings;[80] (2) the proffered resignation of Vernet, which was publicly reported in the daily press;[81] (3) a series of new measures instituted at the Academy in Rome by Quatremère in order to prevent future "abuses"; (4) the eventual deterioration of Quatremère's personal power over architectural thought and practice; and (5) the continued persecution of Labrouste, through the ostracism of his atelier from official recognition by the Academy throughout the tenure of Quatremère as Secrétaire Perpétuel and of his successor from 1840 to 1854, Raoul-Rochette.[82]

Only in the restricted milieu of nineteenth-century French architectural education could such a controversy occur and have such important ramifications. The situation was entirely different, for instance, from the type of controversy incited by A. W. N. Pugin's first publications in England. In France, the attack on the system was waged from within the system itself. For it to be fully understood one must almost read between the lines; it is only as a result of careful attention to details of inflection that one can really grasp the meaning of the changes. So far, it has generally been assumed that the Academy criticized and rejected Labrouste's project over the issue of polychromy;[83] but the Academy had already, as early as 1824, been apprised of and accepted Hittorff's findings on the subject.[84] In fact, aside from their feeling that the "elegance" and "delicacy" of some of the decoration was not "severe" enough, the Academy praised his discreet use of color and considered it absolutely "justified by numerous examples." Furthermore, Labrouste's restoration was hardly polychromatic: only certain details, such as the terracotta decoration of the cornices, the statues of the divinities, and a few inscriptions were rendered in color, and that was fairly muted. Much more significant, no doubt, for the Academy was, first of all, the fact that Labrouste chose to restore a Greek site and, second, that the entire conception of antique architecture evinced by that choice and its explanation were revolutionary.

Labrouste was the first *pensionnaire* at the French Academy in Rome to choose a Greek site as the subject for his fourth-year *envoi.* Between L.-A. Dubut's restoration of the so-called Temple de la Pudicité in Rome of 1801 and Duban's restoration of the Porticus Octaviae of 1827, all the *pensionnaires'* choices were Roman. It was not until 1844, with Théodore Ballu's restoration of the Temple of Athena Polias in Athens, that a *pensionnaire* was again to reconstruct a Greek building. After that date, there was a series of restorations of Greek buildings coincident with the establishment of a branch of the French Academy in Athens.[85]

However, just as the issue of polychromy was not new by 1829, neither was the archaeological investigation of Greek remains. The site of Paestum had been rediscovered in the 1740s, and the temples were published by numerous authors in the later eighteenth century.[86] These included G.-P.-M. Dumont's publication of 1764, based on Soufflot's drawings, and Delagardette's *Ruines de Paestum* of 1799. In contrast with those publications, Labrouste's *Néo-Grec* attitude of specificity was perceived to be radically new. The Neoclassical authors of the eighteenth century had been struck by the dissimilarities in proportion and nature between the newly discovered Greek remains and previously known Roman buildings. As a result of their classical idealism, they tried to find ways of incorporating the Greek examples into their idea of the classical by stretching the boundaries of classicism itself in order to explain away the Greek as the primordial, albeit primitive, type.[87] Labrouste proposed the heretical idea of accepting Greek architecture as Greek architecture. Viollet-le-Duc described his conclusion as a revolutionary discovery: "[Labrouste] did not deign to look at Greek antiquity through the classical lens.... [this] revolution . . . undermined the academic foundations of family, property, and religion."[88] These phrases have profound implications; the final sacred trinity suggests that the debate was raised to the level of a religious controversy.

Nineteenth-century discussions of Labrouste's restoration of Paestum were polemical and consequently most often phrased the issue of its significance in terms of the obviously controversial question of polychromy. In his obituary of Labrouste, Henri Delaborde described his restoration of Paestum as the crucial event in his career. He related the specificity of its conclusions to Labrouste's realistic attitude toward architecture and laid particular stress on the repercussions of its anti-idealistic position:

> Labrouste ... had ... unshakable convictions in matters of art, and though apparently circumspect, he was audacious, and of an independent mind. Thus he would not be disconcerted by the objections his opinions inevitably excited, nor would he fear the consequences of the denials he posed to more generally accepted ideas. Labrouste, in a word, loved truth bravely; he loved it in all its forms and in all its shades of meaning.
>
> Hence, these studies of antiquity that he sent from Rome are strictly faithful portraits of reality—so faithful in fact that they go beyond outward resemblances, and, through the character they derive from certain essential elements, such as the cutting and fitting of the stones, show and explain to us what might be called the organism of each construction. His restorations hardly conformed to the systems and methods normally used by David's architectural contemporaries—he restored the *temple of Neptune* [Hera II] with a covered *cella* and painted tiles and antefixes, the *Basilica* [Hera I] with the unusual profile of its antae, the *temple of Ceres* [Athena],[89] also with polychrome ornaments, and included other such archaeological innovations of a similar nature that the project scandalized some as a heresy and was applauded by others as a promise of emancipation. Never before perhaps had an architectural *envoi* been greeted so passionately. Never had a technical question provoked, even outside the world of art, such animated discussions nor had it preoccupied so many people.... In the heat of the polemic, it

almost reached the point that a political significance was attributed to what was simply a scholarly problem. Labrouste was made to appear either to have courageously upheld the laws, or to have violated them, because he had found traces of painting on some ancient monuments and concluded from this specific fact that the ancients generally made use of polychromy.[90]

The question of polychromy was just a detail, a symptom of a larger, more fundamental change in attitude. Delaborde's reduction of it to the question of polychromy is merely an indication of the Academy's ultimate attempt to chasten Labrouste's reputation by diluting his message. The question of polychromy, like the question of whether the cella of the Temple of Hera II was top-lit or not, upon which Labrouste differed from Quatremère, could be argued in polite archaeological debate. This would not in itself have upset the basic premises of classical idealism. The same could be said for the discrepancies between a number of Labrouste's measurements and those contained in Delagardette's publication. What was at stake was Labrouste's interpretation of the facts. In the *précis historique* that he included with his drawings as an explanation of them, one has to read between the lines in order to arrive at an understanding of how his interpretation differed.

Labrouste's text, as the Academy said, included statements of a very "curious" nature.[91] He proposed that all the facts he had unearthed merely proved that Greek architects had developed their system of proportions, spatial configurations, and decorative surfaces, not as a consequence of imitatively applying the eternal "rules" of architecture, but rather as a locally determined response to specific material, functional, historical, and cultural conditions. To Labrouste, neither were the proportions and physical shape of the Doric Order at Paestum archaically ill-formed nor was the Order, by contrast, to be seen as the primitive prototype for later classical refinement. These had been the parameters within which the debate over the Greek Doric had taken place in the eighteenth century. The problem then merely had been to find a chronological place for the Doric in the "natural" sequence of classical "progress" toward the ideal conception of form. In those terms, the primitive Doric could be accepted simply as another mode. But for Labrouste, Greek art was not simply one term or aspect in the development of a classical style. In his text he made no attempt to justify the "graceless" proportions of the earliest temples at Paestum by reference to later Roman examples, as Delagardette previously had done. Indeed, Delagardette had gone so far as to claim that the originally stubby columns of Hera I were given their more "graceful," cigar-shaped form by later Roman corrective recutting.[92]

Labrouste also made no attempt to explain away the apparent discrepancies between his measurements and rendered profiles and those which Delagardette, the accepted authority, had already given. Labrouste's restoration limited itself to the elaborate and detailed setting forth of each aspect of the Greek temple as a consequence of the specific requirements of material, program, and site. He considered the proportions of the columns, their profiles and those of the antae, as well as the color of the temple surfaces, to be the direct result of the specifically Greek ideals they embody and the material means their builders could call upon at the time. Labrouste did not mention the classical ideal. He offered a radical reinterpretation of Greek architecture as Greek and thus called into question the fundamental tenet of classicism: that supposedly similar forms reappear eternally in certain chosen civilizations.

In the opening paragraph of his *précis historique*, Labrouste categorically denied the opinion claiming the "architecture of these monuments as belonging to the infancy of art, and condemning it as impure and coarse."[93] Furthermore, in contrast with what his readers would have supposed to be a later refinement of the same system of forms, Labrouste claimed that the form of the Greek temples at Paestum "in no way reveals art in its infancy, but rather art having reached its perfection." It is highly significant that throughout his entire text Labrouste never related their style to the later forms of classicism which his readers would have supposed to be the perfected derivatives of Greek architecture. Unlike previous writers on the subject, he never brought any Roman monuments into the argument and thus, by conscious omission, refused to consider the classical as an ideal style.[94]

In reconstructing the missing parts of the temples at Paestum—roofs, doors, gutters, and sculptural decoration—Labrouste did not consider Roman remains a useful source of information. He stated that the real analogies for restoring those missing parts were to be found in other remaining examples of Greek architecture in Italy:

> To have these monuments [at Paestum] appraised *at their true value*, I tried only to represent them exactly and to study them with conscience. . . . I traveled through Sicily and brought back the materials I lacked for my restoration.
>
> . . . One finds the same architecture and the same art of construction in these monuments [of Paestum] as in the monuments of Sicily. . . .
>
> . . . the peoples of Sicily originated in the same country, as can be seen from their both having used the same architectural forms, as well as the same means of constructing monuments [italics added].

Labrouste devoted the main portion of his text to explaining how Greek forms were determined by specific material and cultural circumstances. He described the form of the terminating molding of the entablature of the Temple of Hera II as the inevitable consequence of Greek methods of construction: "Because it supported the last tile of the roof, it required a particular form and thus had to be cut separately."[95] He explained that the degradation of the carved decoration of the temples of Hera I and Athena was a consequence of their builders' astute methods of construction. He claimed that the partially eroded surfaces of these temples gave evidence of the fact that, in employing stones of differing compressive strengths, the architects used the local materials to their fullest advantage. He noted that this had never been previously offered as the explanation:

> The construction of this monument [the Temple of Athena] offers many things of interest, yet it has not been mentioned in any of the works published on the antiquities of Poseidonia.
>
> It should be noted that the stones used in the construction of this temple are of two kinds. The columns, the architraves, the frieze, and the pediment are constructed of hard stone, whereas soft stone was reserved for the parts decorated with moldings, such as the capitals, the moldings of the architrave, the triglyphs, and the cornice of the entablature.... I will simply point out that, although the horizontal cornice is in soft stone, hard stones have been placed at intervals ... to keep the cornice from being crushed by the weight of the pediment.[96]
>
> ... This way of using ... different materials, the mixture of hard and soft stone, ... indicates ... a full knowledge of the materials native to the region.

Labrouste ascribed to this use of different qualities of stone the fact that the temples were originally covered with a coat of painted stucco: "The use of different materials ... necessitated, from the beginning, the use of stucco." This was not his only reason for presuming a polychrome surface. While the material necessity of concealing the surface discontinuity produced by two different kinds of stone was one reason, there was also, in his eyes, a cultural or programmatic determinant. He proposed that the polychrome stucco surface was a direct response to the spiritual program: "We may assume that the ancients customarily renewed the decoration of the monuments at certain consecrated times, or it may be that religion prescribed that custom."[97]

Labrouste ascribed every aspect of the temple forms to a functional rather than an ideal cause. It is for this reason that he interpreted the Temple of Hera I as a "portique" rather than a temple. He thought its plan resulted from and expressed that special function: "This monument is entirely symmetrical in all its parts; ... and its axis is occupied by a row of columns. This disposition led me to consider it as one of those porticoes where the ancients gathered to discuss public affairs."

Labrouste also explained that the novelty of this disposition was a direct consequence of the concern for structural economy, in keeping with the secular and utilitarian purpose of the building: "This disposition ... had perhaps been inspired by the need to cover a large space at little cost, a certain economy being necessary in the erection of these porticoes ... [where] such natural points of support ... carry the whole roof of the building." Labrouste restored the building without pediments, believing that its lowly character

Henri Labrouste. Temple of Hera II ("Temple of Neptune"), Paestum. Restoration. 1828–29. Fourth-year *envoi*. Actual state.

Labrouste was the first nineteenth-century *pensionnaire* at the French Academy in Rome to choose a Greek building as the subject for his fourth-year *envoi*. A constant requirement of the archaeological *envois* was that the actual state of the ruins be carefully delineated in order to show the starting point for the reconstruction.

Labrouste. Temple of Hera II ("Temple of Neptune"), Paestum. Elevation and section.

Not only was Labrouste's study of the Temple of Hera II an unconventional choice of subject for a fourth-year *envoi*, but it was also restored in an unconventional way. A fifth-century Greek temple, it had previously been accepted by some as hypaethral, with an open roof; it was Labrouste's decision to close the roof and to give the building two levels of interior columns standing free, without galleries, which incurred the wrath of the Academy when it reviewed the *envoi*.

precluded such a representational form. "It is this very disposition that made me decide to make the roof *hipped* rather than give it two pediments, for they would have been, I think, less in harmony with the character of the monument."

It is clear from Labrouste's renderings of the restored temples of Hera I and Hera II that he thought the distinctive character of each did not lie in its modal inflection of the Doric Order but rather in each building's overall shape. Labrouste expressed the presumed secular character of the "portique" in his rendering by bringing out its nonhierarchical form and spatial openness (pp. 361–63). His rendering of the Temple of Hera II, by contrast, is absolutely closed. The axis of its internal space is marked on the exterior by its pediments and on the interior, as shown in the section, by the statue of a divinity (p. 373). The statue is framed and the space around it is decidedly concentrated on its image by the existence of two rows of superposed columns. The existence of superposed Orders in the cella of a Greek temple posed a special and extremely thorny problem as to how to interpret their role in the definition of character. Such an unusual internal configuration, "the only example known to be extant," as Labrouste noted, lacking parallels in existing Greek temples, had led some previous architects and archaeologists to suggest parallels in later Roman basilicas. Basing their comparisons on the text of Vitruvius, others concluded that the temple was hypaethral. In restoring Hera II as a Greek temple to the divinity Neptune, Labrouste felt that he had to "reject that opinion as totally unfounded." He rejected all Roman explanations because, as he said, they were "contrary to the nature and character of this monument." The Academy's report specifically criticized his devaluation of the Vitruvian source.

In his effort to define what constituted its specifically Greek character, Labrouste was led to the conclusion that the superposition of the two Orders in the cella of the Temple of Hera II had not issued from a desire on the part of its Greek builders to enhance the structure with an arrangement of decoratively varied forms: "In so arranging these two Orders, the architect, it seems to me, had some other purpose than to decorate the interior of the temple. . . ." He implied that such a manner of providing decorative unity by the harmonic variation resulting from the superposition of two Orders was Roman, not Greek. He related this to what he considered to be the erroneous assumption that the temple was hypaethral; for Labrouste claimed that that misinterpretation of the facts was also based on false comparisons with the Roman text of Vitruvius: "Struck by certain points of resemblance that seem to exist between this monument, as the ruin represents it, and the *hypaethral* [temple] described by Vitruvius, several architects came to see this monument as *hypaethral*." Rather than adopting such an opinion just because Vitruvius seemed to support it, Labrouste felt that he had to "confront the monument's ruins with the text." In doing this, he admitted to the Academy, to whom these remarks were directed, that he was categorically rejecting "this opinion, [which] was shared, I was told, by architects whose judgment is indeed very respectable." He insisted on the need to "dwell on this question" because the occurrence of the superposed Orders had "given rise to an opinion that it is essential to contest."

Labrouste proposed that in order to "restore this monument in its integrity," one had, first of all, to consider the issue from a structural point of view rather than by reference to a later Roman text: "The need to diminish the span of stones covering the cella might have been the first and perhaps the only reason for this disposition" of "two Orders of columns placed one on top of the other." By this method of reasoning, he was also able to account for the obviously non-Roman relationship between the two Orders in which the upper one is simply the telescopic prolongation of the lower one. He asserted that this characteristically rational, Greek solution was solely determined by functional calculations:

> With the upper Order merely the extension of the lower, the two, . . . it seems to me, take the place of a single large Order in holding up the ceiling. This can only be to avoid taking up too much space in the cella, as the necessarily larger diameter of a single Order would do. To gain a smaller diameter, the architect divided the total height between two Orders.[98]

Labrouste was quick to remark that "this singularity, which is not mentioned in any of the published works on the ruins of Poseidonia is, I think, interesting enough for architectural study." One is, of course, led to assume that the divergence from Roman practice is why this was never previously mentioned and why Labrouste found it so interesting.

The explanation of the superposition of two Orders as a mere structural exigency must surely have been anathema to the Academy.[99] Labrouste further asserted that even with such a simple structural explanation in mind, "the span of these ceiling stones may seem excessive." He felt that the primary explanation for the structural prowess of the Greek architects lay in their ability to use local materials to their fullest advantage. He accounted for the extended span of the ceiling beams in the following manner:

> However, I think this method feasible with materials like those used in these monuments, and one can assume the same for the Greeks, whose monuments were of so extraordinary a construction. There are, in the antique quarries of Sicily, columns of stone in one piece and of a prodigious size. . . .

But, as with the question of the polychrome stucco surface, Labrouste's explanation of Greek forms was not simply structural. Starting from a structurally logical basis, he attempted to account for formal appearance on the corollary ground of programmatic requirements. And here is where he felt that in order to restore the Temple of Hera II "in its integrity . . . [and in accord with] the nature and character of the monument," he had to dispute the idea of its having been hypaethral. He stated that the rational articulation of the cornice of the upper Order proved his contention:

> The moldings that make up the cornice of the upper Order seem hardly intended to be outside or to carry the cover or roof of the side aisles of the cella. [For one thing] they exhibit no corona and seem, rather, designed to carry an overall ceiling. [For another] they are similar to those that evidently supported the ceiling of the portico surrounding the temple, and of the pronaos and posticum. If one notes [these things about the moldings], one is led to reject the opinion of those who looked upon the temple of Neptune as hypaethral.

Labrouste asserted that only in this way could the Temple of Hera II be restored in keeping with its specific Greek character: "The character of the monument and the traces [of evidence] still existing naturally indicated to me such a [covered] system."

In Labrouste's mind, the hypaethral idea related to the question of galleries at the level of the entablature of the lower Order. He stated that there was no physical evidence for presupposing the existence of such a gallery level. He implied that previous restorations of the temple with such galleries, meaning Delagardette's, were based on the erroneous assumption that there was some connection between the Greek temple and the Roman basilica. He restored the Temple of Hera II without tribune galleries, thereby contending that the true character of a Greek temple lay in its being a structural carapace for the statue of a divinity, not a place where people might mill about, as in a Roman basilica, prying into all the nooks and crannies of its interior. By extension, Labrouste was also implying that the Christian church, as it had developed in form from the Roman basilica, had no logical connection with the forms of a Greek temple.[100]

Labrouste took Delagardette to task for having assumed that the evidence of stairways to either side of the entrance of the cella meant that these once led to tribune galleries: "They could not lead to interior galleries, as assumed by Delagardette, because similar stairways are placed at the entrance to all the temples of Sicily that certainly had no galleries in the cella."[101] Having thus denied that the stairways were used for access to galleries that did not exist, as well as denying the superposition of the Orders as a means of supporting those purported galleries, Labrouste then offered a more practical reason for the existence of those stairways. His explanation was totally functional. In its apparent simplicity it denied any reference of the temple's character to Vitruvian formulae, and at the same time it reinforced the special "integrity" of the Greek solution to the problem of maintaining a house for a divinity: "One may well imagine that the stone ceilings required constant inspection and special attention. . . . [The] stairways . . . placed at the entrance of . . . [the temple] . . . thus served only for the inspection of the ceilings."

The question of the composition and construction of the ceilings and roofs of the three temples occupied an inordinately large portion of Labrouste's analysis. All the rendered sections show his concern to restore the vanished roofs of the temples as realistically as possible. Within the borders of a number of the sheets, there are even some supplementary details showing how he thought the pieces of wood, stone, and terra cotta were actually fitted and joined (p. 363). But what is even more significant than this is the amount of space Labrouste devoted in his text to the subject. In a text otherwise as dry as bones, as self-consciously prosaic and materially deterministic as it could be, Labrouste let his imagination soar only when it came to a question either of what no longer existed, or of what, when it did exist, was impermanent in material or purely utilitarian in nature. Out of the six pages devoted to the Temple of Hera II, Labrouste gave over a page and a half to a discussion of the presumed design and construction of its wooden roof and stone ceiling and another half-page to ancillary, impermanent features such as the "furniture required for ceremonies." He described how the rafters were joined, how the terra-cotta tiles of the roof were lapped, how all the various parts were picked out by color, and how the interior furniture was arranged to enable the building to function as a temple.

All these considerations are evidence of the Romantic desire to provide local color and thus reconstruct the past as a living reality. In succeeding years, the Academy continually criticized the "nefarious" influence of such a concern for impermanent factors, which, by "masking" the "true nature" of classical temples, distracted the student from the study of what really counted, the proportions of the Orders: "[Students] investigate customs . . . rather than observe the true principles of architecture."[102]

Traditional discussions of the remains of classical architecture usually concentrated on what was believed to be the most significant part of those remains—the Order—and emphasized its measurements, its proportions, its carving, and the character of its capital. In his discussion of Paestum, Labrouste devoted only a few clipped phrases to the peripteral columns of the Temple of Hera II: "The columns of the portico surrounding the temple are built up by means of drums; they are without entasis and they narrow from the bottom up. Their axis inclines toward the center of the temple; they form, that is, so many oblique conical trunks." Labrouste said nothing more. That was it for the columns of Hera II. As for the peripteral Order of the Temple of Athena, he said nothing.[103] Nor did he say anything about the Order of the Temple of Hera I; instead, he chose to discuss the way in which the actual remains gave evidence of the means by which the Greeks constructed the building:

> The construction of the building is no less interesting than its plan. One notices at the socle, under the columns of the entrance to the "portique," some stone

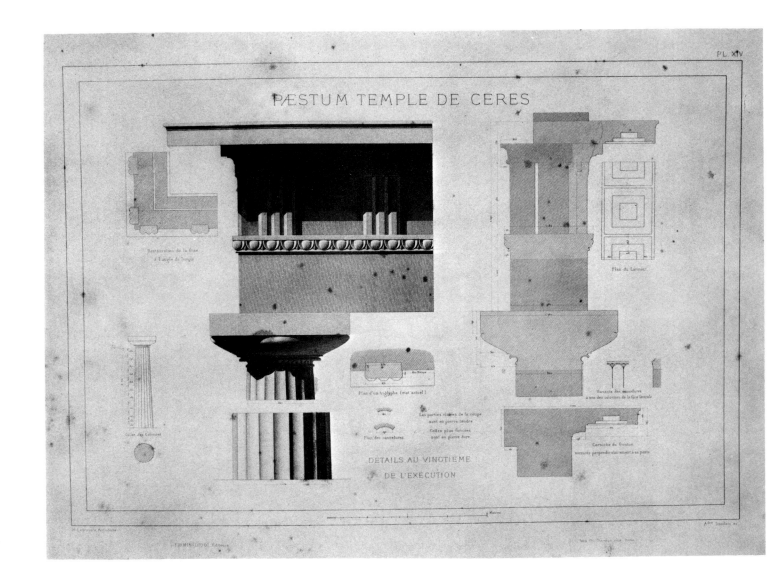

PÆSTUM TEMPLE DE CERES

DETAILS AU VINGTIEME
DE L'EXECUTION

Théodore Labrouste. Temple of Hercules, Cora. Restoration. 1831. Fourth-year *envoi*. Elevation of site and section *(see also pp. 164–65)*.

COUPE TRANSVERSALE RESTAURÉE
SUR UNE ÉCHELLE DE 0.050 P. M.

left to project in order to make it easier to lift up the blocks. . . . One notices, too, on top of these socle stones, the columnar axes traced by the workers, but what is particularly worth attention is the means used to raise and set in place the stones of the frieze of the entablature. One only has to examine the grooves cut into the sides of the stones to understand so simple a means.

It is obvious that Labrouste deliberately concentrated on the matter of means rather than ends. By not discussing the Orders—their relative proportions and their character—he sidestepped the fundamental question of classical architecture, the supposed familial relationship between Greek and Roman forms. This was usually described by a "parallel of the Orders." Any building, Greek or Roman, was supposed to derive its essential character from its choice of mode, or Order. Independent of any other considerations, the Order was thought to carry in itself a form of characteristic expression. Labrouste could not see such a distinction in character between what he called the "portique" and what he called the Temple of Neptune, for they both used the same Order. On the other hand, he did not see that as limiting the characteristic expression of each, for he located the source of the special secular character of the "portique" in the more abstract yet real meaning of its plan.

The denial of characteristic meaning to the Orders was a sacrilege in the Academy's eyes. Furthermore, it was heresy to deny the transference of expressive power from the Greek to the Roman reuse of the same Orders. Although Labrouste took the first step of declaring the perfection of Greek forms, he obviously did not want to be excommunicated at so early an age. He never proposed a parallel of the Orders and therefore never put himself in the position of having to state outright that Roman copies represented a decline. At one or two points, however, such a conclusion does make itself evident in his text. It certainly did not go unnoticed by the Academy.

Labrouste's discussion of the placement of the corner triglyph on the Temple of Hera II surely offered more than just a hint of his disapproval of the way in which Roman architects, according to Vitruvius, had refined the use of that form: "The stonework of the triglyphs and metopes of the frieze, especially at the corner of the monument, is worth remarking. It in no way reveals art in its infancy but rather art having reached its perfection." The case of the Temple of Athena, however, appeared to deny Labrouste's assertion (p. 378). There, according to Delagardette, who had discovered a piece of the corner of the frieze, it was clear that the triglyph had been inset from the edge and located axially over the corner column. Labrouste claimed all sorts of rational excuses for having to restore it in that unfortunate position: "The triglyphs were added and . . . inlaid in the frieze. . . . It was, no doubt, this system of adding rather thin triglyphs to the frieze that prevented one from being placed at the corner of the monument." Despite this justification, he admitted feeling a certain degree of "repugnance" at having to accept such a solution as coming from the hands of Greeks, "but Delagardette found the corner stone of the frieze, which revealed this peculiarity." He could not, however, refrain from evincing some skepticism on the question of Delagardette's discovery, for he added that he accepted Delagardette on his word "although today that stone has disappeared." Labrouste most probably accepted Delagardette's evidence simply so as to be able to declare his repugnance for a peculiarly Roman arrangement without having to state it outright. In allowing for a Greek architect to have placed the corner triglyph axially over the corner column, Labrouste was able to show his disdain for that arrangement while merely blaming it on a structural idiosyncrasy forced upon the Greeks by the use of local materials. Despite that explanation, it must have been obvious to the Academy that Labrouste was aiming his barb at its cherished notion that Roman architecture was the noble and sophisticated version of the classical style, the developed academic model that had to be followed in all cases.

Henry Van Brunt, in recounting the story of Labrouste's censure by the Academy, specified that it was over the question of the placement of the corner triglyph that the Academy witnessed "with pious horror the grave departures from their rules contained in the drawings of their former favorite." He added that "they told him, never did such an absurdity occur in classic architecture as a triglyph on a corner! Palladio and the Italian masters never committed such an obvious crime against propriety, nor could an instance of it be found in all Roman antiquities."[104]

That Labrouste should have singled out this one characteristic of Greek architecture as the touchstone for implying the contradiction between the Greek and Roman understanding of architectural form is indicative. He already understood architectural form as a concatenation of separately responsible parts, each in itself composed in relation to its characteristic function and role in the whole and therefore never, as in the case of the inset corner triglyph, superficially integrated merely for the sake of a preordained, plastic sense of unity. In Labrouste's eyes the Roman idea of placing the corner triglyph axially over the final column belied their academic sense of form. The Greeks, in making the corner triglyph the culminating term of the horizontal frieze, showed a more liberated and elastic sense of composition. The mere existence of similar forms, or what Van Brunt referred to as "outward types," in Greek and Roman architecture could not be accepted as proof of any real familial relationship. In pointing to such formal discrepancies as revealing distinctions of a deeper nature, Labrouste denied the possibility of defining the meaning of classical style by the mere use of the Orders. He obviously felt that any real meaning lay beyond the superficial aspects of style and rather in the spirit in which the parts of a building were put together or composed. Consequently, Labrouste was unable, and indeed unwilling, to define the character of Greek architecture according to its particular inflection of the forms of the so-called classical style. He described the character of Greek expression outside the limits of style as simply an expressive set. He contrasted the "firmness of architecture" in Greek temples with the "extreme delicacy" of their decoration. In separating structural decisiveness from decorative delicacy, Labrouste countered the fundamental classical belief in the unity of construction and decoration in the characteristic forms of the Orders. Whereas classical treatises usually proclaimed that the appropriate expression for any building would be conferred upon it by the choice of the Order (for example, the grave Doric for a court building, the elegant Corinthian for a palace), the use of the same Doric Order for both the secular "portique" and the divine temples at Paestum proved to Labrouste that the Greeks, unlike their followers, never thought that way. "As proved by the Parthenon, the Doric Order is, I believe, capable of richness.... The Doric Order was not formerly reserved for secondary buildings exclusively, and the Greeks preferred it to the other Orders for their temples of the gods."

Labrouste claimed that the Doric was not by nature severe. It was just a structural order for composing a building. Characteristic meaning had to be added by decoration. On one level, the character of the Temple of Hera II and that of the more lowly "portique" were differentiated by their plans and by the resulting structural solutions they determined. On another level, Labrouste surmised that the Greeks had originally given greater distinction to the structurally similar forms of their temples, not by adopting a different Order, but rather by decorating their temples more profusely. Thus, Labrouste explained his restoration of the Temple of Hera II: "In this restoration, I was not afraid, in painting the accessories and by means of several ornaments, to add a certain richness to the architecture of the monument," because "the Doric Order is ... capable of richness." It was thus partially by means of decoration superimposed on an underlying structural order and partially by means of the abstract *parti*, or the plan itself, that the Greeks conferred specific meaning on their buildings. It was not, as classicists would have it, by varying the Orders.

Labrouste's conclusion presented a veiled critique of the entire academic system, which was based on Roman (*i.e.*, Vitruvian) and Renaissance treatises that established that the different Orders represented a progressive development in character from male sturdiness and severity to female refinement and elegance. Furthermore, this idea of progression of character was linked to the historical idea of the progressive development of classical form from an early stage of primitive robustness to a later stage of sophisticated refinement. Since Labrouste refused to entertain such a belief, which his observations of Greek work at Paestum had disproved, he was faced with the almost impossible task of dating the three temples at Paestum. How could he set them in any chronological order if he refused to accept the traditional criteria for the progress of the classical style?

In academic circles, the progressive refinement in the development of the Orders provided the general basis for any discussion of chronology. Indeed, Delagardette had, in conventional fashion, established that the temples of Hera I and Athena were older than Hera II by an examination of the proportions of their Orders. Since the variations at Paestum were somewhat slight, compared with all known forms of the Doric Order, and could thus be attributed to circumstantial rather than historical causes, Delagardette enlarged the scope of his inquiry to include later Roman versions of the Doric. In doing that, Delagardette thought that he was correctly setting forth the full range of the progressive classical development toward more refined and elegant proportions, so that the slighter variations in the stages at Paestum could be convincingly shown to attest to the same general trend. The final chapter of his *Ruines de Paestum* is entitled "A Parallel between the Buildings at Paestum and those of Athens and Rome, whence is deduced the [date of] construction of the Temples of Paestum." Its third section is entitled "A Parallel between the Doric Orders of the Basilica and the little Temple of Paestum and those of the Theater of Marcellus and of the Colosseum in Rome." By comparing the proportions of the Orders of the Greek temples at Paestum with those of Roman buildings, Delagardette arrived at the correct conclusion that both the temples of Hera I and Athena were earlier than Hera II. Seen in the light of the greater and greater refinement of the proportions of the Doric at the hands of Roman architects, the squat proportions of the two earlier temples at Paestum denoted a phase of development preceding the age when Hera II was built. Delagardette, however, was at a loss to explain the quite emphatic entasis and deeply cut, at times relieved, necking of the columns and capitals of the earlier temples. Although the general proportions were stubby, he found a certain *mouvement* and *grâce* in their silhouette, which gave the Order of the earlier temples something of the refinement of the Doric of the Theater of Marcellus and the Colosseum. The only explanation he could offer was that the columns of the two earlier temples at Paestum, which he thought originally had had no entasis and therefore would have appeared even more squat, had been recut by later Roman architects to relieve them of some of their barbaric primitiveness.[105]

Labrouste concluded, by contrast, that the Temple of Hera II was the earliest because it was the most pure of the three! His conclusion was surely a willful act of distortion, similar in its anti-classical intent to his discussion of the corner triglyph of the Temple of Athena. It involves a curious paradox. Whereas Delagardette's conclusion may have been right, his reasons were wrong. His explanation for the shape of the columns of the temples of Hera I and Athena reveals the confusion of his reasoning. Labrouste, however, refused the very idea of a parallel between Greek and Roman forms and thus arrived at a totally erroneous conclusion—but for more rational and realistic reasons. Labrouste claimed that Hera II was the oldest of the three temples because it was constructed from only one variety of stone. He thought that the use of two different grades of stone in both the temples of Hera I and Athena indicated, "if not an improvement" from the point of view of art, "at least a more developed awareness of the materials native to the region." They should be dated later, because they evinced a more developed appreciation of local geological conditions. The Temple of Hera II was the earliest because, in Labrouste's eyes, it was built in the same manner in which temples in Greece were built and thus must have been constructed by Greeks recently emigrated from their homeland. This made the Temple of Hera II a purer expression of Greek art. By this analysis, Labrouste was able to undercut one more academic belief: the equation of technical with artistic progress. Labrouste had implied that the use of differing grades of stone on the part of the later architects of Paestum was a sign of technical progress though it was not, as he said, a sign of artistic progress: "These forms [of the Temple of Athena and of the Temple of Hera I] no longer have the primitive purity that one observes in the Temple of Neptune [Hera]."

Labrouste's miscalculation of the chronological order of the temples at Paestum was radical.[106] That alone, however, could not have accounted for the Academy's displeasure. Since it may be doubted that he really believed what he said, it may also be doubted that the Academy believed it. They must have understood quite well his purpose in reversing the classically defined sequence. Otherwise, his final conclusion for dating the three temples would have seemed simply incredible if not just inscrutable. Labrouste wrote the following in his *précis historique:*

> These observations lead me to consider the temple of Neptune [Hera II] as being Greek architecture . . . and to consider the "portique" [Hera I] and the temple of Ceres [Athena] as . . . *another architecture* . . . and built at a time when the Poseidonians, having become more powerful, *wanted to create for themselves a new architecture* [italics added].

This was heresy. The Academy deleted any reference to it in its report. It was a blasphemy deserving the excommunication that Labrouste in fact received. The very idea of the possibility of "creating by oneself a new architecture" was the Romantic battle cry of the 1820s, '30s, and '40s, which the Academy always vehemently condemned. Furthermore, having interjected the phrase "having become more powerful," Labrouste surely must have seemed to be implying something similar about the "new" architecture of Rome and the Renaissance. The blasphemy lay in equating "newness" with "otherness." Labrouste claimed that the later architecture of Paestum was "another architecture." It was no longer Greek. It could only be classified as "Poseidonian architecture." Labrouste claimed that this later Poseidonian architecture proved that its creators had "forgotten the architectural principles that [their forebears] had brought from Greece."

If within less than a century these principles could be forgotten by architects directly descended from Greek stock and building at the same site with a pure example of Greek art before their eyes, then what real basis existed for claiming a continuity in later Roman and Renaissance classicism, and how could their purported kinship with Greek ideals be justified? What indeed could explain the meaning of the term *classical* in the nineteenth century?

Labrouste's answer offered to the Academy in 1829 still rings loud and clear: such an attempt on the part of the later residents of Paestum (read Italy of Roman or Renaissance times or France of the seventeenth to nineteenth centuries) to create another, new form of architecture, while academically reusing (read imitating) Greek forms in so-called classical ways, could only result in the loss of that "primitive purity" characteristic only of Greek architecture. Any dogmatic insistence on the use of certain forms could only exhibit a "loss of principle." Sterility and decadence were signs of academic old age. There was no ideal in classical idealism. Meaning had nothing to do with the forms themselves. Their blind reuse only betokened spiritual decay. The academic belief in the trinitarian union of the Father Rome, the Son Renaissance, and the Holy Ghost of Greece was indeed, in Labrouste's just opened eyes, like the blind leading the blind. And it was not long before Darcel, Lassus, and Viollet-le-Duc were to believe that they had rediscovered the medieval True Cross.

Once architectural composition was understood as a systematized coordination of rationally ordered parts, then the very nature of architecture's principles would be seen as only an outgrowth of history rather than nature. This undercut the only meaningful basis for the ideal content of classical form that was left to the early nineteenth century: the belief in the hut as the natural prototype of all classical forms. Acceptance of the self-contained prototype of the hut as the source of classical architecture's embodiment of natural laws was inextricably connected with the acceptance of the classical trinity. The belief in the classical trinity was, in turn, contingent upon the belief in the natural prototype of the hut. But it was an abstract, insubstantial prototype in reality. Only by virtue of its abstract image could the relationship between the classical forms of Greek, Roman, and Renaissance architecture be maintained. That involved a metaphysical form of justification that was denied by Labrouste's positive identification of the source of Greek form in Greek culture. To the Neoclassical idealist, the Greek, the Roman, and the Renaissance were just different aspects of a single natural substance.

Charles Blanc, like most others, understood the revolutionary nature of this message and described the significance of Labrouste's work as a *pension-naire* in Italy in the following way:

> [At that time] the great models of Greek architecture existing in Sicily and southern Italy had not been explored, or very little and rather badly. The works published in the eighteenth century, in France by Leroy, in England by Stuart and Revett, were hardly remembered.... As for the *pensionnaires* of the Academy in Rome, they had hardly gone back in their studies beyond the Roman monuments of the Augustan era, when M. Henri Labrouste ... undertook the restoration of the temple[s] of Poestum and made [them] the object[s] of a deeper and more serious piece of work than that of his predecessors.... From Poestum, with his friend M. Duc who had won the prize in 1825 and whose eyes were beginning to open, M. Henri Labrouste went to Sicily.
>
> This trip was for them a second education. The Doric architecture, imported to Sicily by the Greek colonists, appeared to them in the majesty of its colossal ruins. They visited Segesta, Selinus, Agrigentum, Syracuse, and they understood all the changes that this imposing and manly art had undergone, an art whose greatness derived more from the spirit of the people who had invented it than from the size ... of the columns.... *They understood how much this art had been enfeebled, denatured, misunderstood by the Romans of the Empire*, and in measuring these immense and venerable remains that lay in the dust, in their minds' eye re-erecting them, or through study restoring them, they extracted from them the true principles of antique architecture....[107]

How could that which was supposed to be, in all its occurrences, a mimetic idealization of nature be considered in all but its first occurrence to be "denatured"? As a transparent manifestation of ideal laws, how could it be "misunderstood"? As a self-contained progressive principle, how could it become "enfeebled"? Clearly, according to Labrouste, only as a result of imitations more and more abstracted from their historical rather than natural source.

Labrouste's restoration of Paestum sounded the death knell of Neoclassicism in France. His rejection of the classical foundation of academicism showed how questions of architectural substance might be rephrased in less ideal terms than those used in the past. He opened the door to a new and richer understanding of Greek architecture[108] as well as the related understanding of Gothic architecture. Within a decade or so, architects and writers such as Viollet-le-Duc, Lassus, and Alfred Darcel were to redirect Labrouste's basic assumptions toward the task of defining the specific meaning and order of medieval architecture. Their perception of its structural order underlying a decorative surface of descriptive parts was indebted to Labrouste. It was partly as a result of Labrouste's structural definition of the Greek system of proportions and its distinction from classical canonization that later writers saw the more subjective, although no less systematic, order of Gothic proportions as contingent upon local materials and processes of fabrication.[109]

One aspect of Labrouste's restoration offered a positive guideline to how architectural meaning might be achieved, given the disavowal of faith in the classical dogmas. It was this, surely, which most angered the Academy and underlay all its other objections. The critic Gabriel Laviron described the attitude contained in Labrouste's new understanding of Greek architecture as "positivistic," and dissociated it completely from Neoclassical empiricism: "[Around 1830] positive knowledge developed to such an extent that the education of an artist can no longer have anything in common with what it once was . . . [and it] has come to substitute positive data for the empiricism of the old practitioners."[110] The philosophy of positivism rejected the transubstantial classical belief in the inherence of meaning in generic forms and asserted that attributed meaning could only be considered as an abstractly adherent fact.[111] Labrouste's assertion of that idea was contained in his explanation of the Temple of Hera I as a "portique." As that was the final building in terms of his chronology, his critique of it depended on a series of previous negations. Since Labrouste considered that building to have been the last of the three built at Paestum, it necessarily had the least connection with the principles of Greek architecture as embodied in the earliest temple, Hera II. It therefore could be seen as the first instance of a positive assumption of a new and more abstract principle, which in turn would disclose a progressive development toward greater and greater architectural abstraction. In the more abstract means that its architect adopted, it revealed how un-Greek [i.e., unclassical] architectural composition could become and still contain significant expression. This would necessarily have a profound effect on the contemporary revaluation of the architect's understanding of the real determinants of historical evolution.

In proposing that the principles of Greek architecture had been "forgotten" by the architects at Paestum as early as the end of the fifth century B.C., Labrouste dug a deep grave for classicism. However, in his description of the way in which he claimed that the Poseidonian architect of the Temple of Hera I reacted to his own cultural conditions and achieved a form of architectural meaning despite his loss of Greek ideals, he was offering a means for considering how architectural form might gain meaning once again in a similar way. This was surely even more heretical than all the negations on which that was based. He claimed that the final building at Paestum was given its special character by totally abstract means—in fact, by the use of the written word—and that this was both a function of its chronological position and an indication of the loss of the chthonic beliefs that had originally animated the Greek Order.

Labrouste assumed that the original colonizers of Paestum first erected the Temple of Hera II to embody Neptune, the tutelary deity of the place. He thought that this grew out of a primal religious impulse that became weaker and weaker as time went on: "But one is not able to assume . . . that the new colonists set out as zealously to erect temples to other deities." Thus, he stated about the building of the Temple of Athena: "It was only after a number of years of prosperity that the new colonists must have thought to erect a temple to Ceres, in gratitude for the fertility of their lands." And about civic buildings: "It was only after many military successes, and when the colony had acquired a certain degree of stability and power, that the Poseidonians must have thought to construct porticoes where people could gather to discuss communal business."

Labrouste saw the three stages of building at Paestum in terms of the historical progress of humanity as coevally laid out by Auguste Comte in his *Cours de philosophie positive* (1830–42): first, the magical-religious embodiment of the tutelary deity; second, the metaphysical representation of human gratitude; and third, the positive creation of a structure for human intercourse. In his view, this decrease in religious idealism necessarily entailed a loss of purity of form and a devaluation of the meaning of those forms. It also revealed an increased interest in construction over and against the forms of representation. The later architects did not invent new forms but merely reused those they had inherited, with increasing devaluation of their former meaning.

Whereas the entablature of the Temple of Athena could be claimed by Labrouste to be more structurally "ingenious" than its Greek prototype, its pediment already showed a degradation of that original form by the lack of the lower horizontal cornice. Labrouste probably could not bring himself to believe that things had gotten that bad so soon, and he restored the pediment with a slight, lower cornice (p. 379). Still, he acknowledged a fundamental difference between the overall shape of the pediment and that of the pediment of Hera II (p. 372) in making the Temple of Athena look positively proto-Etruscan. Carrying one step further that progressive, Poseidonian devaluation of representational form in the face of more pressing structural concerns, Labrouste restored the Temple of Hera I without any representational frontispiece or pediment at all (p. 361).

Delagardette had likened the Temple of Hera I to a stoa, but preserved for it its traditional designation as a basilica. That still conferred on it some representational imagery, albeit of a Roman sort. Labrouste denied any such ideal association of form and content and saw in its form a real content of an absolutely different sort. He construed it to be a simple "portique," a civic gallery for the functional interaction of people, a structural shelter within which the people of Paestum carried on their daily affairs.[112] It was thus neither a temple, the home of a god, the giver of law, nor a basilica, a monument of public ceremony representing the promulgation of divine laws by men.

Labrouste's renaming it a "portique" literally lowered it in rank to a mere utilitarian structure:

> This building is commonly named a basilica. The arrangement of the plan is sufficient indication that the monument was not a temple; but the name basilica, however, seems to me no more suitable for it, since nothing in the plan indicates any provision for the tribunal . . . ; on the contrary, . . . its axis is occupied by a row of columns. This disposition led me to consider it as one of those porticoes where the ancients gathered to discuss public affairs. . . .
>
> . . . [It is] a building that served as a covered walk . . .; it was inspired by the need to cover a large space at little cost . . . [and by] a certain economy necessary in the erection of these porticoes, which are utilitarian monuments.

Labrouste, however, did not feel that such a functional devaluation necessarily deprived the "portique" of significant expression: "Among the ancients, porticoes were monuments of great importance." It was only that the type of expression and means for achieving it differed from those involved in erecting temples or basilicas. Since the structure itself was meaningless, an architectonic framework only, its characterization had to be conferred upon it by adherent signs, which, when read by the citizens passing through it, would give the structure a meaningful place in their lives: "[Their porticoes often] were decorated with various paintings . . . as well as shields taken . . . from their enemies," that is to say, " with anything that could remind the citizens of the virtues of their ancestors and inspire them with the desire to follow their example."

Labrouste presented his restoration of the interior of the "portique" in two sublimely colored and shaded sections and a contrastingly white, stark perspective (pp. 361–62). They show the interior as an open shell. It has no hung ceiling. The wood rafters of the tile roof are exposed. A blank frieze runs around the entire interior just under the roof line, and it is hung with metal shields and lances. A pilastrade superposed on the central spine of columns is also hung with metal shields and lances and is almost masked by them. Labrouste explained that his intention in doing this was to give some idea of how the building might actually have appeared at the time: "I placed within this 'portique,' as at the Poikile in Athens, enemy shields, with no other intention than to give an idea of how the ancients decorated their porticoes." He claimed that this manner of decoration was justified by Pausanias's description of the one in Athens: "Pausanias tells us that the Athenian Poikile was decorated with various paintings, one of them representing the Battle of Marathon, as well as with shields the Athenians took from their enemies." But, unlike the Athenian prototype, Labrouste's Poseidonian "portique" somehow did not deserve to be ennobled by grand historical paintings. Instead, as may be seen in the perspective, he attempted to make its special character absolutely legible by applying graffiti to its walls and, even more pointedly, to the smooth face of its first column. He admitted that his decision was perhaps a bit outré:

> The decoration I adopted for the interior of the "portique" is not justified by any existing evidence, since the walls are entirely destroyed. It can, however, be given some measure of likelihood by the position of the flutes of the first column of the row forming the axis of the "portique." The fluting is interrupted, and the column remains smooth on the side that faces one upon entering the "portique." This particularity may have been occasioned, I believe, by the need to place in this spot, the most conspicuous of all, some painted inscription concerning the regulations governing the gatherings, and I assume that the walls of the "portique" were also covered with painted inscriptions and were used as an *album.*

Labrouste's perspective of the restored interior of the "portique" is a pure invention of the mind. It is an imaginative description of a container of historical events supported by the wriest form of reasoning. Of the three buildings at Paestum, this is the only interior he represented in perspective. His motive is obvious: sections could describe the unidirectional, hierarchically organized and divinely oriented space of the other two temples; only a perspective could connote the multidirectional, human space of the "portique." Furthermore, only a perspective could exhibit all at once the full intent of Labrouste's use of the inscribed word in stone to describe the building's message: Quatremère and the Academy were presented head-on with the inscriptions on the front face of the first column, while they could see other inscriptions scattered over the side wall.

Was Labrouste seriously proposing to the French Academy that they accept his idea of the Temple of Hera I as merely an *album* for temporary inscriptions? Did he seriously believe that they would agree to his idea of its first internal Order as simply a Colonne Morris *avant la lettre*? Did he really think that they would not balk at the idea of its sacred walls reduced to blank, white pages, covered with graffiti, as impermanent and meaningless as his own marks on the sheet of paper? The Academy must have been perplexed, and surely must have found it difficult to know on what level to take his proposal. It looks unrelievedly serious. Labrouste explained his use of the word *album* and justified his application of it to the building at Paestum by a reference to the lexicon of Suidas: "An album was a wall coated with plaster, suitable for receiving inscriptions dealing with civil matters."[113] He added that even in Rome "such was the name for [inscribed] mural tablets." And yet, on another level, Labrouste's restoration looks willfully naive. Indeed, when one turns to those fourth-year restorations that immediately issued from it—for instance, those by Théodore Labrouste of the early Roman temples at Cora, of 1831 (pp. 164–65), and by M.-A. Delannoy of the Tiber Island, of 1832 (pp. 170–71) —it is hard not to think that all this was a conscious attempt on the part of the youthful Romantics in Rome to poke fun at their doddering elders.

There was, however, a seriousness of purpose in that desire to caricature. There is a message implied in the students' refusal to take the classics seriously. On one level, there can be no doubt that they wanted to review the remains of the past as something other than cold and dry representations of some ideal. They wanted to divest them of their insubstantial idealism and re-invest them with some Romatic local color so that the past could come to life.

Théodore Labrouste's restoration of the Temple of Hercules at Cora draped the whole temple in impermanence and actually dismembered the body of the divinity, rendering him half-substantial and half-insubstantial. His head is a depicted headline on the pediment (p. 165), the rest of his severed body is at the rear of the cella, and a shield hangs in between like a magnified navel. Delannoy's restoration of the island in the Tiber turned the classical image into a storybook illustration. The colored surfaces of the buildings give them a poster-like presence and turn them into descriptions of a specific time and place.

Classical plasticity provided distinctions of a general order that, the Romantics felt, was based on insubstantial grounds. In order to specify, make legible, and name distinct functions, architecture had to call upon the real abstraction of the written word. Labrouste's idea of the "portique" at Paestum as an inscribed *album*, or mural tablet, revealed the historical transference of power from an oral to a written culture. In the nineteenth century, the printed word, through the newspaper, finally achieved total informational hegemony. At such a time the Romantics felt that architecture could no longer be considered, as classical theoreticians had for so long, a rhetorical language articulate in and of itself. The freedom of the individual demanded a readjustment of architecture's place in the hierarchy of communicative tools. That is the task Labrouste outlined for himself, and it is why the Bibliothèque Sainte-Geneviève looks the way it does. Like the "portique" at Paestum, it is no longer classical, and like its forebear its meaning does not simply reside in its style—it is really "another architecture."

"Speaking Architecture" and "Readable Architecture": The *Néo-Grec* at the Ecole des Beaux-Arts

Romanticism, in the form of the *Néo-Grec*, entered the Ecole by the late 1840s. It was not merely a fashionable interlude, but rather showed the first signs of influence of Labrouste's thought as outlined in his restoration of the temples of Paestum. Projects of 1847–53 pick up where Labrouste and his generation left off in 1829 and carry the process of reinvestment of meaning one step further in the Romantic imagination of the past. The direct connection between Labrouste's work as a *pensionnaire* of the French Academy in Rome in 1828–29 and later student work at the Ecole in Paris can be seen by comparing a project of 1847 by Edmond Garrel for a *Pont limitrophe* (Frontier Bridge, *(right)*, in a *concours d'émulation de composition*, with Henri Labrouste's fifth-year *envoi* from Rome of 1829, a *Pont destiné à réunir la France à l'Italie* (Bridge to Unite France and Italy), which was to be situated in the Alps along the Mont Cenis pass over the Guiers River (p. 396). The fifth-year *envoi* had been established by the Academy to allow the student, in his last year, to show off all he had learned during his sojourn in Italy. After four years of studying the Roman monuments of Italy, culminating in a major reconstruction of a particular monument, he was then free, in his final year, to present to the Academy a "public monument of his own composition and appropriate to the customs of France." Throughout the late '20s and '30s, the Academy was bitterly disappointed with all the results. Labrouste's bridge was no exception. The above clause in the Academy's stipulation was obviously the catch. In the composition to end all compositions, the student was to apply what he had learned from antique Roman ruins to what he supposed was demanded by nineteenth-century French conditions of life. A direct connection between the classical past and the present was more than implied. In the academicians' eyes, Labrouste's bridge all too literally bridged the gulf separating the two traditions and countries. It turned its back on the Italic soil, which according to the Academy nurtured the full development of classicism in ancient Rome and in the Renaissance.

Garrel's Frontier Bridge of 1847 is a mirror image of Labrouste's project of 1829. It is a sinister projection of the idea of the gradual debasement of classical forms implicit in Labrouste's project. Both Garrel's and Labrouste's bridges tell a story. Garrel's is a kind of sequel to the events described in Labrouste's. The plot remains the same, only the characters change. Taken together, it is both a "tale of two cities" and a Romantic story of two generations. The tale described by Labrouste's bridge takes place in a distant part of Italy, far removed from the Tiber. Garrel's sequel takes place a generation and a continent away in an even more distant outpost of the Roman Empire, North Africa. It recounts not the incursion into France of Italian ideas, but describes instead the colonization of former Roman territory by French forces. It marks the penultimate event in the establishment of the Pax Gallica in Algeria, the consolidation of the western border with Morocco in 1845.[114]

What I have called the plot of the two bridges is exactly the same. A river on a plateau, with a hill in the distance, is traversed by a double-arched bridge marked by *cippi* in the middle and single-arched triumphal entries at either end. The source of the plot for both can easily be found in the provincial Roman bridges of Spain and Southern France, in particular at Saint Chamas. But in both cases, those were only the most diagrammatic of struc-

Edmond Garrel. *Pont limitrophe* (Frontier Bridge). 1847. *Concours d'émulation, rendu.*

This bridge, reproduced in a radical architectural magazine that published many student projects, was drawn by a student of Léon Vaudoyer who was clearly basing his design on Labrouste's fifth-year *envoi* *(following pages)*. Garrel's project combines North African and Middle Eastern motifs with details derived from classical Italian architecture. It presents a provincial version of a triumphal bridge, which parodies the design proprieties observed at the Ecole.

FRANCE

PROJET D'UN MONUMENT QUE L'ON SUPPOSE PLACE AUX FRONTIERES DE LA FRANCE ET DE L'ITALIE

ON SUPPOSE SUR LE CHEMIN UN PONT DESTINE A REUNIR LA FRANCE A L'ITALIE. LE MILIEU DU TERME EST OCUPE
PAR LES BORNES QUI MARQUENT LES LIMITES DES DEUX PAYS, ET AUX EXTREMITES DU PONT ET EN REGARD SONT
PLACEES DEUX INSCRIPTIONS, D'UN COTE FRANCE ET DE L'AUTRE ITALIA

Henri Labrouste. *Pont destiné à réunir la France à l'Italie* (Bridge to Unite France and Italy). 1829. Fifth-year *envoi*. Perspective, elevation, and section.

This bridge is one of a group of fifth-year *envois* by Romantic students that defied the conventions of the Ecole by introducing non-classical variations on traditional themes. Its provincial location and its sparsely decorated, unmonumental forms prompted severe criticism by the Academy. The literal nature of the decoration presages some of Labrouste's detailing of the Bibliothèque Sainte-Geneviève.

PROJET D'UN MONUMENT QUE L'ON SUPPOSE PLACÉ AUX FRONTIÈRES DE LA FRANCE ET DE L'ITALIE

tures upon which to develop more personal variations. Clearly the real source of Garrel's was Labrouste's and Labrouste's, his imagination. Both bridges are seen in an imagined airless space of the mind. We know from the tremendous number of drawings Labrouste made in Italy that the idea of telling a story architecturally by recomposing historical fragments was closely linked in his mind with the narrative pictorializations of pre-Raphaelite art. In studying and drawing the *trecento* and *quattrocento* frescoes at San Francesco at Assisi and the Campo Santo in Pisa, Labrouste literally removed the architectural structures in the backgrounds of the frescoes from their historical and narrative contexts, and presented them on their own for study.[115] As such, especially those from the frescoes at Assisi then attributed to Giotto, their thinly scaled, airless presence gives a special meaning to the combined elevation-perspective that Labrouste used for his bridge.

In both Labrouste's and Garrel's projects, the forms are severely outlined and the major part of the decorative elaboration is reserved for the internal surfaces. As in Giotto's frescoes, a firm contour outlines the mass, which is rendered meaningful by concisely expressed internal lines of characterization. In his obituary of Labrouste, Henri Delaborde, the Secrétaire Perpétuel of the Academy from 1874 to 1898, remarked on this quality, particularly in his discussion of Labrouste's bridge:

> [What he wanted] to find in the combination of details [was] not a simple decorative expedient but rather a way to define fully the principal forms. Labrouste's last *envoi* especially—the project for a *bridge*...—clearly expressed the wish he had to restore to architecture a scrupulous respect for logic and to reject as an equivocation, if not as a mistake, everything that failed to contribute directly to specify the particular purpose, the requisite physiognomy, the "individuality" of a monument.[116]

Delaborde claimed that such lapidary concision was absolutely new at the time and flew in the face of normal classical practice:

> ... The architects [of] the beginning of the century ... hardly thought of varying their compositions according to the specific characteristics of each subject, and even less of rigorously subordinating the decorative mode to the elements of construction itself. Be it a church, a theater, or a public palace, the same methods for providing order were almost always used, the same pediment atop the same columns, the same portico ... and everywhere the same time-honored ornaments—rinceaux, rosettes, and so on. It could be said of these ornaments, that rather than resulting from thoughtful calculation, they merely depended on ... ingrained habit; that rather than expressing any intention, their only purpose was somehow to cover surfaces.

How, might one then ask, is Labrouste's bridge so different? It too is draped with a classical garland and faced by an engaged Order topped by an entablature. Obviously, Delaborde realized that it was Labrouste's *intention* which differed. This he surely understood from the way in which the traditional classical forms are so skimpy in appearance and so clearly disconnected one from the other so that all traditional meaning has been sapped from them. Their meaning resides only in their syntactical, not in their plastic, connections. Delaborde also realized that this formal reductionism made the meaning less apparent. In commenting on the influence of such designs by Labrouste—and clearly Garrel's bridge would fall into this category—Delaborde said:

> It must however be admitted that if Labrouste's influence . . . on the young school of architecture has been fortunate in the sense that it recognized once again the claims of reason and extended its role in the practice of the art, it has also sometimes led to . . . an excess of reasoning. By attaching an ulterior motive to the slightest combinations of lines and by attempting to condense the meaning of everything, one arrived at the point of making stone speak an almost totally enigmatic language; furthermore, in wanting all too systematically to reduce architectonic forms to the strictly requisite, one expressed dryness rather than accuracy, the pedantry of simple-mindedness rather than a simplicity of intention.

Delaborde found the stones mute when they were no longer intended to speak. He, like most of his contemporaries, did not see that the rhetorical form of classical discourse had been replaced by a new literary form and that what had previously been eloquent, rhetorical figures of speech had been reduced and condensed into marks on a surface that could only be contextually understood.

The context of Garrel's project is Algeria. The surfaces of Roman cut stone are reduced to stucco, the decorative swags to thin ribbons, the panel to an unmolded plaque and the moldings of the extrados of the arches to a thin line or to leafy branches (p. 395). The decoration is all applied with an implication of the poverty of means at the colonizers' disposal. The arches themselves, leanly proportioned but stubbily detailed, were, like those of Labrouste's bridge, based on the so-called Arch of Augustus at Perugia, considered a primitive source because its basis is Etruscan. On the internal face of one of the arches in Garrel's bridge, the three bust-length figures sit in their niches like the figures in the Etruscan Porta Marzia, also in Perugia. Below them are inscribed the names of Louis-Philippe, Maréchal Soult, and Guizot, the figures responsible for France's subjugation of Algeria. Two members of France's cavalry guard the gate, under the winged figures of Victory that tie the horseshoe-shaped bough to the arch's imposts. The cavaliers are of an Assyrian type.[117] On the outside face of the other arch, fluttering ribbons tie the tensile molding of the arch in place, and the winged figures flutter higher up, where they hold in place the hanging, inscribed plaque. There is a mask in the stucco where the keystone would be, and it has a beard of jewels. Its crescent shape, like the turreted, crenellated top of the arch, is Sassanian. The parapet of the bridge is echoed by the curving outline of the crenellations, which in their folkloric simplicity mark the monument as a very distant, provincial relative of Near Eastern forms. Yet this willed primitivism is the key to determining the specific character of the bridge as North African rather than Near Eastern. At both ends of the historical and geographical scale, in its Etruscan and North African character, the bridge is far removed from the great centers of civilization from which the Academy held the monumental art of architecture to have sprung (the Near East) and in which it was supposed to have most fully flourished (Rome).

Garrel's bridge thus describes a specific event in local terms. Situated in Algeria, it uses locally debased forms of Roman colonial architecture to describe that recolonization of North Africa by the self-professed continuer of that Roman tradition, France. On an arch is written: "PAX PAX PAX." The idea of a tradition spreading out from a center of civilization until it is finally realized in forms totally debased is the ultimate *Néo-Grec* significance of Garrel's bridge. The fluttering ribbons, the vegetal moldings, the crescent of jewels, and the lightly relieved winged figures of Victory remove Garrel's bridge one step further from the Italian source for all of Labrouste's decoration. Garrel's figured surfaces clearly depend on the rock-cut arch at Taq-i-Bustan in Iran, of the fifth and sixth centuries, which Pascal Coste had just published as the first set of plates in his *Voyage en Perse* (1843–54).[118] That arch is itself a provincial version of a Roman arch and exhibits the reduced plasticity and revalued meaning implied in such a cultural displacement. Labrouste's bridge of 1829 had told the same story to the Academy but in more direct terms.

The Academy proclaimed against the lack of decorative plasticity in Labrouste's bridge in its report of 1830 on the work of the *pensionnaires* for 1829:

> We think . . . that M. Labrouste could have provided more grandeur to the decoration. . . .
>
> We fail to see why the attic is decorated by a small Ionic Order which seems to take the place of a bas-relief. . . .
>
> The profiles of the project and the garlands placed under the cornice of the bridge [are] treated meagerly and seem to bear little relation or analogy to the gravity of a monument of this sort.
>
> The stone marking the boundary between the States would appear to have been the essential part of such a project. There should have been a large one; one cannot see why there are two small ones.[119]

The Academy felt that not only the decoration but also the entire conception was too inconsequential. The report claimed that in restricting himself to just a bridge, without incorporating into his composition such ancillary structures as fortifications, officers' barracks, customhouses, and warehouses, Labrouste had willfully neglected to consider his project as a "vast composition." As a result, "the limits within which he confined himself have kept him from giving full flight to the imagination and talent of which he is capable," for he "forbade himself the means to develop the full resources of his art." Having made that overall condemnation, the academicians proceeded to criticize the slightness of the bridge itself. They noted that it was much too narrow, that a triple-arched entrance would have been grander. They declared that a large, singly arched span or, even better, a triply arched span should have been used. They criticized the decreased thickness of the attic story of the triumphal arch and questioned its structural stability. They objected to the fact that the attic did not occupy the full depth of the arch and that it did not sit directly over the center of the lower story: "Why he felt he had to deviate from . . . the principle of ponderation, especially in view of the meagerness of the lateral facades, is hard to understand." They would have liked the imposts of the arch to have been wider and to have been faced with an engaged Order in their full height: "When the ancients decorated their gates and their arches with an architectural Order, they usually made of this Order an essential and integral part of the construction."

All the decoration of Labrouste's bridge is obviously applied and not "essential" to its construction. It is classical in a sense but not really Roman. It is etymologically Etruscan. The arches, the proportions of the attic, the diminutive engaged Order, and the *cippi* are all Etruscan. The meagerness of the garland is simply ascetic. Labrouste's decision to place the outer face of the attic nearly flush with the outer face of the arch, thus leaving its inner face inset, was only partially the result of a structural calculation. It reinforced the deliberate blindness of the exterior of the bridge and allowed the interior to be read as more open.

The academicians recognized the relation of such a refusal of outward display to the question of style. Their main criticism was directed at Labrouste's sources. They vehemently objected to their provincial nature: "The *pensionnaire* . . . took as models the antique bridges that the Romans built in the Provinces to cross small rivers." They proclaimed that the lack of grandeur both in conception and in decoration of provincial examples rendered them inconsequential and, indeed, unsuitable as models to be imitated: "They bear, it is true, an original character that is often not without interest to the history of art; but they can only be exceptions to the rules of the beautiful architecture of antiquity; . . . it is in the big cities and principally in the Capitals that the art of architecture has reached its highest degree of richness, taste, and grandeur."

In Labrouste's rejection of Roman sources in favor of pre-Roman (Etruscan) or extra-Roman (provincial) models, the Academy realized the implied criticism of the whole classical tradition. This raised the issue to another level of magnitude for, as the Academy noted, in refusing to look to Rome Labrouste was denying the Rome-Renaissance axis upon which the continuity and value of the classical tradition rested: "Thus the masters of the Renaissance constantly derived their excellent precepts from the unquenchable source of the numerous buildings of Rome." It was, of course, that axis from ancient to Renaissance Rome through Florence and north into France into the heart of Paris, the home of the Academy, that Labrouste's bridge should have grandly marked out: "We think therefore that M. Labrouste could have provided more grandeur to the decoration of a bridge that separates france [sic] from Italy;[120] because it is not, as at . . . Saint Chamas, the meager resources of two provinces sharing the cost of erecting a bridge to serve as a boundary; it is, on the contrary, two great powers rich in resources of every kind."

Labrouste saw the situation in architecture from a different point of view. The Academy was still looking south for rules; he was looking north for more abstract principles. Both his perspective and geometric elevations of the bridge and its arches show only the internal face leading to France. There was no looking back to Italy. By contrast, the Academy specifically remarked first on the arch not described by Labrouste, the one that would be seen toward the south: "The gateway to Italy must . . . prefigure the grandeur of Turin, of Florence, and of Rome, just as that to france [sic] must partake of the grandeur of the Capital."

Whether or not the intended meaning of Labrouste's bridge was actually perceived by the Academy, it is clear that they were not willing to accept the terms in which it was laid out for them, for they were grounded in a revisionist theory of history. The real story the bridge tells is of an autobiographical nature, and such a Romantic use of classical forms for personal reasons was unconscionable in the Academy's view. Labrouste's bridge reads as a kind of thank-you note to Italy for having received him for five years. By its placement, it is an expression of his belief in a certain continuity of tradition. It is the bridge that he might forge between the traditions of the two countries. But, by its established point of view, it is the most humble and really gracious form of thank-you note, for it only points to where his training might lead.

The *cippi* in the middle mark the frontier. The genii of the neighboring countries shake hands at a boundary not too dissimilar from the mark between New York and New Jersey at the center of the Holland Tunnel. And, as in the tunnel, in Labrouste's bridge you would actually have to be on the road to see the sign. The handshaking is a sympathic response, at human scale, to real passage. Only the interior of the bridge reveals the actual meaning. The exterior is abstract. The attics of the triumphal arches are blind. Only after having passed through the first arch would you perceive the sign "FRANCE" on the succeeding "signpost." The keystone of the second triumphal arch is lightly punctuated by a fleur-de-lis. Looking back south, you would obviously see "ITALIA." We are left to imagine what in Labrouste's mind would actually characterize its name. Labrouste simply decided not to look back.

* * *

The Romantic form of the *Néo-Grec* made itself first and most pronouncedly felt in the *concours* of the Ecole des Beaux-Arts as a new manner of rendition rather than composition. In a certain sense, this was only fitting, since the basic idea behind the *Néo-Grec* was the desire for an unconventional, personalized form of expression. It is surely for this reason also that the Romantic attitude toward classicism most fully emerged in the freer *concours d'émulation en esquisses* rather than in the more tradition-bound, conventionalized forms established for the Grand Prix. It should be remembered that the Grands Prix were judged by the Academy, whereas the *concours d'émulation* were judged by the professors of the Ecole and a jury of twenty tenured members chosen by them. As Van Brunt noted, two of the Ecole's hard-line classicists died in 1846. Because of other deaths, five members of the jury were replaced in that year and nine more by the end of 1853. If, as was generally felt, the *esquisse* for the Grand Prix was to be considered the "first draft," the romantically inspired idea for the final rendered project, and if, as was so often said, "the first draft is the student, the final rendering is the *patron*," might it therefore not be said that the project for a sketch competition represented the student's personal rendering of his idea?

From the standpoint of composition, sketch projects such as C.-T. Thomas's *Bains d'eau chaude naturelle et de vapeur* (Natural Hot Water and Steam Baths, 1849), Ancelet's *Rendez-vous de chasse* (1849) or *Pavillon de bains* (Bathing Pavilion, 1850, p. 404), and Edmond Guillaume's *Corps de garde de sapeurs-pompiers* (Firehouse, 1851) are not fundamentally different from those of the '20s and '30s such as Victor Calliat's *Salle d'anatomie* (Surgical Amphitheater, 1825), P.-E. Lequeux's *Cabinet de lecture* (Reading Room, 1832) and A.-I.-E. Godeboeuf's *Bains d'eaux thermales* (Hot Thermal Baths, 1834). They are all little pavilions with pronounced entrances. The superficial rendition of that basic idea is, however, markedly different in the projects of the late '40s and early '50s. The radical shift in expressive surface is most noticeable in the idiosyncratic diminution or subtraction of the Orders as an ordering device, the more pronounced arcading and paneling, the emphasis on a more realistic form of structural articulation at masonry joints, the astringent reduction of openings to fit within the revealed structure, and the application of fluid decorative forms within embedded or incised framed panels. There also emerges a much greater catholicity of sources for the decorative forms. The projects of the '20s and '30s seem stolidly Roman by

Pavillon de Bains

ancelet

Elève de M. Ballard

Gabriel-Auguste Ancelet. *Pavillon de bains* (Bathing Pavilion). 1850. *Concours d'émulation, esquisse.*

The program for this bathing pavilion specified that it would stand in the park of a rich man's house and would serve as a spot to enjoy the freshness and mystery of the woods. Ancelet chose to decorate his compact stone structure with *Néo-Grec* detailing, which in part reflects Labrouste's Bibliothèque Sainte-Geneviève, then nearing completion.

comparison. The sketches of the '40s and '50s reveal a search for poetic surface in the deliberate contrast effected by flat, unmodulated, sectionally sheared off structural members and applied or incised decoration that seems to eat into the material structure and render it insubstantial. The expression is Byzantine and the byzantinism of the statement involves the perceiver in a reading process as complex as that demanded by the historical analogue. Compared with the cold and dry coloration of the earlier projects, even the lush, rich washes of the later sketches gleam with a ductile, metallic, unearthly warmth. No longer rephrased classical figures of speech, they seem to be poetic reveries of the industrialized nineteenth-century world, their surfaces a synthetic version of the dematerializing Byzantine mosaic:

> The néo-Grec style is the epitome of design, its interest a reflection of the tireless mind of the designer, who, having obtained a great many ideas bearing on his subject, melts these very ideas in the crucible of his imagination, refining them again and again until the minted metal gleams refulgent. All material is the same to such a one. By these means, and these alone, is original design possible.[121]

To render an insubstantial idea palpably poetic demanded a revaluation of classical syntax. That was first realized in Labrouste's Bibliothèque Sainte-Geneviève. It was between 1847 and 1850 that Labrouste rendered its idea by decoratively clothing its structure in signifying forms, and it was between 1847 and 1853 that the *Néo-Grec* changed the nature of design at the Ecole and, in fact, reached its most exaggerated form of expression. The period of 1847–53 covers the last year of the July Monarchy, the short-lived Second Republic, and the first year of the Second Empire. It was a period of revolutionary ideas, of a Romantic belief in a utopian future, and of rapid change ending abruptly in the frustration of the aftermath of Napoleon III's *coup d'état.* It was also a period of change at the Ecole itself. In 1845 and 1846, those changes began to be felt when two members of the outer circle of the *Néo-Grec* group were appointed professors.

In 1845 S.-C. Constant-Dufeux became professor of perspective. In 1846 Abel Blouet replaced Louis-Pierre Baltard as professor of theory at the Ecole and, for a period of about seven years, wrote the programs for the monthly *concours* (1846–53). In 1847 Daniel Ramée, known primarily for his restoration of medieval buildings and his historical accounts of medieval architecture, published a second volume of the engravings of Ledoux. And it was during this period, too, that Léon Vaudoyer, in his continuing series of articles on the history of French architecture in *Le Magasin Pittoresque*, first described Ledoux's work as an attempt to create an *architecture parlante,* ("speaking architecture").[122]

The revival of interest in Ledoux's work at this time is curious. The conclusions that can be drawn from such a parallel interest in the possibilities for a poetic and expressive architecture in the two periods are more paradoxical than might appear at first glance. One might suppose that it was natural for those caught up in the revolutionary mood of 1848 to look back to a similar moment in the recent past, indeed, to the Revolution that was felt to have predicated their own. In his article on the architecture of the reign of Louis XVI in the December 1852 issue of *Le Magasin Pittoresque*, however, Léon Vaudoyer denounced Ledoux's buildings as "without purpose or utility," "very luxurious on the exterior . . . very uncomfortable inside, and ordered in the most bizarre of ways." Vaudoyer described the ideas contained in Ledoux's publication as "the extravagances that mistaken and presumptuous minds can be carried away by when, contempuous of all traditions, . . . they have the pretension of creating by themselves alone a wholly new art." Vaudoyer characterized Ledoux as a "supporter of what has since been called 'speaking architecture' " and described his projects with patronizing sarcasm: "He thought he had discovered something marvelous in making the house of a wine grower in the shape of a barrel; no doubt he would have made that of a drinker in the shape of a bottle, etc." In conclusion, Vaudoyer noted a revival of interest in such expressionism: "and even today, the supporters of 'speaking architecture' have made some attempts. . . ."[123]

If, then, we can point to a reawakened interest in the expressive architecture of Ledoux's generation and, indeed, see a correlation in the minds of nineteenth-century architects between the "speaking architecture" of around 1790 and that of around 1850, how then do we explain Vaudoyer's criticism of Ledoux's efforts? First of all, we must differentiate between the preconceptions of the two periods. In describing the silliness of Ledoux's projects for houses in the forms of their owners' occupations, Vaudoyer saw Ledoux's architecture as a version of classical anthropomorphism, the ground against which Ledoux's ideas could only be destructive of the very system which they intended to reinforce. In his attempt to make his buildings describe their functions specifically rather than generically, Ledoux was correctly seen by Vaudoyer as having pushed the classical system beyond its means: "[He] strains all the rules of taste." Vaudoyer understood that Ledoux still believed in the inherent power of his plastic forms to embody meaning and therefore, in Vaudoyer's eyes, to have considered those forms as capable of "speaking." What Vaudoyer could not really understand, and probably did not want to, was that the classical system on which Ledoux's elaborations were based was dead. Thus, while he could sense some connection between the expressive aims of the two periods, he could not really articulate the differences. The main difference lay in the substitution of a mechanomorphic for an anthropomorphic conception of form in which plasticity was devalued as the way to embody meaning. The mid-nineteenth-century *Néo-Grec* type of expressionism was based on a less volitional idea of

Léopold-Amédée Hardy, Juste Lisch, Emile Delange, and Victor Pertuisot. *Phares* (Lighthouses). 1851–52. *Projets de 2ᵉ classe.*

These lighthouse projects by students of Romantic *maîtres d'atelier* were published in the *Revue Générale de l'Architecture* and were hailed by its editor, César Daly, as examples of a significant architecture of feeling that was rare at the Ecole. Unlike the massive, geometric forms of the lighthouse designs of Boullée, these projects use human images to express specific emotions such as anxiety and solicitude.

Revue Générale de l'Architecture et des Travaux Publics. — 4, Rue de Furstemberg, Paris.

Dirigé par Mr CÉSAR DALY, architecte.

Vol. 10.

Pl. 9.

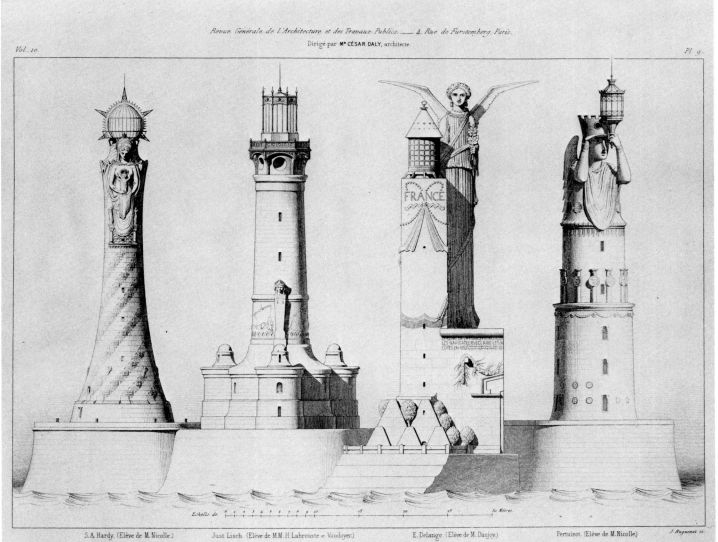

S. A. Hardy. (Elève de M. Nicolle.)   Just Lisch. (Elève de M.M. H. Labrouste et Vaudoyer.)   E. Delange. (Elève de M. Danjoy.)   Pertuisot. (Elève de M. Nicolle)

J. Huguenet sc.

PROJETS DE PHARES.

(CONCOURS DE 2^E CLASSE A L' ÉCOLE DES BEAUX-ARTS. PARIS.)

Imp. de Leisnuage, r. de la Sorbonne, 6, Paris.

form as something to be outlined by the architect and read by the public and not as something that might speak of its own accord. Paradoxically, this becomes most evident in just those student projects that Vaudoyer surely had in mind when he spoke of "the supporters of 'speaking architecture,' " who "even today ... have made some attempts. ..."

The *Néo-Grec* idea of expression, imagistic in a new way, can be examined in four student projects of 1852 for a lighthouse (p. 407).[124] These projects were chosen by César Daly from an exhibition of a *concours* of the *deuxième classe* at the Ecole and published as a group in his *Revue Générale de l'Architecture* (1852) in order to show, as he said, "that one can make poetry in architecture!"[125] He claimed that this poetic content had nothing to do with the classical and eclectic idea of form that was intended to "satisfy exclusively physical needs and to charm the eye by a wholly material harmony of forms." He chose them because he felt that they exhibited "some flashes, some rare outbursts ... amid this ocean of materialism," and that they expressed the poetic quality of a lighthouse by an almost religious transcendence of its material nature:

> A lighthouse is [not] simply a light-holder placed on high so as to be seen from afar and kept sheltered from the assaults of the sea.
>
> ... To respect these considerations is not much more than an effort of pure reason, an application of science to utility; feeling has hardly any part in all this. ... A lighthouse [is a] monument of solicitude and ... interest, [a] monument of love and anxiety, [a] work born both of a need ... and of a spiritual emotion, [a] work of UTILITY and of RELIGION.
>
> Feeling, religion, [that is] ... what constitutes the true *artistic, architectural* character of the monument.

The authors of the projects were Juste Lisch, Emile Delange, Léopold-Amédée Hardy, and Victor Pertuisot. Lisch was a student of Labrouste and Léon Vaudoyer, Delange, of Léon Danjoy. Hardy was a student of Joseph Nicolle, himself a student of Duban, and Pertuisot studied with both Nicolle and Blouet. During the 1840s, the ateliers of Labrouste, Vaudoyer, Danjoy, Nicolle, and Blouet, along with those of Constant-Dufeux, Vasserot, Victor Baltard, and Jaÿ, were the main sources for the development and dissemination of the exaggerated, or high-style, *Néo-Grec*. The four lighthouse projects owe their distinctive similarities to the *Néo-Grec* thought of these teachers. The more developed emphasis on descriptive form in the projects of the students of Danjoy and Nicolle reflects the fact that, as Emile Trélat said, they carried the *Néo-Grec* idea of literary form to its logical conclusion: "Danjoy and some others [including Nicolle], heeding only their imagination, which was excited by the heat of the prevailing atmosphere, yearned, and strove with talent, to make stone speak as a book speaks, to borrow from the writer his ideas and his images, and to clothe our monuments in them."[126]

Each of the four projects offers a readable image descriptive of one abstract emotion attached to the specific idea of the function of a lighthouse. It is clear from Daly's arrangement of the projects as reproduced in his *Revue*, in the same order in which he listed the emotional possibilities of a lighthouse, that Hardy's expresses "solicitude," Lisch's "interest," Delange's "love," and Pertuisot's "anxiety." The lighthouses are weird, their forms individual and strange, as might be expected from attempts to describe a personal emotion in an inanimate object. The students had to find forms of thought outside the traditional architectural vocabulary. The lighthouses are full of solecisms. Their fluency resides only in the stone. Paradoxically, there is a fantastic disproportion between the intrinsic muteness of the masonry carrier of thought and the abstract thought itself. In each lighthouse, the image or idea clings to the stone and yet is read in such an abstract way as to prohibit reading the stone and its image as one. The lighthouses, as literary transcriptions of poetic emotions, demanded a specificity of expression beyond the generically expressive range of classical forms of representation. The images, in fact, transcend the stone and occupy a different realm of perception. As a result of the search to find stone equivalents for human emotions such as solicitude, love, or anxiety, the elusive and disproportionate concatenation of descriptive parts in each project seems to remain unresolved in the different realms of the material and the ideational. The parts only conjoin behind the surface, in the stone, or above the surface, in the mind.

By comparison with Boullée's projects for lighthouses, those four projects of the Ecole of 1852 are more directly symbolic, their meaning less mediated by traditional emblematic means. Boullée's truncated cones rise out of abstract rectangular bases and spew forth smoke from their internal fires like man-made volcanoes.[127] This natural analogy is an aspect of Boullée's own extension of the classical theory of the imitation of nature. The sublime scale, enforced by the "difficult," "terrifying" spacing of tiny articulating details within sheer blank surfaces, declaims the relationship between the minuteness of men and their boats and the immense plane of the sea. Boullée's lighthouses are metaphors hyperbolized. The specific attributes of the program are only rendered in general terms. The lighthouses are only differentiated from projects for cenotaphs and tombs by the light of their fires burning within.[128] The spiraling line of figures in one or the decreasing layers of arcades in another define "tower" generally rather than "lighthouse" specifically.

Both Hardy and Pertuisot used the motifs of spiraling and telescopic layering in their projects. The base of Delange's lighthouse, with its concatenation of five truncated pyramids, also seems related to Boullée's or Lequeu's work. But the unarticulated relationship between the forms, their relationship to the blank wall behind, and the discontinuously detailed corner just above them to the right are much closer in quality to the way in which Labrouste detailed the corner of the facade of his Administration Building for the Bibliothèque Sainte-Geneviève (1846–50). The strange door molding of Delange's lighthouse turns the corner, uselessly adhering to the surface of the stone. The garland above is merely lopped over a block. The gigantic winged figure of safe delivery simply stands on her stone base, having just set down her lantern on its upper ledge. All the real connections are mechanical. The source of that mechanomorphism is spelled out in words. Below her feet, above the garland, the idea of the lighthouse is literally described as the product of Fresnel's invention of the *appareils lenticulaires* that allow for its mechanical functioning. The figure makes the application seductive.

Both Hardy's and Pertuisot's projects, by their enforced metamorphoses of object into personage, seem to belie the actual mechanomorphism of their conception. In Delange's project, the L-shaped stone frame is deliberately opposed to the sculpted body. In Pertuisot's project, the receding cylindrical parts do not so much call to mind the general idea of a tower, as in Boullée's design, as the idea of a lighthouse as telescoped light—light beamed toward the horizon. The abruptly shorn columns on the second story are bolted into place by oversized round paterae, which both hang from them and paradoxically cleave them in two. This demonstration of attachment on both the vertical and horizontal planes of action gives the whole object the sense of a limited extension for a specific, mechanical purpose. The central section reads like a wheel fixed in place by a rachet. The diminutive, coglike columns imply that the telescoped light could be directed to all points on the horizon at 30° intervals in 12 mechanically fixed positions. One's confidence in technological accuracy is undercut by the realization that human beings are responsible for its functioning, and it is the anxiety felt in relation to the higher, human plane of action that informs the upper part of the lighthouse. There, the figure of the anxious eye of France, guiding her seamen, actually holds aloft the enlightening mechanism of safe passage in her left hand. She is the narrow end of the telescope, and her crown marks the point where the human eye would actually look through it. As her left hand holds the lantern vertically at the point where her right hand defines the horizontal beam of the searching eye, she alludes to the act it performs by changing its direction from the vertical to the horizontal, thus clarifying the distinction between the architectural and human planes of action. Her gaze is a salute rendered limp by continual anxiety.

In Hardy's design, the sense of security afforded by a lighthouse is described by the outline of its stone shape. The molten form, rising out of the water into a pair of strong shoulders supporting the head of safeguarding light, seems like a solidified resolution of two waves. Some of the spiraling lines of its lower courses terminate discontinuously in figures of flying, praying angels. The spiraling lines are not imposed on the block, but rather take their internal shape from the contrary direction and nature of the actual blocks of stone coursing. The figures of the Virgin and Child at the top do not so much embody an inherent image of security as determine the stone's overall protective shape. The Virgin's head is reflected in the crowning globe; Her reassuring shoulders are continuous with the haunches of the base of the light; and Her protective lap is but the culmination of the incurving outline of the tower itself. The overall shape of the stone lighthouse gives an emotional sense of stability and permanence, upon which the enlightened invention of science, the reflecting globe of light, sits like a mechanical halo to ensure the return of seafarers.

The lighthouse projects give evidence of an attempt to formulate a new ground on which to figure an abstract idea, indeed, a literary image. The parts, unlike those in late eighteenth-century examples of "speaking architecture," do not add up and pronounce their meaning in unison. The syncretistic fusion of forms literally causes us to read each as a molded stone object, composed of discrete parts like thoughts on paper. The abstract stone ground, like the actual paper it is on, becomes the surface on which the story of its function is told and the surface to which the ascribed emotion just barely adheres. By contrast, Boullée's and Ledoux's projects never seem to adhere to the paper. They preserve a kind of ideal unity of form because they are figured in a transubstantial realm of thought. They thus appear to speak of their own accord and declare their meaning without our having to read meaning into them. In the *Néo-Grec* projects, we have to recompose the parts by the abstract processes of literary analysis and synthesis. In the process of decipherment, one feels the emotional expression directly, as when reading a poem or novel. As Van Brunt remarked:

> The *Romantique* . . . design[s] are distinguished by that tenderness of Love and earnestness of Thought which are the fountains of living Art. . . . every work appears as if its author had something particular to express in it. . . . The ordinary decorations of windows and doors are not made in conventional shape . . . but are highly idiosyncratic. The designer had a distinct thought about this window or that door, and when he would use his thought to ornament these features, he idealized it . . . as a poet attunes *his* thought to . . . verse. . . .
>
> . . . Through the agency of the *Romantique* school, perhaps more new and directly symbolic architectural expressions have been uttered within the last four years than within the last four centuries combined. Like the gestures of pantomime, which constitute an instinctive and universal language, these abstract lines, coming out of our humanity and rendered elegant by the idealization of study [*i.e.*, history], are restoring to architecture its highest capacity of conveying thought in a monumental manner.[129]

* * *

Monument Votif

(left) Gabriel-Auguste Ancelet. *Monument votif* (Votive Monument).
(opposite) Antoine-Jules Vignol. *Monument votif.* 1851. *Concours d'émulation, esquisses.*

According to the program for this competition, an astronomer, a writer, and a ship's captain are rescued after a shipwreck by being washed onto a rock; the rock is later carved into a monument of gratitude with a chapel, which includes tablets on which visitors may inscribe their own names and messages of sympathy. Ancelet's project joins into a single mass the act of being saved and the expression of gratitude. The geyser of waves from which the men are rescued by angels is contained by basaltic shafts emanating from the chapel in the rock. Vignol chose to express his monument as a pilgrimage station with columns above the chapel honoring each of the men.

34

Monument Votif

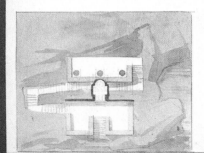

Vignole
Elin de V. Hebod

In the *Néo-Grec*, the tension of the opposing forces of ideational description and material carrier rarely allowed for a smooth and continuous imagistic surface. In the few cases where that almost occurs, it seems to portend the more supple organic continuity of Art Nouveau. In two projects submitted for a *concours* of the *première classe* of February 1851 on the subject of a *Monument votif*, the tension between the materiality of the stone and the discursive immateriality of the idea is stunningly obvious (pp. 412–13). Abel Blouet's program called for a votive monument that would express the pious gratitude of three seafarers—an astronomer, a writer, and a captain—for their deliverance from a shipwreck and that, by its lofty form, would honor their respective talents. According to the story of the program, the three men survived the disaster by reaching a lonely crag along the coast, which they then vowed to consecrate. The program specifically called for a literal rendition of the idea of being saved by stone. Blouet stipulated that the monument should contain blank stone tablets on which visitors to the monument would inscribe their own names. The monument was to be formed of the same rock as that at the place where the shipwrecked men had found their salvation. Visitors to the rock would surely be thankful for reaching it, and their expression of this gratitude would reinforce that of the monument itself as they inscribe their names on its surface. Presumably, in the chapel they would find some crude metal implements with which to scratch their names on the stone tablets. Their graffiti, organized and controlled by the tablets, would thus bear witness to their feelings, and in their active conscription by inscription in the actual stony constitution of the expressive meaning of the work, they would render that expression legible.

The project presented by Ancelet (p. 412), a student of Baltard and Jaÿ and the winner of the Grand Prix in the same year (1851), provides a singular image in stone of a distended rock by the seashore. It is sheared off on its face to reveal an inscription and a votive niche, while its body is impaled by a geyser of congealed water that is staked around its vertical axis. The project by Antoine-Jules Vignol (p. 413), a student of Vasserot, presents an image disrupted by a cliff of uncut rock. As in Ancelet's monument, the smoothly described surface below the rock is seen as if cut in section. In both cases, the literally descriptive surfaces of the lower sections were a direct response to Blouet's program.

Vignol's response to the program emphasizes the rational act of human calculation over and against the idea of divine intervention. It literally emphasizes honor over gratitude. The statuette of the Virgin (gratitude), just above the doorway, almost disappears in the rock that divides the monument in half. The frieze above describes the actual event; and the three columns, each topped by one of the attributes of the three survivors of the wreck, triumphantly honor their intellectual faculties and thus the human source of their salvation. The regularly displayed tablets below reinforce, by their allusion to writing, the rational character of man's powers of abstract thought and calculation. All of these signs are embedded in the stone and are distinctly tiered. The only positive connections are made by us as we scan the surface to reread the story of the event.

Ancelet's response to the program gives the Virgin more credit. Her image in the niche, though more prominent, seems nevertheless to be actually supported by the rational inscriptions of human intervention. These, as in Vignol's project, are carried by an obviously Labroustian device. The inscribed panels of the upper story of the Bibliothèque Sainte-Geneviève are returned to their source in real stone tablets. The flickering floral incisions around the niche can also be read as flames of eternal life.

Ancelet's *Monument votif* is like some strange apparition, surfacing all covered with seaweed and debris. The surface renders the abstract form of the idea legible. The natural stony base takes the form of primordial buttressing; the stone above the niche turns into crystalline pikes that stake the emerging shaft of congealed water; the capital of that shaft reconstitutes the Ionic capital as an undulating feminine image; and above, the guardian angels of the crown modestly lend a divine hand to the grateful survivors. Gratitude, expressed by the prominence of the Virgin in the niche, predominates and is buttressed below and around its perimeter by the harder, male forms of natural power and rational intelligence.

Thus, despite its apparent, indeed, organically derived continuity, Ancelet's monument remains characteristically disjunctive. In its overall form, it conjoins those two basic characteristics of the *Néo-Grec* expressive set—firmness and delicacy, or "Thought" and "Love." That conjunction gives it a characteristic quality that is just the idea of style. It fuses the masculine and the feminine, honor and gratitude, the hard and the soft, the convex and the concave, which were felt to be the abstract order of architectural style as such, underlying the Orders of the classical style.[130] Ancelet's monument exhibits the outward form of no apparent historical style. As just an idea transcribed onto stone, its separate shapes lack that unified sense of continuous relationships that might allow it to speak. Again, its message must be read across the disjointed stone surfaces. Its willed continuity of form can only be barely felt, under the descriptive passages of the surface, to derive its power from the inarticulate stone itself. When such a decoratively applied integument could be organically fused with the abstract linear skeleton underlying Labrouste's Bibliothèque Sainte-Geneviève, then the easier reintegration of structure and decoration, which has generally been seen as the novel quality of Art Nouveau, would come into being.

Organic continuity seems to have been inconsistent with the fundamental *Néo-Grec* impulse toward disjunction and differentiation. This resulted from the desire and felt need to spell out an idea. Continuity could only be romantically achieved in the fictional world open to the perceiving mind. Architecture was, in effect, still conceived on the model of language. It was no longer, however, a fluent spoken language like classical architecture; it was only *like* a language in its written form. The *Néo-Grec* is a "readable architecture," not a "speaking architecture." All its words and punctuation marks therefore had to be reinvented or, at least, reconstituted and reinvested with palpable meaning. This took place in the nature of the materials themselves and thus it is always the joint, the connective tissue of an idea, that marks the intersection of thoughts. This is the real point of *Néo-Grec* articulation—where the material compresses under stress and the surface evaporates upon the impress of thought.

BEAUX-ARTS BUILDINGS IN FRANCE AND AMERICA

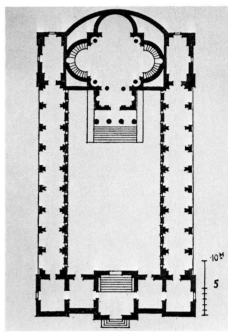

Pierre Fontaine. Chapelle Expiatoire, Paris. 1816–26.

One of the first official acts of Louis XVIII after assuming the throne of France was to direct that the remains of Louis XVI and Marie Antoinette be exhumed from the cemetery of the Madeleine. At the same time he commissioned a chapel of expiation on the site. In 1816, Pierre Fontaine (1762–1853; student of A.-F. Peyre and Heurtier, 2ᵉ Grand Prix 1785) was designated as architect. (Fontaine's associate, Percier, had retired from designing in 1814.) Chateaubriand claimed to be the source of the idea of the chapel and some aspects of its form in his *Memoires d'outre-tombe*; whether this be true or not, Fontaine produced in the Chapelle Expiatoire a work of extraordinary character, which was widely admired at the time of its execution.

Fontaine had been the author of a sepulchral monument in the manner of Boullée when he competed for the Grand Prix in 1785, but thirty years later he conceived of this more modest monument to the dead as an Italian *campo santo*. A simple entrance pavilion and the chapel structure close two ends of a rectangular site, while the long sides are bordered by low arcades with peaked roofs. These create a walled garden on the site of the mass graves of the Revolution, through the center of which the visitor approaches the chapel of expiation. This garden can be entered only through the pavilion, and is thus given an air of privacy and removal, yet the low *arcosilia (opposite)* allow the surrounding park space to seem to blend into the sanctified area.

The chapel structure itself is a plain cube of stone, with three exedrae and a portico joined to it by a single projecting molding. The cube is crowned by a dome, which like the exedrae is pierced by an oculus, to introduce a "religious" light into the interior of the chapel where statuary reminds the visitor of France's atonement for the execution of a king.

At its completion in 1826, the Chapelle Expiatoire was declared by critics to be one of the most remarkable buildings in Paris. Its singular nature is the result of a complex blend of observations and ideas on the part of Fontaine. It at once evokes reminiscences of the Hadrianic and Pompeian planning that were of great interest to a number of architects at the turn of the century; of the Roman Pantheon; and of the *campo santo* at Santa Maria Novella in Florence. These allusions to simple private spaces, glorification, and death are gathered into a cloistered enclosure of great simplicity yet of sensitively considered proportion and detail. Contrasting geometrical forms are joined but not blended: dome and exedra remain distinct from the cubic mass of the chapel, while the arches and gables create separate, continuous rhythms. This is no longer the collection of massive, associative forms that characterized the sepulchral projects of the late eighteenth century, but rather their more elegant descendant, seen as a tableau. Fontaine here undertook an exploration of forms similar to that carried out in England by John Soane, an exploration that benefited from the sensitivity to planning and arrangement of spaces encouraged by his Beaux-Arts education. The Chapelle Expiatoire is a bridge between late eighteenth-century and Napoleonic architecture and the beginnings of Romanticism.

Victor Baltard. Halles Centrales, Paris. 1845–70. Demolished 1973.

The Halles Centrales of Paris were among the most significant urban accomplishments of Napoleon III and his prefect, Georges Haussmann; yet today they are demolished. Les Halles were designed by Victor Baltard (1805–74; student of Louis-Pierre Baltard, Grand Prix 1833), who had been a conservative student at the Ecole des Beaux-Arts, but who nevertheless was one of the principal employers of iron in French architecture of the mid-century.

In August 1845, Baltard and Félix Callet were selected as architects of Les Halles on the basis of a project submitted the year before. Baltard spend the next two years studying markets in other European countries. In mid-1848, he and Callet received approval for a final project, which proposed a group of eight stone pavilions *(left)* for the Napoleonic site bounded by the Halle au Blé and the Rue Saint-Denis.

The first stone was not laid until September 1853, because the Conseil Municipal and the prefect, Berger, had spent the five intervening years in conflict over the site and the plans. In 1847, the architect Hector Horeau revived a project that he had submitted in 1844, calling for a huge iron shed, 100 meters wide, which would face the Seine and extend from the present-day Place du Châtelet to the Marché des Innocents. The prefect and, subsequently, Napoleon III supported this project, but it was finally rejected because of its proposed site. It is unclear whether, in reaction to the whole proposal, the Conseil Municipal then urged Baltard to complete a project entirely in stone, as some of his eulogists claimed, but it seems likely that he had always intended to do just that.

Construction of Baltard's first pavilion proceeded from September 15, 1851, to June 3, 1853, when Napoleon visited the site and ordered that work be halted. The massive, poorly lighted and ventilated building had aroused the anger of the vendors (who called

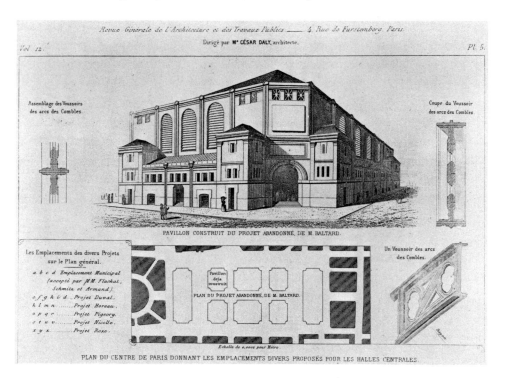

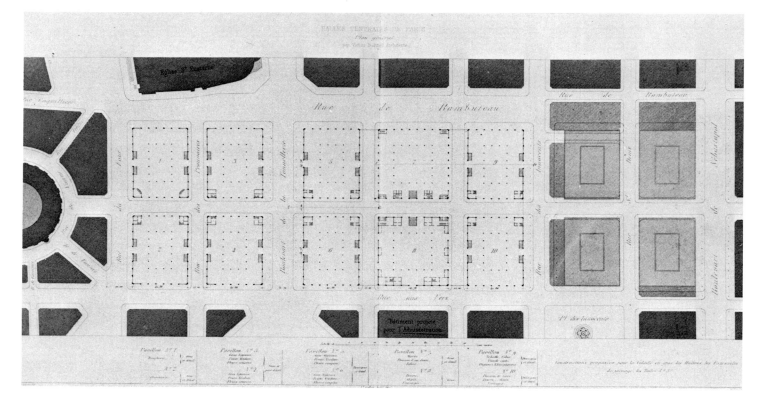

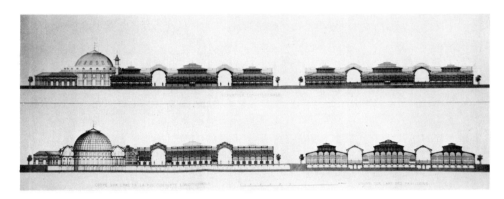

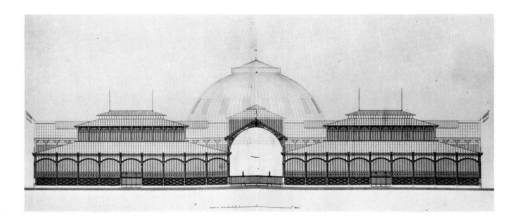

it the *fort de la Halle*, a pun on the name for the brawny market porters), as well as of the emperor, who had admired Horeau's project and was attracted to the appearance of the new Parisian railway stations of iron and glass. Haussmann, appointed Prefect of the Seine in that June of 1853, succeeded in keeping Baltard in his post, but insisted that the architect create the "vast umbrella" that Napoleon desired and that it be entirely in iron. On June 13, Baltard submitted three projects to Haussmann, two of which used much stone and iron, and one of which was all in iron and glass except for a low brick windbreak *(below and right)*. The last was enthusiastically approved by the emperor on June 19. The new project was received by Baltard's contemporaries as a pastiche of the projects of Horeau and of the engineer Eugène Flachat, and indeed it owed much to both, but was far less technically ambitious.

Construction began on the eastern half of the fourteen proposed iron pavilions in May 1854; six were finished by 1858, and ten were in use by 1870. Two more were finished in the 1930s, and two were never built. (The single stone pavilion was used until the late 1860s and then demolished.) The entire market complex, including the surface area of the seven sections of street running through it and of the Halle au Blé, covered 87,790 square meters (approximately the area of the Crystal Palace in London, of 1851). Beneath

HALLES CENTRALES DE PARIS.

almost its entire area were brick-vaulted basements for delivery and storage, a reservoir, and passages for an underground railway connection that was never built. The superstructure, which had gas lighting on account of its early morning hours of use, provided a vast, well-ventilated shelter for all the major markets, which had hitherto been scattered through the area.

What had been controversy over this structure in the 1840s and '50s turned to approbation in the 1860s. Viollet-le-Duc, in the first volume of his *Entretiens sur l'architecture*, of 1863, praised Les Halles for their "absolute respect" for the program and for their honest indication of their means of construction, which qualities made them beautiful, comprehensible, and modern. Several efforts were made after Baltard's death to prove that the conception of the iron structure had been entirely his, though Haussmann's memoirs and a series of letters to the Paris newspapers of 1869 remain as documents to the contrary.

Whatever the sources and motivations of the architect, the buildings of Les Halles, once constructed, were probably the more impressive for having been designed by a former student of the Ecole, because their modest technical innovation was enhanced by the clarity and practicality of their arrangement of regular pavilions and covered streets, which adhered to Beaux-Arts conventions of the separation of circulation from the principal spaces. The huge and functionally successful complex served to establish the role of iron in French construction in a way that no smaller public structure or temporary pavilion had done up to that time. Its progeny were the numerous iron-and-glass market structures in France of the latter part of the century, and it contributed to many other innovative commercial and industrial buildings. The great fault of the Halles Centrales, for which they were demolished, was their location in the crowded center of Paris, of which they were once the commercial heart.

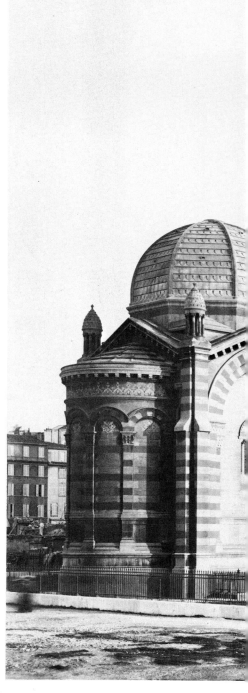

Leon Vaudoyer. Marseilles Cathedral. 1845–93.

To the French Romantic mind the religious building was the fullest statement of a society's values. Marseilles Cathedral, overlooking the new port of the city, was designed by

Léon Vaudoyer (1803–72; student of A.-L.-T. Vaudoyer and Lebas, Grand Prix 1826) as an acknowledgment of the myriad meanings that he perceived in this religious project.

Vaudoyer received the commission in 1845. Possible sites were discussed from 1849 to 1851, until that of the Romanesque church of La Major overlooking the new port was finally chosen. Vaudoyer presented an initial project in 1852, and the cornerstone was laid in that year. A final project was completed in 1855, and by the time of Vaudoyer's death in 1872 the masonry shell was finished. The remaining work, carried out by Vaudoyer's student Henri Espérandieu and, later, Henri-Antoine Revoil, was completed by 1893.

Marseilles Cathedral is principally two things: first, a massive and complex state-

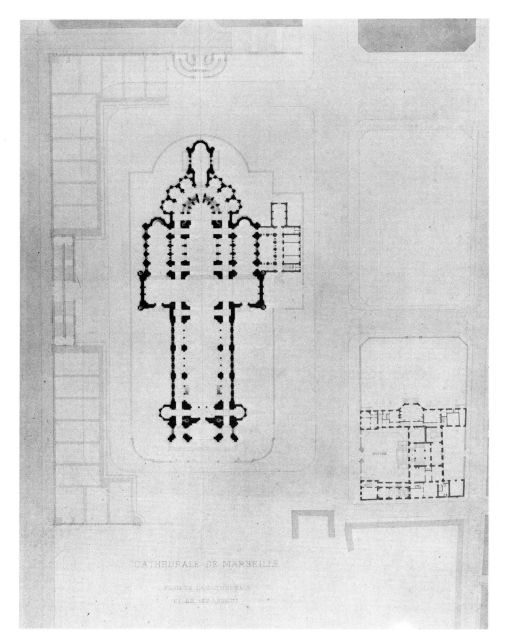

ment of the Romantic eclecticism formulated by the architects of the 1830s and, second, one of the most carefully studied, subtle, and successful productions of French architecture at its peak in the mid-nineteenth century.

As an eclectic building, the Cathedral combines a nave, which is a Roman thermal hall; a crossing, transepts, and a western arm, which form a domed Eastern church; an east facade, which joins a French medieval two-towered elevation with an entry like a Roman triumphal arch; and an elaborated *chevet* of French Romanesque pilgrimage type. The whole is clothed in a Mediterranean structural polychromy, simultaneously Florentine and Cairene, but made up of local materials. The critic Charles Blanc saw the building as a summary of its time and place. In its use of

Roman vaults, as "baptized" by the Byzantines and adapted in France by the architects of the Middle Ages, the Cathedral develops the conception of the architects whom Vaudoyer saw as the last great Christian designers, Arnolfo di Cambio and Filippo Brunelleschi, the builders of Florence Cathedral. In its combination of Mediterranean and Northern European form, it signifies that Marseilles is the seaport link between these two worlds.

Vaudoyer refused to study his design in earnest until the site had been definitively selected, so that he could be certain of the manner in which it would be seen. In spite of the ceremonial laying of the cornerstone, he then took three years to present his finished study. After that he continued to refine his

design, keeping a large model in the *agence*, which periodically he altered slightly (Garnier had a similar model for the Paris Opéra, with interchangeable parts). The exterior of the Cathedral is remarkable for its grouping of three secondary domes around the central, more broadly scaled cupola; the integration of these with the pyramidal terminations of the buttresses and the Islamic turrets on the corner of each transept; and the elaboration of these forms in the contrastingly curved and faceted elements of the west end. In 1875 Espérandieu selected for Charles Blanc photographs from three angles: the east facade, the southern side elevation, "which one must view from the sea," and the three-quarter view of the west end, "especially interesting from the picturesque point of view."

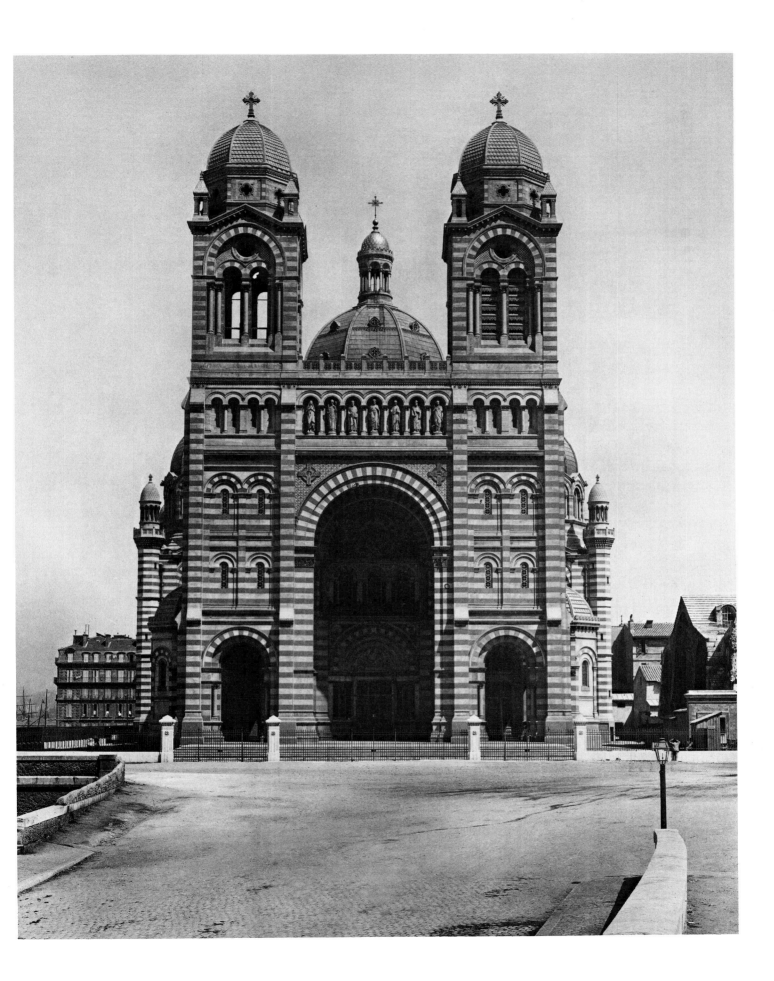

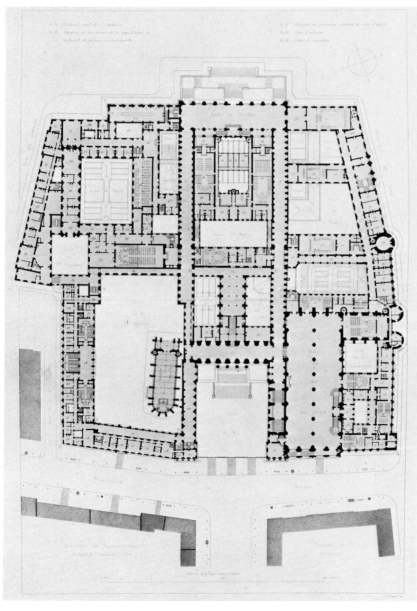

Louis Duc. Salle de Harlay, Palais de Justice, Paris. 1852–69.

In 1869, Napoleon III awarded to the architect of the Palais de Justice in Paris a prize of 100,000 francs for the best work of art produced during the Second Empire. (Baltard's Halles, which almost were selected, were removed from consideration because of a controversy over the authorship of the basic conception.) The architect was Louis Duc (1802–79; student of Chatillon, Grand Prix 1825). The principal facade on the Rue de Harlay *(above)* and the interior space designed by Duc opened in 1869, but he had begun working on the complex of existing buildings in 1840, completing extensive renovations and new construction before his death in 1879. The Salle de Harlay is the most independent and monumental of Duc's work at the Palais de Justice and can be judged beside the great *salle des pas perdus* of Salomon de Brosse or the Cour de Mai of Rousseau.

The object of Duc's work was to fill out the site between the Place Dauphine, the Boulevard du Palais, and the banks of the Ile de la Cité, and to draw existing structures, medieval to eighteenth century, into a unified plan. This plan centers on two parallel corridors, which run from the Cour de Mai at the east to the Salle de Harlay at the west. Because of the tapering form of the Ile de la Cité, Duc's new facade was easily seen from the Seine and thus became the monumental nineteenth-century image of a Palais de Justice, and was frequently copied throughout France.

The Harlay facade is a Romantic translation of classical order. In the 1850s Duc wrote, "Without the Orders, what would our monuments be? Was it not the Order which, by its proportions ruled by those of man, became the unity and the measure of buildings?" And he noted that the Order is the poetic essence that differentiates architecture from mere construction. Yet on the Harlay facade the columns are attached to a plane surface, with high windows, and are carved in such relief that they seem only a screen before a wall, rather than the structural ele-

428

ment of the building. Nor does the deep entablature of this colonnade, with its shields and female heads, serve as a classical entablature, for it is rhythmically broken to make its parts read as vertical extensions of the columns. The historical bases of this facade lie in such monuments as the Temple of Denderah and the temples at Agrigentum, yet the parts have been rearranged by Duc so as to take on a multitude of structural and aesthetic readings. The deep relief of its articulation gives the facade an appearance of strength that dominates its surroundings and

reads particularly well from the angled view along the Seine.

On the interior walls of the vestibule *(above)* Duc continued his reconsidered use of the Orders by running a classical frieze, without colonnade, around the lower walls and by inserting columns in segmental arches on the inner, courtroom wall of the hall. But the most striking element of the vestibule is its vaulting. It is a taut, powerful series of segmental arches separating low domes, with the arches springing from high corbels on which are female heads. The effect of these

arches in fact exaggerates the exigencies of construction. Yet the building moved Duc's contemporaries, and still startles today. In his *Entretiens sur l'architecture*, Viollet-le-Duc wrote admiringly, "The *salle des pas perdus*, on the exterior and the interior, is one of those monuments which will do honor to our times. There, everything holds together, everything is connected by a clear thought. The execution . . . responds to the composition, it is beautiful and pure. One senses an artist, rare thing in our times, who respects his art and the public."

Henri Labrouste. Bibliothèque Nationale, Paris. 1854–75.

After Boullée's project of 1785, dozens of plans had been made to create a new Bibliothèque Impériale (later Nationale), but it was not until 1854, when Henri Labrouste (1801–75; student of Vaudoyer and Lebas, Grand Prix 1824) was appointed architect of the building, that substantial new work began. The plans up to that time had all been intended as conversions of parts of the adjacent Palais Mazarin and Hôtel Chevry-Tubeuf, seventeenth-century structures in what is now the second arrondissement of Paris, and it is this complex that Labrouste had to expand. He spent the first five years of his appointment restoring the buildings and their surrounding gardens. In 1858 he turned to developing a project for new library rooms and a new facade on the Rue de Richelieu. From that time until his death in 1875, Labrouste continued to work on the library, completing the *magasins* (stacks) in 1867, the *salle des imprimés* (main reading room) in 1869, and the new main facade in 1872.

The *magasins (below)* and the *salle des imprimés (opposite and above)* have become famous for their iron structure, as has Labrouste's earlier library, the Bibliothèque Sainte-Geneviève. The *magasins* of the Bibliothèque Nationale are a straightforward framework of iron with glass floors and roof (the roof has been covered by twentieth-century additions). A central hall, open to the roof, is flanked by floors of book stacks, and at one end of this hall is a great, glazed arch, which opens onto the *salle des imprimés* so that the reader there has a constant, distant view of the room from which are drawn the books he has ordered. The *salle des imprimés* is more than simply a great iron structure. As Labrouste's son described his father's professed intentions, the room recalls, by the trees painted in the lunettes of the side walls, a favorite reading spot of students in the Jardin du Luxembourg. When the *salle* is seen thus, as an outdoor reading place, its nine patterned porcelain domes on slender iron columns come to seem like the *velaria* used in Pompeian decorations to suggest a wind-filled tent, or like the *diaeta* (garden study) described by Pliny the Younger. Labrouste reserved utilitarian use of iron for the *magasins* of his library; in the *salle des imprimés* he turned it to the realization of an architectural fantasy that invoked his idea of pleasant hours of reading.

Charles Garnier. Nouvel Opéra de Paris. 1861–75.

The Nouvel Opéra, conceived as the crowning of Second Empire Paris, was the clearest fulfillment of a Beaux-Arts project to be built in nineteenth-century France. Its architect, Charles Garnier (1825–98; student of Lebas, Grand Prix 1848), combined an acute judgment of Parisian society with a newly Romanticized classical sensibility to create the work that has made him the most famous French architect of his century. Garnier was a little-known designer with a promising school career when, on December 30, 1860, a competition for the design of a new opera house was announced. One hundred seventy-one projects were submitted. Five winners were announced, of which the first prize went to Ginain (p. 448) and the fifth to Garnier. These five were instructed to submit a second set of projects to a more precise program; two withdrew, and at the final judging on May 29 Garnier's design was chosen. He began supervising the construction of foundations on August 27, 1861.

The site, chosen by Haussmann, was found to be waterlogged, and a year of clearing and consolidation of the ground and foundations was required before the laying of the first stone could take place on July 21, 1862. Major construction was slowed by the shifting of funds to various other projects of Haussmann and Napoleon III, but by 1865 the building had risen to half its finished height. The scaffolding behind which it was constructed was removed in 1867, at which point the exterior was substantially complete; the masonry and sculpture groups were not entirely finished until 1870, the year in which Napoleon fell from power. The shell of the building served as a hospital during the Franco-Prussian War, and the interiors were completed only in 1874. The Emperor's Pavilion, no longer needed, remains unfinished to this day. The Opéra opened on January 5, 1875, to nearly unanimous applause.

Garnier's design won the competition for the Opéra largely because of its brilliant *parti*, which remains its greatest feature. The organization of the building is exceptionally clear and, as Garnier himself emphasized, is

(continued on p. 436)

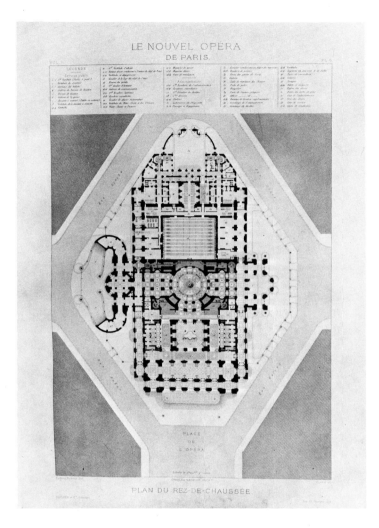

PLAN DU REZ-DE-CHAUSSÉE

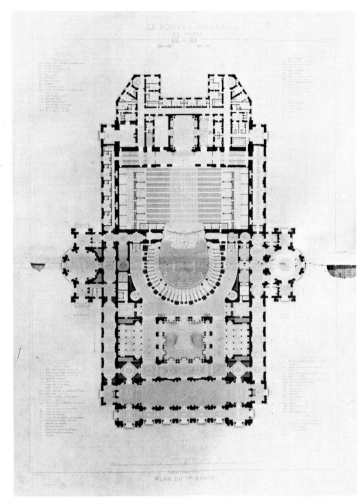

PLAN DU 1er ÉTAGE

(opposite) **Opéra.** Detail of Auditorium and wall of Grand Foyer, from *Le Nouvel Opéra.*

Most of the preliminary color studies for the Opéra are loose and sparkling, while the lithograph plates of the completed building are precise and almost menacing. This surrealist undertone is an aspect of the building itself that has seldom been recognized.

(above) **Opéra.** Plan of *rez-de-chaussée* (ground floor) and of *premier étage* (main floor), from *Le Nouvel Opéra.*

The plan of the site and ground level of the Opéra shows the various means of entry to the building. Operagoers arriving on foot would pass through the main entry *(bottom of plan)* and those arriving by carriage would be taken through the right-hand pavilion where they would enter a central, circular vestibule. These two groups would move up short flights of stairs to meet and mingle on the level above, at the base of the grand staircase—a movement vividly described by Gar-

nier in *Le Théâtre.* At the center left of the building is the base of the ramp to the Emperor's Pavilion. To the rear is the wing for performers, administration, and maintenance.

On the *premier étage,* operagoers had access both to the first level of boxes in the auditorium and to the stairs to upper seating levels *(left and right of grand staircase).* The small balconies appearing on the perimeter of the grand staircase provided the most elegant of viewing stands for the procession of patrons to their seats. On this level also was the *salon* of the emperor *(far left).*

FACADE PRINCIPALE

LE NOUVEL OPÉRA
DE PARIS

COUPES TRANSVERSALES

FAÇADE LATERALE

COUPE LONGITUDINALE

entirely oriented to the ceremony of opera-going and to the practical needs of theatrical production. On the exterior, each portion of the building with a separate function is indicated by its form and its decorative articulation, yet these parts are arranged and proportioned so as to create a continually changing tableau within the urban scene. Garnier's design extends the visual experience of approach through the *foyers* into the great central staircase, where the operagoer is at once aware of his destination and of his place in the center of his own theatrical event, as he mounts the stair surrounded by balconies of spectators. Beyond the ornate level of the *foyers*, stair, and numerous *salons* reserved for the social event of intermissions, more severe and practical staircases lead to the second, more literally theatrical realm of the Grand Salle. Beyond the stage scenery lie the backstage and the rooms of administration, singers, musicians, and *corps de ballet*, which on the exterior are treated as a residential or institutional block.

The organization of the Opéra, and particularly of its visually clear and socially appropriate circulation system, represents the best of Beaux-Arts planning filtered through the social perceptiveness of Charles Garnier. The style and decoration represent another phenomenon, of which Garnier was one of the central figures: the inflection of Ecole des Beaux-Arts classicism by a new Romanticism, derived from the work of the previous three decades and from the influences of archaeological studies. Garnier's delight in motion and contrast of forms produces a dramatic expansion of essentially classical elements into nearly continuous sculptural effects of mass, color, and chiaroscuro.

The forms and decoration Garnier established at the Opéra became models for much Beaux-Arts architecture in the latter part of the century. The influence of the Opéra began from the time that its drawings appeared and its details were carried into school projects, and it did not end until fifty years after its completion.

Opéra. Grand Stair Hall.

Foyer de la Danse.   Grande Salle.

Opéra. Auditorium, with painted curtain.

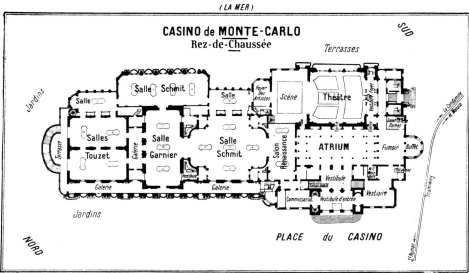

Charles Garnier. Concert Hall (1878–79) and Casino (1881–82), Monte Carlo.

After the construction of the Paris Opéra, one of Garnier's major commissions was for a concert hall and, later, a new gaming room at Monte Carlo. He lived to see these structures extended and altered without his aid or consent. Even before alteration, however, the concert hall and casino formed a far less unified building than the Opéra.

Said to have been fully designed in six months, the concert hall was intended to serve for small musical and theatrical productions and was linked to a large "atrium" (or *salon*), which eventually opened onto the casino. The building had three widely differing entrances. One, on the side facade of the theater, led from a terrace and steps to the palace and was reserved for the royal party. This was heavily decorated and framed by two towers *(opposite above)*. A second entrance, on the opposite side, led to the "atrium" and was intended for the general public. It was less heavily decorated and had two low towers. The third entrance led to the

rear of the concert hall and was centered on its longitudinal axis, but was nevertheless the smallest and most unceremonious (*opposite above*). Because of the position of the "atrium" beside the concert hall, this last facade was thoroughly asymmetrical, and Garnier apparently made some attempt to give it a picturesque tone by introducing a bay window, a varied roofline, and a variety of decorations. The addition of the gaming room next to the main "atrium" facade extended the picturesque confusion. The interior of the concert hall (*right*) brought the luxuriance of the Opéra to a much smaller space and created a room of almost overpowering decoration. Spacial limitations were relieved by huge mirrors along one wall and windows along the opposite wall.

The concert hall complex suggests the tendencies Garnier might have developed after the completion of his finely tuned design for the Opéra. But here, as in his other later buildings, Garnier seems to have carried further his rule of designing by sentiment rather than reason.

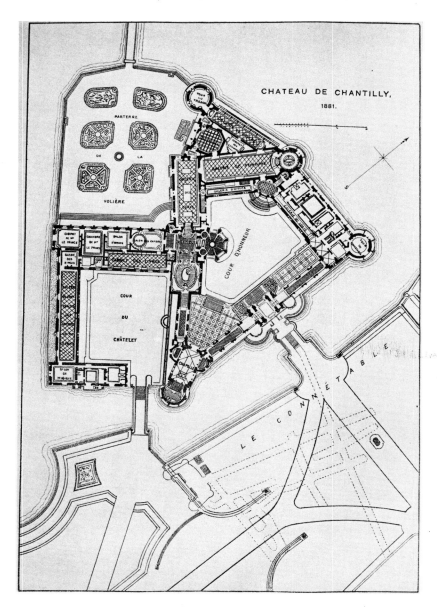

CHATEAU DE CHANTILLY,
1881.

**Honoré Daumet. Château de Chantilly.
1875–82.**

After the fall of Napoleon III and the suppression of the Commune, the duc d'Aumale, fifth son of Louis-Philippe, was allowed to return from exile to his family's Château de Chantilly. It consisted only of a small *châtelet* of the sixteenth century by Jean Bulant and the fourteenth-century foundations of a larger château destroyed in the Revolution of 1789. Félix Duban had designed and built in 1846 a wooden gallery along the side of the châtelet; he also drew up sketches for the restoration of the larger building, but the Revolution of 1848 put an end to that project. When in 1875 the duc d'Aumale was finally able to begin a restoration, it was through a member of the Academy, Gruyer, that he found a new architect, Honoré Daumet (1826–1911; student of Blouet and Gilbert, Grand Prix 1855). Apparently delighted with each other at first meeting, the duc and Daumet became patron and architect in building one of the great houses of France. Construction of the new château began in 1876 and was completed in 1882. The building was extensively published in France and abroad and earned Daumet both commissions and a seat in the Academy.

As in the Second Empire restoration of the Château de Pierrefonds, by Viollet-le-Duc, the central problem at Chantilly was imposed by the boundaries of existing foundations and complete buildings, within which Daumet had to create his new château. Daumet retained two sides of the great fourteenth-century foundations, but suppressed a part of the moat in order to regularize the third side and to join the fourteenth-century structure to the sixteenth-century châtelet. He thus essentially followed the plan of the earlier château, but he shifted certain of its parts, such as the chapel and the entries on the main courtyard. The main entrance across the moat centers on the elevation, while the entrance to the vestibule and stair hall lies across the court on a different axis.

Courtyard entrance *(left)*, chapel *(center)*, entrance to château *(right)*.

The visitor must thus change directions as he proceeds into the château, yet the form of the main entrance pavilion is such as to allow a pivot at the last moment.

Inside the building, the visitor has a choice of two axes. One leads straight ahead to the châtelet, which Daumet restored with small, private *salons* and one long gallery. The other leads, to the left, down the staircase to the private quarters of the duc's art collection. Rather than allow the plan of the foundations to create confusion of circulation, Daumet capitalized upon its angles and its turrets to create a variety of spaces, which are clearly linked and which suggest a comfortable path for the visitor to follow.

As described in the English magazine *The Builder*, the château "forms at the same time a national monument of past ages, a museum of art, and the private residence of an historian of royal race, the heir of Montmorency and of Condé." The principal influence of Chantilly was through its role as a private house, yet the very restrictions of the program brought Daumet to an exceptional solution, which would be difficult to equal in a building with a free program and site.

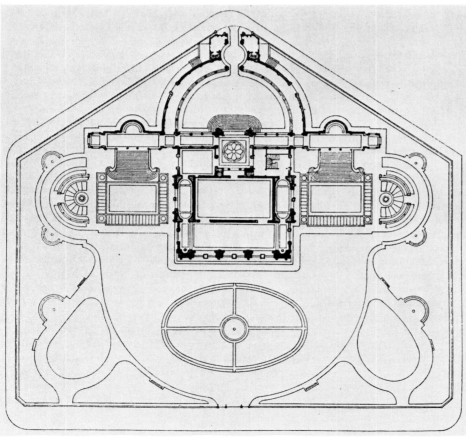

Léon Ginain. Musée Galliera, Paris. 1878–94.

The Musée Galliera in Paris is one of the few examples of late Beaux-Arts style to be fully realized in a French building. It was designed by Léon Ginain (1825–98; student of Huyot and Lebas, Grand Prix 1852) on the commission of the duchesse de Galliera, for a site owned by her family. The duchesse proposed in 1878 to give her art collection, housed in a new museum, to the city of Paris, and it is likely that Ginain was requested to present a design for the museum in late 1878. Construction was underway in 1884 when the duchesse wrote a new will withdrawing the gift of her collection, but guaranteeing that the museum would nevertheless be completed and left to the city. It was substantially complete when it opened in 1890, but interior work continued until 1894. The museum has been devoted to temporary exhibitions since that time.

When he received the commission Ginain was a well respected *maître d'atelier*, architect of clinics and hospitals as well as a recent major addition to the Ecole de Médecine in Paris. He had suffered the great disappointment in 1861 of receiving first prize in the first competition for the Paris Opéra, then losing to Garnier on the second round (after Garnier had tried repeatedly to take him on as a partner). The Opéra had offered Ginain the opportunity to build the great Beaux-Arts project he was capable of designing; the Musée Galliera finally made this possible on a smaller scale.

The collection for which the museum was planned required space to exhibit a great deal of sculpture, both indoors and out, and a much smaller amount of paintings and tapestry, all in a structure to be placed in a pentagonally shaped park. These requirements encouraged a combination of closed galleries, open colonnades and garden *parterres*. Ginain placed the principal entrance to his building at the peak of the pentagonal site, from which point he extended an axis through most of the depth of the building. This axis is paralleled by two major exterior axes, and is crossed by several axes that pass through both building and garden. An open

3190   PARIS. — Le Musée Galliera   X Phot

exedra with an internal colonnade *(opposite)* was used to fill out the angle of the pentagon, thus recalling Pascal's famous Grand Prix project of 1866 (p. 236) and presaging part of Girault's Petit Palais of 1900 (p. 456). At the base of this exedra is a main vestibule, from which extends a long axis that leads to two stairways to the museum's garden. The main part of the building is a simple block broken into several gallery spaces, a library, and a staircase. But the plan of the whole building must be read as extending into the *parterres* around it, for together these form a balanced arrangement of echoing exedrae and inter-

secting axes. In elevation, the open and closed surfaces of the exterior walls are modulated to turn the building in upon itself on its street facade, and to allow its principal axes to flow into the garden.

A contemporary review described the Musée Galliera as *gallo-grec*, and indeed the forms and decoration of the building are rich in references to Hellenic Greek and French Renaissance models, as well as reminiscences of sixteenth-century Italy. The reviewer thought this a new and promising genre, noting that a museum's consecration to the muses required a Greek style, while this

museum was nevertheless also a French building in a French garden. Ginain was adept not only at blending recognizable stylistic motifs in his architecture, but also at creating surfaces that are symphonic arrangements of moldings and their shadows against smooth stone. (It was for this that he was particularly noticed by American students.) Ginain's contemporaries felt that, in the Musée Galliera, he proved himself a master of the detailing of stone, and perhaps for this they overlooked the clumsy handling of scale and intersection between the main block and its flanking galleries.

Ferdinand Dutert. Palais des Machines, Paris. 1886–89. Demolished 1910.

There were two structures at the Paris Exposition of 1889 that attracted wide attention for their appearance and their technical innovations: one was the Tour de 300 Mètres, designed by the engineer Gustave Eiffel, and the other was the Palais des Machines, by the architect Ferdinand Dutert (1845–1906; student of Ginain, Grand Prix 1869). In 1886 Dutert, who had constructed no major buildings up to that time, submitted a project to a competition for the plan of the forthcoming Paris Exposition and was awarded one of three top prizes. This resulted in his receiving the commission for one of the major exhibition buildings, the Palais des Machines, which was to be sited at one end of the Exposition to house the great industrial inventions of recent years. Dutert constructed the building with the aid of the engineers Contamin, Pierron, and Charton, but it is clear from contemporary accounts that the idea of roofing the space with a single span was his.

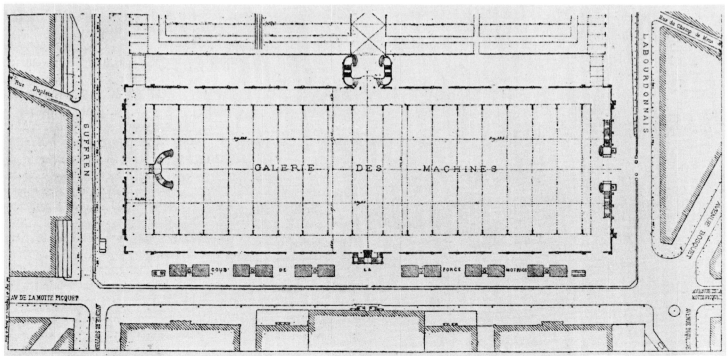

Dutert's first project was presented to the Direction des Travaux of the Exposition in September 1886. It called for an iron-and-glass structure 115 meters wide, 429 meters long, and 43.5 meters high, to be formed by a series of 20 transverse three-hinged arches with their ridge-line carried to the ground through an apse at each end, and with two galleries formed by arcades along each side of the main space. For reasons of expense, the two apses, which gave the building the appearance of a conservatory, were replaced by flat ends. Once this concession was made, Dutert allowed no more alterations in his project. Protestations that the structure was impossible to build seem to have been quelled by the Ministre de l'Instruction Publique et Beaux-Arts, Lockroy, who had already approved the construction of Eiffel's tower.

Construction of the Palais des Machines began with the sinking of piles and the pouring of concrete foundations in July 1887. Part of the site was very sandy, making some of the foundations difficult to lay. Of the 40 bases on which the 20 arches rested, 10 had to consist of groups of 28 piles sunk to a 16-meter depth, over which were poured a series of pyramiding concrete slabs to a thickness of 7.25 meters. The other 30, on more solid ground, were concrete slabs ranging from 1.35 meters to 50 centimeters in thickness. On April 20, 1888, the first arch of the superstructure, an assembly of four pieces, was raised by a crane in about four hours. The raising of the iron structure of the building was completed by September. In the time remaining before the opening of the Exposition, the building was completed and decorated with colored glass, mosaic work, paintings, and ceramic bricks, so that the great metal skeleton became the frame of an enormous jewel box. Particularly interesting is the glass wall, seen from inside, with its arched panelling and linear motifs resembling windows by Frank Lloyd Wright (preceding page). A large traveling car was installed on tracks above the exhibits to carry visitors through the building in a manner suited to its awesome scale.

The Palais des Machines was considered a great technical achievement, for although the three-hinged arch had been developed at least twenty-five years earlier, neither it nor any other metal arch had been used over such a span. It was also thought to be a great economic success, for the price of a usable square meter of its space was 93F, compared with at least 500F per square meter for a stone building. Yet these advances apparently were not thought so important as the aesthetic and even poetic quality of the building. Although the strange, broad proportions of the girders were criticized by some, their delicate contact at the base and center, and the self-regulation of their expansion through hinging, amazed observers. Contemporary accounts conveyed the impression of an extraordinary lightness and a surprisingly pleasing use of iron.

Henri Deglane, Albert Louvet, and A.-F.-T. Thomas. Grand Palais, Paris. 1895–1900. Charles Girault. Petit Palais, Paris. 1895–1900.

Today the two permanent buildings constructed for the Paris Exposition of 1900 testify to the state of architecture in their time. The Petit Palais, by Charles Girault (1851–1932; student of Daumet, Grand Prix 1880), is a last Beaux-Arts expression of elegant planning and classicizing detail. Its companion, the Grand Palais, by Henri Deglane (1855–1931; student of André, Grand Prix 1881), Albert Louvet (1860–1936; student of Louvet and Ginain, 2e Grand Prix 1885, 1886), and A.-F.-T. Thomas (1847–1907; student of Paccard and Vaudoyer, Grand Prix 1870), represents the dilution of that tradition. Nevertheless, seen together the two buildings form one of the great urbanistic ensembles of the end of the century. From well down the Seine or the Champs Elysées, one can see their great roofs above the surrounding park, and from across the Pont Alexandre *(opposite below)* they appear as the covered and decorated extensions of a broad public space.

Site plan of Universal Exposition of 1900.
In the circle at left are the Grand Palais and the Petit Palais; at right the circle encloses the base of the Eiffel Tower.

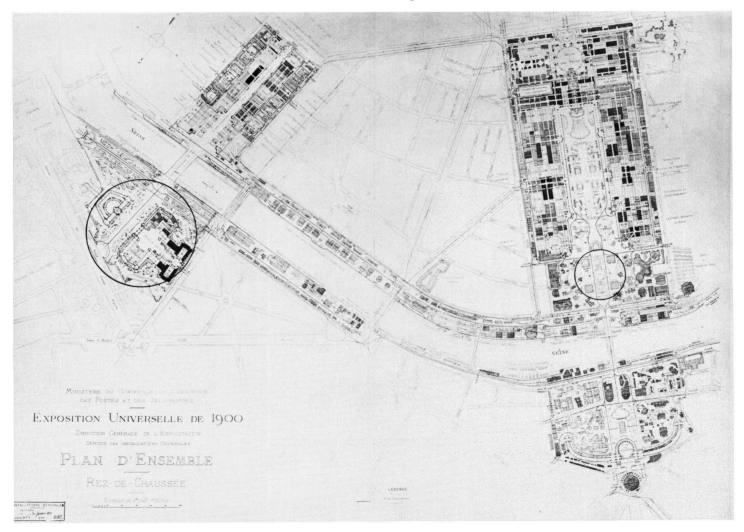

Petit Palais, Paris.

The design of the Petit Palais was an object of critical approbation from the time it was proposed to the Administration de l'Exposition in a competition of 1895. Its author, Girault, was not only given the commission for the Petit Palais, but was also made coordinator of the architects of the Grand Palais. His own building was begun in October 1897, was structurally completed during 1898, and was decorated by early 1900. The plan of the building, particularly admired at the time, consists of four long galleries arranged in a trapezoid, with a broad gallery on the side facing the Grand Palais. Within the trapezoid, on three sides, is a broad, unbroken gallery, and within that is a semicircular colonnade, which opens onto a central garden. Below this was a lower level, lighted by windows in the base of the building. Girault's manner of easing the angles of the trapezoid by introducing shallow bays at the forward corners and circular staircases at the rear is a particularly successful articulation. The plan, with its adaptations to an oddly shaped site, is the descendant of the plans of Pascal's Grand Prix of 1866 (p. 236) and the restoration of the Château de Chantilly by Girault's teacher, Daumet.

In elevation, the Petit Palais succeeds at once in having a principal facade, marked by a low dome and corner pavilions, and in addressing itself to all parts of the site with facades of varying articulation. The transitions between the four facades are skillfully modulated by combinations of their different features at the corners. Contemporary criticism hailed the taste in decoration and the brilliance of the plan as proof of France's continued artistic hegemony, and indeed the building is a notable, though not great, descendant of the school of Garnier.

The Grand Palais is a more complex and less satisfactory building. It suffers from a lack of unity by virtue of its odd site, huge dimensions, and division into three parts by different architects. Nevertheless, the principal part of the building facing the Petit Palais, which was designed by Henri Deglane, is an impressive structure. It combines the exterior visual proprieties of a permanent museum building with the interior and roofline of a *galerie des machines*. The combination is at once awkward and striking. The dimensions of the principal space are so great that the building could contain the base of the Eiffel Tower; thus, the great iron-and-glass roof makes a vast, swelling profile when seen from a distance. The colonnade and the central arch and portico of the facade answer the facade of the Petit Palais, while the indented corner entrances turn to meet the approaching visitor.

As a French answer to the Chicago Exposition of 1893, these buildings of the Exposition of 1900 display far greater originality and strength of design, and a sense of urban ensemble. They lie at the end of the classical Beaux-Arts tradition, but they still convey its capacity to create powerful images.

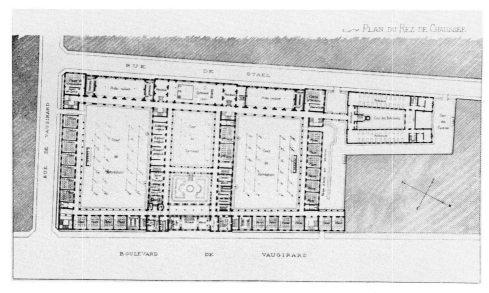

PLAN DU REZ DE CHAUSSÉE

Emile Vaudremer. Lycée Buffon, Paris. 1887–89.

The Lycée Buffon represents an aspect of French architecture that has been largely ignored and has not been thought of as the concern of men who studied at the Ecole des Beaux-Arts. Yet from the 1860s through the '90s its architect, Emile Vaudremer (1829–1914; student of Blouet and Gilbert, Grand Prix 1854), and a few other men who had been students at the Ecole designed a number of schools and institutional buildings in the combination of stone, brick, iron, and terra cotta that characterizes the Lycée Buffon. These buildings came to represent a particular institutional style, which grew from a mingling of Beaux-Arts tenets and the theories of Viollet-le-Duc and his followers (many of whom had studied at the Ecole). They are among the most widespread yet least remarked buildings of Paris and of provincial cities and towns. Eugène Letang, the first professor of design at the Massachusetts Institute of Technology, and Louis Sullivan both studied with Vaudremer.

Through a combination of talent and advantageous friendships, Vaudremer enjoyed a prodigious career, which was already at a peak in 1864 when he received the commission to design the church of Saint-Pierre de Montrouge, today his most famous building. The Lycée Buffon, begun in 1887 and completed in 1889, is thus one of his later works, but it benefits from his previous experience of designing three other lycées and from the contemporary school designs of other architects. It was regarded as a model by such theorists as Julien Guadet. Its clear plan, arranged around three courtyards, was much admired, as was the vertical expression of that plan in the facade with two pavilions flanking the entrance to the central court.

The visual effects and appearance of "rational" organization of the Lycée Buffon are achieved by the combination of carefully chosen materials. The facade is made up of a "framework" of yellowish limestone, filled with light yellow brick and decorated at intervals with medallions and patterns of rose brick and green tiles. The interior courts have similar walls and, on three sides, open loggias with iron roofs borne by stone columns with concrete capitals. Small *tourelles* flanking the entrance were described by a contemporary as giving the roofline "a most agreeable note, at once sympathetic and picturesque." The ability to take the symmetries and reposeful lines of classical architecture, taught at the Ecole, and to infuse these with a "rationalism" of materials and a light decoration of structural polychromy, was the strength of Vaudremer most admired by his contemporaries.

Victor Laloux. Gare de Tours (1895–98) and Gare du Quai d'Orsay, Paris (1898–1900).

The principal public structure built in connection with the Paris Exposition of 1900 was a new terminus for the Paris-Orleans railway lines, at the Quai d'Orsay. Its architect was Victor Laloux (1850–1937; student of André, Grand Prix 1878), who was to have the distinction of being the most popular *maître d'atelier* among American students at the Ecole; ninety-seven went to study with him. (The second most popular, Pascal, had only forty-eight.) Built on the left bank of the Seine, across from the Jardin des Tuileries, the Gare d'Orsay commanded a view of the Ile de la Cité to one side and the buildings of the Exposition of 1900 to the other. It was thus a magnificently placed entryway into the city of Paris. When Laloux received the commission he had already designed a major station on the Orleans railway, at Tours, which was built from 1895 to 1898. The Gare d'Orsay was probably designed in 1896–97, at the time that plans for the Exposition were being prepared, and construction of the station was begun in 1898. The building was finished in 1900 in time to serve, as planned, as one of the urban *foyers* to the Exposition.

Laloux's greatest advantage in the design of the Gare d'Orsay was the recent development of smokeless electric engines, which allowed the incorporation of train shed and waiting rooms into one structure. The Orleans line ran through trenches and tunnels from the edge of the city, and Laloux

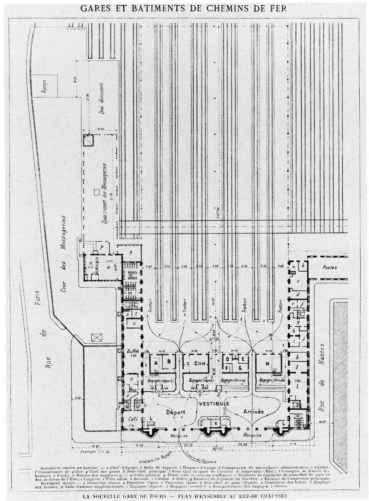

GARES ET BATIMENTS DE CHEMINS DE FER

LA NOUVELLE GARE DE TOURS — PLAN D'ENSEMBLE AU REZ-DE-CHAUSSÉE

Gare du Quai d'Orsay, Paris.

simply continued the tracks under his building, leaving open wells in the floor through which the trains could be observed arriving and departing (p. 462). Above the ground-floor waiting rooms rose a huge vault with iron ribs and strips of porcelain coffers separating large skylights. To the front this butted against a lower, multi-domed vestibule (p. 463), and to the back it rested against several stories of railway offices. The waiting room was the most dramatic public space in Paris, aside from those of the Exposition structures, and it was all the more so for its integration of many functions into a single, open area.

The principal flaw of the Gare d'Orsay lies in the relation of its several parts. The dominant image of the building is its impressive facade, with its broad, glazed archways through which departing travelers pass, and its two enormous clocks in flanking, square-domed pavilions (above). But the powerful articulation and symmetry of this facade are marred by the addition of a hotel block at one end. Arriving passengers passed through one side of this block, below a huge glass canopy. The potential drama of the arrival was lessened by diverting passengers away from the path through the great river facade, and the strength of the building's design was

lessened as well. In this respect, Laloux's earlier station at Tours is much more successful, for its impressive facade is perfectly balanced, and the division of departures and arrivals was made simply by creating two entry pavilions (p. 459). Nevertheless, the Gare d'Orsay was to be more characteristic of Laloux's work and of his times.

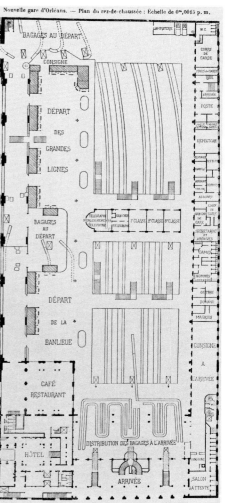

Richard Morris Hunt. Lenox Library, New York. 1869–77. Demolished.

More than five hundred Americans studied architecture at the Ecole des Beaux-Arts between 1846, when Richard Morris Hunt (1827 or 1828–95) was the first to be admitted, and 1968, when the school was reorganized. Hundreds of other Americans not accepted by the Ecole were in architectural ateliers in Paris. By far the largest number of foreigners in the Section d'Architecture before the First World War were the Americans: the Ecole exerted great influence in the United States for more than three-quarters of a century after 1855, when Hunt came home. All across the United States there are buildings that show this influence, but no American building immediately influenced the work of students in Paris.

Hunt had lived in Paris for a decade, and after studying at the Ecole he worked in the office of Hector Lefuel, who enlarged the Louvre for Napoleon III. It was later said that Lefuel made Hunt responsible for the design of the Pavillion de la Bibliothèque (across the Rue de Rivoli from the Palais Royal). By comparison, Hunt's Lenox Library, begun

fourteen years after his return from Paris, was a modest building composed of block-like masses with gently pitched but visible roofs; inside, it consisted mainly of long narrow galleries. The crisp, hard-edged detail and the relatively deep window reveals introduce that "tough" quality Americans are likely to associate with Chicago architecture. The building was demolished after its collections were moved into the newer and larger New York Public Library (p. 479).

Hunt's early works show the strong influence of the *Néo-Grec* architecture of mid-nineteenth–century France, rather than the classicism of his later great houses and his work for the Columbian Exposition of 1893 (pp. 470 *ff*.). His own atelier, in the Tenth Street Studio, produced such architects as Henry Van Brunt, Frank Furness, and George Post, all of whom experimented with the *Néo-Grec* style in their buildings.

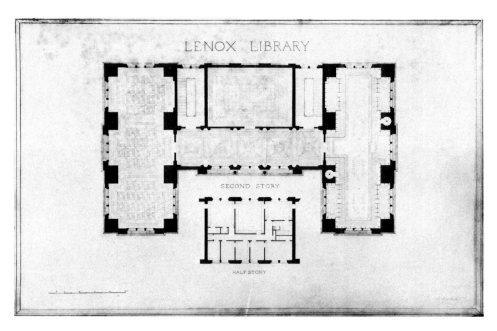

Henry Hobson Richardson. Allegheny County Courthouse, Pittsburgh. 1884–88.

The Allegheny County Courthouse is one of the last designs of Henry Hobson Richardson (1838–86), and it pleased him. In his short career he had changed the appearance of American architecture: in the 1870s he put the Victorian Gothic style out of fashion. The large scale and rough surfaces of his buildings were widely imitated, as were his asymmetrical arrangements and dark materials, often in contrasting colors. The Allegheny County Courthouse has the ruggedness and amplitude one expects to find in Richardson's work, but its granite is of one color, a light gray. Also, the courthouse is symmetrical in both its plan and its front, in accordance with the Ecole's teaching that symmetry in plan adds to ease of circulation within a building and that symmetry of elevation adds to monumentality. The plan of the courthouse looks like work at the Ecole, and the main facade is a personal variation on the type (central tower and corner pavilions) of the northern French, early Renaissance *hôtel de ville*, a type used in the nineteenth century for the *mairies* of several Paris *arrondissements*. Richardson had created a personal style, but when he was entrusted with an important public building in a major city he turned to French precedents.

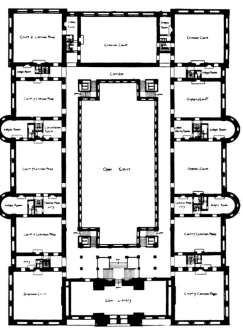

PLAN OF COURT-HOUSE (SECOND STORY), PITTSBURGH.

Charles Follen McKim. Boston Public Library. 1887–95.

The Boston Public Library, by Charles Follen McKim (1847–1909) of the firm McKim, Mead and White, was commissioned in 1887 and opened to the public in 1895. American public libraries in the late nineteenth and early twentieth centuries were meant to embody the democratic ideal of opportunity for all citizens to better their lives through reading. That cities or individual benefactors provided this opportunity was reason enough for these buildings to be monumental; furthermore, public libraries were seen as monuments to the ideal of learning.

McKim's library is obviously derived from Labrouste's Bibliothèque Sainte-Geneviève (p. 335). In each building, above the main entrance, the reading room fills the length of the long front; on both buildings' facades are engraved the names of great writers. But McKim has made his library more monumental than had Labrouste. Inside the reading room of McKim's library, instead of Labrouste's apparently fragile ironwork there is masonry as substantial as in any Italian palazzo. The exterior also seems more massive than does Labrouste's: the deep-cut arches reveal the thickness of the walls, and the whole building is lifted higher above the street and given a more impressive entrance.

McKim's library embodies also the Renaissance assumption that architecture is one of the several fine arts. McKim conceived of his library as including works of painting and sculpture, and among the artists whom he commissioned were Augustus and Louis Saint-Gaudens, John Singer Sargent, Edwin Austin Abbey, and Pierre Puvis de Chavannes.

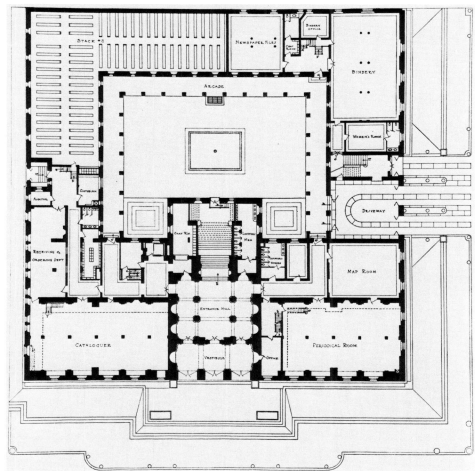

World's Columbian Exposition, Chicago.
1893.

The World's Columbian Exposition of 1893
provided America with a vision of what
public buildings and their surroundings
might be. Such was the intention of its architects; Hunt, their doyen, said, "We consider
this work as an object lesson to the United
States—to our government."

The Exposition by Lake Michigan was a
splendid ensemble of white palaces around a
formal court, within which were a large pool
and monumental sculptures. To the side of
this court of honor was an informal garden
into which, however, extended the axes of
the formal ensemble. Vast crowds had space
enough to circulate easily. The buildings
themselves were awesome in size: the
uniform line of their main cornices was sixty
feet high. Being temporary, they were built
not of stone or brick but of structural frames
surfaced with a strong plaster called staff.

As is well known, the Chicago World's Fair
changed the fashion in American architecture from Richardsonian to classic. This kind
of classicism was a new style in the United
States, and it came via the East Coast; the
members of the board of architects that
determined the appearance of the buildings
on the principal court were largely Eastern-
ers, and the most forceful had been students
at the Ecole des Beaux-Arts. McKim was the
strongest personality; Hunt was the senior
man. A month after the Exposition opened,
when Hunt received the gold medal of the
Royal Institute of British Architects, he
talked to his audience in London about the
board's choice of materials and style: "We
were perfectly well aware that, properly
speaking, iron construction and glass and
tiles were the proper materials to use in such
buildings. But had that problem ever been
satisfactorily solved? In my opinion, none of
the World's Fairs had had the monumental
look about them that they should have.
Furthermore, we insisted that if the problem
could not be satisfactorily solved in the city
of Paris, . . . would it not be foolish and useless for us . . . to undertake it? . . . Thus why
should not we take advantage here of the
very one thing needed in America and give a
monumental character to the principal buildings?"

To Hunt went the honor of designing the
Administration Building, which was at the
land end of the formal court (*opposite above*,
building in center); McKim, Mead and White
did the Agriculture Building nearby (building at left). The Administration Building had
an ornateness that Hunt came to like in his
later years, and it gave the curious impression of being a small building that had grown
big. The work that attracted the most approval was the Fine Arts Building by the
Chicago architect Charles B. Atwood (p. 474).
He had never studied in Paris, but his design
was obviously influenced by the project that
had won the Grand Prix de Rome in 1867,
Emile Bénard's *Palais pour l'exposition des
Beaux-Arts* (p. 241). (It is said that Atwood's
assistant was Alexandre Sandier, a Frenchman who had been in the Section
d'Architecture at the Ecole when Bénard won
the prize.) The facade of Atwood's gallery
was like that of Bénard's palace with most of
the ornament stripped away.

The most brilliant of the Chicago archi-

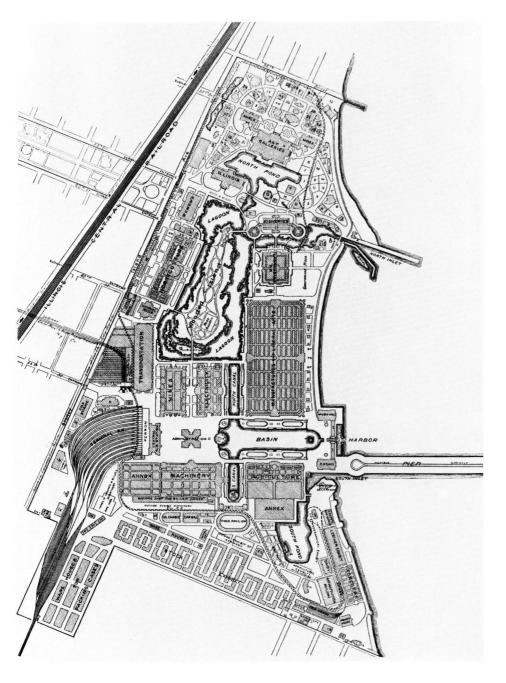

tects, Louis Sullivan, who had also been at the Ecole des Beaux-Arts, was responsible for the Transportation Building (p. 475), located just off the principal court. It was multicolored, not white. And although it was a large building, Sullivan diminished the scale at the entrance by setting arch within arch, as in the entrance to a Gothic church, and by placing on each side of this portal a little kiosk. His somewhat Richardsonian, polychromed architecture was to be put out of fashion by the white classicism of the Fair.

French artists who visited the Fair—and there do not seem to have been many of them—were less impressed by its architecture than by the tall buildings of Chicago. These people were familiar with the *concours* for the Grand Prix de Rome; to their eyes nearly all the Fair's white palaces looked too much like Grand Prix projects. Tall buildings, however, were for them something new and uniquely American. (One French visitor was a goldsmith, André Bouilhet, who belonged to a society named the Union Centrale des Arts Décoratifs, and he published his impressions of the Fair in the Union's periodical, the *Revue des Arts Décoratifs*. He singled out for praise Sullivan's Transportation Building, especially

its colorful doorway. The building had the merit for Bouilhet of recalling nothing European; to him it looked Arab, personal, and even original. He went on to praise the decoration of Sullivan's Auditorium.)

The Fair had perhaps its most lasting effect through the work of Daniel H. Burnham of Chicago, the member of the board of architects in overall charge of construction. Burnham, who had not studied in Paris, was a gifted manager, ready to accept the artistic ideas of his colleagues, and the Fair gave him and his office a national reputation. Because of Burnham, the effect of the World's Columbian Exposition on America was more than a different architectural style: the dream city of 1893 came partly true in the city plans he and his associates later realized. For Chicago he created a master plan, according to which streets were widened into boulevards, the course of the river was straightened, and a system of parks was organized. The lake shore became a place of recreation.

In Washington Burnham revived and enlarged the eighteenth-century plan of the French engineer Pierre-Charles L'Enfant. By removing the railway tracks and station from the Mall, Burnham reopened the vista from the Capitol to the Washington Monument.

Frederick MacMonnies. The Columbian Fountain.

Charles B. Atwood. Fine Arts Building.

Louis Sullivan. Transportation Building.

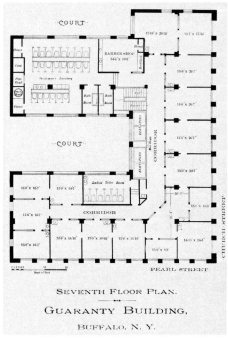

SEVENTH FLOOR PLAN.

GUARANTY BUILDING,

BUFFALO, N. Y.

(above) **Louis Sullivan. Guaranty Building, Buffalo, New York. 1894–95.**

Louis Sullivan's Guaranty Building is one of the masterpieces of that American creation, the skyscraper. Sullivan (1856–1924) had been educated first at Massachusetts Institute of Technology (where the instructor in architectural design was Eugène Letang, a Frenchman from the Ecole des Beaux-Arts) and then briefly at the Ecole itself. In neither school was he trained to design tall buildings: they were just coming into existence in those years. And yet this education influenced him. In fact his partner, Dankmar Adler, commented in 1886, "How American are Sullivan's reminiscences of the training of the Ecole des Beaux-Arts."

The effects of this classical training (and of the classicism in the air in America after the World's Columbian Exposition of 1893) show in the classicism of the Guaranty Building. Sullivan simplifies the appearance of the mass, making it seem more like a single shaft than the extension upward of a U-shaped plan. The building alludes to the first element studied in the Ecole's architectural curriculum—the classical column. Base, shaft, and capital are here translated into two stories near the street, office floors above, and a terminating cornice, all in one of the earth colors Sullivan loved, a light tan.

The ground plan of the building is seldom seen and is troubling. The relationship of the parts—for example, the Church Street vestibule and the elevators—seems more haphazard than composed. Obviously, Sullivan was more interested in organizing the facades.

(opposite) **Ernest Flagg. Singer Building, New York. 1907–08. Demolished 1967.**

The Singer Building was the work of a virtuoso who had studied at the Ecole, Ernest Flagg (1857–1947). Built on Lower Broadway in New York in 1907–08, it set a record for height (47 stories, 612 feet), but was passed a few years later. It looks almost too slim to be stable. Flagg was a master of surprising juxtapositions: a tiny spire above a huge mansarded dome like those of the Louvre of Napoleon III; a giant story above dozens of little ones; glass in the middle of the tower's walls, at the corners masonry (hiding steel bracing). At the entrance and in the ground-floor corridor the building looks very French, with the suave neo–eighteenth-century quality of some Parisian work of this same period.

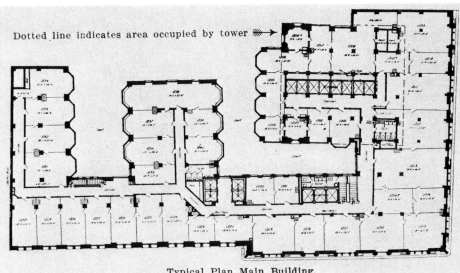

Dotted line indicates area occupied by tower ⟫

Typical Plan Main Building.

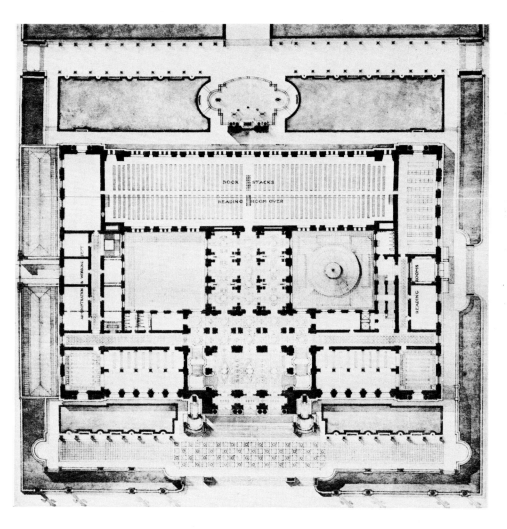

Carrère and Hastings. New York Public Library. 1897–1911.

The New York Public Library was designed by John M. Carrère (1858–1911) and Thomas Hastings (1860–1929) in 1897; construction went on until 1911. Carrère and Hastings both studied at the Ecole des Beaux-Arts and were employed upon their return from Paris in the office of McKim, Mead and White. Younger than their employers by a decade, Carrère and Hastings became the leaders of what could be called the next artistic generation in New York. If McKim's Boston Public Library is in the spirit of the Italian Renaissance, the library of Carrère and Hastings gave substance in New York to the spirit of the World's Columbian Exposition.

The library is white and classical, raised above the hubbub on Fifth Avenue and separated from Sixth by a park that is unified in composition with the building *(below)*. The plan suggests those of many Ecole designs in the last third of the nineteenth century: passage from the entrance to various destinations is orchestrated as a succession of axes, cross-axes, and cross-cross-axes. From Fifth Avenue the visitor climbs up steps straight into the building, finds himself in a tall marble hall, around the side of which he again climbs in order to reach the level of the reading room. He continues on the axis from the street until he enters the paneled and gilded great hall, which extends on both sides of him, its axis at 90° to his approach, a hall that makes opening a book into an event. In such architecture, in which the passage of people is conceived of as a public rite, there reverberates from afar the Opéra of Garnier.

New York Public Library before completion of sculpture.

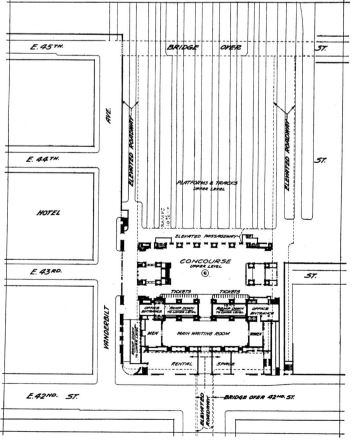

Warren and Wetmore, Reed and Stem. Grand Central Terminal, New York. 1907–13.

Grand Central Station was designed by Reed and Stem, who specialized in railway stations, and Whitney Warren of Warren and Wetmore. Warren (1864–1943), who studied architecture at the Ecole des Beaux-Arts, conceived this building urbanistically. Straddling Park Avenue, the building incorporates in its low perimeter mass rooftop roads for uninterrupted automobile traffic. From streets on three sides of the buildings, people enter and discover below a hall breathtakingly grand (p. 483); beyond it are the trains. The way is obvious, distances are short, and the walk is downward. The result is the greatest passenger terminal in the

world. The building's front can be seen directly from the avenue to the south—on top at the center, giant sculptural figures; in the smooth walls, three huge openings. It is all very large in scale, somewhat eighteenth-century French in feeling. Nearby are tall buildings by Warren and Wetmore: the Biltmore, Commodore, and Vanderbilt hotels, and the Yale Club; to the north, over the tracks, an office building for the New York Central Railroad. Today, the Pan Am Building closes the vista on Park Avenue. These buildings around the station are much taller than it, but smaller in scale. Warren made the terminus of a railroad into the center of a neighborhood. The entire complex is a worthy expression of its great purpose—a gateway between the city and the continent.

Grand Central Terminal, New York, as it originally appeared.

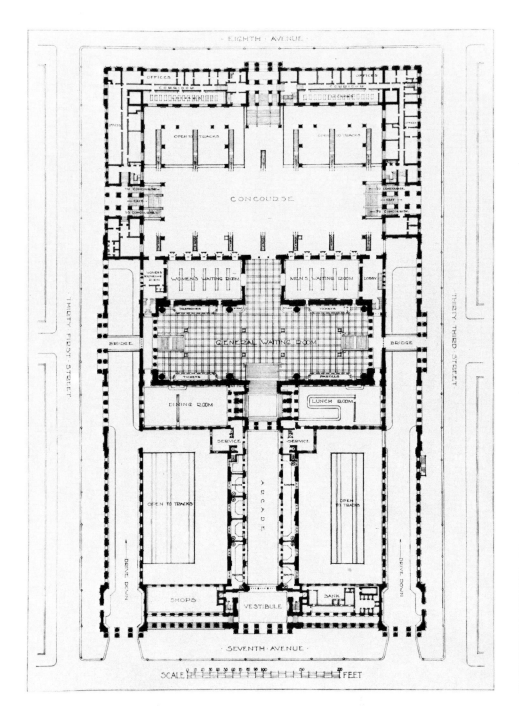

McKim, Mead and White. Pennsylvania Station, New York. 1906–10. Demolished 1964.

Pennsylvania Station was the rival (before its demolition) of Grand Central Terminal, just as the Pennsylvania Railroad competed with the New York Central. McKim, looking for a source of inspiration for public buildings, followed over the years the guidance of his education at the Ecole des Beaux-Arts and arrived finally, after pausing at the Italian Renaissance, at ancient Rome. He was a man of great influence, and with buildings such as this one he set an example of severe classicism that was widely imitated in America. In France at the same time, architectural thinking was moving in a different direction, away from antiquity toward a style more like the Rococo and with hints at Art Nouveau. Inside the giant colonnade of Pennsylvania Station there were Piranesian views, such as in the carriage drive or in the waiting room, which was 107 feet longer than the Baths of Caracalla on which it was modeled. Just beyond was an unforgettable contrast—the concourse, a steel-and-glass train shed that seemed to be as weightlessly voluminous as the waiting room was massive. The building was not as convenient to use as is Grand Central: the distances to walk were longer, although this was put to good use in the shopping arcade that opened onto Seventh Avenue. America is the poorer for its loss.

General waiting room.

Concourse.

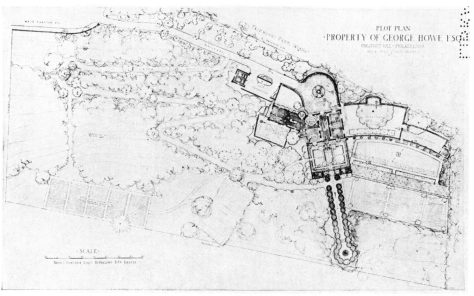

George Howe. Howe House, Chestnut Hill, Pennsylvania. 1913.

The Howe House (also known as High Hollow), which is in the Philadelphia suburb of Chestnut Hill, was designed by George Howe (1886–1955) as his diploma project at the Ecole des Beaux-Arts in 1913 and was constructed immediately thereafter. Nearly all the American architects who had been to the Ecole, like nearly all American architects of the time who had been educated at home, earned their living designing houses, most of which stood surrounded by greenery in new residential neighborhoods or in suburbs. These houses expressed a domestic ideal that remains typically American, however much the appearance of houses has changed and the size of plots of land has shrunk. The Howe House is a relatively luxurious expression of this ideal. What makes it particularly appropriate here is that the jury at the Ecole approved of Howe's drawings of it, and one of the best of the French architects who taught in America, Paul P. Cret, wrote about it in *The Architectural Record* in 1920. Cret thought the house had "the unconscious beauty of the minor domestic architecture of Europe." The house and garden seem to be "an integral part of the hill." The layout, though, has "the quality of the well-planned industrial plant." Cret admired the "feeling of spaciousness" inside, and outside the absence of decoration other than the masonry (of buff, brown, and red stones and lines of brick). The house "is as free from archeological imitation as it is devoid of a pretentious striving for originality." It is an "example of what modern art ought to be: a logical continuation of the best traditions." George Howe, who later abandoned this style, referred to it as "Wall Street Pastorale."

Delano and Aldrich. J. A. Burden House, Syosset, Long Island, New York.

The J. A. Burden House was built in the same decade as the Howe House. By William Adams Delano (1874–1960) and Chester Holmes Aldrich (1871–1940), both of whom had been at the Ecole and in the office of Carrère and Hastings, the house is in the style that many Americans trained in Paris espoused in the early twentieth century—the Colonial Revival. At the Ecole des Beaux-Arts from the early 1890s on, there were lectures on the history of French architecture. Such awareness of a national tradition seems to have put a question into the minds of many of the Americans there, and the answer they found when they came home—an American style—was that of East Coast America in the eighteenth century. This Colonial or Georgian style was used for houses and for larger buildings such as schools or hospitals— buildings for which a small scale was considered fitting, and which could be maintained through delicate wood detailing, small panes of glass, and the size of bricks. In the thinking of Delano and Aldrich (and of McKim, Mead and White), the Colonial style was not appropriate for the most important urban public buildings: they were to be classical. A difference between the American

Colonial Revival and the Georgian Revival occurring at the same time in England is to be seen in the plans, such as of the Burden House: American architects sought the sym-

metry and regularity of eighteenth-century French architecture rather than the haphazard picturesqueness of much English work of that century.

(*left*) **Raymond M. Hood. American Radiator Building, New York. 1923–24.**

The American Radiator Building on West Fortieth Street in New York was designed by Raymond M. Hood (1881–1934). Hood belonged to a generation of individualistic skyscraper designers that changed New York in the 1910s, '20s, and '30s; some of his contemporaries were Harvey Wiley Corbett, Ely Jacques Kahn, William F. Lamb, and William Van Alen. These men, who had been formed at the Ecole des Beaux-Arts, thought of themselves as modern architects, facing the future instead of the past. The skyscraper was for them the building type of the future, and each of them dealt with the problem of its form with gusto. Hood's American Radiator Building is vaguely Gothic—the style that had been set for skyscrapers by Cass Gilbert's Woolworth Building of 1913—but, unlike any Gothic building, shiny black, touched in places with gold. Hood had been partial to the Gothic style at the Ecole; he won a prize there in 1910 for an employment exchange, which has Gothic surfaces of a complicated and ornamental shape (as at the top of the American Radiator Building), rising from a symmetrical plan. The composition of the American Radiator Building is also essentially symmetrical, but as a result of economic necessity the planning has become tighter, more complex, and on the ground floor somewhat less clear in its axial organization. The concern for the careful relation of elements, the predisposition toward symmetry, and the love of ornament that were transmitted in the ateliers in Paris stayed with Hood and his contemporaries all their lives, even when they were conceiving buildings of a height their professors never imagined.

(*opposite*) **Paul P. Cret and Smith and Bassette. Hartford County Building, Hartford, Connecticut. 1926–29.**

The Hartford County Building is by Paul P. Cret (1876–1945) with Smith and Bassette. Cret was a Frenchman who was called to the University of Pennsylvania as professor of architecture in 1903, the year in which he got his diploma at the Ecole des Beaux-Arts. He was the central figure at the university's architecture school for the rest of his life, and unlike most of the other French architects who taught in America, he also established himself in practice. His buildings held other architects' attention. Cret's best early work, the Pan American Union Building of 1907 in Washington, D.C., looks as though it could have been designed at the Ecole. The

Hartford County courthouse, nearly two decades later, shows his allegiance to the kind of planning he had been taught in its clear arrangement of courtrooms, corridors, and secondary spaces. But the character of the building, especially on the outside, has the austere severity of much American early twentieth-century classicism, a severity due ultimately to the vision of Charles F. McKim. The parts that make up the outside have been simplified—for example the piers, square in plan, are without fluting—with the result that the whole becomes a kind of abstract art. Few variations on classicism earned as much contempt from modernists in the '20s and '30s as did this stripped-down style, which seemed to acknowledge an emerging modern idiom and yet refused to give up classical allusions. Cret was much admired as a teacher; perhaps his most distinguished pupil was Louis Kahn, in whose work there are clear references to Beaux-Arts principles.

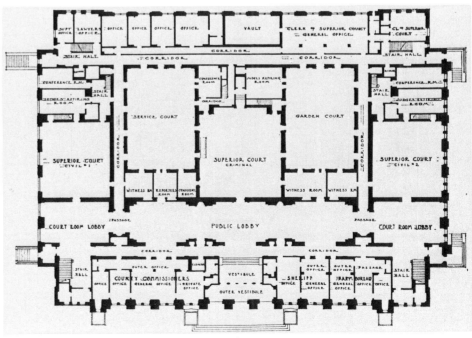

John Russell Pope and Eggers and Higgins. Jefferson Memorial, Washington, D.C. 1934–43.

The Jefferson Memorial is one of the last designs of John Russell Pope (1874–1937); commissioned in 1934, it was built from 1938 to 1943 under the supervision of Pope's former associates, Eggers and Higgins. Pope was the ultimate inheritor of the classicism of Charles F. McKim, under whose personal influence the younger man came after returning from the Ecole des Beaux-Arts. The Jefferson Memorial is the final American

monument in this style. Its allusions are obvious: the Pantheon in Rome, and the building by Jefferson that the Pantheon inspired: the rotunda at the University of Virginia in Charlottesville.

Pope, in his white marble version, screens the wall of the drum with an extension of the colonnade, thus tying the rectangular portico to the cylindrical rotunda. Open to the four directions are views of the standing figure of Jefferson. Unfortunately, Rudolph Evans was not the equal of Daniel Chester French: Evans's statue of Jefferson lacks the quality

of French's Lincoln, at once grand and intimate. Begun one year before The Museum of Modern Art was completed, the Jefferson Memorial seemed at the time not really controversial but merely irrelevant, like the architecture of Pope's nearly contemporary National Gallery. What passed unremarked was the extraordinary suavity of Pope's detail and his masterly handling of the site. Nonetheless, the Jefferson Memorial has become one of the durable images of a public place in America's national consciousness. It is the last of its kind.

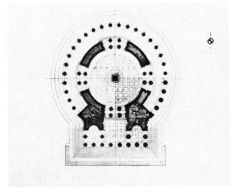

NOTES TO THE ESSAYS

ABBREVIATIONS
USED IN THE NOTES

Delaire.   E. Delaire, *Les Architectes élèves de l'Ecole des Beaux-Arts 1793–1907*, Paris, 1907.

Hautecoeur.   Louis Hautecoeur, *Histoire de l'architecture classique en France*, 7 vols., Paris, 1943–57.

Hitchcock.   Henry-Russell Hitchcock, *Architecture: Nineteenth and Twentieth Centuries*, The Pelican History of Art, Harmondsworth, Middlesex, and Baltimore, 1958.

JSAH.   *Journal of the Society of Architectural Historians.*

RGA.   *Revue Générale de l'Architecture et des Travaux Publics*, Paris, 1840–90.

ENGINEER'S ARCHITECTURE: TRUTH AND ITS CONSEQUENCES
Arthur Drexler

1. From "Picasso Speaks," *The Arts*, May 1923.

2. In its ambiguous religious symbolism, which includes an architectural model, Edward Albee's play *Tiny Alice*, 1964, infuriated drama critics; of the dozens of reviews only one, by Samuel Terrien of Union Theological Seminary *(Christianity and Crisis*, June 28, 1965), offered a serious account of Albee's theology. Max Black's *Models and Metaphors: Studies in Language and Philosophy*, Ithaca, 1962, is perhaps the most instructive examination of linguistic models; Canon Ian T. Ramsay's *Models and Mystery*, Oxford, 1964, examines the idea of the model as an instrument of theological speculation.

3. From "Hochhausprojeckt für Bahnhof Friedrichstrasse in Berlin," *Frühlicht*, 1922, no. 1, pp. 122–24.

4. Paul Valéry, "Reflections on Art," 1935. Translated by Ralph Manheim. From *Aesthetics*, vol. 13 of the Collected Works of Paul Valéry, Bollingen Series XLV, New York, 1964, pp. 134–40.

5. A remark attributed to Mies by German critics, in connection with the Barcelona Pavilion; reported by Philip Johnson.

6. This and the foregoing refer to the title essay of Sir John Summerson's *Heavenly Mansions*, London, 1949; and to "The Mischievous Analogy," 1941, and "Viollet-le-Duc and the Rational Point of View," 1947, both from the same collection. I have run some of the arguments together and added a conclusion Summerson, along with other critics writing thirty years ago, wished to avoid.

7. From "Notre Jeunesse." "To Péguy a *mystique* meant what was noble and fresh and bright in a social or religious conviction: a *politique* represented its degeneration into what was petty and self-seeking." Cited by H. Stuart Hughes in *Consciousness and Society: The Reorientation of European Social Thought 1890–1930*, New York, 1958.

THE TEACHING OF ARCHITECTURE AT THE ECOLE DES BEAUX-ARTS
Richard Chafee

For help with this work, I wish to offer my thanks first to the people at the Ecole Nationale Supérieure des Beaux-Arts whose hospitality made the study possible: to the Directeur, M. Bertin, to the Sous-Directeur, M. Cassenas, and to their secretaries; in the school library, to the former and present Conservateurs, Mme Bouleau-Rabaud and Mlle Jacques, and also to Mme Valentin and the gardiens. At the library of the Royal Institute of British Architects in London, Mr. James C. Palmes and his successor as Librarian, Mr. David Dean, and their staff all have treated me very kindly for years, as have Mr. Adolf K. Placzek and his assistants at the Avery Architectural Library in New York: I am indebted to them. I am grateful to those former students of the Ecole who have shared with me their memories of their education and have answered my many questions: Mssrs M. Abramovitz, J. P. Carlhian, G. Dengler, H. Elarth, D. A. Fletcher, W. K. Harrison. C. Hornbostel, the late E. J. Kahn, M. W. Kley, J. Labatut, the late J. C. Levi, J. C. B. Moore, the late W. G. Perry, H. Sternfeld, and O. Zavaroni. I am obliged to Professor Peter Collins and the late Professor Louis Hautecoeur for their assistance. Finally, I cannot sufficiently thank the supervisor of my doctoral thesis, Sir Nikolaus Pevsner, and my wife, Inge.

1. On the academies in general and the Academy of Painting and Sculpture in particular: Nikolaus Pevsner, *Academies of Art, Past and Present*, Cambridge, 1940, pp. 82–99, esp. pp. 89–92; and Anthony Blunt, *Art and Architecture in France*, Harmondsworth, 1959, pp. 225–30. On the Academy of Architecture in the seventeenth century: Blunt, *op. cit.*, pp. 240–241; and in much greater detail, Hautecoeur, vol. II, pp. 462–91. For a list of all the members of the Academy of Architecture: Delaire, pp. 128–31.

2. These documents were published in the twentieth century: H. Lemmonier (ed.), *Procès-verbaux de l'Académie Royale d'Architecture*, 10 vols., Paris, 1911–26.

3. Hautecoeur, vol. II, p. 465.

4. Hautecoeur, vol. III, pp. 465–66.

5. Blunt, *op. cit.*, pp. 240–41; Hautecoeur, vol. II, pp. 467–91; and basically Lemonnier's edition of the *Procès-verbaux de l'Académie Royale de l'Architecture*.

6. Lemonnier, *Procès-verbaux*, vol. III, p. 216.

7. On the dispute: Hautecoeur, vol. II, pp. 487–91. On Perrault: see Wolfgang Herrmann, *The Theory of Claude Perrault*, London, 1973.

8. François Blondel, *Cours d'architecture enseigné dans l'Académie Royale*, Paris, 1st ed., 1675, 2nd ed., 1698.

9. On J.-F. Blondel: Robin Middleton, "Jacques François Blondel and the *Cours d'Architecture*," *JSAH*, vol. XVIII (1959), pp. 140–49; also (but less perceptive) Hautecoeur, vol. III, pp. 466–72.

10. On the Academy in the eighteenth century before the Revolution: Hautecoeur, vol. III, pp. 457–72; vol. IV, pp. 57–66. Also Marcel Bonnaire (ed.), *Procès-verbaux de l'Académie des Beaux-Arts*, vol. I, Paris, 1937, pp. xxxiv-xxxvi.

11. Delaire, p. 128. Hautecoeur, vol. II, p. 463; vol. III, pp. 458–59.

12. Hautecoeur, vol. III, p. 458.

13. Hautecoeur, vol. IV, pp. 62–66.

14. On the competitions of 1701–02 and of 1703, see Lemonnier, *Procès-verbaux*, vol. III (1697–1711), pp. ix, 120–21, 142–49, 169, 173, and 179. On the beginnings of the annual competition and prize, *ibid.*, vol. IV (1712–26), pp. v and 110, viii, ix, xiv, xv. On the Grand Prix and the Academy in Rome in the first half of the eighteenth century: Hautecoeur, vol. III, pp. 472–76. For a list of subjects and winners of the Grand Prix (with some errors among the second and third prizes, 1827–44): Delaire, pp. 134–40. For illustrations of the designs: H. Rosenau, "The Engravings of the *Grand Prix* of the French Academy of Architecture," *Architectural History*, vol. III (1960), pp. 15–180.

15. On the beginnings of the *prix d'émulation*: Lemonnier, *Procès-verbaux*, vol. VII (1759–67), pp. xxxiv, 146, 150. On student numbers, vol. IV (1712–26), p. viii; vol. VI (1744–58), pp. xiii–xiv.

16. Hautecoeur, vol. IV, pp. 40–41. On the French Academy in Rome during the second half of the eighteenth century: vol. IV, pp. 36–44; vol. V, pp. 50–54.

17. Delaire, pp. 130, 134. LeBon (or Lebon) is not in Thieme-Becker.

18. The most readable general accounts of the struggle are in Pevsner's *Academies of Art*, pp. 197–200, and in Louis Hautecoeur's *Louis David*, Paris, 1954, pp. 133–38. David Lloyd Dowd in *Pageant-Master of the Republic: Jacques Louis David and the French Revolution*, Lincoln, Nebr., 1948, pp. 27–34, 91–93, refers the reader to many relevant published documents, but Dowd's judgment suffers from his limited knowledge of the history of art. Bonnaire's introductions to the *Procès-verbaux de l'Académie des Beaux-Arts*, especially to vol. I (1937) and vol. III (1940), as well as his Appendix II in vol. I, pp. 273–76, carefully report the history of the struggle and the subsequent emergence of the Ecole des Beaux-Arts. Bonnaire cites many sources, published and unpublished. Hautecoeur in *L'Architecture classique* writes at length but somewhat confusingly about the teaching of architecture during the Revolution and the Empire; see vol. V, pp. 93–100, 112–14, 154–55, 263–79.

19. *Voeu des artistes*, Paris (Gueffier), 1789. See Dowd, *op. cit*, pp. 29–30.

20. Quoted in translation by Dowd, *op. cit.*, p. 29.

21. Dowd, *op. cit.*, pp. 30–31; Hautecoeur, *Louis David*, p. 135.

22. Bonnaire, *op. cit.*, vol. I, p. xlvii.

23. Bonnaire, *op. cit.*, vol. I, p. lviii, n. 4. Hautecoeur, *L'Architecture classique*, vol. V, p. 94.

24. Bonnaire, *op. cit.*, vol. I, p. xlvii.

25. Dowd, *op. cit.*, pp. 31–32. J.-L. David and others, *Adresse des représentants des beaux-arts à l'assemblée nationale dans la séance du 28 juin 1790*, Paris (Imprimerie nationale), 1790.

26. Antoine Renou, *Esprit des statuts et règlements de l'Académie royale de Peinture et Sculpture, pour servir de réponse aux détracteurs de son régime*, Paris (Imprimerie Herissant), 1790. Cited by Bonnaire, *op. cit.*, vol. I, p. xlii n.

27. *Adresse et projet de statuts et règlemens pour l'académie centrale de peinture, sculpture, gravure et architecture, présentés à l'assemblée nationale par la majorité des membres de l'académie royale de peinture et sculpture*, Paris (Veuve Valade), 1790. Cited by Bonnaire, *op. cit.*, vol. I, p. xlv, and by Dowd, *op. cit.*, p. 33.

28. Dowd, *op. cit.*, p. 33; Pevsner, *op. cit.*, p. 198.

29. Bonnaire, *op. cit.*, vol. I, pp. xlvii–xlix.

30. Antoine Renou, *Précis motivé par les officiers de l'académie royale de peinture et sculpture, et plusieurs académiciens qui s'y sont joints pour servir de réfutation à un project de statuts d'académie centrale, par quelques académiciens*, Paris (Herissant), March 1791. *Précis sur l'établissement, le régime et le mode d'enseignement de l'académie de peinture et sculpture*, Paris, 1791. Both cited by Bonnaire, *op. cit.*, vol. I, p. xlii n.

31. A.-C. Quatremère de Quincy, *Considérations sur les arts du dessin en France, suivies d'un plan d'académie, ou d'école publique, et d'un système d'encouragemens*, and *Suite aux considérations sur les arts du dessin en France*, both Paris, 1791. Cited by Bonnaire, *op. cit.*, vol. I, p. xxxvii n. See also Pevsner, *op. cit.*, p. 199.

32. Paris (Imprimerie Marat), 1791. Cited by Bonnaire, *op. cit.*, vol. I, p. lxxv.

33. Hautecoeur, *Louis David*, p. 136.

34. Dowd, *op. cit.*, p. 33, n. 35.

35. Bonnaire, *op. cit.*, vol. I, p. xlvii, n. 2.

36. Pevsner, *op. cit.*, p. 199.

37. Hautecoeur (*Louis David*, p. 121) says David was elected September 17, 1792. Pevsner (*op. cit.*, p. 199) says he entered the convention October 17, 1792. Was there a month between election and entry?

38. Dowd, *op. cit.*, p. 88 and n. 45. Dowd's date of October 17, 1793, must be a misprint, for 1792.

39. *Procès-verbaux de la convention nationale*, Paris (Imprimerie nationale), 1792–96, vol. III, pp. 142–43. Dowd, *op. cit.*, pp. 91–92 and n. 61, refers to the incident. Pevsner, *op. cit.*, p. 199, errs in stating that on November 11 David sought to close down all academies.

40. Dowd, *op. cit.*, p. 92; article on Suvée in Thieme-Becker.

41. Quoted by Hautecoeur, *Louis David*, p. 134.

42. *Ibid.*, p. 135; Hautecoeur, *L'Architecture classique*, vol. V, p. 99.

43. *Collection générale des décrets rendu par la convention nationale*, Paris (chez Baudouin, Imprimeur de la Convention Nationale), 1793–95, vol. for September, October, November 1792, p. 235. Henceforth here called Collection Baudouin.

44. Pevsner, *op. cit.*, p. 199.

45. Quoted by Hautecoeur, *Louis David*, p. 137.

46. Collection Baudouin, vol. for May 1793, p. 158.

47. Bonnaire, *op. cit.*, vol. I, p. lix.

48. *Procès-verbaux de la convention nationale*, vol. XV, p. 23.

49. Pevsner, *op. cit.*, p. 199; Hautecoeur, *Louis David*, p. 137.

50. Bonnaire, *op. cit.*, vol. I, p. lxi; Dowd, *op. cit.*, p. 33 and n. 35.

51. A.-L. Lavoisier, *Oeuvres* (E. Grimaux, ed.), Paris, 1862–93, vol. IV, pp. 615–22.

52. Dowd, *op. cit.*, p. 88 and n. 46.

53. Hautecoeur quotes David in *Louis David*, p. 137.

54. Bonnaire, *op. cit.*, vol. I, p. lxi.

55. *Collection générale des lois, proclamations, instructions, et autres actes du pouvoir exécutif*, Paris (Imprimerie nationale), 1792–95, vol. XV, p. 362. The Collection Baudouin (vol. for August 1793, pp. 49–50) prints this decree differently: in Art. I Baudouin replaces the word *jugement* with *paiement*. I believe Baudouin to be in error.

56. Dowd, *op. cit.*, p. 92.

57. J.-L. David, *Discours du citoyen David, député du département de Paris, sur la nécessité de supprimer les Académies*, Paris (imprimé par ordre de la Convention nationale), 1793.

58. "... Toutes les académies et sociétés littéraires, patentés ou dotées par la nation, sont supprimées...." Collection Baudouin, vol. for August 1793, pp. 56–57.

59. Bonnaire, *op. cit.*, vol. I, p. lxii and Appendix I (pp. 263–73).

60. Quoted by Bonnaire, *op. cit.*, vol. I, p. 273.

61. Bonnaire, *ibid.*, mentions the decree of April 3, 1793. The decree of March 8, 1793, may have set a precedent: the Convention then decreed payment to "professeurs et instituteurs" in all establishments of public education. Collection Baudouin, vol. for January, February, March 1793, p. 377.

62. On Julien-David Leroy see Hautecoeur, *L'Architecture classique*, vol. IV, pp. 18–23; vol. V, pp. 263–67. The date of his becoming professor is from Delaire, p. 129.

63. For a plan showing the location of the Royal Academy, see Bonnaire, *op. cit.*, vol. I, page facing p. xlviii. In autumn 1793 David Leroy began using the vestibule from the Jardin de l'Infante into the former apartment of the Queen Mother (Hautecoeur, vol. V, p. 263).

64. Delaire, p. 92, and biographies of Leroy and Vaudoyer; also Eugène Müntz, "Historique de l'Ecole des Beaux-Arts," in H. Guédy, *L'Enseignement à l'Ecole nationale et spéciale des beaux-arts, section d'architecture*, Paris, 1899, pp. xii–xiii; also François Benoit, *L'Art français sous la révolution de l'empire*, Paris, 1897, p. 201, n. 7 (with as reference Thomas de Thomon, *Mémoire pour l'Académie d'architecture*).

65. Collection Baudouin, Vendémaire, an II, Paris, [1793], p. 51. This decree pertains only to the Academy of Painting and Sculpture. Hautecoeur, vol. V, p. 96, mistakenly implies that it maintained all the academic schools. He misdates it September 28, as does Pevsner (*Academies of Art*, p. 93).

66. On David's architect friends, see Hautecoeur, *Louis David*, p. 141, and René Crozet, "David et l'architecture néo-classique," *Gazette des Beaux-Arts*, 6th ser., vol. XLV (1955), p. 214.

67. Two vols. in one, folio, Paris, 1758.

68. James Stuart and Nicholas Revett, *The Antiquities of Athens*, London, 4 folio vols., 1762, 1787, 1794, 1816.

69. Hautecoeur, *L'Architecture classique*, vol. IV, pp. 58–62.

70. See L. D. Ettlinger, "Jacques Louis David and Roman Virtue," *Journal of the Royal Society of Arts*, London, January 1967, pp. 105–23. On the *Horatii* and *The Death of Socrates*, see also the exhibition catalogue, *The Age of Neo-Classicism*, London (The Arts Council of Great Britain), 1972, pp. 40–42.

71. On David's architectural backgrounds, see Crozet, *op. cit.*, pp. 211–20; also Robert Rosenblum, *Transformations in Late Eigh-*

teenth Century Art, Princeton, 1967, pp. 124–26.

72. The sketch, Old Horatius Defending His Son, which is now in the Louvre, is fig. 3 in Ettlinger, op. cit., p. 112. Rosenblum, op. cit., fig. 139, reproduces another (perhaps later) preliminary sketch, now at the Palais des Beaux-Arts in Lille; in this drawing David has made the columns smooth while keeping their bases.

73. David Leroy justifies such smoothness: on p. 1 of the "Seconde Partie" of Ruines des plus beaux monuments . . . , he writes that although fluted columns were generally used by the Greeks, smooth ones were more ancient.

74. For a history of the controversy about its shape, see Nikolaus Pevsner and S. Lang, "The Doric Revival," in Pevsner's Studies in Art, Architecture and Design, vol. I, pp. 197–211.

75. Dowd, op. cit., p. 94.

76. Dowd, op. cit., pp. 94–95; Delaire, p. 137, n. 1. Decrees of 8 brumaire an II (October 29, 1793), 9 brumaire an II (October 30, 1793), and 25 brumaire an II (November 15, 1793) in Collection générale des lois . . . , vol. XVI, pp. 349, 364–65, 365–66. This jury did not endure for many years.

77. The last decree mentioned in the preceding footnote names the fifty-five members of the jury.

78. Hautecoeur, Louis David, pp. 140–41; Dowd, op. cit., pp. 93–94. The decree of 27 nivôse an II (January 16, 1794), in Collection générale des lois . . . , vol, XVII, pp. 207–09, names the members of the committee.

79. On the influence of Durand, see Hitchcock, chap. 2, pp. 20–42.

80. For a twentieth-century history of the Ecole Polytechnique, see P. Tuffrau, "L'Ecole Polytechnique à travers l'histoire," pp. 1–31 in Société des amis de l'Ecole, L'Ecole Polytechnique, Paris, 1932. Tuffrau refers to the two most thorough nineteenth-century books about the school: G. Pinet, Histoire de l'école polytechnique, Paris, 1887, and Ecole Polytechnique, Livre du Centenaire, 3 vols., Paris, 1895–97.

81. Quoted by J.-B. Rondelet, Traité théorique et pratique de l'art de bâtir, in the "Avant-Propos" to "Tome Cinquième" in the 6th ed., Paris, 1832, and in subsequent editions, p. xiii. Rondelet writes somewhat petulantly of his role in the founding of the school on pp. v–xv.

82. Bonnaire, op. cit., p. lxxiv, n. 1.

83. Collection Baudouin, Vendémaire, an IV, Paris, [1795], p. 263.

84. Dates from Hitchcock, p. 20.

85. Durand, Précis . . . , pp. i–ii.

86. Collection Baudouin, Brumarie, an IV, Paris, [1795], pp. 93–100.

87. Quoted by René Schneider, Quatremère de Quincy et son intervention dans les arts (1788–1830), Paris, 1910, p. 160.

88. "Titre IV" of decree of 3 brumaire an IV (October 25, 1795), op. cit.

89. For the names of the architects in both bodies, see Delaire, pp. 129–32.

90. "Titre V," Arts. 5 and 7 of decree of 3 brumaire an IV, op. cit. Also Art. 30 of decree of 15 germinal an IV (April 4, 1796), published in J.-B. Duvergier, Collection complète des lois, décrets, ordonnances, règlements et avis du Conseil d'Etat . . . de 1788 à 1824, Paris, 1825–28, vol. IX, p. 74.

91. On the project for the Left Bank, see Hautecoeur, vol. V, pp. 185–87.

92. Delaire, pp. 13–14.

93. On the course in the Ecole Spéciale, see François Benoit, L'Art français sous la révolution et l'empire, Paris, 1897, pp. 204–05, 207–08.

94. Quoted by Benoit, ibid., p. 208.

95. Delaire, p. 137, n. 2.

96. Quoted by Bonnaire, op. cit., vol III, pp. viii–ix.

97. Decree of 29 ventôse an XIII (March 20, 1805) quoted by Bonnaire, op. cit., vol. III, p. xv.

98. On the moves from the Louvre to the Collège des Quatres Nations, see Bonnaire, op. cit., vol. III, pp. vi–xix.

99. On the changes by Napoleon and Louis XVIII, see Bonnaire, op. cit., vol. II, pp. vii–xiv.

100. Published by Duvergier, op. cit., vol. XIV, pp. 367–68.

101. Duvergier, op. cit., vol. XX, quote on p. 260, whole decree on pp. 260–62.

102. Decree of April 27, 1815, published by Duvergier, op. cit., vol. XIX, p. 414.

103. "Academies," Encyclopedia Britannica, 1962 ed., vol. I, p. 78.

104. "Académie" in section "Arts-Lettres-Sciences," Nouveau Petit Larousse, Paris, 1952, p. 1155.

105. On Dufourny see Hautecoeur, vol. V, especially pp. 264–66, also vol. IV, pp. 17–18. See also Benoit, op. cit., p. 208, and Quatremère de Quincy, Notice sur Dufourny, Paris, 1820.

106. Benoit, op. cit., p. 205; Bonnaire, op. cit., vol. III, p. xvii.

107. Liste chronologique des professeurs et secrétaires de l'école impériale et spéciale des beaux-arts depuis la réorganisation par suite du décret du 28 septembre 1793 jusqu'a ce jour [February 1, 1956]. Volume at Archives Nationales, catalogue number AJ-52-35.

108. On Baltard, see Hautecoeur, vol. V, pp. 268, 270, 271; vol. VI, pp. 158–62, 191, 253, 335.

109. Delaire, pp. 14, 16. These pages about

events during the Revolutionary and Napoleonic eras were written shortly after most of the archives of the Ecole des Beaux-Arts were transferred to the Archives Nationales and before much of the resulting catalogue appeared. That excellent volume—Brigitte Labat-Poussin's Inventaire des archives de l'Ecole Nationale Supérieure des Beaux-Arts—was made public in stages, in 1973–76. It brings to light documents about the suppression of the academies and about the Ecoles Spéciales. I wish I had known of these papers before my writing went to press.

110. On Lenoir's Musée see Courajod, Alexandre Lenoir, son journal et le musée des monuments français, 3 vols., Paris, 1878–87. Hautecoeur shows two views of this romantic place in his vol. V, pp. 112–13.

111. Eugène Müntz quotes the name from the ordonnance of December 18, 1816, in his Guide de l'école nationale des beaux-arts, Paris, [1889], p. 16, and again in his short history, L'Ecole des Beaux-Arts. Souvenir de la visite du 18 avril 1898, Paris, 1898, pp. 14–15. I cannot find the ordonnances of either April 27 or December 18, 1816, in the Collection Duvergier, op. cit., which is said to be incomplete, or in the Bulletin des lois du royaume de France, 7th ser., vol. 2 (1er semestre, 1816), or vol. 3 (2e semestre, 1816).

112. Müntz, . . . Souvenir de la visite . . . , p. 15.

113. Müntz, Guide . . . , "Notice Historique des bâtiments . . . ", pp. 12–25. On the move from the Institut's building, see also Henri Delaborde, L'Académie des beaux-arts depuis la fondation de l'Institut de France, Paris, 1891, pp. 193, 196.

114. This ordonnance is in the collection of Règlements, 1819–1908, in the library of the Ecole des Beaux-Arts. Excerpts from it are in David de Penanrum, Roux and Delaire, Les Architectes élèves de l'Ecole des Beaux-Arts, 1819–94, Paris, 1895, p. 53.

115. Ibid., p. 54.

116. Ibid., pp. 54–58.

117. A collection of twenty-three issues of regulations by the school from 1819 to 1908 is in the Ecole library. The most important of these have been republished. They are: (1) the ordonnance royale of August 4, 1819, and règlement of December 27, 1823, both in David de Penanrun, Roux and Delaire, op. cit., pp. 53–58; (2) the imperial decree of November 13, 1863, and règlement of January 14, 1864, both in RGA, the former in vol. XXI (1863), pp. 294–98, the latter in vol. XXII (1864), pp. 64–68. These documents are also in David de Penanrun, op. cit., pp. 58 ff; (3) the decree of September 30, 1883, and the règlement issued at the same time, both in the Gazette des Architectes et du Bâtiment, 2nd ser., 12th year (1883), pp.

247–51, pp. 254–58, 260–62. Regulations for the current academic year are in David de Penanrun, *op. cit.*, of 1895, pp. 269–87; in Henry Guédy, *L'Enseignement à l'école nationale et spéciale des beaux-arts, section d'architecture,* of 1899, pp. 99–144; and in Delaire of 1907, pp. 94–114.

118. There were only one or two women in ateliers until the school began accepting them. The first woman admitted to the Section d'Architecture was an American, Julia Morgan, in November 1898.

119. A Romanian named Bernhard Horn (born 1895) was admitted in July 1922, after trying eleven times, the first in 1911! (Horn's dossier is in the archives of the Ecole.)

120. The regulations that first state this requirement are not in the collection in the Ecole library, but the addition can be seen by comparing the records of *concours* kept in students' dossiers.

121. *Décret* of September 30, 1883, Art. 21.

121a. More explanation is needed here. The French word for these preliminary sketches is *esquisses,* the same word used for one kind of the *concours d'émulation,* the sketch *concours.* In fact, like the preliminary sketches in the longer architectural competitions, the *concours d'émulation sur esquisses* lasted twelve hours and took place entirely *en loge.* A sketch *concours* thereby challenged the students to solve an architectural problem very quickly and without any help from the *patrons.* So as to avoid confusing preliminary sketches with sketch *concours,* people at the Ecole came to call the latter *esquisses-esquisses.*

122. A few words must be added about the jury, which decided who deserved prizes. It was selected by the people in charge of teaching: by the faculty until the reform of 1863, and thereafter by the Conseil Supérieur d'Enseignement (of which, more later). Before the reform, the jury consisted entirely of faculty members, thereafter largely of them. The medals themselves were designed by a professor at the Ecole. Besides architecture, sculpture, and painting, the Ecole taught engraving to a few students. Some of the medal makers went on to design coinage for the French government.

123. Hautecoeur, vol. V, pp. 153–54; vol. VI, pp. 143–44. The law of December 31, 1940, that regulated the profession of architecture was somewhat due to Professor Hautecoeur himself.

124. In the *Procès-verbaux de l'Académie Royale d'Architecture,* the prize is customarily called *le prix. Grand prix* and *grand prix d'architecture* are the terms used in the regulations published by the Institut in its booklet, *Académie Royale des Beaux-Arts,* Paris, 1822. *Grand Prix de Rome* ap-

pears in the imperial decree of November 13, 1863, and in subsequent decrees. The change in terminology is echoed after a time by a change on the printed sheets on which the Ecole recorded each student's *concours:* until about the mid-1880s, *Concours des Grands Prix* appears; thereafter, *Concours du Grand Prix de Rome.*

125. This summary of the arrangement is based on the "Recueil des Règlements" published by the Institut de France in its booklet entitled *Académie Royale des Beaux-Arts,* Paris, 1822, pp. 29 *ff;* also on "Titre II" of the imperial decree of November 13, 1863; on the imperial decree of February 19, 1870, published in the *Gazette des Architectes et du Bâtiment,* 7th year (1869–70), pp. 115–16; on the decree by the president of the Republic dated November 13, 1871, published in the *RGA,* vol. XXVIII (1870 and 1871), cols. 258–59; and on the various reports of current practice, as reported most years in the architectural press.

126. By the 1880s, the number of competitors in the second trial had been reduced to twenty.

127. A correction: during the first half of the nineteenth century, each Grand Prix *concours* was in two stages; a twelve-hour *concours d'essai* and the long *concours définitif.* Thirty competitors were allowed into the *concours définitif,* but after the preliminary sketch that each of these men made in the first twenty-four hours of this final stage, there was a judgment and the number of competitors was reduced to eight. In 1855 the number of stages, and of programs, was increased to three: a twelve-hour *esquisse,* a twenty-four-hour *esquisse,* and the four-month *concours définitif.* The time for the preliminary sketch in the final stage was increased from twenty-four hours to ten days. (See *RGA,* vol. XIII, 1855, col. 252.) From 1864 until 1968 the Grand Prix *concours* was as described in the paragraph preceeding this note: three stages, each with a different program, and in the final stage a preliminary *esquisse* not of ten days but of a day or two.

128. *RGA,* vol. X (1852), cols. 301–03.

129. The following table arranges ateliers chronologically, shows how long each *patron* was active, and gives the number of winners of the Grand Prix de Rome (abbreviated GP) taught by each *patron.* The criteria used for including an atelier are the jury's recognition, a long life, a large number of students — or, simply, its inescapable importance, as in the case of the atelier Viollet-le-Duc.

TABLE I
IMPORTANT ATELIERS, 1789–1968

1789–1880:

Vaudoyer, Lebas, Ginain

  A.-L.-T. Vaudoyer 1789–c. 1832 (with his

nephew Lebas 1819 *ff.;* perhaps in 1820 Lebas also opened an atelier of his own), about 8 GP (including his son Léon Vaudoyer and Labrouste, both *patrons*).

  Lebas c. 1832–64 (perhaps with Léon Vaudoyer c. 1832–c. 1835), 15 GP (incl. Charles Garnier and the *patrons* Paccard, Jules André, Ginain, Coquart, and Moyaux).

  Ginain 1864–80, 4 GP (incl. the *patron* Paulin); in 1880 to the *atelier officiel* Laisné of 1863 *ff.*

1791–c. 1823:

Percier, about 17 GP (incl. the *patron* Leclère and the professor Lesueur).

c. 1798–c.1819:

A.-F. Peyre (the younger), 2 GP (the *patrons* Guénepin and Huyot). Peyre had conducted an atelier before the Revolution.

1800–c. 1947:

Delespine, Blouet, Gilbert, Questel, Pascal, Recoura

  Delespine 1800–25, 2 GP (incl. Blouet).

  Blouet 1826–53, 2 GP. While he was away, 1829–30, Duban was in charge.

  Gilbert 1853–55, 1 GP (the *patron* Daumet).

  Questel 1856–72, 6 GP (incl. Pascal).

  Pascal 1872–1920 (with Recoura 1917–20, coming from the atelier Duquesne of c. 1904 *ff.* 5 GP (incl. Nénot, Recoura, and Duquesne).

  Recoura 1920–c. 1947 (with Nénot and Duquesne 1922–29, and with Mathon 1932–c. 1947; Duquesne had opened an atelier c. 1904; Mathon brought with him the atelier Douillard of 1860 *ff.*). In c. 1947 Recoura and Mathon merged the atelier into the atelier Blondel of 1881 *ff.*

c. 1814–c. 1854:

Debret, Duban

  Debret c. 1814–c. 1841 (with Duban 1830, coming from the atelier Delespine, Blouet of 1880 *ff.*); 2 GP (the *patrons* Duban and Constant-Dufeux).

  Duban 1830–c. 1854. The students elected to replace Debret with Duban.

1815–53:

Leclère, 3 GP.

c. 1816–c. 1877:

Guénepin

  A.-J.-M. Guénepin c. 1816–c. 1842, 3 GP (incl. his nephew F.-J.-B.).

  F.-J.-B. Guénepin c. 1842–c. 1877.

c. 1822–c. 1840:

L.-P. Baltard, 1 GP (his son Victor, a *patron*).

1823–40:

Huyot, 3 GP. In 1840 most of the atelier joined the atelier Vaudoyer, Lebas of 1789 *ff.*

1830–56:

Labrouste

1832–50 and 1864–72:

Léon Vaudoyer (perhaps also assisting his cousin Lebas, c. 1832–c. 1835 in the atelier Vaudoyer, Lebas of 1789 *ff.*), 1 GP.

c. 1836–c. 1856:

Jäy, 1 GP.

1836 or 1837–71:

Constant-Dufeux. In 1863 he took charge of a new

atelier officiel also.
1842–56:
Nicolle
c. 1844–c. 1856:
Victor Baltard , 1 GP.
1856–57:
Viollet-le-Duc
1856–67:
Jules André. 2 GP (Guadet and Gerhardt, both *patrons*). In 1867 André took charge of the *atelier officiel* Paccard of 1863 *ff*.
1860–1932:
Douillard, Thierry, Deglane, Mathon
    Douillard brothers 1860–89.
    Thierry 1889–94.
    Deglane 1894–1931 (with Nicod 1921–29, and with Mathon 1929–30).
    Mathon 1932; that autumn he merged the atelier into the atelier Delespine, Blouet of 1800 *ff*.
1860–1968:
Vaudremer, Raulin, Héraud, Chappey
    Vaudremer 1860–80.
    Raulin 1880–between 1903 and 1907 (with Sortais c. 1895–c. 1904).
    Héraud between 1903 and 1907 until during World War II (with Boutterin and Chappey 1937–c. 1942), 2 GP (incl. Boutterin).
    Chappey by 1945–68 (with Guth c. 1954–58).
1862–1968:
Daumet, Esquié, Jaussely, Expert, Dengler
    Daumet 1862–c. 1895 (with Girault 1885–c. 1894, and with Esquié 1888–c. 1895), 5 GP (incl. the *patrons* Bernier, Paul Blondel, Girault, Esquié).
    Esquié c. 1895–1909, 3 GP (incl. Jaussely).
    Jaussely 1910–24.
    Expert 1925–52; earlier he had assisted Gromort in that atelier of c. 1919 *ff*.; 1937–52 he was also *patron* of the *atelier officiel* Constant-Dufeux of 1863 *ff*.
    Dengler 1952–68, 2 GP. The atelier in 1955 became *officiel*.
1863–1968, *atelier officiel*:
Constant-Dufeux, Guadet, Paulin, Pierre André, Patouillard, Expert, Beaudouin
    Constant-Dufeux 1863–71, also with his *atelier libre* of c. 1836 *ff*.
    Guadet 1871–94, 1 GP.
    Paulin 1895–1915, 1 GP (the *patron* Nicod).
    Pierre André 1919–30, coming from his *atelier libre* of 1891 *ff*.
    Patouillard 1931–37 (with Grange 1932–37).
    Expert 1937–52, also with the *atelier libre* Daumet of 1862 *ff*.
    Beaudouin 1952–68.
1863–1968, *atelier officiel*:
Laisné, Ginain, Scellier de Gisors, Bernier, Pontremoli, Debat-Ponsan, Leconte, Marot
    Laisné 1863–79.
    Ginain 1880–98, coming from the *atelier libre* Vaudoyer, Lebas of 1789 *ff*., 3 GP (incl. the *patron* Patouillard).
    Scellier de Gisors 1898–1905, also with the *atelier libre* Blondel of 1881 *ff*.

Bernier 1905–19.
    Pontremoli 1919–32 but active a decade after his retirement, 5 GP (incl. the *patrons* Leconte and Beaudoin).
    Debat-Ponsan 1932–42, also with the *atelier libre* Coquart of 1867 *ff*.
    Leconte 1942–c. 1966. 9 GP (incl. the *patrons* Gillet and Marot).
    Marot c. 1966–68.
1863–1968, *atelier officiel*:
Paccard, Jules André, Moyaux, Lambert, Bigot, Nicod, Arretche
    Paccard 1863–67, 1 GP.
    Jules André 1867–90, coming from his *atelier libre* of 1856 *ff*., 7 GP (all *patrons*: Lambert, Laloux, Deglane, Redon, Pierre André, Defrasse, and Tournaire).
    Moyaux 1890–1908.
    Lambert 1908–25, coming from the *atelier libre* Wable of 1875 *ff*.
    Bigot 1925–40, 4 GP (incl. the *patron* Remondet).
    Nicod 1940–48, coming from the *atelier libre* Tournon of 1933 *ff*.
    Arretche 1949–68, also with the *atelier libre* Gromort of c. 1919 *ff*.
1867–1942:
Coquart, Gerhardt, Redon, Tournaire, Debat-Ponsan
    Coquart 1867–82, 1 GP.
    Gerhardt 1882–91.
    Redon 1891–1921, 2 GP (incl. Azéma).
    Tournaire 1921–30 (with Azéma 1925–30), 1 GP (the *patron* Mathon).
    Debat-Ponsan 1931–42, also with the *atelier officiel* Laisné of 1863 *ff*.
1875–1908:
Wable, Lambert
    Wable 1875–80.
    Lambert 1880–1908, 2 GP: in 1908 to the *atelier officiel* Paccard of 1863 *ff*.
1881–1968:
Paul Blondel, Scellier de Gisors, Defrasse, Hilt, Zavaroni, La Mache
    Paul Blondel 1881–97.
    Scellier de Gisors 1897–1905, also in charge of the *atelier officiel* Laisné of 1863 *ff*. (with Defrasse c. 1901–05), 1 GP (Tony Garnier).
    Defrasse 1905–39 (with Madeline 1922–39, also with Marrast 1928–30, Aublet 1930–37, and Hilt 1938–39), 3 GP (incl. the *patrons* Dengler and Hilt).
    Hilt 1939–44. While he was away, c. 1940, Madeline was in charge.
    Zavaroni 1944–57, then to a new *atelier officiel*.
    La Mache 1957–68.
1890–1968:
Laloux, Charles Lemaresquier, Noël Lemaresquier
    Laloux 1890–1937 (with Lemaresquier 1920–37, and with Labro c. 1922–c. 1925), 16 GP (incl. the *patrons* Pontremoli, Bigot, Lefèvre, Debat-Ponsan, and Ferran).
    Charles Lemaresquier 1937–51, 4 GP.

Noël Lemaresquier 1951–68, 6 GP. The atelier in 1953 became *officiel*.
1891–c. 1919 or before:
Pierre André. He then took charge of the *atelier officiel* Constant-Dufeux of 1863 *ff*.
c. 1904–c. 1917 or before:
Duquesne, Recoura
    Duquesne c. 1904–11.
    Recoura 1911–between 1914 and 1917; from 1917 on, he assisted Pascal in the atelier Delespine, Blouet of 1800 *ff*.
c 1909–68:
Umbdenstock, Madelain
    Umbdenstock c. 1909–40 (with Tournon 1923–33, who then opened his own atelier). Umbdenstock had opened an *atelier préparatoire* in 1903 or possibly earlier.
    Madelain c. 1940–68.
c. 1919–c. 1939:
Godefroy, Lefèvre and Ferran
    Godefroy c. 1919–c. 1928. (Godefroy and Freynet had opened an *atelier préparatoire* in 1892 or possibly earlier.)
    Lefèvre and Ferran c. 1928–c. 1939.
c. 1919–68:
Gromort, Arretche
    Gromort c. 1919–37 and c. 1940–before 1961 (with Expert c. 1919–25, who then took charge of the atelier Daumet of 1862 *ff*.; and with Arretche 1937 and c. 1940 *ff*.), 1 GP.
    Arretche 1937–40 and before 1961 until 1968, also *patron* 1949–68 of the *atelier officiel* Paccard of 1863 *ff*.
1924–30 and c. 1945–68:
Perret, Remondet
    Perret 1924–30 and by 1945–54 (with Remondet 1949–54 and Herbé 1951–54), 1 GP.
    Remondet 1954–68 (with Herbé 1951–58, who then conducted a separate atelier until c. 1966).
1933–40:
Tournon, Nicod
    Tournon 1933–40, had earlier assisted Umbdenstock in that atelier of c. 1909 *ff*.
    Nicod 1940, very soon to the *atelier officiel* Paccard of 1863 *ff*.
c. 1936–c. 1966:
Labro, Faugeron
    Labro c. 1936–52, had earlier assisted Laloux in that atelier of 1890 *ff*. (with Gleize 1950 and with Faugeron 1950–52), 1 GP (Gleize).
    Faugeron 1953–c. 1966.
c. 1947–c. 1965:
Lods (with Hermant and Trezzini, c. 1950–c. 1965)
1949–68, *atelier officiel*:
Vivien 1949–68 (with Lagneau 1950–52, who then directed his own atelier until 1958), 1 GP.
c. 1949–c. 1965:
Pingusson
1957–68, *atelier officiel*:
Zavaroni, coming from an *atelier libre* Blondel of 1881 *ff*.
1958–68:
Gillet (with Johannet).

The table is an enlargement and correction of the list of ateliers Delaire published in 1907 (pp. 122–25). Comparable lists are in David de Penanrun's book of 1895 (p. 266), in the *Annuaire* of the S.A.D.G. of 1931 (pp. 330–35), and in the *Annuaire des Architectes D.P.L.G.* published by the *Grand Masse*, Paris, 1966 (pp. 125 *ff.*). More specific evidence comes from Delaire's "Repetoire Biographique," from the *dossiers* of individual students in the archives at the Ecole, from the catalogues of *esquisses, projets rendus*, and construction projects kept by the Ecole, from Guerinet's annual *Les Médailles des concours ...* of 1898–99 *ff.*, and from Vincent's annual *Les Concours d'architecture ...* of 1906–07 *ff.*, from the *Liste chronologique des professeurs ...*, 1793–1956, that is now AJ-52-35 at the Archives Nationales, and from the *Procès-verbaux* of the assemblies of professors. Also, the Ecole kept (incomplete) records of registrations in ateliers: 1863–74 in the volume that is now Archives Nationales AJ-52-246, 1874–75 in AJ-52-248, 1945–56 in a volume still at the Ecole. The identification of the atelier of each Grand Prix is from Delaire and from Vincent's annual volumes, with confirmation from Pré Lampué, *Programmes des concours d'architecture pour le grand prix de Rome*, [1823–80], Paris, 1881, and from current periodicals.

Further sources of information about some of the ateliers are as follows. Atelier Blondel, Scellier de Gisors, Defrasse: *L'Architecture*, June 17, 1905, p. 215, and October–December 1939, p. 294. Atelier *libre* Constant-Dufeux: *RGA*, vol. XXIV (1866), col. 127. Atelier Daumet, Esquié . . . Expert: letter from Daumet dated November 15, 1879, in his Ecole *dossier*; H. Deverin, *Petit Histoire d'un atelier 1862–1911*, Paris, n.d.; *NIAE Golden Jubilee Journal*, p. 52; *La Const. mod.*, May 1955, p. 171. Atelier Debret, Duban: *La Const. mod.*, vol. X (1895), pp. 253–54. Atelier Delespine, Blouet, Gilbert, Questel . . . Recoura: *RGA*, vol. XI (1853), col. 225, and vol. XIV (1856), col. 98; *La Const. mod.*, vol. X (1894), p. 62; R. Middleton, *Viollet-le-Duc and the Rational Gothic Tradition*, chap. 4, p. 13; conversation with O. Zavaroni. Atelier Duquesne. Recoura: *The Builder*, April 13, 1962, p. 752; *Harvard University: Quinquennial Catalogue ...*, Cambridge, Mass., 1930, "Duquesne." Atelier Labrouste: *RGA*, vol. XIV (1856), col. 98; *La Const. mod.*, vol. X (1895), pp. 253–55; L. Labrouste, *Esthétique monumentale*, Paris, 1902, pp. 214–15. Atelier Laisné . . . Pontremoli, Debat-Ponsan: S.A.D.G. *Bulletin*, 50 (October 1956), p. 9. Atelier Laloux, Lemaresquier: *Am. Arch.*, 31 (May 1890), p. 126; conversation with N.

Lemaresquier. Atelier Nicolle: *RGA*, vol. XLIV (1887), cols. 244–46; Atelier Percier: Middleton, *op. cit.*, chap. 1, p. 144. Atelier Perret: *Arch. Asso. Jrnl.*, January 1955, p. 146; Perret Centenary Exhibit, Paris, 1974. Atelier Vaudoyer, Lebas, Ginain: *RGA*, vol. XXVII (1869), cols. 244–49. Atelier Vaudremer, Raulin: *RGA*, vol. XXXVIII (1881), col. 22. Atelier Viollet-le-Duc: Middleton, *op. cit.*, chap. 7, pp. 6–13.

130. Walter Cook, "Emile Vaudremer," *AIA Journal*, vol. III (July 1915), p. 298; Louis Sullivan, *The Autobiography of an Idea*, New York, 1924, p. 238.

131. Letter of December 7, 1874, to Albert Sullivan quoted by Willard Connely in *Louis Sullivan as He Lived*, New York, 1960, p. 62.

132. William Graves Perry in a conversation on September 29, 1971.

133. Charles Collens, "The Beaux-Arts in 1900," *AIA Journal*, vol. VII (1947), pp. 80–86, 144–51, 187–97.

134. Walter D. Blair, "Student Life at the Ecole des Beaux-Arts," *The Brickbuilder*, vol. XVIII (March 1909), pp. 52–54.

135. *RGA*, vol. XXVIII (1870–71), cols. 188–89. At the Ecole, the dossiers of all students in the *atelier officiel* Bernier held a receipt of this payment.

136. In a conversation on September 24, 1971, E. J. Kahn remembered being accepted into the atelier Redon early in 1908 by the *massier*.

137. So J. C. Levi said in a conversation on August 12, 1969.

138. F. L. V. Hoppin, "An Architectural Knockabout," *The American Architect*, vol. XXVI (August 24, 1889), p. 89.

139. Donald A. Fletcher, in a letter of November 23, 1974.

140. Emmanuel Pontremoli, "Mirages et réalités," dated 1951, in *Propos d'un solitaire*, Paris, [1959], pp. 62–63.

141. Harry Sternfeld in the *NIAE Golden Jubilee Journal*, New York, 1964, p. 53.

142. John J. Burnet, "Jean Louis Pascal: An Old Pupil's Appreciation," *R.I.B.A. Journal*, 3rd ser., vol. XXVII (June 26, 1920), p. 400.

143. Williams Adams Delano, *A Letter To My Grandson*, privately printed [New York, 1944], pp. 35–36. I wish to thank Mr. Richard Delano for letting me read this memoir.

144. Alexis Lemaistre, *L'Ecole des Beaux-Arts dessinée et racontée par un élève*, Paris, 1886, p. 39.

145. *RGA*, vol. XI (1853), col. 225.

146. *RGA*, vol. XIV (1856), col. 98; vol. XXXVI (1879), col. 36; vol. XLV (1888–90), cols. 152–59 by J. Guadet.

147. Delaire, p. 123.

148. *The American Architect*, vol. XXVIII (May 31, 1890), p. 126; *The Architectural Journal*, April–June 1920, p. 640.

149. Erno Goldfinger, "The Work of Auguste Perret," *The Architectural Association Journal*, vol. LXX (January 1955), p. 145.

150. Occasionally such moves had occurred in the nineteenth century, but in the 1930s they became usual. For examples, "Grand Prix de Rome, 1934," *Pencil Points*, vol. XV (July 1934), p. 370.

151. Pentremoli, *op. cit.*, pp. 63, 67.

152. "Hommage à Laloux," *Pencil Points*, vol. XVIII (October 1937), especially Jean Labatut, p. 624; William E. Parsons, p. 628; Charles Butler, p. 623.

153. Francis Swales, *Pencil Points*, vol. IX (November 1928), pp. 689, 693.

154. E. J. Kahn, "Fragment 2," dated 8/7/68, 26 typed pages of an incomplete autobiography, p. 16, generously loaned to the author on September 24, 1971.

155. Arthur L. Tuckerman in a letter of March 20, 1884, to the secretary of the R.I.B.A., *R.I.B.A. Transactions*, 1st ser., vol. XXXIV, session 1883–84, p. 113.

156. On Labrouste these are two Ph.D. dissertations: Renée Plouin, "Henri Labrouste: sa vie, son oeuvre," Faculté des Lettres et Sciences Humaines, Université de Paris, 1965; and Neil Levine, "Architectural Reasoning in the Age of Positivism: The *Néo-Grec* Idea of Henri Labrouste's Bibliothèque Sainte-Geneviève," Yale University, 1975. On Viollet-le-Duc these are two Ph.D. dissertations: John Maxwell Jacobus, Jr., "The Architecture of Viollet-le-Duc," Yale University, 1956; and Robin Middleton, "Viollet-le-Duc and the Rational Gothic Tradition," Cambridge University, 1957. Also on Labrouste see Hautecoeur, vol. VI, pp. 242–48. Also on Viollet-le-Duc see Nikolaus Pevsner, *Ruskin and Viollet-le-Duc*, London, 1969, and "Viollet-le-Duc and Reynaud" in *Some Architectural Writers of the Nineteenth Century*, Oxford, 1972; and Hautecoeur, vol. VI, pp. 295–98, and vol. VII, pp. 337–60. I have not yet seen the dissertations of Plouin, Levine, or Jacobus.

157. Quatremère made his rebuke not in his speech about the *envois* at the public meeting of the Académie des Beaux-Arts but rather in a letter to the director of the Académie de France à Rome. The letter remains in the latter academy's archives. The episode is dealt with at length by Neil Levine in his dissertation on Labrouste, and also, more briefly, by René Schneider on pp. 300–05 of his *Quatremère de Quincy et son intervention dans les arts (1788–1830)*, Paris, 1910.

158. On the beginnings of these two ateliers, see the letters by Labrouste of 1830 in *La Construction Moderne*, vol. X (1894–95), pp. 252–55.

159. In the archives of the Institut de France

is a copy of this petition, signed by Duban, Labrouste, Abel Blouet, Antoine Garnaud, Alfred Frommiers, Debaisne, Guillelaud, and Cudriet. The events of the summer of 1830 are documented in the archives of the Institut, in the *Procès-verbaux* of the Ecole des Beaux-Arts, and in the pages of contemporary periodicals, notably the weekly *Journal des Artistes*. David Van Zanten has gathered this material together. See also Henry Lapauze, *Histoire de l'Académie de France à Rome*, Paris, 1924, vol. II, chap. 7.

160. About this commission see Schneider, *op. cit.*, pp. 271–73.

161. Most of the information about Viollet-le-Duc in the following pages comes from Middleton, *op. cit.*, especially chap. 3, "Viollet-le-Duc: childhood and youth, 1814–1837"; chap. 4, "Viollet-le-Duc and the Gothic Revival: his reaction to the architectural movement of the 1830s"; chap. 6, "Viollet-le-Duc: under new tutorships"; chap. 8, "The Atelier Viollet-le-Duc and the 'Entretiens sur l'Architecture' Volume I"; chap. 9, "The Ecole des Beaux-Arts and the Ecole Viollet-le-Duc."

162. On this memoir and the dispute it provoked, see Pevsner, *Architectural Writers*, pp. 200–02, and Hautecoeur, vol. VI, pp. 335–41.

163. The memoir, "Considérations sur la question de savoir s'il est convenable, au XIXᵉ siècle, de bâtir des églises en style gothique," was reprinted in the *Annales Archéologiques*, vol. IV (1846), pp. 326 *ff.*, and in the *RGA*, vol. VI (1845–46), cols. 313–21.

164. *RGA*, vol. X (1852), cols. 371–79.

165. They were announced, as was the new atelier, in the *RGA*, vol. XIV (1856), cols. 391–92, and in the *Encyclopédie d'architecture*, vol. VII (January 1857), cols. 1-3, which reported that the lectures would be published. The first *Entretien* appeared in either 1858 or 1860; the first volume of ten *Entretiens* in 1863.

166. "Les Mandarins à Paris" in the first issue of Charles Blanc's *Gazette des Beaux-Arts*, 1859.

167. "L'Enseignement des arts: il y a quelque chose à faire," *Gazette des Beaux-Arts*, May, June, July, and September 1862.

168. The documents were reprinted in *RGA*, vol. XXI (1863), cols. 290–99, and in the *Gazette des Architectes et du Bâtiment*, 1863, pp. 192–96. On the reform see also Middleton, *op. cit.*, chap. 9; Hautecoeur, vol. VII, pp. 293–99; Henri Delaborde, *L'Académie des beaux-arts depuis la fondation de l'institut de France*, Paris, 1891, pp. 310–39; and Julien Guadet, "A l'école des beaux-arts: souvenirs de 1863," in *S.A.D.G., recueil publié à l'occasion de la millième adhésion à la société des architectes diplomés par le*

gouvernement, Paris, 1911, pp. 23–37. Middleton and Hautecoeur are detached, Delaborde and Guadet (who was in 1863 a student at the school) are hostile to Viollet-le-Duc.

169. *RGA*, vol. XXII (1864), cols. 44–45.

170. *Ibid.*, cols. 45–49.

171. *Ibid.*, cols. 49–63, 149, 259–60; and *Gazette des Architectes*, 1864, pp. 105–08, 116–20.

172. The decree was reprinted in *RGA*, vol. XXI (1863), cols. 297–98.

173. Delaborde, *op. cit.*, p. 313.

174. *RGA*, vol. XXII (1864), cols. 64–68.

175. His forenames may have been Charles-Jean.

176. On these three patrons, see Middleton, *op. cit.*, chap. 9, p. 27, and Guadet, *op. cit.*, p. 28. On Constant-Dufeux see also *RGA*, vol. XXVIII (1870–71), cols. 188–89; and Hautecoeur, vol. VI, pp. 249–53. On Paccard see also *Gazette des Architectes*, 1867, p. 136.

177. Decree of November 18, 1863, Art. 13.

178. For an example of critical comment on the first lecture, see *RGA*, vol. XXII (1864), cols. 68–70. For a summary of the series, see the *Gazette des Architectes*, 1863, pp. 304–06, 314, 316–17, 324–28; 1864, pp. 6, 8–9, 14, 16–17, 37–38, 54–56.

179. Guadet, *op. cit.*, pp. 35–36.

180. *Décret* of November 18, 1863, Art. 13; *règlement* of January 14, 1864, Art. 28; *RGA*, vol. XXII (1864), col. 149.

181. "Le professeur chargé du service du concours" is the phrase used on the programs, which are now at the Archives Nationales, catalogued AJ-52-129.

182. For the legal decision, see *RGA*, vol. XXII (1864), cols. 259–60, and *Gazette des Architectes*, 1864, pp. 105–06.

183. *Gazette des Architectes*, 1864, p. 180.

184. *Ibid.*, p. 180; *RGA*, vol. XXII (1864), cols. 260–61.

185. *RGA*, vol. XXII (1864), col. 279.

186. *RGA*, vol. XXIII (1865), cols. 141–42.

187. *Gazette des Architectes*, 1869–70, pp. 115–16.

188. *RGA*, vol. XXVIII (1870–71), col. 259.

189. *RGA*, vol. XXI (1874), cols. 135–38.

190. *Ibid.*, col. 221, n. 1.

191. The following table lists lectures regularly offered to students of architecture, with the names and tenures of the professors. Courses primarily for painters and sculptors are omitted. The table is arranged according to the government's regulations of 1819 and its decrees of 1863 and 1874, which organized and reorganized the lecture courses at the Ecole. The names and tenures of the professors are from the Ecole's register: *Liste chronologique des professeurs et secrétaires de l'école impériale et spéciale des beaux-arts depuis la réorganisation par*

suite de décret du 28 septembre 1793 jusqu'à ce jour, [February 1, 1956]. This register is now at the Archives Nationale with the catalogue number AJ-52-35.

TABLE II
PROFESSORS RESPONSIBLE FOR
LECTURE COURSES,
1793 UNTIL AFTER 1955

SEPTEMBER 29, 1793–AUGUST 4, 1819
Architecture
  J.-D. Leroy 1774–c. 1803
  L. Dufourny 1804–18
  L.-P. Baltard 1818–19 *ff.*
Stéréotomie
  Rieux
  J.-B. Rondelet 1806–19 *ff.*
Perspective
  P.-A. de Machy 1786–1807
  C.-P. Dandrillon 1807–12
  P.-H. Valenciennes 1812–19
  J.-T. Thibault 1819 *ff.*
Mathématiques
  A.-R. Mauduit 1768–1815
  J.-B.-A. Lavit 1815–19 *ff.*

AUGUST 4, 1819–NOVEMBER 13, 1863
Théorie de l'architecture
  L.-P. Baltard before 1819–46
  G.-A. Blouet 1846–53
  J.-B.-C. Lesueur 1853–63
Histoire de l'architecture
  J.-N. Huyot 1819–40
  L.-H. Lebas 1840–63
Construction
  J.-B. Rondelet before 1819–26 (Professor of *Stéréotomie*)
  A.-M.-F. Jäy 1826–63
Perspective
  J.-T. Thibault 1819–26
  L.-J. Girard 1827–44
  S.-C. Constant-Dufeux 1845–63
Mathématiques
  J.-B.-A. Lavit before 1819–36
  M. Courtial 1837–43
  I. Francoeur 1843–63 *ff.*

NOVEMBER 13, 1863–MAY 6, 1874
Histoire de l'art et esthétique
  E.-E. Viollet-le-Duc 1863–64
  Hippolyte Taine 1864–74 *ff.*
Histoire et archéologie (Established in 1828 as a course mainly for painters and sculptors and called *Histoire et antiquités* until 1863, it was taught by A. Jarry de Mancy in 1828–62 and L.-A. Heuzey from January 1863 on.)
  L.-A. Heuzey 1863–74 *ff.*
Administration et comptabilité, construction et application sur les chantiers
  E. Millet 1863–65
  Baron P.-J.-E. Baude 1865–71
  E.-J. Brune 1871–74 *ff.*
Perspective
  J.-A. Chevillard 1863–74 *ff.*
Mathématiques élémentaires
  I. Francoeur 1863–67

504

J.-H.-J. Caqué 1867–74 *ff.* (Professor of *Mathématiques*)

A.-P.-A. Dessignes 1867–71

Géométrie descriptive

A.-D.-A. Amyot 1863–65

P. Ossian Bonnet 1865–74 *ff.*

Géologie, physique et chimie élémentaires

Louis Pasteur 1863–67

E.-S. Cloëz 1867–74 *ff.*

Stéréotomie (from 1868 on)

A.-A. Durand Claye 1868–74 *ff.*

Histoire de l'architecture (from 1870 on)

Albert Lenoir 1870–74 *ff.*

Législation du bâtiment (from 1872 on)

P.-J.-B. Delacroix 1872–74 *ff.*

Dessin ornemental (from 1873 on; not lectures, instruction in the galeries)

G.-A. Ancelet 1873–74 *ff.*

MAY 6, 1874 *ff.*

FOR THE SECTION D'ARCHITECTURE:

Théorie de l'architecture (chair reestablished January 15, 1873)

J.-.B.-C. Lesueur again 1874–83

E.-J.-B. Guillaume 1884–94

Julien Guadet 1894–1908

V.-A. Blavette 1908–27

Louis Madeline 1928–37

Georges Gromort 1937–40

Paul Tournon 1940–42

Michel Roux-Spitz 1942–44

Louis Madeline 1944–49

André Gutton 1949–57

Louis Aublet 1957–64

Jean Fayeton 1965 *ff.* (*Professeur chargé de la direction des études d'architecture*)

Histoire de l'architecture (from 1891 on called *Histoire générale de l'architecture*)

Albert Lenoir before 1874–91

L. Magne 1891–1916

L. Jaussely 1917–24

Louis Hautecoeur 1925–40

Pierre Lavedan 1940–after 1951

Construction

E.-J. Brune before 1874–86

P.-L. Monduit 1886–1919

E. Arnaud 1920–34

F.-J.-S. Vitale 1934–47

N.-P. Untersteller 1947–48

F.-J.-S. Vitale 1948 *ff.*

G.-H. Pingusson 1951–62

Jean Fayeton 1962 *ff.* (from 1965 on, *Professeur chargé de la direction des études d'architecture*)

Perspective

J.-A. Chevillard before 1874–86

P.-F. Julien 1886–1914

P. Guadet 1914–31

P.-E. Olmer 1932–48

R.-M. Limouse 1948–64

A. Flocon 1964 *ff.*

Mathématiques (from 1913 on, called *Statique et théorie de la résistance des matériaux*)

J.-H.-J. Caqué before 1874–77

C.-M. Brisse 1877–96

C. Bourlet 1896–1913

P.-A.-A. Montel 1913–38

J.-J.-C. Pérès 1938–48

R. Siestrunck 1948 *ff.*

Géométrie descriptive

P. Ossian Bonnet before 1874–83

J.-J.-D. Pillet 1883–c. 1912

J.-E.-R. Brandon 1912–17

E. Cartan 1917–31

H. Béghin 1932–c. 1942

L.-C. Malavard 1942–after 1953

Physique et chimie (from 1883 on, called *Physique, chimie, et géologie*; from 1941 on, called *Physique et chimie*)

F.-S. Cloëz before 1874–83

A.-J. Riban 1883–1906

F.-G. Maneuvrier 1906–19

E. Bloch 1920–41

J. Cabannes 1941–55

H.-J. Boiteux 1955 *ff.*

Stéréotomie (from 1955 on, called *Eléments et matériaux de construction*)

A.-A. Durand-Claye before 1874–88

Marcel Lambert 1888–1908

L.-A. Masson 1908–15

J.-E.-R. Brandon 1917–39

P. de Lagarde 1940–53

J. Gauthier 1955 *ff.*

Législation du bâtiment (Professorship abolished 1934)

P.-J.-B. Delacroix before 1874–89

E.-J. Mulle 1889–1904

E.-M.-J. Cassagnade 1904–24

P. Coutant 1925–34

Dessin ornemental (instruction in the galeries: post evidently renamed in 1955 *Correcteur des dessins de la Section d'Architecture*)

G.-A. Ancelet before 1874–95

H. d'Espouy 1895–1926

L. Roger 1928–34

H.-J.-T. Rapin 1935–39

J. Hardy 1941–c. 1953

B.-E. Bouret 1953–55

R. Veysset 1955 *ff.*

Histoire de l'architecture française (from 1892 on: professorship abolished 1934)

P.-L. Boeswillwald 1892–1928

Marcel Aubert 1929–34

FOR ALL SECTIONS OF THE ECOLE:

Histoire générale

J.-H. Lemonnier 1874–1912

P.-M. Levi 1912–40

J.-M.-L. Baillon 1941–44

P.-M. Levi 1944–47

J.-M.-L. Baillon 1947–after 1951

Littérature (from 1877 on: Professorship transformed in 1934 to *maitrise de conférances*)

E.-L. Ruel 1877–96

E.-S. Rocheblave 1896–1919

P. Gautier 1919–34

Enseignement simultanée des trois arts (from 1883 on: instruction in *dessin, modelage, architecture élémentaire*, and *composition décorative*)

Histoire de l'art et esthétique and *Histoire et archéologie* continued to be part of the curriculum after 1874 as lecture courses for painters and sculptors.

192. Articles 70–75 of the regulations of November 27, 1867, reprinted in *RGA*, vol. XXVI (1868), cols. 82–90.

193. *RGA*, vol. XXVII (1869), col. 206; *Gazette des Architectes*, 1868–69, p. 248.

194. For a list of all these prizes as of 1907, see Delaire, pp. 82–90, 107–11, 140–46.

195. *RGA*, vol. X (1852), col. 301; *The Architectural Record*, special issue of January 1901 on the Ecole des Beaux-Arts, p. 15; Delaire, p. vi.

196. For a recent study of Guadet see Sandor Kuthy, "Julien Guadet et l'enseignement de l'architecture," *Architecture, mouvement, continuité* (Bulletin de la S.A.D.G.), no. 176 (1970), pp. 26–32; and also Kuthy's Ph.D. thesis, Institut d'Art et d'Archéologie de la Faculté des Lettres et Sciences Humaines, Université de Paris, 1968.

197. See the monument in the Cour du Murier of the school or *La Construction Moderne*, vol. XXXIX (1924), p. 521.

198. See *L'Architecture*, vol. XLVII (1934), pp. 351–54.

199. The figures for 1920–21 are from *La Construction Moderne*, vol. XXXVI (February 13, 1921), p. 158; those for 1967–68 are from the secretariat of the Ecole Nationale Supérieure des Beaux-Arts.

200. The cash values of the awards are from the regulations of 1907 and 1963; the rates of exchange from Baedeker's *Southern France* of 1907 and *The Times*, London, of 1963.

201. For writings in the English language on the events of May that pertain to the Ecole and on French architectural education since then, see Martin Pawley's and Bernard Tchumi's polemic, "The 'Beaux-Arts' since '68," *Architectural Design*, vol. XLI (September 1971), pp. 533–66; and see Donald Drew Egbert's calmer and less biased article, "The Rise of a New Architectural Education in France," *AIA Journal*, vol. LVI (October 1971), pp. 44–47. For a recent official statement of purpose, see Ministère des Affaires Culturelles, Service des Enseignements de l'Architecture et des Arts Plastiques, *La Reforme de l'enseignement de l'architecture en France*, Paris, 1973.

ARCHITECTURAL COMPOSITION AT THE ECOLE DES BEAUX-ARTS FROM CHARLES PERCIER TO CHARLES GARNIER
David Van Zanten

I should like to express my gratitude to the two scholars who introduced me to this subject: Neil Levine of Harvard University and the late Donald Drew Egbert of Princeton University. Many of the ideas expressed in this essay evolved during conversations with Neil Levine. For my initial factual knowledge of the subject I am indebted to Donald Drew Egbert, and to his widow, Mrs. Virginia Egbert Kilborne, who kindly made available to me his unpublished manuscript history of the *Concours du Grand Prix de Rome*. (The Egbert manuscript is being prepared for publication by the Princeton University Press in the near future.) I should also like to express my thanks to the University of Pennsylvania, which provided me a year's leave of absence to do this work, and to the Department of Fine Arts of Harvard University, which gave me access to its library during that year. I am, of course, deeply indebted to the librarians of the Ecole des Beaux-Arts, Mlle Annie Jacques and Mme Bouleau-Rabaud, whose help was indispensable. I must also thank my wife, Ann Lorenz Van Zanten, for all her assistance, both scholarly and practical.

1. Guadet, *Eléments et théorie de l'architecture*, Paris, [1901–04], vol. 1, p. 80.
2. *Ibid.*, vol. I, p. 82.
3. When, for example, composition began to appear in the titles of a number of books explaining what were believed to be the principles of architecture: John Vreedenburgh Van Pelt, *A Discussion of Composition*, 1902; Thomas Hastings, "Principles of Architectural Composition" (Bragdon, Cram, Hastings, *Six Lectures on Architecture*, 1917); David Varron, *Architectural Composition*, 1923; Nathaniel Cortlandt Curtis, *Architectural Composition*, 1923; Howard Robertson, *Principles of Architectural Composition*, 1924; and Albert Ferran, *Philosophie de la composition*, 1954.
4. F.-L. Reynaud, *Traité d'architecture*, Paris, 1850–57, vol. II, pp. 3–4.
5. G. Boffrand, *Livre d'architecture*, Paris, 1745, p. 11.
6. J.-F. Blondel, *Cours d'architecture*, Paris, 1771–77, vol. IV, chap. 2.
7. A.-C. Quatremère de Quincy, *Architecture, Encyclopédie méthodique*, Paris, 1788–1825, vol. II, "Distribution."
8. *Dictionnaire de l'Académie française*, Paris, 1835, "Distribuer," "Disposer," "Composer."

9. Georges Gromort, *Essai sur la théorie de l'architecture*, Paris, 1946, pp. 143–45.
10. Quatremère de Quincy, *op. cit.*, "Composition."
11. Guadet, *op. cit.*, vol. I, p. 80.
12. A point often emphasized by Colin Rowe ("Character and Composition; or Some Vicissitudes of Architectural Vocabulary in the Nineteenth Century," *Oppositions IV*, January 1974, pp. 41–60).
13. *Op. cit.*, vol. IV, chap. 2.
14. MS "Architecture" read before the Académie des Beaux-Arts, January 21, 1832: Bibliothèque Nationale, Paris. Cabinet des Manuscrits. fr. 12340, p. 24.
15. *Le Théâtre*, Paris, 1871, p. 402.
16. The importance of Vanvitelli's plan for late eighteenth-century French planning seems to have been great. See Quatremère de Quincy, *op. cit.*, "Palais," "Unité," "Vanvitelli" (he calls the building the most important of the century); Charles Percier and P.-F.-L. Fontaine, *Résidences de souverains: parallèle entre plusieurs résidences des souverains de France, d'Allemagne, de Suède, de Russie, et d'Italie*, Paris, 1833.
17. Gromort, *op. cit.*, p. 154.
18. This project owes much to the project by Huyot (Lefuel's master) of 1835–36 for the Palais de Justice.
19. J. V. Van Pelt, *A Discussion of Composition, Especially as Applied to Architecture*, New York, 1902, p. 192.
20. J. Mondain-Monval, *Soufflot: sa vie, son oeuvre, son esthétique (1743–1780)*, Paris, 1918; M. Petzet, *Soufflots Ste.-Geneviève und der französische Kirchenbau des 18. Jahrhunderts*, Berlin, 1961.
21. Guadet, *op. cit.*, vol. I, pp. 120 *ff*.
22. *Op. cit.*, "Basilique." Clémence's version of the type is a correction of the composite form adopted by Mathurin Crucy in his Bourse at Nantes (begun in 1791) and the filter through which the Palladian paradigm was converted into Thomas de Thomon's Saint Petersburg Bourse (1804–16), Brongniart's Paris Bourse (1808–25), and Durand's model *bourse* published in his *Précis*, vol. II, pl. 14.
23. Petzet, *op. cit.*; Robin Middleton, "The Abbé Cordemoy and the Greco-Gothic Ideal: A Prelude to Romantic Classicism," *Journal of the Warburg and Courtauld Institutes*, vol. XXV (1962), pp. 278–320; vol. XXVI (1963), pp. 90–123.
24. *Op. cit.*, "Basilique."
25. *Ibid.*, "Cupole."
26. *Ibid.*, "Clocher."
27. See the annual reports on the *envois* of the *pensionnaires* at Rome during the years 1828–36: *Rapport sur les ouvrages des élèves pensionnaires de l'Ecole Royale de France à Rome . . . à Paris.*

28. A. Guerinet, *Les Grands Prix de Rome d'architecture, 1er série*, Paris, n.d.; P. Lampué, *Programmes des concours d'architecture pour le Grand Prix de Rome*, Paris, 1881. Both start with Duban's design of 1823.
29. Students of Percier, A.-F. Peyre, Percier, and Percier and Vaudoyer, respectively.
30. *Op. cit.*, vol. 1, p. 128.
31. *Op. cit.*, "Conclusion," especially pp. 330–36.
32. *Op. cit.*, vol. IV, chap. 2.
33. David Leroy, *Histoire de la disposition et des formes différentes que les Chrétiens ont données à leurs Temples, depuis le règne de Constantin le Grand, jusqu'à nos jours*, Paris, 1764, pp. 61–62, 85.
34. Etienne-Louis Boullée, *architecture, essai sur l'art*, edited by J.-M. Pérouse de Montclos, Paris, 1968.
35. *Ibid.*, pp. 67–68.
36. *Ibid.*, pp. 73–74, 133.
37. Roger de Piles records these words as the exclamation of Correggio upon first encountering the art of Raphael (*Abrège de la vie des peintres*, Paris, 1699, p. 297).
38. See the lengthy text of their *Résidences des souverains*, 1833, or their earlier *Choix des plus célèbres maisons de plaisance de Rome et ses environs*, 1809, or the books of their students Grandjean de Marigny (*Architecture toscane*, 1815, with A. Famin) and M.-P. Gauthier (*Les Plus Beaux Edifices de la ville de Gênes*, 1818–32).
39. These are preserved in the Bibliothèque Nationale, Paris, Cabinet des Manuscrits, in the Royal Institute of British Architects, London, and in the hands of the Vaudoyer family. The passages quoted are from the Bibliothèque Nationale MS.
40. Cf. the lengthy text volume of Percier and Fontaine's *Résidences de souverains*.
41. They were recorded in the *Registre des concours*, now in the Archives of the Institut de France, during the years 1817–63, 1871–1968.
42. The Section d'Architecture awarded Vaudremer the Premier Grand Prix and Paul-Emile Bonnet the Second Premier but the Académie des Beaux-Arts then voted to reverse the awards, giving Bonnet the Premier and Vaudremer the Second Premier. Vaudremer was to prove the better architect.
43. The four months permitted the competitors to render their original sketches were evidently meant to be spent refining the proportions. *Revue Générale de l'Architecture*, vol. XIII (1855), col. 186.
44. Hatzfeld-Darmesteter-Thomas, *Dictionnaire générale de la langue française*, Paris, [1890–1900].
45. J. B.-B. Boutard, *Dictionnaire des arts de dessin*, 2nd ed., Paris, 1832, "Ligne." The word had appeared earlier in Boullée's MS

"Essai sur l'art": "La simple inspection des plans fera apercevoir une distribution dont la marche devient facile, noble et désormais vaste au-dela de ce qu'on pouvait espérer" (op. cit., p. 130).

46. Quatremère de Quincy, op. cit., vol. II, "Parti." There he also uses it in the sense of tirer parti (take advantage of). This weaker meaning appears elsewhere from time to time.

47. Cf. Encyclopédie d'architecture, November 1860, p. 162.

48. Cf. Revue Encyclopédique, vol. XXX (1826), p. 580.

49. Charles Garnier, op. cit., p. 73.

50. Namely his volumes already cited, his dissertation Quel fut l'Etat de l'architecture egyptienne et qu'est-ce que les Grecs en ont empruntés? written in 1785 and published in 1803, and his eulogies of deceased architect members of the Academy read at public meetings of that body. See René Schneider, Quatremère de Quincy et son intervention dans les arts (1788-1830) and L'Esthétique classique chez Quatremère de Quincy, both Paris, 1910.

51. Architecture, vol. 1, "Caractère."

52. Ibid.

53. Ibid., vol. II, "Moderne," "Grecque."

54. Notice historique sur la vie et les ouvrages de M. Dufourny, Paris, 1833.

55. M. Pellet, Variétés révolutionnaires, Paris, 1885-90, vol. I, chap. 12.

56. Précis, vol. 1, p. 15.

57. Cf. Ibid., pp. 18-20.

58. Ibid., vol. I, p. 24; cf. vol. III, p. 25.

59. Ibid., 2nd ed., Paris, 1817, Avis au lecteur.

60. The stony silence of French authorities during the nineteenth century on the subject of Durand's ideas contrasts with his popularity in Germany and England—at least as a purveyor of a simple method of planning (Engelhard, "Schinkels Architekturschule in Norddeutschland," Allgemeine Bauzeitung, 1847, pp. 271-82; J. Gwilt, The Rudiments of Architecture, London, 1839, pp. 144-46; The Architectural Magazine, vol. IV, pp. 251-53). In his Architecture: Nineteenth and Twentieth Centuries, H.-R. Hitchcock suggested that Durand's influence was immense during the first half of the nineteenth century.

61. This particular period of French architecture is the subject of Neil Levine's Ph.D. dissertation. It was also the subject of my own dissertation, "The Architectural Polychromy of the 1830s," Harvard University, 1970; published in 1977 by Garland Publishing. Mr. Levine and I have worked together since 1968 and I am deeply indebted to his ideas at many points.

62. A fact emphasized by his two contemporary biographers and evident in the quite heterogeneous approaches of his students. A. Lance, Abel Blouet, architect, membre de l'Institut: sa vie et ses travaux, Paris, 1854; Achille Hermant, Abel Blouet, Paris, 1857.

63. For example, in 1883 of the six Grand Prix submissions for a Nécropole published in the journal Intime Club (1.3-4.4), only two were strongly Néo-Grec, and those two won the Premier and the Deuxième Grands Prix.

64. Davioud had won the Deuxième Grand Prix in 1849.

65. Ludovic Vitet, Etudes sur les beaux-arts, Paris, 1846, vol. I, pp. 265-70. To see just how both Davioud and Villain treated the program, its first four paragraphs should be read in the original:

Une bourse pour une des grandes villes de commerce maritime du Midi de la France.

Cette bourse à laquelle seraient réuni le tribunal de commerce serait située sur une place publique et formerait un des principaux ornements du port sur la rive duquelle se trouvait la place.

Tout l'édifice serait élevé sur un haut soubassement contenant des magasins et des dépôts à l'usage de commerce. Il se composerait: de très vastes portiques ou de promennoirs couverts sous lesquels, suivant l'usage du Midi, se réuniraient les négociants pour traiter de leurs affaires; de la bourse où s'opéreraient les transactions; et du tribunal de commerce où se jugeraient les différents.

Sous les portiques se trouveraient de petits bureaus d'écriture, des cabinets pour la lecture des journaux, des bancs pour le repos, et des parties de murs destinées à recevoir les affiches relatives au commerce. . . .

Signed: Abel Blouet, 9 January, 1849.

66. Neil Levine has documented this building in great detail in his dissertation.

67. RGA, vol. X (1852), col. 382.

68. Théodore de Banville, Le Quartier Latin et la Bibliothèque Sainte-Geneviève, Paris, 1926, p. 30.

69. An early and caustic discussion of the Néo-Grec, using that term to designate the fashion: Gazette des Architectes et du Bâtiment, 1863, pp. 79-80. "In general aspect, this recalls simultaneously the cemetery and the prison, but the cemetery dominates. Flat moldings in the upper parts [of facades], flat wall strips surrounding and joining the windows, flat sepulchral pediments surmounting the entrances, here and there flat rosettes accompanied by meager rinceaux; these are the ordinary details."

70. Encyclopédie d'architecture, August 1856, col. 123.

71. Paul Nénot, Notice sur M. Gabriel-Auguste Ancelet, Paris, 1896, pp. 5-6.

72. RGA (1879), col 80.

73. Notes de voyage d'un architecte, Paris, 1876, p. 279. The church, as Narjoux noted somewhat obliquely, imitates Viollet-le-Duc's Notre-Dame-de-l'Estrée in Saint-Denis.

74. In the atlas, published in 1872, of his Entretiens sur l'architecture, Paris, 1863-72.

75. Ibid., vol. II, p. 95.

76. Le Massif de Mont Blanc, Paris, 1876.

77. Ibid., pp. xv-xvi. His geodesy appears again as the basic principle of structural geometry in his Histoire d'un dessinateur, Paris, n.d.

78. Dictionnaire raisonné, vol. VIII, p. 482, "Style."

79. Only the fourth-year envois have been preserved at the Ecole. The most interesting projects among the envois, those of the fifth year, must be traced through the families of the architects concerned.

80. Les Thermes d'Antonin Caracalla à Rome, Paris, 1828.

81. L. Cernesson, "Emile Gilbert, sa vie, ses oeuvres: notice biographique," Annales de la société centrale des architectes, 1st ser., vol. II (1874).

82. The pertinent correspondence survives in the Archives of the Institut de France. Neil Levine has documented this fully in his dissertation.

83. Labrouste's drawings and explanatory text were published after his death: Les Temples de Paestum: restauration executée en 1829 [sic] . . . , Paris, 1884.

84. I discussed this matter at length in my dissertation, cf. note 61, and shall publish shortly an updated study of it.

85. Rapport sur les ouvrages des élèves pensionnaires à l'Ecole de France à Rome . . . à Paris, Paris, 1833.

86. Léon Vaudoyer, Discours prononcé aux funérailles de M. Duban, Paris, 1871. Protestanism was very much an issue around 1830, especially in the thinking of Edgar Quinet.

87. Rapport sur les ouvrages . . . , Paris, 1831. Cf. L'Artiste, 1831, p. 89.

88. Rapport sur les ouvrages . . . , Paris, 1832, 1833, 1834. Théodore Labrouste's project was bequeathed to the Ecole, where it is preserved. The description of Delannoy's project is very thorough in the Journal des Artistes, vol. II (1834), pp. 242-43.

89. Rapport sur les ouvrages . . . , Paris, 1835. The project was published after Constant-Dufeux's death as part of a series of loose plates lithographed from his drawings.

90. Rapport sur les ouvrages . . . , Paris, 1836. The exclamation point is the Academy's.

91. Journal des Artistes, vol. II (1836), p. 133.

92. Le Siècle, August 25, 1836.

93. H. J. Hunt, Le Socialisme et le roman-

tisme en France; études de la presse socia-liste de 1830 à 1848, Oxford, 1935.

94. All three worked together on Pierre Leroux and Jean Reynaud's *Encyclopédie nouvelle* (1835–41, 2nd ed. 1839–42 — Léonce Reynaud was Jean's brother). Then with help from Albert Lenoir, Vaudoyer wrote his "Etudes d'architecture en France" for the *Magasin Pittoresque* (1839–54) as well as his "Histoire d'architecture en France" for the compendium *Patria*, both edited by participants in the *Encyclopédie nouvelle* project. Fourtoul meanwhile published his *De l'art en Allemagne* (1841–42), with help from Vaudoyer on the architectural sections, while Léonce Reynaud, professor of architecture at the Ecole Polytechnique, published his massive *Traité d'architecture* (1850), with advice from Labrouste. See Delaire, *Les Architectes élèves de l'Ecole des Beaux-Arts 1793–1907*, Paris, 1907, "Labrouste, Henri." See also D. A. Griffiths, *Jean Reynaud; encyclopédiste de l'époque romantique*, Paris, 1965.

95. P. Leroux and J. Reynaud, *Encyclopédie nouvelle*, Paris, 1835–41, vol. I, "Architecture," 2nd ed. (1839), pp. 770–78.

96. *Ibid.*, vol. I, p. 775.

97. "Etudes d'architecture en France," *Magasin Pittoresque*, 1842, p. 122.

98. Reynaud, *loc. cit.*, p. 776; Vaudoyer, "Etudes," 1839, pp. 334–36; Fourtoul, *De l'art en Allemagne*, Paris, 1841–42, vol. II, chap. 20, "De l'architecture curviligne" (his term for post-Constantinian architecture, based on the arch). Cf. Prosper Mérimée, "Essai sur l'architecture religieuse du moyen age particulièrement en France," *L'Annuaire Historique pour l'Année 1838* of the Société de l'Histoire de France, Paris, 1837. Neil Levine writes at length of this Byzantine "revival," which I believe secondary to the Renaissance crisis in terms of which Reynaud, Vaudoyer, and Fortoul seem to have viewed it.

99. Reynaud, *loc. cit.*, p. 777.

100. "Etudes," 1842, pp. 123–24.

101. There is a cryptic remark made both by and of the members of the circle of Duban, Labrouste, and Vaudoyer that they were "Romantiques à la façon d'Ingres" (L. Vaudoyer, "Discours prononcé . . . "; E. Beulé, *Eloge de Duban*, Paris, 1872). Duban and Ingres were friends, having worked together at Dampierre around 1840.

102. "Etudes," 1842, p. 123.

103. *Loc. cit.*, p. 777.

104. These ideas, in fact, show up in the writings of young architects all over Europe around the middle of the 1830s: G. Semper, *Vorläufige Bemerkungen über die bemalte Architektur und Plastik bei den Alten*, Altona, 1834; O. Jones, "On the Influence of Religion upon Art," *Lectures on Architecture and the Decorative Arts*, London, 1863 (a lecture delivered originally in 1834). See M. Darby and D. Van Zanten, "Owen Jones' Iron Buildings of the 1850s," *Architectura, Zeitschrift für Geschichte der Architektur*, no. 1 (1974), pp. 53–75. These notes on French Romantic architectural theory are far from complete. I hope in the next few years to continue this research.

105. *Op. cit.*, vol. II, p. 323.

106. Immediately after Vaudoyer's death, his former student, assistant for the construction of the Cathedral, and successor as architect, Henri Espérandieu, wrote Charles Blanc a series of letters about Vaudoyer and the building. The letters are preserved among the Blanc papers at the Institut de France.

107. Léon Vaudoyer, "Histoire d'architecture en France," *Patria* (J. Aicard, editor), Paris, 1847, p. 2195; Reynaud, *loc. cit.*, p. 778.

108. Paul Sédille published a letter by Duc explaining his use of the Order, in *Joseph-Louis Duc, architecte*, Paris, 1879.

109. Both Labrouste and Viollet-le-Duc insisted on doing perspective studies, a policy greatly developed at the Ecole Spéciale d'Architecture founded by Emile Trélat in the 1860s to rival the Ecole des Beaux-Arts. Charles Chipiez, a professor at that school, in particular devoted himself to evolving methods of perspective projection. The ultimate solution was found by the engineer Auguste Choisy, professor at the Ecole des Ponts et Chaussées, in the uptilted isometric sections with which he illustrated his *Histoire de l'Architecture* of 1899.

110. Donald Drew Egbert emphasized its importance, as did Van Pelt (*op. cit.*, p. 84) and Curtis (*op. cit.*, pp. 80–82).

111. The program in its entirety:

1866

A TOWN HOUSE IN PARIS
FOR A RICH BANKER

The plot on which one would have to arrange the plan of this town house is situated in one of the districts of Paris most sought after for vast and splendid habitations.

It is of a rather irregular shape, determined by the opening of new streets and the creation of a boulevard 40 meters wide, on which the plot fronts for about 170 meters. The plot is further enlarged by the contiguity on one of its sides, AB [the back], with an immense public square, an old park planted with magnificent trees. Not only has it two rights of exit into the square (no more than two), but also the right of unobstructed view over the full extent of the property lines. In fact, except for two sections of 27 meters each, marked CD and EF on the plan, which according to the disposition of the buildings and of the lots still to be sold, can be occupied by the party walls of the adjoining properties, the whole lot on this side must be enclosed by a light, low grill that should do little to spoil the view. Thus in the deed of sale it has been stipulated that the part contiguous to the square would be laid out in such a manner to continue and expand the view from the garden of the town house, while naturally respecting the general plan of the public promenade and not causing any harm to come to the front of the properties facing it.

It must also be noted that aside from the condition mentioned above of the two party walls, CD and EF, there exist no easements of any sort, except that one must take into account all the regulations currently in force and that the competitors, in their sketches as well as in their renderings, will be held rigorously accountable, any violation of these regulations affecting the judgment of the work.

The general plan of the town house is to consist of: 1. the banker's residence; 2. his offices; 3. two private houses for the use of his children.

1. The house of the banker is to provide, on one of the two main floors, his apartments and those of his wife, the salons and an intimate room for receptions, and his business office with all its attendant facilities, among which are to be included the offices for three secretaries whose lodgings will be located in the upper parts of the house.

On the other floor would be the great reception rooms, including a ballroom, conversation rooms, winter garden, dining room, banquet hall, anteroom, vestibule, grand stairway, a vast porte cochère, etc., etc., a waiting room, cloakroom, and dressing rooms.

Adjoining the reception rooms would be a library, a gallery for objects of art (sculpture and painting), rooms for the display of collections of rare and precious objects, auxiliary rooms for all these functions, in a word, all the refinements and accommodations permitted to the rich, indispensable to those of an enlightened taste.

We must, however, caution the competitors against the harm that would result from arrangements too vast for these last elements of the project: they must keep in mind that what is involved here is the residence of a rich private individual, nothing more.

The kitchens are to consist of everything necessary in a house of this importance: both a large and a small kitchen, a grill, a baking room, a butler's pantry, a laundry room, a storeroom, staff quarters, cellars, etc. The stables are to contain at least thirty horses, half of them in stalls, storage for twenty car-

riages; saddlery, forge, feed preparation facilities, a cesspit, fodder storage, etc.; three lodgings for married couples; seven lodgings, each with two or three rooms; at least thirty rooms will be needed to lodge the numerous domestics.

2. The offices, consisting of three main divisions, at the head of each a separate manager; each of these divisions will consist of an office for the manager, with waiting room, anteroom, and secretarial offices, as well as two offices for office managers, four offices for five clerks each, the cashier's office, and two offices for ten forwarding agents.

Separate from these three divisions, two big rooms for the meetings of the board of directors would also be required, as well as an anteroom, vestibules, and secretarial offices.

Entrances to the offices should be separate from the main entrance of the house. They should also not be the same as those leading to the yards of the kitchens and stables.

3. The two private houses are to be linked by convenient passageways with the main house, still they offer a complex of rooms for habitation and for holding intimate receptions, as well as auxiliary rooms of all kinds to make them totally independent: they are to consist principally of five bedrooms for the master's family, including two for children, two salons, a dining room, anteroom, vestibule, porte cochère, kitchen and its annexes, stable for eight horses, storage for six carriages.

In the rendering one could impart a very special character to the plan of one of these two houses, left in outline in the sketch; the house could, for instance, be more especially destined for a bachelor and show in its composition a large room serving as both office and workroom, providing facilities also for fencing, a small gallery for objects of art, as well as a smoking room, etc., etc.

For the sketches one will make the general plan in outline with the drawing of the gardens and a cutaway projection of the square at a scale of 1000:1.

A plan of all the buildings, with the exception of the plan of one of the private houses, at 500:1 (this plan at the reception room level); a special plan of the main house on the banker's residence floor at the same scale, 500:1.

An elevation of the main house at 250:1.

A general section (which can be broken) at the same scale, 250:1.

For the rendered drawings one will make: An overall plan (detailed) with the cutaway of the square at 400:1.

A plan of the reception rooms and a plan of the residence floor of the main house at

200:1.

A general facade and a general section at 1000:1.

A detail at the discretion of the competitor either of the facade or of the section at a scale of 500:1.

112. J. Bouchet, *RGA*, vol. XXIV (1866), col. 80.

113. *Gazette des Architectes et du Bâtiment*, 1866, p. 178.

114. The various *partis* are discussed and several plans shown in outline in *Intime Club*, vol. I (1866–67), 5.1-5.2. The photographs of Weyland's and Laynaud's projects, preserved at the Harvard School of Design, were identified by comparing them with these plans.

115. For example, J.-B.-B. Boutard, "Grands Prix d'architecture," *Journal des Débats*, September 16, 1808.

116. Guadet, *op. cit.*, vol. I, pp. 90 *ff*.

117. Batigny also chose to render the street facade.

118. Between 1863 and 1871 the jury's membership was different each year. That of 1866 was E.-T. Dommey, J.-U. Clerget, A.-I.-E. Godeboeuf, T.-F.-J. Uchard, Joseph Nicolle, Emile Boeswillwald, Edmond Guillaume, and A.-F.-J. Girard. It is interesting that Pascal placed last when his *esquisse* was judged (Bénard, fifth; Mayeux, first).

119. *RGA*, vol. XXIV (1866), cols. 70–71.

120. *Moniteur des Architectes*, 1866, col. 143.

121. Both as a design and as a rendering—Normand compliments the "rendu brilliant" and predicts "de grands envois," but wishes that "M. Pascal met un peu plus de tranquilité et d'harmonie dans les tons qu'il emploi." (*Ibid.*, col 142.)

122. See a letter to his brother, Théodore, of July 12, 1830, published in *Souvenirs d'Henri Labrouste, architecte, membre de l'Institut: notes recueillies et classées par ses enfants*, Fontainebleau, 1928, p. 24.

123. *RGA*, vol. I (1840), cols. 543–47. Auguste Thoumeloup answered him in cols. 595–601 of that volume.

124. Adolphe Lance hailed Duban's election in the *Encyclopédie d'architecture*, vol. IV (1854), col. 57, and predicted the victory of his and Labrouste's ideas. Louis Duc, Henri Labrouste, and Léon Vaudoyer were, however, not elected to the Academy until 1866, 1867, and 1868, respectively.

125. The *Registre des concours* in the Archives of the Institut de France documented this process. Indeed, in 1862 the final program was chosen by vote rather than by lottery.

126. The authors of the other programs of this period were Lebas (1854), de Gisors (1855 and 1857), Caristie (1859), and Lefuel

(1860 and 1861).

127. See, for example, the review of the Grand Prix projects by J.-B.-B. Boutard: *Journal des Débats*, September 21, 1807; September 16, 1808; September 21, 1812.

128. *RGA*, 1855, cols. 186, 251–56. Both Daly, in the *RGA*, and Adolphe Lance, in the *Encyclopédie d'architecture* (1857, vol. VII, cols. 129–34), attribute the impetus to Duban.

129. *Gazette des Beaux-Arts*, vol. II (1862), pp. 477–78.

130. *Moniteur des Architectes*, 1866, col. 142.

131. The only lengthy review of the projects of 1867 is by Anatole de Baudot, *Gazette des Architectes et du Bâtiment*, vol. IV (1867), pp. 105–06 (the Exposition Universelle of 1867 overshadowed all other events). See also the plates in *Intime Club*, 1867, 5.6, 6.4-6.5, 7.1, 8.1, 9.1; 1868, 1.1, 4.5, 8.1, 10.1; 1869, 3.3 (unusually extensive publication of Grand Prix projects for that journal).

132. Fritz Walch, "Das Gebäude der Pariser Weltaustellung," 1867, Ph.D. dissertation, Karlsruhe, 1967, chap. 4. LePlay had been a member of the *Encyclopédie nouvelle* group.

133. A student of Nicolle and the most successful of that radical group.

134. The projects submitted in the competition for the buildings were published in extenso in the *Encyclopédie d'architecture*, 1876.

135. A. Guerinet, *Supplément aux médailles des concours d'architecture*, Paris, n.d., pls. 96-99.

136. As is well known, the frontispiece of Bénard's project was copied in the Fine Arts Building at the Columbian Exposition in Chicago in 1893 (now moved and transformed into the Field Museum of Natural History), and then copied again in the Museum of Science and Industry.

137. By Viollet-le-Duc's son in the *Gazette des Architectes et du Bâtiment*, vol. I (1863), p. 29.

138. Emmanuel Brune, winner of the Premier Grand Prix in 1863, was a student of Charles Questel; Julien Guadet, 1864, of Louis-Jules André; Louis Noguet and Gustave-Adolphe Gerhardt, both of 1865, students of Questel and André, respectively; Pascal, a student of Questel; Bénard, a student of Alexis Paccard. Among the runners-up, Jules-Louis Batigny was a student of Hippolyte Lebas and Léon Ginain; Henri Mayeux a student of Paccard.

139. Garnier published a list of his most significant assistants in *Le Nouvel Opéra de Paris*, Paris, 1878–80, vol. II, pp. 501–03.

140. Jean-Louis Pascal, "Notice sur la vie et les oeuvres de Julien Guadet," preface to the

2nd ed. of Guadet's *Eléments et théorie de l'architecture*, Paris, 1909; J.-L. Pascal, *Charles Garnier*, Paris, 1899; Julien Guadet, *Charles Garnier, notice historique*, Paris, 1899; Paul Nénot, *L'Architecture*, 1925 (writing in the special issue devoted to Charles Garnier, n. 21).

141. *Le Nouvel Opéra de Paris*, vol. II, p. 503.

142. *Ibid.*, p. 505.

143. Sets survive at the Bibliothèque Nationale, Paris, and the Boston Public Library. They bear no author, title, or date.

144. *Le Théâtre*, pp. 42–43. A recent study has documented the building: M. Steinhauser, *Die Architektur der Pariser Oper*, Munich, 1969.

145. *Le Théâtre*, p. 44.

146. *Ibid.*, p. 49.

147. *Ibid.*, p. 59.

148. *Ibid.*, p. 104.

149. "Le Nouvel Opéra," *Gazette des Architectes et du Bâtiment*, vol. I (1863), pp. 29–30.

150. *A travers les Arts*, Paris, 1867, p. 49.

151. *Le Théâtre*, p. 404.

152. *Ibid.*, p. 401.

153. *Ibid.*, pp. 1–2.

154. *Le Nouvel Opéra de Paris*, vol. I, p. 341.

155. *Ibid.*, vol. I, p. 24.

156. *Ibid.*, vol. I, p. 16.

157. *A travers les Arts*, p. 69.

158. *Le Théâtre*, p. vi.

159. *Le Nouvel Opéra de Paris*, vol. I, pp. 121–22. Cf. pp. 339–40.

160. *Le Théâtre*, p. 413.

161. The most interesting—but secondhand—remark is in an American source: a reminiscence of André's atelier methods by "a former pupil of Richardson's" quoted in M. G. Van Rensselaer, *Henry Hobson Richardson and His Works*, New York, 1888, p. 128, n. 1. See also J.-L. Pascal, *Notice sur Jules André, architecte*, Paris, 1891; J. Guadet, "Notice sur la vie et les ouvrages de M. André," *L'Architecture*, vol. III (1890), pp. 419–21, 429–31.

162. See *RGA*, vol. XLI (1883), XLII (1884), XLIII (1855).

163. F. Monmory, "Le Nouvel Musée zoologique au Jardin des Plantes," *RGA*, vol. XLI (1883), cols. 16–22.

164. F. Monmory, "Le Nouvel Musée de l'historie naturelle au Jardin des Plantes," *RGA*, vol. XLIII (1885), cols. 248–51.

165. E.-J. Delécluze, *Louis David, son école et son temps*, Paris, 1855, p. 5.

166. Tony Garnier around 1900 seems to have been the bridge between the Ecole and this renewed philosophical and social revolution. See Anthony Vidler, "The New Industrial World: The Reconstruction of Urban Utopia in Late Nineteenth Century France,"

Perspecta XIII–XIV, New York, 1971, pp. 242–57.

167. Emile Kaufmann, *Von Ledoux bis Le Corbusier*, Vienna, 1933; Rowe, *op. cit.*

168. Kaufmann, *op. cit.*, p. 42.

169. *Ibid.*, pp. 61–63.

170. *Op. cit.*

171. *Ibid.*, p. 54, quoting *The Ecclesiologist*, vol. VI (1846), p. 129.

172. Cf. C. Beutler, "St. Eugène und die Bibliothèque Nationale," *Miscellanea Pro Arte, Festschrift für Hermann Schnitzler*, Dusseldorf, n.d. See the explanation of Labrouste's intent published by his son, Léon, who assisted his father on the building: *La Bibliothèque Nationale: ses bâtiments et ses constructions*, Paris, 1885, as well as the reviews of the opening of the Salle des Imprimés: Henri Crozic, *L'Illustration*, May 30, 1868, p. 341; Henri Lacroix, *Le Moniteur Universel*, June 12, 1868, p. 825.

THE ROMANTIC IDEA OF ARCHITECTURAL LEGIBILITY: HENRI LABROUSTE AND THE *NEO-GREC*
Neil Levine

I am deeply grateful to Vincent Scully for his constant advice and encouragement over the past decade. Many of the ideas developed here were also suggested by or worked out in numerous discussions of the subject with David Van Zanten, Sheldon Nodelman, and George Hersey. For the help afforded my research in France and Italy I should like to thank Mme Henri Labrouste; M. Léon Malcotte; Mlle Madeleine Boy and the staff of the Bibliothèque Sainte-Geneviève; M. Jean Adhémar and Mme Bertrand Jestaz of the Cabinet des Estampes of the Bibliothèque Nationale; Mme Wanda Bouleau-Rabaud and Mlle Annie Jacques of the Ecole des Beaux-Arts; Mme Paul René-Bazin, former archivist of the Académie des Beaux-Arts of the Institut de France; Mme Louis Hautecoeur-Milliez of the library of the Institut de France; Mlle Renée Plouin of the Institut d'Art et d'Archéologie; M. Pierre Le Moël and Mme Labat of the Archives Nationales; and Mme Janine Calisti at the library of the French Academy in Rome. My research in France was partially funded by a Harvard Graduate Society Fund Fellowship from Harvard University. Charles Rosen and Henri Zerner provided generous assistance in the preparation of the manuscript. And to Arthur Drexler goes my warmest appreciation for his patience and acumen.

1. John Ruskin, *Lectures on Architecture and Painting, Delivered at Edinburgh, in November, 1853*, New York, 1854, pp. 172–73. The words "structures" and "architecture" in brackets are my substitutions for the original "sculptures and pictures" and "paintings." I feel that Ruskin would hardly have disapproved of the additional sense his exhortation has been made to bear.

2. Sigfried Giedion, *Space, Time and Architecture*, orig. pub. 1941; 4th ed., enl., Cambridge, Mass., 1962, p. 219.

3. From a letter to his brother Théodore dated November 20, 1830, in *Souvenirs d'Henri Labrouste, architecte, membre de l'Institut: notes recueillies et classées par ses enfants*, Fontainebleau 1928, p. 24.

4. Eugène-Emmanuel Viollet-le-Duc, *Entretiens sur l'architecture*, 2 vols. text, 1 vol. pls., Paris, 1863–72, vol. II (1872), pp. 61, 47, 64.

5. E.-E. Viollet-le-Duc, "Lettres extra-parlementaires," *Le XIXe Siècle* (Paris), 21 arts., January 29–August 1, 1877, art. IX, March 21, 1877, pp. 1–2.

6. Viollet-le-Duc, "Lettres extra-parlementaires," art. VII, March 5, 1877, p. 1.

7. Viollet-le-Duc, "Lettres extra-parlementaires," March 5, 1877, p. 1 and March 21, 1877, pp. 1–2.

8. Ibid.

9. Giedion, op. cit., p. 218.

10. E.-E. Viollet-le-Duc, Dictionnaire raisonné de l'architecture française du XIe au XVIe siècle, 10 vols., orig. pub. 1854–68; Paris, 1875, vol. VIII, p. 494.

11. Viollet-le-Duc, Entretiens sur l'architecture, vol. I (1863), p. 24.

12. César Daly, "Discours prononcé au nom des anciens élèves de Félix Duban," in Funérailles de Félix Duban, ed. César Daly, Paris, 1871, p. 33.

13. César Daly, Architecture funéraire contemporaine: spécimens de tombeaux, Paris, 1871, col. 3.

14. Daly, "Discours prononcé . . . ," pp. 32–33.

15. Julien Guadet, Eléments et théorie de l'architecture, 4 vols., orig. pub. 1901–04; Paris, [1905], vol. I, pp. 84–85, 97.

16. Julien Guadet, "Notice sur la vie et les oeuvres de M. André," L'Architecture, 3d year, no. 35 (August 30, 1890), p. 419.

17. Emile Trélat, "L'Architecture contemporaine," La Nouvelle Revue, vol. III (March–April 1880), p. 88.

18. Charles Garnier, A travers les arts: causeries et mélanges, Paris, 1869, p. 85.

19. Cf. Henry Van Brunt, "Greek Lines," The Atlantic Monthly, vol. VII, no. 44 (June 1861), pp. 654–67 and vol. VIII, no. 45 (July 1861), pp. 76–88; and Montgomery Schuyler, "The Works of the Late Richard Morris Hunt," in American Architecture and Other Writings, eds. William Jordy and Ralph Coe, 2 vols., Cambridge, Mass., 1961, vol. II, pp. 502 ff.

20. See, for example, Alexandre Sandier, "Neo-Grec," in A Dictionary of Architecture and Building, ed. Russell Sturgis, 3 vols., New York, 1901–02, vol. II (1901), cols. 1025–26.

21. See, for example, Prosper Mérimée, "Essai sur l'architecture religieuse du moyen âge, particulièrement en France," Annuaire Historique pour l'Année 1838, Société de l'Histoire de France, Paris, 1837, pp. 283–327; Ludovic Vitet, "Des monumens de Paris," La Revue Française, vol. V (February–March 1838), pp. 218–33 and "De l'architecture lombarde," orig. pub. 1830, reprinted in his Etudes sur les beaux-arts: essais d'archéologie et fragments littéraires, 2 vols., Paris, 1847, vol. II, pp. 1–25; and Louis Batissier, Histoire de l'art monumental dans l'antiquité et au moyen âge, Paris, 1845.

22. This is the opinion expressed by Viollet-le-Duc in the sixth discourse of the first volume of his Entretiens sur l'architecture (1863).

23. This point, as well as numerous others to be touched on here, have been developed much more fully in my Ph.D. dissertation, "Architectural Reasoning in the Age of Positivism: The Néo-Grec Idea of Henri Labrouste's Bibliothèque Sainte-Geneviève," Yale University, 1975.

24. Henry Van Brunt, Greek Lines and Other Architectural Essays, Boston and New York, 1893, pp. 82–83, 86. In his original article of 1861, Van Brunt referred to the new style as "the Romantique." In its revised form, published in 1893, he usually changed that to "neo-Grec."

25. Van Brunt, "Greek Lines," The Atlantic Monthly, vol. VIII, no. 45 (July 1861), p. 86. The word "Order" has been capitalized here and, when necessary for reasons of consistency, in all succeeding quotations.

26. Ibid., p. 85.

27. Cf. Daly, "Discours prononcé. . . ," pp. 33–34; and Trélat, op. cit., pp. 86–88 and his obituary of Labrouste, in Ecole Spéciale d'Architecture. Séance d'ouverture, 9 Novembre 1875, Paris, n.d., esp. pp. 13–22.

28. Van Brunt, "Greek Lines," p. 85.

29. Ibid., pp. 84–85.

30. Van Brunt, Greek Lines, pp. 81–82.

31. Van Brunt, "Greek Lines," p. 86.

32. Ibid., p. 86 (italics added).

33. My chronology of the design and construction of the Bibliothèque Sainte-Geneviève is based primarily on the drawings in the collection of the Labrouste family and the following documents: Paris, Archives Nationales, F21 751, F21 1362-64, N III Seine 1135 and Versement de la Direction de l'Architecture, Album 45; and Paris, Bibliothèque Sainte-Geneviève, MSS. 3910-39. Although the letter from the Minister of the Interior officially commissioning the design is dated November 29, 1838, it is more than likely, based on other documents, that Montalivet had informally told Labrouste during the preceding month that he intended to sponsor the construction of a new library.

34. Henri Labrouste, "A M. le Directeur de la Revue d'Architecture," Revue Générale de l'Architecture et des Travaux Publics, vol. X (1852), col. 382.

35. Ibid., col. 382.

36. Auguste Bossel de Saint-Martin to Labrouste, MS. 3911, Bibliothèque Sainte-Geneviève, Paris.

37. Henri Labrouste, "Bibliothèque de Ste. Geneviève. Projet d'un bâtiment à ériger sur l'Emplacement de l'ancienne prison de Montaigu et destiné à recevoir la bibliothèque de Ste. Geneviève," [December 1839], n. pag., fasc. 1, F21 1362, Archives Nationales, Paris. Note explaining the project submitted in December 1839.

38. Achille Hermant, "La Bibliothèque Sainte-Geneviève," L'Artiste, 5th ser., vol. VII (December 1, 1851), p. 129.

39. César Daly, "Bibliothèque Sainte-Geneviève," RGA, vol. X (1852), col. 380.

40. Félix Pigeory, "Théorie de l'architecture religieuse au XIXe siècle," Revue des Beaux-Arts, vol. II (1851), p. 217.

41. Théodore de Banville, "Le Quartier Latin et la Bibliothèque Sainte-Geneviève," in Paris Guide par les principaux écrivains et artistes de la France, 2 vols., Paris 1867, vol. II, pp. 1358–59.

42. F. Barrière, "Embellissemens de Paris," Journal des Débats, December 31, 1850, p. 1.

43. "Promenades in Paris," The Builder, vol. VIII, no. 370 (March 9, 1850), p. 111.

44. Henry Trianon, "Nouvelle Bibliothèque Sainte-Geneviève," L'Illustration, vol. XVII, no. 411 (January 10–17, 1851), p. 30.

45. Ibid., p. 30.

46. Antoine-Nicolas Bailly, Notice sur M. Henri Labrouste, Paris, 1876, p. 14.

47. Trélat, obituary of Labrouste, Ecole Spéciale d'Architecture . . . , pp. 20–21.

48. Hermant, op. cit., pp. 129–31.

49. Quoted in Paul Sédille, "Joseph Louis Duc, architecte (1802–79)," Encyclopédie d'Architecture, 2d ser., vol. VIII (1879), pp. 70, 68.

50. Ibid., p. 68.

51. "Conseil des Bâtiments civils. Rapport fait au Conseil par Mr. Caristie Inspecteur général," January 23 and 25, 1840, n. pag., fasc. 1, F21 1362, Archives Nationales, Paris. Caristie suggested, with a certain degree of insistence, that Labrouste heighten the ground floor, vault in stone both the ground floor and the first floor, and substitute stone or marble columns for the proposed cast-iron ones. The effect of this would clearly have been a more traditionally plastic articulation of the whole, for such a fundamental revision of the structure would certainly have entailed basic alterations to the overall design. In its conclusion to the report, the Conseil did not back Caristie up on these points and left the decision up to Labrouste.

52. Victor Hugo, "Préface," Cromwell, orig. pub. 1827; Paris, 1968, pp. 81–82.

53. Labrouste, "A M. le Directeur. . . ," col. 383.

54. The calendar as first published in April 1849 was simply a series of thirteen consecutive pages, each one listing the names of one month's days. In 1852, Comte recast it in tabular form on two pages, one containing the first seven months of the new positivistic year, the other the final six months. In this form, it was published in the fourth edition of the Calendrier positiviste in May 1852 and

was also included in his *Catéchisme positiviste* of the same year.

55. Auguste Comte, *Catéchisme positiviste*, orig. pub. 1852; Paris, 1966, p. 264.

56. Léon Danjoy (1806–62) was a friend of Labrouste. He visited the library a number of times while it was still under construction. The drawing, given to Labrouste for his *album amicorum*, is dedicated "à son camarade Labrouste." Danjoy entered the Ecole des Beaux-Arts in 1827 as a student of Huyot. He was never promoted to the *première classe*. As an architect he built very little. He began the construction of the seminary at Coutances in 1852 and was responsible for the decoration of the base of the Demidoff tomb at Père-Lachaise cemetery (ca. 1850). Aside from that, he was mostly involved in the restoration of medieval buildings and conducted an important atelier in the late 1840s and '50s.

Danjoy was particularly known for a kind of visionary approach to architecture, more poetic than practical, which pushed the *Néo-Grec* idea to its most extreme and fantastic conclusion. Ten years after his death, Adolphe Lance described his work in the following way:

Danjoy, perhaps more radical than practical in his method of architectonic composition, sought to break free, if need be, from any form sanctioned by science or by tradition, and wanted feeling to dominate everything, even matter. On that basis, he had imagined a kind of imitative architecture that would have been like a poetic painting in relief of everyday things, like a new art midway between dream and reality. Endowed with great talent as a draftsman, he knew so well how to translate onto paper the seductive daydreams of his imagination that, while never convincing you, he almost always fascinated you.... [His] sketchbooks ... contained ... charming fantasies, ingeniously conceived.... Unfortunately ... all that was imagined for a world which is not ours. Architecture, being above all an art of reality and material substance, cannot be treated like painting or poetry. (Dictionnaire des architectes français, 2 vols., Paris, 1872, vol. I, pp. 178–79.)

Lance claimed that Danjoy was more adept at constructing with "ideas" than with "stones," and that he "gladly took flight into ... the world of the impossible ... with his eyes closed." (p. 156.) He added that Danjoy's dreamlike *compositions* revealed "a sort of invisible reality predominating the visible reality." Such would appear to be the case for his impression of Labrouste's library.

57. Victor Hugo, *Notre-Dame de Paris 1482*, 8th ed; orig. pub. 1832; Paris, 1967, p. 32. See below note 129.

58. *Ibid.*, pp. 198, 199, 207, 209.

59. Victor Hugo summarized his theory of "real history" as opposed to "mythological history" in his *William Shakespeare*, published in 1864. He defined "real history" as a history written "au point de vue du principe" and not "au point de vue misérable du fait." Labrouste's readjustment of certain facts in his restoration of Paestum in order to accord more precisely with what he felt to be the principles of Greek architecture can be seen to reflect this Romantic idea of history.

60. The facts relating to this interchange of thought between Hugo and Labrouste in 1831–32 are documented in my dissertation (see note 23) and will form the basis of an article on the subject.

61. "Etudes obligatoires pour chaque Pensionnaire architecte," May 15, 1820, Registre des procès-verbaux de l'Académie des Beaux-Arts, 1819–25, p. 93, 2 E 7, Archives de l'Académie des Beaux-Arts, Institut de France, Paris. Rules adopted by the Academy in the meeting of April 1, 1820, and sent to the Minister of the Interior for approval on May 15, 1820.

62. "Rapport sur les ouvrages des élèves de l'Ecole de france à Rome pour l'année 1834," [1835], p. 1, Pièces annexes des procès-verbaux de l'Académie des Beaux-Arts, 1835, 5 E 24, Archives de l'Académie des Beaux-Arts, Institut de France, Paris. Draft of report.

63. "Rapport de la Section d'Architecture sur les travaux des Pensionnaires-Architectes de l'Ecole française à Rome. Année 1831," November 24, 1832, p. 8, in "Rapports sur les ouvrages des architectes de l'Académie de France à Rome," vol. III (1825–34), p. 190, MS. 630, Library, Ecole des Beaux-Arts, Paris.

64. "Etudes obligatoires ...," Registre des procès-verbaux ..., 1819–25, p. 92, 2 E 7, Archives de l'Académie des Beaux-Arts, Institut de France, Paris.

65. "Rapport fait par la Section d'architecture à l'Académie royale des Beaux-Arts de l'Institut sur les ouvrages des Pensionnaires de l'académie de france à Rome pour l'année 1828," November 15, 1829, p. 13, in "Rapports ...," vol. III, p. 104, MS. 630, Library, Ecole des Beaux-Arts, Paris. All following references to the Academy's criticism of Labrouste's fourth-year *envoi* are to this report.

66. Horace Vernet–Quatremère de Quincy correspondence, May–June 1829, and "Rapport sur les voyages des Architectes pensionnaires," June 6, 1829, Pièces annexes des procès-verbaux de l'Académie des Beaux-Arts, 1829, 5 E 19; and Procès-verbaux de l'Académie des Beaux-Arts, 1829, passim, Registre des procès-verbaux ..., 1826-36, 2 E 8; Archives de l'Académie des Beaux-Arts, Institut de France, Paris.

67. Trélat, obituary of Labrouste, *Ecole Spéciale d'Architecture ...*, pp. 13–14.

68. "Rapport de la Section d'Architecture sur les travaux envoyés de Rome, pour l'année 1833, par MM les Pensionnaires-Architectes de l'Ecole de France," September 20, 1834, p. 4, in "Rapports ...," vol. III, p. 218, MS. 630, Library, Ecole des Beaux-Arts, Paris.

69. In its report on the *pensionnaires'* work of 1830–31, with particular reference to the *envois* of Théodore Labrouste and Louis Duc, the Academy strongly condemned the study of Etruscan and Roman Republican architecture and warned against the "unfortunate influence" it was already exerting. The report describes those forms of architecture as being "in their infancy, and not having been cultivated by skillful masters." ("Rapport de la Section d'Architecture sur les Ouvrages envoyés de Rome par Messieurs les Pensionnaires-Architectes," December 10, 1831, pp. 7–8, 21–22, Pièces annexes des procès-verbaux de l'Académie des Beaux-Arts, 1831, 5 E 21, Archives de l'Académie des Beaux-Arts, Institut de France, Paris.)

70. Quatremère to the Director of the Academy in Rome [1835], quoted in René Schneider, *Quatremère de Quincy et son intervention dans les arts (1788–1830)*, Paris, 1910, p. 311. The letter cited by Schneider, and surely misdated by him 1833, is missing from the archives of the Académie des Beaux-Arts. There exist, however, two rough drafts which contain more or less the same wording and which were written in late 1835, rejecting Victor Baltard's request of November of that year to visit Greece in order to find a subject for his fourth-year *envoi*. (Pièces annexes des procès-verbaux de l'Académie des Beaux-Arts, 1835, 5 E 24, Archives de l'Académie des Beaux-Arts, Institut de France, Paris.)

71. "Rapport ... pour l'année 1834," p. 2, Pièces annexes des procès-verbaux ..., 1835, 5 E 24, Archives de l'Académie des Beaux-Arts, Institut de France, Paris.

72. Alfred Darcel, "De l'architecture ogivale: architecture nationale et religieuse," *La Revue Française* (Paris), vol. VIII (1857), p. 551.

73. Beulé's remarks were contained in the opening lecture of his course on archaeology given at the Bibliothèque Nationale on January 6, 1857 and published as "Archéologie. D'une architecture nationale et religieuse," *Revue des Cours Publics et des Sociétés Savantes de la France et de l'Etranger*, 3d year, no. 4 (January 25, 1857), pp. 44–49. In this lecture, Beulé specifically related Labrouste's teaching to the rise of interest in Gothic architecture (pp. 47–48). The complete text

of Beulé's lecture was also published in the *RGA* (vol. XIV, 1856, cols. 373–83), with a response from one of Labrouste's students, Edmond Bailly, in the following issue (vol. XV, 1857, cols. 80–81).

74. Daly, "Discours prononcé. . . ," pp. 33–34 (italics, except for "*absolute*" and "*Romanticism*," added).

75. This controversy is too complicated to go into here and will have to await a future study devoted to Labrouste's career and the events surrounding his student years. Although the names of Labrouste, Duban, Duc, and Vaudoyer were usually linked by architects and critics in nineteenth-century France, and their effort to overthrow Neoclassicism was usually seen as a group effort, one member of the group or another was often cited as being the "instigator" of reform. This depended on the point of view of the critic. Viollet-le-Duc and Trélat, for instance, singled out Labrouste as the radical force. Beulé, on the other hand, saw Duban as the leader. These differences of opinion resulted from what it was that later writers wanted to see as the message contained in their work. They reflect the breach between radical and conservative points of view in the second half of the nineteenth century and, in turn, reveal certain dissensions that had grown up within the ranks of the original *Néo-Grecs* themselves.

Whether the ideas of the *Néo-Grecs* were in fact ever that cohesive must be studied in more detail; whether or not their ideas were really developed in common study at the Ecole in Paris and the Academy in Rome must also be more fully investigated. Generally speaking, it was usually presumed that Duban and Labrouste, the two oldest members of the group, were its original leaders; and that Duc and Vaudoyer, who followed them to Rome in 1826 and 1827, picked up and developed their ideas. Once having returned to Paris, the four architects seem to have remained quite close throughout the 1830s and '40s. This may simply reflect the fact that they were then still the outsiders, a youthful force rebelling against the establishment. By the mid-1850s, however, after each one had had the chance to build a building and show what he could do on his own, splits began to appear in the group. This was made most obvious by the "schools" that had begun to form around each of the four mainly as a result of what they taught in their ateliers. Labrouste's atelier was the most radical. It produced almost solely "medievalists." All this was exacerbated by the relative success, or lack of success, which the *Néo-Grecs* had in entering the Academy itself, and this was clearly related to the reputation of their ateliers as much as their

buildings. Duban was elected to the Academy in 1854, thirteen years before Labrouste. Lefuel, Victor Baltard, and Duc all preceded Labrouste into the Academy. Vaudoyer gained entrance one year after Labrouste; but the fact that Duc had won the Grand Prix a year after Labrouste, yet entered the Academy a year before him, seemed to most critics to be an indication of something more political at hand. Indeed, Duc's letter of 1856, probably written to Duban and quoted above, shows to what an extent their opinions on architecture had diverged by that point. It was in the summer of 1856, directly following his first rejection by the Academy, that Labrouste felt compelled to close his atelier. As he told his students, Labrouste did this for their own good. Up to then his teaching had been relentlessly opposed by the Academy. In seeing his old friends Duban and Duc adopt the more conservative line of the Academy itself, Labrouste surely felt that no student of his stood any greater chance for success than before. Duban and Duc were, in effect, to become the figureheads, if not the leaders, of the new establishment. It would appear from all accounts that Léon Vaudoyer always occupied a kind of mediatory position between the more radical and more conservative factions of the original *Néo-Grecs*.

The above-mentioned disagreements tended to remain unaired until the 1870s, when, in a series of obituaries published on the occasions of the successive deaths of Duban (1870), Vaudoyer (1872), and Labrouste (1875), their respective roles in the *Néo-Grec* revolution were necessarily discussed. By this time, the Academy, which had already received Labrouste as one of its members (1867), had to find some way of incorporating him into their historical exegesis without, however, allowing him to appear as the radical force. Thus, his role was made to appear as coequal with that of Vaudoyer and of Duc, if not in fact subsidiary to that of Duban. It was to this question that Viollet-le-Duc addressed himself in his series of "Lettres extra-parlementaires" of 1877, published in *Le XIXe Siècle*. In his seventh article of March 5, 1877, he described the relationship between Duban and Labrouste in terms of La Fontaine's fable of "The Monkey and the Cat." Labrouste was portrayed as the cat, independent yet self-effacing, who stole the chestnuts from the fire while Duban the monkey, his fast-talking imitator, underhandedly took them from him. In the process, Labrouste's hands were burned (meaning he took the blame for stealing the chestnuts), while Duban "ate, with certain marks of a mysterious respect, the chestnuts pulled from the fire by [Labrouste]. . . ." (p. 1.) Thus Duban, in

Viollet-le-Duc's view, received all the credit but none of the blame.

While Viollet-le-Duc did not reveal the real names of the characters in his *fable à clef*, they were obvious at the time. So much so that a member of Labrouste's family felt it incumbent upon herself to rephrase her father's position more politely. Under her pseudonym, Léon Dassy, Labrouste's daughter Laure published a *Protestation contre l'épithète de Bertrand donné à un maître* (n.d.), in which she both managed to deprecate what she felt to be the ill-intentioned tone of Viollet-le-Duc's interpretation yet uphold his conclusion of the preeminent role her father played.

76. Viollet-le-Duc, "Lettres extra-parlementaires," March 5, 1877, p. 1.

77. Van Brunt, "Greek Lines," pp. 84–85 (initial italics added).

78. For a description of these events, see A. de Baudot, *L'Architecture: le passé—le présent*, Paris, 1916, pp. 196–97.

79. For a summary of the issues raised by Labrouste's restoration, see L. Dassy [pseud.], *Compte rendu sur la restauration de Paestum exécutée en 1829 par Henri Labrouste*, Paris, 1879.

80. This is recounted in René Schneider, *op. cit.*, pp. 301–05.

81. See the *Journal des Débats*, October 22, 1830 (p. 3) and November 17, 1830 (p. 2). In a number of letters throughout the first six months of 1830, Vernet had asked the Academy to review their conclusions about Labrouste's work. When they categorically refused to hear Labrouste's own letter of "justification," Vernet informed the Academy, on September 7, that he was submitting his resignation to the Minister of the Interior, Guizot. On October 5, however, Guizot replied to Vernet, refusing to accept it.

82. During the twenty-six years of its existence, Labrouste's atelier produced not a single Grand Prix winner. Furthermore, almost none of his students were promoted to the *première classe* of the Ecole and none ever won a *médaille* in a *concours* of the *première classe*.

83. Cf. Louis Hautecoeur, *Histoire de l'architecture classique en France*, 7 vols., Paris, 1943–57, vol. VI (1955), pp. 228–32 and 238 *ff.*

84. J.-I. Hittorff, "Mémoire sur mon voyage en Sicile. Lu à l'académie des beaux-arts de l'Institut, avec l'extrait du procès-verbal de la Séance du 24 Juillet 1824, où cette lecture eut lieu," MS. 4641, Institut de France, Paris.

85. In 1846, Philippe-Auguste Titeux restored the Erectheion and the Propylaea; in 1847 Alexis Paccard restored the Parthenon; in 1848 Jacques-Martin Tétaz did the Erectheion again; in 1849 Prosper

Desbuisson did the Propylaea again; in 1850 Félix Thomas restored the Temple of Hera II (Neptune) at Paestum; in 1852 Jules André chose the Hephaisteion in Athens; in 1853 Garnier did the Temple of Apollo at Aegina; in 1854 Denis Lebouteux restored the Temple of Apollo at Bassae; and in 1855 Louis-Victor Louvet did the Sounion acropolis. This spate of Greek restorations coincided with that moment of liberalism of ca. 1846–53 already spoken of in relation to the *concours* of the Ecole itself.

86. See S. Lang, "The Early Publications of the Temples at Paestum," *Journal of the Warburg and Courtauld Institutes* (London), vol. XIII (1950), pp. 48–64.

87. Cf. Nikolaus Pevsner and S. Lang, "Apollo or Baboon," *Architectural Review* (London), vol. CIV, no. 624 (December 1948), pp. 271–79.

88. Viollet-le-Duc, "Lettres extra-parlementaires," March 5, 1877, p. 1.

89. These were the names traditionally given to the three temples at Paestum. Hereafter, I shall refer to them by their present appellations: the Temple of Neptune as Hera II; the Basilica as Hera I; and the Temple of Ceres as Athena.

90. Henri Delaborde, *Notice sur la vie et les ouvrages de M. Henri Labrouste*, Paris, 1878, pp. 7–9.

91. The text and engravings of his drawings were published by the French government in 1877 as *Les Temples de Paestum: restauration exécutée en 1829 par Henri Labrouste*, Restaurations des monuments antiques par les architectes pensionnaires de l'Académie de France à Rome depuis 1788 jusqu'à nos jours, Paris, 1877. Along with the original drawings, there is a manuscript copy of Labrouste's text in the library of the Ecole des Beaux-Arts ("Mémoire explicatif de la restauration des Temples de Poestum près Naples," 1829, pp. 1–45, MS. 240). All citations here, except where otherwise noted, are from the published text. The differences between the manuscript and published text are of an editorial rather than substantive nature. Since the proofs of Labrouste's text were ready just a few months after his death, there can be no doubt that he was responsible for the changes. For references to the Academy's report dealing with Labrouste's restoration, see above note 65.

92. C.-M. Delagardette, *Les Ruines de Paestum, ou Posidonia, ancienne ville de la Grande Grèce*, Paris, An VII [1799], pp. 67–72. This may reflect the opinion previously published by Paulantonio Paoli, in his *Paesti Quod Posidoniam Etiam Dixere Rudera* (Rome, 1784), that the "lightness" and "elegant" entasis of the columns of the Temple of Hera I give evidence that it was probably built after the two other temples (p. 141). He claimed that all three temples were Etruscan.

93. Labrouste, *Les Temples de Paestum*, p. 3. Here, of course, Labrouste could hardly have been referring to Piranesi's *Différentes vues de quelques restes de trois grand édifices qui subsistent encore dans le milieu de l'ancienne ville de Pesto, autrement Posidonia* (Rome, 1778). This, of all previous publications, and for special reasons, was most outspoken in favor of the superiority of "Poseidonian," if not of all Greek, architecture.

94. While Labrouste often referred to Greek buildings, either extant or known through surviving texts, he never specified any Roman buildings. For certain parts of his restoration, such as the painted roof tiles or some pieces of movable furniture, he noted that there were analogies in Roman architecture but that these remains were not justifications in and of themselves and merely showed that the Romans still carried on some Greek practices. In Labrouste's eyes, the evidence for restoring certain decorative or impermanent features that could be gleaned from the wall paintings at Pompeii were of this sort. Much of the decorative painting, especially of the temples of Athena and Hera I, was based on the recently discovered Etruscan tombs at Tarquinia, which Labrouste claimed "could be attributed to the Greeks" (*Les Temples de Paestum*, p. 11). The only substantive comparison that Labrouste made with Roman architecture was in connection with his restoration of the Temple of Hera I as a "portique" rather than a temple. He justified his decoration of its interior with inscriptions by reference to both Greek stoas and Roman civic buildings. The significance of his restoration of the Temple of Hera I as a "portique" will be discussed below.

95. Such a willful desire to see architectural form as directly reflecting the materials and methods of construction is clearly what lay behind Viollet-le-Duc's later writings. The relationship is most evident in Viollet-le-Duc's own explanation of the forms of Greek architecture, where, in the second discourse of his *Entretiens sur l'architecture*, he made a specific point of refuting the classical theory of imitation.

96. Previous writers, such as Delagardette and Piranesi, had, of course, remarked on the different types of stone used but offered very different explanations. Viollet-le-Duc's later explanation of the rationality of the Gothic architect's use of columns and stones *en délit* was similar to Labrouste's.

97. Labrouste did not assume that the Temple of Hera II was originally covered with a coat of polychrome stucco. It is built of only one type of stone which, as shall be seen, indicated to Labrouste that it was earlier in date and totally different in conception.

98. Again, the reasoning is analogous to that later used by Lassus and Viollet-le-Duc to describe how medieval proportions resulted from structural considerations. In his sixth discourse, Viollet-le-Duc illustrated the similar telescopic means by which the Romanesque architect of Saint-Rémi at Reims articulated the engaged columns of that building's side facade. He described the conception as un-Roman and related it to Greek architecture:

Here in the West, as early as the tenth century (and perhaps before), we see architects omitting the intermediate entablatures of those superposed Orders and, out of the two, three, or four columns that the Romans placed one on top of the other, making but a single cluster or a single column, or a single cylindrical buttress having only a single capital with an entablature at the top of the building. When several stories are superposed, they are indicated by stringcourses between the columns, and these [columns] rise up from the base either indefinitely elongated or reduced in thickness at each story. Here we have a new principle born of sound reasoning. Among the Greeks of antiquity, we have already seen that, when two Orders were superposed, the upper Order was but the extension of the lower column as, for example, in the temple of Neptune [Hera II] at Paestum.... (*Entretiens sur l'architecture*, vol. I pp. 230–32.)

Viollet-le-Duc reproduced two sections of the Temple of Hera II to illustrate his point. He asserted that the medieval architect was able to revive this rational Greek principle despite his ignorance of Greek architecture for, aside from being acquainted with Roman buildings, he also knew the *néo-grec* architecture of Byzantium which, in Viollet-le-Duc's eyes, was in itself a revival of the Greek genius: "... in having recourse to the Byzantine arts, the West gave birth to principles of its own...." (p. 232.)

99. The Academy refused even to consider Labrouste's contention that such a structural concern could have been the sole reason for the superposition of the Orders. In paraphrasing his conclusion, the report stated: "Could not the use of two Orders, one above the other, lead one to believe that *aside from simply being a decorative motif*, the upper Order could also have been useful in relieving the great span of the roof structure in the event that this temple were entirely covered, as Mr. Henri Labrouste thinks...." ("Rapport ... pour l'année 1828," p. 10, in "Rapports...," vol. III, p.

102, MS. 630, Library, Ecole des Beaux-Arts, Paris [italics added].)

100. The reference, of course, would have been to that prime model of classical architecture of the previous generation, Labrouste's own teacher Lebas's Notre-Dame de Lorette (1822–36).

101. Labrouste added: "... and I noted in Sicily, that only the temple of Olympian Jupiter, at Agrigentum, has no staircases, and we know that it was hypaethral or without ceilings." (*Les Temples de Paestum*, p. 10.)

102. This is from the Academy's report of 1834 dealing with the *envois* of Pierre-Joseph Garrez and Marie-Antoine Delannoy of 1833–34 ("Rapport ... pour l'année 1833 ...," pp. 3, 5, in "Rapports ...," vol. III, pp. 217, 219, MS. 630, Library, Ecole des Beaux-Arts, Paris). In its report of the previous year, the Academy had already criticized the "archaeological investigations" of Delannoy as tending to mask the true nobility of character of Roman architecture ("Rapport de la Section d'Architecture sur les ouvrages de MM. les Pensionnaires-architectes à l'Académie de france à Rome (Envoi de 1832)," September 24, 1833, pp. 5–6, in *ibid.*, pp. 201–02); and in 1832, the Academy had even more vehemently censured Théodore Labrouste's restorations of Cora on the same grounds ("Rapport ... Année 1831," pp. 6–7, in *ibid.*, pp. 188–89). The Academy felt his drawings revealed that he had not been able to see the forest for the trees.

103. Labrouste only referred to the various elements composing the peripteral Order of the Temple of Athena when discussing the different varieties of stone used in its construction. Significantly, he chose rather to talk about the character of the Order of the pronaos that no longer existed, which he presumed to have been Ionic. The Academy rejected his conclusion by referring to the early Roman Doric temple at Cora where the Order also has a base.

104. Van Brunt, "Greek Lines," p. 84. Delagardette had previously remarked that, to his knowledge, this was the only example of such an occurrence in Greek architecture and suggested, once again, the possibility of Roman restoration (*op. cit.*, pp. 50, 70).

105. Delagardette, *op. cit.*, pp. 70–72.

106. Labrouste was, in effect, adopting the by then totally discredited chronology proposed by Paoli in 1784 (*op. cit.*, pp. 112, 141). In the opening section of his *précis historique*, however, Labrouste denied Paoli's contention that the temples were Etruscan. In rejecting Delagardette's explanation, he thus ended up agreeing with Paoli's conclusion if not his reasons.

107. Charles Blanc, "Félix Duban, 1797–1870," *in Les Artistes de mon temps*, Paris, 1876, pp. 3–4 (italics added).

108. See, for example, Gabriel Laviron, "Architecture," *L'Artiste*, 2d ser., vol. I (1839), pp. 393–95.

109. Labrouste's student Lassus's discussion of the "human scale" of Gothic proportions in his series of articles, "De l'art et de l'archéologie," in the *Annales Archéologiques* (vol. II, 1845, esp. pp. 72–75 and 201–02), was clearly dependent on Labrouste's explanation of Greek proportions. In defending Lassus's conclusions against the classicist Beulé (see above note 73), Alfred Darcel explicitly stated that the new understanding of Greek architecture had informed that opinion:

St. Peter's in Rome! that model of bad taste, the most flagrant example of the oblivion of antique traditions along with a pretension to express grandeur by preserving the module of the temples of antiquity!

Why do the temples of Pestum, Agrigentum, Selinus ... seem to have such an appearance of grandeur, which they are far from really possessing? It is because of that perfect concordance of their forms, the rules that presided over their construction and the dimensions of the materials of which they are composed. The powerful architrave of these buildings astonishes me without frightening me, because I have the feeling that its length and its height enable it to support its own weight and the weight it carries; besides, in seeing it so frankly set on top of the capitals of the solid columns that hold it up, I immediately grasp the method of construction, and the total harmony of the building is revealed to my mind through my senses and through my intellect. I understand that the strength of the materials used has set certain limits to the length of the architrave and to the spacing of the columns; that a precise feeling for harmony has regulated the height of the latter and, consequently, their diameter. But when these requisites of construction no longer exist, when I see an architrave divided up into a multitude of little voussoirs tied together by iron [as at the Panthéon], when I no longer see an agreement between form and execution, I am amazed that proportions which nothing any longer justifies have been retained, and I see nothing but an aberration of the mind just where I am supposed to see an intelligent respect for the classical tradition. I then come to admire the barbarians of the eleventh and twelfth centuries who broke up the antique module, and who led the architects of the thirteenth century to substitute number for grandeur. ... [In Gothic] architecture the parts are multiplied according to need, leaving each one of them

*dependent upon the materials at hand. If the church is large, it will have more bays than if it is small; if the weight that the columns have to support is greater, they will be thicker, while next to them, a thinner column, though taller if need be, will support a lesser weight. ... [And since] these columns no longer support an architrave but rather an arch, the diameter of the arch alone will regulate their spacing. ("De l'architecture ogivale," pp. 556–57.)

110. Laviron, *op. cit.*, p. 393.

111. Cf. John Stuart Mill, *The Positive Philosophy of Auguste Comte*, orig. pub. 1865; Boston, 1866, esp. pp. 16–19.

112. Some eighteenth-century writers such as Dumont and Thomas Major, basing their interpretation on David Leroy's discussion of the primordial nature of temples having a central spine of internal columns ("Essai sur l'histoire de l'architecture," in *Les Ruines des plus beaux monuments de la Grèce*, 2d ed., Paris, 1770, vol. I, pp. ix–xiv), allowed that Hera I could have been either a temple or a basilica. Major, like Delagardette, also suggested that if indeed it were a basilica it also could have been used for "transacting the Affairs of Commerce," but he preferred to think of it as a temple (*The Ruins of Paestum, otherwise Posidonia, in Magna Graecia*, London, 1768, p. 28). Piranesi countered with the idea that it might have been a "Gymnasium," and, perhaps most relevant to Labrouste's conclusion, Paoli suggested that it was an "Etruscan atrium" or "portico," specifically designed for commercial use and public gatherings (*op. cit.*, pp. 131–48).

113. This citation is from the manuscript copy of Labrouste's text in the library of the Ecole des Beaux-Arts ("Mémoire explicatif de la restauration des Temples de Poestum ...," p. 34, MS. 240). In the published text, the discussion of antique sources for the walls of a building functioning as an *album* was greatly reduced in length. In 1829 the idea of a building's walls as surfaces for recording events in words was clearly of much more immediate interest. In that same year, the third volume of François Mazois's *Les Ruines de Pompéi* (Paris, 1829), which was devoted to public buildings other than temples or theaters, included as its frontispiece (pl. I) one of the tablets from the lateral facade of the Building of Eumachia. It was described in the accompanying text, which was revised and completed by François-Christian Gau after Mazois's death in 1826, as part of the "*album* on which were written public and private notices" (p. 11). The Building of Eumachia was presented in seven other plates (pls. XXII–XXVIII), with a descriptive text (pp. 42–46) in which the function of the building as an *album* was related to the antique "custom of writing with a paint brush, in red or black, on the wall of the most frequented places, everything which we customarily make known by means of printed posters" (p. 46). Gau noted that this included announcements of "sales, rentals, public festivals and performances." One can assume that Labrouste was aware of the text before it was published, if indeed he did not contribute some thoughts to it, for Gau had asked him, in 1828, to supply drawings of the Forum Baths as well as a description of them, which were credited to Labrouste in the publication of 1829 (pls XLVII–L and p. 67).

114. Garrel (1823–67) in his bridge project, which was his first following his promotion to the *première classe*, departed from the somewhat abstract program for the competition which called for a "monument . . . to be erected in commemoration of a peace treaty the result of which would have been the delimitation of two countries. . . ." That boundary-line was to be "established on a little river or deep ravine which, it is to be assumed, separates France from Italy. . . ." ("Ecole des Beaux-Arts. Architecture 1^erre Classe. Concours d'Emulation. Programmes rédigés par L.-P. Baltard, Blouet et Lesueur, professeurs à l'Ecole, 1831–1854," March 2, 1847, AJ 52 143, Archives Nationales, Paris.) Garrel obviously felt that a more relevant response to the program would be to rewrite it in terms of an actual current event which it could be made to fit almost precisely. Just two years prior to the competition, France and Morocco had signed the Convention of Lalla Maghnia (March 18, 1845). This, following the treaty of Tangier of the previous September which ended the hostilities between the two countries, having culminated in the French victory in the Battle of Isly on August 14, 1844, established the boundary between Morocco and Algeria. More importantly, it contained the proviso that the Sultan of Morocco, Abd-er-Rahman, would thenceforth refrain from giving aid or sanctuary to the Algerian rebel leader, Abd-el-Kader. As a result of that, Abd-el-Kader's movements were restricted and he was forced to move south toward the Sahara, where he was finally captured in December 1847. Marshal Bugeaud, who led the French cavalry in the Battle of Isly, referred to that battle, in his report of August 17, 1844, as "the consecration of our conquest of Algeria."

Artists in Paris immediately reacted to the events. In response to a request from the magazine *L'Illustration*, Delacroix supplied four illustrations culled from the sketches made during his trip to Morocco in 1832. The final one, published on September 21, 1844,

in the same issue announcing the Treaty of Tangier, was a portrait of Abd-er-Rahman. In the following March, Delacroix exhibited in the Salon of 1845 the painting of *Mouley Abd-er-Rahman, Sultan of Morocco*, seen against the background of his palace and surrounded by his guards. In the same Salon, Horace Vernet exhibited his seventy-foot-long painting of the *Capture of the Retinue of Abd-el-Kader at Taguin (May 16, 1843)*. In the Salon of 1846, Vernet exhibited the *Battle of Isly (August 14, 1844)*. Both of Vernet's paintings were destined for the Palace of Versailles where they were hung in Louis-Phillipe's African rooms, which already included Vernet's paintings of French victories in Algeria during the 1830s.

Given the contemporary importance attached to the events in North Africa of 1844–45, it is clear why an imaginative young architect like Garrel might have turned to them for inspiration. Since the program of the Ecole actually called for a bridge between France and Italy, it is also clear why Garrel might have immediately turned to Labrouste's project of 1829 as a model to be transformed in terms of those events. Despite the fact that Labrouste's drawings, as his fifth-year *envoi*, were not kept by the Ecole and remained in his possession, it can be assumed that since Garrel had been a member of E.-T. Dommey's atelier from 1842 to 1844 and was currently in Léon Vaudoyer's atelier, he could have had access to Labrouste's project, since both Dommey and Vaudoyer were close friends of Labrouste. Significantly, Vaudoyer had visited Algeria in the late 1830s as a member of a French mission to report on the artistic and archaeological treasures of Algeria.

Garrel's transformation of Labrouste's bridge answered, in general terms, all the requirements of the program while at the same time it related them to the specific North African situation. The Isly, where the French victory took place, is a wadi or ravine that runs between the Algerian border town of Lalla Maghnia and the Moroccan border town of Oujda. Since the program called for the inclusion of "signs" which might "characterize" the cause for the treaty and the establishment of a frontier, Garrel stationed members of the French cavalry, who were responsible for the French victory at Isly, in front of the piers of his arch. One of the figures in the niche above the far arch is holding a peace treaty, referring no doubt both to the Treaty of Tangier and the Convention of Lalla Maghnia.

The one remaining question is to prove that Garrel's project, based on his revised program, is indeed the one he submitted in the competition of March 1847. Since his

project was not premiated, it was not kept by the Ecole and is known to me only in the engravings published by F. Thierry-Ladrange, after Garrel's death (1867), in his short-lived magazine, *Architecture: revue contemporaine d'oeuvres inédites de l'atelier*, 1st year, installments VII–VIII [1870], pls. 23–27. Aside from the perspective (p. 395), these include an elevation of the internal face of an arch, a site plan, a plan of the bridge itself, a longitudinal section and a *partial* elevation of the lateral facade. The program had called for just such renderings but stipulated that the lateral elevation should be of its full extent. The judging of the competition took place on May 7, 1847, two months after the program was given out and the preliminary sketches were made. A *première médaille* was awarded to L.-F. Douillard and a *deuxième médaille* to J.-A.-C. Scheffer. The records of the Ecole show that one project was eliminated by the jury for having not only departed too radically from the original sketch but also for having failed to provide a complete lateral elevation! ("Registre des procès-verbaux des jugements des prix délivrés dans l'Ecole d'architecture, Janvier 1846–Septembre 1850," AJ 52 107, Archives Nationales, Paris.) This project was only referred to by its number (5), since all projects were entered anonymously. The only way to ascertain whether Garrel's project was in fact No. 5 would be either to see the actual drawings or to examine the register which each student signed the morning of the competition, at which time he was assigned a number. Unfortunately, that register is missing. Significantly, however, in his description of Garrel's project, Thierry-Ladrange noted that Garrel had told him that one of the professors on the jury (probably Constant-Dufeux) had commended him for having been "able to form judiciously a new ideal on a new subject." Furthermore, the question of the partial elevation noted by the jury and reproduced by Thierry Ladrange should leave no doubt as to the fact that Garrel's North African bridge was the one submitted in the competition, based on a revision of the program and his sketch after having seen Labrouste's project between the morning of March 2, 1847, and the time he handed in his renderings on May 7. Curiously the problems of revision do not end there, for in his own explanation of the program for Garrel's bridge, Thierry-Ladrange claimed that it was to have been situated over the Rhine! In late 1870, this was as current an emendation as was Garrel's own in 1847.

I should like to thank David Van Zanten for bringing Thierry-Ladrange's publication and Garrel's bridge to my attention.

115. These are among the approximately 750

drawings by Labrouste, done while a *pensionnaire* in Italy, which are now in the Cabinet des Estampes of the Bibliothèque Nationale in the topographical series, Vb 132.

116. Delaborde, *op. cit.*, p. 10.

117. The first major excavation of an Assyrian site, the palace of Sargon II at Khorsabad, had just been completed by Paul-Emile Botta between 1842 and 1844. Although Botta's five-volume *Monument de Ninive*, produced in collaboration with Eugène Flandin, was only published in Paris in 1849–50, the *Lettres de M. Botta sur ses découvertes à Khorsabad, près de Ninive*, edited by Jules Mohl, had appeared in 1845 and included fifty-five plates. Flandin, who was responsible for the drawings, had returned to Paris with them by June 1845, and the sculptural fragments which Botta removed from the site and had sent back arrived at the Louvre in January 1847.

118. See Pascal Coste and Eugène Flandin, *Voyage en Perse: Perse ancienne*, 5 vols., Paris [1843-54], text vol., pp. 1–6 and pl. vol. I, pls. 1–14. I should like to thank my colleague Oleg Grabar, Professor of Fine Arts at Harvard University, for pointing out this source to me.

119. "Rapport sur les ouvrages des élèves de l'Ecole de france à Rome pour l'année 1829," December 1830, n. pag., MS., Archives de l'Académie de France à Rome, Rome. All following references to the Academy's criticism of Labrouste's fifth-year *envoi* are to this report.

120. The Academy consistently spelled Italy with a capital "I" but France with a lower-case "f."

121. A. E. Richardson, "The Style of Néo-Grec," *Architectural Review*, vol. XXX, no. 176 (July 1911), p. 28.

122. Léon Vaudoyer, "Etudes d'architecture en France," *Le Magasin Pittoresque*, vol. XX (December 1852), p. 388. This article was the forty-fifth and final one in a series that began in 1839. In the first article it was noted that the survey was to be co-authored by Léon Vaudoyer and Albert Lenoir. Although no mention was subsequently made of any change in that arrangement, it is clear from external evidence that Vaudoyer was solely responsible for the latter articles, if not for almost all of them. Indeed, in 1847, he published a somewhat shorter version of the articles, under his own name, as "Histoire de l'architecture en France," in the encyclopedia *Patria. La France ancienne et moderne, morale et matérielle* (Paris, vol. II, ch. XXVI, cols. 2113–2200). While he criticized Ledoux's style in 1847 for being "bizarre and often even ridiculous," he only applied the term "architecture parlante" to it in the expanded version of 1852.

123. It should, in all fairness to Vaudoyer's position, be added that he completed this statement in saying ". . . that we hope will meet with little success." (p. 388.) Why Vaudoyer arrived at this conclusion is difficult to say, given the fact that he was a close friend of Labrouste and given my supposition that much of what he considered to be "architecture parlante" was a direct issue from Labrouste's work and teaching. It could be that Vaudoyer was already aligning himself with Duc and Duban, the more conservative wing of the original *Néo-Grecs*, against the more radical tendencies that were seen to be emerging from Labrouste's faction. Indeed, what Vaudoyer meant by "architecture parlante" can be seen, in the work of Danjoy, Nicolle, Labrouste, Constant-Dufeux, and their students, to be an exaggerated, extremist form of *Néo-Grec* expression. It is interesting that César Daly always gave a tremendous amount of coverage to the work of Danjoy, Nicolle, and Constant-Dufeux in his *Revue* but, of the original four *Néo-Grecs*, only to that of Labrouste.

124. The program was actually given out on December 3, 1851; the projects were submitted on February 6, 1852.

125. César Daly, "Ecole des Beaux-Arts de Paris. Concours mensuel de 2ᵉ classe," *RGA*, vol. X (1852), cols. 42–43 and pl. 9. These projects are only known to me in the engraving published by Daly. Despite the fact that the jury awarded eight *premières mentions* and four *deuxièmes mentions*, none of the four chosen by Daly was amongst the prize-winners. However, J.-J. Huguenet's engraving of them was exhibited in the Salon of 1853!

126. Trélat, "L'Architecture contemporaine," p. 89.

127. See Jean-Marie Pérouse de Montclos, *Etienne-Louis Boullée (1728–1799)*, Paris, 1969, figs. 129–30.

128. Cf. *ibid.*, fig. 131.

129. Van Brunt, "Greek Lines," pp. 85–87.

130. It was in the same year, 1851, that Ruskin, in the first volume of *The Stones of Venice*, provided a description of the abstract basis of architectural style as lying in the existence and reconciliation of polar opposites in what are surely some of the most beautiful and moving passages ever written on architecture. He categorically dismissed the idea of there being three, not to speak of five, Orders and postulated only two: the "Doric" convex and the "Corinthian" concave, the one being the mirror reflection of the other (ch. I, pars. XVII–XIX; ch. VI, pars. IV–V; ch. XXVII, pars. XXXV–XXXVII; Appendix 7; and pls. XVII–XVIII). The straight line drawn diagonally from the top of the shaft to the abacus was to be considered "the line of origin," the "center or root of both" the concave and convex Orders which are "distinguished . . . by circular curves drawn on opposite sides of the same line." The resulting two Orders are the "roots" of all possible variants and give a sense of massiness and strength, on the one hand, and elegance and lightness, on the other. For Ruskin, "these two great and real orders are representative of the two great influences which must forever divide the heart of man: the one of Lawful Discipline, with its perfection and order . . . ; the other of Lawful Freedom, with its vigour and variety. . . ." (ch. XXVII, par. XL.) While the Venetian ogee arch presented the most obvious form of reconciliation, it was, for Ruskin, in the Byzantine synthesis of Classical form that the opposed characters of each of the Orders was made most explicit and in the efflorescence of the Venetian Gothic in the Ducal Palace that "the glacier torrent and the lava stream . . . met and contended over the wreck of the Roman Empire; and . . . [at] the point of pause of both" these were reconciled in "the central building of the world" (ch. I, par. XXIV).

Ruskin's sense of architectural form as a unifying or reconciling of the mirror reflections of concavity and convexity was so all-consuming that he saw the same forces at work not only in the character of the two Orders themselves but in all parts of a building. In his eyes, the capital was but the "gathered" or "concentrated" cornice, the cornice an unrolled capital; the column or shaft was but the "gathered" or "concentrated" expanse of "wall veil"; the base, either unrolled or gathered, was but an upside-down version of the cornice or capital (ch. IX, par. I). All the parts of a building, from the contrast of "roll" and "recess" mouldings to his consideration of the pointed arch as simply a "curved gable" (ch. X, par. X), were felt to stem from that one basic dichotomy of the convex and the concave. The building itself then emerges, at least theoretically, as a malleable, plastic construct in which all the parts, by expansion, contraction or reversal, form an organically continuous whole, rendered expressive in actual contour by the application of "abstract natural lines."

Ruskin's sense of architectural form as conveying emotional significance through its abstract linear outlines was something which was equally shared by César Daly and was passed on by both of them to such Americans as Henry Van Brunt. It should also not be forgotten that Ruskin, like Daly and the other *Néo-Grecs*, felt most deeply the connection between such lapidary conciseness and the idea of architecture as a legible, readable form of expression. In the second volume of *The Stones of Venice* (1853), Ruskin described the Byzantine Basilica of St. Mark's in absolutely Hugolian terms:

. . . the whole church [was] . . . a great Book of Common Prayer; the mosaics were its illuminations and the common people of the time were taught their Scripture history by means of them. . . . The walls of the church necessarily became the poor man's Bible. . . . (ch. IV, par. LXII.)

Never had a city a more glorious Bible. . . . for her [Venice], *the skill and the treasures of the East had gilded every letter, and illumined every page, till the Book-Temple shone from afar off like the star of the Magi.* (ch. IV, par. LXXI.)

Ruskin claimed that in medieval times such "legible imagery" was understood, for "every one who at any time entered [the church], was supposed to look back and to read this writing. . . ." (ch. IV, par. LXVI.) Echoing Hugo, he related the architectural impotence of the nineteenth century to the growth in power of the printed word:

Our eyes are now familiar and wearied with writing. . . . But the old architect was sure of his readers. He knew that every one would be glad to decipher all that he wrote; that they would rejoice in possessing the vaulted leaves of his stone manuscript. . . . (ch. IV, par. LXIV.)

In *Notre-Dame de Paris*, Hugo had, twenty years previously, described the process of understanding the "hermetic" content of pre-Gutenberg buildings as a laborious act of reading:

I will not tell you . . . to go visit the sepulchral chambers of the pyramids . . . nor the temple of Solomon. . . . We will content ourselves with the fragments of the book of Hermes that we have here. I will explain to you the statue of saint Christopher, the symbol of the Sower, and that of the two angels who are on the portal of the Sainte-Chapelle. . . . I will have you read, one after the other, the marble letters of the alphabet, the granite pages of the book. We will go to the Sainte-Chapelle. . . . We will spell out the facades together. . . . (pp. 196–97.)

For Ruskin, as for Hugo, it was essential that the nineteenth century perceive architecture in terms of the written word:

We must take some pains, therefore, when we enter [a building], *. . . to read all that is inscribed, or we shall not penetrate into the feeling either of the builder or his times.* (*op. cit.*, vol. II, ch. IV, par. LXIV.)

For us in the final quarter of the twentieth century, such reading may prove to be a relief and a release from all sorts of other considerations that have, for so long, made nineteenth-century architecture seem to be a closed book.

LISTS OF ARCHITECTS AND THEIR WORKS

The list immediately following refers the reader to illustrations both of student drawings from the Ecole des Beaux-Arts and of built buildings by architects who had trained at the Ecole. It is followed by lists of the buildings according to location and of works by other architects.

PHOTOGRAPH CREDITS

Berenice Abbott, courtesy Museum of the City of New York: 487; Alinari, Florence: 31 bottom; *American Architect and Building News* (New York), 1907: 478 top; Courtesy American Academy of Arts and Letters: 478 bottom left; *Architects' and Builders' Magazine* (New York), 1908: 477 bottom right; *The Architectural Forum* (New York), 1929: 491 bottom; *Architectural Record* (New York), 1920: 488 bottom; *L'Architecture* (Paris), vol. I, 1888: 451 bottom; vol. II, 1898: 448 bottom; vol. XII, 1899: 459 bottom; *L'Architecture à L'Exposition Universelle de 1900*, Paris, 1902: 455; Archives Photographiques, Centre de Recherches sur les Monuments Historiques, Palais de Chaillot, Paris: 282–85; C. D. Arnold, courtesy Avery Architectural Library, Columbia University, New York: 471–75; James Austin, Cambridge, England: 80, 324, 335, 341, 345, 429–30; Courtesy Avery Architectural Library, Columbia University, New York: 485 bottom left; L.-P. Baltard and A.-L.-T. Vaudoyer, *Les Grands Prix d'architecture*, Paris, 1834, courtesy D. D. Egbert: 125 bottom, 133; V. Baltard and F. Callet, *Monographie des Halles Centrales de Paris*, Paris, 1863: 421; Hubert Howe Bancroft, *The Book of the Fair*, vol. I: 470; Courtesy John Barrington Bayley: 47–48; Bibliothèque Nationale, Paris: 371, 395; W. Boesiger and H. Girsberger, *Le Corbusier 1910–65*, Frederick A. Praeger, New York, 1967: 26; Courtesy Boston Public Library: 468 top, (Print Department) 468 bottom; Brown Bros.: 483; *The Builder* (London), 1884: 444 top; J.-E. Bulloz, Paris: 32, 114, 119, 120, 121 center, 131, 132, 146–49, 153–56, 164–65, 165, 188, 194–95, 215–16, 262–67, 270–71, 273, 275–77, 280–81, 289, 291–97, 306–08, 361, 363, 372–73, 404, 412, 426 left (courtesy J.-L. Vaudoyer); Byron, New York, courtesy The Singer Company: 477 left; Cartographic Archives Division of the National Archives, Washington, D.C.: 493 bottom left; Chevojon Frères, Paris: 110, 113 center and bottom, 116, 117, 122 bottom, 123 top, 125 top, 145, 150–51, 157, 166 top, 236–39, 255–57, 298–99, 300 bottom, 301–03, 312, 314–19, 422–23, 431 top, 436 top, 437 top, 438–41, 450, 451 top, 452–53, 461 right, 462 left top and bottom; Auguste Choisy, *Histoire de l'architecture*, Paris, 1899, vol. II: 18; C. Collens, "The Beaux-Arts in 1900," *AIA Journal*, 1947, vol. VII: 92 bottom; Baldwin Coolidge, courtesy Boston Public Library Print Department: 469 top; *Constant-Dufeux*, Paris 1872–75: 178–79; *La Construction Moderne* (Paris), 1890, vol. V: 458 bottom; 1900–01, vol. XVI: 462 bottom right; E. H. Denby, "The Ecole des Beaux-Arts Revisited," *Légion d'Honneur*, January 1933, vol. III: 78; Courtesy Library, Ecole Nationale Supérieure des Beaux-Arts, Paris: 90; *Encyclopédie d'Architecture*, Paris, 1860, vol. VI: 420 bottom; Sigmund Fischer, courtesy John F. Harbeson: 491 top; Fondation Le Corbusier, Paris: 25; Charles Garnier, *Le Nouvel Opéra de Paris*, Paris, 1878–80: 269, 274, 433–35; John Wallace Gillies: 488 top left; Giraudon, Paris: 60; Romaldo Giurgola and Jaimini Mehta, *Louis I. Kahn*, Westview Press, Boulder, Colorado, 1975: 57 top; George P. Hall, courtesy Museum of the City of New York: 485 bottom right; Bob Hauser Photographers, Hugh Morrison Collection, The Museum of Modern Art, New York: 476 left; Louis Hautecoeur, *Histoire de l'architecture classique en France*, Paris, 1955, vol. VI: 418 right; Hedrich-Blessing, Chicago: 16 top; David Holbrook, New Haven, Connecticut: 378, 407; Horydczak, courtesy Library of Congress, Washington, D.C.: 492, 493 top; *Inception and Creation of the Grand Central Terminal*, priv. printed for A. Stem and A. Fellheimer: 480 bottom; Kate Keller, The Museum of Modern Art, New York: 19; *Le Corbusier: Architect, Painter, Writer*, Macmillan, New York, 1948: 44–45; A. Lemaistre, *L'Ecole des Beaux-Arts dessinée et racontée par un élève*, Paris, 1889: 93 bottom; Neil Levine, Cambridge, Massachusetts: 336–37, 339–40, 344, 354, 380–81, 396–97; Library of Congress, Washington, D.C.: 485 top; James Mathews, New York: 17 top, 30, 31 top and center, 113 top, 121 top and bottom, 122 top, 123 bottom, 126 bottom, 128, 135–37, 139, 140–41, 143–44, 158, 160–61, 163, 166 bottom, 167–69, 172–75, 177, 180–84, 186–87, 189–90, 192, 198–203, 205–06, 209–10, 212–13, 218, 220–21, 224–25, 240–41, 243–49, 258–60, 300 top, 304–05, 309–11, 313, 320–22, 379; *Richard Meier, Architect*, Oxford University Press, New York, 1976: 21 bottom; *A Monograph of the Work of McKim, Mead, and White 1879–1915*, New York [1915–19]: 469 bottom, 484 left; The Museum of Modern Art, New York: 22, 466 top; Courtesy New York Public Library: 465 top, 479 bottom; Manuscripts and Archives Division, The New York Public Library, Astor, Lenox, and Tilden Foundations: 464; Ed Nowak, New York: 480 top, 481 top; Penanrun, Roux and Delaire, *Les Architectes Elèves de l'Ecole des Beaux-Arts 1819–94*, Paris, 1895: 84; *Les Architectes Elèves ... 1793–1907*, Paris, 1907: 92 top; Rolf Peterson, The Museum of Modern Art, New York: 17 bottom, 54; *Pol's Practical Guide to Monte Carlo*, Lyons, 1918: 442 bottom; *Portraits of Ten Country Houses Designed by Delano & Aldrich*, Garden City, New York, 1924: 489 bottom; *Revue Générale de l'Architecture et des Travaux Publics* (Paris), vol. XII: 420 top; vol. XXXIX, 1882: 428 bottom; 1885: 286; Roger-Viollet, Paris: 81, 342, 418 left, 419, 424–25, 426–27, 428 top, 431 bottom, 436 bottom, 437 bottom, 442 top, 443, 444 bottom, 445–47, 448 top, 449, 454, 456–57, 459 top, 460; *S.A.D.G. Recueil publié à l'occasion de la millième adhésion à la Société des Architectes Diplômés par le Gouvernement*, Paris, 1911: 91; Mrs. Schuyler Van Rensselaer, *Henry Hobson Richardson and His Works*, Boston–New York, 1888: 466 bottom left; Courtesy Paul Sprague: 476 right; Luke Swank: 467; Tebbs Hymans, Ltd., courtesy Wank, Adams, Slavin Assoc.: 481 bottom; *Transactions of the R.I.B.A.*, vol. XXXIV, 1883–84: 79; Trouchard, *L'Ecole Nationale Supérieure des Beaux-Arts*, Paris, 1937: 93 left; United States Department of the Interior, National Park Service: 493 bottom right; David Van Zanten, Philadelphia: 458 top; Malcolm Varon, New York: 126, 127 top, 170–71, 362, 413, 432; E.-E. Viollet-le-Duc, *Entretiens sur l'architecture*, vol. II: 227 left top and bottom, 227 right (courtesy Virginia Egbert); Wurts Bros., courtesy Richard Wurts, Litchfield, Connecticut: 465 bottom, 478 bottom right, 479 top, 490.